Get a FREE eBook

To register this book, scan the code or go to
www.manning.com/freebook/deruiter

By registering you get

- **FREE eBook copy**
  download in PDF and ePub

- **FREE online access**
  to Manning's liveBook platform

- **FREE audio**
  read and listen online in liveBook

- **FREE AI Assistant**
  it knows the book and what you are reading when it answers

- **FREE in-book testing**
  fun tests to lock in your knowledge

In Manning's liveBook platform you can share discussions and comments with other readers, add your own bookmarks and highlights, insert personal notes anywhere on the page, see color versions of all the book's graphics, download source code and other resources, and more!

To register, scan the code or go to www.manning.com/freebook/deruiter

MANNING

Data Pipelines with Apache Airflow

ORCHESTRATION FOR DATA AND AI
SECOND EDITION

JULIAN DE RUITER
ISMAEL CABRAL
KRIS GEUSEBROEK
DANIEL VAN DER ENDE
BAS HARENSLAK

MANNING
SHELTER ISLAND

Manning Publications Co.
20 Baldwin Road
PO Box 761
Shelter Island, NY 11964

Development editor:	Elesha Hyde
Technical editor:	Arthur Zubarev
Review editor:	Radmila Ercegovac
Production editor:	Keri Hales
Copy editor:	Keir Simpson
Proofreader:	Katie Tennant
Technical proofreader:	Anant Agarwal
Typesetter:	Tamara Švelić Sabljić
Cover designer:	Marija Tudor

ISBN 9781633436374

brief contents

contents

vii

preface

The world of data is never dull, and much has changed since the original release of this book. Whereas large language models (LLMs) used to be a niche research topic, nowadays everyone—even our mothers—has heard of AI tools such as ChatGPT. For better or worse (depending on who you ask), this shift has led to a huge boom in companies adopting AI to optimize their processes and shift to more data-driven decision making. Besides this technological acceleration, global challenges such as geopolitical strife and climate change add even more pressure to adapt to an ever-changing environment, making high-quality data more critical than ever.

In response to these developments, the landscape of data tooling has not stood still. There is more contention than ever in the space of data orchestrators, trending toward more integrated, secure, and developer-friendly platforms. Accordingly, Airflow has evolved considerably since the first edition of this book was released, adding several new features and culminating in the recent release of a new major milestone: Airflow 3.

Working on this second edition, we found that we needed to make substantial changes to bring the book up to date with all the changes since Airflow 2.0, including the following:

- An entirely new UI
- Significant changes in Airflow's scheduling logic
- New features such as data-aware (event-based) scheduling, new executor types, and the option to combine multiple executors
- Changes in deployment, shifting to managed solutions or Kubernetes
- New use cases, such as generative AI (GenAI)–related workloads (e.g., RAG)

To incorporate all these changes, we reworked the book considerably, adding many new sections, screenshots, and chapters and restructuring the code examples to make them easier to use and enable them to run in a generic way across all chapters. We hope that these additions do justice to the incredible amount of work that the community has put into developing this new release.

Altogether, this updated book aims to provide a comprehensive introduction to Airflow 3, covering everything from building simple workflows and developing custom components to designing and managing Airflow deployments. We intend to complement the many excellent blogs and other online documentation by consolidating various topics into a single, concise, easy-to-follow resource. Through our combined years of experience working with Airflow, we hope to give you a strong foundation to begin your journey with this powerful tool.

acknowledgments

This book would not have been possible without the support of many amazing people. Colleagues from GoDataDriven and personal friends supported us and provided valuable suggestions and critical insights. In addition, Manning Early Access Program (MEAP) readers posted useful comments in the online forum.

Reviewers from the development process also contributed helpful feedback: Al Krinker, Clifford Thurber, Daniel Lamblin, David Krief, Eric Platon, Felipe Ortega, Jason Rendel, Jeremy Chen, Jiri Pik, Jonathan Wood, Karthik Sirasanagandla, Kent R. Spillner, Lin Chen, Philip Best, Philip Patterson, Rambabu Posa, Richard Meinsen, Robert G. Gimbel, Roman Pavlov, Salvatore Campagna, Sebastián Palma Mardones, Thorsten Weber, Ursin Stauss, and Vlad Navitski.

Thanks also go to the reviewers of the second edition: Akshay Phadke, Albert Okiri, Aliaksandra Sankova, Anant Agarwal, Ansam Yousry, Arun Chandramouli, Ashish Bhatia, Aushim Nagarkatti, Bas Harenslak, Ben McNamara, Bonnie Why, Denise Sison, Dhruv Seth, Dmitry Maletin, Gregor Zurowski, Harsh Daiya, Karthik Rajashekaran, Kushal Bohra, Maja Ferle, Manohar Sai Jasti, Matt Housley, Matthew Copple, Moises Baltazar, Monica G, Najeeb Arif, Oleksii Segeda, Pavan Emani, Pavel Filatov, Prabhu Patel, Prashanth Josyula, Rambabu Posa, Rohini Uppuluri, Roman Volozhanin, Sanchit Srivastava, Sandeep Singh Sandhu, Sanjana Balain, Shankar Govri, Srujan Jabbireddy, Sujay Kulkarni, Szymon, Venkata Karthik Penikalapati, Venkatraman Umbalacheri Ramasamy, and Vinicios Wentz. Your suggestions helped make this book better.

At Manning, we owe special thanks to Brian Sawyer and Jonathan Gennick, our acquisitions editors, who helped us shape the initial book proposal and believed in our ability to see it through, and to the rest of the staff: Elesha Hyde, our development editor; Arthur Zubarev, our technical editor; Keir Simpson, our copyeditor; Katie Tennant, our proofreader; Anant Agarwal, our technical proofreader; and the entire production department for making the production process proceed smoothly.

Julian de Ruiter—First and foremost, I'd like to thank my wife, Anne Paulien, and my kids, Dexter and Zoë, for their endless patience during the many hours I spent doing "just a little more work" on the book. This book would not have been possible without their unwavering support. In the same vein, I'd like to thank our family and friends for their support. And of course, thanks go to my colleagues at Xebia Data for their advice and encouragement; I've also learned an incredible amount from them in the past few years. Last but definitely not least, special thanks go to our new coauthors, for without you, this second edition would never have made it to the finish line.

Ismael Cabral—I want to give a big thanks to my parents for always guiding me and cheering me on along the way. To Florien: thank you for your patience and support, even when my focus on this book made our trips a little less fun at times. You've been amazing! And of course, a huge shout-out goes to Xebia Data for creating such a creative and inspiring space that made it possible to invest time and energy in this second edition of the book. Writing this book has been a journey of learning and sharing, and I'm thrilled to have been part of it!

Kris Geusebroek—Special thanks go to my wife, Gita, and my kids, Lieke and Bas, for leaving me alone during all the hours I spent hidden behind my laptop writing that almost-final piece of text or adjusting that last piece of code to run the examples. I'm also grateful for the support of the kids' sports clubs, who allowed me to sit in the sports accommodation during their practice sessions to squeeze in an extra couple of hours. Finally, I'd like to thank our colleagues at Xebia Data for their advice and encouragement; I've also learned an incredible amount from them in the past few years. Our jobs can be done right only if we keep learning. Writing down what you know to educate others makes you do some extra research and increases your knowledge of a topic even more, which makes writing this book even more rewarding.

Daniel van der Ende—I would like to extend deep gratitude to my wife, Chantalle, and my children, Julia and Max, for their unwavering support and patience during the countless hours I dedicated to writing this book. It truly wouldn't have been possible without them, especially during those hour-long sessions of "putting the kids to bed," which I often used to write text, code, and refine images and examples. I am also thankful to Xebia Data for providing me the time and opportunity to pursue this project. I appreciate my colleagues, who were always willing to brainstorm with me and share their insights. More broadly, my colleagues at Xebia Data have been instrumental in sharing their knowledge over the years, and I am proud to continue that tradition through this book.

Bas Harenslak—Writing the first edition of *Data Pipelines with Apache Airflow* was a humbling and energizing experience. The overwhelming feedback from family and friends, colleagues at Astronomer and GoDataDriven, and the vibrant Airflow community was both inspiring and deeply motivating. This second edition of *Data Pipelines with Apache Airflow* is dedicated to my dad, who is always in my thoughts and my work. A special thanks goes to my coauthors for carrying forward the work on this edition. It's exciting to witness the thriving Apache Airflow community and the release of Airflow 3.

about this book

Data Pipelines with Apache Airflow, Second Edition, was written to help you implement data-oriented workflows (or pipelines) using Airflow. The book begins with the concepts and mechanics involved in programmatically building workflows for Airflow using the Python programming language. Then the book switches to more in-depth topics such as extending Airflow by building custom components and comprehensively testing your workflows. The final part of the book focuses on designing and managing Airflow deployments, touching on topics such as security and cloud platforms.

Who should read this book

Data Pipelines with Apache Airflow, Second Edition, was written for data professionals looking to develop basic workflows in Airflow and for those interested in advanced topics such as building custom components for Airflow and managing Airflow deployments. Because Airflow workflows and components are built primarily in Python, we do expect readers to have intermediate experience with programming in Python—that is, have a good working knowledge of building Python functions and classes, understanding concepts such as *args, **kwargs, and so on. Some experience with Docker is also beneficial because most of our code examples are run using Docker (though you can run them locally if you want to).

How this book is organized: A road map

The book consists of four parts, covering 17 chapters. Part 1 focuses on the basics of Airflow, explaining what Airflow is and outlining its basic concepts:

- Chapter 1 discusses data workflows/pipelines and how to build them with Airflow. It also discusses the advantages and disadvantages of Airflow compared with other solutions and sets forth some situations in which you may not want to use Airflow.

- Chapter 2 goes into the basic structure of pipelines in Airflow (also known as *directed acyclic graphs*, or DAGs), explaining the components involved and how they fit together.
- Chapter 3 shows how to use Airflow to schedule your pipelines to run at recurring time intervals so you can, for example, build pipelines that incrementally load new data over time. The chapter also dives into some intricacies in Airflow's scheduling mechanism, which is often a source of confusion.
- Chapter 4 looks at Airflow's asset-aware scheduling options, which allow you to schedule DAGs to run when certain data asset events take place. This includes both consuming and producing data asset events and defining complex interdependencies based on these events.
- Chapter 5 demonstrates how to use templating mechanisms in Airflow to dynamically include variables in your pipeline definitions. This allows you to reference variables such as schedule execution dates within your pipelines.
- Chapter 6 describes various approaches for defining relationships between tasks in your pipelines, allowing you to build more complex pipeline structures with branches, conditional tasks, and shared variables.

Part 2 dives deeper into more complex Airflow topics, including interfacing with external systems, building your own custom components, and designing tests for your pipelines:

- Chapter 7 shows how you can trigger workflows based on external input.
- Chapter 8 demonstrates workflows using operators that orchestrate various tasks on external systems, allowing you to develop a flow of events across systems that aren't connected.
- Chapter 9 explains how to build custom components for Airflow that allow you to reuse functionality across pipelines or integrate with systems that Airflow's built-in functionality doesn't support.
- Chapter 10 discusses various options for testing Airflow workflows, touching on several properties of operators and showing how to approach them during testing.
- Chapter 11 demonstrates how to use container-based workflows to run pipeline tasks within Docker or Kubernetes and discusses the advantages and disadvantages of these container-based approaches.

Part 3 focuses on applying Airflow in practice, including following best practices, running/securing Airflow, and exploring two demonstrative use cases:

- Chapter 12 highlights several best practices to use when building pipelines, which will help you design and implement efficient, maintainable solutions.

- Chapter 13 is an example Airflow project in which you periodically process rides from New York City's Yellow Cab and Citi Bike services to determine the fastest means of transportation between neighborhoods.
- Chapter 14 takes things a step further by showing you how to use Airflow in a GenAI setting, building a RAG solution that allows you to ask questions about a database of family recipes.

Part 4 explores how to run Airflow in production, discussing topics such as security, configuration options for production, and deployment options:

- Chapter 15 covers several aspects of running Airflow in a production setting, such as architectures for scaling out, monitoring, logging, and alerting.
- Chapter 16 discusses how to secure your Airflow installation to prevent unwanted access and minimize the effects in case a breach occurs.
- Chapter 17 shows how to get Airflow up and running in a Kubernetes environment.
- Appendix A provides more detailed instructions on running the code examples, and appendix B contains a mapping for converting metrics from StatsD format to Prometheus format, which is discussed in chapter 15.

People who are new to Airflow should read chapters 1 and 2 first to get a good idea of what Airflow is and what it can do. Chapters 3 through 6 provide important information about Airflow's key functionality. The rest of the book discusses topics such as building custom components, testing, best practices, and deployments; these chapters can be read out of order, based on the reader's particular needs.

About the code

This book contains many examples of source code, both in numbered listings and inline with normal text. In both cases, source code is formatted in a `fixed-width font` `like this` to separate it from ordinary text. Sometimes, code is also **in bold** to highlight code that has changed from previous steps in the chapter, such as when a new feature adds to an existing line of code.

In many cases, the original source code has been reformatted; we've added line breaks and reworked indentation to accommodate the available page space in the book. In some cases, even this was not enough, and listings include line-continuation markers (➥). Additionally, comments in the source code were removed from the listings when the code is described in the text. Code annotations accompany many of the listings, highlighting important concepts.

Source code for all examples and instructions for running them using Docker and Docker Compose are available in our GitHub repository (https://github.com/godatadriven/data-pipelines-with-airflow-2nd-ed) and can be downloaded via the book's website (https://www.manning.com/books/data-pipelines-with-apache-airflow-second-edition). You can get executable snippets of code from the liveBook (online)

version of this book at https://livebook.manning.com/book/data-pipelines-with
-apache-airflow-second-edition.

All code samples were tested with Airflow 3. Most examples should also run in older
versions of Airflow (2.11) with small modifications.

liveBook discussion forum

Purchase of *Data Pipelines with Apache Airflow, Second Edition*, includes free access to a
private web forum run by Manning Publications where you can make comments about
the book, ask technical questions, and receive help from the authors and other users.
To access the forum and subscribe to it, go to https://livebook.manning.com/#!/
book/data-pipelines-with-apache-airflow-second-edition/discussion.

Manning's commitment to our readers is to provide a venue where meaningful dia-
logue between individual readers and between readers and authors can take place. It is
not a commitment to any specific amount of participation on the part of the authors,
whose contributions to the forum remain voluntary (and unpaid). We suggest that you
try asking the authors some challenging questions lest their interest stray! The forum
and the archives of previous discussions will be accessible on the publisher's website as
long as the book is in print.

about the authors

JULIAN DE RUITER is Field CTO Data + AI at Xebia Data, with a background in computer and life sciences and a PhD in computational cancer biology. He enjoys helping clients design and build AI solutions and platforms, as well as the teams that drive them. From this work, he has extensive experience in deploying and applying Airflow in production in diverse environments.

ISMAEL CABRAL is a machine learning engineer and Airflow trainer with experience spanning Europe, the United States, Mexico, and South America, where he has worked with market-leading companies. He has vast experience implementing data pipelines and deploying machine learning models in production.

Kris Geusebroek is a data engineering consultant with extensive hands-on experience with Airflow at several clients and is the maintainer of Whirl (the open source repository for local testing with Airflow), where he is actively adding new examples based on new functionality and new technologies that integrate with Airflow.

Daniel van der Ende is a data engineer who started using Airflow in 2016. Since then, he has worked in many Airflow environments, both on premises and in the cloud. He has actively contributed to the Airflow project and to related projects such as Astronomer Cosmos.

Bas Harenslak, author of the first edition, is a staff architect at Astronomer. In his daily job, he helps large-scale Airflow users worldwide get the most out of Airflow by supporting complex use cases and running production deployments at large scale. He is also a committer on the Apache Airflow project. He is passionate about open source software that is relied upon by users and organizations around the world.

about the cover illustration

The figure on the cover of *Data Pipelines with Apache Airflow, Second Edition*, is "Femme de l'Isle de Siphanto" ("Woman from Siphanto Island"), taken from a collection by Jacques Grasset de Saint-Sauveur published in 1797. Each illustration is finely drawn and colored by hand.

In those days, it was easy to identify where people lived and what their trade or station in life was by their dress alone. Manning celebrates the inventiveness and initiative of the computer business with book covers based on the rich diversity of regional culture centuries ago, brought back to life by pictures from collections such as this one.

Part 1

Getting started

This part of the book sets the stage for your journey into building pipelines for all kinds of wonderful data processes using Apache Airflow. The first two chapters are aimed at giving you an overview of what Airflow is and what it can do for you.

First, in chapter 1, we'll explore the concepts of data pipelines and sketch the role Airflow plays in helping you implement these pipelines. To set expectations, we'll also compare Airflow with several other technologies and discuss when it may (or may not) be a good fit for your specific use case. Next, chapter 2 will teach you how to implement your first pipeline in Airflow. After building the pipeline, we'll examine how to run this pipeline and monitor its progress using Airflow's web interface.

Chapters 3–6 dive deeper into key concepts of Airflow to give you a solid understanding of Airflow's underpinnings. Chapters 3 and 4 focus on scheduling semantics, which allow you to configure Airflow to run your pipelines at regular intervals or based on events. This lets you, for example, write pipelines that load and process data efficiently on a daily, weekly, or monthly basis or write pipelines that respond to data set updates. Next, in chapter 5, we'll discuss templating mechanisms in Airflow, which allow you to dynamically reference variables such as execution dates in your pipelines. Finally, in chapter 6, we'll dive into different approaches for defining task dependencies in your pipelines, which allow you to define complex task hierarchies, including conditional tasks and branches.

If you're new to Airflow, we recommend that you understand the main concepts described in chapters 3–6 because these concepts are key to using it effectively.

Airflow's scheduling semantics (described in chapters 3 and 4) can be especially confusing for new users as they can be somewhat counterintuitive when first encountered.

After finishing part 1, you should be well equipped to write your own basic pipelines in Airflow and be ready to dive into more advanced topics in parts 2–4.

Meet Apache Airflow

This chapter covers

- Representing data pipelines in workflows as graphs of tasks
- Seeing how Airflow fits into the ecosystem of workflow managers
- Determining whether Airflow is a good fit

Enterprises are becoming more reliant on high-quality data to make data-driven decisions and optimize their business processes. Data volumes involved in these business processes have increased substantially over the years, from megabytes per day to gigabytes per minute. Though handling this data deluge may seem like a considerable challenge, these increasing data volumes can be managed with the appropriate tooling.

Apache Airflow helps you tackle this challenge by building data pipelines that coordinate data operations in an efficient, structured manner. In this process, Airflow is best thought of as an orchestrator conductor; it connects to your systems and coordinates work between them to ensure a harmonious result: high-quality data.

This work can include a wide variety of operations, from loading data from a source system to transforming data through queries, training a model, and more.

After reading this book, you'll be equipped not only to use Airflow to build data pipelines but also to use it in a structured, well-considered way. This will enable you to use Airflow in production contexts to orchestrate different types of workflows in different ways. We'll take a hands-on approach: each concept and part of Airflow is explained not only in text but also in (real-world) examples onto which you can map your situation.

Let's start with a short introduction to data pipelines in Airflow. Then we'll discuss several considerations to keep in mind when evaluating whether Airflow is right for you and demonstrate how to take your first steps with Airflow.

1.1 Introducing data pipelines

Data pipelines generally consist of several tasks or actions that must be executed to achieve the desired result. Suppose that we want to build a small weather dashboard that tells us what the weather will be like in the coming week (figure 1.1). To implement this live weather dashboard, we need to perform something like the following steps:

1. Fetch weather forecast data from a weather API.
2. Clean or otherwise transform the fetched data (e.g., convert temperatures from Fahrenheit to Celsius or vice versa) so that it suits our purpose.
3. Push the transformed data to the weather dashboard.

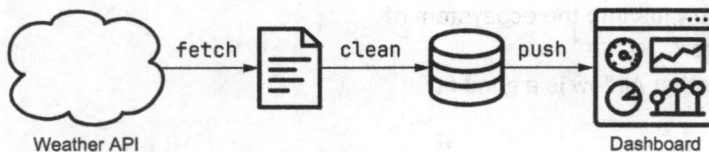

Figure 1.1   For this weather dashboard, weather data is fetched from an external API and fed into a dynamic dashboard.

As you can see, this relatively simple pipeline consists of three tasks, each performing part of the work. Moreover, these tasks need to be executed in a specific order; it doesn't make sense to try transforming the data before fetching it, for example. Similarly, we can't push any new data to the dashboard until it has undergone the required transformations. As such, we need to make sure that we enforce the implicit task order when running this data process.

1.1.1 Drawing a pipeline as a graph

One way to make dependencies between tasks more explicit is to draw the data pipeline as a graph. In this graph-based representation, tasks are represented as nodes in the graph, and dependencies between tasks are represented by directed edges between the task nodes. The direction of the edge indicates the direction of the dependency, with an edge pointing from task 1 to task 2 indicating that task 1 needs to be completed before task 2 can start.

Applying this graph representation to our weather dashboard pipeline, we see that the graph provides a relatively intuitive representation of the overall pipeline (figure 1.2). Just by glancing at the graph, we see that our pipeline consists of three tasks, each corresponding to one of the outlined tasks. The direction of the edges clearly indicates the order in which the tasks need to be executed; we can simply follow the arrows to trace the execution.

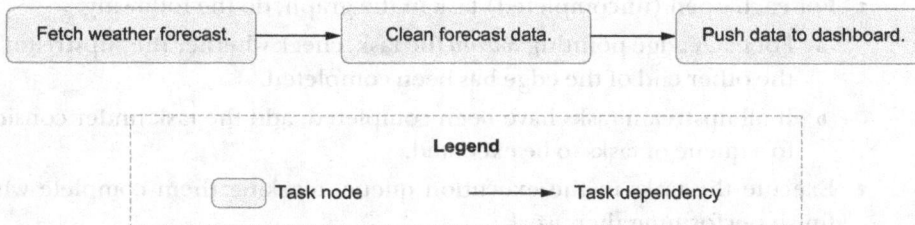

Figure 1.2   Graph representation of the data pipeline for the weather dashboard. Nodes represent tasks, and directed edges represent dependencies between tasks (with an edge pointing from task 1 to task 2, indicating that task 1 needs to be run before task 2).

This type of graph is typically called a *directed acyclic graph* (DAG) because the graph contains *directed* edges and does not contain any loops or cycles (*acyclic*). This acyclic property is extremely important as it prevents us from running into circular dependencies between tasks, where task A depends on task B and vice versa (figure 1.3). These circular dependencies become problematic when we try to execute the graph; we run into a situation where task 2 can execute only when task 3 has been completed, and task 3 can execute only when task 2 has

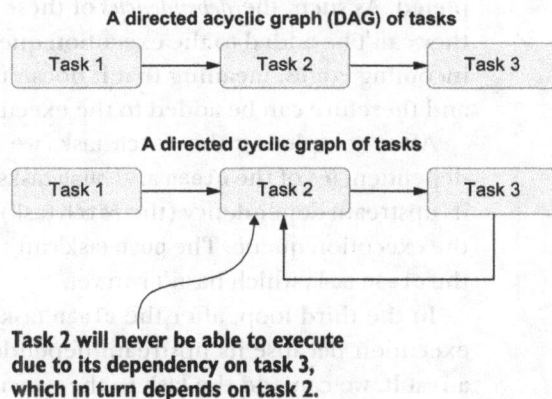

Figure 1.3   Cycles in graphs prevent task execution due to circular dependencies. Acyclic graphs (top) have a clear path to execute the three tasks. But cyclic graphs (bottom) no longer have a clear execution path due to the interdependency between tasks 2 and 3.

been completed. This logical inconsistency leads to a deadlock in which neither task 2 nor 3 can run, preventing us from executing the graph.

Cyclic graph representations can contain cycles to illustrate iterative parts of algorithms, for example, which are common in many machine learning (ML) applications; they're notably different from the acyclic graphs used in Airflow. But Airflow and many other workflow managers use the acyclic property of DAGs to resolve and execute these graphs of tasks efficiently.

1.1.2 Executing a pipeline graph

A nice property of the DAG representation in general is that it provides a relatively straightforward algorithm we can use to run the pipeline. Conceptually, this algorithm consists of the following steps:

1 For each open (uncompleted) task in the graph, do the following:

    a For each edge pointing *toward* the task, check whether the "upstream" task on the other end of the edge has been completed.

    b If all upstream tasks have been completed, add the task under consideration to a queue of tasks to be executed.

2 Execute the tasks in the execution queue, marking them complete when they finish performing their work.

3 Jump back to step 1 and repeat until all tasks in the graph have been completed.

To see how this works, let's trace a small execution of our dashboard pipeline (figure 1.4). On our first iteration (loop) through the steps of our algorithm, we see that the clean and push tasks still depend on upstream tasks that have not yet been completed. As such, the *dependencies* of these tasks have not been satisfied, so at this point, they can't be added to the execution queue. The fetch task, however, doesn't have any incoming edges, meaning that it doesn't have any unsatisfied upstream dependencies and therefore can be added to the execution queue.

After completing the fetch task, we can start the second loop by examining the dependencies of the clean and push tasks. Now the clean task can be executed because its upstream dependency (the fetch task) has been completed, so we can add the task to the execution queue. The push task can't be added to the queue because it depends on the clean task, which hasn't run yet.

In the third loop, after the clean task is complete, the push task is finally ready for execution because its upstream dependency on the clean task has been satisfied. As a result, we can add the task to the execution queue. When the push task finishes executing, we have no more tasks to execute, thus finishing the execution of the overall pipeline.

1.1.3 Pipeline graphs vs. sequential scripts

Although the graph representation of a pipeline provides an intuitive overview of the tasks in the pipeline and their dependencies, you may wonder why we wouldn't use a simple script to run this linear chain of three steps. To illustrate some advantages of the graph-based approach, let's jump to a slightly bigger example.

Loop 1

Task ready for execution; no unsatisfied dependencies

| Fetch weather forecast. | → | Clean forecast data. | → | Push data to dashboard. |

Loop 2

Task has finished execution.

Task is ready for execution as its upstream dependency is satisfied.

Not ready for execution yet; still has unsatisfied dependencies

| Fetch weather forecast. | ----> | Clean forecast data. | → | Push data to dashboard. |

Loop 3

Task has finished execution.

Task is ready for execution.

| Fetch weather forecast. | ----> | Clean forecast data. | ----> | Push data to dashboard. |

End state

| Fetch weather forecast. | ----> | Clean forecast data. | ----> | Push data to dashboard. |

Legend

| Open task | → Unsatisfied dependency |
| Completed task | ----> Satisfied dependency |

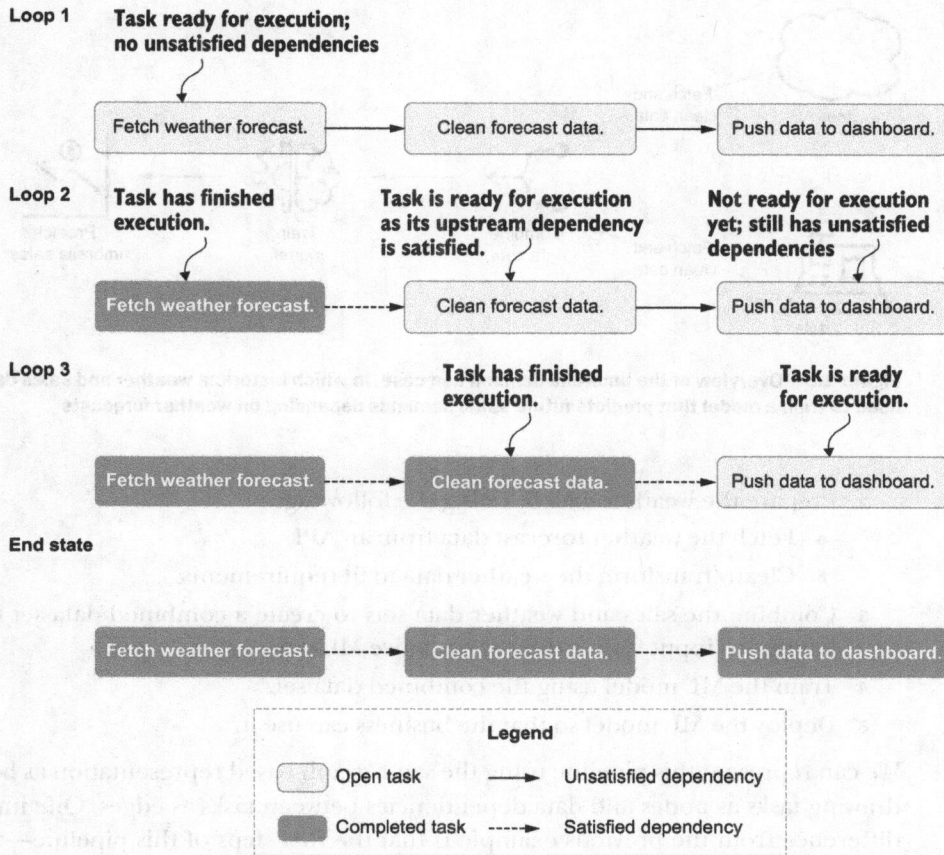

Figure 1.4 Using the DAG structure to execute tasks in the data pipeline in the correct order. The figure depicts each task's state during each loop through the algorithm, demonstrating how it leads to the completed execution of the pipeline (end state).

In this new use case, we've been approached by the owner of an umbrella company, who was inspired by our weather dashboard and wants to try to use ML to increase the efficiency of their operation. To do so, the company owner wants us to implement a data pipeline that creates an ML model correlating umbrella sales with weather patterns. This model can be used to predict how much demand there will be for the company's umbrellas in the coming weeks, depending on the weather forecasts for those weeks (figure 1.5).

To build a pipeline for training the ML model, we need to implement something like the following steps:

1 Prepare the sales data by doing the following:

 a Fetch the sales data from the source system.

 b Clean/transform the sales data to fit requirements.

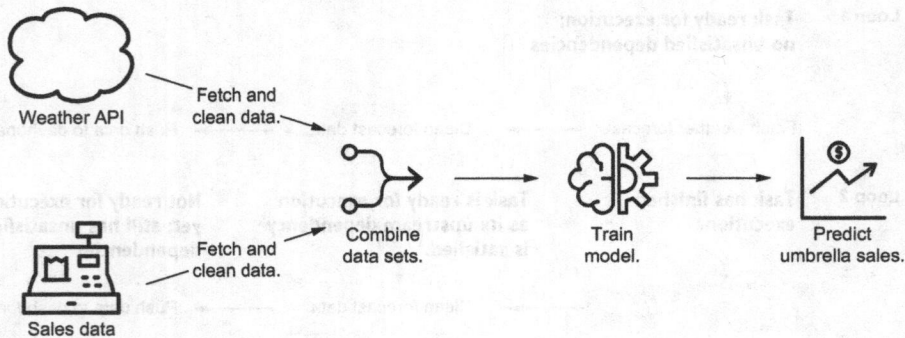

Figure 1.5   Overview of the umbrella-demand use case, in which historical weather and sales data are used to train a model that predicts future sales demands depending on weather forecasts

2 Prepare the weather data by doing the following:

  a Fetch the weather forecast data from an API.

  b Clean/transform the weather data to fit requirements.

3 Combine the sales and weather data sets to create a combined data set that can be used as input for creating a predictive ML model.

4 Train the ML model using the combined data set.

5 Deploy the ML model so that the business can use it.

We can represent this pipeline using the same graph-based representation as before by drawing tasks as nodes and data dependencies between tasks as edges. One important difference from the previous example is that the first steps of this pipeline—fetching and cleaning the weather/sales data—are in fact independent because they involve two separate data sets. This is clearly illustrated by the two separate branches in the graph representation of the pipeline (figure 1.6), which can be executed in parallel if we apply our graph execution algorithm, making better use of available resources and potentially decreasing the running time of a pipeline compared with executing the tasks sequentially.

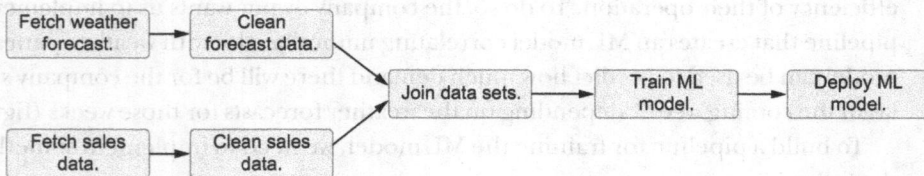

Figure 1.6   Independence between sales and weather tasks in the graph representation of the data pipeline for the umbrella-demand forecast model. The two sets of fetch/clean tasks are independent because they involve two different data sets (weather and sales). This independence is indicated by the lack of edges between the two sets of tasks.

Another useful property of the graph-based representation is that it clearly separates pipelines into small incremental tasks rather than having one monolithic script or process do all the work. Although having a single monolithic script may not initially seem like much of a problem, it can introduce inefficiencies when tasks in the pipeline fail because we'd have to rerun the entire script. By contrast, in the graph representation, we need to rerun only tasks that failed (and any downstream dependencies).

1.1.4 Running pipelines using workflow managers

The challenge of running graphs of dependent tasks is hardly a new problem in computing. Over the years, many workflow management solutions have been developed to tackle this problem, generally allowing you to define and execute graphs of tasks as workflows or pipelines. Table 1.1 lists some well-known workflow managers you may have heard of.

Table 1.1 Well-known workflow managers and their key characteristics

Name	Originated at[a]	Workflows defined in	Written in	Scheduling	Backfilling	User interface[b]	Installation platform	Horizontally scalable
Airflow	Airbnb	Python	Pythonn	Yes	Yes	Yes	Anywhere	Yes
Argo	Applatix	YAML	Go	Yes	No	Yes	Kubernetes	Yes
Azkaban	LinkedIn	YAML	Java	Yes	No	Yes	Anywhere	N/A
Conductor	Netflix	JSON	Java	Third party[c]	No	Yes	Anywhere	Yes
Dagster	Elementl	Python	Python	Yes	Yes	Yes	Anywhere	Yes
Luigi	Spotify	Python	Python	Yes	Yes	Yes	Anywhere	Yes
Make	Bell Labs	Custom DSL	C	No	No	No	Anywhere	No
Metaflow	Netflix	Python	Python	Third party[d]	No	No	Anywhere	Yes
Nifi	NSA	UI	Java	Yes	No	Yes	Anywhere	Yes
Oozie	Yahoo	XML	Java	Yes	Yes	Yes	Hadoop	Yes
Prefect	Prefect Technologies	Python	Python	Yes	Yes	Yes	Anywhere	Yes
Temporal	Uber (Cadance)	Multiple languages	Go	Yes	Yes	Yes	Anywhere	Yes
ControlM	BMC	Python/ JSON	Multiple languages	Yes	Yes	Yes	Anywhere	N/A

[a] Some tools were created by (ex-)employees of a company, but all tools are open source and not represented by a single company.
[b] The quality and features of user interfaces vary widely.
[c] https://github.com/jas34/scheduledwf.
[d] Managed with Argo Workflows.

Although these workflow managers have their own strengths and weaknesses, they all provide similar core functionality that allows you to define and run pipelines containing multiple tasks with dependencies. One key difference between these tools is how they define their workflows. Tools such as Oozie use static (XML) files to define workflows; they provide legible workflows but limited flexibility. Other solutions, such as Luigi and Airflow, allow you to define workflows as code, which provides greater flexibility but can be more challenging to read and test (depending on the coding skills of the person implementing the workflow).

Other key differences lie in the extent of features provided by the workflow manager. Tools such as Make and custom scripts don't provide built-in support for scheduling workflows, meaning that you'll need an extra tool like cron if you want to run your workflow on a recurring schedule. Other tools provide extra functionality, such as monitoring and user-friendly web interfaces built into the platform, so you don't have to stitch together multiple tools to get these features.

All in all, picking the right workflow management solution for your needs requires some careful consideration of the key features of the solutions and how they fit your requirements. In the next section, we'll dive into Airflow and explore the key features that make it particularly suitable for handling data-oriented workflows or pipelines.

1.2 Introducing Airflow

Airflow is an open source solution for developing and monitoring workflows. Let's take a bird's-eye view of what Airflow does, after which we'll jump into a detailed examination of whether it's a good fit for your use case.

1.2.1 Defining pipelines flexibly in (Python) code

Like other workflow managers, Airflow allows you to define pipelines or workflows as DAGs of tasks. These graphs are similar to the examples sketched earlier in this chapter, with tasks defined as nodes in the graph and dependencies defined as directed edges between tasks.

In Airflow, you define your DAGs using Python code in *DAG files*, which are essentially Python scripts that describe the structure of the corresponding DAG. Airflow 3 introduced the option of using programming languages other than Python. (An experimental SDK for Golang is available with the Airflow 3 release.) Python, however, is still Airflow's primary language and the language in which most of Airflow itself is written. For this reason, we will use Python as the primary language throughout this book.

Each DAG file typically describes the set of tasks for a given DAG and the dependencies between the tasks, which Airflow parses to identify the DAG structure (figure 1.7). DAG files also typically contain some metadata about the DAG telling Airflow how and when it should be executed. We'll dive into scheduling more in section 1.2.3.

One advantage of defining Airflow DAGs in code is that this programmatic approach gives you a lot of flexibility for building DAGs. As you'll see in chapter 12, you can use Python code to generate optional tasks dynamically depending on certain conditions

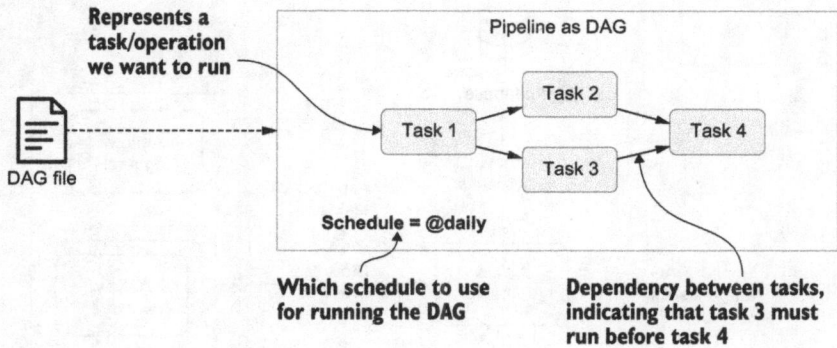

Figure 1.7 Airflow pipelines are defined as DAGs using Python code in DAG files. Each DAG file typically defines one DAG, which describes the tasks and their dependencies. The DAG also defines a schedule interval that determines when Airflow executes the DAG.

or even generate entire DAGs based on external metadata or configuration files. This flexibility allows you to fit Airflow to your needs when building arbitrarily complex pipelines.

1.2.2 Integrating with external systems

In addition to the flexibility of using code to define pipelines, another advantage of Airflow's Python foundation is that tasks can execute any operation you can implement in Python. Over time, this has led to the development of many Airflow external providers. These providers enable you to execute tasks across a wide variety of systems, including external databases, big data technologies, and various cloud services. They allow you to build complex data pipelines that bring together data processes from many systems.

1.2.3 Scheduling and executing pipelines

After you've defined the structure of your pipeline as a DAG, Airflow allows you to define a schedule for your DAG to determine exactly when Airflow will run your pipeline. This way, you can tell Airflow to execute your DAG every hour, every day, every week, and so on or even use more complicated schedules based on cron-like expressions.

To see how Airflow executes your DAGs, let's briefly look at the overall process involved in developing and running Airflow DAGs. At a high level, Airflow is organized into five main components (figure 1.8):

- *DAG processor*—Parses DAGs and serializes them into the Airflow metastore (metadata database) via the Airflow API server.
- *Scheduler*—Checks DAGs' schedule and, if the DAGs' scheduled time has passed, starts scheduling the DAGs' tasks for execution by passing them to the Airflow workers.

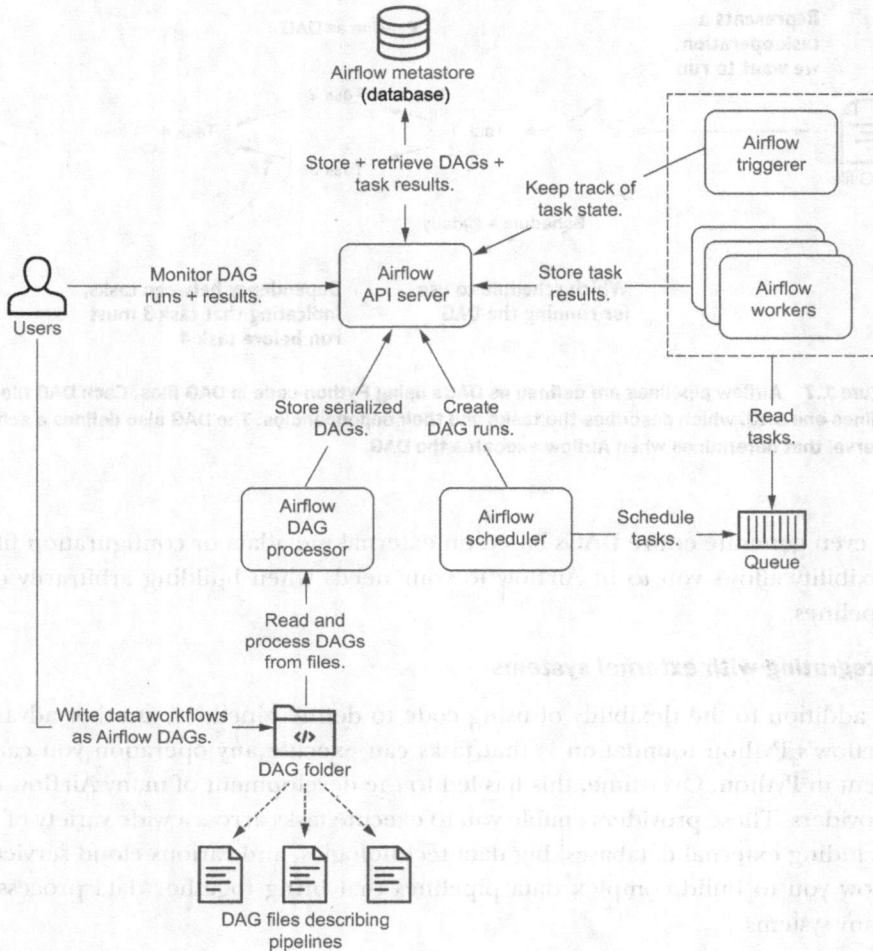

Figure 1.8   The main components involved in Airflow are the API server, scheduler, DAG processor, triggerer, and workers.

- *Workers*—Picks up tasks that are scheduled for execution and execute them. The workers are responsible for doing the actual work.

- *Triggerer*—Checks task-completion status for tasks that support asynchronous processing, allowing Airflow to check for specific conditions in the background.

- *API server*—Serves as the main interface where users can visualize DAGs and monitor DAG runs and their results. In addition, the API server functions as the gateway for other Airflow components that need to read or write from/to the Airflow metastore. All database interaction should be done via the Airflow API server.

The heart of Airflow is arguably the scheduler, which is where most of the magic happens that determines when and how your pipelines are executed. The scheduler is a continuously running process that, at a high level, runs through the following steps (figure 1.9):

1 When users have written their workflows as DAGs, the DAG processor reads the files containing these DAGs to extract the corresponding tasks, dependencies, and schedule interval for each DAG. The result is stored in the Airflow metastore.

2 For each DAG, the scheduler checks whether the schedule interval has passed since the previous time check. If so, the tasks in the DAG are scheduled for execution.

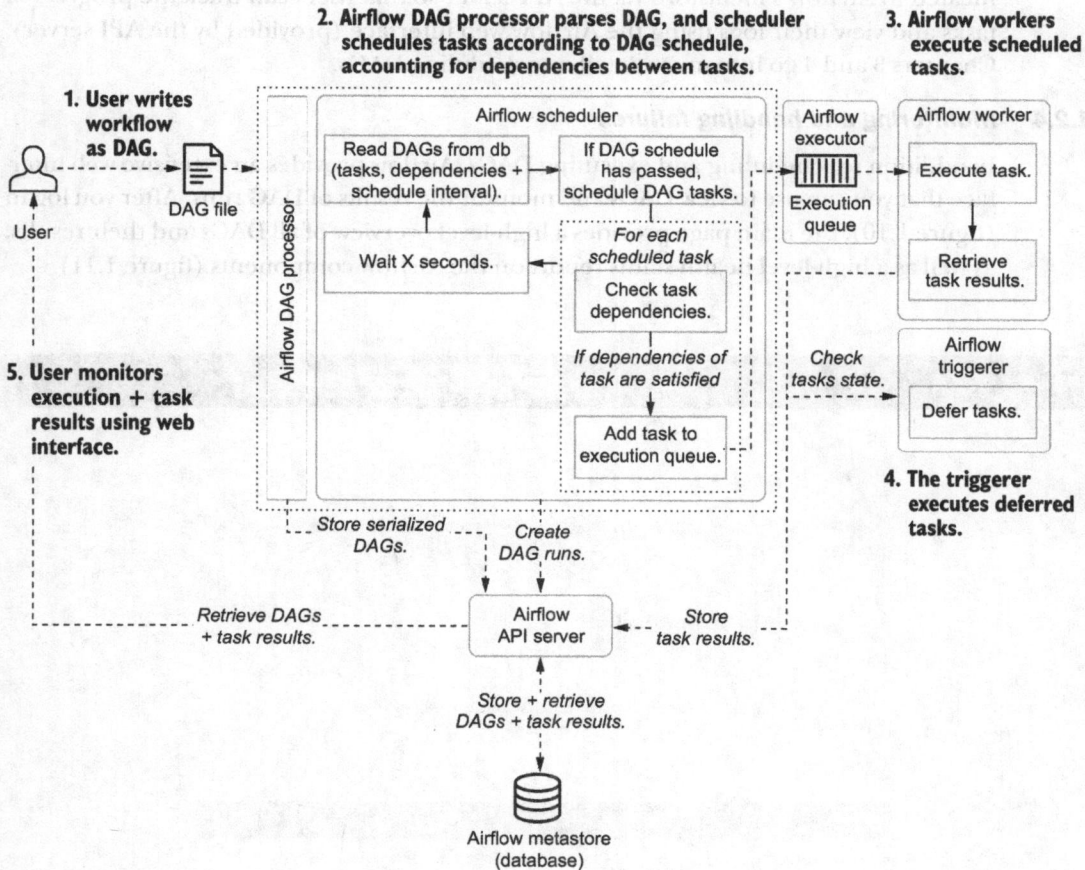

Figure 1.9 Developing and executing pipelines as DAGs using Airflow. When the user has written the DAG, the DAG processor and scheduler ensure that it is run at the right moment. The user can monitor progress and output at all times while the DAG is running.

3 For each scheduled task, the scheduler checks whether the dependencies (upstream tasks) of the task have been completed. If so, the task is added to the execution queue.

4 If tasks depend on external resources to complete, some of them can be deferred to the triggerer, making workers available for tasks that are ready to run.

5 The scheduler starts a new loop by jumping back to step 2.

The astute reader may have noticed that the steps followed by the scheduler are similar to the algorithm introduced in section 1.1. This similarity is no accident. Airflow is essentially following the same steps, adding some extra logic on top to handle its scheduling logic.

When tasks have been queued for execution, they're picked up by a pool of Airflow workers that execute tasks in parallel and track their results. These results are communicated to Airflow's metastore via the API server so that users can track the progress of tasks and view their logs using the Airflow web interface (provided by the API server). Chapters 3 and 4 go into more detail on scheduling DAGs.

1.2.4   *Monitoring and handling failures*

In addition to scheduling and executing DAGs, Airflow provides an extensive web interface that you can use to view DAGs and monitor the results of DAG runs. After you log in (figure 1.10), the main page provides a high-level overview of all DAGs and their results, as well as a high-level health status report on the Airflow components (figure 1.11).

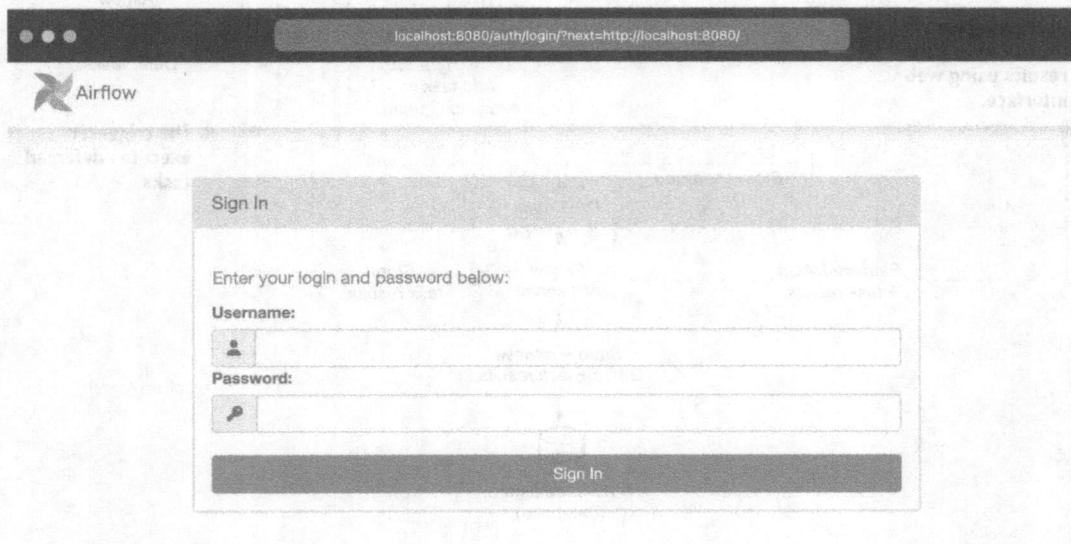

Figure 1.10   The login page for the Airflow web interface. In the code examples accompanying this book, a default user airflow is provided with the password *airflow*.

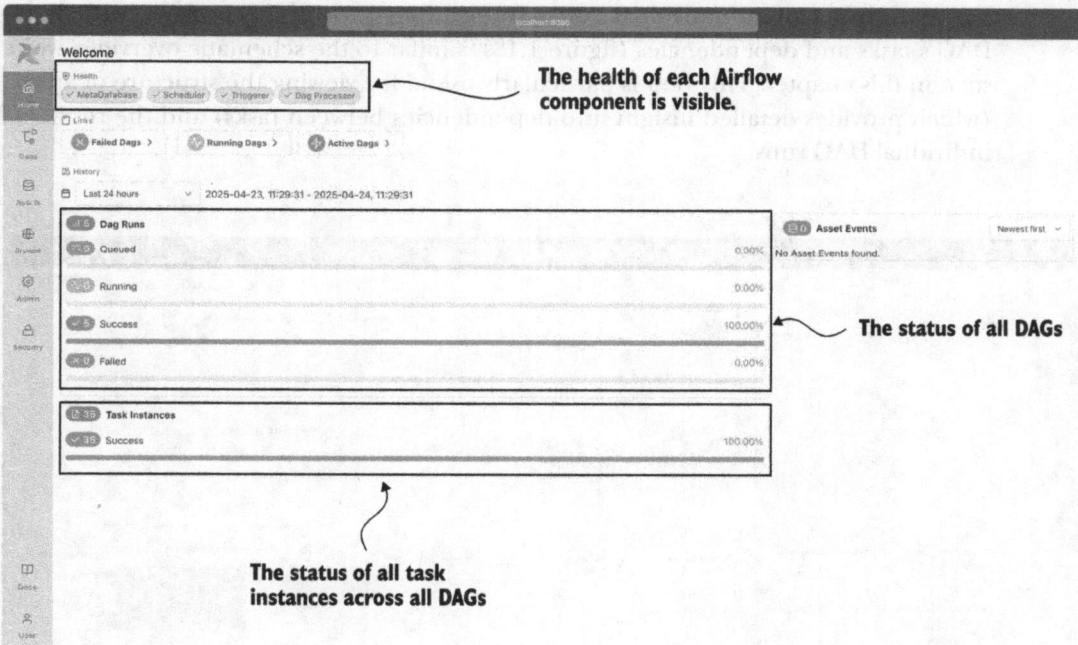

The health of each Airflow component is visible.

The status of all DAGs

The status of all task instances across all DAGs

Figure 1.11 The main page of Airflow's web interface, showing a high-level overview of all DAGs and their recent results

When you click the Dags tab in the left menu bar, you see the overview page of all DAGs in Airflow (figure 1.12). On this page, you can click a specific DAG to get information about its runs.

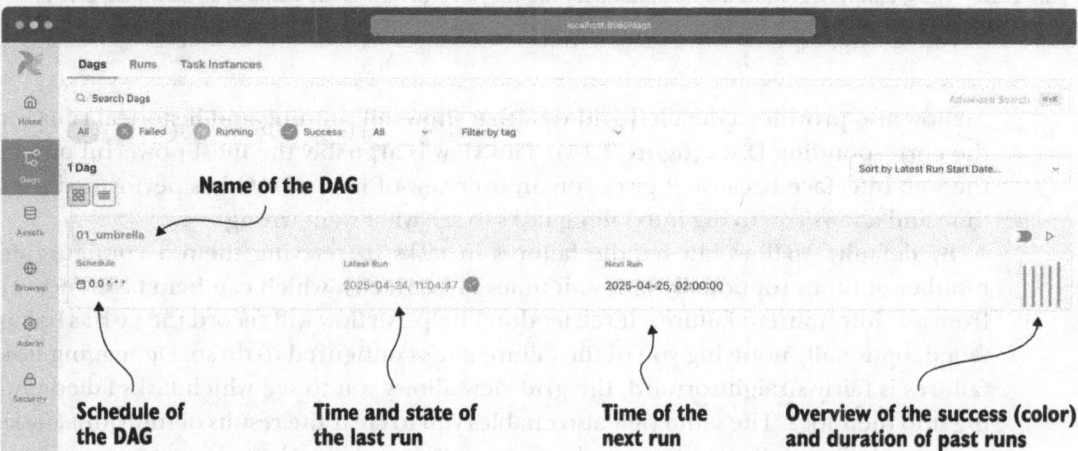

Name of the DAG

Schedule of the DAG

Time and state of the last run

Time of the next run

Overview of the success (color) and duration of past runs

Figure 1.12 The Dags tab of Airflow's web interface, showing a high-level overview of all DAGs and their recent results

The graph view of an individual DAG, for example, provides a clear overview of the DAG's tasks and dependencies (figure 1.13), similar to the schematic overviews we've seen in this chapter. This view is particularly useful for viewing the structure of a DAG (which provides detailed insight into dependencies between tasks) and the results of individual DAG runs.

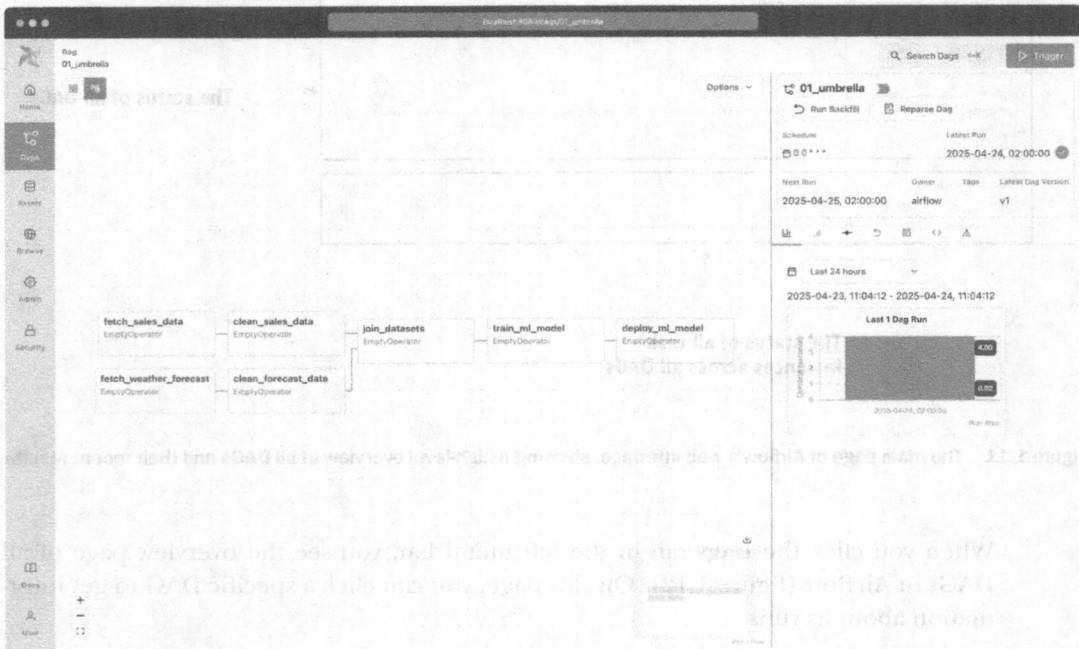

Figure 1.13   The graph view in Airflow's web interface, showing an overview of the tasks in an individual DAG and the dependencies between these tasks

Airflow also provides a detailed grid view that shows all running and historical runs for the corresponding DAG (figure 1.14). This view is arguably the most powerful one in the web interface because it gives you an overview of how a DAG has performed over time and allows you to dig into failing tasks to see what went wrong.

By default, Airflow can handle failures in tasks by retrying them a configurable number of times (optionally with wait times in between), which can help tasks recover from any intermittent failures. If retries don't help, Airflow will record the task as being failed, optionally notifying you of the failure if it's configured to do so. Debugging task failures is fairly straightforward; the grid view allows you to see which tasks failed and dig into their logs. The same view also enables you to clear the results of individual tasks to rerun them together with any tasks that depend on that task, making it easy to rerun tasks after you make changes in their code.

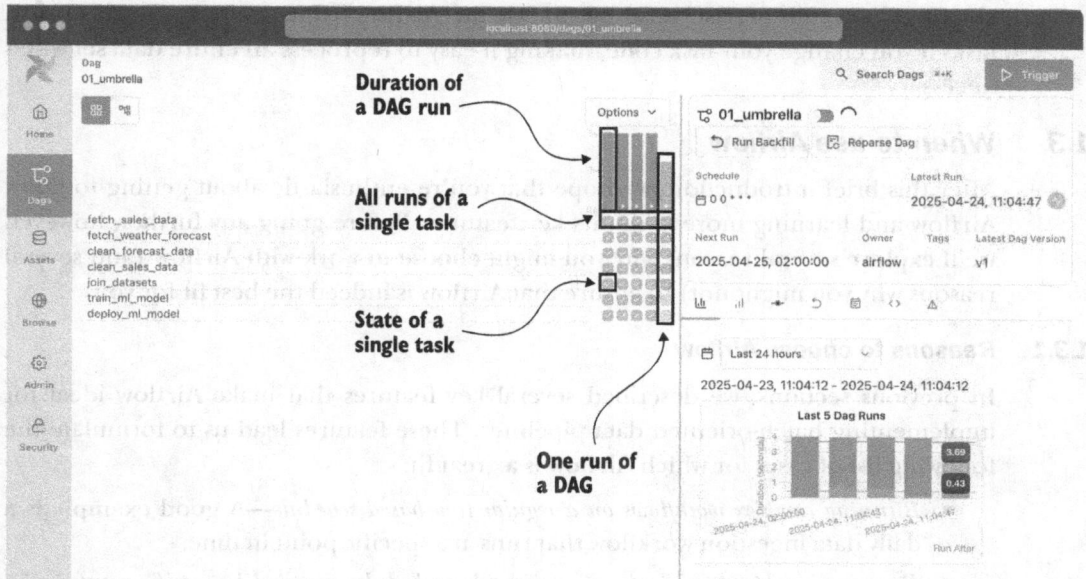

Figure 1.14   Airflow's grid view, showing the results of multiple runs of the umbrella sales model DAG (most recent plus historical runs). The columns show the status of one execution of the DAG, and the rows show the status of all executions of a single task. Colors (which you can see in the e-book version) indicate the result of the corresponding task. Users can also click the task squares to see details on a given task instance or to manage the state of a task so that Airflow can rerun it.

1.2.5   *Incremental loading and backfilling*

One powerful feature of Airflow's scheduling semantics is that the schedule not only triggers DAGs at specific time points (similar to `cron`, for example) but also provides details about the last and next (expected) schedule intervals. This essentially allows you to divide time into discrete intervals (e.g., every day, week, and so on) and run your DAG for each of these intervals. If this sounds a bit abstract to you now, don't worry; we provide more detail on these concepts later in the book.

This property of Airflow's schedule intervals is invaluable for implementing efficient data pipelines because it allows you to build incremental data pipelines. In these incremental pipelines, each DAG run processes only data for the corresponding time slot (the data's *delta*, which is data that changed since the last interval) instead of reprocessing the entire data set every time. Especially for larger data sets, this can provide significant time and cost benefits by eliminating expensive reprocessing of existing results.

Schedule intervals become even more powerful when combined with the concept of *backfilling*, which allows you to execute a DAG for schedule intervals that occurred in the past. This feature makes it easy to create (or *backfill*) new data sets with historical data simply by running your DAG for these past schedule intervals. Moreover, by clearing the results of past runs, you can use this Airflow feature to rerun any historical tasks if you change your task code, making it easy to reprocess an entire data set when necessary.

1.3   When to use Airflow

After this brief introduction, we hope that you're enthusiastic about getting to know Airflow and learning more about its key features. Before going any further, however, we'll explore several reasons why you might choose to work with Airflow (and several reasons why you might not) to ensure that Airflow is indeed the best fit for you.

1.3.1   Reasons to choose Airflow

In previous sections, we described several key features that make Airflow ideal for implementing batch-oriented data pipelines. These features lead us to formulate the following list of cases for which Airflow is a great fit:

- *Running complex workflows on a regular time-based schedule*—A good example is a daily data ingestion workflow that runs at a specific point in time.
- *Running complex workflows on an irregular schedule, triggered by specific events rather than exact moments*—Good examples include data transfers that run erratically and workflows that need to run during specific holidays.
- *Using predefined intervals of time to interact with data sets*—This concept is a powerful one. Airflow provides time intervals to your workflow, allowing you to bucket your data into discrete intervals.
- *Integrating with a wide variety of external systems*—Airflow has a large set of integrations and extensions for all kinds of systems. With its Python foundation, Airflow also makes it relatively easy to extend and customize these integrations if necessary. Good examples are integrations with various database systems (such as PostgreSQL) and cloud provider services (such as Google's BigQuery).
- *Applying software engineering best practices to your workflows*—Airflow's base idea is that workflows in which multiple pieces of software are defined and run are code themselves too.
- *Backfilling previous workflow executions*—This task is easy to handle with Airflow, allowing you to recompute any data sets after making changes to your code.

An additional advantage of Airflow is that it is open source, which guarantees that you can build your work in Airflow without getting stuck with any vendor. Also, Airflow has been around for a while and is an actively maintained open source solution that many reputable companies use in production. It has proved to scale well for enterprise workloads and is designed for production use cases. Managed Airflow solutions are available from several companies (should you desire some technical support), giving you a lot of flexibility in how you run and manage your Airflow installation.

1.3.2 Reasons not to choose Airflow

Although Airflow has many rich features, several of its design choices may make it less suitable for certain cases, including the following:

- *Use of streaming pipelines*—Airflow is designed primarily to run recurring or batch-oriented tasks rather than streaming workloads. An example is processing website click streams containing user clicks on a website. Airflow is a great fit for processing that kind of data set in bulk but not for processing individual events in real time.

- *Teams with little or no programming experience*—Implementing DAGs in code can be daunting. For such teams, using a workflow manager with a graphical interface (such as Microsoft Azure Data Factory) or a static workflow definition may make more sense.

- *Large use cases*—Similarly, code in DAGs can quickly become complex for larger use cases. Implementing and maintaining Airflow DAGs requires proper engineering rigor to keep things maintainable in the long run. Examples include using reusable DAGs and modularizing tasks, which are Airflow versions of common software engineering best practices such as DRY (Don't Repeat Yourself) and SRP (Single Responsibility Principle). Also, Airflow is primarily a workflow/pipeline management platform and currently doesn't include extensive features such as maintaining data lineages and data versioning. Should you require these features, you'll probably need to look at combining Airflow with specialized tools that provide those capabilities.

NOTE Recent versions of Airflow support OpenLineage (https://mng.bz/gm9G).

1.4 The rest of this book

By now, we hope that you have a good idea of what Airflow is and how its features can help you implement and run data pipelines. In the remainder of part 1, we'll introduce the basic components of Airflow that you need to be familiar with to start building your own data pipelines. These chapters should be broadly applicable and appealing to a wide audience. We expect you to have intermediate experience with programming in Python (about one year of experience), meaning that you're familiar with basic concepts such as string formatting, comprehensions, and args/kwargs. You should also be familiar with the basics of the Linux terminal and have a basic working knowledge of databases (including SQL) and data formats.

In parts 2 and 3, we'll dive into advanced features of Airflow, such as generating dynamic DAGs, implementing your own operators, and running containerized tasks. These chapters require more understanding of the technologies involved, including custom Python classes, basic Docker concepts, file formats, and data partitioning. We expect these parts to be of special interest to the data engineers in the audience.

Finally, part 4 focuses on topics surrounding the deployment of Airflow, including deployment patterns, monitoring, security, and cloud architectures. We expect these chapters to be of special interest to people who are interested in rolling out and managing Airflow deployments, such as system administrators and DevOps engineers.

Summary

- DAGs are visual tools that represent data workflows in data processing pipelines. A node in a DAG denotes the task to be performed, and edges define the dependencies between them. This system is not only more understandable visually but also enables better representation, easier debugging and rerunning, and the use of parallelism instead of single monolithic scripts.

- In Airflow, DAGs are defined using Python files. Airflow 3 introduced the option of using other languages. This book focuses on Python, however. These scripts outline the order of task execution and their interdependencies. Airflow parses these files to construct and understand the DAG's structure, enabling task orchestration and scheduling.

- Although many workflow managers have been developed for executing graphs of tasks, Airflow has several key features that make it uniquely well suited to implement efficient, batch-oriented data pipelines.

- Airflow excels as a workflow orchestration tool due to its intuitive design, scheduling capabilities, and extensible framework. It provides a rich user interface for monitoring and managing tasks in data processing workflows.

- Airflow has five key components:
  - *DAG processor*—Reads and parses the DAGs and stores the resulting serialized version of these DAGs in the metastore for use by (among others) the scheduler
  - *Scheduler*—Reads the DAGs parsed by the DAG processor, determines whether their schedule intervals have elapsed, and queues their tasks for execution
  - *Workers*—Executes the tasks assigned by the scheduler
  - *Triggerer*—Handles the execution of deferred tasks, which are waiting for external events or conditions
  - *API server*—Presents a user interface for visualizing and monitoring the DAGs and their execution status; also acts as the interface between Airflow components

- Airflow enables you to set a schedule for each DAG, specifying when the pipeline should be executed. In addition, Airflow's built-in mechanisms manage task failures automatically.

- Airflow is well suited for batch-oriented data pipelines, offering sophisticated scheduling options that enable regular, incremental data processing jobs. On the other hand, Airflow is not the right choice for streaming workloads or highly dynamic pipelines in which the DAG structure changes from day to day.

Anatomy of an Airflow DAG

This chapter covers

- Running Airflow on your own machine
- Writing and running your first workflow
- Examining the first view in the Airflow interface
- Handling failed tasks in Airflow

By now, you have a decent overview-level understanding of what data pipelines are and how Airflow can help you manage them. To get a feeling for how this works in practice, let's get our hands dirty on a small example pipeline that demonstrates the basic building blocks of many workflows.

2.1 *Collecting data from numerous sources*

Rockets are among humanity's engineering marvels, and every rocket launch attracts attention around the world. Our friend John is a rocket enthusiast who tracks and follows every rocket launch. News about rocket launches appears in many news sources that John keeps track of, and ideally, he'd like all his rocket news aggregated in a single location. John recently picked up programming and wants an automated way to collect information about all rocket launches and eventually gain some personal insight into the latest rocket news. To start small, he decided to collect images of rockets first.

For the data, we'll use Launch Library 2 (https://thespacedevs.com/llapi), an online repository of data about both historical and future rocket launches from various sources. It's a free API, open to anybody on the planet (subject to rate limits).

Currently, John is interested only in upcoming rocket launches. Luckily, Launch Library provides exactly the data he's looking for (https://ll.thespacedevs.com/2.0.0/launch/upcoming). It provides data about upcoming rocket launches and URLs to images of the respective rockets. The following listing shows the data this URL returns.

Listing 2.1   Example curl request and response to the Launch Library API

The response is a JSON document, as you see by the structure.

Inspects the URL response with curl from the command line

```
$ curl -L "https://ll.thespacedevs.com/2.0.0/launch/upcoming"

{
  ...
  "results": [
    {
      "id": "9603b3c2-da94-41c6-8012-30e990fdc999",
      "url": "https://.../9603b3c2-da94-41c6-8012-30e990fdc999/",
      "launch_library_id": null,
      "slug": "falcon-9-block-5-starlink-group-7-14",
      "name": "Falcon 9 Block 5 | Starlink Group 7-14",
      "status": { "id": 2, "name": "TBD"},
      "net": "2024-02-13T22:17:00Z",
      "window_end": "2024-02-14T02:46:00Z",
      "window_start": "2024-02-13T22:17:00Z"
      "image": "https://spacelaunchnow-prod-east.nyc3.digitaloceanspaces.com
/media/launcher_images/falcon_9_image_20230807133459.jpeg",
      ...
    },
    {
      "id": "d9a3c8e1-bc0d-4fab-a04c-218ffe44a026",
      "url": "https://.../d9a3c8e1-bc0d-4fab-a04c-218ffe44a026/",
      "launch_library_id": null,
      "slug": "gslv-mk-ii-insat-3ds",
      "name": "GSLV Mk II | INSAT-3DS",
      "status": { "id": 1, "name": "Go" },
      "net": "2024-02-17T12:00:00Z",
      "window_end": "2024-02-17T15:30:00Z",
      "window_start": "2024-02-17T11:30:00Z",
      "image": "https://spacelaunchnow-prod-east.nyc3.digitaloceanspaces.com
/media/launcher_images/gslv2520mk2520ii_image_20190825171642.jpg",
      ...
    },
    ...
  ]
}
```

The square brackets indicate a list.

All values within these curly braces refer to a single rocket launch.

Here, we see information such as rocket ID and start and end time of the rocket-launch window.

URL to an image of the launching rocket

As you see, the data is in JSON format and provides rocket-launch information, and for every launch, there's information about the specific rocket, such as ID, name, and image URL. This data is exactly what John needs. Initially, he draws the plan in figure 2.1 to collect the images of upcoming rocket launches (e.g., to point his screensaver to the directory that holds these images).

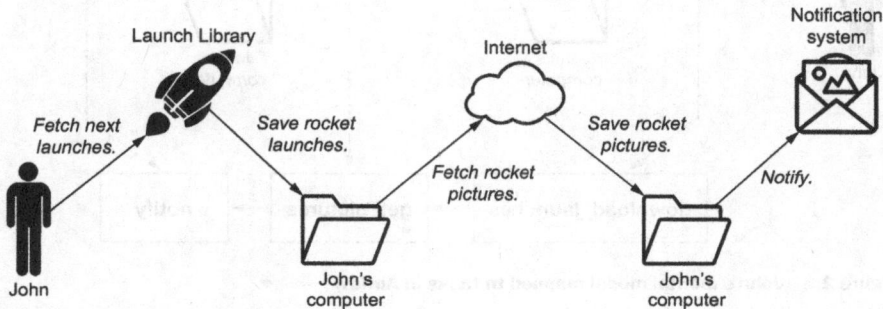

Figure 2.1 John's mental model of downloading rocket pictures

Based on the example in figure 2.1, we see that at the end of the day, John's goal is to have a directory filled with rocket images, such as the image in figure 2.2 of the Ariane 5 ECA rocket.

2.2 *Writing your first Airflow DAG*

John's use case is nicely scoped, so let's check out how to program his plan. It's only a few steps, and in theory, with some Bash-fu, you could work it out in a one-liner. So why would we need a system like Airflow for this job?

The nice thing about Airflow is that it lets us split a large job, consisting of one or more steps, into individual tasks that together form a directed acyclic graph (DAG). Multiple tasks can be run in parallel, and tasks can run different technologies. We could run a Bash script first and then a Python script, for example. Figure 2.3 breaks John's mental model of his workflow into three logical tasks in Airflow.

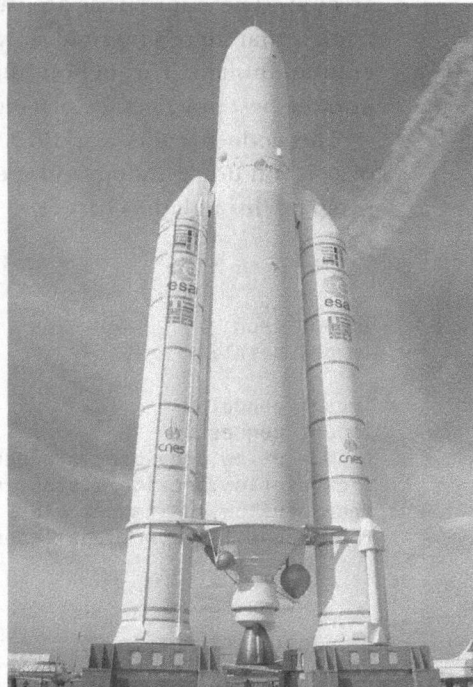

Figure 2.2   Example image of the Ariane 5 ECA rocket

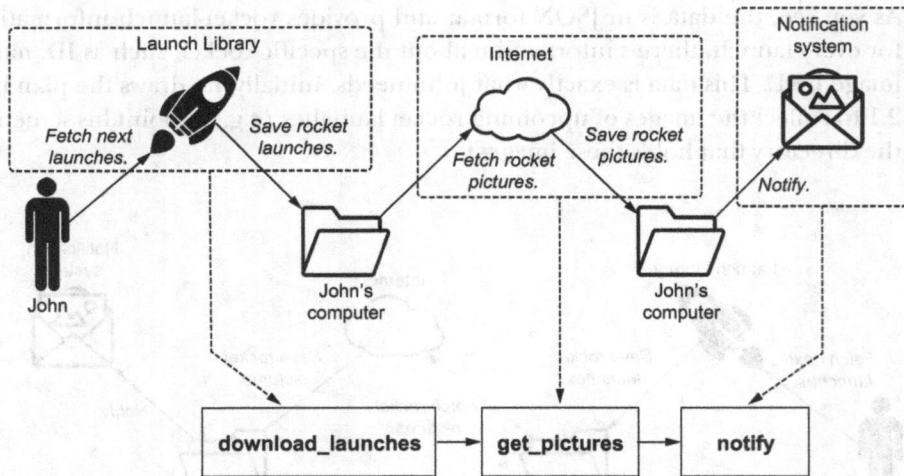

Figure 2.3   John's mental model mapped to tasks in Airflow

Why these three tasks, you ask? Why not download the launches and corresponding pictures in one single task or split them into five tasks (because John's plan has five arrows)? These questions are valid ones to ask while developing a workflow, but the truth is that there's no right or wrong answer. We must take several points into consideration, though. Throughout this book, we'll work out many use cases to gain insight into the best practices for placing task boundaries when defining a new data pipeline.

The code for this workflow follows (dags/01_download_rocket_launches.py). It's okay if you don't understand every part of this code. We'll provide explanations as we progress through the chapter.

Listing 2.2   DAG for downloading and processing rocket-launch data

```
import json
import pathlib

import pendulum
import requests
from airflow.providers.standard.operators.bash import BashOperator
from airflow.providers.standard.operators.python import PythonOperator
from airflow.sdk import DAG
from requests.exceptions import ConnectionError, MissingSchema


def _get_pictures():
    # Ensure directory exists
    pathlib.Path("/tmp/images").mkdir(parents=True, exist_ok=True)

    # Download all pictures in launches.json
```

Python function that parses the response and downloads all rocket pictures

```
with open("/tmp/launches.json") as f:
    launches = json.load(f)
    image_urls = [launch["image"] for launch in launches["results"]]
    for image_url in image_urls:
        try:
            response = requests.get(image_url)
            image_filename = image_url.split("/")[-1]
            target_file = f"/tmp/images/{image_filename}"
            with open(target_file, "wb") as f:
                f.write(response.content)
            print(f"Downloaded {image_url} to {target_file}")
        except MissingSchema:
            print(f"{image_url} appears to be an invalid URL.")
        except ConnectionError:
            raise ConnectionError(f"Could not connect to {image_url}.")
```

```
with DAG(                                          ◀──  Instantiates a DAG object. This is
    dag_id="01_download_rocket_launches",               the starting point of any workflow.
    start_date=pendulum.today('UTC').add(days=-14),  ◀──
    schedule=None,          ◀── The interval at which      The name
):                              the DAG should run          of the DAG
                                                        The date on which the
                                                        DAG should start running
    download_launches = BashOperator(
        task_id="download_launches",     ◀── The name of the task
        bash_command="curl -o /tmp/launches.json
            -L 'https://ll.thespacedevs.com/2.0.0/launch/upcoming'",
    )

    get_pictures = PythonOperator(
        task_id="get_pictures",          Task that calls the Python
        python_callable=_get_pictures,   function _get_images
    )

    notify = BashOperator(
        task_id="notify",
        bash_command='echo "There are $(ls /tmp/images/ | wc -l) images."',
    )
                                         Airflow syntax that sets the
    download_launches >> get_pictures >> notify  ◀──  execution order of the tasks
```

Task that uses Bash to download the URL response with curl

Let's break down the workflow. The DAG is the starting point of any workflow. All tasks within the workflow reference this DAG object so that Airflow knows which tasks belong to which DAG.

In broad terms, three mainstream methods define a DAG in Airflow: the explicit definition, the context-manager approach, and the Taskflow API. Each method has advantages and disadvantages; the choice often depends on the user's specific needs and preferences.

The explicit definition of a DAG (figure 2.4) offers a straightforward approach, making it clear (especially to users who have no Python knowledge) which task is linked to the DAG. But this method is more verbose because it requires passing the DAG object to each task, which can lead to cluttered code and expose us to the risk of forgetting to provide the DAG argument, potentially causing errors in the workflow.

Explicit definition	Context manager
| ```
dag = DAG(…):
task1 = PythonOperator(…,dag=dag)
task2 = BashOperator(…,dag=dag)
task3 = HttpOperator(…,dag=dag)
``` | ```
with DAG(…):
    task1 = PythonOperator(…)
    task2 = BashOperator(…)
    task3 = HttpOperator(…)
``` |

Figure 2.4   Explicit definition of a DAG compared with the same definition in a context manager

On the other hand, using a context manager to define a DAG leads to less verbose code, reducing the risk of errors because there's no need to remember to pass the DAG object to each task. This option isn't without disadvantages, however. The scope of a context manager is limited to defining one DAG, which can be restrictive if multiple workflows must be defined. Also, it may be less clear to those who are unfamiliar with this Python feature.

NOTE   A context manager in Python is identifiable because it starts with the 'with' keyword. It's a Python class that manages resources using two methods: __enter__() to set up resources and __exit__() to release them. It ensures safe handling of resources even when errors occur and is commonly used to manage files, threads, or database connections.

A third method of defining a DAG in Airflow is the newer Taskflow API, which we cover in detail in chapter 6. For the purposes of this book, we'll primarily take the context-manager approach. The following listing defines the DAG object for our project using context-manager syntax (dags/02_download_rocket_launches.py).

Listing 2.3   Instantiating a DAG object

```
with DAG(
    dag_id=02_download_rocket_launches",
    start_date=pendulum.today('UTC').add(days=-14),
    schedule=None,
):
```

The DAG class takes two required arguments.

The name of the DAG displayed in the Airflow user interface (UI)

The datetime at which the workflow should start running

Let's break the DAG code into pieces to explain the important parts. First, we need to name our DAG. We can do this by providing a `dag_id`. Also note that we set `schedule` to `None`, so the DAG won't run automatically. For now, we can trigger it manually from the Airflow UI. We discuss scheduling in section 2.4.

Next, an Airflow workflow script consists of one or more tasks that perform the actual work. In the next listing, we apply the `BashOperator` to run a Bash command to download upcoming launches by calling the API (`dags/03_BashOperator.py`).

Listing 2.4 Instantiating a `BashOperator` to run a Bash command

```
download_launches = BashOperator(
    task_id="download_launches",                    ◄──┤ The name of the task
    bash_command="curl -o /tmp/launches.json
    ,https://ll.thespacedevs.com/2.0.0/launch/upcoming'",  ◄──┐ The Bash command
)                                                              │ to execute
```

Each task performs a single unit of work, and multiple tasks together form a workflow or DAG in Airflow. Tasks run independently, although we can define the order of execution, called *dependencies* in Airflow. After all, John's workflow wouldn't be useful if he tried downloading pictures while there's no data about the locations of the pictures. To make sure that the tasks run in the correct order, we can set dependencies between tasks.

Listing 2.5 Defining the order of task execution

```
download_launches >> get_pictures >> notify      ◄──┐ Arrows set the order
                                                     │ of execution of tasks.
```

In Airflow, we can use the *bitwise right shift operator* (`rshift [>>]`) or *bitwise left shift operator* (`lshift [<<]`) to define dependencies between tasks. This operator ensures that the `get_pictures` task runs only after `download_launches` has completed successfully, and the `notify` task runs only after `get_pictures` has completed successfully.

NOTE In Python, the `rshift (>>)` and `lshift (<<)` operators are used to shift bits, which is a common operation in cryptography libraries. In Airflow, there is no use case for bit shifting, so the operators are overridden to provide a readable way to define dependencies between tasks.

2.2.1 Tasks vs. operators

You may wonder about the difference between tasks and operators because they both execute a bit of code. In Airflow, *operators* have a single responsibility: they exist to perform one single piece of work. Some operators perform generic work, such as the `BashOperator` (used to run a Bash script) and the `PythonOperator` (used to run a Python function); others have specific use cases, such as the `EmailOperator` (used to send an email) and the HTTPOperator (used to call an HTTP endpoint or API). Either way, an operator performs a single piece of work.

> NOTE   For a complete list of operators, consult Airflow's Operators reference (https://mng.bz/eB0q).

The role of a DAG is to orchestrate the execution of a collection of operators, including starting and stopping operators, starting consecutive tasks when an operator is done, and ensuring that dependencies between operators are met. In this context and throughout the Airflow documentation, the terms *operator* and *task* are used interchangeably. From a user's perspective, they refer to the same thing, and the terms are often used interchangeably in discussions. Operators provide the implementation of a piece of work. Airflow has a class called BaseOperator, and many subclasses inherit from the BaseOperator, such as the PythonOperator, the EmailOperator, and the OracleOperator.

There's a difference, though. Tasks in Airflow manage the execution of an operator; they can be thought of as small wrappers around an operator or managers that ensure that the operator executes correctly. The wrapper role of a task involves handling errors, managing dependencies, and scheduling the execution of the operator. This separation of concerns allows users to focus on designing the work to be done by defining operators, whereas Airflow takes care of the execution details by using tasks (figure 2.5).

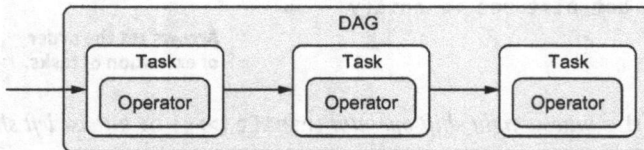

Figure 2.5   Airflow users employ both DAGs and operators. Tasks are internal components that manage operator state and display state changes (e.g., started/finished) to the user.

2.2.2   *Running arbitrary Python code*

Fetching the data for the next rocket launch is a single curl command in Bash, easily executed with the BashOperator. But the tasks of parsing the JSON result, selecting the image URLs from it, and downloading the respective images require a bit more effort. Although you can still perform all these tasks in a Bash one-liner, it's often easier (and more readable) to use a few lines of Python or the language of your choice. Because Airflow code is defined in Python, it's convenient to keep the workflow and execution logic in the same script. We implemented the following code to download the rocket pictures (dags/04_PythonOperator_get_pictures.py).

Listing 2.6 Running a Python function using the `PythonOperator`

```
def _get_pictures():                    ⬅── Python function to call      Creates pictures directory
    # Ensure directory exists                                            if it doesn't exist
    pathlib.Path("/tmp/images").mkdir(parents=True, exist_ok=True)   ⬅──

    # Download all pictures in launches.json      Opens the result from
    with open("/tmp/launches.json") as f:    ⬅──  the previous task
        launches = json.load(f)
        image_urls = [l["image"] for l in launches["results"]]
        for image_url in image_urls:
            try:
                response = requests.get(image_url)          ⬅── Downloads each image
                image_filename = image_url.split("/")[-1]
                target_file = f"/tmp/images/{image_filename}"
                with open(target_file, "wb") as f:          Stores each image
                    f.write(response.content)          ⬅──
                print(f"Downloaded {image_url} to {target_file}")   ⬅──
            except MissingSchema:
                print(f"{image_url} appears to be an invalid URL.")
            except ConnectionError:
                raise ConnectionError(f"Could not connect to {image_url}.")

                                    Instantiates a PythonOperator        Prints to
                                    to call the Python function          stdout. This
get_pictures = PythonOperator(   ⬅──                                     will be
    task_id="get_pictures",                                             captured in
    python_callable=_get_pictures,   ⬅──                               Airflow logs.
)                                       Points to the Python
                                        function to execute
```

The `PythonOperator` in Airflow is responsible for running any Python code. Like the `BashOperator`, this operator and all other operators require a `task_id`. The `task_id` serves as the primary task identifier across all Airflow operations (logging, dependencies, API calls, and so on) and is displayed in the UI. The use of a `PythonOperator` is always twofold:

- We define the operator (`get_pictures`).
- The `python_callable` argument points to a callable, typically a function (`_get_pictures`).

When we run the operator, the Python function is called and executes the function. Let's break it down. The basic use of the `PythonOperator` always looks like figure 2.6.

```
def _get_pictures():          ─┐
    # do work here ...         ├─ PythonOperator callable
get_pictures = PythonOperator(   ─┐
    task_id="get_pictures",       ├─ PythonOperator
    python_callable =_get_pictures,─┘
)
```

Figure 2.6 The python_callable argument in the PythonOperator points to a function to execute.

Although doing so isn't required, for convenience, we'll keep the variable name `get_pictures` equal to `task_id`. It's also good practice to keep the name of the Python function that is being called similar to the variable name. Because you can't name a variable and a function the same way, we use the underscore (`_`) as a prefix. The first step in the callable ensures that the directory in which the images will be stored exists.

Listing 2.7   Ensuring that the output directory exists and creating it if it doesn't

```
# Ensure directory exists
pathlib.Path("/tmp/images").mkdir(parents=True, exist_ok=True)
```

Next, we open the result downloaded from the Launch Library API and extract the image URLs for every launch.

Listing 2.8   Extracting image URLs for every rocket launch

```
with open("/tmp/launches.json") as f:          ◄─── Opens the rocket-launches JSON
    launches = json.load(f)
    image_urls = [l["image"] for l in launches["results"]]   ◄───  Reads as a
                                                                   dict so we
                                         For every launch, fetches   can mingle
                                         the element "image"         the data
```

Each image URL is called to download the image and save it in `/tmp/images`.

Listing 2.9   Downloading all images from the retrieved image URLs

```
                                                         Gets only the filename by selecting
                                                         everything after the slash. https://
                                                         host/RocketImages/Electron
                                        Loops over all   .jpg_1440.jpg, for example,
for url in image_urls:      ◄───        image URLs       becomes Electron.jpg_1440.jpg.
    try:                                      Gets the
        response = requests.get(url)    ◄───  image
        image_name = url.split("/")[-1]             ◄───
        target_file = f"/tmp/images/{image_name}"   ◄───  Constructs the
        with open(target_file, "wb") as f:                target file paths
            f.write(response.content)                 ◄───      Opens the
        print(f"Downloaded {url} to {target_file}")   ◄───      target file
    except MissingSchema:                                       handle
        print(f"{url} appears to be an invalid URL.")
    except ConnectionError:                                 Writes the
        raise ConnectionError(f"Could not connect to {url}.")   image to the
                                                                file path
                                    Catches and processes
                                    potential errors        Prints result
```

2.3   *Running a DAG in Airflow*

Now that we have our basic rocket-launch DAG, let's get it up and running and then view it in the Airflow UI. The bare-minimum Airflow consists of five core components: a DAG processor, a scheduler, an API server, a triggerer, and a database. To get Airflow up and running, you can install Airflow in your Python environment or use Docker.

2.3.1 Running Airflow in a Python environment

The initial approach is to use the Airflow package in Python. To do so, we'll use a virtual environment. When working on Python projects, it's desirable to keep each project in its own Python environment to create a reproducible installation and prevent dependency clashes. Virtual environments are created with tools such as these:

- pyenv (https://github.com/pyenv/pyenv)
- Conda (https://docs.conda.io)
- virtualenv (https://virtualenv.pypa.io)
- Poetry (https://python-poetry.org)
- uv (https://github.com/astral-sh/uv)

When you have a Python environment, you can use a package installer to start the Airflow installation. If you're using virtualenv, you can use pip to install Airflow. Make sure to activate the environment you created earlier before running the following command:

```
pip install apache-airflow
```

> **WARNING** Be sure to install apache-airflow, not just airflow. After joining the Apache Foundation in 2016, the PyPi airflow repository was renamed apache-airflow. Because many people were still installing airflow instead of removing the old repository, it was kept as a placeholder to provide everybody a message pointing to the correct repository.

When Airflow is installed in the virtual environment, start running Airflow using the handy standalone command:

```
airflow standalone
```

This command performs several tasks behind the scenes: it initializes the metastore (the database that stores all Airflow states); creates a user; and launches the api -server, scheduler, dag-processor, and triggerer. After you're set up, go to http:// localhost:8080 and log in with username admin and the generated password from the log output to access the Airflow UI:

```
standalone | Starting Airflow Standalone
Simple auth manager | Password for user 'admin': FBzzMdy6BYNM97zZ
standalone | Checking database is initialized
standalone | Database ready
```

2.3.2 *Running Airflow with Docker*

Although using a Python environment is an easy way to run Airflow, it may not be the best choice when the Airflow configuration grows more complicated. To achieve a smoother, more flexible learning experience, we advise using Docker to run Airflow. Docker is a popular way to create isolated environments for running reproducible code. It creates an isolated environment on the operating system level. As a result, you can create Docker containers that contain not only a set of Python packages but also other dependencies, such as database drivers or a compiler. To run a Docker container, you must have Docker Engine installed on your machine, which you typically accomplish by installing Docker Desktop (https://www.docker.com/products/docker-desktop).

In this book, we'll primarily use Docker to run Airflow in the examples. To define the Airflow installation setup, we'll use Docker Compose, a tool that helps us manage and define multicontainer Docker applications with YAML files. It's particularly relevant for the Airflow setup because we'll define different services (database, workers, scheduler, and so on) and configurations.

> **NOTE** YAML (https://yaml.org) is a so-called human-friendly data serialization language that's widely used to create configuration files.

Docker Compose helps us organize these configurations efficiently. See the configuration file (`official-airflow-docker-compose.yml`) provided by Apache Airflow in the root of the book's repository. Also, each chapter includes an extra configuration in the repository (`compose.override.yaml`) that adds functionality to the base configuration.

The initial step in running Airflow is navigating to the chapter folder. When there, run Airflow using the following command.

Listing 2.10 Running docker compose up to get Airflow ready to run

```
@user $ cd chapter02

@user $ docker compose up
```

This command initializes the database, creates the first user account, and configures all the services so Airflow can run. You'll need to wait a couple of minutes to let Docker finish the configuration. When the services are successfully set up, you'll be able to view them by running the `docker.ps` command shown in the following listing.

Listing 2.11 List of the Airflow services running

```
@user $ docker ps

CONTAINER ID    IMAGE                  NAMES
8e2d4649dfbd    apache/airflow:3.1.0   chapter02-airflow-worker-1
2229516745e6    apache/airflow:3.1.0   chapter02-airflow-apiserver-1
1e9ee7e33ec6    apache/airflow:3.1.0   chapter02-airflow-dag-processor-1
```

```
1f57735aa785    apache/airflow:3.1.0    chapter02-airflow-scheduler-1
ac23f91faab2    apache/airflow:3.1.0    chapter02-airflow-triggerer-1
7cd704c8fce4    postgres:16             chapter02-postgres-1
5b867091e894    redis:7.2-bookworm      chapter02-redis-1
```

Now you have an Airflow instance set and ready to use. You can view Airflow at `http://localhost:8080` and log in with username *airflow* and password *airflow*.

2.3.3 Inspecting the DAG in Airflow

After logging in, you can inspect the rocket-launches DAGs, shown in figure 2.7. The figure shows the DAGs that are available to Airflow in the `dags` directory. The main view provides a lot of information, but let's inspect the `01_download_rocket_launches` DAG first. Click the DAG's name to open it, and inspect the graph view (figure 2.8).

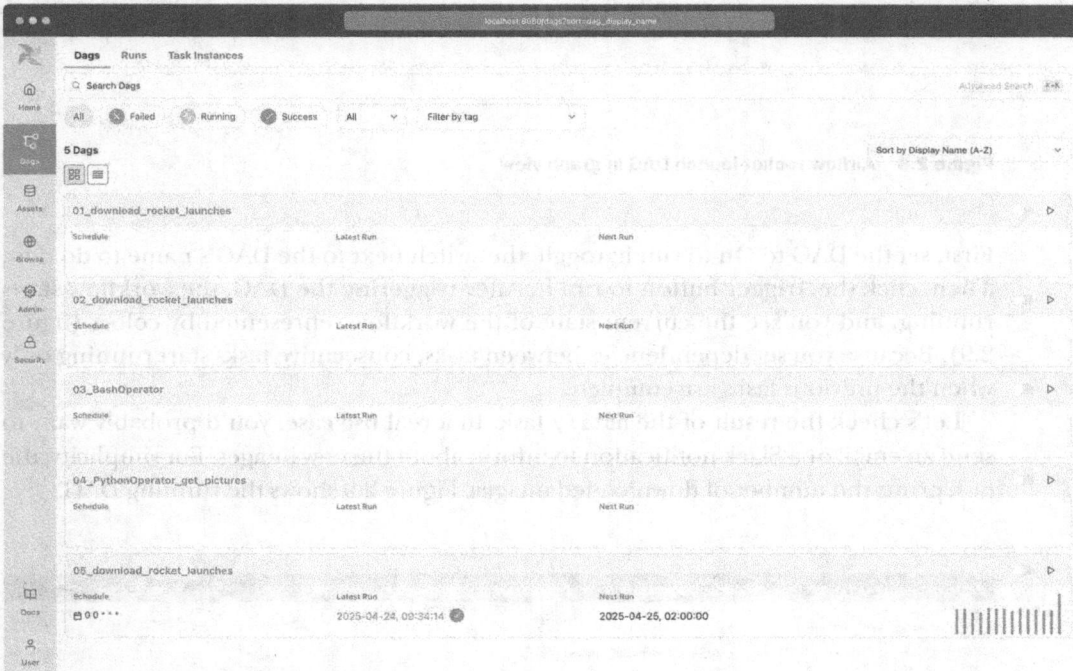

Figure 2.7   Airflow's DAG overview screen

This view shows the structure of the DAG script provided to Airflow. When the script is placed in the `dags` directory, Airflow will read it and pull out the bits and pieces that form a DAG so that it can be visualized in the UI. The graph view shows the structure of the DAG, including how and in which order all tasks in the DAG are connected and will be run. This view is the one you'll probably use most often while developing workflows.

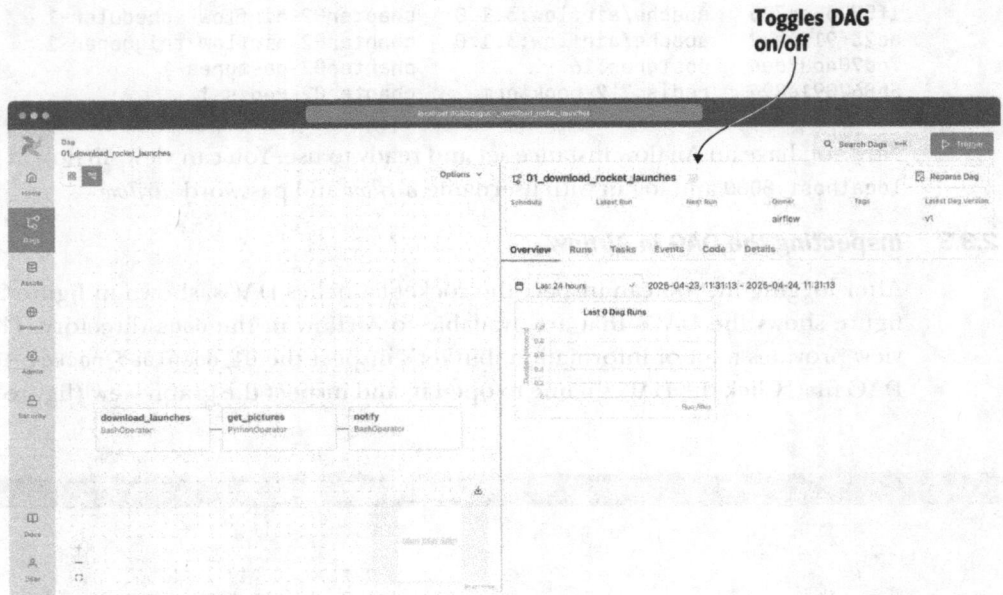

Figure 2.8   Airflow rocket-launch DAG in graph view

First, set the DAG to On to run it; toggle the switch next to the DAG's name to do that. Then, click the Trigger button to run it. After triggering the DAG, the workflow starts running, and you see the current state of the workflow represented by colors (figure 2.9). Because you set dependencies between tasks, consecutive tasks start running only when the previous tasks are complete.

Let's check the result of the notify task. In a real use case, you'd probably want to send an email or a Slack notification to inform about the new images. For simplicity, the task prints the number of downloaded images. Figure 2.9 shows the running DAG.

Figure 2.9   Graph view displaying a running DAG

All task logs are collected in Airflow, so you can check the UI for output or potential issues in case of failure. Click a completed `notify` task, and you see the resulting logs in the task detail screen (figure 2.10).

Figure 2.10 Task detail screen

Click the Logs button to inspect the logs (if they're not selected by default), as shown in figure 2.11. The logs are verbose by default but display the number of downloaded images. Finally, open the `/tmp/images` directory and view the images. When you're running in Docker, this directory exists only inside the worker Docker container, not on your host system. Therefore, first you must get into the worker Docker container, as shown in the next listing. After that, you get a Bash terminal in the container and can view the images in `/tmp/images` (figure 2.12).

Listing 2.12 Accessing the worker instance to explore the filesystem

```
# to get the name of the worker
@user $ docker ps

CONTAINER ID    IMAGE                 NAMES
8e2d4649dfbd    apache/airflow:3.1.0  chapter02-airflow-worker-1
2229516745e6    apache/airflow:3.1.0  chapter02-airflow-apiserver-1
1e9ee7e33ec6    apache/airflow:3.1.0  chapter02-airflow-dag-processor-1
1f57735aa785    apache/airflow:3.1.0  chapter02-airflow-scheduler-1
ac23f91faab2    apache/airflow:3.1.0  chapter02-airflow-triggerer-1
7cd704c8fce4    postgres:16           chapter02-postgres-1
5b867091e894    redis:7.2-bookworm    chapter02-redis-1

@user $ docker exec -it chapter02-airflow-worker-1 /bin/bash
    default@8e2d4649dfbd:/opt/airflow$
```

es=["/opt/airflow/logs/dag_id=01_download_rocket_launches/run_id=manual__2025-04-24T09:45:00.185495+00:0
- DAG bundles loaded: dags-folder: source="airflow.dag_processing.bundles.manager.DagBundlesManager"
- Filling up the DagBag from /opt/airflow/dags/01_download_rocket_launches.py: source="airflow.models.da
- Tmp dir root location: /tmp: source="airflow.task.hooks.airflow.providers.standard.hooks.subprocess.Su
- Running command: ['/usr/bin/bash', '-c', 'echo "There are now $(ls /tmp/images/ | wc -l) images."']: s
- Output:: source="airflow.task.hooks.airflow.providers.standard.hooks.subprocess.SubprocessHook"
- There are now 7 images.: source="airflow.task.hooks.airflow.providers.standard.hooks.subprocess.Subpro
- Command exited with return code 0: source="airflow.task.hooks.airflow.providers.standard.hooks.subproc
- Pushing xcom: ti="RuntimeTaskInstance(id=UUID('0196672f-ae31-72bc-8c01-502275b46aa0'), task_id='notify
ne='59e64e21ce60', context_carrier={}, task=<Task(BashOperator): notify>, bundle_instance=LocalDagBundle(
ate=None, is_mapped=False)": source="task"

Figure 2.11   Print statement displayed in logs

long2520march25202d_image_
20190222031211.jpeg

falcon25209_image_
20190224025007.jpeg

h-iia2520202_image_
20190222031201.jpeg

falcon2520heavy_image_
20190224025007.jpeg

long2520march25203_image_
20200102181012.jpg

ariane252052520eca_image_
20190224012333.jpeg

kuaizhou_image_
20191027094423.jpeg

soyuz25202.1b_image_
20190520165337.jpg

electron_image_
20190705175640.jpeg

firefly_alpha_image_
20200817170720.jpg

Figure 2.12   Resulting rocket pictures

2.4 *Running at regular intervals*

Rocket enthusiast John is happy now that he has a workflow up and running in Airflow; he can trigger it every now and then to collect the latest rocket pictures. He can see the status of his workflow in the Airflow UI, which is already an improvement on the command-line script he was running before. But he still needs to trigger his workflow by hand periodically—a task that could be automated. After all, nobody likes doing repetitive tasks that computers are good at doing themselves.

In Airflow, we can schedule a DAG to run at certain intervals, such as once an hour, day, or month. This interval is controlled in the DAG by the `schedule` argument, as shown in the following listing. In addition to fixed-interval scheduling, Airflow supports more complex scheduling approaches such as using `cron` expressions, scheduling irregular events with timetables, and triggering a workflow when an external database updates. Chapter 3 covers these advanced scheduling features in Airflow.

Listing 2.13 Running a DAG once a day (dags/05_download_rocket_launches.py)

```
with DAG(
    dag_id="L11_download_rocket_launches",
    start_date=pendulum.today('UTC').add(days=-14),
    schedule="@daily",          ◄──  Airflow alias for 0 0 * * *
    catchup=True,                    (i.e., midnight)
):
```

Setting `schedule` to `@daily` tells Airflow to run this workflow once a day so that John doesn't have to trigger it manually. This behavior is best viewed in the grid view (figure 2.13).

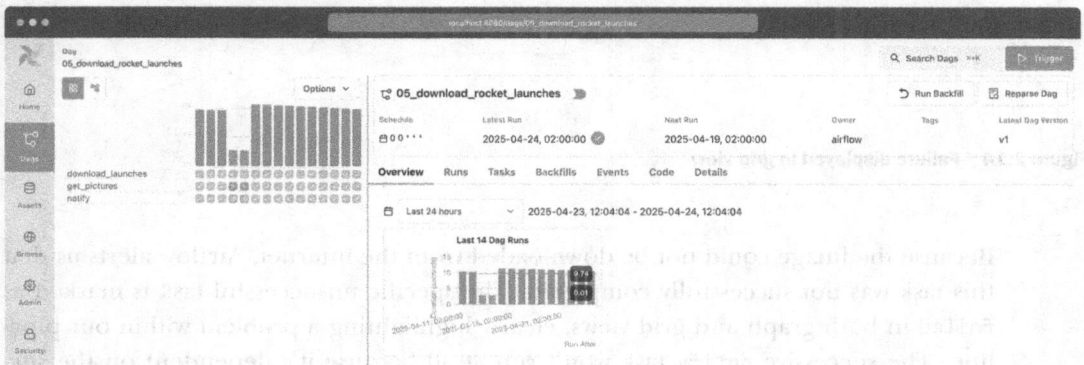

Figure 2.13 Relationship between graph view and grid view

The structure of the DAG is displayed in a rows-and-columns layout—specifically, the status of all runs of the specific DAG in which each column represents a single run at some point in time. When we set the `schedule` to `@daily`, Airflow knew that it had to run this DAG once a day. Given the `start_date` provided to the DAG 14 days ago, the time from 14 days ago to now can be divided into 14 equal intervals of one day. Because both the start and end dates of these 14 intervals lie in the past, they'll start running after we provide a `schedule` to Airflow. Chapter 3 covers the semantics of the schedule interval and various ways to configure it.

2.5   *Handling failing tasks*

So far, we've seen only green in the Airflow UI. But what happens if something fails? It's not uncommon for tasks to fail, which they may do for a multitude of reasons (e.g., an external service is down, the code contains an error, network connectivity issues occurred, or a disk broke).

Suppose that at some point, we experience a network interruption while getting John's rocket pictures. As a consequence, we see in the Airflow UI that the `get_picture` task failed (figure 2.14).

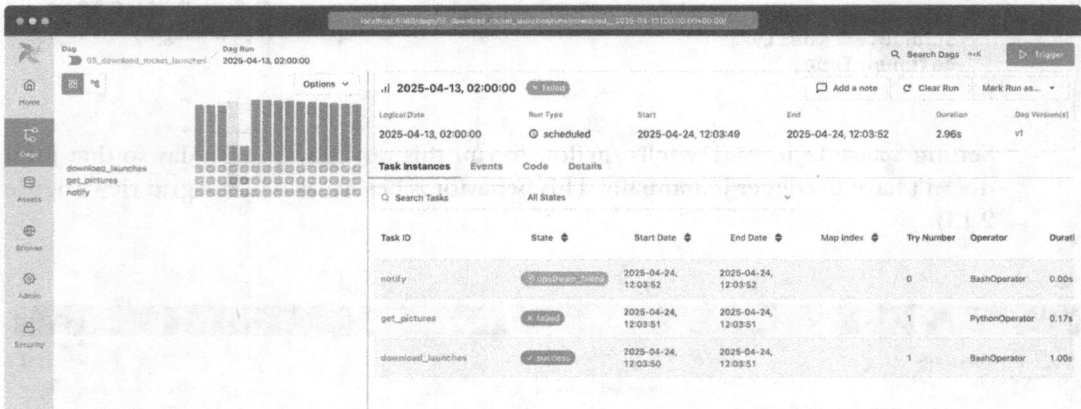

Figure 2.14   Failure displayed in grid view

Because the image could not be downloaded from the internet, Airflow alerts us that this task was not successfully completed. The specific unsuccessful task is marked as `failed` in both graph and grid views, clearly highlighting a problem within our pipeline. The successive `notify` task won't run at all because it's dependent on the successful state of the `get_pictures` task, and it's marked as `upstream_failed`. Such task instances are displayed in orange. By default, all previous tasks must run successfully; any successive tasks of the failed task won't run.

Let's figure out the issue by inspecting the logs again. Open the logs of the `get_pictures` task (figure 2.15).

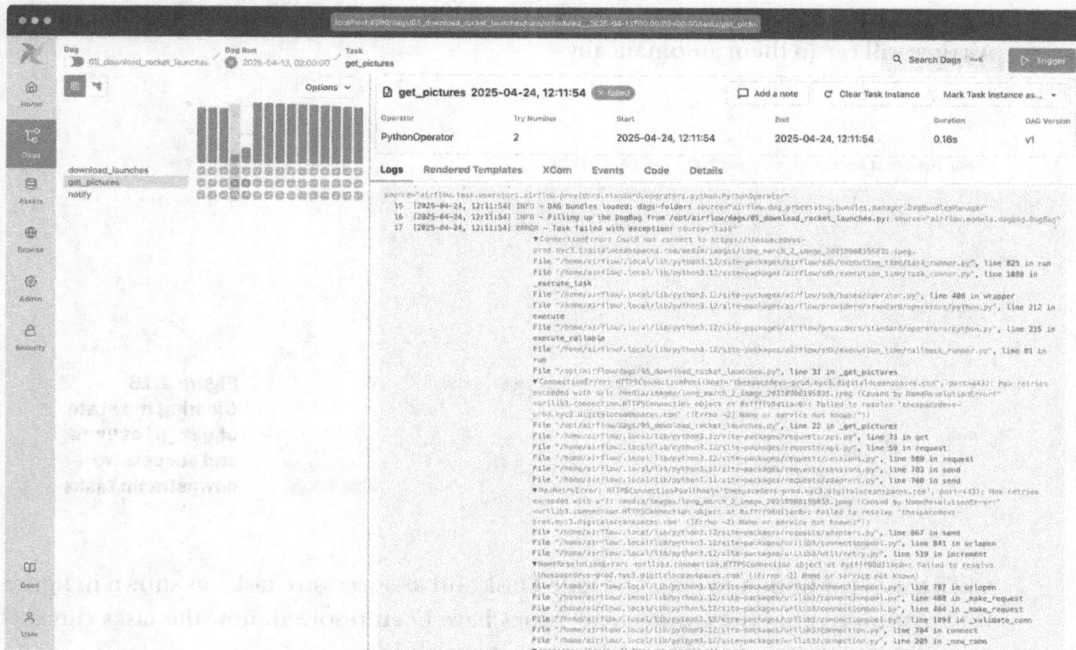

Figure 2.15 Stack trace of the failed `get_pictures` task

In the stack trace, we uncover the potential cause:

```
ConnectionError: Could not connect to https://thespacedevs-
    prod.nyc3.digitaloceanspaces.com/media/images/
    long_march_2_image_20210908195835.jpeg.
```

This message indicates that the task is trying to establish a connection but can't do so, which could hint at a firewall rule blocking the connection or a lack of internet connectivity. Assuming that we can fix the problem (by plugging in the internet cable, for example), let's restart the task.

> **NOTE** Restarting the entire workflow isn't necessary. Airflow lets you restart from the point of failure and onward without restarting any previously successful tasks.

Click the failed task; then click the Clear Task Instance button in the top-right corner of the task information view (refer to figure 2.15). When you do, a selection menu pops up, giving you options for the tasks you're about to clear.

You can clear only one specific task, but you also have the option to select tasks that come before or after it in the same run by choosing Upstream and Downstream from the pop-up menu (figure 2.16). Or you can clear the same task from a different run in the past or future. By doing this, you're essentially resetting the tasks, which means that Airflow will rerun them automatically.

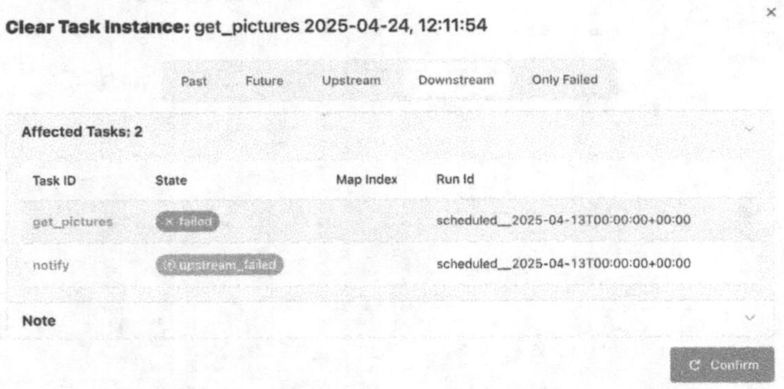

Clear Task Instance: get_pictures 2025-04-24, 12:11:54   ×

	Past	Future	Upstream	Downstream	Only Failed

Affected Tasks: 2

Task ID	State	Map Index	Run Id
get_pictures	× failed		scheduled__2025-04-13T00:00:00+00:00
notify	⊗ upstream_failed		scheduled__2025-04-13T00:00:00+00:00

Note

↻ Confirm

Figure 2.16 **Clearing the state of `get_pictures` and successive downstream tasks**

Click the Clear button to clear the failed task and its successive tasks, as shown in figure 2.17. Assuming that the connectivity issues have been resolved, now the tasks run successfully, and the whole grid view is green (figure 2.18).

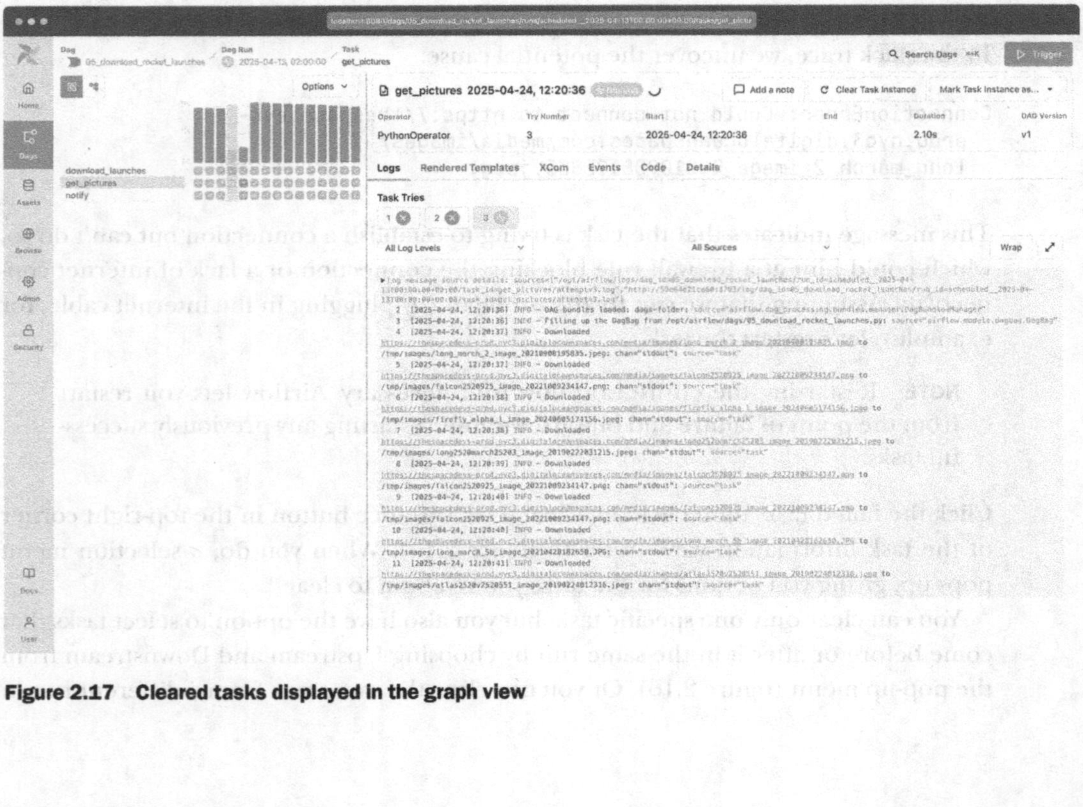

Figure 2.17   Cleared tasks displayed in the graph view

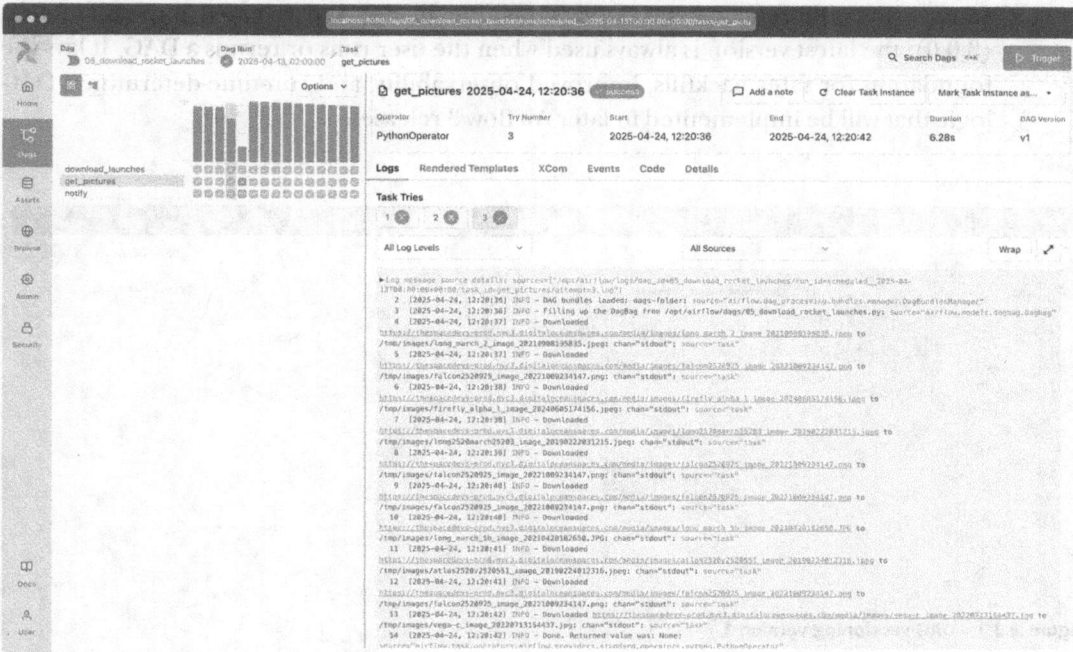

Figure 2.18 Successfully completed tasks after failed tasks are cleared

Any piece of software can have many reasons for failure. In Airflow workflows, sometimes failure is accepted, sometimes it isn't, and sometimes it is, but only under certain conditions. The criteria for dealing with failure can be configured on any level in the workflow, as discussed in detail in chapter 6.

After you clear the previously failed tasks, Airflow automatically reruns these tasks. If all goes well, John will download the rocket images resulting from the failed tasks. The called URL in the download_launches task simply requests the next rocket launches, meaning that it will return the next rocket launches when the API is called. Chapter 5 discusses how to incorporate the run-time context in which a DAG was run into your code.

2.6 *DAG versioning*

A new feature introduced in Airflow 3 is DAG versioning. Now DAG structure changes (renamed tasks, dependency shifts, and so on) are tracked directly in the metadata database, allowing users to inspect historical DAG structures through the UI and API.

The DAG processor understands when changes to the code have been made and automatically creates a new version for you. By default, Airflow runs the DAG with the latest version of the code. But you can view previous versions of the code and task runs by choosing them from the Versions drop-down menu in the UI (figure 2.19). Currently, the DAG versioning feature introduced in Airflow 3 has only limited implications. You can see the differences between versions, but in the first released implementation (3.0.0), the latest version is always used when the user runs or reruns a DAG. It lays the foundation for safer backfills, improved observability, and run-time-determined DAG logic that will be implemented in later Airflow 3 releases.

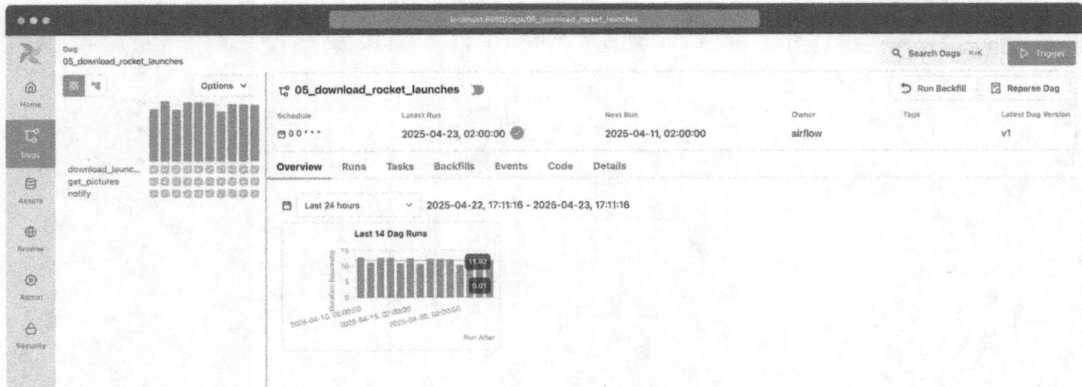

Figure 2.19   DAG versioning version 1

To show a new version of this DAG in the Airflow UI, you need to make some manual changes to the DAG. First, make sure the DAG has run at least once with the v1 version so you can clearly see the difference when adding an extra task to the DAG. An easy manual change is adding a new task after the `notify` task.

Listing 2.14   Adding an extra task to the DAG

```
...
versioning_example = BashOperator(
    task_id="versioning_example_task",
    bash_command='echo "Hey Airflow DAG versioning is here!"',
)

download_launches >> get_pictures >> notify >> versioning_example
```

After the DAG processor processes the new DAG file(s), you see a new version (v2) indicated in the top-right corner of the DAG page in the UI. To see the differences more clearly, look at the Code tab in the UI; a drop-down menu shows all available versions (figure 2.20). If you scroll down, you see the manual changes you made to the code.

To show how the difference affects the DAG runs, you can trigger the DAG by clicking the Trigger button to execute the latest version of the DAG code. That result is visible in figure 2.21, with the added task that ran only in the latest DAG run.

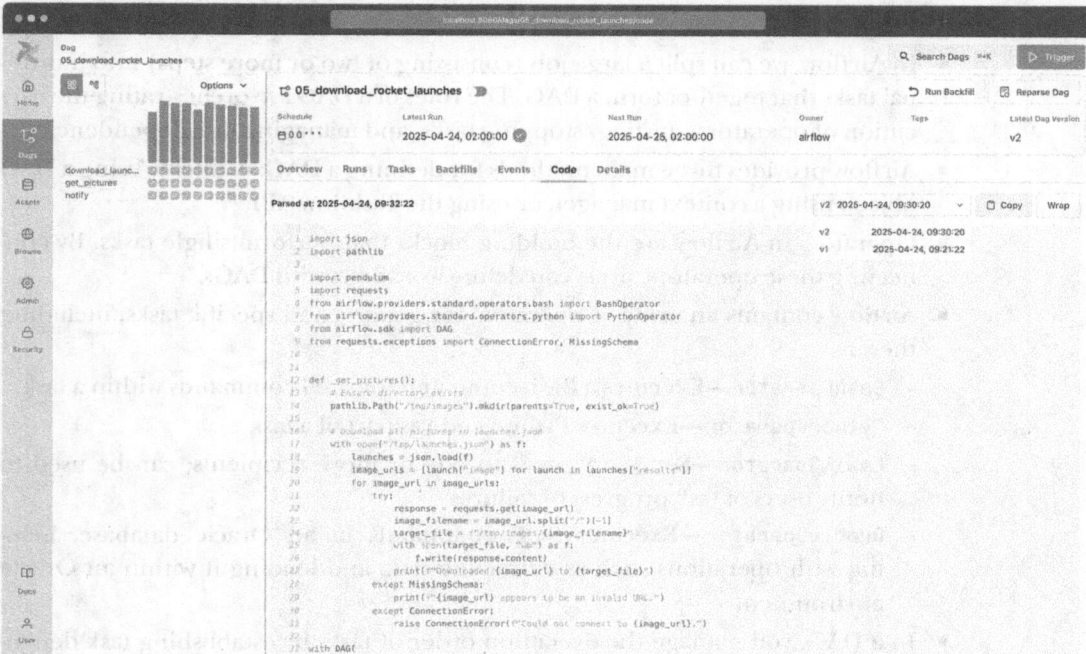

Figure 2.20 DAG versioning version selector in code view

NOTE DAG versioning operates based on the new concept of DAG bundles. For backward compatibility, the local `dag` folder is a converted DAG bundle of type `LocalDagBundle`. Another built-in option is `GitDagBundle`. Chapter 17 describes in detail how to set up and use DAG bundles.

Figure 2.21 DAG versioning, with a new task visible in the latest run

Summary

- In Airflow, we can split a large job (consisting of two or more steps) into individual tasks that together form a DAG. The roles of a DAG are orchestrating the execution of operators, starting/stopping tasks, and managing task dependencies.

- Airflow provides three main methods for defining a DAG: explicitly using a DAG object, using a context manager, or using the Taskflow API.

- Operators in Airflow are the building blocks that perform single tasks. By connecting these operators, users can define workflows with DAGs.

- Airflow contains an array of operators for generic and specific tasks, including these:
  - `BashOperator`—Executes a Bash command for shell commands within a task
  - `PythonOperator`—Executes Python code as part of a task
  - `EmailOperator`—Sends an email to one or more recipients; can be used to notify users of task progress or failures
  - `OracleOperator`—Executes SQL commands in an Oracle database, helping with operations such as extracting data and loading it within an Oracle environment

- In a DAG, you manage the execution order of tasks by establishing task dependencies. The most common way to define task-execution order in Airflow is to set task dependencies with the `rshift` (>>) and `lshift` (<<) operators. The Airflow UI displays a list of all created DAGs; allows users to trigger DAG executions; and provides detailed insights into each task's execution status (success or failure), along with logs to help users diagnose and troubleshoot any issues.

- In Airflow, task failure management is a critical aspect of workflow execution. When a task fails, Airflow provides mechanisms to handle such events gracefully. Users can configure retries to rerun a task after a failure. If manual intervention is required, users can clear the failed task state, prompting Airflow to reschedule and execute the task again.

- Airflow 3 introduces DAG versioning. At the time of writing, the effect is cosmetic, but it lays the foundation for safer backfills, improved observability, and run-time-determined DAG logic.

Time-based scheduling

This chapter covers

- Running DAGs at regular or irregular points in time
- Processing data incrementally using data intervals
- Loading and reprocessing previously processed data using backfilling
- Applying best practices to enhance task reliability

In the first two chapters, we explored Airflow's UI and learned how to define a basic Airflow directed acyclic graph (DAG) and run it every day by defining a scheduled interval. In this chapter, we'll dive a bit deeper into scheduling in Airflow and explore how it allows us to process data incrementally at regular intervals. First, we'll introduce a small use case scenario focused on analyzing user events from our website and explore how to build a DAG to analyze these events at regular points in time. Next, we'll explore ways to make this process more efficient by taking an incremental approach to analyzing our data and seeing how it ties into Airflow's concept of schedule intervals. We'll also look at a scheduling option based on specific event times. Finally, we'll show how to fill gaps in our data set by using backfilling and discuss important properties of proper Airflow tasks.

3.1 Processing user events

To understand how Airflow's scheduling works, consider a small example. Suppose that we have a service that tracks user behavior on our website and allows us to analyze which pages users (identified by IP addresses) accessed. For marketing purposes, we want to know how many pages users access and how much time they spend on the site during each visit. To get an idea of how this behavior changes over time, we want to calculate these statistics daily so we can compare changes across days and larger time periods. The events look something like this:

```
{"user":"132.242.6.226","timestamp":"2025-08-01T23:51:38.739617945"}
{"user":"220.187.70.44","timestamp":"2025-08-01T23:55:58.075215591"}
{"user":"30.147.208.138","timestamp":"2025-08-01T23:58:41.352037055"}
```

For practical reasons, the external tracking service doesn't store data for more than 30 days. We must store and accumulate this data ourselves because we want to retain our history for longer periods. Normally, because the raw data may be quite large, it would make sense to store this data in a cloud storage service such as Amazon's S3 or Google's Cloud Storage, which combine high durability with relatively low costs. For simplicity's sake, however, we'll store our data locally.

To simulate this example, we created a simple (local) API that allows us to retrieve user events. We can retrieve the full list of available events from the past seven days using the following API call:

```
curl -o /tmp/events.json http://events-api:8081/events/latest
```

This call returns a JSON-encoded list of user events we can analyze to calculate our user statistics. Using this API, we can break our workflow into two tasks: fetching user events and calculating the statistics. We can download the data itself by using the BashOperator, as we saw in chapter 2. To calculate the statistics, we can use a PythonOperator, which allows us to load the data into a pandas DataFrame and calculate the number of events using a groupby and an aggregation. This approach gives us the DAG shown in the following listing (dags/01_unscheduled.py).

Listing 3.1   Initial unscheduled event-processing DAG

```python
from pathlib import Path

import pandas as pd
from airflow.providers.standard.operators.bash import BashOperator
from airflow.providers.standard.operators.python import PythonOperator
```

```
from airflow.sdk import DAG


def _calculate_stats(input_path, output_path):
    """Calculates event statistics."""
    events = pd.read_json(input_path)
    stats = events.groupby(["date", "user"]).size()
    .reset_index()
    Path(output_path).parent.mkdir(exist_ok=True)
    stats.to_csv(output_path, index=False)

with DAG(
    dag_id="01_unscheduled",
    schedule=None,
):

fetch_events = BashOperator(
    task_id="fetch_events",
    bash_command=(
    "mkdir -p /data && "
    "curl -o /data/events.json
    http://events-api:8081/events/latest"
    ),
)

calculate_stats = PythonOperator(
    task_id="calculate_stats",
    python_callable=_calculate_stats,
    op_kwargs={
    "input_path": "/data/events.json",
    "output_path": "/data/stats.csv",
    },
)

fetch_events >> calculate_stats
```

Loads the events and calculates the required statistics

Makes sure that the output directory exists and writes the statistics to CSV

Specifies that this DAG is unscheduled

Fetches and stores the events from the API

Sets the execution order of the tasks

3.2　*The basic components of an Airflow schedule*

We have our basic DAG, but we need to make sure that Airflow runs it regularly. We'll schedule it so we get daily updates. In Airflow, schedules are defined by four parameters: `start_date` (required), `end_date` (optional), `schedule` (required), and `catchup` (optional). These parameters essentially define the boundaries within which a DAG operates.

The `start_date` and `end_date` parameters specify the time window during which Airflow will consider executing the DAG (figure 3.1). Within that window, the `schedule` parameter determines precisely when the DAG executes (daily, hourly, and so on). These schedules can be time-based (discussed in this chapter) or asset-based (discussed in chapter 4). By default, a DAG doesn't have a schedule (`schedule=None`), so it won't run unless it's triggered manually.

Executions determined by the schedule

First	Second	Third	*Future*
execution	execution	execution	*execution*

Start
date

End date
(optional)

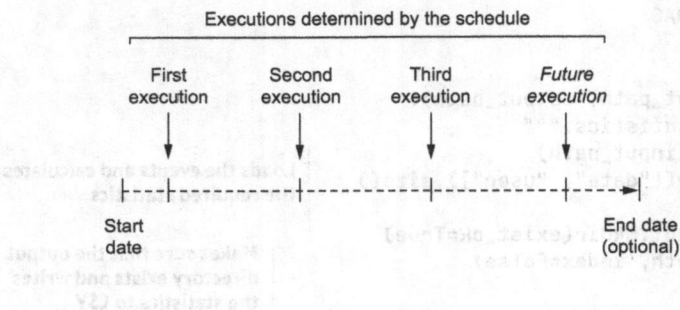

Figure 3.1　Example of a regular time-based schedule in Airflow, in which the pipeline is executed at regular intervals (the schedule) between the given start and end dates. If no end date is given, the pipeline executes indefinitely.

The `catchup` parameter determines whether Airflow should also execute the DAG for missed time points in the past. By default (`catchup=False`), Airflow doesn't execute the DAG for missed time points in the past; it considers only the future, starting from when the DAG was enabled (figure 3.2A). If you enable `catchup` on a DAG, Airflow also executes DAG runs for time points in the past, starting from the start date (figure 3.2B).

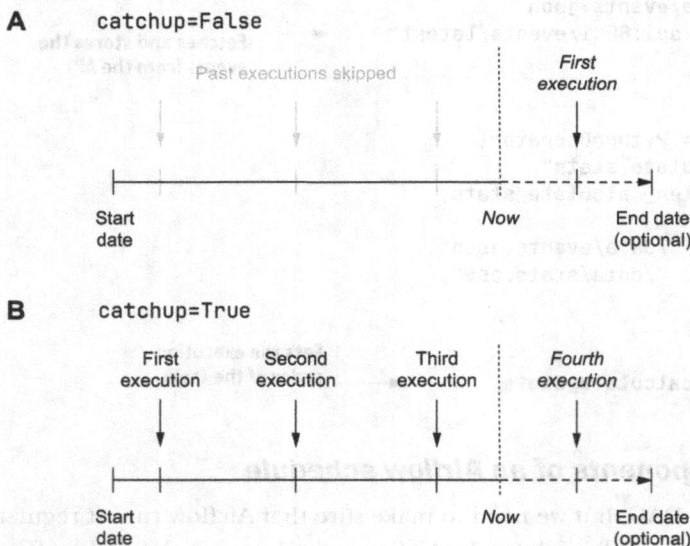

A　`catchup=False`

Past executions skipped

*First
execution*

Start
date

Now

End date
(optional)

B　`catchup=True`

First	Second	Third	*Fourth*
execution	execution	execution	*execution*

Start
date

Now

End date
(optional)

Figure 3.2　The effect of the catchup parameter on scheduling in Airflow. With catchup=False (A), Airflow won't execute the pipeline for any historical time points before the pipeline was enabled. With catchup=True (B), Airflow does schedule runs for past time points.

3.3　*Running regularly using trigger-based schedules*

To see how this example works in practice, we'll use Airflow 3's default time-based schedule type: trigger-based schedules. We'll start by making our DAG run once a day so we get daily updates of our user statistics.

> **WARNING**　Scheduling behavior changed significantly between Airflow 2 and 3. See the sidebar "Changes in scheduling behavior between Airflow 2 and 3" for details.

Changes in scheduling behavior between Airflow 2 and 3

The default behavior for scheduling changed significantly between Airflow 2 and 3 when defining schedules as string `cron` expressions (e.g., `schedule="5 4 * * *"`) or Airflow presets (e.g., `schedule="@daily"`).

In Airflow 3, these string expressions result in trigger-based schedules (discussed in section 3.3.1); in Airflow 2, they result in interval-based schedules (discussed in section 3.4). To eliminate confusion, we'll avoid string expressions and explicitly refer to timetable classes (such as `CronTriggerTimetable` in section 3.3.1) wherever possible, which should exhibit the same behavior in Airflow 2 and Airflow 3.

Another significant change is that `catchup`, which is enabled by default in Airflow 2, is disabled by default in Airflow 3. To enable `catchup` in Airflow 3, you must explicitly pass `catchup=True` to your DAGs or change the default using the `scheduler.catchup_by_default` setting in the Airflow configuration.

3.3.1 Defining a daily schedule

To schedule our DAG for daily executions, we need to specify a start date for the DAG together with a daily schedule, as shown in the next listing (`dags/02_trigger_cron.py`). We can define this daily schedule using the `CronTriggerTimetable` class, which requires a time zone and a `cron` expression. For more details on `cron` expressions, see section 3.3.2. In this case, we'll start with the Coordinated Universal Time (UTC) time zone, which is Airflow's default setting, and the `cron` expression `"0 0 * * *"`, which runs the DAG every day at midnight.

Listing 3.2 Defining a daily schedule

```
from airflow.timetables.trigger import CronTriggerTimetable

with DAG(
    dag_id="02_daily_schedule",
    start_date=pendulum.datetime(year=2025, month=1, day=1),      # Starts running the DAG on January 1, 2025
    end_date=pendulum.datetime(year=2025, month=1, day=5)         # Stops running the DAG on January 5, 2025
    schedule=CronTriggerTimetable("0 0 * * *", timezone="UTC"),   # Schedules the DAG to run every day at midnight
    ...
):
```

Together with the start and end dates, this code effectively starts running our DAG once a day at midnight (00:00 UTC), starting January 1 at 00:00 (the start date) and ending January 5 (the end date), as shown in figure 3.3.

You can omit the end date to keep the DAG running indefinitely (figure 3.4). For now, however, keep the end date to avoid generating a potentially large number of DAG runs.

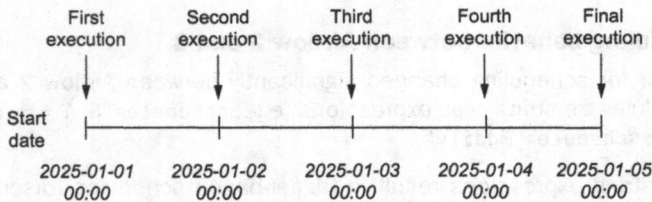

Figure 3.3   Executions for a daily scheduled DAG with specified start (2025-01-01) and end dates (2025-01-05) that prevent the DAG from executing beyond those dates

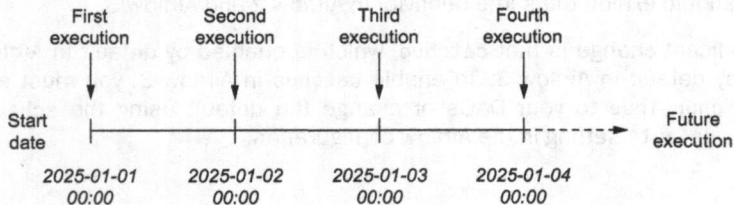

Figure 3.4   By omitting the end date, you can keep the DAG running indefinitely.

If you enable this DAG now, Airflow won't execute any runs because all the executions are in the past and `catchup` is disabled by default in Airflow 3. (In Airflow 2, `catchup` is enabled by default.) You can change this behavior by enabling `catchup` as shown in the following listing (`dags/02_trigger_cron.py`), after which Airflow should start executing runs for past dates as well.

Listing 3.3   Enabling `catchup` for past runs

```
with DAG(
    dag_id="02_daily_schedule",
    start_date=pendulum.datetime(year=2025, month=1, day=1),
    schedule=CronTriggerTimetable("@daily", timezone="UTC"),
    catchup=True,
):
```
> Enables catchup to execute past runs

This code ensures that our DAG will run every day between January 1 and January 5, 2025, executing at 00:00 UTC. One limitation of this DAG is that we're still saving the output of every run to a single file (`/data/events.json`). Every DAG run overwrites the results of the previous run, preventing us from building up a history of results.

One way to solve this issue is to modify the DAG to write the outputs under the date for which the DAG is being executed (e.g., `/data/2025-01-01.json`). Fortunately, Airflow provides these details in the task's execution context, which we'll examine in chapter 5. For now, it's sufficient to know that this context contains a parameter called `logical_date` that contains the date of the DAG execution. We can insert these parameters into our Bash command dynamically using Airflow's Jinja-based templating functionality (chapter 5), as shown in the following listing (`dags/02_trigger_cron.py`).

Listing 3.4 Using templating to specify dates

```
fetch_events = BashOperator(
    task_id="fetch_events",
    bash_command=(
        "mkdir -p /data/events && "
        "curl -o /data/events/{{ logical_date | ds }}.json"
        "'http://events-api:8081/events/latest"
    ),
)
```

References the logical date to store output in a file named after the date

When the DAG runs, this code effectively inserts the execution date (logical date) of the DAG into the filename before calling the API, ensuring that the output of the `curl` command is written to a file named after the date. To calculate statistics for each daily set of events, we can modify the `calculate_stats` task to read the daily events file only when calculating statistics, as shown in the next listing (`dags/02_trigger_cron.py`).

Listing 3.5 Calculating statistics per execution

```
calculate_stats = PythonOperator(
    task_id="calculate_stats",
    python_callable=_calculate_stats,
    op_kwargs ={
        "input_path": "/data/events/{{logical_date | ds}}.json",
        "output_path": "/data/stats/{{logical_date | ds}}.csv",
    },
)
```

Reads only the events from the current execution's JSON file

Writes the results to a CSV file partitioned by the execution date

Great! We've ensured that we get daily extracts of the latest events and calculated statistics for that daily extract. This approach still has a couple of limitations, however: we have no control of the time range of events returned by `latest` (which may be a problem if we rerun the DAG later), and our statistics aren't quite daily because the events extract contains more events than those of the past day. We'll tackle these issues with interval-based scheduling in section 3.4. First, though, we'll dive into different flavors of trigger-based schedules.

3.3.2 Using cron expressions

As shown in section 3.3.1, Airflow allows us to define schedules with the same syntax as cron, a time-based job scheduler used by UNIX-like computer operating systems such as macOS and Linux. This syntax consists of five components and is defined as follows:

```
# ┌───────── minute (0 - 59)
# │ ┌─────── hour (0 - 23)
# │ │ ┌───── day of the month (1 - 31)
# │ │ │ ┌─── month (1 - 12)
# │ │ │ │ ┌─ day of the week (0 - 6) (Sunday to Saturday;
# │ │ │ │ │    7 is also Sunday on some systems)
# * * * * *
```

In this definition, a cron job is executed when the time/date specification fields match the current system time/date. We can use asterisks (*) instead of numbers to define unrestricted fields, meaning that cron selects all possible values.

Although this cron-based representation may seem convoluted, it gives us considerable flexibility in defining time intervals. We can define hourly, daily, and weekly intervals using the following cron expressions:

- 0 * * * *—Hourly (running on the hour)
- 0 0 * * *—Daily (running at midnight)
- 0 0 * * 0—Weekly (running at midnight on Sunday)

We can also define more complicated expressions like these:

- 0 0 1 * *—At midnight on the first of every month
- 45 23 * * SAT—At 23:45 every Saturday

Also, cron expressions allow us to define collections of values using a comma (,) to define a list of values or a dash (-) to define a range of values. Using this syntax, we can build expressions to run jobs on multiple weekdays or multiple sets of hours during a day:

- 0 0 * * MON,WED,FRI—Run every Monday, Wednesday, and Friday at midnight
- 0 0 * * MON-FRI—Run every weekday at midnight
- 0 0,12 * * *—Run every day at 00:00 and 12:00

TIP Although cron expressions are extremely powerful, they can be difficult to work with, so it may be a good idea to test your expressions before trying them in Airflow. Fortunately, many online tools can help you define, verify, or explain cron expressions in plain English. (The website https://crontab .guru, for example, translates cron expressions to human-readable language.) Further, it doesn't hurt to document the reasoning behind complicated cron expressions in your code. This documentation may help other people (including future you) understand the expression when revisiting your code.

3.3.3   *Using shorthand expressions*

Airflow provides several built-in shorthand expressions that you can use to describe common cron schedules. In our use case, we can use Airflow's @daily shorthand, which runs the DAG every night at midnight and is equivalent to the cron expression 0 0 * * * that we used earlier. We can pass this shorthand to the CronTriggerTimetable instead of the cron expression (listing 3.6; dags/03_trigger_preset.py) or directly to the DAG as a schedule. In the latter case, passing the @daily shorthand is equivalent to using a CronTriggerTimetable with a @daily schedule and UTC time zone (Cron-TriggerTimetable("@daily", timezone="UTC")). We prefer the more explicit approach, though, especially given the recent changes between Airflow 2 and 3 (see the previous sidebar "Changes in scheduling behavior between Airflow 2 and 3" for details).

Listing 3.6 Using a preset instead of a cron expression

```
with DAG(
    dag_id="03_trigger_preset",
    start_date=pendulum.datetime(year=2025, month=1, day=1),
    schedule=CronTriggerTimetable("@daily", timezone="UTC"),   ◄───┐
    catchup=True,
):                                                    Passes an Airflow shorthand
                                                      instead of a cron expression
```

Besides the @daily shorthand expression, Airflow provides shorthands for common cases such as hourly and weekly runs. Table 3.1 provides an overview of available shorthands.

Table 3.1 Airflow shorthand expressions for frequently used schedules

Preset	Meaning
@hourly	Run once an hour at the end of the hour.
@daily	Run once a day at midnight.
@weekly	Run once a week at midnight on Sunday.
@monthly	Run once a month at midnight on the first day of the month.
@quarterly	Run once a quarter at midnight on the first day.
@yearly	Run once a year at midnight on January 1.

3.3.4 *Using frequency-based timetables*

A limitation of cron expressions is that they can't represent certain frequency-based schedules. How would you define a cron expression that runs a DAG once every two days, for example? You could write an expression that runs on every first, third, fifth, and so on day of the month, but this approach would run into problems at the end of the month: the DAG would run consecutively on the last day of the current month and the first day of the following month, violating the desired schedule.

This limitation stems from the nature of cron expressions, which define a pattern that is continuously matched against the current time to determine whether a job should be executed. This has the advantage of making the expressions stateless, meaning that you don't have to remember when a previous job was run to calculate the next execution. As you can see, this advantage comes at the price of some expressiveness.

What if you want to run your DAG once every two days? To support this type of schedule, Airflow allows you to define schedules in terms of relative time frequencies. To use such a frequency-based schedule, you can pass a Duration instance from the pendulum module as a schedule, as shown in the following listing (dags/04_trigger_frequency.py).

Listing 3.7   Defining a frequency-based schedule

```
import pendulum
...

with DAG(                                              Defines a frequency-based schedule
    dag_id="04_trigger_frequency",                     to run the DAG once every two days
    start_date=pendulum.datetime(year=2025, month=1, day=1),
    schedule=DeltaTriggerTimetable(pendulum.duration(days=2)),
    ...
):
    ...
```

This approach results in your DAGs running every two days after the start date (on January 3, 5, and so on, 2025). You can also use this approach to run your DAG every 10 minutes (using `duration(minutes=10)`) or every two hours (using `duration(hours=2)`).

By default, frequency-based schedules operate in the UTC time zone. To use a different time zone, you can supply a time zone in the `start_date` parameter (dags/04_trigger_frequency.py).

Listing 3.8   Specifying time zones for frequency-based schedules

```
import pendulum
...

with DAG(                                              Defines a time zone for a
    dag_id="03_timedelta",                             frequency-based schedule
    schedule=DeltaTriggerTimetable(pendulum.duration(days=2)),
    start_date=pendulum.datetime(2024, 1, 1, tz="Europe/Amsterdam"),
    end_date=pendulum.datetime(2024, 1, 5),
    catchup=True,
):
    ...
```

3.3.5   *Summarizing trigger timetables*

Because scheduling is such an important concept in Airflow, let's summarize trigger timetables and make sure that we fully understand when the execution of a DAG occurs. As we've seen, we can control when Airflow runs a DAG with two or three parameters: `start_date`, `schedule`, and (optional) `end_date`. Airflow uses these parameters to identify when a DAG is available for execution (between the start and end dates) and when it should be triggered (the schedule).

With trigger-based schedules, the schedule defines discrete points in time at which the DAG should be executed. When time passes such a point, Airflow immediately schedules an execution of the DAG so that it is executed as quickly as possible after that time (refer to figure 3.3). Trigger schedules work similarly to tools such as cron.

During a DAG run, Airflow provides a variable called `logical_date` that identifies the date and/or time for which the DAG is being executed. You can use this variable in your commands/code to query data specific to that date, define filenames for output, and so on.

3.4 Incremental processing with data intervals

Even with our DAG running every day and the output being stored in separate files, we haven't achieved our goal. For one thing, our DAG is downloading and calculating statistics for the entire catalog of user events every day, which is hardly efficient. Also, even though we're storing the outputs in separate files, these files contain many duplicate rows because we're including the entire catalog of events every time.

3.4.1 Processing data incrementally

One way to solve these issues is to change our DAG to load data incrementally so that we load only events from the corresponding day in each schedule interval and calculate only statistics for the new events. In this approach, we also write both the daily events and their statistics to different files named by the date (partitions) to avoid overwriting previous results and accumulate results over time (figure 3.5).

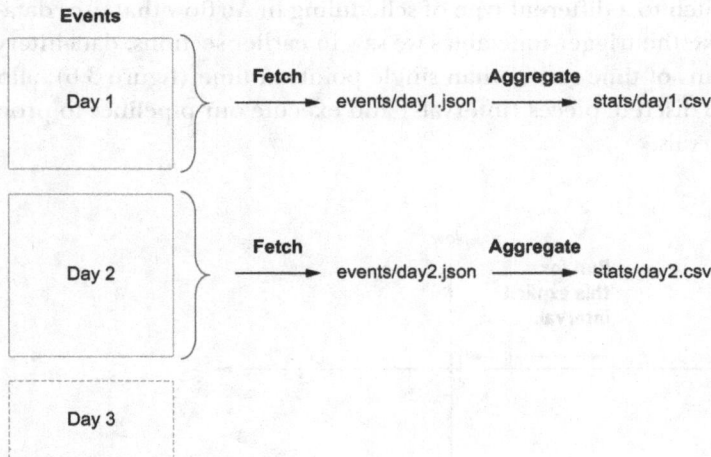

Figure 3.5 Fetching and processing data incrementally by splitting time into daily blocks and having each execution process the data of a specific day

This incremental approach is much more efficient than fetching and processing the entire data set; it significantly reduces the amount of data that must be processed in each schedule interval. Also, because now we're storing our data in separate files each day, we can start building a history of files over time—way past the seven-day limit of our API.

3.4.2 Defining incremental schedules with data intervals

To implement incremental processing in our workflow, we must modify our DAG to download only data for a specific day. Fortunately, we can adjust our API call to fetch events from the /events/range endpoint, which takes the start and end dates as parameters and returns events within this interval, as shown in listing 3.9 (dags/05_ interval_cron.py). In this example, start_date is inclusive and end_date is exclusive, so we're effectively fetching events that occur between 2024-01-01 00:00:00 and 2024 -01-01 23:59:59.

Listing 3.9   Fetching events for a specific time interval

```
fetch_events = BashOperator(
    task_id="fetch_events",
    bash_command=(
        "mkdir -p /data && "
        "curl -o /data/{{ logical_date | ds }}.json "
        "'http://events-api:8081/events/range?"      ◁─┐ Fetches dates for a
        "start_date=2024-01-01&"                        │ specific time range
        "end_date=2024-01-02'"                        ◁─┘
    ),
)
```

To fetch data for any date other than January 1, 2024, we need to change the command to use start and end dates that reflect the day for which the DAG is being executed. To do so, we can switch to a different type of scheduling in Airflow that uses data-interval timetables. Unlike the trigger timetables we saw in earlier sections, data-interval timetables define spans of time rather than single points in time (figure 3.6), allowing us to slice time into discrete pieces (intervals) and execute our pipelines to process data inside those intervals.

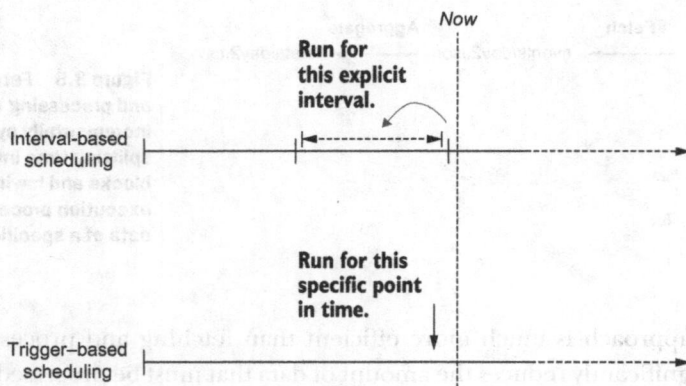

Figure 3.6   Incremental processing in interval-based scheduling windows versus windows derived from trigger schedules. For incremental (data) processing, time is typically divided into discrete time intervals that are processed as soon as the corresponding interval has passed. The interval-based scheduling approach explicitly schedules tasks to run for each interval while providing exact information to each task concerning the start and end of the interval. By contrast, trigger–based scheduling approaches execute tasks only at given times, leaving it up to each task itself to determine the incremental interval for which the task is executing.

To see how this works, we'll switch our DAG to use a `CronDataIntervalTimetable` instead of the trigger-based version (listing 3.10; dags/05_interval_cron.py). This switch changes a couple of things:

- The DAG will no longer execute at the start of the interval but at the end. This makes sense because can't process any data that lies in the future; we must wait until the end of the interval for all data to be available.
- Airflow provides two extra parameters in the execution context, `data_interval_start` and `data_interval_end`, that respectively indicate the start and end times of the interval for which our DAG is being executed (figure 3.7).

Listing 3.10 Using a data-interval-based timetable

```python
import pendulum
...

with DAG(
    dag_id="05_interval_cron",
    schedule=CronDataIntervalTimetable("@daily", timezone="UTC"),
    start_date=pendulum.datetime(2024, 1, 1),
    end_date=pendulum.datetime(2024, 1, 5),
    catchup=True,
):
    ...
```

Changes the DAG to use an interval-based timetable

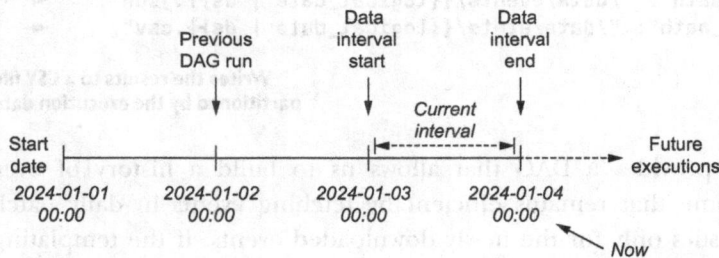

Figure 3.7 Illustration of schedule interval values in Airflow. DAGs are triggered at the end of the given interval, with `data_interval_start` pointing to the start of the interval and `data_interval_end` pointing to the end.

We can insert these parameters into our Bash command dynamically using Airflow's templating functionality (covered in chapter 5), as shown in listing 3.11 (dags/05_interval_cron.py). Now when the DAG runs, it effectively inserts the start/end dates of the execution interval (formatted as YYYY-MM-DD by the `ds` macro) into the URL before calling the API, ensuring that we fetch only events for that interval. Combined with our earlier change of writing results to separate JSON files (e.g., /data/events/2025-01-01.json), now each data file will include only events from the corresponding day.

Listing 3.11   Using templating to specify dates

```
fetch_events = BashOperator(
    task_id="fetch_events",
    bash_command=(
        "mkdir -p /data && "
        "curl -o /data/events/{{logical_date | ds}}.json"
        "'http://events-api:8081/events/range?"
        "start_date={{data_interval_start | ds}}&"
        "end_date={{data_interval_end | ds}}'"
    ),
)
```

Inserts the query start/end dates dynamically using the data_interval_start and _end variables

Dividing a data set into smaller, more manageable pieces is a common strategy in data storage and processing systems. This strategy is commonly referred to as *partitioning*, with the smaller pieces of a data set called *partitions*. An additional advantage of partitioning our data set is that the second task in our DAG (`calculate_stats`) also calculates statistics for only the new events we just downloaded (dags/05_interval_cron.py).

Listing 3.12   Calculating statistics per execution interval

```
calculate_stats = PythonOperator(
    task_id="calculate_stats",
    python_callable=_calculate_stats,
    op_kwargs ={
        "input_path": "/data/events/{{logical_date | ds}}.json",
        "output_path": "/data/stats/{{logical_date | ds}}.csv",
    },
)
```

Reads only the events from the current execution's JSON file

Writes the results to a CSV file partitioned by the execution date

This approach provides a DAG that allows us to build a history of events and statistics over time that remains efficient by fetching events in daily batches and computing statistics only for the newly downloaded events. If the templating in the example (`{{logical_date | ds}}`) went a bit too quickly, don't worry; we'll discuss the task context in more detail in chapter 5. In chapter 12, we'll take a closer look at partitioning scenarios and best practices for handling them. The important point here is that these changes allow us to compute our statistics incrementally per schedule interval by processing only a small subset of our data each day. This setup would also work if we wanted to use a slightly different interval—say, the @hourly preset. We might need to modify the statistics computing code to accommodate this interval, but the fundamental principles would still apply.

3.4.3   *Defining intervals using frequencies*

As with the trigger-based variant, you can define data intervals using a frequency instead of a cron expression. You can do so by switching your schedule to use a

`DeltaIntervalTimetable` and passing in a pendulum `Duration` instance (dags/06_interval_delta.py).

```
import pendulum
...

with DAG(
    dag_id="03_timedelta",
    schedule=DeltaIntervalTimetable(pendulum.duration(days=2)),  ◄──┐
    ...                                            Defines a frequency-based schedule
):                                                 to run the DAG once every two days
    ...
```

Like its trigger-based counterpart, this interval-based schedule executes the DAG once every two days, starting from the provided `start_date`. But this schedule follows interval-scheduling semantics, giving us the data interval start/end variables and executing our DAG at the end of an interval rather than the beginning.

3.4.4 *Summarizing interval-based schedules*

Because data intervals can be confusing, let's take a minute to fully understand how intervals are defined and how they differ from the trigger-based approach. As we've seen, we can control when Airflow runs a DAG with three parameters: `start_date`, `schedule`, and (optional) `end_date`. With data-interval-based timetables, Airflow uses these three parameters to divide time into a series of schedule intervals, starting from the given start date and optionally ending at the end date (figure 3.8).

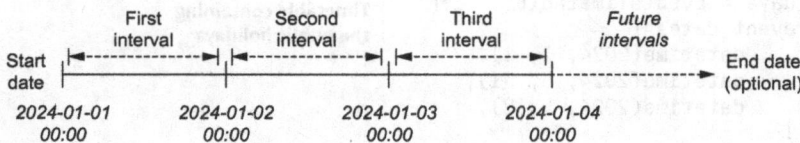

Figure 3.8 Time represented in terms of Airflow's scheduling intervals, assuming a daily interval with a start date of 2024-01-01. Execution happens at the end of the interval (e.g., the DAG run for the first interval is executed at 2024-01-02 00:00).

In this interval-based representation of time, a DAG is executed at the end of the interval when the time slot of that interval has passed. The first interval in figure 3.8, for example, would be executed as soon as possible after 2024-01-01 23:59:59 because, by then, the last time point in the interval has passed. Similarly, the DAG would execute for the second interval shortly after 2024-01-02 23:59:59, and so on until we reach our optional end date.

The interval-based approach is ideal for performing the type of incremental data processing we saw earlier in this chapter because we know exactly which interval of time a task is executing for: the start and end of the corresponding interval. We can access the start and end of each interval using the `data_interval_start` and `data_interval_end` variables. A `logical_date` variable is also provided, generally pointing to the start of the interval; we can use it as an identifier for our run if necessary.

3.5   *Handling irregular intervals*

Although regular schedule intervals are powerful and the most common form of scheduling, they don't allow us to trigger workflows based on irregular events that don't occur at a fixed interval (e.g., sports matches, holidays, festivals, space launches, and elections). An alternative would be to schedule our DAG to run every day and add a condition in the DAG to check the date, but this approach is hardly efficient if our events are sporadic.

Fortunately, Airflow provides support for irregular events through its `Events-Timetable` class, which allows us to define a schedule interval based on a list of specific dates/times rather than a recurring time schedule. Suppose that we want to calculate event statistics only for specific public holidays in the year (perhaps because we expect more traffic on these days). We can trigger the DAG for these public holidays by creating an `EventsTimetable` object with the corresponding dates and passing this object as the DAG's schedule interval (dags/07_events_timetable.py).

> Listing 3.14   Defining `EventsTimetable` to process data for public holidays

```
from pendulum import datetime
from airflow import DAG
from airflow.timetables.events import EventsTimetable

holiday_days = EventsTimetable(          ◄──  Timetable containing
        event_dates=[                         the public holidays
            datetime(2024, 1, 1),
            datetime(2024, 3, 31),
            datetime(2024, 5, 2),
        ]
)

with DAG(
        dag_id="07_events_timetable",        Passes the timetable
        schedule=holiday_days,          ◄──  as a schedule interval
        start_date=datetime(2024, 1, 1),
):
        ...
```

It's important to note that the list of events must be finite; you can't define custom logic to generate lists of potentially unknown length. Moreover, the list should be of a reasonable size because longer lists result in longer load times for the DAG. With this schedule, this DAG executes three times, once for each of these three dates:

- 2024-01-01 00:00
- 2024-03-31 00:00
- 2024-05-02 00:00

In terms of behavior, the EventsTimetable is like the trigger-based schedules discussed in earlier sections. It triggers DAGs to run exactly at the specified date time (e.g., 2024-01-01 00:00:00) and provides a logical_date but doesn't define any data intervals, so data_interval_start and data_interval_end don't have meaningful values. This means we can't use the EventsTimetable for incremental processing unless we calculate the required date offsets ourselves.

Finally, it's worthwhile to mention one additional, less obvious behavior. Typically, regardless of your scheduling settings, you can always trigger a manual run of your DAG from the Airflow UI. You can disable this functionality for the EventsTimetable by passing an additional flag, restrict_to_events. The following code (dags/07_events_timetable.py) forces manual runs to use the most recent EventsTimetable entry or the first entry if none of the events has taken place yet.

> **Listing 3.15 Setting the right behavior for manual runs with** EventsTimetable

```
...
public_holidays = EventsTimetable(
    event_dates=[
        pendulum.datetime(year=2024, month=1, day=1),
        pendulum.datetime(year=2024, month=3, day=31),
        pendulum.datetime(year=2024, month=5, day=2),
    ],
    restrict_to_events=True
)
...
```

3.6   *Managing backfilling of historical data*

As we've seen, Airflow allows us to define schedule intervals from an arbitrary start date in the past. We can use this property to perform historical runs of our DAG for loading or analyzing past data sets—a process typically referred to as *backfilling*. This process works particularly well when combined with interval-based schedules (section 3.4).

Backfilling behavior (figure 3.9) is controlled by the catchup parameter, which can be enabled or disabled explicitly for a given DAG. As mentioned earlier, in Airflow 3, catchup is disabled by default, so historical runs won't be processed unless you explicitly enable catchup. By contrast, Airflow 2 enables catchup by default. We strongly advise you to explicitly set the catchup behavior for your DAG.

Although backfilling is a powerful concept, it's limited by the availability of data in source systems. In our example use case, we can load past events from our API by specifying a start date up to seven days in the past. Because the API provides no more than seven days of history, however, we can't use backfilling to load data from earlier days.

catchup=True

**Airflow starts processing, including
past intervals (= backfilling).**

Start
date

*Current
interval*

Now

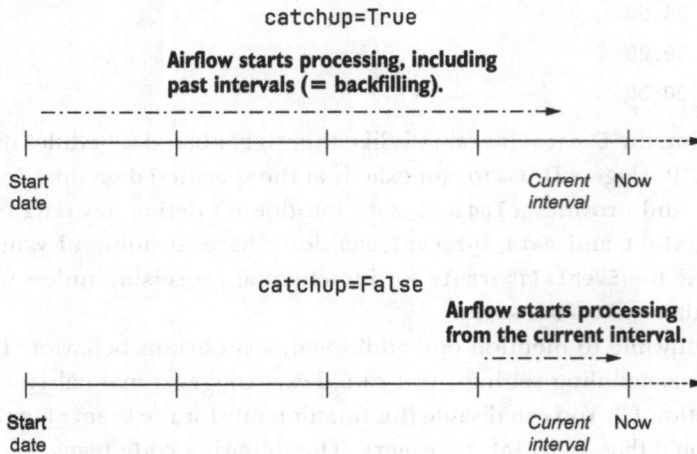

**Figure 3.9   Backfilling
in Airflow. By default,
Airflow 3 won't run
tasks for all past
intervals up to the
current time. You can
change this behavior
by setting the** catchup
parameter of a DAG to
True, **in which case
Airflow will also include
historical runs.**

catchup=False

**Airflow starts processing
from the current interval.**

Start
date

*Current
interval*

Now

We can also use backfilling to reprocess data after we make changes in our code or find corrupted data in historic DAG runs. Suppose that we change our calc_statistics function to add a new statistic. Using backfilling, we can clear past runs of our calc_statistics task to reanalyze our historical data using the new code. In this case, we aren't restricted by the seven-day limit of our data source because we loaded these earlier data partitions as part of our past runs.

One thing to consider is the load that backfilling will place on Airflow and on any external systems it interacts with. When you start backfilling, Airflow tries to catch up as quickly as possible, which can lead to the creation of hundreds (or more) of parallel DAG runs. As a result, other DAG runs may be crowded out or external systems may be overloaded.

You have ways to control this behavior a little. One way is to use pools. (See chapter 12 for details.) But you can also change some other configurations at the DAG level:

- You can use the max_active_tasks parameter of a DAG to set the maximum number of parallel task instances of this DAG that can run in parallel. This setting defaults to Airflow's value for core.max_active_tasks_per_dag (16 by default) if you don't set anything explicitly.

NOTE   In Airflow 2 this parameter was named concurrency (with core.dag_concurrency being the global setting).

- You can use the max_active_runs parameter of a DAG to set the maximum number of active runs for a DAG. Especially in backfilling scenarios, this approach can be useful. When Airflow hits this maximum, it won't create new DAG runs until previous ones have completed. If this parameter is left unset, the value is set to core.max_active_runs_per_dag (by default, 16).

The DAG definition

```
dag = DAG('my_dag', max_active_tasks=10, max_active_runs=2)
```

means this DAG could have at most 10 tasks running in parallel, spread out over at most two DAG runs.

3.7 *Designing well-behaved tasks*

Although Airflow does much of the heavy lifting in backfilling and rerunning tasks, we have to ensure that our tasks fulfill certain key properties for proper results. In this section, we dive into two of the most important properties of proper Airflow tasks: atomicity and idempotency.

3.7.1 *Atomicity*

The term *atomicity* is frequently used in database systems, where an atomic transaction is considered to be an indivisible, irreducible series of database operations: everything occurs, or nothing occurs. Similarly, in Airflow, tasks should be defined so that they succeed and produce some proper result or fail in a manner that doesn't affect the state of the system (figure 3.10).

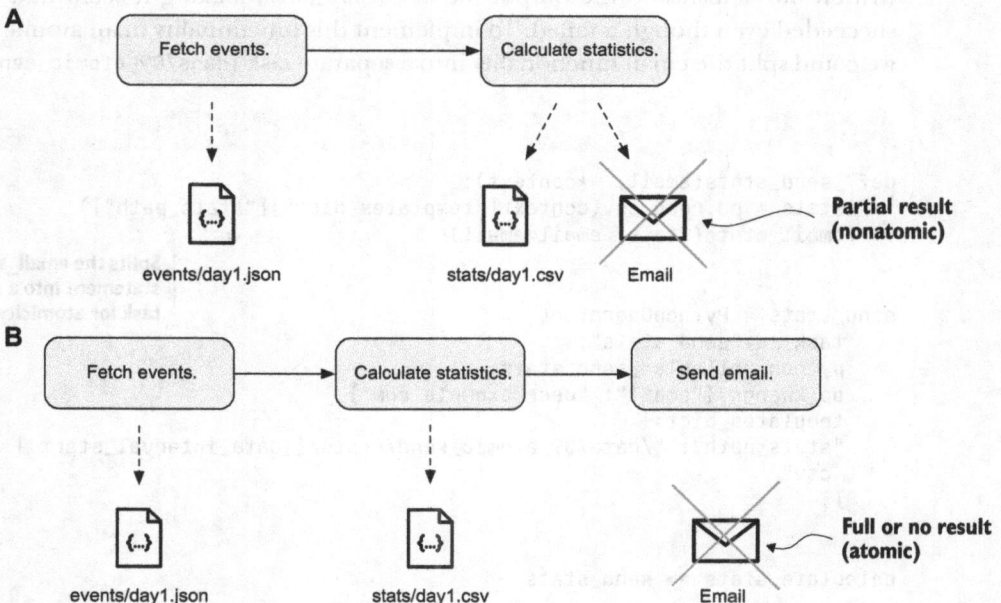

Figure 3.10 Atomicity means operations either fully complete or don't happen at all, preventing incomplete or incorrect work. (a) This non-atomic Airflow DAG shows a single task handling two jobs. If one job fails, the task is left in failed state, hiding the fact that data may still have been written. (b) In this atomic Airflow DAG, each job is a separate task. This ensures each job fully finishes or doesn't run, correctly reflecting the result of each task.

Consider a simple extension to our user-event DAG. We want to add some functionality that sends an email to our top 10 users at the end of each run. One simple way to add this extension is to extend our previous function with a call to some function that sends an email containing our statistics (dags/08_non_atomic_send.py).

Listing 3.16   Two jobs in one task, breaking atomicity

```
def _calculate_stats(**context):
    """Calculates event statistics."""
    input_path = context["templates_dict"]["input_path"]
    output_path = context["templates_dict"]["output_path"]

    events = pd.read_json(input_path)
    stats = events.groupby(["date", "user"]).size().reset_index()
    stats.to_csv(output_path, index=False)

    email_stats(stats, email="user@example.com")    ◀── Sends an email after writing to
                                                         CSV creates two pieces of work
                                                         in a single function, breaking
                                                         the atomicity of the task
```

Unfortunately, a drawback to this approach is that the task is no longer atomic. Can you see why? If not, consider what happens if the email_stats function fails (which is bound to happen if the email server is a bit flaky). In this case, we'll already have written our statistics to the output file at output_path, making it seem that our task succeeded even though it failed. To implement this functionality in an atomic fashion, we could split the email functionality into a separate task (dags/09_atomic_send.py).

Listing 3.17   Splitting functionality into multiple tasks to improve atomicity

```
def _send_stats(email, **context):
    stats = pd.read_csv(context["templates_dict"]["stats_path"])
    email_stats(stats, email=email)    ◀── Splits the email_stats
                                           statement into a separate
                                           task for atomicity

send_stats = PythonOperator(
    task_id="send_stats",
    python_callable=_send_stats,
    op_kwargs={"email": "user@example.com"},
    templates_dict={
    "stats_path": "/data/09_atomic_send/stats/{{data_interval_start | ds}}.
     csv"
    },
)

calculate_stats >> send_stats
```

This way, failing to send an email no longer affects the result of the calculate_stats task; only send_stats fails, making both tasks atomic. Based on this example, you may think that separating all operations into individual tasks is sufficient to make all your tasks atomic. This isn't necessarily true, however. To understand why, think about what would happen if your event API required you to log in before querying for events. You'd generally need an extra API call to fetch some authentication token, after which you could start retrieving events.

Following your previous reasoning of one operation = one task, you'd have to split these operations into two separate tasks. Doing so, however, would create a strong dependency between them because the second task (fetching the events) would fail if the first one didn't run shortly before. This strong dependency between tasks means that you're likely to be better off keeping both operations within a single task, allowing the task to form a single, coherent unit of work.

Most Airflow operators are designed to be atomic, which is why many operators include options for performing tightly coupled operations such as authentication internally. But more flexible operators, such as the Python and Bash operators, may require you to think carefully about your operations to make sure that your tasks remain atomic.

3.7.2 Idempotency

Another important property to consider when writing Airflow tasks is idempotency. Tasks are said to be *idempotent* if calling the same task multiple times with the same inputs has no additional effect. This means that rerunning a task without changing the inputs shouldn't change the overall output. The easy way to perform such a rerun is to click the Clear Task button in the UI. That triggers Airflow to run the task again, but with the same schedule interval's variable values (as opposed to triggering a new run manually). Consider the following implementation of the fetch_events task (dags/06_interval_delta.py), which fetches the results for a single day and writes them to our partitioned data set.

Listing 3.18 Existing implementation for fetching events

```
fetch_events = BashOperator(
    task_id="fetch_events",
    bash_command=(
        "mkdir -p /data/events && "
        "curl -o  /data/events/{{ logical_date | ds }}.json "
        "'http://events-api:8081/events/range?"
        "start_date={{data_interval_start | ds}}&"        Partitions by setting
        "end_date={{data_interval_end | ds}}'"            templated filename
    ),
)
```

If we rerun this task for a given date, the task fetches the same set of events as it did during its previous execution (assuming that the date is within our 30-day window) and overwrites the existing JSON file in the /data/events folder, producing the same result. This implementation of the fetch_events task is clearly idempotent.

To see an example of a nonidempotent task, consider using a single JSON file (/data/events.json) and simply appending events to this file. In this case, if you rerun a task, the events would be appended to the existing data set, thus duplicating the day's events (figure 3.11). This implementation is not idempotent because additional executions of the task change the overall result.

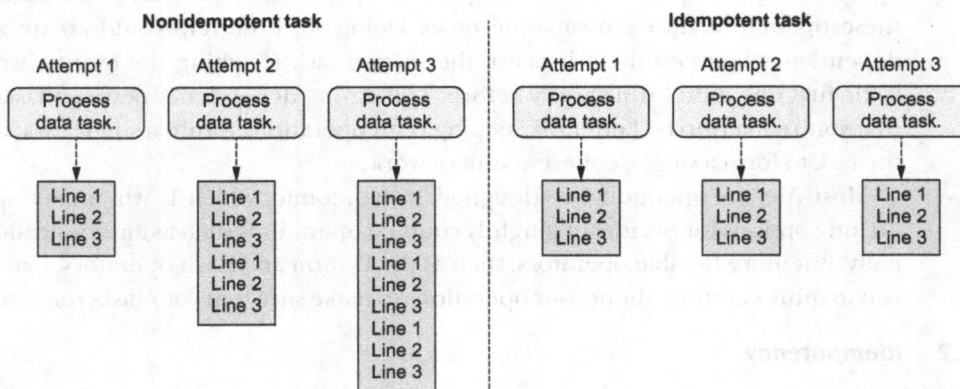

Figure 3.11   An idempotent task produces the same result no matter how many times you run it. Idempotency ensures consistency and ability to deal with failure.

In general, we can make tasks that write data idempotent by checking for existing results or making sure that previous results are overwritten by the task. In time-partitioned data sets, this process is relatively straightforward: we overwrite the corresponding partition. Similarly, for database systems, we can use upsert operations to insert data, allowing us to overwrite existing rows that were written by previous task executions. In more general applications, however, we should carefully consider all side effects of our task and make sure that they're performed in an idempotent fashion.

Summary

- In Airflow, scheduling is a fundamental feature that allows the automated triggering of workflows.
- Two main types of scheduling are used to trigger DAGs in Airflow. Time-based schedules (covered in this chapter) trigger DAGs at regular or irregular intervals at given points in time. Asset-based schedules (discussed in chapter 4) take a different approach.
- Time-based schedules are defined with four main parameters: start_date (marks when scheduling begins), schedule (defines the frequency of runs), an optional end_date (marks when scheduling ends), and catchup (determines whether executions will be scheduled for past time points).
- Trigger-based time schedules allow you to execute DAGs at regularly occurring points in time. Execution of a DAG occurs at the specific point in time defined by the schedule (e.g., midnight). During execution, the schedule provides

the `logical_date` parameter with the exact point in time for which the DAG is executing.

- Data-interval-based schedules are ideal for incremental processing because they divide time into discrete intervals. DAG execution for a given date happens at the end of an interval. Information about the start and end of the interval is provided by the `data_interval_start` and `data_interval_end` parameters.

- You can define trigger- and data-interval-based schedules using `cron` expressions, frequencies (e.g., using `pendulum.duration`), and Airflow shorthand expressions (e.g., `@daily`).

- You can implement irregular time schedules using the `EventsTimetable`, which allows you to trigger DAGs at an arbitrary list of moments in time.

- Backfilling (controlled by the `catchup` parameter) enables the execution of workflows for past intervals to process historical data by running DAGs retrospectively from a chosen start date.

- Atomicity ensures that operations in a series are treated as a single unit, completing entirely or not at all, whereas idempotency ensures that rerunning a task with unchanged inputs doesn't alter the result.

- Airflow 3 made considerable changes to the default scheduling behavior, moving from data-interval-based schedules to trigger-based schedules as the default and switching the default `catchup` behavior from `True` to `False`. We recommend being explicit in your schedules to prevent nasty surprises, especially when migrating from Airflow 2 to 3.

Asset-aware scheduling

This chapter covers

- Splitting DAGs into producer and consumer DAGs
- Defining dependencies between DAGs using assets
- Updating assets in producer DAGs and triggering consumer DAGs
- Passing information between producers and consumers
- Defining complex dependencies on multiple assets

In chapter 3, we focused on time-based scheduling for tasks that are executed at predefined times or intervals. This method works well in many situations but can be problematic for scaling beyond individual directed acyclic graphs (DAGs). In this chapter, we'll dive into an alternative event-driven approach called *asset-aware scheduling*, which explicitly models dependencies between DAGs as assets and triggers DAGs whenever the assets they depend on are updated.

4.1 Challenges of scaling time-based schedules

In chapter 3, we scheduled a DAG to ingest user events from an API at regular time intervals. But what happens when multiple teams—perhaps for analytics, marketing, and performance monitoring—need access to the same data?

We could allow each team to build its own pipeline to fetch the data (figure 4.1A). But this approach introduces several problems:

- The load increases when multiple DAGs request the same data from an API, which can lead to performance issues or extra costs.
- If the API endpoints change, the logic would have to be updated in multiple places.
- If teams implement the data retrieval logic differently, they could create data inconsistencies and conflicting business insights.

A better approach would be to have a single team prepare the data in a producer DAG, which downstream teams can then use in consumer DAGs (figure 4.1B). This solves the data consistency problem but introduces a new challenge: how do the consumer DAGs know when to run?

A   *Every team fetching its own data*   **B**   *Central producer with multiple consumers*

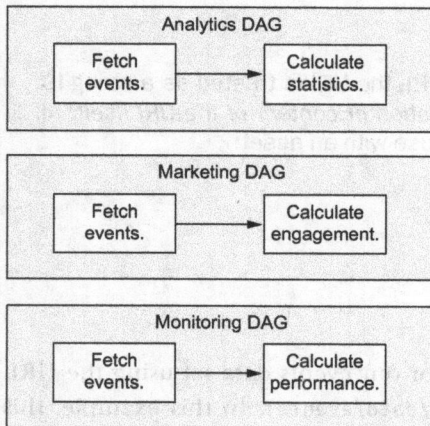 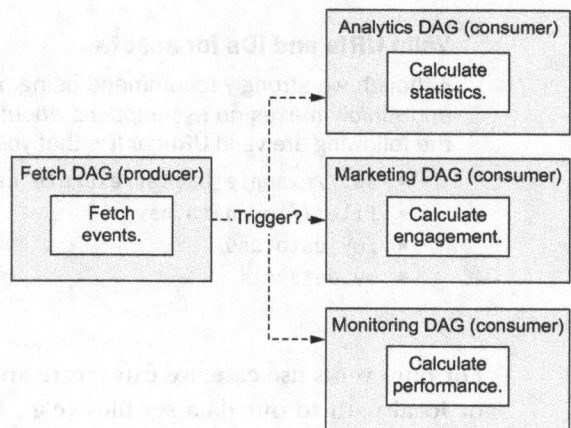

Figure 4.1 When multiple teams rely on the same data, each team can do its own ingestion (A), but this is hardly efficient and can lead to inconsistencies. In this case, it's more efficient to have a single team ingest the data and trigger the other teams' workloads whenever new data is ingested (B). But how do we align the schedules of the producer and consumer DAGs?

We could try to align the schedules, running the consumer DAGs shortly after the producer DAG is scheduled to finish, but this approach is both inefficient and brittle. The consumer DAGs would run on a fixed schedule even if the source data hasn't changed, wasting resources. Furthermore, if the data engineering team changes its schedule or its DAG's run time is unpredictable, the consumer DAGs may run with incomplete or outdated data.

Another option could be for the producer DAG to trigger the consumer DAGs directly. But this would create tight coupling between the workflows. The producer DAG needs to know about all its consumers, which doesn't scale well because the DAG would have to keep a manually curated list of all the downstream consumers as more teams start using the data set (an error-prone process). Fortunately, asset-aware scheduling offers a more robust and efficient solution.

4.2   Introducing asset-aware scheduling

Asset-aware scheduling allows you to define relationships between DAGs in terms of the assets they consume and produce. As you'll see, this explicit modeling of relationships is a powerful concept, allowing us to easily couple producer and consumer DAGs without the drawbacks outlined in the preceding section.

An *asset* is a virtual reference and can be anything depending on your use case: a data set, a data table, a machine learning model, and so on. An asset is identified by its Uniform Resource Identifier (URI), which generally reflects the unique location of the asset. For a data set stored on Amazon's S3 service, for example, you could use a URI that points to the data set: s3://example_bucket/example.csv.

> ### Valid URIs and IDs for assets
>
> Although we strongly recommend using a valid URI, the URI is treated as a string ID, and *Airflow makes no assumptions about the location or content of the URI itself*. All the following are valid URIs or IDs that you could use with an asset:
>
> - s3://example_bucket/example.csv
> - file://tmp/data.csv
> - /my_data.csv
> - my_dataset

For our events use case, we can create an asset for our events data set using the URL or local path to our data set files (e.g., file:///data/events). In this example, this identifier is unique enough, though in a broader setting, we may want to use a cloud bucket or other shared storage that uniquely identifies the data set and all consumers can access.

With this asset in hand, we can split our original events DAG into two parts: a producer DAG, which fetches and stores the events, and a consumer DAG, which processes new events and calculates event statistics (figure 4.2). Both DAGs are connected to the data set asset. For the producer DAG, the asset is an output of the DAG, meaning that it will generate an asset event whenever it updates the data set. For the consumer DAG, the asset is an input, which means that Airflow will trigger the DAG automatically

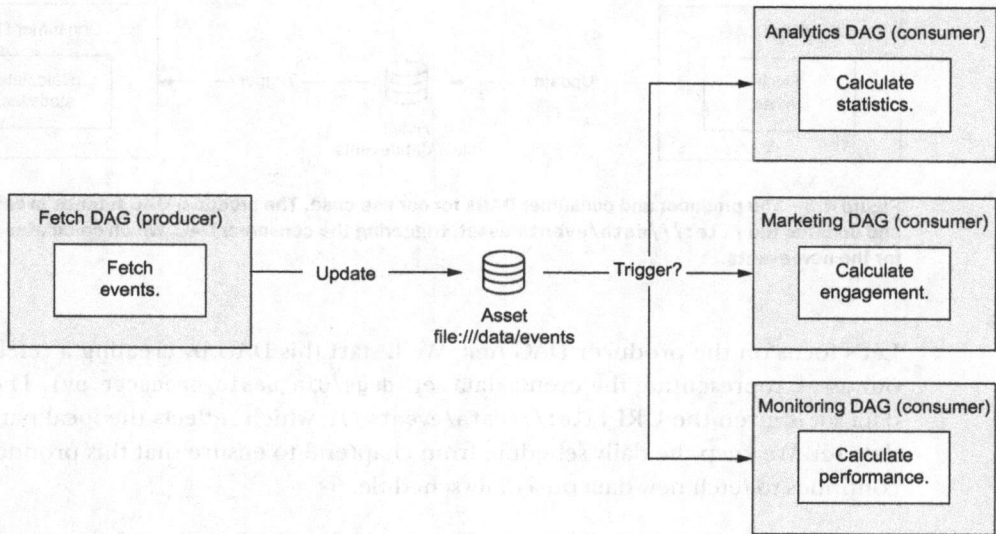

Figure 4.2 Splitting the events DAG into separate producer and consumer DAGs that different teams own. The producer DAG creates and updates an asset representing the event data set, which is consumed by the downstream DAGs owned by the other teams. Airflow ensures that these downstream DAGs are triggered automatically whenever the asset is updated.

whenever the asset is updated, passing the relevant asset events to the consumer DAG in the process.

If necessary, we can easily extend this example to multiple consumers by adding more consumer DAGs that reference the same asset. This option gives us a powerful approach to scaling workloads across multiple DAGs—one that is much less brittle than time-based scheduling.

NOTE Asset-aware scheduling doesn't provide any notion of time; therefore, it's less suitable for DAGs that need to run on a fixed schedule. Together, however, the two approaches are quite powerful: combined, they allow you to both fetch data daily using a time-based schedule and trigger downstream DAGs dynamically using asset-aware scheduling.

4.3 Producing asset events

Now that you know the basics of asset-aware scheduling, it's time to put this knowledge into practice. In this section, you'll modify the existing event-processing DAG from chapter 3 to apply the producer/consumer pattern described in section 4.1. This process effectively creates two DAGs: a producer DAG that creates and updates the events data set asset and a consumer DAG that reacts to any updates to the asset and calculates statistics for new data (figure 4.3).

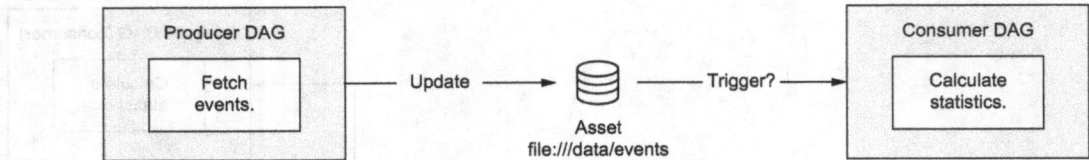

Figure 4.3   The producer and consumer DAGs for our use case. The producer DAG fetches event data and updates the `file:///data/events` asset, triggering the consumer DAG, which calculates statistics for the new events.

Let's focus on the producer DAG first. We'll start this DAG by creating a reference to our asset, representing the events data set (dags/01a_basic_producer.py). The events data set is given the URI `file:///data/events_01`, which reflects the local path to the data set. We keep the daily schedule from chapter 3 to ensure that this producer DAG continues to fetch new data on a daily schedule.

Listing 4.1   Defining an asset for the events data set

```
from airflow.sdk import DAG, Asset
from airflow.timetables.interval import CronDataIntervalTimetable
...

events_dataset = Asset("file:///data/events_01")    ◄──  Defines the data set asset, with
                                                          the URI as the only parameter
with DAG(
    dag_id="01_producer",
    schedule=CronDataIntervalTimetable("0 0 * * *", timezone="UTC"),    ◄──
    start_date=pendulum.yesterday(),
    catchup=True                                      Keeps running this
):                                                    DAG on a daily schedule
    ...
```

Next, to emit an event whenever the events data set is updated, we connect the asset instance to the Airflow task that updates the data set. We can make this connection by passing the asset to the `outlets` argument of the corresponding operator (dags/01a_basic_producer.py). The code for the `fetch_events` function itself is unchanged from chapter 3 and omitted from the following listing for brevity.

Listing 4.2   Adding the asset as an output of the `fetch_events` task

```
fetch_events = PythonOperator(
    task_id="fetch_events",
    python_callable=_fetch_events,
    op_kwargs={
        "start_date": "{{ data_interval_start | ds }}",
        "end_date": "{{ data_interval_end | ds }}",
        "output_path": "/data/events/{{ data_interval_start |
    ds }}.json",
```

```
    },
    outlets=[events_dataset],
)
```

Adds a reference from our task to the events_dataset asset

Now we run the DAG by enabling it in the Airflow UI. Airflow should trigger a run for the previous day, fetching data for that day and emitting an asset event to indicate that the data set was updated.

We can check which asset events were generated by opening the Assets tab in the Airflow UI and selecting the `file:///data/events_01` asset we created. This view (figure 4.4) shows our producing DAG together with the data set it creates (left) as well as the list of asset events that was generated (right).

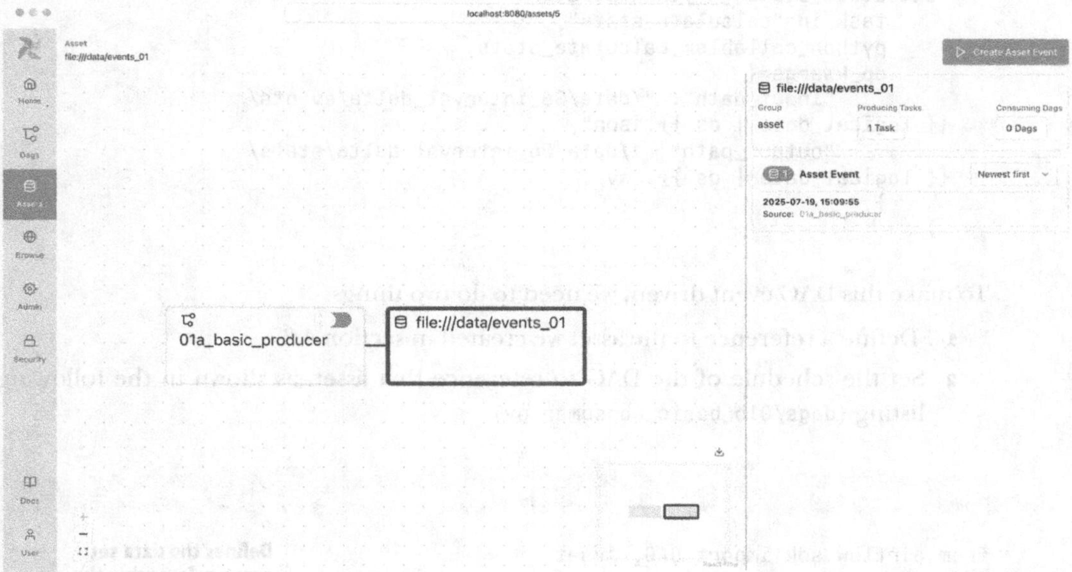

Figure 4.4 Asset view in the Airflow UI. On the left, you see the relationship between the asset and the producer DAG. On the right, you see the event(s) produced by runs of the producer DAG.

4.4 Consuming asset events

Now that we have a DAG that updates the data set for us, let's connect the downstream consumer DAG, which calculates statistics whenever the data set is updated. This DAG won't have a fixed schedule but will be triggered by updates to the events data set asset.

As you may remember from chapter 3, the code for calculating event statistics reads a day's worth of events, calculates some statistics for these events, and writes the result to a CSV file named after the same date, as shown in the next listing (`chapter03/dags/06_ interval_delta.py`).

```
def _calculate_stats(input_path, output_path):
    """Calculates event statistics."""
    ...

with DAG(
    dag_id="06_interval_delta",
    schedule=CronDataIntervalTimetable("@daily", timezone="UTC"),
    start_date=pendulum.datetime(year=2024, month=1, day=1, tz="Europe/
     Amsterdam"),
    end_date=pendulum.datetime(year=2024, month=1, day=5),
    catchup=True,):
    ...

    calculate_stats = PythonOperator(
        task_id="calculate_stats",
        python_callable=_calculate_stats,
        op_kwargs={
            "input_path": "/data/06_interval_delta/events/
 {{ logical_date | ds }}.json",
            "output_path": "/data/06_interval_delta/stats/
 {{ logical_date | ds }}.csv",
        },
    )
```

To make this DAG event driven, we need to do two things:

1 Define a reference to the asset we created in section 4.3.

2 Set the schedule of the DAG to reference that asset, as shown in the following listing (dags/01b_basic_consumer.py).

```
from airflow.sdk import DAG, Asset                    ← Defines the data set
                                                         asset, referencing the
events_dataset = Asset("file:///data/events_01")  ←     same URI as before

with DAG(
    dag_id="01b_consumer",                           ← Sets the schedule of
    schedule=[events_dataset],                          the DAG to this asset
    start_date=pendulum.datetime(year=2024, month=1, day=1),
):
    ...
```

That's it. Now every time the producer DAG updates the asset with the URI file:///
data/events, the consumer DAG is triggered. You can test this by enabling the consumer DAG and clearing one task of the producer DAG. This clearing ensures that the task is rerun, thus producing a new event to trigger the DAG. Unfortunately, you'll get the following error message, indicating that you're not quite done:

```
Exception rendering Jinja template for task 'calculate_stats', field
    'op_kwargs'. Template: {'input_path': '/data/events/{{ logical_date |
    ds }}.json', 'output_path': '/data/stats/{{ logical_date | ds
    }}.csv'}: source="airflow.sdk.definitions._internal.abstractoperator"
UndefinedError: 'logical_date' is undefined
```

This error occurs because event-driven DAGs don't define any date- or interval-related parameters, unlike their time-based counterparts from chapter 3. Conceptually this makes sense: asset-driven DAGs don't follow a time-based schedule, so these concepts therefore don't apply.

This situation poses an interesting conundrum: how do we know which slice of our data set to load if we don't know the day for which our DAG is executing? One way to get this information would be to inspect the DAG run that generated the event; the producing DAG is scheduled and therefore should have this information.

Airflow allows us to access this information using the `triggering_asset_events` variable in the Airflow context, which provides the collection of the events that triggered our DAG. This variable is a dictionary of events, with keys reflecting the assets (we can have more than one triggering asset) and the values being a list of events (DAGs can generate more than one event per asset). In this case, we have only one triggering asset and expect only a single event, so we can fetch the logical date of our triggering DAG as shown in the next listing (`dags/01b_basic_consumer.py`). Here, the expression `| first | first` ensures that we grab the first (and only) event of our asset, whereas the `source_dag_run` attribute allows us to reference the `logical_date` of the producer DAG run that generated the event.

Listing 4.5 Defining the `input_path`/`output_path` parameters based on source DAG

```
calculate_stats = PythonOperator(
    task_id="calculate_stats",
    python_callable=_calculate_stats,
    op_kwargs={
        "input_path": "/data/events/{{
    (triggering_asset_events.values() | first |
    first).source_dag_run.logical_date }}.json",
        "output_path": "/data/stats/{{
    (triggering_asset_events.values() | first |
    first).source_dag_run.logical_date }}.csv",
    },
)
```

Defines the input path and output paths based on the logical date of the source DAG run (the run of the producer DAG)

Defines the output path to read from using the producer DAG's values and variable values from the producer DAG run

Broken behavior in Airflow 3: The missing source_dag_run attribute

Unfortunately, this example doesn't work in Airflow 3 as of this writing because the `source_dag_run` attribute seems to have been removed accidentally in the switch from Airflow 2 to 3 (see https://github.com/apache/airflow/issues/52932 for details). Because the example is still present in the Airflow documentation, we expect the issue to be fixed in the near future. In the meantime, you can use the metadata approach discussed in section 4.5 as a workaround.

Now if you rerun the consuming DAG (by clearing the consumer DAG task or the upstream producer DAG task), you should see the task successfully reading the correct file and generating the corresponding set of statistics. If you open the asset view, you should also see the consumer DAG linked to the asset in the view on the left (figure 4.5).

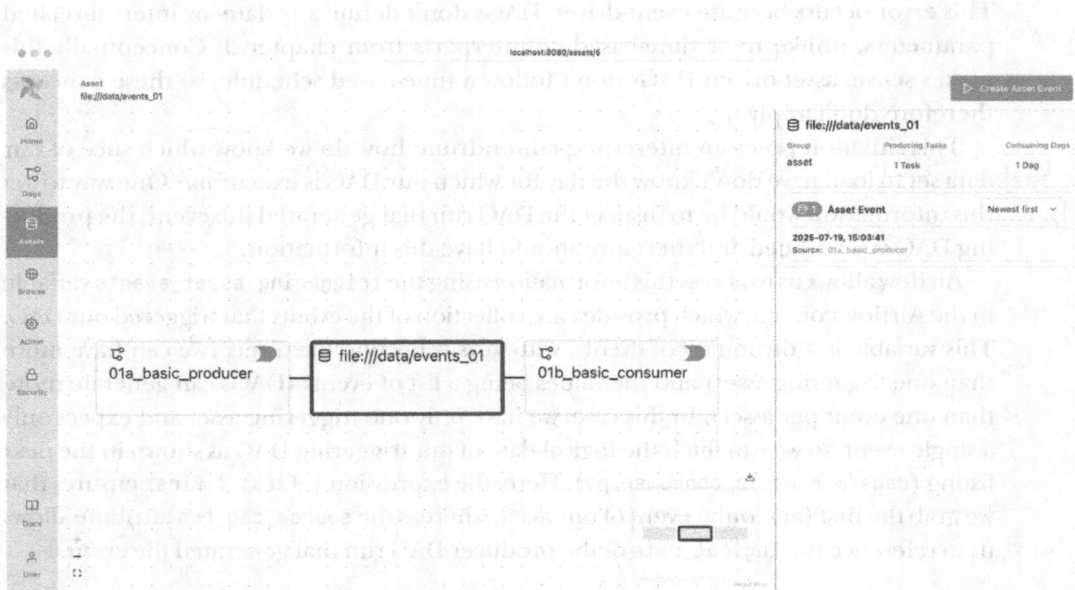

Figure 4.5   View of the events data set asset, now including the relationship with the consumer DAG

> **WARNING**   The `logical_date` you use to generate the file paths is available only because the producer has a time-based schedule. If this DAG were also triggered on an event or had a manual trigger, it would not contain this information. You must take this dependency into account when setting up relationships between DAGs using event-driven scheduling because changing the schedule type of the producing DAG will also affect its consumers if they rely on this schedule information.

4.5   *Adding extra information to events*

As an alternative, Airflow allows you to add metadata to an asset event. This metadata is reflected in the `extra` field of an event, which is essentially a dictionary of arbitrary values depending on your needs.

In our use case, we could decide to add a `date` metadata field to the event that contains the date for which data was loaded. To do so, we modify the `fetch_events` task to generate a `Metadata` object containing the required information, as shown in the following listing (`dags/02a_metadata_producer`).

Listing 4.6 Adding a `Metadata` object to an asset event

```
from airflow.sdk import DAG, Asset, Metadata
...
def _fetch_events(start_date, end_date, output_path, logical_date):
    ...
    yield Metadata(events_dataset, extra={"date": logical_date.strftime("%Y-
%m-%d")}})
```

→ Imports the Metadata class

→ Modifies the function to include the logical date from the Airflow context

→ Returns a Metadata instance referencing the asset and defining a date metadata attribute based on the logical date

You can test this by running the new DAG and inspecting the generated events from the UI on the Assets tab. The new events include an extra `metadata` field in the UI, which (if you expand the field) shows the corresponding date of each run (figure 4.6).

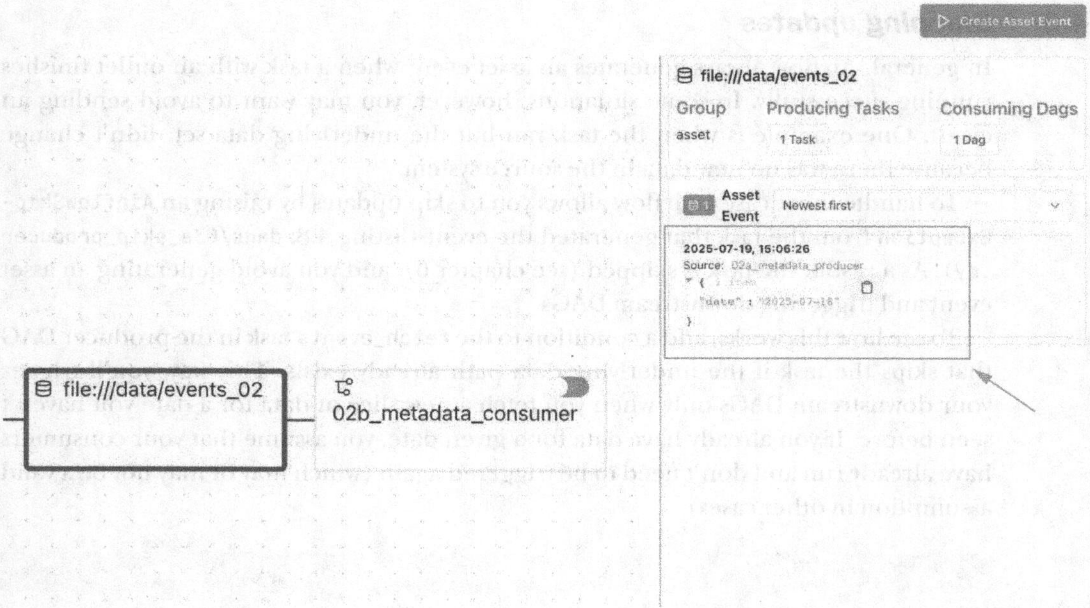

Figure 4.6 View of the asset event, now including the data from the extra `metadata` field

We can reference the new metadata value in our consumer DAG via the `extra` field of the asset event. This metadata value allows us to generate the input and output paths for reading input data and writing our output (`dags/02b_metadata_consumer.py`).

```
calculate_stats = PythonOperator(
    task_id="calculate_stats",
    python_callable=_calculate_stats,
    op_kwargs={
        "input_path": "/data/events_02/{{
(triggering_asset_events.values() | first | first).extra.date
}}.json",
        "output_path": "/data/stats_02/{{
(triggering_asset_events.values() | first |
first).extra.date }}.csv",
    },
)
```

WARNING   When you define metadata attributes, it's important to agree with your downstream consumers which attributes will be provided and what values they contain. It's tempting to see these fields as extra information you provide, but they're an important part of the data contract with your consumers because changes to these fields will potentially break their pipelines.

4.6 *Skipping updates*

In general, Airflow always generates an asset event when a task with an outlet finishes running successfully. In some situations, however, you may want to avoid sending an event. One example is when the task ran but the underlying data set didn't change because there was no new data in the source system.

To handle these cases, Airflow allows you to skip updates by raising an `AirflowSkip-Exception` from the task that generated the event (listing 4.8; `dags/03a_skip_producer.py`). As a result, the task is skipped (see chapter 6), and you avoid generating an asset event and triggering downstream DAGs.

To see how this works, add a condition to the `fetch_events` task in the producer DAG that skips the task if the underlying data path already exists. This way, you'll trigger your downstream DAGs only when you fetch a new slice of data for a date you haven't seen before. If you already have data for a given date, you assume that your consumers have already run and don't need to be triggered again (which may or may not be a valid assumption in other cases).

```
from pathlib import Path
from airflow.exceptions import AirflowSkipException
...

def _fetch_events(start_date, end_date, output_path):
    if Path(output_path).exists():
    raise AirflowSkipException()
    else:
    ...
```

Now if you run the DAG for the first time, you'll see the DAG fetching data and triggering downstream consumer DAGs. Then if you clear the run task (in the producer DAG), the task runs again but this time is skipped because the underlying data file already exists (figure 4.7). Likewise, any downstream DAGs will not be triggered in this case.

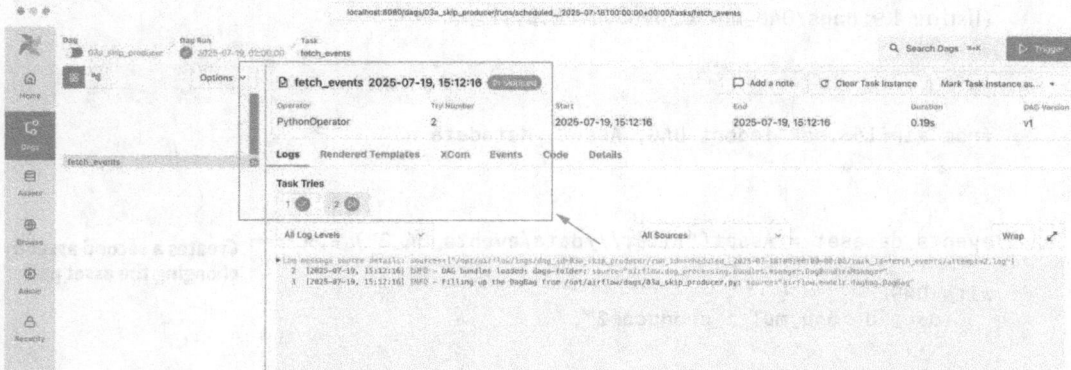

Figure 4.7   The second run of the task is skipped because the data file already exists, ensuring that any DAGs downstream listening to the asset aren't triggered because no new data is available to process.

4.7   *Consuming multiple assets*

For more complex workflows, Airflow allows you to generate or consume multiple assets in a single DAG. A common example is a consumer DAG that takes multiple input data sets and combines (joins) them to generate one or more outputs. To see how this works, extend your events DAG to consume two input data sets (figure 4.8).

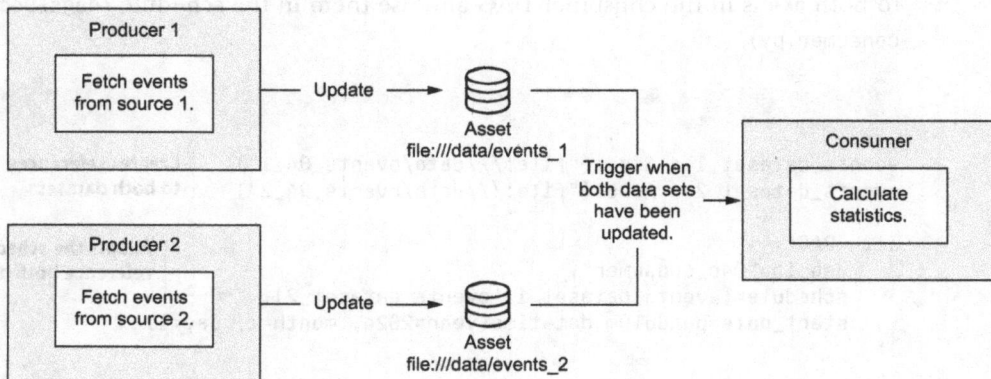

Figure 4.8   Adding a second producer that conceptually fetches additional event data from a different source.

This situation could arise if, for example, you suddenly have multiple sources generating events that need to be combined to a single output.

To simulate this case, we'll add an extra producer DAG that generates events. For simplicity, we'll create a copy of our existing DAG and change only the DAG ID and the path to which data is written. In reality, this DAG would also pull events from a different source (such as an API), but we'll keep the API the same for both producers for now (listing 4.9; dags/04b_multi_producer2.py).

Listing 4.9   Creating a second producer DAG

```
from airflow.sdk import DAG, Asset, Metadata

...

events_dataset = Asset("file:///data/events_04_2")          ◀── Creates a second asset by
                                                                changing the asset path
with DAG(
    dag_id="04b_multi_producer2",
    ...
):

    fetch_events = PythonOperator(
        ...
        op_kwargs={
            ...
            "output_path": "/data/events_04_2/
 {{ data_interval_start | ds }}.json",          ◀── Changes the data
        },                                              path to match
        ...
    )
```

With this extra DAG, we have two producer DAGs: one for each event source and one consumer DAG. To consume events from both these producers, we add references to both assets in the consumer DAG and use them in the schedule (dags/04c_multi_consumer.py).

Listing 4.10   Consumer DAG with multiple assets

```
events_dataset_1 = Asset("file:///data/events_04_1")     Creates references
events_dataset_2 = Asset("file:///data/events_04_2")     to both datasets

with DAG(                                                        Adapts the schedule to
    dag_id="04c_consumer",                                       reference both datasets
    schedule=[events_dataset_1, events_dataset_2],       ◀──
    start_date=pendulum.datetime(year=2024, month=1, day=1)
):
```

Next, we need to ensure that our consumer DAG will process data from both data sources. To achieve this, we can modify the _calculate_stats function to take a list of input files instead of a single input file, as shown in the following listing (dags/04c_ multi_consumer.py).

Listing 4.11 Processing data from multiple assets

```python
def _calculate_stats(input_paths, output_path):
    """Calculates event statistics."""
    events = pd.concat(
        pd.read_json(input_path, convert_dates=["timestamp"],
            lines=True) for input_path in input_paths
    )

    stats = (
        events.assign(date=lambda df: df["timestamp"].dt.date).
            groupby(["date", "user"]).size().reset_index()
    )

    Path(output_path).parent.mkdir(exist_ok=True)
    stats.to_csv(output_path, index=False)
```

Modifies the function signature to accept multiple paths

Reads the files and concatenates their contents

This modified function reads data from one or more input files and combines them into a single data set. Afterward, it continues to calculate statistics as it did before.

Finally, we need to adjust the PythonOperator task to pass an input_paths argument that references both data sets. We can do this by using the same triggering_dataset_ events variable we used before, but this time, we explicitly select the event for each of the data sets. To help with this task, we've created a small macro function, get_event, that fetches the first event in each data set for us. (For more details on templating and macros, see chapter 5.) We can use this macro function in the DAG by calling it inside the path templates, passing the URI of the corresponding asset to make sure we get the right event (dags/04c_multi_consumer.py).

Listing 4.12 Extracting specific events from specific assets

```python
def _get_event(triggering_asset_events, uri):
    return triggering_asset_events[Asset(uri)][0]

with DAG(
    ...
    user_defined_macros={"get_event": _get_event},
):

    ...
    calculate_stats = PythonOperator(
        task_id="calculate_stats",
        python_callable=_calculate_stats,
        op_kwargs={
            "input_paths": [
                "/data/events_04_1/{{get_event(triggering_asset_events,
'file:///data/events_04_1').extra.date }}.json",
                "/data/events_04_2/{{get_event(triggering_asset_events,
```

Defines a custom macro function to get the first event for a specific asset

Passes the macro to the DAG

Uses the macro to extract the date from the extra field of the asset events

```
      'file:///data/events_04_2').extra.date }}.json",
            ],
            "output_path":
    "/data/stats_04/{{get_event(triggering_asset_events,
      'file:///data/events_04_1').extra.date }}.csv",
        },
    )
```

Now that we've modified the DAG to handle multiple input data sets, let's try running it. If we open the DAGs view in the Airflow UI, we see that our new DAG (04c_multi_consumer) is waiting for events from both of our assets (figure 4.9). Similarly, if we open the Assets view and select either of the assets (e.g., file:///data/events_04_1) we'll get a view of the two assets and their relationship with our producer and consumer DAGs (figure 4.10).

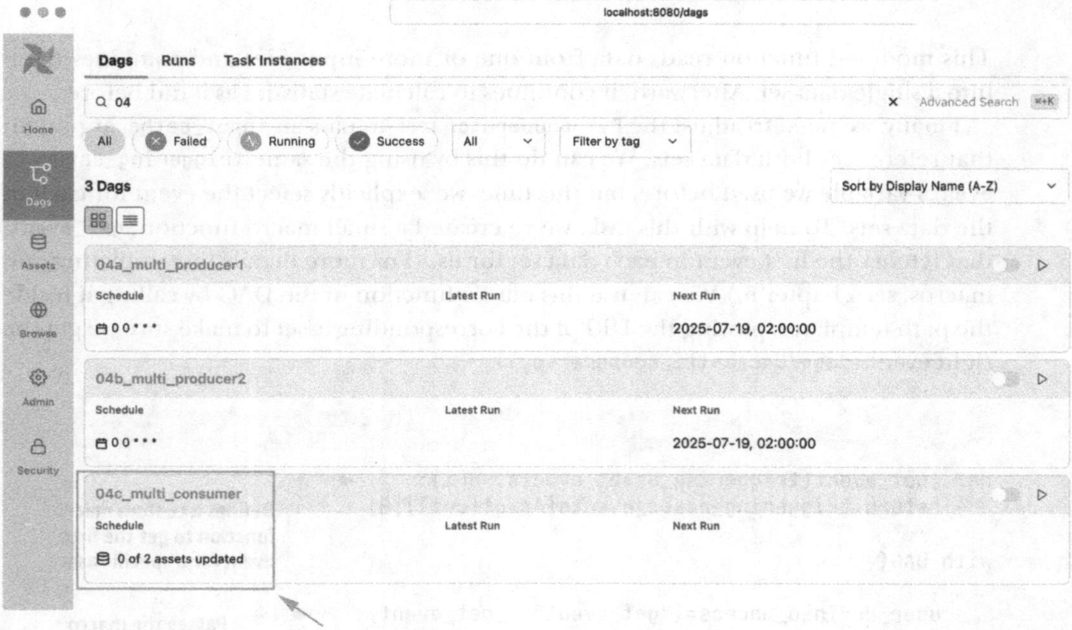

Figure 4.9 The DAG listing view, showing that the new DAG is waiting for events from two different assets. The first number updates when events occur and resets after each run of the consumer DAG.

To generate the first event, we enable the consumer DAG (04c_multi_consumer) and then enable the first producer DAG (04a_multi_producer). The producer DAG starts running and generates an event. This should be reflected in the status of the consumer DAG but shouldn't trigger the consumer DAG because we have only one event.

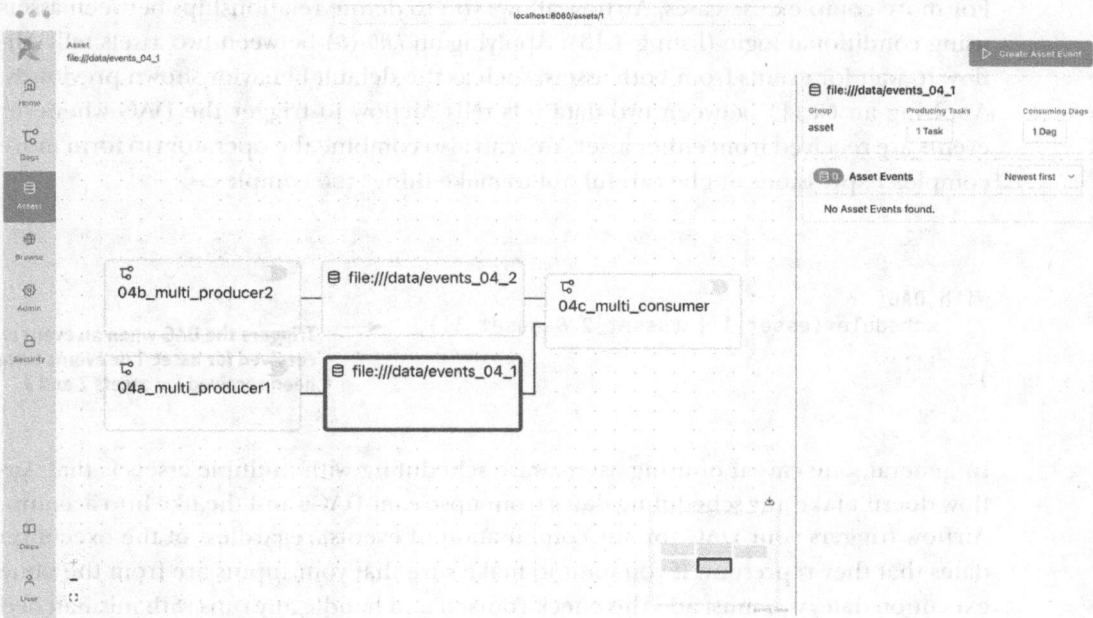

Figure 4.10 The asset view showing the two assets and their relationship with the two producer and single consumer DAGs

Next, we enable the second producer DAG (`04b_multi_producer`) to generate a second event. This second event should trigger the consumer DAG because now we have events from both input DAGs.

By default, Airflow triggers DAGs with multiple input assets whenever all input assets had an event since the last time the DAG was run. In this case, it happened when the second producer generated an event, triggering the DAG. Events don't necessarily need to come in pairs; multiple events coming from one asset won't trigger the consumer until the second asset also has an event. Figure 4.11 summarizes this behavior.

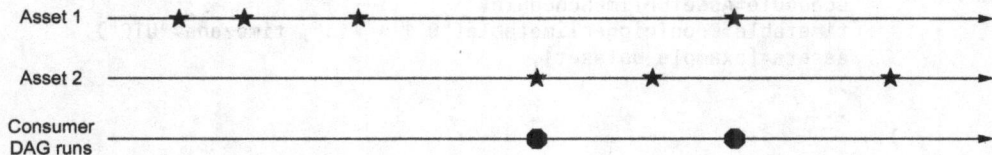

Figure 4.11 Every star icon indicates an asset update for either the first or second data set. Only when both data sets have been updated is a DAG run for our consumer DAG triggered. The order in which the assets are updated doesn't matter.

For more complex use cases, Airflow allows you to define relationships between assets using conditional logic (listing 4.13). Applying an AND (&) between two assets tells Airflow to wait for events from both assets, such as the default behavior shown previously. Applying an OR (|) between two data sets tells Airflow to trigger the DAG whenever events are received from either asset. You can also combine the operators to form more complex expressions but be careful not to make things too complex.

Listing 4.13   Example of complex conditional logic between assets

```
with DAG(
    schedule=(asset_1 | (asset_2 & asset_3)),    ◄─── Triggers the DAG when an event is
    ...,                                              received for asset 1 or events have
):                                                    been received for assets 2 and 3
    ...
```

In general, one caveat of using asset-aware scheduling with multiple assets is that Airflow doesn't take any scheduling dates from upstream DAGs and the like into account. Airflow triggers your DAG for any combination of events, regardless of the execution dates that they represent. If you want to make sure that your inputs are from the same execution date, you must add this check yourself and handle any runs with mismatched input files accordingly.

4.8   Combining time- and asset-based schedules

For some use cases, you want to ensure that your DAG responds quickly to any changes in upstream data sets but also executes consistently at regular intervals. You can implement this kind of hybrid schedule using the AssetOrTimeSchedule class, which accepts both a time-based timetable and an asset expression.

Listing 4.14   Combining time- and asset-based schedules

```
from airflow.sdk import DAG, Asset
from airflow.timetables.assets import AssetOrTimeSchedule
from airflow.timetables.trigger import CronTriggerTimetable

example_dataset = Asset("file:///data/example")

with DAG(
    schedule=AssetOrTimeSchedule(
    timetable=CronTriggerTimetable("0 1 * * 3", timezone="UTC"),
    assets=[example_dataset],
    ),
    ...
):
    ...
```

This feature can be particularly useful for DAGs that must be responsive to changes but also must run regular checks or updates. Be careful when combining the different schedules, however. Different timetables have different semantics (such as data intervals), which you have to handle accordingly in your DAG.

Summary

- Airflow's asset feature allows event-driven (or asset-aware) scheduling, in which task execution is triggered by data availability or changes as opposed to strict time intervals.
- In data pipelines, asset-aware scheduling is useful for splitting concerns between DAGs. Producer DAGs focus on fetching/transforming data to produce one or more output data sets, and consumer DAGs are triggered by updates to these data sets, potentially producing their own data sets in turn.
- You can access information about upstream DAGs (e.g., a DAG's scheduling interval) via the `triggering_asset_events` variable provided to a consumer DAG.
- Producer DAGs can include extra information in an asset event via the `extra` field. Any downstream DAGs triggered by the event can access this information.
- A producer DAG can skip downstream updates by raising an `AirflowSkip-Exception`. This approach is useful when a DAG run didn't modify an asset and therefore shouldn't trigger any dependent consumer DAGs.
- Consumer DAGs can depend on multiple assets, in which case they're executed by default whenever all input assets have seen at least one event. You can use conditional logic for more complicated relationships between assets. Either way, this functionality doesn't take scheduling semantics of upstream DAGs into account.
- DAGs can combine time- and asset-based scheduling if they need to react in a timely fashion to data set updates and run periodically.

Templating tasks using the Airflow context

This chapter covers

- Rendering variables at run time with templating
- Mastering variable templating with the PythonOperator
- Rendering templated variables for debugging purposes
- Performing operations on external systems

Static data pipelines are hardly useful if they always perform the same operations and can't adapt to changes between executions (e.g., loading data for a given day). We've seen some examples of how Airflow allows us to make pipelines more dynamic by referencing the execution date of a DAG. In this chapter, we'll dive a bit deeper into how this templating functionality works.

5.1 Inspecting data for processing with Airflow

Throughout this chapter, we'll work out several components of operators with the help of a (fictitious) stock-market-prediction tool that applies sentiment analysis. We'll call this tool StockSense.

Wikipedia is one of the largest public information resources on the internet. In addition to the wiki pages, items such as page-view counts are publicly available. For the examples in this chapter, we'll apply the axiom that an increase in a company's page views shows positive sentiment, so the company's stock is likely to increase, and that a decrease in page views shows loss of interest, so the stock price is likely to decrease.

The Wikimedia Foundation (the organization behind Wikipedia) provides all page views since 2015 in machine-readable format. The page views (https://dumps.wikimedia .org/other/pageviews) can be downloaded in `.gzip` format and are aggregated per hour per page. Each hourly dump is approximately 50 MB in gzipped text files and is between 200 MB and 250 MB unzipped.

NOTE The structure and technical details of Wikipedia page-views data are documented at https://mng.bz/pZ5w and https://mng.bz/OwNa.

These details are essential for work with any sort of data. Data, both small and big, can be complex, so it's important to have a technical plan of approach before building a pipeline. The solution always depends on what you or other users want to do with the data, so getting answers to questions such as these will help you address the technical details:

- Will we want to process the data again in the future?
- How do we receive the data (frequency, size, format, source type, and so on)?
- What are we going to build with the data?

Let's download one single hourly dump and inspect the data by hand. To develop a data pipeline, we must understand how to load it in an incremental fashion and work with the data (figure 5.1).

The URLs follow a fixed pattern, which we can use when downloading the data in batch fashion (touched on in chapters 3 and 4). As a thought experiment and to validate the data, let's see what the most-used domain codes are for January 1, 20:00–21:00 (figure 5.2).

The top results, `1061202` `en` and `995600` `en.m`, tell us that the most-viewed domains between 20:00 and 21:00 January 1 are `en` and `en.m` (the mobile version of `.en`). This makes sense, given that English is the most-used language in the world. Also, results are returned as we expect to see them. This confirms that there are no unexpected characters or misalignment of columns, so we don't have to perform any additional processing to clean up the data. Often, cleaning and transforming data into a consistent state is a large part of the work.

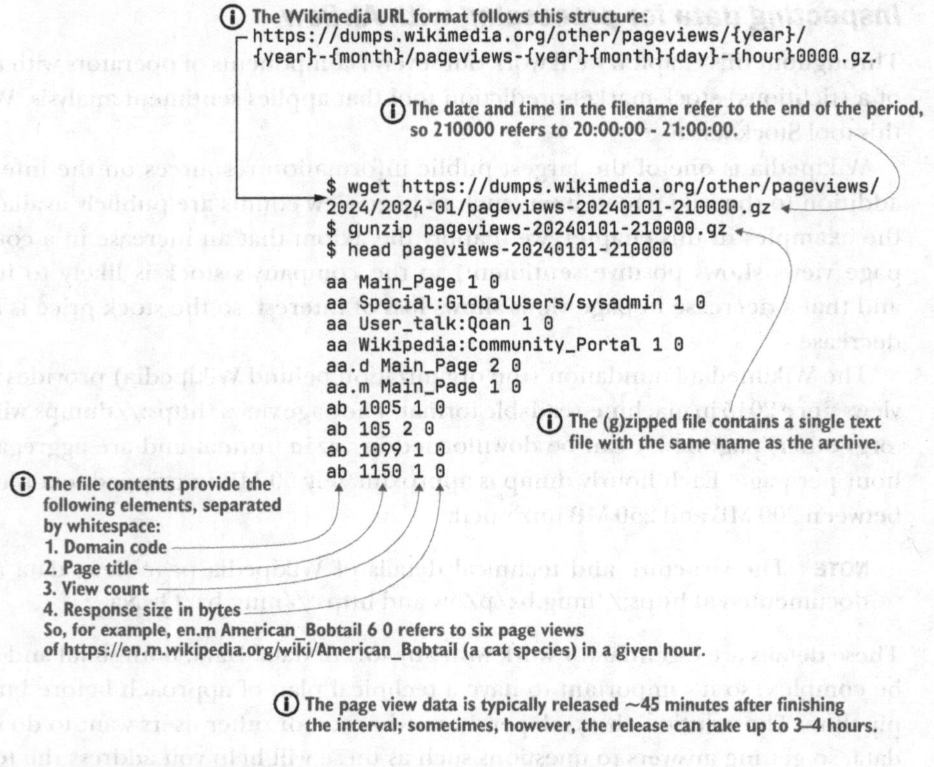

(i) The Wikimedia URL format follows this structure:
```
https://dumps.wikimedia.org/other/pageviews/{year}/
{year}-{month}/pageviews-{year}{month}{day}-{hour}0000.gz.
```

(i) The date and time in the filename refer to the end of the period,
so 210000 refers to 20:00:00 - 21:00:00.

```
$ wget https://dumps.wikimedia.org/other/pageviews/
2024/2024-01/pageviews-20240101-210000.gz
$ gunzip pageviews-20240101-210000.gz
$ head pageviews-20240101-210000

aa Main_Page 1 0
aa Special:GlobalUsers/sysadmin 1 0
aa User_talk:Qoan 1 0
aa Wikipedia:Community_Portal 1 0
aa.d Main_Page 2 0
aa.m Main_Page 1 0
ab 1005 1 0
ab 105 2 0
ab 1099 1 0
ab 1150 1 0
```

(i) The (g)zipped file contains a single text
file with the same name as the archive.

(i) The file contents provide the
following elements, separated
by whitespace:
1. Domain code
2. Page title
3. View count
4. Response size in bytes
So, for example, en.m American_Bobtail 6 0 refers to six page views
of https://en.m.wikipedia.org/wiki/American_Bobtail (a cat species) in a given hour.

(i) The page view data is typically released ~45 minutes after finishing
the interval; sometimes, however, the release can take up to 3–4 hours.

Figure 5.1   Downloading and inspecting Wikimedia page-views data

```
$ wget https://dumps.wikimedia.org/other/pageviews/024/2024-01/pageviews-20240101-210000.gz
$ gunzip pageviews-20240101-210000.gz
$ awk -F' ' '{print $1}' pageviews-20190101-210000    | sort | uniq -c | sort -nr | head

1061202 en
 995600 en.m              Example:
 300753 ja.m              aa Main_Page 3 0
 286381 de.m              af Ford_EcoSport 1 0
 257751 de                ab 1911 1 0
 226334 ru                ab 2009 1 0
 201930 ja
 198182 fr.m              aa
 193331 ru.m              af
 171510 it.m              ab
                          ab
                          aa
                          ab
                          ab
                          af
                          1 aa
                          2 ab
                          1 af
                          2 ab
                          1 af
                          1 aa
```

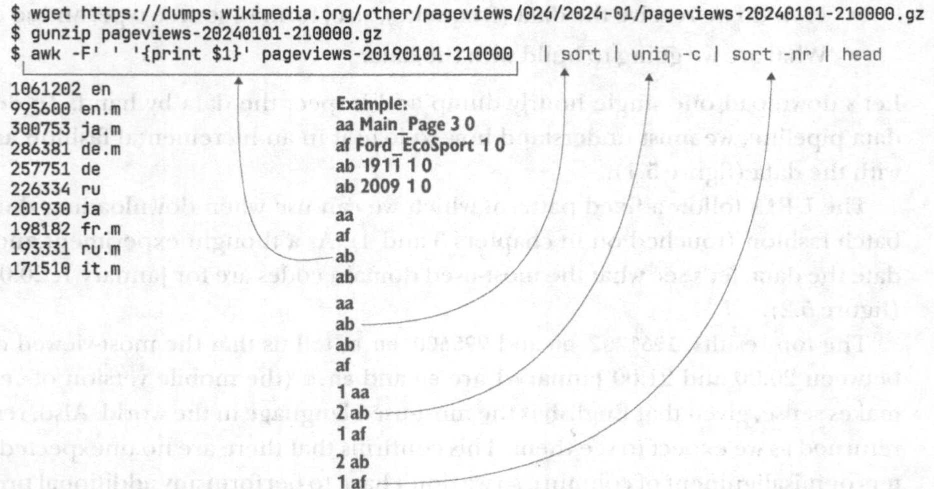

Figure 5.2   First simple analysis on Wikimedia page-views data

5.2 Task context and Jinja templating

In this section, we'll create the first version of a DAG that pulls in the Wikipedia page-view counts. We'll start by downloading, extracting, and reading the data. We've selected five companies—Amazon, Apple, Facebook, Google, and Microsoft—to track initially so we can validate the hypothesis (figure 5.3).

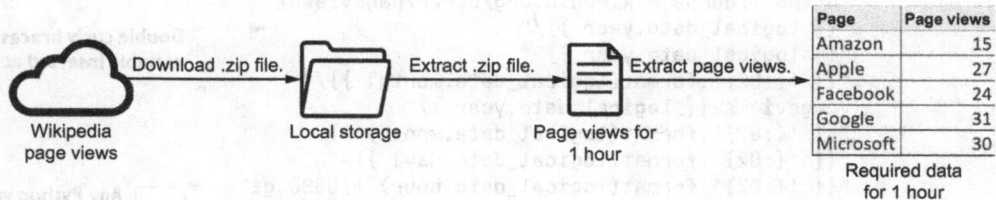

Page	Page views
Amazon	15
Apple	27
Facebook	24
Google	31
Microsoft	30

Required data
for 1 hour

Figure 5.3   First version of the StockSense workflow

The first step is downloading the `.zip` file for every interval. The URL is constructed of various date and time components:

```
https://dumps.wikimedia.org/other/pageviews/
{year}/{year}-{month}/pageviews-{year}{month}{day}-{hour}0000.gz
```

We have to insert the date and time for each specific interval in the URL. In chapters 3 and 4, we briefly touched on scheduling and discussed how to use the `data_interval_start` variable in our code to execute a task for a specific interval. Here, we'll see how that process works.

5.2.1 Templating operator arguments

To start, download the Wikipedia page views using the `BashOperator`, which takes a `bash_command` argument. The value for this argument is a Bash command to execute. All components of the URL where we want to insert a variable at run time start and end with double curly braces, as shown in the following listing (`dags/01_stocksense_bashoperator.py`).

Listing 5.1   Downloading Wikipedia page views with the `BashOperator`

```
import pendulum
from airflow.sdk import DAG
from airflow.providers.standard.operators.bash import BashOperator
from airflow.timetables.trigger import CronTriggerTimetable

with DAG(
    dag_id="01_stocksense_bashoperator",
```

```
    start_date=pendulum.today("UTC").add(hours=-3),
    schedule=CronTriggerTimetable("@hourly", timezone="UTC"),
    catchup=True
):

get_data = BashOperator(
    task_id="get_data",
    bash_command=(
        "curl -o /tmp/wikipageviews.gz "
        "https://dumps.wikimedia.org/other/pageviews/"
        "{{ logical_date.year }}/"
        "{{ logical_date.year }}-"
        "{{ '{:02}'.format(logical_date.month) }}/"
        "pageviews-{{ logical_date.year }}"
        "{{ '{:02}'.format(logical_date.month) }}"
        "{{ '{:02}'.format(logical_date.day) }}-"
        "{{ '{:02}'.format(logical_date.hour) }}0000.gz"
    ),
)
```

We subtract 3 hours here for demonstration purposes to ensure that we always have some DAG runs created.

We set catchup to True to ensure that DAG runs are created from the start date, not only the last interval before activating the DAG.

Double curly braces denote a variable inserted at run time.

Any Python variable or expression can be provided.

Chapters 3 and 4 mentioned that the variable logical_date becomes available at a task's run time. Using the logical_date variable is a practical example of a concept called *string interpolation*, which allows you to insert variables into strings in real time—particularly useful when the value of a variable is unknown while the code is being written but will be defined at run time.

Consider a form in which a user can enter their name. With string interpolation, the code can print the user's name dynamically even though that name was unknown when the code was written (figure 5.4).

Insert name here:

```
print("Hello {{ name }}!")
```

The double curly braces tell Jinja there's a variable or expression inside to evaluate.

Figure 5.4   You won't know all variables up front while writing code, such as when you're using interactive elements, for example, forms.

The value of name is not known during programming because the user will enter their name in the form at run time. What we do know is that the inserted value is assigned to a variable called name, and we can provide a string, "Hello {{ name }}!", to render and insert the value of name at run time.

In Airflow, this type of string interpolation is supported by Jinja templating. Jinja (https://jinja.palletsprojects.com) is a templating engine used in programming environments to generate dynamic content. It uses a straightforward syntax with double curly braces ({{variable}}) for variable interpolation, which allows the creation of reusable templates. We can use several variables that are available at run time from the task context by using the double-curly-braced templating string. One of these variables is `logical_date`. Airflow uses the Pendulum library (https://pendulum.eustace.io) for datetimes, and `logical_date` is a Pendulum datetime object. This object is a drop-in replacement for a native Python datetime, so all methods that can be applied to Python can also be applied to Pendulum. As the following listing shows, you can use `datetime` `.now().year` or get the same result with `pendulum.now().year`.

Listing 5.2   Pendulum behavior equal to native Python datetime

```
>>> from datetime import datetime
>>> import pendulum
>>> datetime.now().year
2024
>>> pendulum.now().year
2024
```

The Wikipedia page-views URL requires zero-padded months, days, and hours (e.g., `07` for hour 7). Within the Jinja-templated string, therefore, we apply string formatting for padding:

```
{{ '{:02}'.format(data_interval_start.hour) }}
```

> **Which arguments are templated?**
>
> It's important to know that not all operator arguments can be templates. Every operator can keep an allowlist of attributes that can be made into templates. By default, the attributes are not Jinja templated, so Jinja will interpret a string {{ name }} literally as {{ name }} and not template it unless it's included in the list of attributes that can be templated. This list is set by the attribute `template_fields` of every operator. You can check these attributes in the documentation (https://airflow.apache.org/docs); go to the operator of your choice and view the `template_fields` item.
>
> The elements in `template_fields` are names of class attributes. Typically, the argument names provided to `__init__` match the class attributes' names, so everything listed in `template_fields` maps 1:1 to the `__init__` arguments. But technically, it's possible that the argument names provided to `__init__` won't be identical to the class attributes' names, so you should document the class attributes that an argument maps.

5.2.2   Templating the PythonOperator

The `PythonOperator` is an exception to the templating shown in section 5.2.1. With the `BashOperator` (and all other operators in Airflow), you provide a string to the `bash_command` argument (or whatever the argument is named in other operators), and the string is automatically templated at run time. The `PythonOperator` uses a different convention; instead of taking arguments that can be templated with the run-time context, it takes a `python_callable` argument that's passed to the run-time context when the corresponding function is executed. To illustrate this idea, we'll convert our code for downloading the Wikipedia page views from the `BashOperator` (refer to listing 5.1) to use the `PythonOperator` instead, as shown in the following listing (dags/02_stocksense.py).

> **Listing 5.3   Downloading Wikipedia page views with the `PythonOperator`**

```python
from urllib import request

import pendulum
from airflow.sdk import DAG
from airflow.providers.standard.operators.python import PythonOperator
from airflow.timetables.trigger import CronTriggerTimetable

def _get_data(**kwargs):
    year, month, day, hour, * = kwargs["logical_date"].timetuple()
    url = (
        "https://dumps.wikimedia.org/other/pageviews/"
        f"{year}/{year}-{month:0>2}/"
        f"pageviews-{year}{month:0>2}{day:0>2}-{hour:0>2}0000.gz"
    )
    output_path = "/tmp/wikipageviews.gz"
    request.urlretrieve(url, output_path)


with DAG(
    dag_id="02_stocksense",
    start_date=pendulum.today("UTC").add(hours=-3),
    schedule=CronTriggerTimetable("@hourly", timezone="UTC"),
    catchup=True
):

    get_data = PythonOperator(
        task_id="get_data",
        python_callable=_get_data,
    )
```

The PythonOperator takes a Python function, whereas the BashOperator takes a Bash command as a string to execute.

In this approach, we provide a *callable* (a function is a callable object) to the `python_callable` argument of the `PythonOperator`. On execution, the `PythonOperator` executes the provided callable, which could be any function. Because the callable is a function, not a string (as it is to all other operators), the code within the function can't be templated automatically. Instead, the `PythonOperator` passes along any task context variables that are referenced as input arguments of the function (such as `data_interval_start` in this case). Then we can use the values of these variables inside the callable.

NOTE   In Python, any object implementing `__call__()` , such as a function or method, is considered a callable.

Instead of referencing specific context variables, you can capture the entire context using Python's **kwargs syntax, which effectively captures all context variables in a Python dictionary (or *dict*; figure 5.5). This syntax can be useful if you don't know up front which context variables you need or want to avoid explicitly writing out all expected keyword argument names.

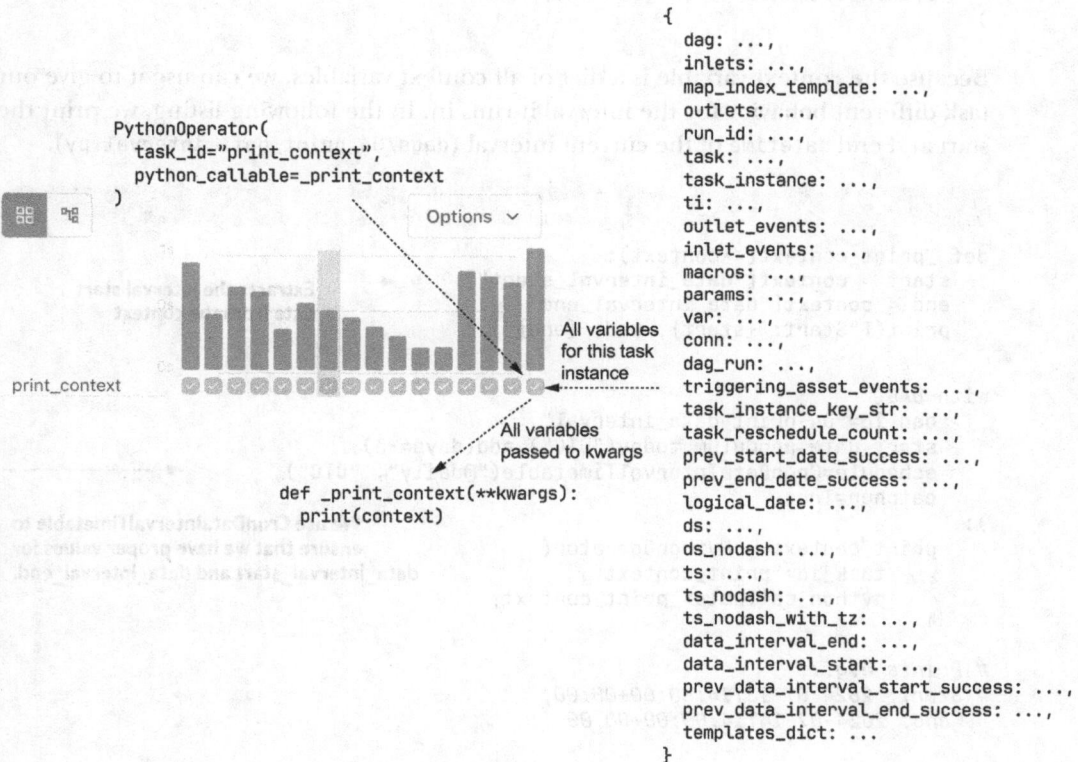

```
PythonOperator(
    task_id="print_context",
    python_callable=_print_context
)
```

All variables for this task instance

print_context

All variables passed to kwargs

```
def _print_context(**kwargs):
    print(context)
```

```
{
    dag: ...,
    inlets: ...,
    map_index_template: ...,
    outlets: ...,
    run_id: ...,
    task: ...,
    task_instance: ...,
    ti: ...,
    outlet_events: ...,
    inlet_events: ...,
    macros: ...,
    params: ...,
    var: ...,
    conn: ...,
    dag_run: ...,
    triggering_asset_events: ...,
    task_instance_key_str: ...,
    task_reschedule_count: ...,
    prev_start_date_success: ...,
    prev_end_date_success: ...,
    logical_date: ...,
    ds: ...,
    ds_nodash: ...,
    ts: ...,
    ts_nodash: ...,
    ts_nodash_with_tz: ...,
    data_interval_end: ...,
    data_interval_start: ...,
    prev_data_interval_start_success: ...,
    prev_data_interval_end_success: ...,
    templates_dict: ...
}
```

Figure 5.5 Providing task context with the PythonOperator

Listing 5.4 Keyword arguments stored in kwargs

```
def _print_context(**kwargs):
    print(kwargs)
```

Keyword arguments can be captured with two asterisks (**). The convention is to name the capturing argument kwargs.

You want to tell your future self and other readers of your Airflow code your intentions for capturing the Airflow task context variables in the keyword arguments. A good practice is to name this argument appropriately (e.g., context), as in the next listing (dags/03_print_context_with_intent.py).

Listing 5.5   Renaming kwargs to context for expressing intent to store task context

```
def _print_context(**context):
    print(context)

print_context = PythonOperator(
    task_id="print_context",
    python_callable=_print_context,
)
```

Naming this argument
context indicates that we
expect Airflow task context.

Because the context variable is a dict of all context variables, we can use it to give our task different behavior for the interval it runs in. In the following listing, we print the start and end datetime of the current interval (dags/04_print_data_interval.py).

Listing 5.6   Printing start and end dates of interval

```
def _print_context(**context):
    start = context["data_interval_start"]
    end = context["data_interval_end"]
    print(f"Start: {start}, end: {end}")

with DAG(
    dag_id="04_print_data_interval",
    start_date=pendulum.today("UTC").add(days=-3),
    schedule=CronDataIntervalTimetable("@daily", "UTC"),
    catchup=True
):
    print_context = PythonOperator(
        task_id="print_context",
        python_callable=_print_context,
    )

# Prints e.g.:
# Start: 2024-07-13T14:00:00+00:00,
  end: 2024-07-14T14:00:00+00:00
```

Extracts the interval start
date from the context

We use CronDataIntervalTimetable to
ensure that we have proper values for
data_interval_start and data_interval_end.

Now that we've seen a few basic examples, let's dissect the PythonOperator, as shown in figure 5.6, by downloading the hourly Wikipedia page views (listing 5.5).

The _get_data function called by the PythonOperator takes one argument: **context. As we've seen, we could accept all keyword arguments in a single argument named **kwargs. (The double asterisk indicates all keyword arguments; kwargs is the variable's name.) To indicate that we expect task context variables, we could rename it **context. But the following listing shows yet another way to accept keyword arguments in Python.

Listing 5.7   Explicitly selecting the variable data_interval_start

```
def _get_data(data_interval_start, **context):
    year, month, day, hour, *_ = data_interval_start.timetuple()
    # ...
```

Tells Python we expect to receive an argument named
data_interval_start, which won't be captured in the context argument

Task context
variables

Extract datetime components
from data_interval_start.

```
def _get_data(**context):
    year, month, day, hour, *_ = context["data_interval_start"].timetuple()
    url = (
        "https://dumps.wikimedia.org/other/pageviews/"
        f"{year}/{year}-{month:0>2}/pageviews-{year}{month:0>2}{day:0>2}-{hour:0>2}0000.gz"
    )
    output_path = "/tmp/wikipageviews.gz"
    request.urlretrieve(url, output_path)
```

Format URL with datetime components.

Retrieve data.

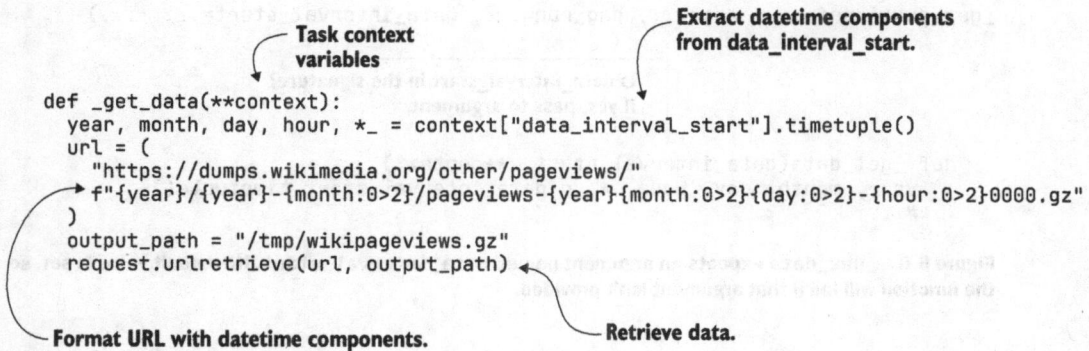

Figure 5.6 The `PythonOperator` **takes a function instead of string arguments, so it can't be Jinja templated. In this called function, we extract datetime components from the** `data_interval_start` **to construct the URL dynamically.**

Under the hood, the `_get_data` function is called with all context variables as keyword arguments. Then Python checks whether any of the given arguments is expected in the function signature (figure 5.7).

Listing 5.8 Passing all context variables as keyword arguments

```
_get_data(conf=..., dag=..., dag_run=..., data_interval_start=..., ...)
```

```
_get_data(conf=..., dag=..., dag_run=..., data_interval_start=..., ...)
```

Is conf in the signature?

If not, add to **context.

```
def _get_data(data_interval_start, **context):
    year, month, day, hour, *_ = data_interval_start.timetuple()
    # ...
```

Figure 5.7 Python determines whether a given keyword argument is passed to one specific argument in the function or to the `**context` **argument if no matching name was found.**

The first argument, `conf`, is checked and not found in the signature (expected arguments) of `_get_data`, so it's added to `**context`. This process is repeated for `dag` and `dag_run` because these arguments aren't in the function's expected arguments. Next is `data_interval_start`, which we expect to receive, so its value is passed to the `data_interval_start` argument in `_get_data()` (figure 5.8). The result is that a keyword with the name `data_interval_start` is passed to the `data_interval_start` argument, and all other variables are passed to `**context` because they're not explicitly expected in the function signature (figure 5.9).

```
_get_data(conf=..., dag=..., dag_run=..., data_interval_start=..., ...)
```

Is data_interval_start in the signature?
If yes, pass to argument.

```
def _get_data(data_interval_start, **context):
    year, month, day, hour, *_ = data_interval_start.timetuple()
    # ...
```

Figure 5.8   _get_data expects an argument named `data_interval_start`. No default value is set, so the function will fail if that argument isn't provided.

```
_get_data(conf=..., dag=..., dag_run=..., data_interval_start=..., ...)
```

```
def _get_data(data_interval_start, **context):
    year, month, day, hour, *_ = data_interval_start.timetuple()
    # ...
```

Figure 5.9   Any named argument can be given to `_get_data()`. `data_interval_start` must be provided explicitly because it's listed as an argument; all other arguments are captured by `**context`.

Now we can use the `data_interval_start` variable directly instead of extracting it from `**context` with `context["data_interval_start"]`. In addition, our code will be more self-explanatory, and tools such as linters and type hinting will benefit from the explicit argument definition.

5.2.3   *Passing additional variables to the PythonOperator*

Now that we've seen how the task context works in operators and how Python deals with keyword arguments, suppose that we want to download data from more than one data source. We could duplicate the `_get_data()` function and alter it slightly to support a second data source. The `PythonOperator`, however, also supports supplying additional arguments to the callable function. Suppose that we start by making the `output_path` configurable so that, depending on the task, we can configure the `output_path` instead of duplicating the entire function only to change the output path (figure 5.10).

We can provide the value of `output_path` in two ways. The first way is via an argument (`op_args`).

Listing 5.9   Providing user-defined variables to the `PythonOperator` callable

```
get_data = PythonOperator(
    task_id="get_data",
    python_callable=_get_data,
    op_args=["/tmp/wikipageviews.gz"],
)
```

Provides additional variables to the callable with op_args

```
def _get_data(output_path, **context):
  year, month, day, hour, *_ = context["data_interval_start"].timetuple()
  url = (
    "https://dumps.wikimedia.org/other/pageviews/"
    f"{year}/{year}-{month:0>2}/pageviews-{year}{month:0>2}{day:0>2}-{hour:0>2}0000.gz"
  )
  request.urlretrieve(url, output_path)
```

**output_path now
configurable via argument**

Figure 5.10 Now the `output_path` is configurable via an argument.

On execution of the operator, each value in the list provided to `op_args` is passed to
the callable function, which has the same effect as calling the function directly (`_get_data("/tmp/wikipageviews.gz")`). Because `output_path` in figure 5.10 is the first argument in the `_get_data` function, its value will be set to `/tmp/wikipageviews.gz` when it's
run. (We call arguments of this type *nonkeyword arguments*.) A second approach is to use
the `op_kwargs` argument, as shown in the following listing.

Listing 5.10   Providing user-defined kwargs to the callable

```
get_data = PythonOperator(
    task_id="get_data",
    python_callable=_get_data,
    op_kwargs={"output_path": "/tmp/wikipageviews.gz"},
)
```

**A dict given to op_
kwargs will be passed
as keyword arguments
to the callable.**

As in `op_args`, all values in `op_kwargs` are passed to the callable function, this time as
keyword arguments. The equivalent call to `_get_data` is

```
_get_data(output_path="/tmp/wikipageviews.gz")
```

Note that these values can contain strings and thus can be templated. This means we
could avoid extracting the datetime components inside the callable function itself and
instead pass templated strings to our callable function (`dags/05_retrieve_data.py`).

Listing 5.11   Providing templated strings to the callable

```
def _get_data(year, month, day, hour, output_path, **_):
    url = (
        "https://dumps.wikimedia.org/other/pageviews/"
        f"{year}/{year}-{month:0>2}/"
        f"pageviews-{year}{month:0>2}{day:0>2}-{hour:0>2}0000.gz"
    )
    request.urlretrieve(url, output_path)
```

```
get_data = PythonOperator(
    task_id="get_data",
    python_callable=_get_data,
    op_kwargs={
        "year": "{{ logical_date.year }}",
        "month": "{{ logical_date.month }}",
        "day": "{{ logical_date.day }}",
        "hour": "{{ logical_date.hour }}",
        "output_path": "/tmp/wikipageviews-
{{ logical_date.format('YYYYMMDDHH') }}.gz",
    },
)
```

User-defined keyword arguments are templated before being passed to the callable.

5.2.4 *Inspecting templated arguments*

The Airflow UI is a useful tool for debugging issues in templated arguments. You can inspect the templated-argument values after running a task by selecting it in the graph or grid view and then clicking the Rendered Template button (figure 5.11). The rendered template view displays all attributes of the given operator that are renderable, along with their values. This view is visible per task instance. Consequently, a task must be scheduled by Airflow before you can inspect the rendered attributes for the given task instance—that is, you must wait for Airflow to schedule the next task instance. During development, however, this process can be impractical. The Airflow command-line interface (CLI) allows you to render templated values for any given datetime.

📄 get_data 2025-04-25, 17:28:23 ✓ success

Operator	Start	End
PythonOperator	2025-04-25, 17:28:23	2025-04-25, 17:28:39

Logs   **Rendered Templates**   XCom   Events   Code   Details

op_args	[] 📋
op_kwargs	{"year":"2025","month":"4","day":"24","hour":"22","output_path":"/tmp/wikipageviews-2025042422.gz"} 📋

Figure 5.11   Inspecting the rendered template values after running a task

The CLI provides the same information shown in the Airflow UI without requiring you to run a task, which makes inspecting the result easier. The command to render templates using the CLI is

```
airflow tasks render [dag id] [task id] [desired execution date]
```

You can enter any datetime, and the Airflow CLI will render all templated attributes as though the task would run for the desired datetime. Using the CLI doesn't register anything in the metastore, so this option is more lightweight and flexible. The following listing shows the output of running the render command for a specific task.

Listing 5.12 Rendering templated values for any given execution date

```
# airflow tasks render 05_retrieve_data get_data 2025-04-24T22:00:00
# ------------------------------------------------------------
# property: templates_dict
# ------------------------------------------------------------
None


# ------------------------------------------------------------
# property: op_args
# ------------------------------------------------------------
[]


# ------------------------------------------------------------
# property: op_kwargs
# ------------------------------------------------------------
{'year': '2025', 'month': '4', 'day': '24', 'hour': '22', 'output_path':
    '/tmp/wikipageviews 2025042422.gz'}
```

5.3 *What is available for templating*

We understand which arguments of an operator can be templated, but which variables do we have at our disposal for templating? We've seen `logical_date` used in several examples, but more variables are available. With the help of the `PythonOperator`, we can print the full task context and inspect it (`dags/06_print_context.py`).

Listing 5.13 Printing the task context

```python
import pendulum
from airflow.sdk import DAG
from airflow.providers.standard.operators.python import PythonOperator
from airflow.timetables.trigger import CronTriggerTimetable

def _print_context(**context):
    print(context)


with DAG(
    dag_id="06_print_context",
    start_date= pendulum.today("UTC").add(days=-3)),
    schedule=CronTriggerTimetable("@daily", timezone="UTC"),
    catchup=True
):


    print_context = PythonOperator(
```

```
        task_id="print_context",
        python_callable=_print_context,
    )
```

Running this task prints a dict of all available variables in the task context, as shown in the next listing. Table 5.1 was printed using a PythonOperator run manually in a DAG with execution date 2024-01-01T00:00:00, @daily interval.

Listing 5.14   All context variables for the given date interval

```
{
    'dag': <DAG: 06_print_context>,
    'inlets': [],
    'map_index_template': None,
    'outlets': [],
    'run_id': 'manual__2025-04-25T17:36:14.198033+00:00',
    'task': <Task(PythonOperator): print_context>,
    'task_instance': RuntimeTaskInstance(id=UUID(...),
    ...
}
```

Table 5.1   All task context variables, with deprecated variables omitted

Key	Description	Example
conn	Information about the connections accessed by the task.	Connection object
dag	The current DAG object.	DAG object
dag_run	The current DagRun object.	DagRun object
data_interval_end	The end of the schedule interval for a DAG run.	pendulum.datetime.DateTime object
data_interval_start	The start of the schedule interval for a DAG run.	pendulum.datetime.DateTime object
ds	logical_date formatted as %Y-%m-%d.	"2024-01-01"
ds_nodash	logical_date formatted as %Y%m%d.	"20240101"
expanded_ti_count	The number of subtasks a given task was split into. If the task isn't mapped into subtasks, it's equal to None.	Int | None
inlets	Shorthand for task.inlets, a feature that tracks input data sources for data lineage and data assets.	[]
logical_date	Timestamp when a task is scheduled to run.	pendulum.datetime.DateTime object

Table 5.1 All task context variables, with deprecated variables omitted (*continued*)

Key	Description	Example
macros	airflow.macros module	macros module
map_index_template	A map of names to apply to mapped tasks instead of the default integer indexed version. (Dynamic Task Mapping is discussed in chapter 12.)	{}
outlets	Shorthand for task.outlets, a feature that tracks output data sources for data lineage and data assets.	[]
params	User-provided variables for the task context.	{}
prev_data_interval_end_success	End of the data interval of the previous successful DAG run.	pendulum.datetime.DateTime object
prev_data_interval_start_success	Start of the data interval of the previous successful DAG run.	pendulum.datetime.DateTime object
prev_start_date_success	Date and time on which the last successful run of the same task (only in past) was started.	pendulum.datetime.DateTime object
run_id	The DagRun's run_id (a key typically composed of a prefix plus datetime).	"manual__2024-01-01T00:00:00+00:00"
task	The current operator.	PythonOperator object
task_instance	The current TaskInstance object	TaskInstance object
task_instance_key_str	A unique identifier for the current TaskInstance ({dag_id}__{task_id}__{ds_nodash}).	"dag_id__task_id__20240101"
task_reschedule_count	The number of times this task has been rescheduled.	0
templates_dict	User-provided variables for the task context.	{}
test_mode	Boolean indicating whether a task was run in test mode (e.g., run with airflow test in the CLI).	False
ti	The current TaskInstance object; same as task_instance.	TaskInstance object
triggering_asset_events	If the DAG was triggered by a a data asset event, provides a dictionary with all the events that trigger the DAG.	{}

Table 5.1 All task context variables, with deprecated variables omitted (*continued*)

Key	Description	Example
ts	execution_date formatted according to ISO8601 format.	"2024-01-01T00:00:00+00:00"
ts_nodash	execution_date formatted as %Y%m%dT%H%M%S.	"20240101T000000"
ts_nodash_with_tz	ts_nodash with time zone information.	"20240101T000000+0000"
var	Helper objects for dealing with Airflow variables.	{}

Deprecated context variables

After you print all the context variables, you realize that Airflow might provide more variables than the ones mentioned in table 5.1. In the evolving landscape of Airflow, certain variables and parameters that once were important for defining workflows have been deprecated. Deprecation is a natural progression in software development, given the continuous evolution toward new features, improved performance, and clearer variable-naming conventions. With the release of Airflow 3, several previously deprecated variables have been removed.

5.4   Bringing it all together

Now that we've worked out how templating works, let's continue the use case by processing the hourly Wikipedia page views. The two operators in the following listing (dags/07_wikipedia_pageviews.py) extract the archive and process the extracted file by scanning it and selecting the page-view counts for the given page names. The result is printed in the logs.

Listing 5.15   Reading page views for given page names

```
def _fetch_pageviews(pagenames, logical_date, **_):
    result = dict.fromkeys(pagenames, 0)
    with open(f"/tmp/wikipageviews-{ data_interval_start
.format('YYYYMMDDHH') }", "r") as f:          ◄─── Opens the file written
        for line in f:                              in the previous task
            domain_code, page_title, view_counts, _ =
line.split(" ")                      ◄─── Extracts the elements of a line
            if domain_code == "en"
and page_title in pagenames:         ◄─── Filters only domain en and
                                             checks whether page_title is
                result[page_title] = view_counts    in the given pagenames

    print(result)
```

```
    # Prints e.g. "{'Facebook': '778', 'Apple': '20',
'Google': '451',  'Amazon': '9', 'Microsoft': '119'}"


extract_gz = BashOperator(
    task_id="extract_gz",
    bash_command="gunzip --force /tmp/wikipageviews-
    {{ logical_date.format('YYYYMMDDHH') }}.gz",
)

fetch_pageviews = PythonOperator(
    task_id="fetch_pageviews",
    python_callable=_fetch_pageviews,
    op_kwargs={
        "pagenames": {
            "Google",
            "Amazon",
            "Apple",
            "Microsoft",
            "Facebook",
        }
    },
)
```

This listing prints, for example, {'Apple': '31', 'Microsoft': '87', 'Amazon': '7',
'Facebook': '228', 'Google': '275'}. As a first improvement, we'll write these counts
to our own database. This improvement will allow us to query with SQL and ask questions such as "What is the average hourly page-view count on the Google Wikipedia
page?" (figure 5.12).

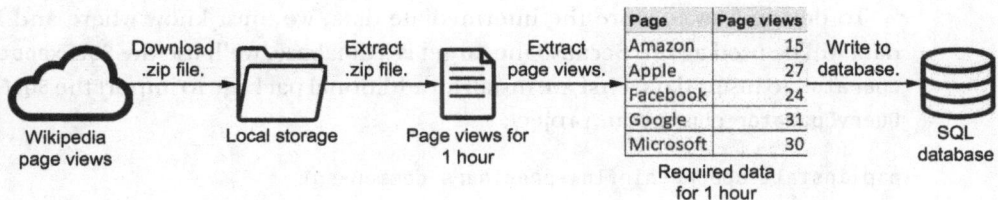

Page	Page views
Amazon	15
Apple	27
Facebook	24
Google	31
Microsoft	30

**Figure 5.12 Conceptual idea of workflow. After extracting the page views, write the page-view counts
to a SQL database.**

We'll use PostgreSQL (https://www.postgresql.org) to store the hourly page views. The
table that stores the data contains three columns, as shown in the next listing.

Listing 5.16   CREATE TABLE statement for storing output

```
CREATE TABLE pageview_counts (
    pagename VARCHAR(50) NOT NULL,
```

```
    pageviewcount INT NOT NULL,
    datetime TIMESTAMP NOT NULL
);
```

The `pagename` and `pageviewcount` columns hold the name of the Wikipedia page and the number of page views for that page for a given hour, respectively. The datetime column holds the date and time for the count, which equals Airflow's `data_interval_start`. The following listing shows an example INSERT query.

Listing 5.17   INSERT statement storing output in the `pageview_counts` table

```
INSERT INTO pageview_counts VALUES ('Google', 333, '2024-01-01T00:00:00');
```

This code currently prints the found page-view count. Next, we want to connect the dots by writing those results to the PostgreSQL table. The PythonOperator currently prints the results but doesn't write to the database, so we'll need a second task to write the results. In Airflow, we have two ways to pass data between tasks:

- Use the Airflow metastore to write and read results between tasks. (This approach, called *XCom*, is covered in chapter 6.)
- Write results to and from a persistent location (such as a disk or database) between tasks.

Airflow tasks run independently, possibly on different physical machines depending on your setup; therefore, Airflow can't share objects in memory. Data between tasks must be persisted elsewhere, where it will reside after a task finishes and can be read by another task. Note that this persistent location must be accessible to all machines involved to avoid having the same problem with persistent storage.

To decide how to store the intermediate data, we must know where and how the data will be used again. Because the target is a database, we'll use the `SQLExecuteQuery-Operator` to insert data. First, we install an additional package to import the `SQLExecute-QueryOperator` class in our project:

```
pip install apache-airflow-providers-common-sql
```

The `SQLExecuteQueryOperator` will run any query we provide it. Because the `SQL-ExecuteQueryOperator` doesn't support inserts from CSV data, first we'll write SQL queries as our intermediate data, as shown in the following listing (`dags/08_writing_insert_statements.py`).

Listing 5.18   Writing INSERT statements to feed to the `SQLExecuteQueryOperator`

```
def _fetch_pageviews(pagenames, logical_date, **_):
    result = dict.fromkeys(pagenames, 0)          ◄── Initializes result for all
    with open(f"/tmp/wikipageviews-{ logical_date         page views with zero
    .format('YYYYMMDDHH') } ", "r") as f:
```

```
    for line in f:
        domain_code, page_title, view_counts, _ =
line.split(" ")
        if domain_code == "en"
and page_title in pagenames:
            result[page_title] = view_counts     ◄──┘ Stores page-view count.

    with open("/tmp/postgres_query.sql", "w") as f:
        for pagename, pageviewcount in result.items():    ◄──
            f.write(                                            For each result,
                "INSERT INTO pageview_counts VALUES ("          writes SQL query
                f"'{pagename}', {pageviewcount},
'{ data_interval_start }'"
                ");\n"
            )

fetch_pageviews = PythonOperator(
    task_id="fetch_pageviews",
    python_callable=_fetch_pageviews,
    op_kwargs={"pagenames": {"Google", "Amazon",
"Apple", "Microsoft", "Facebook"}},
)
```

Running this task produces a file (/tmp/postgres_query.sql) for the given interval, containing all the SQL queries to be run by the SQLExcuteQueryOperator. The following listing shows these queries.

Listing 5.19   Multiple INSERT queries to feed to the SQLExecuteQueryOperator

```
INSERT INTO pageview_counts VALUES ('Facebook', 275,
 '2024-01-18T02:00:00+00:00');
INSERT INTO pageview_counts VALUES ('Apple', 35,
 '2024-01-18T02:00:00+00:00');
INSERT INTO pageview_counts VALUES ('Microsoft', 136,
 '2024-01-18T02:00:00+00:00');
INSERT INTO pageview_counts VALUES ('Amazon', 17,
 '2024-01-18T02:00:00+00:00');
INSERT INTO pageview_counts VALUES ('Google', 399,
 2024-01-18T02:00:00+00:00');
```

Although this straightforward method of adding new entries works, executing the DAG repeatedly could cause problems with atomicity and idempotency because it would result in duplicate records being inserted into the database. To adhere to best practices, we advise including the clause ON CONFLICT (date), DO UPDATE SET, or DO NOTHING in the insertion command and ensuring that the date column is designated as a primary key within the table.

Now that we've generated the queries, it's time to connect the last piece of the puzzle (dags/09_postgres_call.py). Figure 5.13 shows the corresponding graph view.

Listing 5.20   Calling the `SQLExecuteQueryOperator`

```
from airflow.providers.common.sql.operators.sql import
    SQLExecuteQueryOperator

with DAG(..., template_searchpath="/tmp"):          ◄──── Path to search for SQL file

    write_to_postgres = SQLExecuteQueryOperator(
        task_id="write_to_postgres",
        conn_id="my_postgres",          ◄──── Identifier to credentials
                                               to use for connection
        sql="postgres_query.sql",       ◄──── SQL query or path to file
        Return_last=False,                     containing SQL queries
    )
```

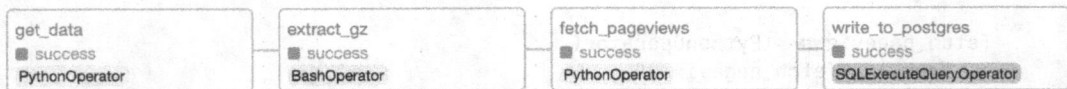

```
┌────────────────────┐   ┌────────────────────┐   ┌────────────────────┐   ┌────────────────────────┐
│ get_data           │   │ extract_gz         │   │ fetch_pageviews    │   │ write_to_postgres      │
│ ■ success          │──▶│ ■ success          │──▶│ ■ success          │──▶│ ■ success              │
│ PythonOperator     │   │ BashOperator       │   │ PythonOperator     │   │ SQLExecuteQueryOperator│
└────────────────────┘   └────────────────────┘   └────────────────────┘   └────────────────────────┘
```

Figure 5.13   DAG fetching hourly Wikipedia page views and writing results to PostgreSQL

To run a query against a database, the `SQLExecuteQueryOperator` requires only that we fill in a task ID (`task_id`) and a connection ID (`conn_id`). Intricate operations such as setting up a connection to the database and closing it after completion are handled under the hood. The `conn_id` argument points to an identifier holding the credentials in the database. Airflow can manage such credentials (stored encrypted in the metastore), and operators can fetch one of the credentials when required. Without going into detail, we can add the `my_postgres` connection in Airflow with the help of the CLI.

Listing 5.21   Storing credentials in Airflow with the CLI

```
airflow connections add \
--conn-type postgres \
--conn-host localhost \
--conn-login postgres \
--conn-password mysecretpassword \     ◄──── The connection identifier that operators
my_postgres                                   will use to reference the connection
```

Now the connection is visible in the UI (and can also be created there). Choose Admin > Connections to view all connections stored in Airflow (figure 5.14).

When several DAG runs are complete, the table in the PostgreSQL database holds a few counts:

```
"Amazon",12,"2024-01-17 00:00:00"
"Amazon",11,"2024-01-17 01:00:00"
"Amazon",19,"2024-01-17 02:00:00"
"Amazon",13,"2024-01-17 03:00:00"
"Amazon",12,"2024-01-17 04:00:00"
```

```
"Amazon",12,"2024-01-17 05:00:00"
"Amazon",11,"2024-01-17 06:00:00"
"Amazon",14,"2024-01-17 07:00:00"
"Amazon",15,"2024-01-17 08:00:00"
"Amazon",17,"2024-01-17 09:00:00"
```

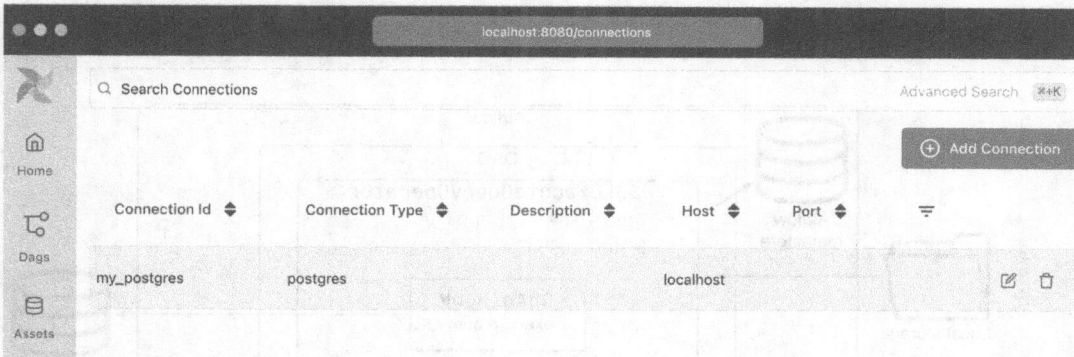

Figure 5.14   Connection listed in Airflow UI

Let's point out several things in this last step. The DAG has an additional argument: `template_searchpath`. In addition to the string `INSERT INTO ...`, the content of files can be templated. Each operator can read and template files with specific extensions by providing the file path to the operator. In the case of the `SQLExecuteQueryOperator`, the argument `SQL` can be templated, so a path to a file holding a SQL query can also be provided. Any file path ending in `.sql` will be read, templates in the file will be rendered, and the queries in the file will be executed by the `SQLExecuteQueryOperator`. Again, refer to the operator documentation, and check the field `template_ext`, which holds the file extensions that the operator can template.

> **NOTE** Jinja requires us to provide the path to search for files that can be templated. By default, only the path of the DAG file is searched for, but because we stored it in `/tmp`, Jinja won't find it. To add paths for Jinja to search, we set the argument `template_searchpath` on the DAG as we did in listing 5.20; then Jinja will traverse the default path plus additional provided paths to search for.

PostgreSQL is an external system, and Airflow supports connecting to a wide range of external systems with the help of many operators in its ecosystem. This support does have an implication, however: connecting to an external system often requires installing specific dependencies that allow connection and communication with the external system. PostgreSQL has the same requirement: we must install the `apache-airflow-providers-common-sql` package to install additional dependencies in our Airflow installation. Many dependencies are characteristic of any orchestration system; if we want to communicate with many external systems, we inevitably must install many dependencies.

Upon execution of the SQLExecuteQueryOperator, several things happen (figure 5.15). The SQLExecuteQueryOperator instantiates a so-called hook to communicate with Postgres. The hook deals with creating a connection, sending queries to the database, and then closing the connection. The operator is merely passing the request from the user to the hook in this situation.

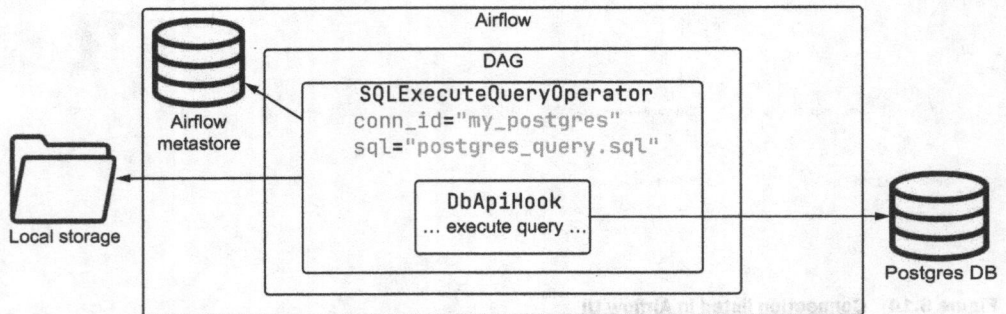

Figure 5.15   Running a SQL script against a PostgreSQL database involves several components. Provide the correct settings to the SQLExecuteQueryOperator, and the DbApiHook will do the work under the hood.

NOTE   An operator determines what has to be done; a hook determines how to do something.

When you build pipelines like these, you deal only with operators and have no notion of hook, because hooks are used internally in operators. After several DAG runs, the PostgreSQL database will contain a few records extracted from the Wikipedia page views. Then, once an hour, Airflow will automatically download the new hourly page-views data set, unzip it, extract the desired counts, and write these counts to the PostgreSQL database. Now we can ask questions such as "At which hour is each page most popular?"

Listing 5.22   SQL query asking which hour is most popular per page

```sql
SELECT x.pagename, x.hr AS "hour", x.average AS "average pageviews"
FROM (
  SELECT
    pagename,
    date_part('hour', datetime) AS hr,
    AVG(pageviewcount) AS average,
    ROW_NUMBER() OVER (
      PARTITION BY pagename ORDER BY AVG(pageviewcount)
    DESC)
```

```
FROM pageview_counts
 GROUP BY pagename, hr
) AS x
WHERE row_number=1;
```

The result of this query tells us the most popular time to view given pages. That time is between 16:00 and 21:00, as shown in table 5.2.

Table 5.2 Query results showing which hour is most popular per page

Page name	Hour	Average page views
Amazon	18	20
Apple	16	66
Facebook	16	500
Google	20	761
Microsoft	21	181

With this query, we have completed the envisioned Wikipedia workflow, which performs a full cycle of downloading the hourly page-view data, processing the data, and writing results to a PostgreSQL database for future analysis. Airflow is responsible for orchestrating the correct time and order of starting tasks. With the help of the task run-time context and templating, code is executed for a given interval using the date-time values that come with that interval. If everything is set up correctly, the workflow can run until infinity.

Summary

- In Airflow, templating allows the dynamic parameterization of tasks at run time. This enables the creation of more generic and reusable workflows because values such as dates and file paths can be determined when the DAG is executed rather than being hardcoded.
- Jinja templating lets you create flexible workflows in Airflow operators. You can generate a SQL 'SELECT' statement dynamically using Jinja templating, for example, by including {{ logical_date }} in the query. Airflow replaces it with the current interval (e.g., 20240101).
- The PythonOperator in Airflow is unique when it comes to templating. The PythonOperator variables and run-time information aren't templated with Jinja; instead, all variables are passed as a dictionary directly to the function that the python_callable points to during execution.
- By using op_args (a list of positional arguments) and op_kwargs (a dictionary of keyword arguments), you can pass additional parameters to the Python callable of a PythonOperator.

- The airflow tasks render command allows you to test and verify the output of the templated arguments before running the actual tasks in a workflow.
- Operators describe what to do; hooks define how, handling the interaction with external systems and services. Hooks are connection interfaces to external systems such as databases, cloud services, and filesystems.

Defining dependencies between tasks

This chapter covers

- Defining task dependencies in an Airflow DAG
- Implementing joins using trigger rules
- Making tasks execute on certain conditions
- Seeing how trigger rules affect task execution
- Using XComs to share state between tasks
- Simplifying DAGs with the Airflow Taskflow API

We've seen how to build a basic directed acyclic graph (DAG) and define simple dependencies between tasks. In this chapter, we'll dive a bit deeper into how dependencies are defined and explore how to define more complex constructs, such as conditional tasks, branches, and joins. Toward the end of the chapter, we'll investigate XComs, which allow passing data between different tasks in a DAG run, and discuss the merits and drawbacks of this approach. We'll also show how the Airflow Taskflow API can simplify DAGs.

6.1   *Basic dependencies*

Before going into complex task dependency patterns such as branching and conditional tasks, let's examine the task dependencies we've already encountered, including linear chains of tasks (tasks that are executed one after another) and fan-out/fan-in patterns (which involve one task linking to multiple downstream tasks, or vice versa).

6.1.1   *Linear dependencies*

So far, we've focused mainly on DAGs that consist of a single linear chain of tasks. Our rocket-launch picture-fetching DAG from chapter 2 (figure 6.1), for example, consisted of a chain of the three tasks shown in the following listing: one for downloading launch metadata, one for downloading the images, and one for notifying us when the entire process is complete.

Listing 6.1   Tasks in the rocket-picture-fetching DAG

```
download_launches = BashOperator(...)
get_pictures = PythonOperator(...)
notify = BashOperator(...)
```

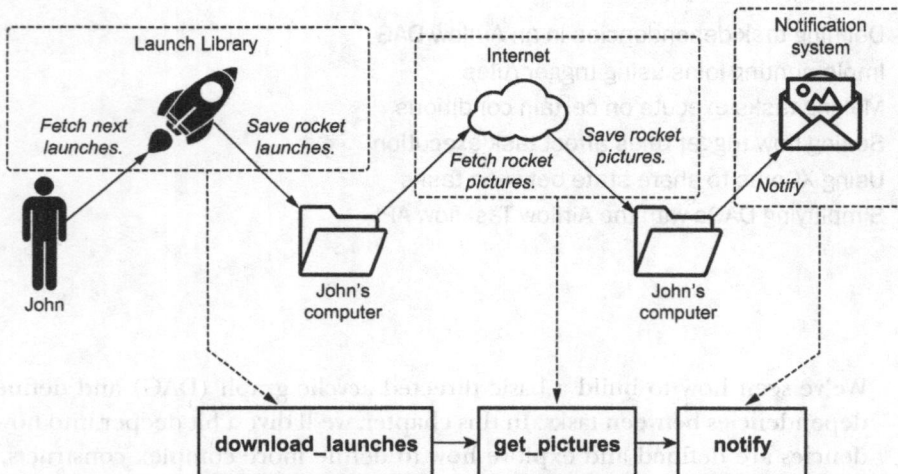

Figure 6.1   Our rocket-picture-fetching DAG from chapter 2 (originally shown in figure 2.3) consists of three tasks: downloading metadata, fetching the images, and sending a notification.

This type of DAG must complete each task before going to the next because the result of the preceding task is required as input for the next. As we've seen, Airflow allows us to indicate this type of relationship between two tasks by creating a dependency between them, using the bitwise right shift operator (>>).

Listing 6.2   Adding dependencies between tasks

```
download_launches >> get_pictures
get_pictures >> notify

download_launches >> get_pictures >> notify
```

Set task dependencies one by one . . .

. . . or set multiple dependencies in one go.

Task dependencies effectively tell Airflow that it can start executing a given task only when its upstream dependencies have executed successfully. In our example, this means `get_pictures` can start executing only when `download_launches` has run successfully. Similarly, `notify` can start only when the `get_pictures` task is complete without error.

One advantage of explicitly specifying task dependencies (listing 6.2) is that it clearly defines the implicit ordering of our tasks. This enables Airflow to schedule tasks only when their dependencies have been met, which is more robust than, say, scheduling individual tasks one after another using cron and hoping that preceding tasks will be complete by the time the next task starts. Moreover, Airflow will propagate any errors to downstream tasks, effectively postponing their execution. In the case of a failure in the `download_launches` task, Airflow won't try to execute the `get_pictures` task until the issue with `download_launches` has been resolved. In the case of an ephemeral problem, such as temporary network failure, it's possible to use Airflow's task-retry mechanism to retry a specific task a configurable number of times to cope with the problem automatically.

6.1.2   Fan-in/fan-out dependencies

We can also use Airflow's task dependencies to create more complex dependency structures between tasks. Let's revisit the umbrella use case from chapter 1, in which we wanted to train a machine learning (ML) model to predict demand for our umbrellas in the upcoming weeks based on the weather forecast.

As you may remember, the main purpose of the umbrella DAG was to fetch weather and sales data daily from two different sources and combine the data into a data set for training our model. The DAG (figure 6.2) starts with two sets of tasks for fetching and cleaning the input data: one for the weather data (`fetch_weather` and `clean_weather`) and one for the sales data (`fetch_sales` and `clean_sales`). These tasks are followed by a task (`join_datasets`) that joins the resulting cleaned sales and weather data into

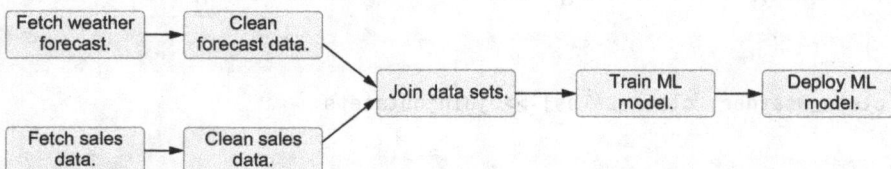

Figure 6.2   Overview of the DAG from the umbrella use case in chapter 1

a combined data set for training a model. Then this data set is used to train the model (`train_model`), and the final task deploys it (`deploy_model`).

If you think about this DAG in terms of dependencies, you see a linear dependency between the `fetch_weather` and `clean_weather` tasks: you need to fetch the data from your remote data source before you do any data cleaning. Because the fetching and cleaning of the weather data are independent of the sales data, there's no cross-dependency between the weather and sales tasks, so you can define the dependencies for the `fetch` and `clean` tasks as follows.

Listing 6.3   Adding linear dependencies that execute in parallel

```
fetch_weather >> clean_weather
fetch_sales >> clean_sales
```

Upstream of the two `fetch` tasks, we could have added an empty `start` task representing the start of our DAG. In this case, that task isn't strictly necessary, but it illustrates the implicit fan-out at the beginning of our DAG, in which the start of the DAG kicks off both the `fetch_weather` and `fetch_sales` tasks. This fan-out dependency, linking one task to multiple downstream tasks, could be defined as follows.

Listing 6.4   Adding a fan-out (one-to-multiple) dependency

```
from airflow.providers.standard.operators.empty import EmptyOperator

start = EmptyOperator(task_id="start")     ◀——————  Creates an empty start task
start >> [fetch_weather, fetch_sales]      ◀——┐
                                              Creates a fan-out (one-to-
                                              multiple) dependency
```

In contrast to the parallelism of the `fetch`/`clean` tasks, building the combined data set requires input from both the weather and sales branches. Therefore, the `join_datasets` task has a dependency on both the `clean_weather` and `clean_sales` tasks and can run only when both these upstream tasks have completed successfully. This type of structure, in which one task has a dependency on multiple upstream tasks, is often referred to as a *fan-in structure* because it consists of multiple upstream tasks that fan into a single downstream task. In Airflow, fan-in dependencies can be defined as shown in listing 6.5. After fanning in with the `join_datasets` task, the remainder of the DAG is a linear chain of tasks for training and deploying the model (listing 6.6). Combined, this should give us something similar to the DAG shown in figure 6.3.

Listing 6.5   Adding a fan-in (multiple-to-one) dependency

```
[clean_weather, clean_sales] >> join_datasets
```

Listing 6.6   Adding the remaining dependencies

```
join_datasets >> train_model >> deploy_model
```

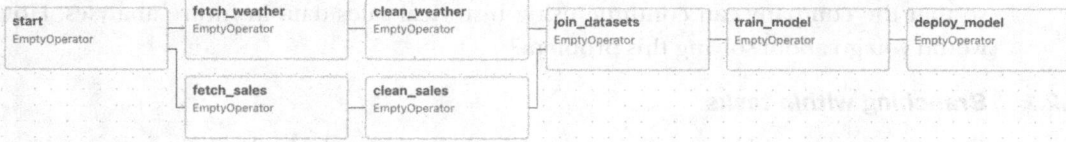

Figure 6.3 The umbrella DAG, rendered by Airflow's graph view. This DAG performs several tasks, including fetching and cleaning sales data, combining the data into a data set, and using the data set to train an ML model. Sales and weather data are handled in separate branches of the DAG because these tasks aren't directly dependent on each other.

What do you think would happen if you started executing this DAG now? Which tasks would start running first, and which tasks wouldn't run in parallel?

As you might expect, if you run the DAG now, Airflow starts by running the start task (figure 6.4). When the start task completes, it initiates the fetch_sales and fetch_weather tasks, which run in parallel (assuming that you've configured Airflow for multiple workers). Completion of either fetch task results in the start of the corresponding clean task (clean_sales or clean_weather). Only when both clean tasks are complete can Airflow start executing the join_datasets task. The rest of the DAG executes linearly, with train _model running as soon as the join_datasets task is complete and deploy_ model running when the train_model task is complete.

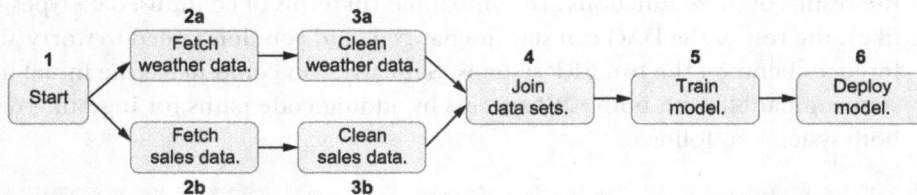

Figure 6.4 The execution order of tasks in the umbrella DAG, with numbers indicating the order in which tasks are run. Airflow starts by executing the start task, after which it can run the sales/weather fetch and clean tasks in parallel (as indicated by the a/b suffixes). This means that the weather/sales paths run independently; 3b, for example, might start executing before 2a. When both clean tasks are complete, the rest of the DAG proceeds linearly, executing the join, train, and deployment tasks.

6.2 Branching

Suppose that you just finished writing the ingestion of sales data in your DAG when your coworker comes in with some news. Apparently, management has decided to switch enterprise resource planning (ERP) systems, which means that your sales data will be coming from a different source (and in a different format, of course) in one or two weeks. This change shouldn't disrupt the training of your model. Moreover, management wants you to keep the flow compatible with both the old and new systems so that the company can continue using historical sales data in future analyses. How would you go about solving this problem?

6.2.1 Branching within tasks

One approach could be to rewrite your sales ingestion tasks to check the current data_interval_start and use it to decide between two code paths for ingesting and processing the sales data. You could rewrite the sales cleaning task as something like the following listing.

Listing 6.7   Branching within the clean task

```
def _clean_sales(**context):
    if context["data_interval_start"] < ERP_CHANGE_DATE:
        _clean_sales_old(**context)
    else
        _clean_sales_new(**context)
...
clean_sales_data = PythonOperator(
    task_id="clean_sales",
    python_callable=_clean_sales,
)
```

In this example, _clean_sales_old is a function that performs the cleaning for the old sales format, and _clean_sales_new does the same thing for the new format. As long as the results of these functions are compatible (in terms of columns, data types, and the like), the rest of the DAG can stay unchanged, and you don't need to worry about differences between the two ERP systems. Similarly, you could make the initial ingestion step compatible with both ERP systems by adding code paths for ingesting data from both systems, as follows.

Listing 6.8   Branching within the fetch task

```
def _fetch_sales(**context):
    if context["data_interval_start "] < ERP_CHANGE_DATE:
        _fetch_sales_old(**context)
    else:
        _fetch_sales_new(**context)
    ...
```

Combined, these changes would allow the DAG to handle data from both systems in a relatively transparent fashion. The initial fetch/clean tasks ensure that the sales data arrives in the same processed format, independent of the corresponding data source.

An advantage of the approach in listing 6.8 is that it allows you to incorporate some flexibility into DAGs without modifying the structures of the DAGs themselves. This approach, however, works only when the branches in the code consist of similar tasks.

Here, for example, you effectively have two branches in the code, both of which perform `fetch` and `clean` operations with minimal differences. But what if loading data from the new data source requires a very different chain of tasks (figure 6.5)? In that case, you might be better off splitting data ingestion into two separate sets of tasks.

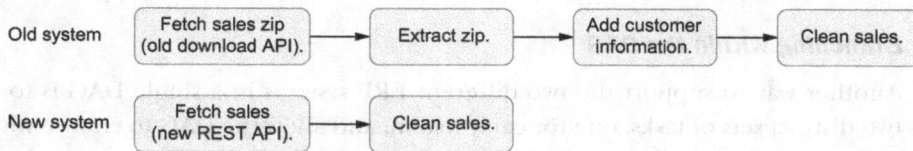

Figure 6.5   An example of different sets of tasks between two ERP systems. If different flows have a lot of commonalities, you may be able to get away with using a single set of tasks and some internal branching. If there are many differences between the two flows, however (such as shown here for the two ERP systems), you may be better off taking a different approach.

Another drawback of this approach is that it's difficult to see which code branch Airflow is using during a specific DAG run. In figure 6.6, can you guess which ERP system was used for this specific DAG run? This seemingly simple question is quite difficult to answer using only this view because the actual branching is hidden within the tasks. One way to solve this problem is to include better logging in tasks. But as you'll see later in this chapter, there are other ways to make branching more explicit in the DAG itself.

Finally, you can encode this type of flexibility into tasks only by falling back to general Airflow operators such as the `PythonOperator`. This prevents you from using functionality provided by more specialized Airflow operators, which allow you to perform more complicated work with minimal coding effort. If one of your data sources happens to be a SQL database, for example, simply

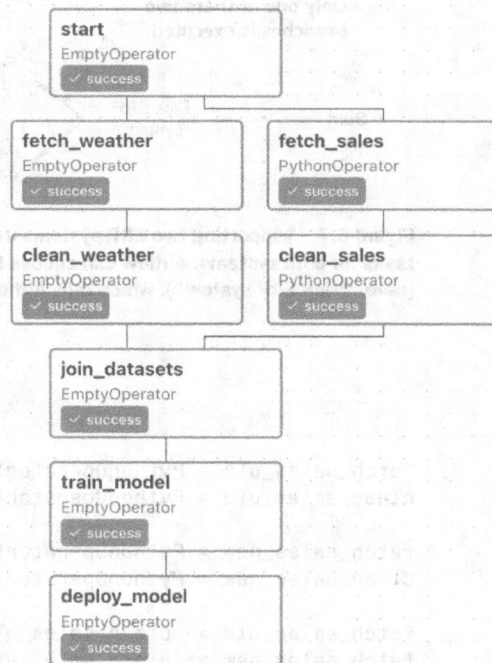

Figure 6.6   Example run for a DAG that branches between two ERP systems within the `fetch_sales` and `clean_sales` tasks. Because this branching happens within these two tasks, it's impossible to see which ERP system was used in this DAG run. You'd need to inspect your code (or possibly your logs) to identify the ERP system.

using the `SqlExecuteQueryOperator` to execute a SQL query would save you a lot of work because this operator allows you to delegate the actual execution of the query (along with authentication, configuration, connectivity, and so on) to the provided operator.

Fortunately, checking for conditions within tasks isn't the only way to perform branching in Airflow. The following subsection shows how to weave branches into a DAG structure, which provides more flexibility than the task-based approach.

6.2.2   *Branching within the DAG*

Another way to support the two different ERP systems in a single DAG is to develop two distinct sets of tasks, one for each system, and allow the DAG to choose whether to execute the tasks by fetching data from either the old or new ERP system (figure 6.7). Building the two sets of tasks is relatively straightforward: we simply create tasks for each ERP system separately, using the appropriate operators, and link the respective tasks (listing 6.9).

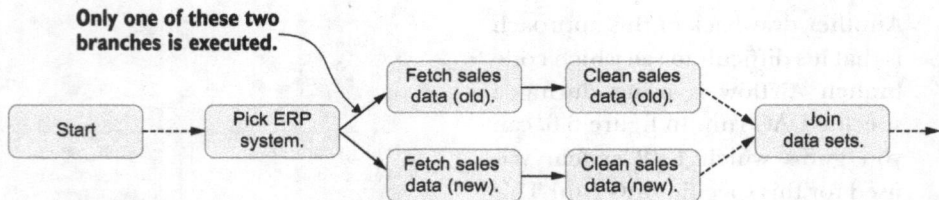

Figure 6.7   Supporting two ERP systems using branching within the DAG, implementing different sets of tasks for both systems. Airflow can choose between these two branches using a specific branching task (here, "Pick ERP system"), which tells Airflow which set of downstream tasks to execute.

Listing 6.9   Adding extra `fetch`/`clean` tasks

```
fetch_sales_old = PythonOperator(...)
clean_sales_old = PythonOperator(...)

fetch_sales_new = PythonOperator(...)
clean_sales_new = PythonOperator(...)

fetch_sales_old >> clean_sales_old
fetch_sales_new >> clean_sales_new
```

We still need to connect these tasks to the rest of our DAG and make sure that Airflow knows which task it should execute when. Fortunately, Airflow provides built-in support for choosing between sets of downstream tasks by using the `BranchPythonOperator`. As its name suggests, this operator is similar to the `PythonOperator` in the sense that it takes a Python callable as one of its main arguments, as shown in the next listing.

```
Listing 6.10    Branching with the BranchPythonOperator
```

```python
def _pick_erp_system(**context):
    ...

pick_erp_system = BranchPythonOperator(
    task_id="pick_erp_system",
    python_callable=_pick_erp_system,
)
```

In contrast to the PythonOperator approach, however, callables passed to the Branch-PythonOperator are expected to return the ID of a downstream task as a result of their computation. The returned ID determines which downstream task will be executed when the branch task is complete.

We can also return a list of task IDs, in which case Airflow will execute all referenced tasks. In this case, we can implement our choice between the two ERP systems by using the callable to return the appropriate task_id depending on the execution date of the DAG.

```
Listing 6.11    Adding the branching condition function
```

```python
def _pick_erp_system(**context):
    if context["data_interval_start "] < ERP_CHANGE_DATE:
        return "fetch_sales_old"
    else:
        return "fetch_sales_new"

pick_erp_system = BranchPythonOperator(
    task_id="pick_erp_system",
    python_callable=_pick_erp_system,
)

pick_erp_system >> [fetch_sales_old, fetch_sales_new]
```

This way, Airflow will execute our set of old ERP tasks for dates that occur before the switch date while executing the new tasks that occur after that date. Now all we need to do is connect these tasks with the rest of our DAG. To connect our branching task to the start of the DAG, we can add a dependency between our previous start task and the pick_erp_system task.

```
Listing 6.12    Connecting the branch to the start task
```

```python
start_task >> pick_erp_system
```

Similarly, connecting the two clean tasks is as simple as adding a dependency between them and the join_datasets task (similar to the earlier situation in figure 6.7, where clean_sales was connected to join_datasets). If you do this, running the DAG would result in Airflow's skipping the join_datasets task and all its downstream tasks. (You can try it if you want to.) The reason is that, by default, Airflow requires all tasks upstream of a given task to complete successfully before that task itself can be executed. By connecting both of your `clean` tasks to the `join_datasets` task, as shown in the following listing, you create a situation in which this can never occur because only one of the cleaning tasks is executed. As a result, the `join_datasets` task can never be executed, so Airflow skips it (figure 6.8).

Listing 6.13 Connecting the branch to the `join_datasets` task

```
[clean_sales_old, clean_sales_new] >> join_datasets
```

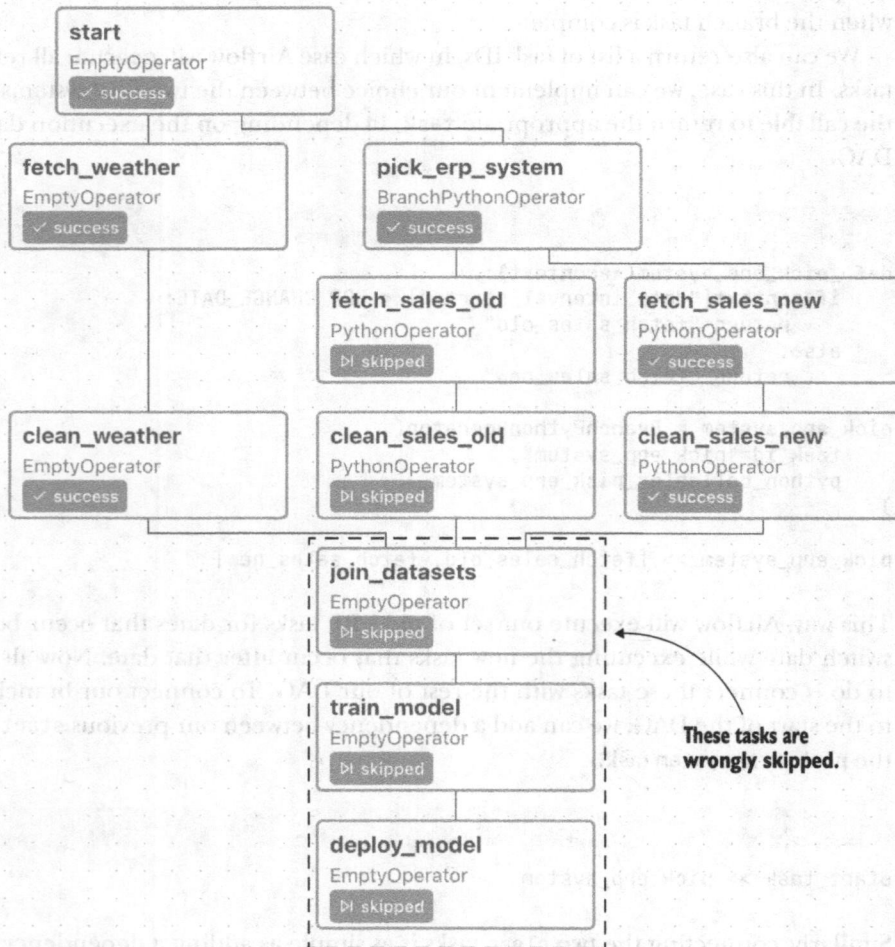

Figure 6.8 Combining branching with the wrong trigger rules causes Airflow to skip downstream tasks. In this example, Airflow skips the `fetch_sales_old` task, which results in skipping all tasks downstream of that task, which is not what we want.

This behavior that defines when tasks are executed is controlled by trigger rules in Airflow. (Section 6.4 discusses these rules in detail.) We can define trigger rules for individual tasks by using the `trigger_rule` argument, which can be passed to any operator. By default, trigger rules are set to `all_success`, meaning that all parents of the corresponding task need to succeed before the task can be run. This never happens when we use the `BranchPythonOperator`; it skips any tasks not chosen by the branch, which explains why Airflow skipped the `join_datasets` task and all its downstream tasks.

To fix this problem, we can change the trigger rule of `join_datasets` so that it still triggers if Airflow skips one of its upstream tasks. The following listing changes the trigger rule to `none_failed`, which specifies that a task should run as soon as all its parents have executed without failures. (Skipping doesn't count as failure.) This way, `join_datasets` starts executing as soon as all its parents finish executing without failures, allowing it to continue its execution after the branch (figure 6.9).

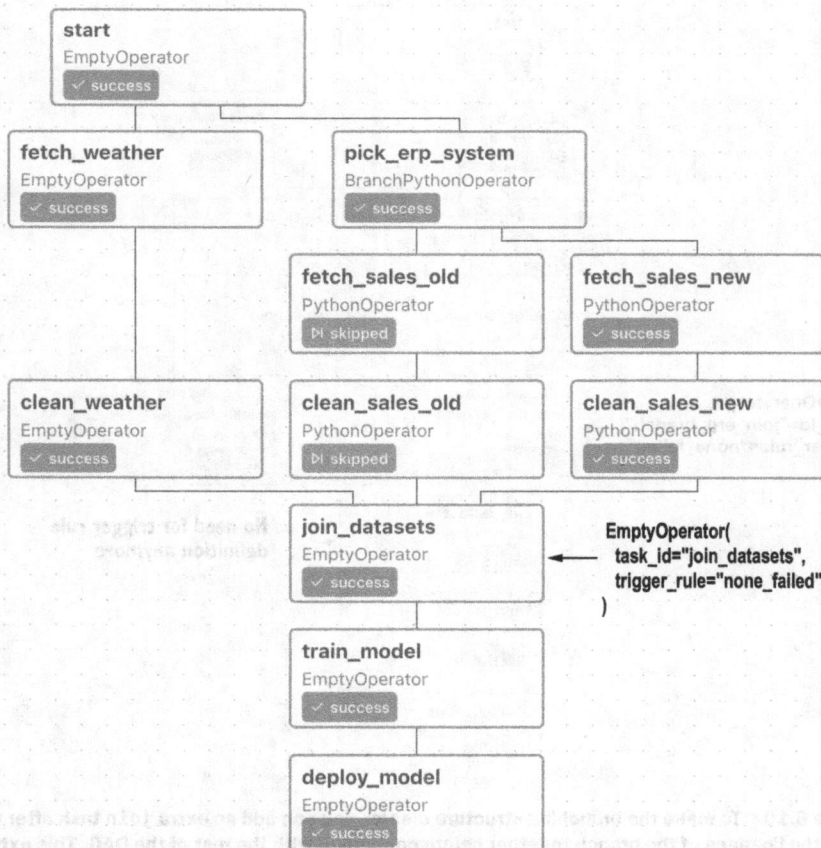

Figure 6.9 Branching in the umbrella DAG using trigger rule `none_failed` for the `join_datasets` task, which allows it and its downstream dependencies to execute after the branch

```
join_datasets = PythonOperator(
    ...,
    trigger_rule="none_failed",
)
```

One drawback of this approach is that now we have three edges—`clean_weather`, `clean_sales_old`, and `clean_sales_new`—in the `join_datasets` task. This structure doesn't reflect the nature of our flow; we essentially want to fetch sales/weather data (choosing between the two ERP systems first) and then feed these two data sources into `join_datasets`. For this reason, many people choose to make the branch condition more explicit by adding an empty task that joins the branches before continuing with the DAG (figure 6.10). To add an empty task to our DAG, we can use Airflow's

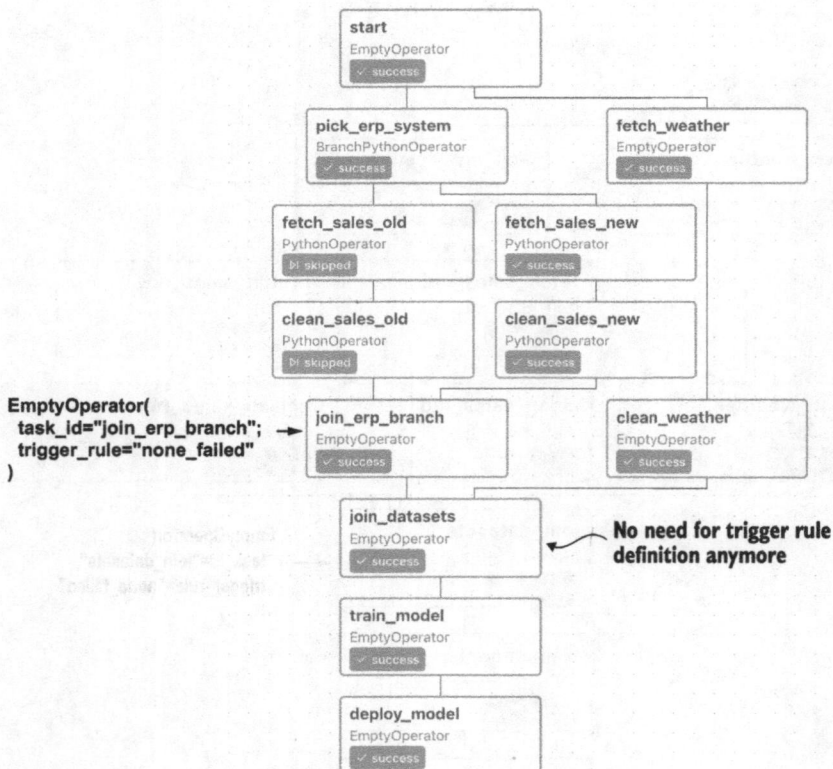

Figure 6.10   To make the branching structure clearer, you can add an extra `join` task after the branch, tying the lineages of the branch together before continuing with the rest of the DAG. This extra task has an added advantage: you don't have to change trigger rules for other tasks in the DAG because you can set the required trigger rule on the `join` task. That is, you no longer need to set the trigger rule for the `join_datasets` task.

built-in EmptyOperator, shown in listing 6.15. This change also means that we no longer need to change the trigger rule for the join_datasets task, making our branch more self-contained than the original.

Listing 6.15 Adding an empty join task for clarity

```
from airflow.providers.standard.operators.empty import EmptyOperator

join_branch = EmptyOperator(
    task_id="join_erp_branch",
    trigger_rule="none_failed"
)

[clean_sales_old, clean_sales_new] >> join_branch
join_branch >> join_datasets
```

6.3 Conditional tasks

Airflow also provides other mechanisms for skipping specific tasks in your DAG depending on certain conditions. These mechanisms allow you to make certain tasks run only if certain data sets are available or only if your DAG is executing for the most recent data interval.

6.3.1 Conditions within tasks

In the umbrella DAG (refer to figure 6.3), for example, we have a task that deploys every model we train. But consider what would happen if a colleague changes the clean code and wants to use backfilling to apply these changes to the entire sales and weather data sets. In this case, backfilling the DAG would also result in running all the train_model and deploy_model tasks on the changed data and with that run deploying many nonrelevant instances of our model, which we certainly aren't interested in doing.

We can eliminate this issue by changing the DAG to deploy the model for only the most recent DAG run, which ensures that we deploy only one version of our model: the one trained on the most recent data set. One way is to implement the deployment using the PythonOperator and explicitly check that the deployment task is executed only for the most recent run. To achieve this functionality, we should deploy the model only when the task execution happens between the data_interval_end of the current execution interval and before the data_interval_end of the next execution interval.

As you may have noticed, the next_data_interval_end parameter isn't available in the Airflow context. Fortunately, this problem has a workaround: use the next_dagrun_info function of the DAG's timetable instance in the Airflow context to get this parameter, as shown in the following listing.

Listing 6.16 Implementing a condition within a task

```
def _deploy_model(dag, data_interval_start, data_interval_end, **_):

    task_exec_start = pendulum.now("UTC")
```

```
time_restriction = TimeRestriction(earliest=None, latest=None,
    catchup=True)
current_interval = DataInterval(start=data_interval_start, end=data_
    interval_end)

next_info = dag.timetable.next_dagrun_info(
            last_automated_data_interval=current_interval,
            restriction=time_restriction,
        )
if next_info is None:
    # Last scheduled execution
    return True

next_info_start, next_info_end = next_info.data_interval
if next_info_start < task_exec_start <= next_info_end:
    print("Deploying model")
```

Although this implementation should have the intended effect, it has the same drawbacks as the corresponding branching implementation. It confounds the deployment logic with the condition that we can no longer use any built-in operators other than the `PythonOperator`, and tracking task results in the Airflow UI becomes less explicit (figure 6.11).

6.3.2   *Making tasks conditional*

Another way to implement conditional deployments is to make the `deploy_model` task itself conditional, meaning that it's executed only based on a predefined condition (in this case, whether the DAG run is the most recent). In Airflow, we can make tasks conditional by adding a task to the DAG that tests the condition and ensures that any downstream tasks are skipped if the condition fails. Also, we can make our deployment conditional by adding a

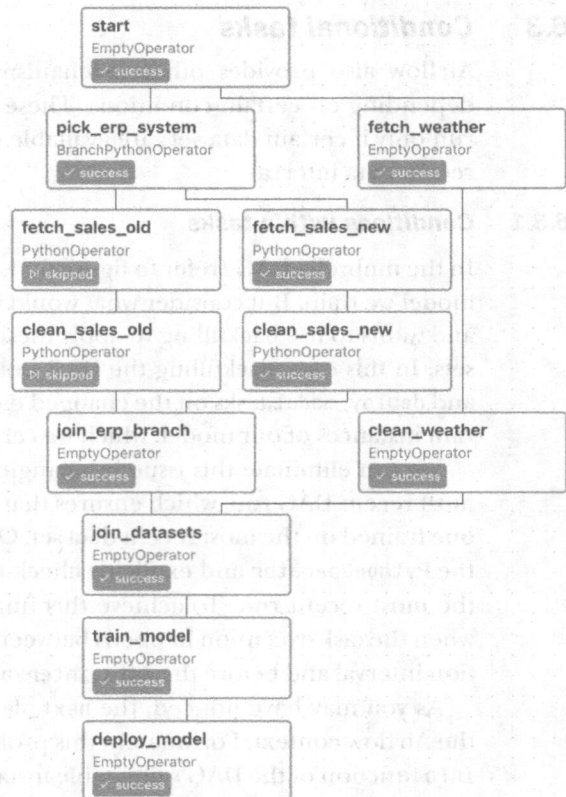

Figure 6.11   Example run for the umbrella DAG with a condition inside the `deploy_model` task, which ensures that the deployment is performed only for the latest run. Because the condition is checked internally within the `deploy_model` task, we can't discern from this view whether the model was actually deployed.

task that checks whether the current execution is the most recent DAG execution and adding our deployment task downstream of this task, as shown in the next listing. Now our DAG should look something like figure 6.12, with the train_model task connected to our new task and the deploy_model task downstream of this new task.

Listing 6.17 Building the condition into the DAG

```
def _latest_only(**context):
    ...

latest_only = PythonOperator(
    task_id="latest_only",
    python_callable=_latest_only,
)

latest_only >> deploy_model
```

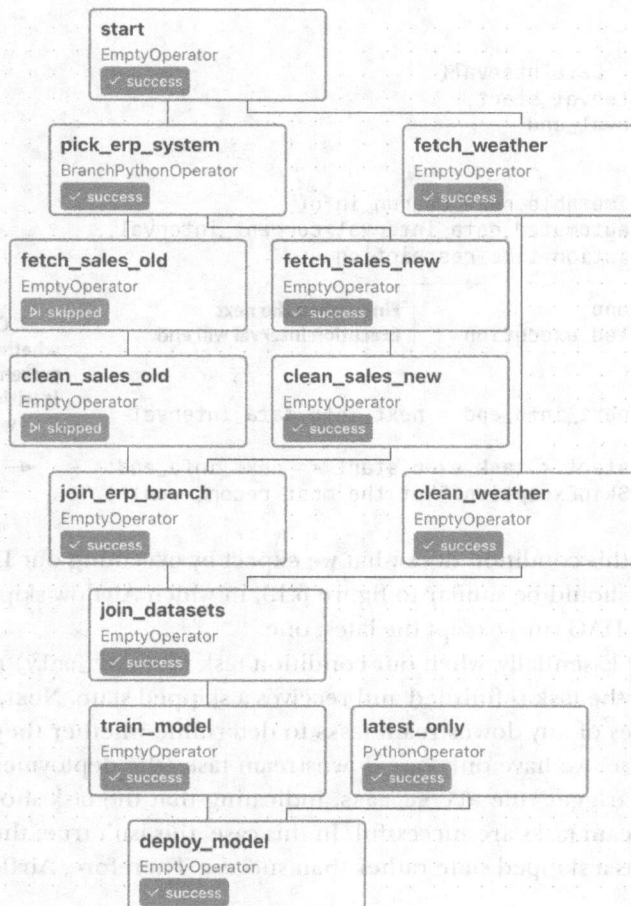

Figure 6.12 An alternative implementation of the umbrella DAG with conditional deployment. The condition is included in the DAG as a task, making the condition much more explicit than in our previous implementation.

Next, we need to fill in the `latest_only` function to make sure that Airflow skips downstream tasks if the `data_interval_start` doesn't belong to the most recent run. To do so, we check our data interval start and, if necessary, raise an `AirflowSkipException` from our function, which is Airflow's way of allowing us to indicate that the condition and all its downstream tasks should be skipped, thus skipping the deployment, which gives us something like the following implementation for our condition.

Listing 6.18   Implementing the `_latest_only` condition

```python
from airflow.exceptions import AirflowSkipException
from airflow.timetables.base
➥  import DataInterval, TimeRestriction

def _latest_only(dag, data_interval_start, data_interval_end, **_):
    task_exec_start = pendulum.now("UTC")
    time_restriction = TimeRestriction(
        earliest=None,
        latest=None,
        catchup=True
    )
    current_interval = DataInterval(
        start=data_interval_start,
        end=data_interval_end
    )

    next_info = dag.timetable.next_dagrun_info(
            last_automated_data_interval=current_interval,
            restriction=time_restriction,
        )
    if next_info is None:
        # Last scheduled execution
        return True

    next_info_start, next_info_end = next_info.data_interval

    if not next_info_start < task_exec_start <= next_info_end:
        raise AirflowSkipException("Not the most recent run!")
```

Finds when the next execution interval will end

Checks whether our current time is within the window

We can check whether this condition does what we expect by executing our DAGs for a few dates. The result should be similar to figure 6.13, in which Airflow skipped our `deploy_model` task in all DAG runs except the latest one.

How does this work? Essentially, when our condition task (`latest _only`) raises an `AirflowSkipException`, the task is finished and receives a skipped state. Next, Airflow looks at the trigger rules of any downstream tasks to determine whether they should be triggered. In this case, we have only one downstream task (the deployment task), which uses the default trigger rule `all_success`, indicating that the task should execute only if all its upstream tasks are successful. In this case, this isn't true: the parent (the condition task) has a skipped state rather than success. Therefore, Airflow skips the deployment.

latest_only
start
fetch_weather
pick_erp_system
clean_weather
fetch_sales_new
fetch_sales_old
clean_sales_new
clean_sales_old
join_erp_branch
join_datasets
train_model
deploy_model

Figure 6.13 Result of our `latest_only`
**condition for three runs of our umbrella DAG.
This tree view shows that our deployment task
was run only for the most recent execution
window; the** `deploy_model` **task was skipped
on previous executions. This shows that our
condition indeed functions as expected.**

**The deployment task
is skipped in all runs
except the last one.**

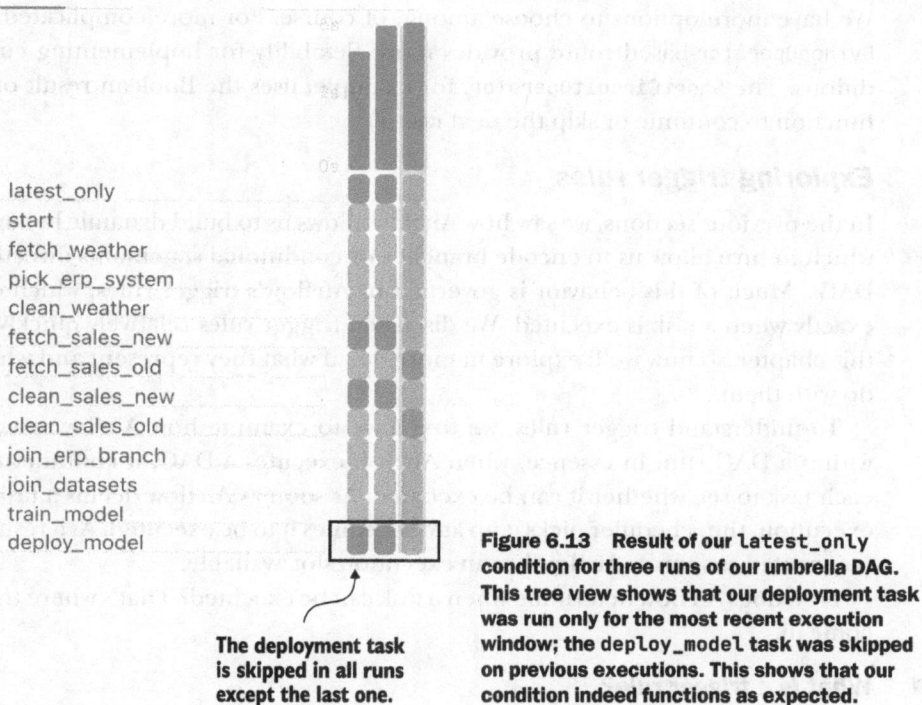

Conversely, if the condition task doesn't raise an `AirflowSkipException`, it completes
successfully and receives a success status. Therefore, the deployment task is triggered
because all its parents completed successfully, and we get our deployment.

6.3.3 Using built-in operators

Because running tasks for only the most recent DAG run is a common use case, Airflow
provides the built-in `LatestOnlyOperator` class, which effectively performs the same job
as our custom-built implementation based on the `PythonOperator`. Using the `Latest-
OnlyOperator`, we can implement our conditional deployment as follows, which saves
us from writing our own complex logic.

Listing 6.19 Using the built-in `LatestOnlyOperator`

```
from airflow.providers.standard.operators.latest_only
    import LatestOnlyOperator

latest_only = LatestOnlyOperator(
    task_id="latest_only",
)

train_model >> latest_only >> deploy_model
```

We have more options to choose among, of course. For more complicated cases, the PythonOperator-based route provides more flexibility for implementing custom conditions. The ShortCircuitOperator, for example, uses the Boolean result of a Python function to continue or skip the next task(s).

6.4 *Exploring trigger rules*

In the previous sections, we saw how Airflow allows us to build dynamic behavior DAGs, which in turn allow us to encode branches or conditional statements directly into our DAGs. Much of this behavior is governed by Airflow's trigger rules, which determine exactly when a task is executed. We discussed trigger rules relatively quickly earlier in this chapter, so now we'll explore in more detail what they represent and what you can do with them.

To understand trigger rules, we first have to examine how Airflow executes tasks within a DAG run. In essence, when Airflow executes a DAG, it continuously checks each task to see whether it can be executed. As soon as Airflow deems a task ready for execution, the scheduler picks it up and schedules it to be executed. As a result, the task is executed as soon as Airflow has an execution slot available.

How does Airflow determine when a task can be executed? That's where trigger rules come in.

6.4.1 *What is a trigger rule?*

Trigger rules are essentially the conditions that Airflow applies to tasks to determine whether they're ready to execute, based on the execution status of their dependencies (meaning the preceding tasks in the DAG). Airflow's default trigger rule is all_success, which states that all a task's dependencies must complete successfully before the task itself can execute.

To see what this means, let's jump back to our initial implementation of the umbrella DAG (refer to figure 6.4), which uses no trigger rules other than the default all_success rule. If we started executing this DAG, Airflow would start looping over its tasks to determine which tasks can be executed (i.e., which tasks have no dependencies that have not completed successfully).

In this case, only the start task satisfies the condition by not having dependencies. Therefore, Airflow starts executing the DAG by running the start task (figure 6.14). When the start task completes successfully, the fetch_weather and fetch_sales tasks become ready for execution because now their only dependency satisfies their trigger rule (figure 6.14). By following this pattern of execution, Airflow continues to the remaining tasks until it has executed the entire DAG.

6.4.2 *The effect of failures*

This example only sketches the situation for a happy flow, in which all tasks complete successfully. What happens if, say, one of our tasks encounters an error during execution?

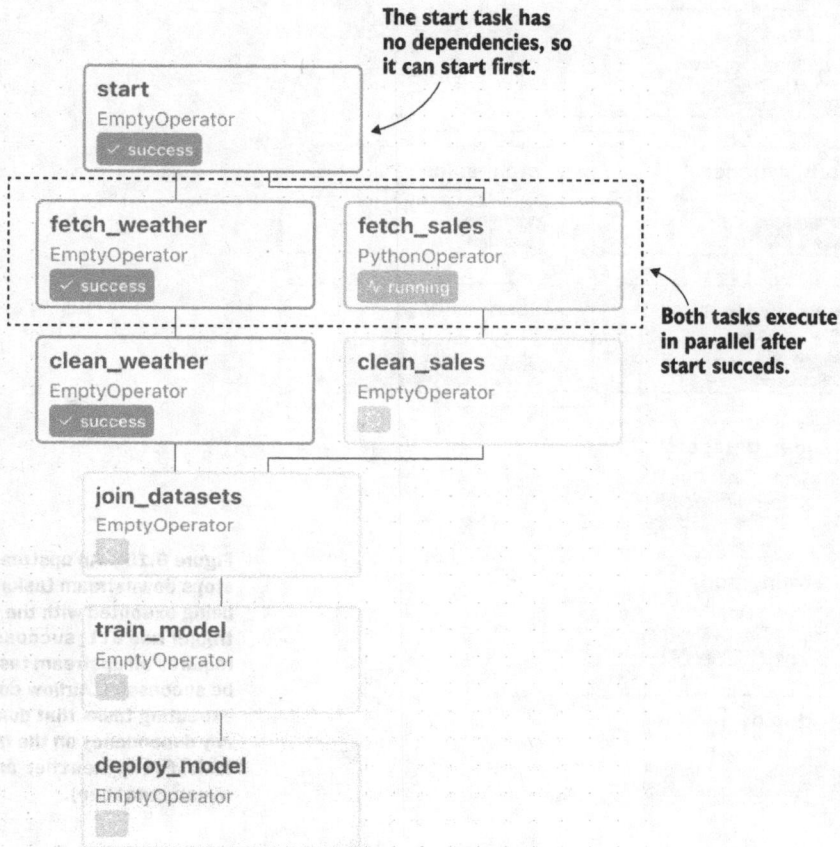

Figure 6.14 Tracing the execution of the basic umbrella DAG (figure 6.4) using the default trigger rule `all_success`. Airflow starts executing the DAG by running the only task with no preceding tasks that didn't complete successfully: the `start` task. When the `start` task completes successfully, other tasks become ready for execution, and Airflow picks them up.

We can easily test this situation by simulating a failure in one of the tasks. By simulating a failed `fetch_sales` task, for example, we see that Airflow records the failure by assigning `fetch_sales` the failed state rather than the success state (figure 6.15). This means that the downstream `clean_sales` task can no longer be executed because it requires `fetch_sales` to be successful. As a result, the `clean_sales` task is assigned the state `upstream_failed`, which indicates that it can't proceed because of the upstream failure.

This type of behavior, in which the result of upstream tasks affects downstream tasks, is referred to as *propagation*. In this case, the upstream failure is *propagated* to the downstream tasks. The effects of skipped tasks can also be propagated downstream by the default trigger rule, resulting in Airflow's skipping all tasks downstream of a skipped task. This propagation is a direct result of the definition of the `all_success` trigger rule,

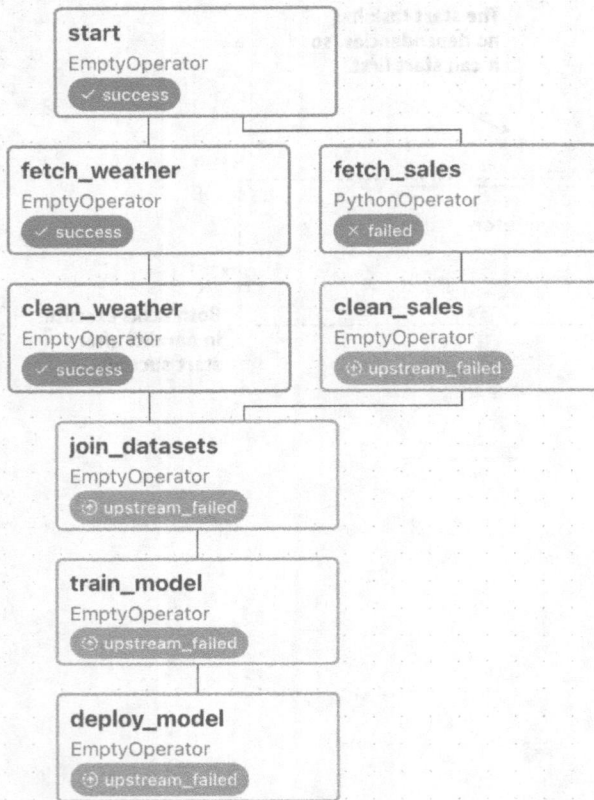

Figure 6.15   An upstream failure stops downstream tasks from being executed with the default trigger rule all_success, which requires all upstream tasks to be successful. Airflow continues executing tasks that don't have any dependency on the failed task (fetch_weather and clean_weather).

which requires all of its dependencies to complete successfully. Therefore, if Airflow encounters a skip or failure in a dependency, it has no option other than to fail in the same manner, propagating the skip or failure.

6.4.3   *Other trigger rules*

Airflow supports several other trigger rules, which allow different types of behavior in response to successful, failed, or skipped tasks. Let's look back at our branching pattern between the two ERP systems in section 6.2. In this case, we had to adjust the trigger rule of the task joining the branch (done by the join_datasets or join_erp_branch tasks) to avoid skipping downstream tasks because, with the default trigger rule, the skips resulting from the branch would be propagated downstream. As a result, Airflow would skip all tasks after the branch as well. By contrast, the none_failed trigger rule checks only whether all upstream tasks have completed without failure. This means it tolerates both successful and skipped tasks while waiting for all upstream tasks to complete before continuing, making the trigger rule suitable for joining the two branches. In terms of propagation, the rule doesn't propagate skips, but it still propagates failures, meaning that any failures in the `fetch`/`clean` tasks will still halt the execution of downstream tasks.

We can use other trigger rules to handle other situations. The `all_done` rule, for example, enables us to define tasks that execute as soon as their dependencies finish executing, regardless of their results. We could use this rule to execute cleanup code (e.g., shutting down our machine or cleaning up resources) that we want to run regardless of what happens. Another category of trigger rules includes eager rules such as `one_failed` and `one_success`, which don't wait for all upstream tasks to complete before triggering; they require only one upstream task to satisfy their condition. We could use these rules to signal early failure of tasks or respond as soon as one task in a group of tasks completes successfully.

Although we won't go any deeper into trigger rules here, we hope this section gives you an idea of the role of trigger rules in Airflow and how to use them to introduce more complex behavior into DAGs. For a complete overview of trigger rules and some potential use cases, see table 6.1.

WARNING   Remember this common pitfall: using the wrong trigger rule when working with branching can lead Airflow to skip tasks unexpectedly.

Table 6.1   Overview of the trigger rules Airflow supports

Trigger rule	Behavior	Example use case
`all_success` (default)	Triggers when all parent tasks have completed successfully	The default trigger rule for a normal workflow
`all_failed`	Triggers when all parent tasks have failed (or failed as a result of a failure in their parents)	Triggers error-handling code to clean up temporary resource or aid in alerting scenarios
`all_done`	Triggers when all parents are done executing, regardless of the resulting state	Executes cleanup code that you want to execute when all tasks have finished (e.g., shutting down a machine or stopping a cluster)
`all_done_setup_success`	Triggers when all setup tasks have succeeded and other upstream tasks are done	Is configured automatically by teardown tasks; you wouldn't set this rule yourself
`all_skipped`	Triggers when all parent tasks have been skipped	Executes code that would replace the logic of skipped tasks upstream
`one_failed`	Triggers as soon as at least one parent fails; doesn't wait for other parent tasks to finish executing	Quickly triggesr some error-handling code, such as notifications or rollbacks
`one_success`	Triggers as soon as one parent succeeds; doesn't wait for other parent tasks to finish executing	Quickly triggers downstream computations/notifications as soon as one result becomes available
`one_done`	Triggers if at least one upstream task succeeds or fails	Quickly continues with the DAG logic when one task completes execution, whether that task succeeded or failed

Table 6.1 Overview of the trigger rules Airflow supports (*continued*)

Trigger rule	Behavior	Example use case
`none_failed`	Triggers if no parents failed but were completed successfully or skipped	Joins conditional branches in Airflow DAGs (section 6.2)
`none_failed_min_one_success`	Triggers when upstream tasks have not failed (they could have been skipped) but at least one upstream task has succeeded	Joins conditional branches in Airflow DAGs (section 6.2)
`none_skipped`	Triggers if no parents have been skipped but have completed successfully or failed	Triggers a task if all upstream tasks were executed, ignoring their result(s)
`always`	Triggers regardless of the state of any upstream tasks	Performs testing

6.5   *Sharing data between tasks*

Airflow also allows you to share small pieces of data between tasks using XComs. (*XCom* is an abbreviation of *cross-communication.*) XComs essentially enable you to exchange messages between tasks, enabling some level of shared state.

6.5.1   *Sharing data using XComs*

To see how this works, let's look back at our umbrella use case (refer to figure 6.3). Suppose that when we train our model (in the `train_model` task), the trained model is registered in a model registry using a randomly generated identifier. To deploy the trained model, we need to pass this identifier to the `deploy_model` task somehow so that it knows which version of the model to deploy.

One way to solve this problem is to use XComs to share the model identifier between the `train_model` and `deploy_model` tasks. In this case, the `train_model` task is responsible for pushing the XCom value, which essentially publishes the value and makes it available for other tasks. We can publish XCom values explicitly within our task using the `xcom_push` method, which is available on the task instance in the Airflow context.

Listing 6.20   Pushing Xcom values explicitly using `xcom_push`

```
def _train_model(**context):
    model_id = str(uuid.uuid4())
    context["task_instance"].xcom_push(key="model_id", value=model_id)

train_model = PythonOperator(
    task_id="train_model",
    python_callable=_train_model,
)
```

This call to `xcom_push` tells Airflow to register our `model_id` value as an XCom value for the corresponding task (`train_model`) and the corresponding DAG and execution date. After running this task, we can view these published XCom values in the web interface by choosing Browse > XComs. The resulting page (figure 6.16) shows an overview of all published XCom values. To retrieve the XCom value in other tasks, use the xcom_pull method, which is the inverse of xcom_push (listing 6.21).

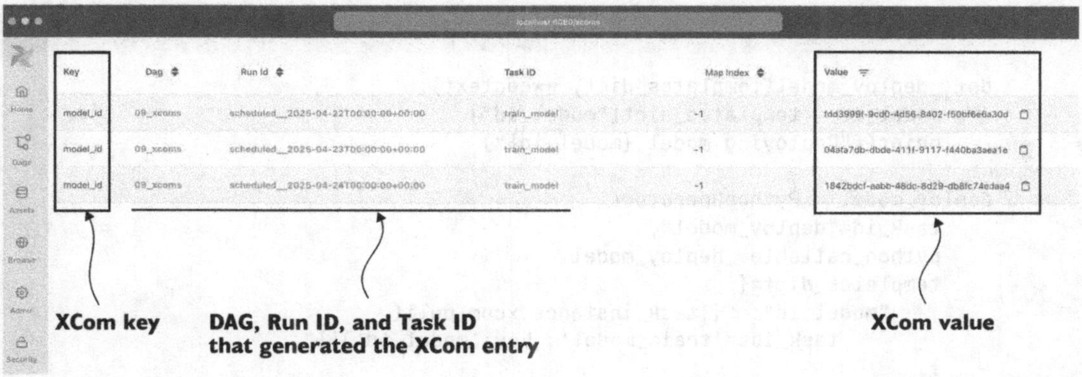

XCom key   **DAG, Run ID, and Task ID**   **XCom value**
               that generated the XCom entry

Figure 6.16   Overview of registered XCom values

Listing 6.21   Retrieving XCom values using xcom_pull

```
def _deploy_model(**context):
    model_id = context["task_instance"].xcom_pull(
        task_ids="train_model", key="model_id"
    )
    print(f"Deploying model {model_id}")

deploy_model = PythonOperator(
    task_id="deploy_model",
    python_callable=_deploy_model,
)
```

This method tells Airflow to fetch the XCom value with key model_id from the train_model task, which matches the model_id we pushed in the train_model task. xcom_pull also allows us to define the dag_id and execution date when fetching XCom values. By default, these parameters are set to the current DAG and current (logical) date so that xcom_pull fetches only values published by the current DAG run.

NOTE   You can specify other values for dag_id and/or logical_date to fetch XCom values from other DAGs or other execution dates, but we strongly recommend against doing this unless you have an extremely good reason.

We can verify that this method works by running the DAG, which should give us something like the following result for the deploy_model task, and we can reference XCom variables in templates, as shown in listing 6.22:

```
[2025-04-25, 14:04:31] INFO - Deploying model
  fdd3999f-9cd0-4d56-8402-f50bf6e6a30d: chan="stdout": source="task"
[2025-04-25, 14:04:31] INFO - Done. Returned value was: None:
  source="airflow.task.operators.airflow.providers
  .standard.operators.python.PythonOperator"
```

Listing 6.22   Using XCom values in templates

```python
def _deploy_model(templates_dict, **context):
    model_id = templates_dict["model_id"]
    print(f"Deploying model {model_id}")


deploy_model = PythonOperator(
    task_id="deploy_model",
    python_callable=_deploy_model,
    templates_dict={
        "model_id": "{{task_instance.xcom_pull(
            task_ids='train_model', key='model_id')}}"
    },
)
```

Finally, many operators provide support for pushing XCom values automatically, depending on the value of the Boolean argument `do_xcom_push`, which by default is `True` in the `BaseOperator`. The `BashOperator` pushes the last line written to stdout by the Bash command as an XCom value. Similarly, the `PythonOperator` will publish any value returned from the Python callable as an XCom value, so we can also write our example as shown in the listing 6.23. This method works by registering the XCom under the default key `return_value`, as we can see by choosing Browse > XComs in the web interface (figure 6.17).

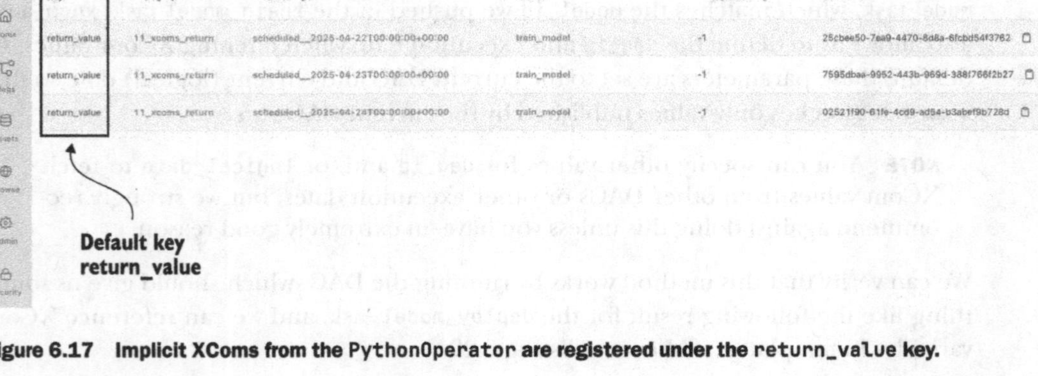

Figure 6.17   Implicit XComs from the `PythonOperator` are registered under the `return_value` key.

Listing 6.23 Using `return` to push XComs

```
def _train_model(**context):
    model_id = str(uuid.uuid4())
    return model_id
```

6.5.2 When and when not to use XComs

Although XComs may seem useful for sharing state between tasks, they also have some drawbacks. For one, they add a hidden dependency between tasks because the pulling task has an implicit dependency on the task pushing the required value. In contrast to explicit task dependencies, this dependency isn't visible in the DAG, and Airflow won't take it into account when scheduling the tasks; you're responsible for making sure that tasks with XCom dependencies are executed in the correct order. These hidden dependencies become even more complicated when you share XCom values between different DAGs or execution dates—another practice that we don't recommend.

XComs can also be a bit like antipatterns when they break the atomicity of an operator. (Chapter 3 discusses atomicity in detail.) We've seen people use an operator to fetch an API token in one task and then use an XCom to pass the token to the next task. In that case, one drawback was that the token expired after a couple of hours, so any rerun of the second task failed. A better approach might have been to combine the fetching of the token with the use in an API call because, this way, refreshing the API token and performing the associated work happen at the same time, keeping the task atomic.

A technical limitation of XComs is that any value stored by an XCom needs to support serialization. This means that some Python types, such as `lambdas` and many multiprocessing-related classes, generally can't be stored in an XCom (though you probably shouldn't do that anyway). Also, the size of an XCom value may be limited by the backend used to store them. By default, XComs are stored in the Airflow metastore and are subject to the following size limits:

- *SQLite*—Stored as `BLOB` type, 2 GB limit
- *PostgreSQL*—Stored as `BYTEA` type, 1 GB limit
- *MySQL*—Stored as `BLOB` type, 64 KB limit

These size limits are fairly big in some cases, but that doesn't mean you should store huge values with XCom. That said, XComs can be powerful tools when used appropriately. Just make sure that you consider their use carefully and clearly document the dependencies they introduce between tasks to prevent any surprises down the road.

6.5.3 Using custom XCom backends

A limitation of using the Airflow metastore to store XComs is that it generally doesn't scale well for larger data volumes. Typically, you want to use XComs to store individual values or small results, not large data sets.

To make XComs more flexible, you can specify a custom XCom backend for your Airflow deployment, like the one in the next listing. This option essentially allows you to define a custom class that Airflow will use for storing/retrieving XComs. The only requirement is that this class must inherit from the `BaseXCom` base class and implement two static methods for serializing and deserializing values, respectively.

Listing 6.24   Skeleton for a custom XCom backend

```python
from typing import Any
from airflow.sdk.bases.xcomimport BaseXCom

class CustomXComBackend(BaseXCom):

    @staticmethod
    def serialize_value(value: Any):
        ...

    @staticmethod
    def deserialize_value(result) -> Any:
        ...
```

In this custom backend class, the `serialize` method is called whenever an XCom value is pushed within an operator, whereas the `deserialize` method is called when XCom values are pulled from the backend. When you have the desired backend class, you can configure Airflow to use the class with the `xcom_backend` parameter.

TIP Custom XCom backends greatly expand your options for storing XCom values. If you want to store large XCom values in relatively cheap and scalable cloud storage, Airflow has built-in support for object storage backends; see https://mng.bz/Mwz8.

6.5.4   XCom cleanup

Because the default storage for XCom values is the Airflow metastore database, be careful not to overflow the database storage by storing huge values or a lot of Xcom values. You can use the `airflow db clean` command to clean up old XCom values (and more). For custom XCom backends, you have to implement monitoring and cleaning yourself.

6.6   Chaining Python tasks with the Taskflow API

Although you can use XComs to share data between Python tasks, the API can be cumbersome to use, especially if you're chaining a large number of tasks. To solve this issue, Airflow has a decorator-based API for defining Python tasks and their dependencies: the Taskflow API. Although it's not without flaws, this API can simplify your code considerably.

6.6.1 Simplifying Python tasks with the Taskflow API

To see how to use the Taskflow API, let's revisit our tasks for training and deploying the ML model. In our previous implementation (listings 6.20 and 6.21), these tasks and their dependencies were defined as follows.

Listing 6.25 Defining `train`/`deploy` tasks using the regular API

```python
def _train_model(**context):
    model_id = str(uuid.uuid4())                      ◄──  Defines the train/
    context["task_instance"].xcom_push(                    deploy functions
        key="model_id",
        value=model_id
    )

def _deploy_model(**context):                         ◄──  Shares the model
    model_id = context["task_instance"].xcom_pull(         ID using XComs
        task_ids="train_model", key="model_id"
    )
    print(f"Deploying model {model_id}")

with DAG(...):
    ...

    train_model = PythonOperator(
        task_id="train_model",
        python_callable=_train_model,                  ◄──  Creates the train/deploy tasks
    )                                                       using the PythonOperator

    deploy_model = PythonOperator(
        task_id="deploy_model",
        python_callable=_deploy_model,
    )

    ...
    join_datasets >> train_model >> deploy_model       ◄──┐ Sets dependencies
                                                          └  between the tasks
```

One drawback of this approach is that it requires us to define a function (e.g., `_train _model` and `_deploy_model`) outside the context manager defining our DAG, which we then need to wrap in a `PythonOperator` to create the Airflow task. Moreover, to share the model ID between the two tasks, we need to use `xcom_push` and `xcom_pull` explicitly within the functions to send/retrieve the model's ID value. Defining this data dependency is cumbersome and prone to breakage if we change the key of the shared value, which is referenced in two locations.

The Taskflow API aims to simplify the definition of these tasks by making it easier to convert Python functions to tasks and making the sharing of variables via XComs between these tasks more explicit in the DAG definition. To see how this works, let's convert these functions to use the alternative API. First, we'll change the definition of our `train_model` task to a relatively simple Python function decorated with the `@task` decorator added by the Taskflow API (table 6.2). Listing 6.26 shows the code changes.

NOTE   Table 6.2 includes many operators that we haven't covered yet. We'll delve into most of them in subsequent chapters.

Table 6.2   An overview of decorators in the Taskflow API

Decorator	Use
@dag	Defines an Airflow DAG
@task	Defines a PythonOperator
@task_group	Defines a TaskGroup
@task.branch	Defines a BranchPythonOperator
@task.sensor	Defines a PythonSensor
@task.short_circuit	Defines a ShortCircuitOperator
@task.bash	Defines a BashOperator
@task.external_python @task.virtualenv	Defines a PythonVirtualenvOperator to execute code in a Python virtual environment
@task.docker	Defines a DockerOperator
@task.branch_external_python	Defines an ExternalBranchPythonOperator, which combines the functionality of the BranchPythonOperator and the ExternalPythonOperator to create a Python branch within an existing virtual environment
@task.branch_virtualenv	Defines a BranchPythonVirtualenvOperator, which combines the functionality of the BranchPythonOperator and the PythonVirtualenvOperator to create a Python branch within a new virtual environment
@task.kubernetes	Defines a KubernetesPodOperator
@task.pyspark	Wraps a Python function in a PythonOperator to be run in a SparkSession
@task.run_if	Runs a task only if the given condition is met
@task.skip_if	Opposite of @task.run_if; skips a task if the given condition is met

Listing 6.26   Defining the train_model task using the Taskflow API

```
...
from airflow.sdk import task
...

with DAG(...):
    ...
    @task
```

```
def train_model():
    model_id = str(uuid.uuid4())
    return model_id
```

This code tells Airflow to wrap our `train_model` function so that we can use it to define Python tasks with the Taskflow API. We're no longer explicitly pushing the model ID as an XCom—simply returning it from the function so that the Taskflow API can take care of passing it on to the next task. Similarly, we can define our `deploy_model` task as follows.

Listing 6.27 Defining the `deploy_model` task using the Taskflow API

```
@task
def deploy_model(model_id):
    print(f"Deploying model {model_id}")
```

Here, the model ID is no longer retrieved using `xcom_pull`; it's passed to our Python function as an argument. Now the only thing left to do is connect the two tasks, which we can do using syntax that looks suspiciously like normal Python code, as shown in the following listing. This code should result in a DAG with two tasks—`train_model` and `deploy_model`—and a dependency between the two tasks (figure 6.18).

Listing 6.28 Defining dependencies between Taskflow tasks

```
model_id = train_model()
deploy_model(model_id)
```

Figure 6.18 Subset of our previous DAG containing the `train_model` and `/deploy_model` tasks, in which tasks and their dependencies are defined with the Taskflow API

Comparing the new code with our previous implementation, we see that the Taskflow-based approach provides similar results, with code that's easier to read and looks more like normal Python code. But how does it work?

In essence, when we call the decorated `train_model` function, it creates a new operator instance for the `train_model` task (shown as @Task in figure 6.18). From the return statement in the `train_model` function, Airflow sees that we're returning a value that will automatically be registered as an XCom returned from the task. For the `deploy_model` task, we call the decorated function to create an operator instance, but now we also pass the `model_id` output from the `train_model` task. By doing so, we're telling Airflow that the `model_id` output from `train_model` should be passed as an argument to the decorated `deploy_model` function. This way, Airflow realizes that a dependency exists between the two tasks and takes care of passing the XCom values between the two tasks.

6.6.2   *Using the Taskflow API to define a new DAG*

In section 6.6.1, we defined our tasks by using the Taskflow API inside a context manager. But we can also define a DAG with the Taskflow API. To set up our DAG this way, we create a Python function and define the operators of our DAG inside that function, just as we did when we defined our DAG with a context manager. Then we can decorate our Python function with @dag, telling Airflow that this function is defining a DAG. In the decorator, we can set the DAG parameters: dag_id, start_date, schedule, and any other parameters required to define our DAG.

> **NOTE** If dag_id is missing in the decorator definition, the name of the function becomes dag_id.

Finally, it's important to call the decorated function at the end of the script to allow Airflow to pick it up as a new DAG. We can rewrite the train/deploy DAG we defined in section 6.6.1 by using the Taskflow API as follows.

Listing 6.29   Defining a DAG with a Taskflow API decorator

```
import uuid
from airflow.sdk import task, dag

@dag(                              ◄──────  The decorator takes care
    start_date=...,                         of defining the DAG.
    schedule=...,
)                                           The function name becomes dag_id because
def taskflow_api_decorator():      ◄──────  it wasn't defined in the decorator.

    @task                          ◄──────
    def train_model():
        model_id = str(uuid.uuid4())
        return model_id

    @task                          ◄──────
    def deploy_model(model_id: str):        Everything inside the function
        print(f"Deploying model {model_id}")   will be part of the DAG.

    model_id = train_model()
    deploy_model(model_id)

taskflow_api_decorator()                    We make the decorated function
                                            available in Airflow by calling it.
```

6.6.3   *When and when not to use the Taskflow API*

The Taskflow API provides a simple approach to defining Python tasks and their dependencies, using syntax that is closer to regular Python functions than the more object-oriented operator API. This syntax allows the API to simplify DAGs dramatically by reducing boilerplate code. Furthermore, the Taskflow API addresses one of our previous criticisms of using XComs by ensuring that values are passed explicitly, not hiding dependencies between tasks within the corresponding functions.

One drawback of the Taskflow API is that it's available to a limited number of operators (refer to table 6.2), so tasks involving any other Airflow operators require using the regular API to define tasks and their dependencies. Although this situation doesn't prevent you from mixing and matching the two styles, the resulting code can become confusing if you're not careful. When you combine the new train/deploy tasks back into the original DAG (figure 6.19), for example, you must define a dependency between the join_datasets task and the model_id reference, which may not be intuitive immediately because of the different syntax used to define the dependency.

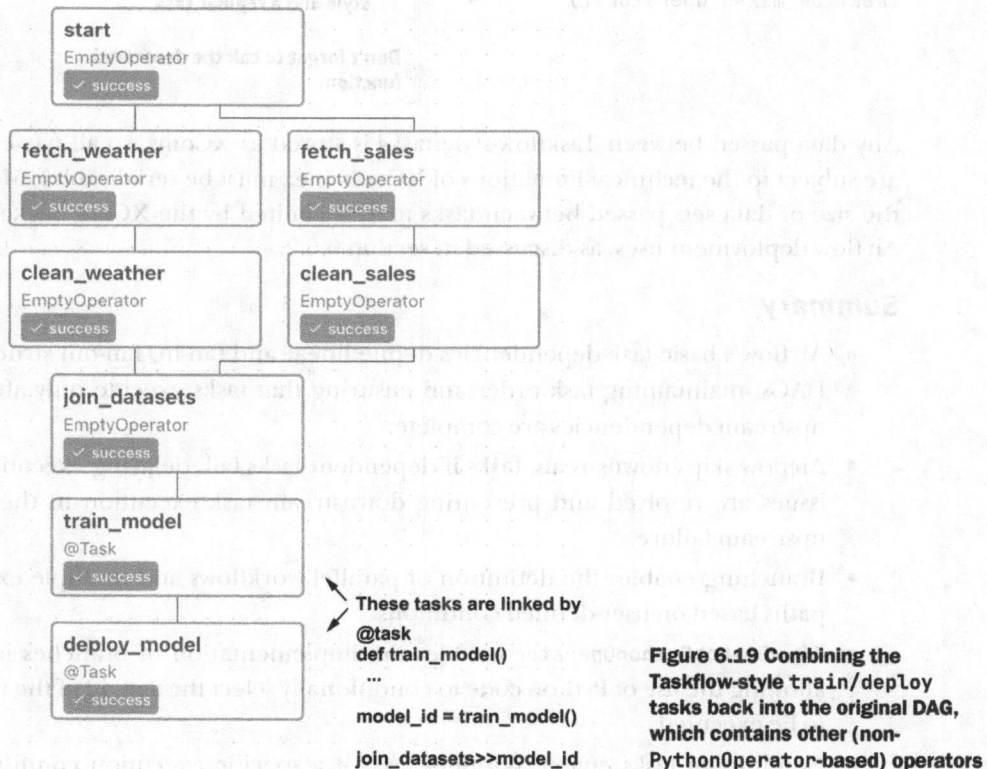

These tasks are linked by
```
@task
def train_model()
...
model_id = train_model()
join_datasets>>model_id
```

Figure 6.19 Combining the Taskflow-style train/deploy tasks back into the original DAG, which contains other (non-PythonOperator-based) operators

Listing 6.30 Combining other operators with Taskflow

```
@dag(...)
def taskflow_mixed_operators():
    start = EmptyOperator(task_id="start")
    ...
    [clean_sales, clean_weather] >> join_datasets
```

Defines tasks and dependencies using the regular API

```
@task
def train_model():
    model_id = str(uuid.uuid4())
    return model_id

@task
def deploy_model(model_id: str):
    print(f"Deploying model {model_id}")

model_id = train_model()
deploy_model(model_id)

join_datasets >> model_id

taskflow_mixed_operators()
```

Uses the Taskflow API for Python tasks and dependencies

Mixes the two styles with a dependency between a Taskflow style and a regular task

Don't forget to call the decorated function.

Any data passed between Taskflow-style tasks is stored as XComs, so all passed values are subject to the technical limitations of XComs (i.e., must be serializable). Moreover, the size of data sets passed between tasks may be limited by the XCom backend your Airflow deployment uses, as discussed in section 6.6.2.

Summary

- Airflow's basic task dependencies define linear and fan-in/fan-out structures in DAGs, maintaining task order and ensuring that tasks execute only after their upstream dependencies are complete.
- Airflow skips downstream tasks if dependent tasks fail, delaying execution until issues are resolved and preventing downstream task execution in the case of upstream failure.
- Branching enables the definition of parallel workflows and multiple execution paths based on user-defined conditions.
- The BranchPythonOperator enables the implementation of branches in DAGs, allowing the use of Python code to conditionally select the dag_id of the next task to be executed.
- Conditional tasks enable skipping tasks if a specific execution condition isn't met, offering flexibility in task execution.
- Explicitly encoding branches/conditions in your DAG structure provides substantial benefits in terms of the interpretability of how your DAG was executed.
- The execution of Airflow tasks is governed by trigger rules, which dictate the consequences if an upstream task is skipped or fails. By changing the default all_success rule to none_failed, for example, you can continue with the DAG workflow even if an upstream task was skipped.

- XComs facilitate sharing small data chunks among tasks, which is particularly useful when the output of one task is relevant to the execution of downstream tasks.

- XComs aren't suitable for sharing large amounts of data among tasks but are ideal for sharing filenames, paths, and small API responses. For larger data sets, we recommend using external resources such as external databases or blob storage.

- The Taskflow API simplifies DAGs by converting Python functions to Airflow tasks using decorators, which streamline task creation.

Part 2

Beyond the basics

Now that you're familiar with Airflow's basics and able to build some of your own data pipelines, you're ready to learn some advanced techniques that allow you to build complex cases involving external systems, custom components, and more.

In chapter 7, we'll examine how to trigger workflows with external input. This allows you to trigger pipelines in response to certain events, such as new files or a call from an HTTP service.

Chapter 8 demonstrates how to use Airflow's built-in functionality to run tasks on external systems. This extremely powerful feature of Airflow allows you to build pipelines that coordinate data flows across many systems, such as databases, computational frameworks such as Apache Spark, and storage systems.

Next, chapter 9 shows how to build custom components for Airflow, allowing you to execute tasks on systems that aren't supported by Airflow's built-in functionality. You can also use this functionality to build components that you can easily reuse across pipelines to support common workflows.

To help increase the robustness of your pipelines, chapter 10 elaborates on strategies you can use to test your data pipelines and custom components. This topic commonly recurs in the Airflow community, so we'll spend some time exploring it.

Finally, chapter 11 dives into using container-based approaches to implement tasks in your pipelines. We'll show how to run tasks using both Docker and Kubernetes, and we'll discuss several advantages and drawbacks of using containers for your tasks.

After completing part 2, you should be well on your way to becoming an advanced Airflow user because you'll be able to write complex (and testable) pipelines that optionally involve custom components and/or containers. Depending on your interests, however, you may want to pick specific chapters to focus on; not all chapters in this part may be relevant to your use case.

Triggering workflows with external input

This chapter covers

- Waiting for certain external conditions to be met with sensors
- Setting dependencies between tasks in different directed acyclic graphs (DAGs)
- Executing workflows via the REST API and the command-line interface (CLI)
- Triggering DAGs when messages are published on a message queue

In previous chapters, we saw how to trigger pipelines based on time intervals (chapter 3) and asset updates (chapter 4). In this chapter, we'll explore ways to trigger workflows in response to events that occur outside Airflow, such as files being uploaded to a shared drive, developers pushing their code to a repository, and messages being published on a message bus. Any of these events could be reasons to start running your pipeline in a modern enterprise.

7.1   *Polling conditions with sensors*

One common use case for starting a workflow is the arrival of new data. Suppose that a third party delivers a daily dump of its data on a storage system it shares with your company. Further suppose that you're developing a popular mobile couponing app and are in contact with all supermarket brands, which deliver a daily export of their promotions to be displayed in your couponing app. Currently, the promotion process is mostly manual; most supermarkets employ pricing analysts who study the competition and take many factors into account to deliver accurate promotions. Some promotions are well thought out weeks in advance; others are spontaneous one-day flash sales or are made late at night. Hence, daily promotions data often arrives at random times. Generally speaking, you observe the data arriving in the shared storage between 16:00 and 2:00 the next day. There is no guarantee, however, that this will always be the case: the daily data can be delivered at any time of day.

Let's develop the initial logic for such a workflow (figure 7.1). In this workflow, we copy the delivered data from supermarkets 1–4 to our own raw storage, from which we can always reproduce results. The process_supermarket_{1,2,3,4} tasks transform and store all raw data in a results database that our app can read. Finally, the create_metrics task computes and aggregates several metrics that give us insights into the promotions for further analysis. With data from the supermarkets arriving at varying times, the timeline of this workflow could look like figure 7.2.

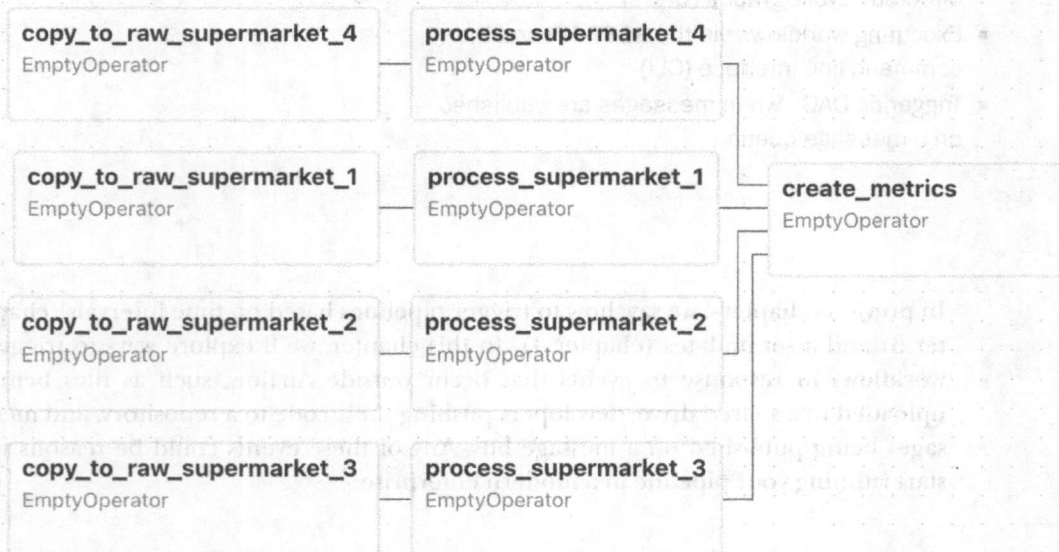

Figure 7.1   Initial logic for processing supermarket promotion data

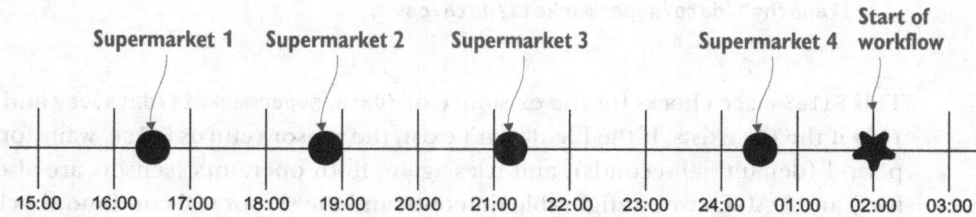

Figure 7.2 **Timeline of processing supermarket promotion data**

In figure 7.2, we see the data delivery times of the supermarkets and the start time of our workflow. Because supermarkets sometimes deliver data as late as 2:00, a safe bet would be to start the workflow at 2:00 to make certain that all supermarkets have delivered their data. This approach results in lots of waiting time, however. Supermarket 1 delivered its data at 16:30, and the workflow started processing it at 2:00 but did nothing for 9.5 hours (figure 7.3).

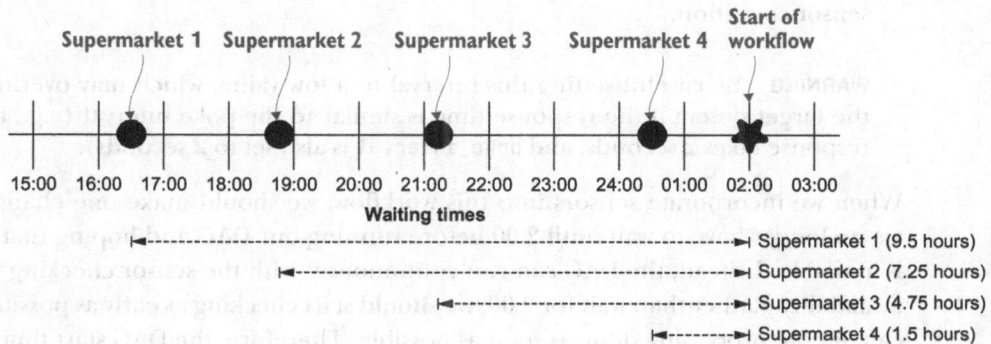

Figure 7.3 **Timeline of supermarket promotion workflow with waiting times**

One way to solve this problem in Airflow is to employ *sensors*, a special type (subclass) of operators. Sensors continuously poll for certain conditions to be `True`. When the condition holds, the task in the Airflow DAG moves to a `Success` state. If a condition is `False`, the sensor waits and tries again when the condition is `True` or a timeout is reached, as shown in the following listing.

Listing 7.1   A `FileSensor` waits for a file path to exist

```
from airflow.providers.standard.sensors.filesystem import FileSensor

wait_for_supermarket_1 = FileSensor(
    task_id="wait_for_supermarket_1",
```

```
    filepath="/data/supermarket1/data.csv",
)
```

This `FileSensor` checks for the existence of `/data/supermarket1/data.csv` and returns `True` if the file exists. If the file doesn't exist, the sensor returns `False`, waits for a given period (default: 60 seconds), and tries again. Both operators (sensors are also operators) and DAGs have configurable timeouts, and the sensor will continue checking the condition until a timeout is reached. We can inspect the output of sensors in the task logs:

```
{file_sensor.py:60} INFO - Poking for file /data/supermarket1/data.csv
{file_sensor.py:60} INFO - Poking for file /data/supermarket1/data.csv
{file_sensor.py:60} INFO - Poking for file /data/supermarket1/data.csv
{file_sensor.py:60} INFO - Poking for file /data/supermarket1/data.csv
{file_sensor.py:60} INFO - Poking for file /data/supermarket1/data.csv
```

Here, we see that, once a minute, the sensor pokes for the availability of the given file. We can configure the poke interval using the `poke_interval` argument.

DEFINITION   *Poking* is Airflow's name for running the sensor and checking the sensor condition.

WARNING   Be careful setting this interval to a low value, which may overload the target system if the response time is similar to the poke interval (e.g., the response takes 2 seconds, and `poke_interval` is also set to 2 seconds).

When we incorporate sensors into this workflow, we should make one change. Now we no longer have to wait until 2:00 before running our DAG and hoping that all data is available. Instead, the DAG can run continuously, with the sensor checking for data availability. Rather than wait for 2:00, we should start checking as early as possible so we can get the processing done as soon as possible. Therefore, the DAG start time should be placed at the start of the data arrival boundaries (i.e., right before the first data usually arrives), as shown in figure 7.4. From this moment on, the `FileSensors` check for the existence of files. The corresponding DAG has a task (`FileSensor`) added to the start of processing each supermarket's data (figure 7.5).

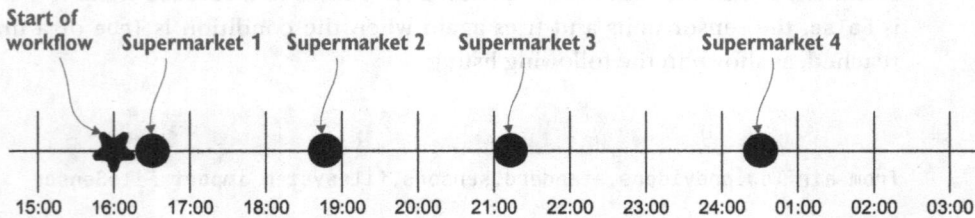

Figure 7.4   Supermarket promotion timeline with sensors

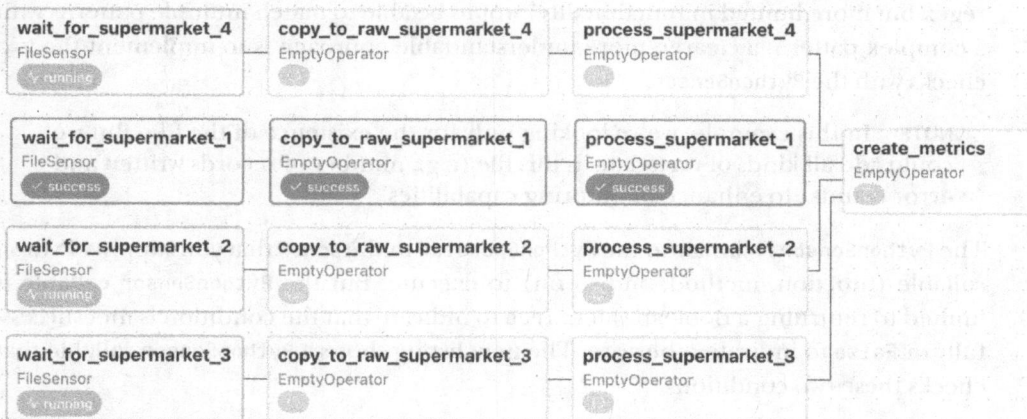

Figure 7.5 Supermarket promotion DAG with sensors in Airflow

In figure 7.5, sensors were added at the start of the DAG, and the DAG's `schedule` was set to start *before* the expected delivery of data. This way, sensors at the start of the DAG continuously poll for the availability of data and continue to the next task when the condition is met (i.e., the data is available in the given path).

Here, supermarket 1 has already delivered data, which sets the state of its corresponding sensor to success, and the DAG continues processing its downstream tasks. As a result, data was processed directly after delivery without an unnecessary wait for the expected delivery time to end.

TIP By polling some external system continuously, sensors introduce load on both Airflow and on the external system. Whenever you start using a sensor this way, it's a good idea to verify that polling every 60 seconds (or at whatever interval you configure) won't overload any system involved.

7.1.1 Polling custom conditions

Some data sets are large and consist of multiple files (e.g., `data-01.csv`, `data-02.csv`, `data-03.csv`, and so on). Airflow's `FileSensor` supports wildcards to match, for example, `data-*.csv`, which matches any file with that pattern. If the first file `data-01.csv` is delivered while the supermarket is still uploading other files to shared storage, for example, the `FileSensor` would return `True`, and the workflow would continue to the `copy_to_raw` task, which is undesirable because only part of the data for a given interval would have been processed.

Therefore, we agree with the supermarkets to write a file named `_SUCCESS` as the last part of uploading to indicate that the full daily data set was uploaded. The data team wants to check for the existence of one or more files named `data-*.csv` and one file named `_SUCCESS`. Under the hood, the `FileSensor` uses *globbing* (https://mng.bz/oZjy) to match patterns against filenames or directory names. Although globbing (similar to regex but more limited in functionality) would be able to match multiple patterns with a complex pattern, a clearer, more understandable approach is to implement the two checks with the PythonSensor.

> **NOTE** In this example, we're looking only for the existence of the file. But we could add all kinds of metadata in this file (e.g., number of records written and error counts) to enhance monitoring capabilities.

The PythonSensor is similar to the PythonOperator in the sense that you supply a Python callable (function, method, and so on) to execute. But the PythonSensor callable is limited to returning a Boolean value: True to indicate that the condition is met successfully or False to indicate otherwise. The next listing shows a PythonSensor callable that checks these two conditions.

> **Listing 7.2   Implementing a custom condition with the PythonSensor**

```
from pathlib import Path
from datetime import timedelta
from airflow.providers.standard.sensors.python
    import PythonSensor

def _wait_for_supermarket(supermarket_id):
    supermarket_path = Path("/data/" + supermarket_id)      ◄─── Initializes Path object
    data_files = supermarket_path.glob("data-*.csv")        ◄─── Collects data-*.csv files
    success_file = supermarket_path / "_SUCCESS"
    return data_files and success_file.exists()             ◄─── Collects _SUCCESS file
                                                                 Returns whether both
wait_for_supermarket_1 = PythonSensor(                           data and success files exist
    task_id="wait_for_supermarket_1",
    python_callable=_wait_for_supermarket,
    op_kwargs={"supermarket_id": "supermarket1"},
    timeout=timedelta(minutes=5),                           ◄─── Default timeout (seven
)                                                                days) changes to 5 minutes
```

The callable supplied to the PythonSensor is executed and expected to return a Boolean True or False. Then the callable now checks two conditions: whether both the data and the _SUCCESS file exist. Other than rendering slightly differently, the PythonSensor tasks appear the same way in the UI (figure 7.6).

7.1.2   *Working with sensors outside the happy flow*

We've seen sensors running successfully. But what happens if, one day, a supermarket doesn't deliver its data? By default, sensors will fail just like operators (figure 7.7).

Sensors accept a timeout argument, which holds the maximum number of seconds a sensor is allowed to run. If at the start of the next poke, the number of running seconds turns out to be higher than the number set to timeout, the sensor will fail:

```
INFO - Poking for file /data/supermarket4/data.csv
INFO - Poking for file /data/supermarket4/data.csv
```

```
ERROR - Task failed with exception: source="task"AirflowSensorTimeout:
    Sensor has timed out; run duration of 600.075443316 seconds exceeds
    the specified timeout of 600.0.
```

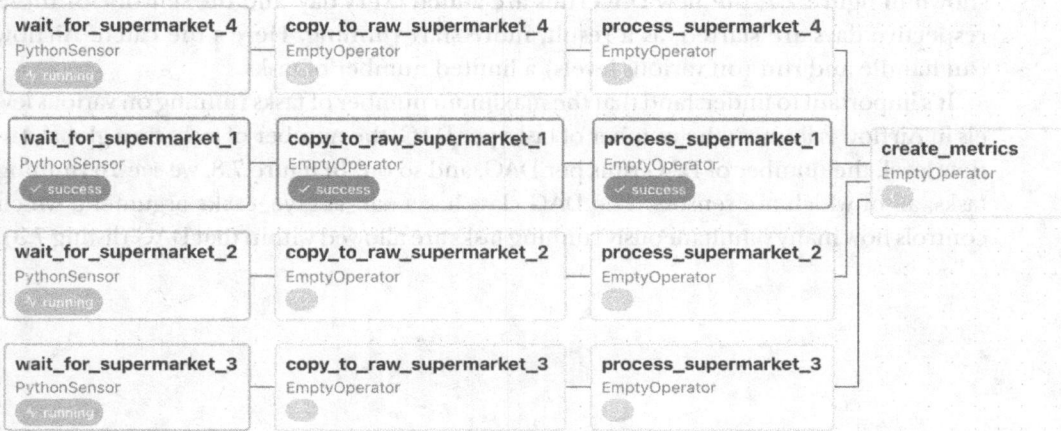

Figure 7.6   Supermarket promotion DAG using `PythonSensors` for custom conditions

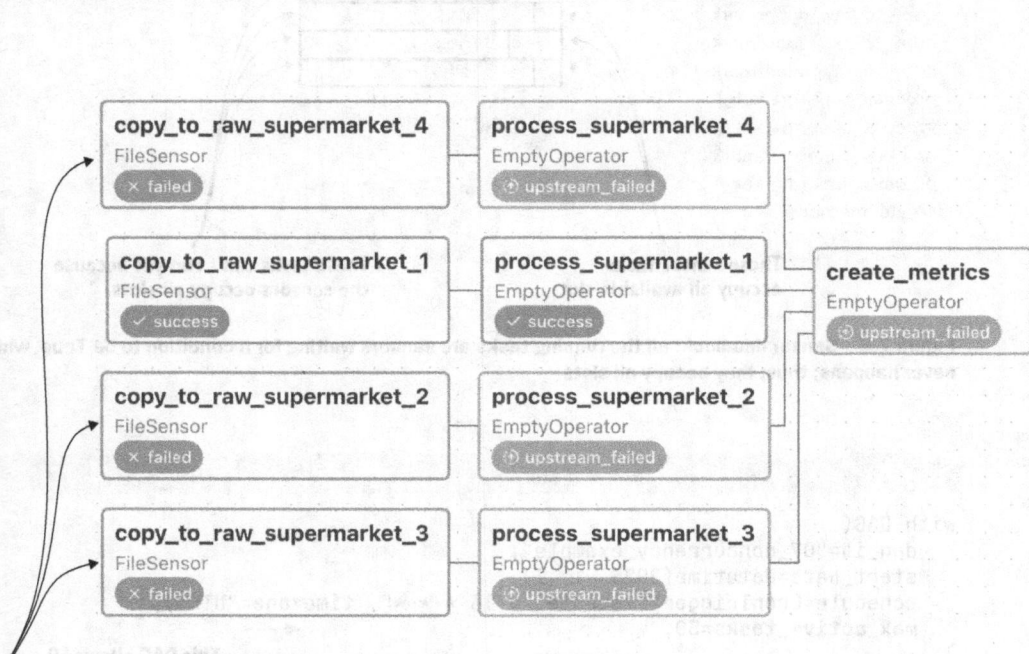

These sensors did not complete within the maximum time frame.

Figure 7.7   Sensors that exceed the maximum time frame will fail.

By default, the sensor timeout is set to seven days. (In the example log in listing 7.2, we set it to 5 minutes to avoid waiting a long time.) If the DAG schedule is set to once a day, it creates an undesirable snowball effect, which is surprisingly common in DAGs! The DAG runs once a day, and supermarkets 2, 3, and 4 will fail after seven days, as shown in figure 7.7. But new DAG runs are added every day, and the sensors for those respective days are started; as a result, more start running. Here's the catch: Airflow can handle and run (on various levels) a limited number of tasks.

It's important to understand that the maximum number of tasks running on various levels in Airflow is limited: the number of tasks per DAG, the number of tasks on a global Airflow level, the number of DAG runs per DAG, and so on. In figure 7.8, we see 16 running tasks, all of which are sensors. The DAG class has a max_active_tasks argument, which controls how many simultaneously running tasks are allowed within that DAG (listing 7.3).

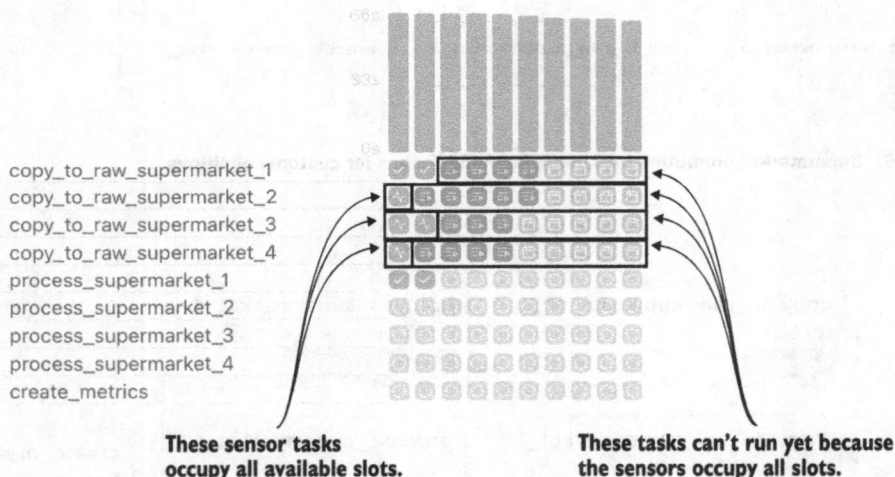

These sensor tasks occupy all available slots.

These tasks can't run yet because the sensors occupy all slots.

Figure 7.8   Sensor deadlock: all the running tasks are sensors waiting for a condition to be True, which never happens; thus, they occupy all slots.

Listing 7.3   Setting the maximum number of concurrent tasks in a DAG

```
with DAG(
    dag_id="07_concurrency_example",
    start_date=datetime(2025, 1, 1),
    schedule=CronTriggerTimetable("0 16 * * *", timezone="UTC"),
    max_active_tasks=50,
):
```

This DAG allows 50 concurrently running tasks.

In figure 7.8, we ran the DAG with all defaults, which is 16 concurrent tasks per DAG. The following snowball effect happened:

- *Day 1*—Supermarket 1 succeeded; supermarkets 2, 3, and 4 are polling, occupying 3 tasks.
- *Day 2*—Supermarket 1 succeeded; supermarkets 2, 3, and 4 are polling, occupying 6 tasks.
- *Day 3*—Supermarket 1 succeeded; supermarkets 2, 3, and 4 are polling, occupying 9 tasks.
- *Day 4*—Supermarket 1 succeeded; supermarkets 2, 3, and 4 are polling, occupying 12 tasks.
- *Day 5*—Supermarket 1 succeeded; supermarkets 2, 3, and 4 are polling, occupying 15 tasks.
- *Day 6*—Supermarket 1 succeeded; supermarkets 2, 3, and 4 are polling, occupying 16 tasks; two new tasks can't run, and any other task trying to run is blocked.

This behavior is often referred to as *sensor deadlock*. In this example, the maximum number of running tasks in the supermarket couponing DAG is reached; thus, the impact is limited to that DAG, and other DAGs can still run. When the global Airflow limit of maximum tasks is reached, however, the entire system is stalled, which is obviously undesirable.

You can solve this problem in various ways. For one, the sensor class takes a mode argument, which you can set to poke or reschedule. By default, it's set to poke, leading to the blocking behavior: the sensor task occupies a task slot as long as it's running. Once in a while, it pokes the condition and then does nothing but still occupies a task slot. The sensor reschedule mode releases the slot when it's done poking, so it occupies a slot *only* while it's doing actual work (figure 7.9). You can also control the number of concurrent tasks with several configuration options on the global Airflow level, as discussed in chapter 15.

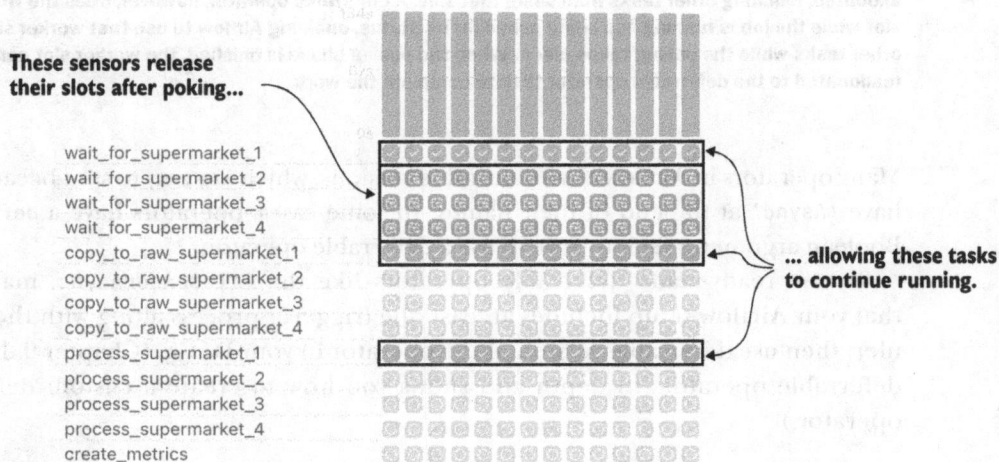

These sensors release their slots after poking...

wait_for_supermarket_1
wait_for_supermarket_2
wait_for_supermarket_3
wait_for_supermarket_4
copy_to_raw_supermarket_1
copy_to_raw_supermarket_2
copy_to_raw_supermarket_3
copy_to_raw_supermarket_4
process_supermarket_1
process_supermarket_2
process_supermarket_3
process_supermarket_4
create_metrics

... allowing these tasks to continue running.

Figure 7.9 Sensors with mode="reschedule" release their slot after poking, allowing other tasks to run.

Another way to avoid the dreaded sensor deadlock is to use deferrable operators. These operators can free the workers when they're idling so that they can take care of other tasks. When an operator defers, it hands the job over to the triggerer, which starts handling any necessary polling or waits for the task to complete in an external system. When the triggerer is done waiting, it lets the operator know that it's time to get back to work.

NOTE You can find more information on deferrable operators at https://mng.bz/a9XX.

Triggers run asynchronous Python code, which means they can wait without blocking anything else. They're made to run in the triggerer, which is a part of Airflow designed to handle lots of these triggers at the same time. The triggerer is an optional component for Airflow in general but a requirement for using deferrable operators. Essentially, it's an `asyncio` event loop that can run tasks when necessary. Figure 7.10 shows the difference between using deferrable operators and standard operators.

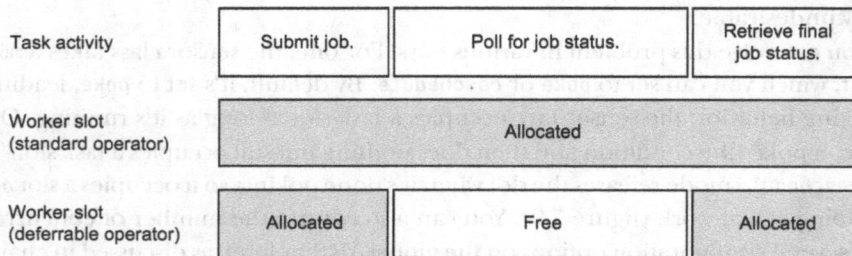

Task activity	Submit job.	Poll for job status.	Retrieve final job status.
Worker slot (standard operator)	Allocated		
Worker slot (deferrable operator)	Allocated	Free	Allocated

Figure 7.10 When you use a standard operator, during the entire task duration, a worker slot is allocated, blocking other tasks from using that slot. A deferrable operator, however, frees the worker slot while the job is running and being polled for its status, enabling Airflow to use that worker slot for other tasks while the polling takes place. When the polling phase is finished, the worker slot can be reallocated to the deferrable operator task to complete the work.

Many operators in Airflow have deferrable versions, which are easy to spot because they have `'Async'` at the end of their names. In some cases, operators have a `deferrable` Boolean argument; set it to `True` to use a deferrable operator.

To use ready-made deferrable operators like the `FileSensorAsync`, make sure that your Airflow setup includes at least one triggerer process along with the scheduler; then use deferrable version of the operator in your DAGs. (Chapter 9 discusses deferrable operators in depth and shows you how to create a custom deferrable operator.)

NOTE Python and Taskflow API Python operators can't be deferred. These operators are intended to be used to write straightforward, imperative-style

Python code that a worker executes when the task is scheduled. These executions are synchronous by nature: the task runs to completion after it starts, and during its execution, it occupies a worker slot. Deferrable operators, on the other hand, are designed to work asynchronously.

7.2 Starting workflows with the REST API and CLI

In addition to triggering DAGs based on external events or based on a schedule, you can trigger them via the REST API and CLI. This technique can be useful if you want to start workflows from outside Airflow as part of a continuous integration/continuous delivery (CI/CD) pipeline. Also, you can process data that arrives at random times in an AWS S3 bucket by setting a lambda function to call the REST API, triggering a DAG, instead of running sensors that poll all the time. Using the Airflow CLI, you can trigger a DAG as follows.

Listing 7.4 Triggering a DAG using the Airflow CLI

```
airflow dags trigger dag1
```

```
conf | dag_id | dag_run_id          | data_interval_start  |
=====+========+=====================+======================+
{}   | dag1   | manual__2024-04     | 2024-04-18T16:00:00+0 |
     |        | -19T16:37:19+00:00  | 0:00                 |


                     |          | external_ | last_scheduling_ |
data_interval_end    | end_date | trigger   | decision         |
=====================+==========+===========+==================+
2024-04-19T16:00:    | None     | True      | None             |
00+00:00             |          |           |                  |

 logical_date                | run_type | start_date | state
=============================+==========+============+=========
2024-04-19T16:37:19+00:00    | manual   | None       | running
```

This code triggers `dag1` with the execution date set to the current date and time. The DAG `run_id` is prefixed with `manual_` to indicate it was triggered manually or from outside Airflow. The CLI accepts additional configuration to the triggered DAG, as shown in the following listing. Then this piece of configuration is available in all tasks of the triggered DAG run via the task context variables (listing 7.6).

Listing 7.5 Triggering a DAG with additional configuration

```
airflow dags trigger -c '{"supermarket_id": 1}' dag1
airflow dags trigger --conf '{"supermarket_id": 1}' dag1
```

Listing 7.6   Using DAG run configuration in a DAG

```python
import pendulum
from airflow.sdk import DAG
from airflow.providers.standard.operators.python import PythonOperator

def print_conf(**context):
    print(context["dag_run"].conf)          ◄──── Configuration supplied when
                                                  triggering DAGs is accessible
                                                  in the task context

with DAG(
    dag_id="11_inspect_dag_run_config",
    start_date=pendulum.today("UTC").add(days=-3),
    schedule=None,
):

process = PythonOperator(
    task_id="process",
    python_callable=print_conf,
)
```

These tasks print the conf provided to the DAG run, which can be applied as a variable throughout the task:

```
...
{task_command.py:423} INFO - Running <TaskInstance:
⇒ 19_inspect_dag_run_configuration.process
⇒ manual__2024-04-20T07:11:47+00:00 [running]> on host
⇒ aa69e3a53421
{logging_mixin.py:188} INFO - {'supermarket_id': 1}
{python.py:201} INFO - Done. Returned value was: None
(taskinstance.py:1138) INFO - Marking task as SUCCESS.
⇒ dag_id=11_inspect_dag_run_configuration, task_id=process,
⇒ execution_date=20240420T071147, start_date=20240420T071149,
⇒ end_date=20240420T071149
{local_task_job_runner.py:234} INFO - Task exited with return code 0
{taskinstance.py:3281} INFO - 0 downstream tasks scheduled from
⇒ follow-on schedule check
```

As a result, if you have a DAG in which you run copies of tasks simply to support different variables, it becomes a lot more concise with the DAG run conf, which allows you to insert variables into the pipeline (figure 7.11). The DAG in listing 7.6, however, has no defined schedule; it runs only when triggered. If the logic in your DAG relies on a DAG run conf, it won't be possible to run on a schedule because a scheduled run doesn't provide any DAG run conf.

Similarly, you can use the REST API to get the same result if you have no access to the CLI but can reach your Airflow instance over HTTP. This approach could be convenient for triggering DAG from outside Airflow, such as from your CI/CD system, as shown in listing 7.7.

Without DAG run conf

copy_to_raw_supermarket_3 EmptyOperator	—	process_supermarket_3 EmptyOperator	—	create_metrics_3 EmptyOperator
copy_to_raw_supermarket_4 EmptyOperator	—	process_supermarket_4 EmptyOperator	—	create_metrics_4 EmptyOperator
copy_to_raw_supermarket_1 EmptyOperator	—	process_supermarket_1 EmptyOperator	—	create_metrics_1 EmptyOperator
copy_to_raw_supermarket_2 EmptyOperator	—	process_supermarket_2 EmptyOperator	—	create_metrics_2 EmptyOperator

With DAG run conf

| copy_to_raw
PythonOperator | — | process
PythonOperator | — | create_metrics
PythonOperator |

Figure 7.11 Simplifying DAGs by providing a payload at run time

---

Listing 7.7   Triggering a DAG using the Airflow REST API

```
# URL is /api/v1

curl \
-u airflow:airflow \
-X POST \
"http://localhost:8080/api/v1/dags/11_inspect_dag_run_config/dagRuns" \
-H  "Content-Type: application/json" \
-d '{"conf": {}}'

{
  "conf": {},
  "dag_id": "11_inspect_dag_run_config",
  "dag_run_id": "manual__2024-04-20T08:10:59.817154+00:00",
  "data_interval_end": "2024-04-20T00:00:00+00:00",
  "data_interval_start": "2024-04-19T00:00:00+00:00",
  "end_date": null,
  "execution_date": "2024-04-20T08:10:59.817154+00:00",
  "external_trigger": true,
  "last_scheduling_decision": null,
  "logical_date": "2024-04-20T08:10:59.817154+00:00",
  "note": null,
  "run_type": "manual",
  "start_date": null,
```

Sending a plain-text username/password is undesirable. Consult the Airflow API authentication documentation for information on other authentication methods.

The endpoint requires a piece of data even if no additional configuration is given.

```
  "state": "running"
}

curl \
-u airflow:airflow \
-X POST \
"http://localhost:8080/api/v1/dags/11_inspect_dag_run_config/dagRuns" \
-H "Content-Type: application/json" \
-d '{"conf": {"supermarket": 1}}'

{
  "conf": {
    "supermarket_id": 1
  },
  "dag_id": "11_inspect_dag_run_config",
  "dag_run_id": "manual__2024-04-20T08:10:46.623540+00:00",
  "data_interval_end": "2024-04-20T00:00:00+00:00",
  "data_interval_start": "2024-04-19T00:00:00+00:00",
  "end_date": null,
  "execution_date": "2024-04-20T08:10:46.623540+00:00",
  "external_trigger": true,
  "last_scheduling_decision": null,
  "logical_date": "2024-04-20T08:10:46.623540+00:00",
  "note": null,
  "run_type": "manual",
  "start_date": null,
  "state": "running"
}
```

You can also prompt a DAG to run by updating a data set through the Airflow REST API; send a POST request to the data set's endpoint. When Airflow receives this update, it can automatically trigger any DAGs that rely on the data set. The following listing shows how to send this POST request.

Listing 7.8   Triggering a DAG updating a data set via the Airflow REST API

```
POST datasets/events/

Payload:
{
    "dataset_uri": "string",
    "extra": { }
}
```

7.3   *Triggering workflows with messages*

Many environments use near-real-time message queues containing messages that represent a single piece of information. A simple example is bank transactions. Each transaction represents some amount of money being transferred from one bank account to another and could be represented by a message published on a message queue. Consumers of this data receive such messages relatively quickly, making message queues attractive solutions for near-real-time systems. Examples include Apache Kafka, RabbitMQ, and cloud-specific systems such as Google Cloud Pub/Sub and Microsoft's Azure Event Hubs.

In the context of Airflow, we can also use message queues to trigger workflows to run. This approach could be useful if some or all messages in a queue are signals that a DAG must be executed. Let's see how this works in practice. Returning to the supermarket example, recall from section 7.1.1 that the supermarkets write a _SUCCESS file when they finish writing the data so that we'll know when data extraction is complete. Instead of writing such a file and checking for the existence of the file with a FileSensor, we could use a message queue. Each supermarket could post a message on the queue indicating that its data upload is complete. Using these messages, we can trigger our DAG automatically using an asset.

For this example, we'll focus on a single supermarket with data to be processed. The message queue in this example is Apache Kafka (https://kafka.apache.org), but any provider with an implementation for the MessageQueueTrigger in Airflow should work similarly. First, we define a trigger that points at the Kafka broker and topic.

Listing 7.9 Defining a MessageQueueTrigger

```
from airflow.providers.common.messaging.triggers.msg_queue import
    MessageQueueTrigger

trigger = MessageQueueTrigger(
    queue="kafka://kafka:9092/events",
    apply_function="custom.kafka_util.apply_function",
)
```

Points the trigger to the message queue. In Kafka, the topic name is provided in the URL (events, in this case).

Passes the apply_function into the trigger

In addition to the trigger itself, an apply_function is defined and passed to the trigger. This function is used to filter published messages; we may not want all messages to trigger the DAG to run, only messages that contain a specific value. In this example, we don't apply filtering and always return True. The exact syntax will vary depending on the message queue used.

Listing 7.10 The MessageQueue apply_function

```
def apply_function(message):
    print(f"Value in message is {message.value()}")
    return True
```

Defines the apply function. This function returns a Boolean indicating whether a DAG run should be triggered. The logic for this may depend on the value of the message.

Next, we set this trigger as the trigger for a data Asset, as shown in listing 7.11. Now that we have a data Asset object, we can use this object in the schedule attribute of the DAG (listing 7.12).

Listing 7.11   Defining the `Asset` for a `MessageQueueTrigger`

```
from airflow.sdk import Asset, AssetWatcher

asset = Asset("kafka_queue_asset", watchers=[
AssetWatcher(name="kafka_watcher", trigger=trigger)
])
```

Listing 7.12   A full example using `MessageQueueTrigger` in Kafka

```
from airflow.sdk import DAG, AssetWatcher, Asset
from airflow.providers.standard.operators.empty import EmptyOperator
from airflow.providers.common.messaging.triggers.msg_queue
➥ import MessageQueueTrigger
from airflow.timetables.trigger import CronTriggerTimetable

trigger = MessageQueueTrigger(
    queue="kafka://kafka:9092/events",
    apply_function="custom.kafka_util.apply_function",
)

asset = Asset("kafka_queue_asset", watchers=[AssetWatcher(name="kafka_
watcher", trigger=trigger)])

with DAG(
        dag_id="12_kafka_trigger",
        schedule=[asset]
):
    create_metrics = EmptyOperator(task_id="create_metrics")

    copy = EmptyOperator(task_id=f"copy_to_raw_supermarket_1")
    process = EmptyOperator(task_id=f"process_supermarket_1")
    copy >> process >> create_metrics
```

The resulting DAG is similar to what we've seen before, as you see in figure 7.12. The only real difference is the schedule, which now points to a kafka_queue_asset.

To run the DAG, you must produce a message and put it on the Kafka topic. To do this, use the Kafka CLI:

```
$ /opt/kafka/bin/kafka-console-producer.sh --bootstrap-server kafka:9092
    --topic events
>
```

When the > appears on your terminal, type some text and press Enter. This text is sent to the Kafka topic as a message. There may be some delay in starting the DAG run because the Kafka consumer has a fixed (configurable) interval at which it fetches new messages.

Although this approach requires additional infrastructure in the form of a message queue, it can be a powerful way to trigger DAGs. It could be particularly interesting for

Dag

12_kafka_trigger

copy_to_raw_supermarket_1	process_supermarket_1	create_metrics
EmptyOperator	EmptyOperator	EmptyOperator

Options ∨

⌇° **12_kafka_trigger**

Schedule

🗄 kafka_queue_asset

Overview   Runs   Tasks

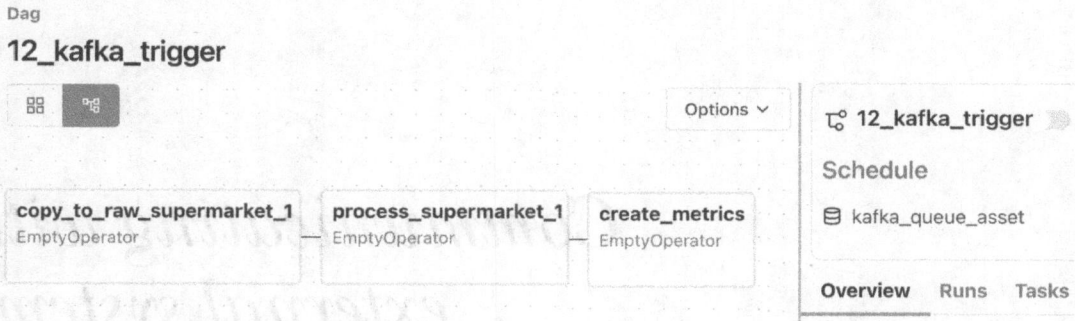

Figure 7.12   A DAG triggered by messages published on a Kafka topic. The schedule is set to kafka_queue_ asset.

triggering workflows across instances. You can imagine a DAG in Airflow instance A pushing a message to the message queue when it completes, triggering another DAG in Airflow instance B to run. The message queue acts as the interface between the Airflow instances, allowing easy communication without exposing the Airflow API or requiring sensors.

Summary

- Sensors are special types of operators in Airflow that continuously check whether certain conditions are met. If a condition is True, the sensor completes successfully. If not, it pauses and retries after a specified amount of time, continuing this cycle until the condition becomes True or a timeout limit is reached.
- Airflow offers a variety of sensors tailored to different systems and use cases. These sensors are designed to monitor specific conditions or events in external systems. The FileSensor, for example, checks whether a file exists in a specified path. If the file is present, the sensor returns True. If the file isn't there, the sensor returns False and pauses; then, after a set interval (by default, 60 seconds), it checks again.
- The PythonSensor works similarly to the PythonOperator in that you provide custom logic to a Python function. This function should return a Boolean value based on the outcome of the checks it performs.
- You can trigger DAGs from outside Airflow by using the REST API and/or CLI. You can also initiate the execution of a DAG by using the REST API to notify Airflow that a data set update has occurred, which you do through the datasets/ events/ endpoint.
- By using a MessageQueueTrigger, you can run DAGs in Airflow whenever certain messages are published on a message queue, allowing Airflow to respond to events in near-real-time. This approach also enables inter-Airflow instance communication without exposing APIs between the Airflow instances involved.

Communicating with external systems

This chapter covers

- Working with Airflow operators performing actions on systems outside Airflow
- Applying operators specific to external systems
- Implementing Airflow operators to perform A-to-B operations
- Testing tasks connecting to external systems

In previous chapters, we used mainly generic operators such as the BashOperator and the PythonOperator to keep the focus on understanding the basics of Airflow. This is hardly the best use of Airflow, however. Airflow's main power lies in its capability to connect to a broad variety of systems (e.g., an Apache Spark cluster, a Google BigQuery data warehouse, and a PostgreSQL database) and orchestrate workloads between them.

To demonstrate, this chapter explores how to install and use additional operators from the Airflow ecosystem to integrate with external systems without having to write custom integration logic. For illustration, we'll develop two use cases connecting to

164

different external systems and see how specific operators help us move and transform data between these systems.

> **NOTE** Operators are always under development. By the time you read this chapter, there may be new operators that suit your use case but are not described here.

8.1 Installing additional operators

A large portion of software runs on cloud services nowadays. Generally, you can control these services via an API—an interface that enables you to connect and send requests to your cloud provider. The API typically comes with a client in the form of a Python package. The Amazon Web Services (AWS) client, for example, is named boto3 (https://github.com/boto/boto3); the Google Cloud Platform (GCP) client is named Cloud SDK (https://cloud.google.com/sdk); and Microsoft Azure's client is appropriately named Azure SDK for Python (https://docs.microsoft.com/azure/python). Such clients provide convenient functions that let you enter the required details for a request; the clients handle the technical internals of the request and response.

Airflow allows you to interface with a wide variety of external systems via operators. Operators are the convenience classes to which you can provide the required details to make a request to a cloud service; the operators handle the technical implementation internally. In the case of GCP, these operators use the Cloud SDK internally to send requests and provide a small layer around the Cloud SDK, allowing you to call a wide variety of GCP services (figure 8.1).

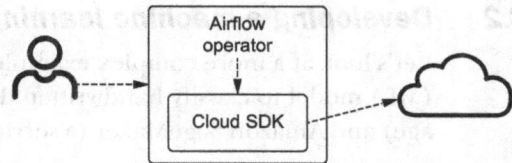

Figure 8.1   An Airflow operator translates given arguments to operations on the Cloud SDK.

The apache-airflow Python package includes a few essential operators but no components that connect with any cloud. For the cloud services, you can install the provider packages in table 8.1.

Table 8.1   Extra packages to install for additional cloud-provider Airflow components[a]

Cloud	pip install **command**
AWS	pip install apache-airflow-providers-amazon
GCP	pip install apache-airflow-providers-google
Azure	pip install apache-airflow-providers-microsoft-azure

[a] The list of cloud provider packages is limited to the three most popular cloud providers for brevity.

This holds not only for the cloud providers but also for other external services. To install operators and corresponding dependencies required to run the PostgresOperator, for example, install the apache-airflow-providers-postgres package. For a full list of all available additional packages, see the Airflow documentation (https://airflow.apache .org/docs).

Let's use the S3CopyObjectOperator to perform an action on AWS. This operator copies an object from one bucket to another. It accepts several arguments (but we've skipped the irrelevant arguments for this example).

Listing 8.1   The S3CopyObjectOperator with only the necessary details

```
from airflow.providers.amazon.aws.operators.s3 import S3CopyObjectOperator

S3CopyObjectOperator(
    task_id="...",
    source_bucket_name="databucket",          ◄──── The bucket to copy from
    source_bucket_key="/data/{{ ds }}.json",  ◄──── The object name to copy
    dest_bucket_name="backupbucket",          ◄──── The bucket to copy to
    dest_bucket_key="/data/{{ ds }}-backup.json",  ◄──── The target object name
)
```

This operator makes copying an object on S3 to a different location on S3 a simple task of filling in the blanks; you don't have to dive into the details of AWS's boto3 client. If you check the implementation of the operator, internally it calls copy_object() on boto3.

8.2   Developing a machine learning model

Let's look at a more complex example. In this section, we develop a machine learning (ML) model to classify handwritten digits in AWS using AWS services such as S3 (storage) and Amazon SageMaker (a service for developing and deploying ML models).

8.2.1   Use case: Classifying handwritten digits

As a starting point for our model, we'll use the MNIST dataset (s3://sagemaker-sample -data-eu-west-1/algorithms/kmeans/mnist), containing approximately 70,000 handwritten digits from 0–9 (figure 8.2). After training the model, we should be able to feed it a new, previously unseen handwritten number, and the model should classify that number (figure 8.3).

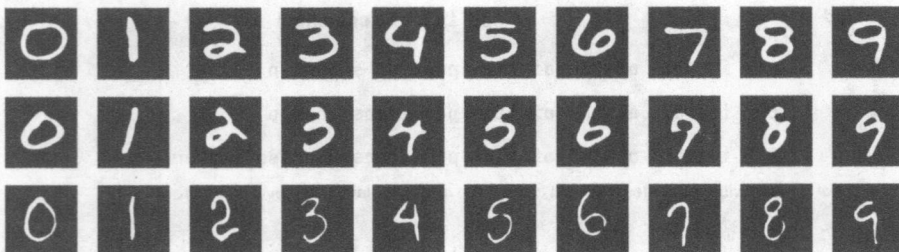

Figure 8.2   Example handwritten digits in the MNIST data set

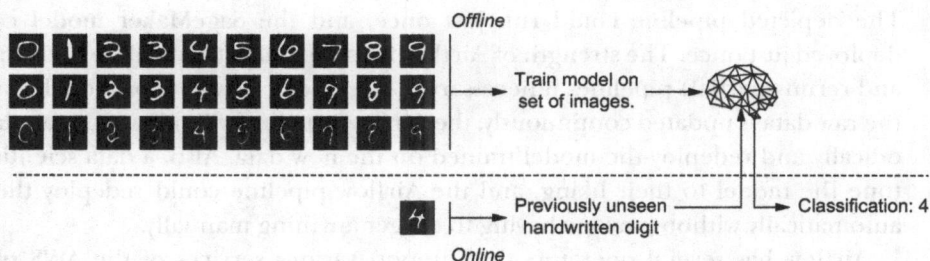

Figure 8.3 Rough outline of how an ML model is trained in one stage and classifies previously unseen samples in another

The model has two parts: one offline and one online. The offline part takes a large set of handwritten digits, trains a model to classify these handwritten digits, and stores the result (a set of model parameters). This process can be done periodically when new data is collected. The online part is responsible for loading the model and classifying previously unseen digits. It should run instantaneously because users expect direct feedback.

Airflow workflows are typically responsible for the offline part of a model. Training a model comprises loading data, preprocessing it into a format suitable for the model, and training the model, which can become complex. Also, retraining the model periodically fits nicely with Airflow's batch-processing paradigm. The online part is typically an API, such as a REST API or HTML page with REST API calls under the hood. Such an API is typically deployed only once or as part of a continuous integration/continuous delivery (CI/CD) pipeline. There's no use case for redeploying an API every week; therefore, it's typically not part of an Airflow workflow.

8.2.2 Setting up the pipeline

In this section, we'll develop an Airflow pipeline to train a handwritten-digit classifier. The pipeline will use SageMaker, an AWS service that facilitates the development and deployment of ML models. In the pipeline, first we copy sample data from a public location to our own S3 bucket. Next, we transform the data into a format that the model can use and train the model with SageMaker. Finally, we deploy the model to classify a given handwritten digit. The pipeline will look like figure 8.4.

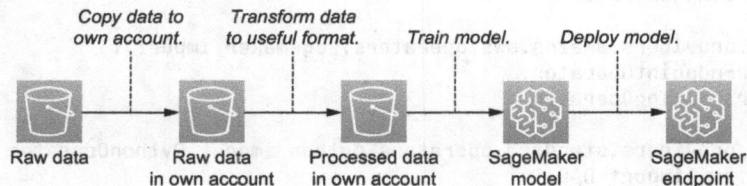

Figure 8.4 Logical steps for creating a handwritten-digit classifier

The depicted pipeline could run just once, and the SageMaker model could be deployed just once. The strength of Airflow is its capability to schedule such a pipeline and rerun (partial) pipelines if necessary in the case of new data or model changes. If the raw data is updated continuously, the Airflow pipeline will reload the raw data periodically and redeploy the model trained on the new data. Also, a data scientist could tune the model to their liking, and the Airflow pipeline could redeploy the model automatically without anyone having to trigger anything manually.

Airflow has several operators that support various services of the AWS platform. Although the list is never complete because services are continuously added, changed, and removed, most AWS services are supported by an Airflow operator. AWS operators are provided by the `apache-airflow-providers-amazon` package. Figure 8.5 shows the pipeline.

Figure 8.5   Logical steps implemented in the Airflow directed acyclic graph (DAG)

Even though the pipeline has only four main tasks, the first two of which are just setting up a fresh bucket and making sure that SageMaker can read data from it, we have quite a lot to configure in SageMaker. Hence, the DAG code (shown in the following listing) is lengthy. No worries, though; we'll break it down.

Listing 8.2   DAG to train and deploy a handwritten-digit classifier

```
import gzip
import io
import json
import os
import pickle

import pendulum
from airflow.providers.amazon.aws.hooks.s3 import S3Hook
from airflow.providers.amazon.aws.operators.s3 import (
    S3CopyObjectOperator,
    S3CreateBucketOperator
)
from airflow.providers.amazon.aws.operators.sagemaker import (
    SageMakerEndpointOperator,
    SageMakerTrainingOperator,
)
from airflow.providers.standard.operators.python import PythonOperator
from airflow.sdk import DAG
from sagemaker import image_uris
from sagemaker.amazon.common import write_numpy_to_dense_tensor
```

```python
BUCKET_NAME=os.environ.get("MNIST_BUCKET")
REGION_NAME=os.environ.get("AWS_REGION")
SAGEMAKER_ROLE=os.environ.get("SAGEMAKER_EXEC_ROLE_ARN")


def _add_bucket_policy():
    # Create a bucket policy
    bucket_policy = {
        "Version": "2012-10-17",
        "Id": "ExamplePolicy01",
        "Statement": [
            {
                "Sid": "ExampleStatement01",
                "Effect": "Allow",
                "Principal": {
                    "AWS": SAGEMAKER_ROLE
                },
                "Action": "s3:*",
                "Resource": [
                    f"arn:aws:s3:::{BUCKET_NAME}/*",
                    f"arn:aws:s3:::{BUCKET_NAME}"
                ]
            }
        ]
    }

    # Convert the policy from JSON dict to string
    bucket_policy = json.dumps(bucket_policy)

    # Set the new policy
    s3hook = S3Hook()
    session = s3hook.get_session(region_name=REGION_NAME)
    s3_client = session.client("s3")
    s3_client.put_bucket_policy(Bucket=BUCKET_NAME, Policy=bucket_policy)

def _extract_mnist_data():
    s3hook = S3Hook()
    # Download S3 dataset into memory
    mnist_buffer = io.BytesIO()
    mnist_obj = s3hook.get_key(
        bucket_name=BUCKET_NAME,
        key="mnist.pkl.gz",
    )

    mnist_obj.download_fileobj(mnist_buffer)
    # Unpack gzip file, extract dataset,
    # convert, upload back to S3
    mnist_buffer.seek(0)

    with gzip.GzipFile(fileobj=mnist_buffer, mode="rb") as f:
        train_set, _, _ = pickle.loads(f.read(), encoding="latin1")
        output_buffer = io.BytesIO()

        write_numpy_to_dense_tensor(
            file=output_buffer,
```

Sometimes, your desired functionality isn't supported by any operator, and you have to implement the logic yourself.

We can use the S3Hook for operations on S3.

Downloads the S3 object

```
            array=train_set[0],
            labels=train_set[1],
    )

    output_buffer.seek(0)                    Uploads the extracted
    s3hook.load_file_obj(        ◀──────┐    data back to S3
        output_buffer,
        key="mnist_data",
        bucket_name=BUCKET_NAME,
        replace=True,
    )

with DAG(
    dag_id="01_aws_handwritten_digits_classifier",
    schedule=None,
    start_date=pendulum.today("UTC").add(days=-3),
):
    create_bucket = S3CreateBucketOperator(
        task_id="create_mnist_bucket",
        bucket_name=BUCKET_NAME,
        region_name=REGION_NAME
    )

    add_bucket_policy = PythonOperator(
        task_id="add_sagemaker_bucket_policy",
        python_callable=_add_bucket_policy,
    )                                              The S3CopyObjectOperator
                                                   copies objects between two
    download_mnist_data = S3CopyObjectOperator(  ◀ S3 locations.
        task_id="download_mnist_data",
        source_bucket_name="sagemaker-sample-data-eu-west-1",
        source_bucket_key="algorithms/kmeans/mnist/mnist.pkl.gz",
        dest_bucket_name=BUCKET_NAME,
        dest_bucket_key="mnist.pkl.gz",         Sometimes, your desired functionality
    )                                           isn't supported by any operator, and
                                                you have to implement it yourself and
    extract_mnist_data = PythonOperator(  ◀──── call it with the PythonOperator.
        task_id="extract_mnist_data",
        python_callable=_extract_mnist_data,
    )                                              The SageMakerTraining-
                                                   Operator creates a
    sagemaker_train_model = SageMakerTrainingOperator(  ◀─┘ SageMaker training job.
        task_id="sagemaker_train_model",
        config={                                  ◀──────   The config is a JSON
            "TrainingJobName":                               containing the training-job
➡ "mnistclassifier-{{ logical_date | ts_nodash }}",         configuration.
            "AlgorithmSpecification": {
                "TrainingImage":
➡ image_uris.retrieve(framework="kmeans",region=REGION_NAME),
                "TrainingInputMode": "File",
            },
            "HyperParameters": {"k": "10", "feature_dim": "784"},
            "InputDataConfig": [
                {
                    "ChannelName": "train",
```

```
                    "DataSource": {
                        "S3DataSource": {
                            "S3DataType": "S3Prefix",
                            "S3Uri": f"s3://{BUCKET_NAME}/mnist_data",
                            "S3DataDistributionType": "FullyReplicated",
                        }
                    },
                }
            ],
            "OutputDataConfig": {"S3OutputPath": f"s3://{BUCKET_NAME}/
    mnistclassifier-output"},
            "ResourceConfig": {
                "InstanceType": "ml.c4.xlarge",
                "InstanceCount": 1,
                "VolumeSizeInGB": 10,
            },
            "RoleArn": SAGEMAKER_ROLE,
            "StoppingCondition": {"MaxRuntimeInSeconds": 24 * 60 * 60},
        },
        wait_for_completion=True,          The operator conveniently waits until the training job is
        print_log=True,                    complete and prints CloudWatch logs during training.
        check_interval=10,
    )

    sagemaker_deploy_model = SageMakerEndpointOperator(
        task_id="sagemaker_deploy_model",
        wait_for_completion=True,                      The SageMakerEndpointOperator
        config={                                    deploys the trained model, which makes
            "Model": {                               it available behind an HTTP endpoint.
                "ModelName":
    "mnistclassifier-{{ logical_date | ts_nodash }}",
                "PrimaryContainer": {
                    "Image": image_uris.
        retrieve(framework="kmeans",region=REGION_NAME),
                    "ModelDataUrl": (
                        f"s3://{BUCKET_NAME}/mnistclassifier-output/"
                        "mnistclassifier-{{ logical_date | ts_nodash }}/"
                        "output/model.tar.gz"
                    ), # this will link the model and the training job
                },
                "ExecutionRoleArn": SAGEMAKER_ROLE,
            },
            "EndpointConfig": {
                "EndpointConfigName":
    "mnistclassifier-{{ logical_date | ts_nodash }}",
                "ProductionVariants": [
                    {
                        "InitialInstanceCount": 1,
                        "InstanceType": "ml.t2.medium",
                        "ModelName": "mnistclassifier-{{ logical_date | ts_nodash
    }}",
                        "VariantName": "AllTraffic",
                    }],
            },
            "Endpoint": {
```

```
            "EndpointConfigName":
    "mnistclassifier-{{ logical_date | ts_nodash }}",
            "EndpointName": "mnistclassifier",
        },
    },
)
```

```
    create_bucket >> add_bucket_policy >> download_mnist_data >>
    extract_mnist_data >> sagemaker_train_model >> sagemaker_deploy_model
```

When you work with external services, the complexity isn't always in Airflow; it's in ensuring the correct integration of various components of your pipeline. SageMaker requires a lot of configuration, such as input and output parameters and resource types to use. We'll break down the tasks piece by piece in the following code listings.

Listing 8.3   Copying data between two S3 buckets

```
download_mnist_data = S3CopyObjectOperator(
    task_id="download_mnist_data",
    source_bucket_name="sagemaker-sample-data-eu-west-1",
    source_bucket_key="algorithms/kmeans/mnist/mnist.pkl.gz",
    dest_bucket_name="[your-bucket]",
    dest_bucket_key="mnist.pkl.gz",
)
```

After the DAG is initialized, the first task copies the MNIST data set from a public bucket to our own bucket. (We store the data set in our own bucket for further processing.) The S3CopyObjectOperator asks for both the bucket and object name of the source and destination and copies the selected object for us. While developing, how do we verify that this process works correctly without coding the full pipeline first and keeping our fingers crossed to see whether it works in production?

8.2.3   *Developing locally with external systems*

Specifically for AWS, if you have access to the cloud resources from your development machine with an access key, you can run Airflow tasks locally. With the help of the command-line interface (CLI) command airflow tasks test, you can run a single task for a given execution date or run ID. Because the download_mnist_data task doesn't use the logical date, you don't need to provide the date parameter for this task; it's optional. But if the dest_bucket_key were given as mnist-{{ ds }}.pkl.gz, you'd have to think wisely about what date to test with.

From the command line, complete the steps in the following listing. This code runs the download_mnist_data task and display logs (listing 8.5).

Listing 8.4   Setting up to locally test AWS operators

```
# Add secrets in ~/.aws/credentials:
  # [myaws]
```

```
# aws_access_key_id=AKIAEXAMPLE123456789
# aws_secret_access_key=supersecretaccesskeydonotshare!123456789

export AWS_PROFILE=myaws
export AWS_DEFAULT_REGION=eu-west-1
export AIRFLOW_HOME=[your project dir]
airflow db init
airflow tasks test \
  01_aws_handwritten_digits_classifier \
  download_mnist_data \
  2024-01-01
```

Initializes a local Airflow metastore ◄

Runs a single task ◄

dag_id ◄

task_id ◄

execution_date or run_id ◄

Using secrets in Airflow

Listing 8.4 uses AWS keys to gain access to cloud services. In a production environment, it's important to handle sensitive credentials with care. Therefore, we advise using a secret manager (such as HashiCorp Vault, Azure Key Vault, AWS SSM, and Google Cloud Secrets Manager). Doing this prevents secrets from being spread across different systems and consolidates them in one system specifically designed for storage and management of secrets. For a more in-depth look at managing secrets and security best practices in Airflow, see chapter 16.

Listing 8.5 Verifying a task manually with `airflow tasks test`

```
$ airflow tasks test 01_aws_handwritten_digits_classifier download_mnist_data
2024-01-01

INFO - Filling up the DagBag from .../chapter08/dags
INFO - Found credentials in shared credentials file: ~/.aws/credentials
INFO - Dependencies all met for dep_context=non-requeueable deps
  ti=<TaskInstance:
  01_aws_handwritten_digits_classifier.download_mnist_data
  __airflow_temporary_run_2024-07-01T19:43:12.947336+00:00__ [None]>
INFO - Dependencies all met for dep_context=requeueable deps
  ti=<TaskInstance:
  01_aws_handwritten_digits_classifier.download_mnist_data
  __airflow_temporary_run_2024-07-01T19:43:12.947336+00:00__ [None]>
INFO - Starting attempt 1 of 1
INFO - Executing <Task(S3CopyObjectOperator): download_mnist_data> on
  2024-01-01 00:00:00+00:00
INFO - Exporting env vars: AIRFLOW_CTX_DAG_OWNER='airflow'
  AIRFLOW_CTX_DAG_ID='01_aws_handwritten_digits_classifier'
  AIRFLOW_CTX_TASK_ID='download_mnist_data'
  AIRFLOW_CTX_EXECUTION_DATE='2024-01-01T00:00:00+00:00'
  AIRFLOW_CTX_TRY_NUMBER='1'
  AIRFLOW_CTX_DAG_RUN_ID='__airflow_temporary_run_2024-07-
  01T19:43:12.947336+00:00__'
INFO - ::endgroup::
INFO - Using connection ID 'aws_default' for task execution.
```

```
INFO - Found credentials in shared credentials file: ~/.aws/credentials
INFO - ::group::Post task execution logs
INFO - Marking task as SUCCESS.
   dag_id=01_aws_handwritten_digits_classifier, task_id=download_mnist_data,
   run_id=__airflow_temporary_run_2024-07-01T19:43:12.947336+00:00__,
   execution_date=20240101T000000, start_date=, end_date=20240701T194316
```

After this, the data is copied to our own bucket (figure 8.6). What just happened? We configured the AWS credentials so we could access the cloud resources from our local machine.

Although this method is specific to AWS, similar authentication methods apply to GCP and Azure. The AWS boto3 client used internally in Airflow operators, for example, will search for credentials in various places on the machine where a task is run.

	Name	▲	Type	▽	Last modified	▽	Size	▽	Storage class
☐	🗋 mnist.pkl.gz		gz		July 1, 2024, 21:43:14 (UTC+02:00)		15.4 MB		Standard

Figure 8.6   After we run the task locally with `airflow tasks test`, the data is copied to our own AWS S3 bucket.

In listing 8.4, we set the `AWS_PROFILE` environment variable, which the boto3 client picks up for authentication. Then we set another environment variable: `AIRFLOW_HOME`. This location is where Airflow will store logs and the like. Inside this directory, Airflow will search for a `/dags` directory. If that directory happens to live elsewhere, you can point Airflow there with another environment variable: `AIRFLOW__CORE__DAGS_FOLDER`.

Next, run `airflow db init`. First, however, make sure that you haven't set `AIRFLOW__CORE__SQL_ALCHEMY_CONN` (a URI that points to a database for storing all state) or set it to a database URI specifically for testing purposes. If `AIRFLOW__CORE__SQL_ALCHEMY_CONN` isn't set, `airflow db init` initializes a local SQLite database (a single-file, no-configuration-required database) inside `AIRFLOW_HOME`. `airflow tasks test` runs and verifies a single task. It doesn't record any state in the database, but it requires a database for storing logs, so you must initialize one with `airflow db init`.

> **NOTE**   The database that `airflow db init` initializes is generated in a file named `airflow.db` in the directory set by `AIRFLOW_HOME`. You can open and inspect it with, for example, DBeaver.

After all this, we can run the task from the command line with `airflow tasks test 01_aws_handwritten_digits_classifier extract_mnist_data 2024-01-01`. After we've copied the file to our own S3 bucket, we need to transform it into a format that the SageMaker K-Means model expects, which is recordIO.

NOTE The documentation for MIME type application/x-recordio-protobuf is available at https://mng.bz/gmpG.

Listing 8.6 Transforming MNIST data to recordIO for SageMaker's K-Means model

```python
import gzip
import io
import pickle

from airflow.operators.python import PythonOperator
from airflow.providers.amazon.aws.hooks.s3 import S3Hook
from sagemaker.amazon.common import write_numpy_to_dense_tensor


def _extract_mnist_data():            Initializes S3Hook to
    s3hook = S3Hook()                 communicate with S3

    # Download S3 dataset into memory
    mnist_buffer = io.BytesIO()       Downloads data into
    mnist_obj = s3hook.get_key(       in-memory binary stream
        bucket_name="your-bucket",
        key="mnist.pkl.gz",
    )
    mnist_obj.download_fileobj(mnist_buffer)

    # Unpack gzip file, extract dataset, convert, upload back to S3
    mnist_buffer.seek(0)                                          Unzips and
    with gzip.GzipFile(fileobj=mnist_buffer, mode="rb") as f:     unpickles
        train_set, _, _ = pickle.loads(f.read(), encoding="latin1")
        output_buffer = io.BytesIO()
        write_numpy_to_dense_tensor(         Converts NumPy array
            file=output_buffer,              to recordIO records
            array=train_set[0],
            labels=train_set[1],
        )
        output_buffer.seek(0)
        s3hook.load_file_obj(           Uploads result to S3
            output_buffer,
            key="mnist_data",
            bucket_name="your-bucket",
            replace=True,
        )


extract_mnist_data = PythonOperator(
    task_id="extract_mnist_data",
    python_callable=_extract_mnist_data,
)
```

Airflow in itself is a general-purpose orchestration framework with a manageable set of features to learn. When you work in the data field, however, it often takes time and experience to learn about all technologies and know which dots to connect in which way. You never develop Airflow alone; often, you're connecting to other systems and reading the documentation for those systems. Airflow will trigger the job for such a task, but the difficulty in developing a data pipeline often lies outside Airflow; it's in the system you're communicating with. Although this book focuses solely on Airflow, due to the nature of working with other data processing tools, we try to demonstrate via these examples what developing a data pipeline is like.

For this task, no existing functionality in Airflow allows us to download data and extract, transform, and upload the result back to S3. Therefore, we must implement our own function. The function downloads the data into an in-memory binary stream (`io.BytesIO`) so that the data is never stored in a file on the filesystem and no remaining files are left after the task. The MNIST data set is small (15 MB) and therefore will run on any machine. Think wisely about the implementation, however. For larger data, it may be wise to opt for storing the data on disk and processing in chunks. Similarly, this task can be run/tested locally with the following code, after which the data will be visible in S3 (figure 8.7):

```
airflow tasks test 01_aws_handwritten_digits_classifier
  extract_mnist_data 2024-01-01
```

	Name ▲	Type ▽	Last modified ▽	Size ▽	Storage class
☐	🗋 mnist_data	-	July 1, 2024, 22:04:15 (UTC+02:00)	151.8 MB	Standard
☐	🗋 mnist.pkl.gz	gz	July 1, 2024, 21:43:14 (UTC+02:00)	15.4 MB	Standard

Table Selection Select mnist_data

Figure 8.7   Gzipped and pickled data was read and transformed into a usable format.

Airflow Object Storage

Airflow 2.8.0 introduced a new experimental feature called Object Storage. This feature simplifies the implementation of object-storage systems like S3, GCS, and Azure Blob Storage. This new approach makes it easier to work with object storage systems. Because it simplifies the syntax of your code, the Object Storage feature lets you shift between object storage systems without altering your DAG code. It also helps with moving data between different storage systems and transferring large files. For additional details, see the Airflow documentation.

The next two tasks train and deploy the SageMaker model. The SageMaker operators take a `config` argument, which entails configuration specific to SageMaker and beyond the scope of this book. Let's focus on the other arguments in the next listing.

> **Listing 8.7   Training an AWS SageMaker model**

```
sagemaker_train_model = SageMakerTrainingOperator(
    task_id="sagemaker_train_model",
    config={
        "TrainingJobName":
"mnistclassifier-{{ logical_date | ts_nodash }}",
        ...
    },
    wait_for_completion=True,
    print_log=True,
    check_interval=10,
)
```

Many of the details in `config` are specific to SageMaker; you can find out more by reading the SageMaker documentation (https://mng.bz/nZ9V). Two lessons apply to working with any external system, however.

First, AWS restricts the `TrainingJobName` to be unique within an AWS account and region. Running this operator with the same `TrainingJobName` twice returns an error. Suppose that we provided a fixed value, `mnistclassifier`, to the `TrainingJobName`. Running it a second time would result in failure:

```
botocore.errorfactory.ResourceInUse: An error occurred (ResourceInUse) when
    calling the CreateTrainingJob operation: Training job names must be
    unique within an AWS account and region, and a training job with this
    name already exists (arn:aws:sagemaker:eu-west-1:[account]:
    training-job/mnistclassifier)
```

The `config` argument can be templated, so if you plan to retrain your model periodically, you must give it a unique `TrainingJobName`, which you can do by templating it with the `logical_date`. This way, you ensure that the task is idempotent and that existing training jobs don't have conflicting names.

Second, note the arguments `wait_for_completion` and `check_interval`. If `wait_for_completion` were set to `false`, the command would *fire and forget* (which is how the boto3 client works): AWS would start a training job, but you'd never know whether it completed successfully. Therefore, all SageMaker operators wait (default: `wait_for_completion=True`) for the given task to complete. Internally, the operators poll every X seconds, checking to see whether the job is still running. This ensures that Airflow tasks complete only when the SageMaker training job is finished (figure 8.8). If you have

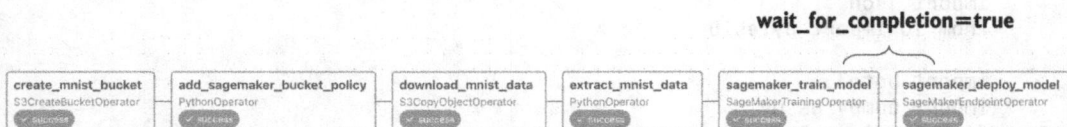

wait_for_completion=true

create_mnist_bucket	add_sagemaker_bucket_policy	download_mnist_data	extract_mnist_data	sagemaker_train_model	sagemaker_deploy_model
S3CreateBucketOperator	PythonOperator	S3CopyObjectOperator	PythonOperator	SageMakerTrainingOperator	SageMakerEndpointOperator
✓ success	✓ success	✓ success	✓ success	✓ success	✓ success

Figure 8.8   The SageMaker operators succeed only when the job is completed successfully in AWS.

downstream tasks and want to ensure the correct behavior and order of your pipeline, you'll want to wait for completion.

When the full pipeline is complete, we've successfully deployed a SageMaker model and endpoint to expose it (figure 8.9). In AWS, however, a SageMaker endpoint isn't exposed to the outside world. It's accessible via the AWS APIs, but not, for example, via a worldwide-accessible HTTP endpoint. To complete the data pipeline, we'd like to have a nice interface or API that allows us to feed handwritten digits and receive a result. In AWS, to make the pipeline accessible to the internet, we could deploy Lambda (https://aws.amazon.com/lambda) to trigger the SageMaker endpoint and API Gateway (https://aws.amazon.com/api-gateway) to create an HTTP endpoint forwarding requests to Lambda, so why not integrate them into our pipeline (figure 8.10)?

Name	▽	ARN	▽	Creation time	▽	Status	▽	Last updated	▽
○ mnistclassifier		arn:aws:sagemaker:eu-central-1:640799725937:endpoint/mnistclassifier		8/9/2024, 1:32:32 PM		⊘ InService		8/9/2024, 1:39:58 PM	

Figure 8.9   The SageMaker model menu shows that the model was deployed and the endpoint is operational.

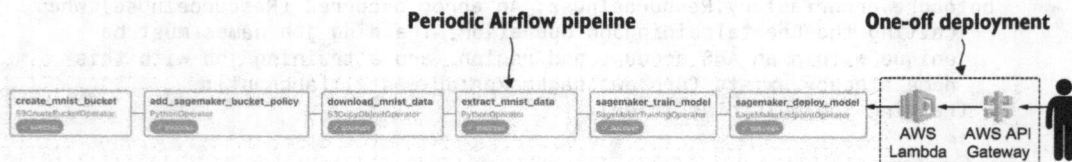

Figure 8.10   The handwritten-digit classifier consists of more components than the Airflow pipeline.

The reason for not deploying infrastructure is that Lambda and API Gateway will be deployed as one-offs, not periodically. They operate in the online stage of the model and therefore are better deployed as part of a CI/CD pipeline. For the sake of completeness, we can implement the API with Chalice. Chalice (https://github.com/aws/chalice) is a Python framework similar to Flask for developing an API and automatically generating the underlying API Gateway and Lambda resources in AWS.

Listing 8.8   An example user-facing API using Chalice

```
import json
from io import BytesIO

import boto3
import numpy as np
from PIL import Image
from chalice import Chalice, Response
from sagemaker.amazon.common import numpy_to_record_serializer
```

```
app = Chalice(app_name="number-classifier")

@app.route("/", methods=["POST"], content_types=["image/jpeg"])
def predict():
    """
    Provide this endpoint an image in jpeg format.
    The image should be equal in size to the training images (28x28).
    """
    img = Image.open(
        BytesIO(app.current_request.raw_body)
    ).convert("L")
    img_arr = np.array(img, dtype=np.float32)
    runtime = boto3.Session().client(
        service_name="sagemaker-runtime",
        region_name="eu-west-1",
    )
    response = runtime.invoke_endpoint(
        EndpointName="mnistclassifier",
        ContentType="application/x-recordio-protobuf",
        Body=numpy_to_record_serializer()(img_arr.flatten()),
    )
    result = json.loads(response["Body"].read().decode("utf-8"))
    return Response(
        result,
        status_code=200,
        headers={"Content-Type": "application/json"},
    )
```

Converts input image to grayscale NumPy array

Invokes the SageMaker endpoint deployed by the Airflow DAG

The SageMaker response is returned as bytes.

The API holds a single endpoint that accepts a JPEG image. The result, if the model is trained correctly, looks like figure 8.11. The API transforms the given image into recordIO format, which the SageMaker model was trained on. Then the recordIO object is forwarded to the SageMaker endpoint deployed by the Airflow pipeline and returns a prediction for the given image.

Listing 8.9 Classifying a handwritten image by submitting it to the API

```
curl --request POST \
  --url http:/ /localhost:8000/ \
  --header 'content-type: image/jpeg' \
  --data-binary @'/path/to/image.jpeg'
```

```
{
    "predictions": [
        {
            "distance_to_cluster": 2284.0478515625
            "closest_cluster": 2.0
        }
    ]
}
```

Figure 8.11 Example API input and output. A real product could display a nice UI for uploading images and displaying the predicted number.

8.3 Moving data from between systems

A classic use case for Airflow is a periodic extract, transform, load (ETL) job in which data is downloaded daily and transformed elsewhere. Such a job is often performed for analytical purposes when data is exported from a production database and stored elsewhere for processing later. Many production databases (depending on the data model) aren't capable of returning historical data, such as the state of the database one month ago. Therefore, a periodic export is often created and stored for later processing. Historic data dumps grow your storage requirements quickly and require distributed processing to crunch all data. This section explores how to orchestrate such a task with Airflow.

8.3.1 Use case: Analyzing Airbnb listings

As an example, let's explore a small use case in which we analyze a small data set involving Airbnb places in Amsterdam. The data comes from Inside Airbnb (http://insideairbnb.com), a website and public data collection containing records on listings, reviews, and more. Once a day, we'll download the latest data from a PostgreSQL database containing the Airbnb listings to our AWS S3 bucket. From there, we'll run a pandas job inside a Docker container to determine the price fluctuations and save the result back to S3.

> **NOTE** Inside Airbnb is a mission-driven project that provides data and advocacy about Airbnb's effect on residential communities.

We developed a GitHub repository with code examples to go along with this book. It contains a Docker Compose file for deploying and running the next use case, in which we extract Airbnb listings data and process it in a Docker container with pandas. In a large-scale data processing job, the Docker container could be replaced by a Spark job that distributes the work over multiple machines. The Docker Compose file contains the following:

- One PostgreSQL container holding the Airbnb Amsterdam listings.
- One container compatible with AWS S3 API. Because there is no such thing as AWS-S3-in-Docker, we created a MinIO container (S3 API–compatible object storage) for reading/ writing data.
- One Airflow container.

Visually, the flow will look like figure 8.12. The PostgreSQL container is a custom-built PostgreSQL image holding a database filled with Inside Airbnb data, available inside the Docker Compose file as `insideairbnb`. The database holds a single table named `listings`, which contains records of places in Amsterdam listed on Airbnb between June 2024 and March 2025. We add a column called `download_date` and act as though the data is from different days in March 2025 to enable some analytics on the data (figure 8.13).

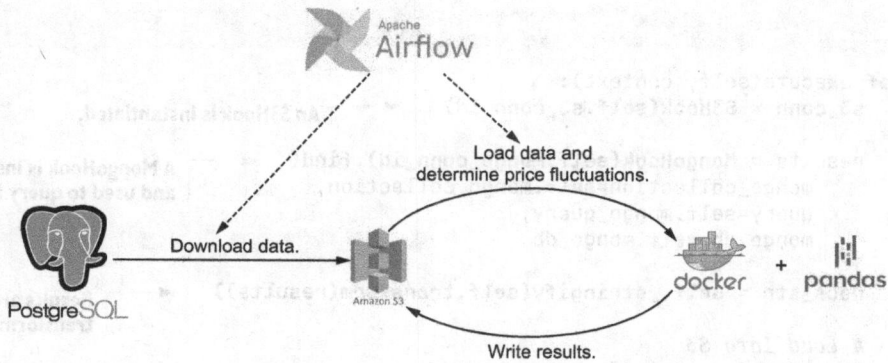

Figure 8.12 **Airflow managing jobs that move data between various systems**

First, we'll query the database and export data to S3. Then we'll read and process the data with pandas.

A common task in Airflow is data transfer between two systems, possibly with a transformation in between. Querying a MySQL database and storing the result in Google Cloud Storage, copying data from a Secure File Transfer Protocol (SFTP) server to your data lake on AWS S3, or calling an HTTP REST API and storing the output have one thing in common: they deal with two systems (one for input and one for output).

In the Airflow ecosystem, this has led to the development of many such A-to-B operators. For these examples, we have the `MySqlToGoogleCloudStorage-Operator`, the `SFTPToS3operator`, and the `SimpleHttp-Operator`. Although the operators in the Airflow ecosystem can cover many use cases, no `Postgres -query-to-AWS-S3` operator is available at the time of writing. What do we do?

Figure 8.13 **Table structure of example Inside Airbnb database**

8.3.2 *Implementing a PostgresToS3Operator*

First, we could note how similar operators work and develop our own `Postgres-ToS3Operator`. (For in-depth information about creating custom operators, see chapter 9.) Let's look at an operator closely related to our use case: the `MongoToS3Operator` in `airflow.providers.amazon.aws.transfers.mongo_to_s3` (after `apache-airflow-providers-amazon` is installed). This operator runs a query on a MongoDB database and stores the result in an AWS S3 bucket. Let's inspect it and figure out how to replace MongoDB with PostgreSQL. The `execute()` method is implemented as follows. (Some code was omitted.)

Listing 8.10   Implementation of the `MongoToS3Operator`

```
def execute(self, context):
    s3_conn = S3Hook(self.s3_conn_id)          ◄──── An S3Hook is instantiated.

    results = MongoHook(self.mongo_conn_id).find(   ◄──── A MongoHook is instantiated
        mongo_collection=self.mongo_collection,            and used to query for data.
        query=self.mongo_query,
        mongo_db=self.mongo_db
    )
    docs_str = self._stringify(self.transform(results))   ◄──── Results are
                                                                 transformed.
    # Load Into S3
    s3_conn.load_string(            ◄──── load_string() is called on the S3Hook
        string_data=docs_str,             to write the transformed results.
        key=self.s3_key,
        bucket_name=self.s3_bucket,
        replace=self.replace
    )
```

It's important to note that this operator doesn't use any of the filesystems on the Airflow machine; it keeps all results in memory. The flow is basically

```
MongoDB -> Airflow in operator memory -> AWS S3.
```

Because this operator keeps the intermediate results in memory, think wisely about the memory implications when running large queries; a large result could potentially drain the available memory on the Airflow machine. For now, let's keep the `Mongo-ToS3Operator` implementation in mind and look at one other A-to-B operator: the `S3ToSFTPOperator`.

Listing 8.11   Implementation of the `S3ToSFTPOperator`

```
def execute(self, context):
    ssh_hook = SSHHook(ssh_conn_id=self.sftp_conn_id)
    s3_hook = S3Hook(self.s3_conn_id)

    s3_client = s3_hook.get_conn()
    sftp_client = ssh_hook.get_conn().open_sftp()

    with NamedTemporaryFile("w") as f:        ◄──── NamedTemporaryFile is used to
        s3_client.download_file(                     temporarily download a file, which
            self.s3_bucket,                          is removed when the context exits.
            self.s3_key,
            f.name
        )
        sftp_client.put(f.name, self.sftp_path)
```

This operator instantiates two hooks: SSHHook (SFTP is FTP over SSH) and S3Hook. In this operator, however, the intermediate result is written to a Named-Temporary-File, which is a temporary place on the local filesystem of the Airflow instance. In this situation, we don't keep the entire result in memory, but we must ensure that enough disk space is available.

Both operators have two hooks in common: one for communicating with system A and one for communicating with system B. How data is retrieved and transferred between systems A and B is different, however, and the process is up to the person who implements the specific operator. In the case of PostgreSQL, database cursors can iterate to fetch and upload chunks of results. This implementation detail is beyond the scope of this book, however. Keep things simple, and assume that the intermediate result fits within the resource boundaries of the Airflow instance. The following listing shows a possible minimal implementation of the `PostgresToS3Operator`.

Listing 8.12 Example implementation of the `PostgresToS3Operator`

```
def execute(self, context):
    postgres_hook = PostgresHook(
        postgres_conn_id=self._postgres_conn_id
    )
    s3_hook = S3Hook(aws_conn_id=self._s3_conn_id)

    results = postgres_hook.get_records(self._query)   #  Fetches records from the PostgreSQL database
    s3_hook.load_string(                                #  Uploads records to S3 object
        string_data=str(results),
        bucket_name=self._s3_bucket,
        key=self._s3_key,
    )
```

Let's inspect this code. The initialization of both hooks is straightforward; you initialize both of them by providing the name of the connection ID. While doing that, you may notice that the S3Hook takes the argument `aws_conn_id`—not `s3_conn_id`, which might be a more fitting parameter name. To understand why, you must dive into the source code or carefully read the documentation to view all available arguments and see how things are propagated into classes. Because the S3Hook is a subclass of the AwsBaseHook, it inherits several methods and attributes, such as `aws_conn_id`.

The PostgresHook is also a subclass, in this case, of the DbApiHook. As a subclass, it inherits several methods, such as `get_records()`, which executes a given query and returns the results. The return type is a sequence of sequences (more precisely, a list of tuples as specified in PEP 249, the Python Database API Specification). Then we stringify the results and call `load_string()`, which writes encoded data to the given bucket/key on AWS S3.

You may think this process isn't practical, and you're correct. Although this example is a minimal flow to run a query on PostgreSQL and write the result to AWS S3, the list of tuples is stringified, which no data processing framework is able to interpret as an ordinary file format such as CSV or JSON (figure 8.14).

PostgreSQL

123 id ⇅	abc name
2.818	Quiet Garden View Room & Super Fast WiFi
20.168	Studio with private bathroom in the centre 1
25.428	Lovely apt in City Centre (w.lift) near Jordaan

AWS S3

```
"[(2818, 'Quiet Garden View Room&Super Fast WiFi'),
(20168, 'Studio with private bathroom in the centre 1'),
(25428, 'Lovely apt in City Centre (w.lift) near Jordaan')]"
```

Figure 8.14   Exporting data from a PostgreSQL database to stringified tuples

The tricky part of developing data pipelines isn't always orchestrating jobs with Airflow, but ensuring that all bits and pieces of various jobs are configured correctly and fit together like puzzle pieces. Let's write the results to CSV, which will allow data processing frameworks such as pandas and Spark to interpret the output data easily.

The S3Hook provides various convenient methods for uploading data to S3. For filelike objects (that is, in-memory objects with file-operation methods for reading/writing), we can apply load_file_obj().

Listing 8.13   In-memory conversion of PostgreSQL query results to CSV and upload to S3

```
def execute(self, context):
    postgres_hook = PostgresHook(
        postgres_conn_id=self._postgres_conn_id
    )
    s3_hook = S3Hook(aws_conn_id=self._s3_conn_id)

    results = postgres_hook.get_records(self.query)

    data_buffer = io.StringIO()
    csv_writer = csv.writer(data_buffer, lineterminator=os.linesep)
    csv_writer.writerows(results)
    data_buffer_binary = io.BytesIO(data_buffer.getvalue().encode())
    s3_hook.load_file_obj(
        file_obj=data_buffer_binary,
        bucket_name=self._s3_bucket,
        key=self._s3_key,
        replace=True,
    )
```

> For convenience, first we create a string buffer, which is like a file in memory to which we can write strings. After writing the buffer, we convert it to binary.

> Requires a filelike object in binary mode

> Ensures idempotency by replacing files if they already exist

Buffers live in memory, which can be convenient because memory leaves no remaining files on the filesystem after processing. We have to realize, however, that the output of the PostgreSQL query must fit into memory. The key to idempotency is setting replace=True, which ensures that existing files are overwritten. We can rerun our pipeline after a code change, for example; then the pipeline will fail without replace=True because of the existing file.

With these few extra lines, we can store CSV files on S3. Let's see this operation in practice. With this code, we have a convenient operator that makes querying PostgreSQL and writing the result to CSV on S3 a simple exercise of filling in the blanks.

Listing 8.14   Running the `PostgresToS3Operator`

```
download_from_postgres = PostgresToS3Operator(
    task_id="download_from_postgres",
    postgres_conn_id="inside_airbnb",
    query="SELECT * FROM listings WHERE download_date BETWEEN '{{ data_
        interval_start | ds }}' AND '{{ data_interval_end | ds }}'",
    s3_conn_id="s3",
    s3_bucket="inside_airbnb",
    s3_key="listing-{{ ds }}.csv",
    dag=dag,
)
```

8.3.3   Outsourcing the heavy work

A common discussion in the Airflow community is whether to view Airflow as not only a task-orchestration system but also a task-execution system because many DAGs are written with the BashOperator and the PythonOperator, which execute work within the same Python runtime as Airflow. Opponents of this mindset argue for viewing Airflow as only a task-triggering system and suggest that no actual work should be done inside Airflow. Instead, they say, all work should be offloaded to a system designed to deal with data, such as Spark.

Suppose that we have a large job that would take all resources on the machine where Airflow is running. In this case, it's better to run the job elsewhere; Airflow will start the job and wait for it to complete. The idea is that there should be strong separation between orchestration and execution, which we can achieve by having Airflow start the job and wait for completion and having a data processing framework such as Spark perform the actual work. We have various ways to start a job in Spark:

- *Using the* SparkSubmitOperator—Requires a spark-submit binary and YARN client config on the Airflow machine to find the Spark instance
- *Using the* SSHOperator—Requires Secure Shell (SSH) access to a Spark instance but doesn't require Spark client config on the Airflow instance
- *Using the* SimpleHTTPOperator—Requires running Livy, a REST API for Spark

The key to working with any operator in Airflow is reading the documentation and figuring out which arguments to provide. Let's look at the DockerOperator, which starts the Docker container for processing the Inside Airbnb data with pandas. (For more information about running tasks in containers, see chapter 11.)

Listing 8.15   Running a Docker container with the `DockerOperator`

```
crunch_numbers = DockerOperator(
    task_id="crunch_numbers",
    image=" manning-airflow/numbercruncher",
    api_version="auto",
    auto_remove="success",                    ◄─┐  Removes the container
    docker_url="unix://var/run/docker.sock",    │  after successful completion
```

```
    network_mode="host",          ◄──────────────
    environment={                              ◄──
        "S3_ENDPOINT": "localhost:9000",
        "S3_ACCESS_KEY": "[insert access key]",
        "S3_SECRET_KEY": "[insert secret key]",
    },
)
```

> To connect to other services on the host machine via http://localhost, we must share the host network namespace by using host network mode.

The DockerOperator wraps around the Python Docker client and, given a list of arguments, enables starting Docker containers. In listing 8.15, the docker_url is set to a UNIX socket, which requires Docker running on the local machine. It starts the Docker image manning-airflow/numbercruncher, which includes a pandas script that loads the Inside Airbnb data from S3, processes it, and writes the results back to S3.

Listing 8.16   Sample results from the numbercruncher script

```
[
    {
        "id": 5530273,
        "download_date_min": 1428192000000,
        "download_date_max": 1441238400000,
        "oldest_price": 48,
        "latest_price": 350,
        "price_diff_per_day": 2
    },
    {
        "id": 5411434,
        "download_date_min": 1428192000000,
        "download_date_max": 1441238400000,
        "oldest_price": 48,
        "latest_price": 250,
        "price_diff_per_day": 1.3377483444
    },
    ...
]
```

Airflow manages starting the container, fetching logs, and eventually removing the container if necessary. The key is ensuring that no state is left behind so your tasks can run idempotently and no remainders are left.

Summary

- Operators for external systems expose functionality by calling the client for a given system.
- Sometimes, these operators merely pass arguments to the Python client. At other times, they provide additional functionality, such as the SageMaker-Training -Operator, which continuously polls AWS and blocks until completion.
- If access to external services from the local machine is possible, you can test tasks using the CLI command airflow tasks test.

- Think wisely about what task to create in your pipeline. One-off infrastructure setup tasks are better deployed as part of a CI/CD pipeline, for example.
- The Airflow ecosystem has a lot of operators that transfer data between two systems (A-to-B operators). If one isn't available for your use case, you can write it yourself.
- Separate orchestration from execution, especially for large jobs.

Extending Airflow
with custom operators
and sensors

This chapter covers

- Making DAGs more modular and concise with custom components
- Designing and implementing custom hooks, operators, sensors, and deferrable sensors
- Distributing custom components as a basic Python library

As we've seen, one strong feature of Airflow is the ecosystem of operators that allow you to coordinate jobs across many types of systems. At some point, however, you may want to execute a task on a system that Airflow doesn't support. Or you may have a task that you can implement using the PythonOperator, but it requires a lot of boilerplate code, which prevents others from reusing your code easily across DAGs. How should you go about it?

Fortunately, Airflow makes it easy to create new operators to implement your custom operations so you can run jobs on otherwise unsupported systems or make common operations easy to apply across DAGs. In fact, many of the operators in Airflow were implemented because someone had to run a job on a certain system and built an operator to do it.

In this chapter, we'll show you how to build your own operators and use them in DAGs. We'll also explore how to package your custom components into a Python package, making them easy to install and reuse across environments.

9.1 Starting with a PythonOperator

Before building any custom components, let's try solving a problem using the by-now-familiar PythonOperator. In this case, we're interested in building a recommender system that recommends new movies based on our view history. In the initial pilot project, we decide to focus on getting the data, which concerns users' past ratings for a given set of movies and recommending the movies that seem most popular overall based on those ratings.

The movie-ratings data will be supplied via an API, which we can use to obtain user ratings in a certain time period. We can fetch new ratings daily, for example, and use this data to train our recommender. For our pilot, we want to set up a daily import process and create a ranking of the most popular movies, which will be used downstream to start recommending popular movies (figure 9.1).

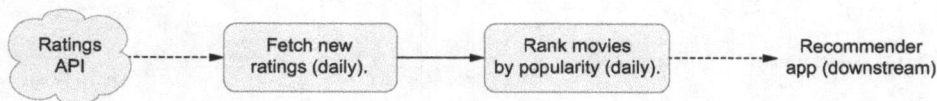

Figure 9.1   Building a simple pilot MVP for the movie-recommender project

9.1.1 Simulating a movie-rating API

To simulate data for this use case, we use data from the MovieLens data set (https://grouplens.org/datasets/movielens), which is freely available and contains close to 34 million ratings by 330,000 users for around 86,000 movies. Because the data set is provided as a flat file, we built a small REST API using Flask, which serves parts of the data set at different endpoints.

NOTE   The code for the API is available in the code repository that accompanies this book (https://mng.bz/vZBm).

To get you started serving the API, we've provided a Docker Compose file that creates multiple containers. including one for the REST API and a couple for running Airflow itself. You can start the containers with the following commands:

```
$ cd chapter09
$ docker-compose up
```

After both containers start up, you should be able to access our movie-rating API at port 8081 on localhost (http://localhost:8081). When you do, you should see a hello message from the API (figure 9.2).

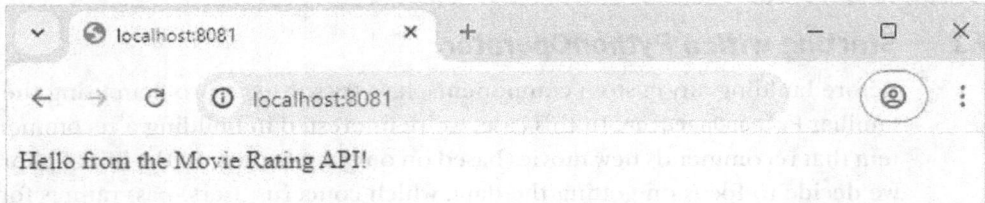

Figure 9.2   Hello message from the API

For this use case, we're interested mainly in obtaining movie ratings, which are provided by the API's /ratings endpoint. To access this endpoint, visit http://localhost:8081/ratings. This result should be an authentication prompt (figure 9.3) because this part of the API returns data that could contain sensitive user information. By default, we use airflow/airflow as a username/password combination.

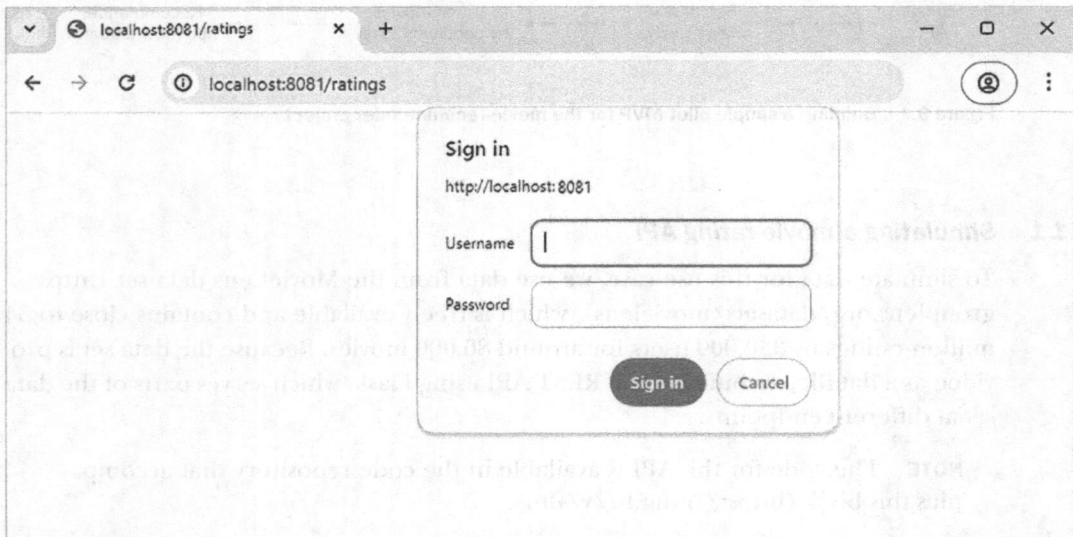

Figure 9.3   Authenticating to the ratings endpoint

After you enter the credentials, you should get an initial list of ratings. As you see in figure 9.4, the ratings are returned in JSON format. In this JSON, the actual ratings are contained in the result key. Two additional fields, limit and offset, indicate that we're looking at only a single page of the results (the first 100 ratings) and that more ratings may be available, indicated by the total field, which describes the total records available for a query.

Figure 9.4 Ratings returned by the ratings endpoint of the API

To step through the paginated result of a query, you can use the offset parameter of the API. To fetch the next set of 100 records, for example, add the offset parameter with a value of 100:

```
http://localhost:8081/ratings?offset=100
```

You can also increase the number of records retrieved in a single query using the limit parameter:

```
http://localhost:8081/ratings?limit=1000
```

By default, the /ratings endpoint returns all ratings available in the API. To fetch ratings for a specific time period, you can select ratings between given start and end dates using the start_date and end_date parameters:

```
http://localhost:8081/ratings?start_date=2023-01-01&end_date=2023-01-02
```

NOTE   The API goes back only 30 days, so make sure that you update the start_date and end_date parameters to more recent dates than the ones in this example.

This API filtering functionality allows you to load data from the API on an incremental (daily) basis without having to load the full data set.

9.1.2   *Fetching ratings from the API*

Now that we've seen the basics of the MovieLens API, we want to start fetching ratings programmatically so that we can use Airflow later to automate this fetching. To access our API from Python, we can use Requests (https://requests.readthedocs.io/en/latest), a popular, easy-to-use library for performing HTTP requests in Python. To start firing requests at our API, first we need to create a requests session using the Session class:

```
import requests
session = requests.Session()
```

This session allows us to fetch ratings from our API by using its get method, which performs a GET HTTP request on our API:

```
response = session.get("http://localhost:8081/ratings")
```

The get method also allows us to pass extra arguments, such as parameters (e.g., start_date and end_date), to include in the query:

```
response = session.get(
    "http://localhost:8081/ratings",
    params={
        "start_date": "2023-01-01",
        "end_date": "2023-01-02",
    },
)
```

Our call to get returns a response object that represents the result of the request. We can use the response object to check whether the query was successful by using the raise_for_status method, which raises an exception if the query returned an unexpected status code. We can access the result of the query using the content attribute or, in this case, the json method (because we know that our API returns JSON):

```
response.raise_for_status()
response.json()
```

If we perform this query, our requests should fail because we forgot to include any authentication in the request. Because our API uses basic HTTP authentication, we can configure our session to include our authentication details as follows:

```
movielens_user = "airflow"
movielens_password = "airflow"

session.auth = (movielens_user, movielens_password)
```

This configuration ensures that the `requests` session includes our username/password authentication. Let's encapsulate this functionality in a `_get_session` function. This function, shown in the following listing, handles setting up the session with authentication so that we don't have to worry about it in other parts of our code. We'll also let this function return the base URL of the API so that it's also defined in a single place. To make the code a bit more configurable, we can specify our username and password and the parts of our URL using environment variables (listing 9.2; `dags/01_python.py`).

Listing 9.1 Function that builds the API HTTP session

```
def _get_session():
    """Builds a requests Session for the Movielens API."""

    session = requests.Session()         ◄─── Creates a requests session
    session.auth = ("airflow", "airflow")    ◄─── Configures the session for basic
                                                  HTTP authentication with this
    base_url = "http://localhost:8081"            username and password

    return session, base_url     ◄─── Returns the session with the API's base URL
                                      so we also know where to reach the API
```

Listing 9.2 Making `_get_session` configurable

Retrieves the API configuration details
from optional environment variables

```
MOVIELENS_HOST = os.environ.get("MOVIELENS_HOST", "movielens")
MOVIELENS_SCHEMA = os.environ.get("MOVIELENS_SCHEMA", "http")     ◄───
MOVIELENS_PORT = os.environ.get("MOVIELENS_PORT", "8081")

MOVIELENS_USER = os.environ["MOVIELENS_USER"]                    ◄─── Fetches the username/
MOVIELENS_PASSWORD = os.environ["MOVIELENS_PASSWORD"]                password from two
                                                                    required environment
def _get_session():                                                 variables
    """Builds a requests Session for the Movielens API."""

    session = requests.Session()
    session.auth = (MOVIELENS_USER, MOVIELENS_PASSWORD)    ◄───
                                                                Uses the retrieved
    base_url = f"{MOVIELENS_SCHEMA}://{MOVIELENS_HOST}:      configuration to build
  ➥ {MOVIELENS_PORT}"                                       our session and base URL

    return session, base_url

session, base_url = _get_session()
```

By using environment variables, we can easily change the values of the parameters when running this script without having to change the script itself. Now that we have a rudimentary setup for our requests session, we need to implement some functionality that will handle the pagination of the API transparently. One way is to wrap our call to `session.get` with some code that inspects the API response and keeps requesting new pages until we reach the total number of rating records, as shown in the following listing (dags/01_python.py).

Listing 9.3   Helper function for handling pagination

```
def _get_with_pagination(session, url, params, batch_size=100):
    """
    Fetches records using a GET request with given URL/params,
    taking pagination into account.
    """

    offset = 0                                                    Keeps track of how many records we've
    total = None                                                  retrieved and how many we should expect
    while total is None or offset < total:
        response = session.get(                                   Keeps looping until
            url,                                                  we've retrieved all
            params={                                              records. The None
                **params,                                         check is for the first
                **{"offset": offset, "limit": batch_size}         loop because the total
            }                                                     number of records is
        )                                                         unknown until after
        response.raise_for_status()                               the first loop.
        response_json = response.json()                           Fetches a new
                                                                  page, starting from
        yield from response_json["result"]                        the given offset

        offset += batch_size                                      Checks the result status and
        total = response_json["total"]                            parses the resulting JSON

            Updates our current offset and          Yields any retrieved
            the total number of records             records to the caller
```

By using `yield from` to return results, this function effectively returns a generator of individual rating records, meaning that we don't have to worry about pages of results anymore. An additional advantage of this implementation is that it's lazy: it fetches a new page only when the records from the current page have been exhausted. The only thing missing is a function that ties everything together and allows us to perform queries to the ratings endpoint while specifying start and end dates for the desired date range. The following listing (dags/01_python.py) gives us a nice concise function for fetching ratings that we can start using in our DAG.

Listing 9.4   Tying things together in `_get_ratings`

```
def _get_ratings(start_date, end_date, batch_size=100):
    session, base_url = _get_session()       Gets the requests session (with
                                             authentication) plus a base URL for the API
```

```
    yield from _get_with_pagination(
        session=session,
        url=base_url + "/ratings",
        params="start_date": start_date, "end_date": end_date},
        batch_size=batch_size,
    )

ratings = _get_ratings(session, base_url + "/ratings")
next(ratings)
list(ratings)
```

Uses our pagination function to fetch a collection of records transparently

Makes sure that we're using the ratings endpoint

Fetches records between the given start and end dates

Limits pages to a specific batch size

Fetches a single record . . .

. . . or the entire batch

Example use of the _get_ratings function

9.1.3 Building the actual DAG

Now we can call our `_get_ratings` function with the PythonOperator to fetch ratings for each schedule interval. When we have the ratings, we can dump the results into a JSON output file, partitioned by date so that we can rerun fetches easily if necessary. We can implement this functionality by writing a small wrapper function that supplies the start/end dates and writes the ratings to an output function, as shown in the next listing (dags/01_python.py).

Listing 9.5 Using the `_get_ratings` function

```
def _fetch_ratings(templates_dict, batch_size=1000, **_):
    logger = logging.getLogger(__name__)

    start_date = templates_dict["start_date"]
    end_date = templates_dict["end_date"]
    output_path = templates_dict["output_path"]

    logger.info(f"Fetching ratings for {start_date} to {end_date}")
    ratings = list(
        _get_ratings(
            start_date=start_date,
            end_date=end_date,
            batch_size=batch_size,
        )
    )
    logger.info(f"Fetched {len(ratings)} ratings")

    logger.info(f"Writing ratings to {output_path}")

    output_dir = os.path.dirname(output_path)
    os.makedirs(output_dir, exist_ok=True)

    with open(output_path, "w") as file_:
```

Uses logging to provide some useful feedback about what the function is doing

Extracts the templated start/end dates and output path

Uses the _get_ratings function to fetch rating records

Creates the output directory if it doesn't exist

Writes the output data as JSON

```
        json.dump(ratings, fp=file_)

fetch_ratings = PythonOperator(                      Creates the task using
    task_id="fetch_ratings",                         the PythonOperator
    python_callable=_fetch_ratings,
    templates_dict={
        "start_date": "{{data_interval_start | ds}}",
        "end_date": "{{data_interval_end | ds}}",
        "output_path":
            "/data/python/ratings/{{data_interval_start | ds}}.json",
    },
)
```

The start_date/end_date/output_path parameters are passed using templates_dict, which allows us to reference context variables such as the execution date in their values. After fetching our ratings, we include another step, rank_movies, to produce our rankings (listing 9.6; dags/custom/ranking.py). This step uses the PythonOperator to apply our rank_movies_by_rating function, which ranks movies by their average rating, optionally filtering for a minimum number of ratings (listing 9.7; dags/01_python.py).

Listing 9.6 Helper function for ranking movies

```
import pandas as pd
def rank_movies_by_rating(ratings, min_ratings=2):          Calculates the average
    ranking = (                                             rating and the total
        ratings.groupby("movieId")                          number of ratings
        .agg(
            avg_rating=pd.NamedAgg(column="rating", aggfunc="mean"),
            num_ratings=pd.NamedAgg(column="userId", aggfunc="nunique"),
        )
        .loc[lambda df: df["num_ratings"] > min_ratings]
        .sort_values(["avg_rating", "num_ratings"], ascending=False)
    )
    return ranking                                    Sorts by average rating

                                                      Filters for the minimum
                                                      number required ratings
```

Listing 9.7 Adding the rank_movies task

```
                                                           Uses the helper
def _rank_movies(templates_dict, min_ratings=2, **_):      function to rank movies
    input_path = templates_dict["input_path"]
    output_path = templates_dict["output_path"]
                                                  Reads ratings from the given
    ratings = pd.read_json(input_path)            (templated) input path
    ranking = rank_movies_by_rating(ratings, min_ratings=min_ratings)
    output_dir = os.path.dirname(output_path)
    os.makedirs(output_dir, exist_ok=True)
    ranking.to_csv(output_path, index=True)       Creates the output
                                                   directory if it doesn't exist

                                                   Writes ranked movies to CSV
```

```
rank_movies = PythonOperator(          ◄────┐  Uses the _rank_movies function
    task_id="rank_movies",                   │  within a PythonOperator
    python_callable=_rank_movies,
    templates_dict={
        "input_path":
        "/data/python/ratings/{{data_interval_start | ds}}.json",
        "output_path":
        "/data/python/rankings/{{data_interval_start | ds}}.csv",
    },
)
fetch_ratings >> rank_movies  ◄───────┘  Connects the fetch and rank tasks
```

This listing results in a DAG comprising two steps: one for fetching ratings and one for ranking movies. By scheduling this DAG to run daily, it provides a ranking of the most popular movies for that day. (A smarter algorithm might take some history into account, but we have to start somewhere, right?)

9.2 Building a custom hook

As you can see, it takes some effort (and code) to start fetching ratings from our API and use them for our ranking. Most of the code you've seen so far concerns interaction with the API: we must get the API address and authentication details, set up a session for interacting with the API, and include extra functionality such as pagination.

Typically in Airflow, this kind of code for interacting with an external service is implemented in a utility class called an *Airflow hook*. This way, Airflow hooks contain all the logic for interacting with that service, allowing the functionality to be reused across operators. Hooks also provide additional magic that allow us to use Airflow to manage connection credentials via the database and UI; we don't have to hardcode our API credentials in our DAG. If we implement our previous logic in an Airflow hook, we can reduce the effort of fetching ratings to something like the following listing. In the next few sections, we'll explore how to write a custom hook and set about building a hook for our movie API.

> **Listing 9.8   Using a `MovielensHook` to fetch ratings**

```
hook = MovielensHook(conn_id="movielens")      ◄───┐  Creates the hook
ratings = hook.get_ratings(start_date, end_date)  ◄─┐
hook.close()  ◄────────────┐                        │  Uses the hook to
                           │                        │  do some work
              Closes the hook, freeing
                any used resources
```

9.2.1 Designing a custom hook

In Airflow, all hooks are created as subclasses of the abstract `BaseHook` class. The following listing shows a skeleton custom hook.

Listing 9.9   Skeleton for a custom hook

```
from airflow.hooks.base import BaseHook

class MovielensHook(BaseHook):
    ...
```

To start building a hook, we need to define an `__init__` method that specifies which connection the hook uses (if applicable) and any extra arguments our hook might need, as shown in the next listing (dags/custom/hooks.py). In this case, we want our hook to get its connection details from a specific connection, but we don't need any extra arguments.

Listing 9.10   Start of the `MovielensHook` class

```
from airflow.hooks.base import BaseHook

class MovielensHook(BaseHook):
    def __init__(self, conn_id):        ◄——   The parameter conn_id tells the
        super().__init__()              ◄——   hook which connection to use.
        self._conn_id = conn_id         ◄——   Calls the constructor of
                                               the BaseHook class

                                               Don't forget to store
                                               the connection ID.
```

Most Airflow hooks are expected to define a `get_conn` method, which is responsible for setting up a connection to an external system. In this case, we can reuse most of our previously defined `_get_session` function, which already provides a preconfigured session for the movie API. As a result, a naive implementation of `get_conn` could look something like the next listing.

Listing 9.11   Initial implementation of the `get_conn` method

```
class MovielensHook(BaseHook):

    ...

    def get_conn(self):
        session = requests.Session()
        session.auth = (MOVIELENS_USER, MOVIELENS_PASSWORD)

        schema = MOVIELENS_SCHEMA
        host = MOVIELENS_HOST
        port = MOVIELENS_PORT

        base_url = f"{schema}://{host}:{port}"

        return session, base_url
```

Instead of hardcoding our credentials, however, we prefer to fetch them from the Airflow credentials store, which is more secure and easier to manage. Follow these steps:

1. Add the connection to the Airflow metastore by choosing Admin > Connections in the Airflow web UI and clicking Create.
2. In the resulting Add Connection screen (figure 9.5), fill in the API's connection details. For this example, call the connection movielens. (You'll use this ID later to refer to the connection.)
3. In the Connection Type section, select HTTP as the REST API.
4. In the Host section, enter the hostname of the API in our Docker Compose setup, which is movielens.
5. Enter the required login credentials: user airflow and password airflow.

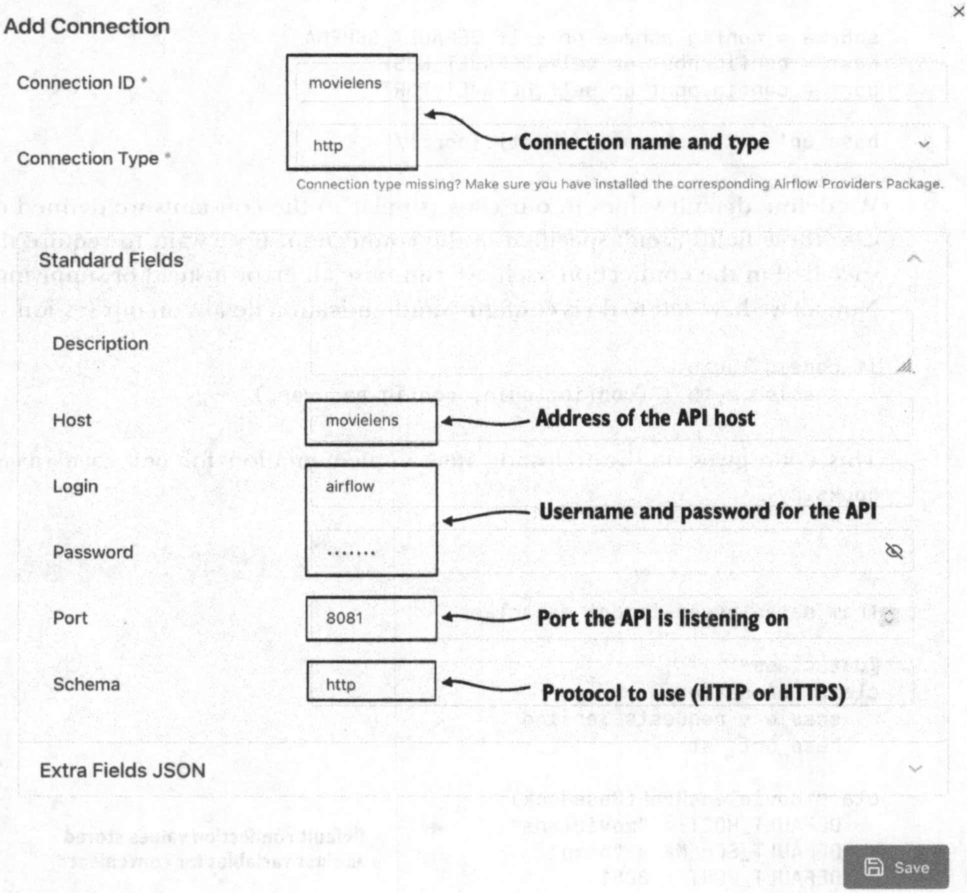

Add Connection   ×

Connection ID *   movielens

Connection Type *   http   ←   **Connection name and type** ˅

Connection type missing? Make sure you have installed the corresponding Airflow Providers Package.

Standard Fields   ˄

Description

Host   movielens   ←   **Address of the API host**

Login   airflow

                                      ←   **Username and password for the API**

Password   •••••••   ⊘

Port   8081   ←   **Port the API is listening on**

Schema   http   ←   **Protocol to use (HTTP or HTTPS)**

Extra Fields JSON   ˅

💾 Save

Figure 9.5 Adding our movie API connection in the Airflow web UI

6 In the Port section, enter the port on which the API will be available—in this case, port 8081 in our Docker Compose setup (as we saw in section 9.1.1 when accessing the API manually).

7 (Optional) Indicate the schema to use for the connection (HTTP).

Now we need to modify get_conn to fetch the connection details from the metastore. The BaseHook class provides a convenience method called get_connection, which can retrieve the connection details for a given connection ID from the metastore:

```
config = self.get_connection(self._conn_id)
```

This connection configuration object has fields that map to the details we provided when creating the connection, so we can use the config object to start determining the host/port and user/password for our API. First, we use the schema, host, and port fields to determine our API's URL as before:

```
schema = config.schema or self.DEFAULT_SCHEMA
host = config.host or self.DEFAULT_HOST
port = config.port or self.DEFAULT_PORT

base_url = f"{schema}://{host}:{port}/"
```

We define default values in our class (similar to the constants we defined earlier) in case these fields aren't specified in the connection. If we want to require them to be specified in the connection itself, we can raise an error instead of supplying defaults. Now all we have left to do is configure authentication details on our session:

```
if config.login:
    session.auth = (config.login, config.password)
```

This code gives us the following new implementation for get_conn (dags/custom/hooks.py).

Listing 9.12 Making get_conn configurable

```
from dataclasses import dataclass

@dataclass
class Connection:
    session: requests.Session
    base_url: str

class MovielensHook(BaseHook):
    DEFAULT_HOST = "movielens"        ◄──  Default connection values stored
    DEFAULT_SCHEMA = "http"                as class variables for convenience
    DEFAULT_PORT = 8081
    def __init__(self, conn_id:str):
        super().__init__()
```

```
        self._conn_id = conn_id

    def get_conn(self):
        config = self.get_connection(self._conn_id)    ◀──── Fetches the connection
                                                              configuration using the
                                                              given ID
        schema = config.schema or self.DEFAULT_SCHEMA  ◀────
        host = config.host or self.DEFAULT_HOST              Builds the base URL
        port = config.port or self.DEFAULT_PORT             using the connection
                                                            config and defaults
        base_url = f"{schema}://{host}:{port}"

                                                         Creates the
        session = requests.Session()              ◀──── requests session
                                                         using the login and
                                                         password from the
        if config.login:                                 connection config
            session.auth = (config.login, config.password)  ◀──

        return Connection(session=session, base_url=base_url)  ◀──

                                              Returns the requests
                                              session and base URL
```

One drawback of this implementation is that each call to get_conn results in a call to
the Airflow metastore because get_conn has to fetch the credentials from the database.
We can avoid this limitation by caching session and base_url in our instance as protected variables, as shown in the next listing (dags/custom/hooks.py).

Listing 9.13   Adding caching for the API session

```
from dataclasses import dataclass

@dataclass
class Connection:
    session: requests.Session
    base_url: str

class MovielensHook(BaseHook):

    def __init__(self, conn_id:str, retry=3):
        ...
        self._session = None        Two extra instance variables used for
        self._base_url = None       caching the session and base URL

    def get_conn(self):
        """
        Returns the connection used by the hook for querying data.
        Should in principle not be used directly.
        """
                                      Checks whether we already have an
                                      active session before creating one
        if self._session is None:  ◀──
            config = self.get_connection(self._conn_id)
            ...
            self._base_url = f"{schema}://{config.host}:{port}"
```

```
        self._session = requests.Session()
        ...

    return Connection(session=self._session, base_url=self._base_url)
```

This way, the first time get_conn is called, self._session is None, so we end up fetching our connection details from the metastore and setting up our base URL and session. By storing these objects in the _session and _base_url instance variables, we make sure that these objects are cached for later calls. A second call to get_ conn will see that self._session no longer is None and will return the cached session and base URL.

> **NOTE**   We're not fans of using the get_conn method directly outside the hook, even though it's publicly exposed, because this method exposes the internal details of how the hook accesses the external system, breaking encapsulation. This creates substantial headaches if we ever want to change this internal detail because our code will be strongly coupled to the internal connection type. This situation is an issue in the Airflow codebase as well. In the case of the HdfsHook, for example, the implementation of the hook was tightly coupled to a Python 2.7–only library (snakebite).

Now that we can build an authenticated connection to our API, we can finally start building some useful methods into our hook and do something useful with our API. To fetch ratings, we can reuse the code from our previous implementation (listing 9.4), which retrieved ratings from the /ratings endpoint of the API and used the get_ with_ pagination function to handle pagination. The main difference is that now we use get_conn within the pagination function to get our API session, as shown in the next listing (dags/custom/hooks.py).

> **Listing 9.14   Adding a get_ratings method**

```
class MovielensHook(BaseHook):
    ...

    def get_ratings(
        self,
        start_date:str=None,
        end_date:str=None,
        batch_size:int=100,
    )-> Generator[Dict[str, Any], None, None]:    ◁──── Public method that will be
        """                                                called by users of the hook
        Fetches ratings between the given start/end date.
        Parameters
        ──────────
        start_date : str
        Start date to start fetching ratings from (inclusive). Expected
        ➥ format is YYYY-MM-DD (equal to Airflow's ds formats).
        end_date : str
    ➥ End date to fetching ratings up to (exclusive). Expected
```

```
            format is YYYY-MM-DD (equal to Airflow's ds formats).
        batch_size : int
        Size of the batches (pages) to fetch from the API. Larger values
        mean less requests, but more data transferred per request.
        """

        yield from self._get_with_pagination(
            endpoint="/ratings",
            params={"start_date": start_date, "end_date": end_date},
            batch_size=batch_size,
        )

    def _get_with_pagination(
        self,
        endpoint:str,
        params:dict,
        batch_size:int=100,
    ) -> Generator[Dict[str, Any], None, None]:
        """
```

Internal helper method that
handles pagination (same
implementation as before)

```
        Fetches records using a get request with given url/params,
        taking pagination into account.
        """

        connection = self.get_conn()
        url = connection.base_url + endpoint

        offset = 0
        total = None
        while total is None or offset < total:
            response = connection.session.get(
                url, params={
                    **params,
                    **{"offset": offset, "limit": batch_size}
                }
            )
            response.raise_for_status()
            response_json = response.json()

            yield from response_json["result"]

            offset += batch_size
            total = response_json["total"]
```

Altogether, this code gives us a basic Airflow hook that handles connections to the MovieLens API. We can add functionality (other than fetching ratings) easily by adding extra methods to the hook.

Although building a hook may seem like a lot of effort, most of the work involves shifting the functions we wrote earlier into a single consolidated hook class. An advantage of our new hook is that it provides nice encapsulation of the MovieLens API logic in a single class, which is easy to use across DAGs.

9.2.2   *Building a DAG with the MovielensHook*

Before we start using our hook to fetch ratings in our DAG, we have to save our hook class somewhere so that we can import it into our DAG. One way is to create a package in the same directory as our dags folder and save our hook in a hooks.py module inside this package. (We'll show another package-based approach in section 9.6.)

> **Listing 9.15   Structure of a DAG directory with a custom package**

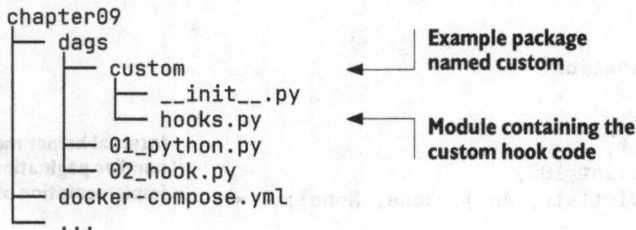

```
chapter09
├── dags
│   ├── custom                    ◀─── Example package
│   │   ├── __init__.py                 named custom
│   │   └── hooks.py              ◀─── Module containing the
│   ├── 01_python.py                    custom hook code
│   └── 02_hook.py
├── docker-compose.yml
└── ...
```

When we have this package, we can import our hook from the new custom package, which contains our custom hook code:

```
from custom.hooks import MovielensHook
```

After we import the hook, fetching ratings is quite simple. All we have to do is instantiate the hook with the proper connection ID and then call the hook's get_ratings method with the desired start and end dates.

> **Listing 9.16   Using our MovielensHook to fetch ratings**

```
hook = MovielensHook(conn_id=conn_id)
ratings = hook.get_ratings(
    start_date=start_date,
    end_date=end_date,
    batch_size=batch_size
)
```

This code returns a generator of rating records, which we write to an output JSON file. To use the hook in our DAG, we still need to wrap this code in a PythonOperator that supplies the correct start and end dates for the given DAG run and writes the ratings to the desired output file. For this task, we can use the _fetch_ratings function we defined for our initial DAG, changing the call to _get_ratings with the call to our new hook, as shown in the next listing (dags/02_hook.py).

> **Listing 9.17   Using the MovielensHook in the DAG**

```
def _fetch_ratings(
    conn_id:str,
    templates_dict:dict,
```

```
        batch_size:int=1000,
        **_
    ):
        logger = logging.getLogger(__name__)

        start_date = templates_dict["start_date"]
        end_date = templates_dict["end_date"]
        output_path = templates_dict["output_path"]

        logger.info(f"Fetching ratings for {start_date} to {end_date}")
        hook = MovielensHook(conn_id=conn_id)
        ratings = list(
            hook.get_ratings(
                start_date=start_date, end_date=end_date,
                batch_size=batch_size
            )
        )
        logger.info(f"Fetched {len(ratings)} ratings")

        logger.info(f"Writing ratings to {output_path}")

        output_dir = os.path.dirname(output_path)
        os.makedirs(output_dir, exist_ok=True)

        with open(output_path, "w") as file_:
            json.dump(ratings, fp=file_)

PythonOperator(
    task_id="fetch_ratings",
    python_callable=_fetch_ratings,
    op_kwargs={"conn_id": "movielens"},
    templates_dict={
        "start_date": "{{data_interval_start | ds}}",
        "end_date": "{{data_interval_end | ds}}",
        "output_path":
        "/data/custom_hook/{{data_interval_start | ds}}.json",
    },
)
```

Creates an instance of the
MovielensHook with the
appropriate connection ID

Uses the hook to fetch
ratings from the API

Writes the fetched
ratings like before

Specifies which
connection to use

We added the parameter `conn_id` to `fetch_ratings`, which specifies the connection to use for the hook. We must include this parameter when calling `_fetch_ratings` from the `PythonOperator` because the hook will use this ID to fetch the address and authentication details of the API from the Airflow metastore. This change gives us the same behavior as before but with a much simpler and smaller DAG file because most of the complexity in the MovieLens API is outsourced to the `MovielensHook`.

9.3 Building a custom operator

Although building a `MovielensHook` allowed us to move a lot of complexity from our DAG into the hook, we still have to write a considerable amount of boilerplate code to define start and end dates and write the ratings to an output file. If we want to reuse this functionality in multiple DAGs, considerable code duplication and extra effort are involved.

Fortunately, Airflow allows us to build custom operators, which we can use to perform repetitive tasks with a minimal amount of boilerplate code. In our case, we could use this functionality to build a `MovielensFetchRatingsOperator`, which would allow us to fetch movie ratings using a specialized operator class.

9.3.1   *Defining a custom operator*

In Airflow, all operators are built as subclasses of the `BaseOperator` class. The following listing shows a bare-bones implementation of a custom operator as a subclass of the `BaseOperator`.

Listing 9.18   Skeleton for a custom operator

```
from airflow.sdk import BaseOperator


class MyCustomOperator(BaseOperator):
    def __init__(self, conn_id:str, **kwargs):
        super.__init__(self, **kwargs)
        self._conn_id = conn_id
        ...
```

Inherits from the BaseOperator class

Passes any extra keyword arguments to the BaseOperator constructor

Any arguments specific to your operator (such as `conn_id` in this example) can be specified explicitly in the `__init__` constructor method. How you use these arguments is up to you. Operator-specific arguments vary between operators but typically include connection IDs (for operators that involve remote systems) and any details required for the operation (start and end dates, queries, and so on).

The `BaseOperator` class takes a large number of mostly optional generic arguments that define the basic behavior of the operator. Examples include the `task_id` the operator created for the task, as well as arguments such as `retries` and `retry_delay` that affect the scheduling of the resulting task. To avoid listing all these generic tasks explicitly, we use Python's `**kwargs` syntax to forward the generic arguments to the `__init__` of the `BaseOperator` class.

Thinking back to earlier DAGs in this book, you may remember that Airflow provides the option of defining certain arguments as default arguments for the entire DAG. You can do this using the `default_args` parameter of the DAG object itself, as shown in the following listing.

Listing 9.19   Applying default arguments to operators

```
default_args = {
    "retries": 1,
    "retry_delay": timedelta(minutes=5),
}
```

```
with DAG(
    ...,
    default_args=default_args
):
    MyCustomOperator(
        ...
    )
```

Next, we define what our operator does by implementing the `execute` method, the main method Airflow calls when the operator is executed as part of a DAG run.

Listing 9.20 The operator's execute method

```
class MyCustomOperator(BaseOperator):
    ...

    def execute(self, context:Context):  ◄────  Main method called when
        ...                                       executing the operator
```

As you see, the `execute` method takes a single parameter, `context`, which is a dictionary (*dict*) containing all the Airflow context variables. Then the method can continue to perform whatever function the operator was designed to do, taking variables from the Airflow context (such as execution dates) into account.

9.3.2 Building an operator to fetch ratings

Now that we know the basics of building an operator, let's see how to build a custom one to fetch ratings. This operator will fetch ratings from the MovieLens API between given start and end dates and write these ratings to a JSON file, similar to what the `_fetch_ratings` function did in our previous DAG. We start by filling in the operator's required parameters in its `__init__` method, including the start and end dates, the connection to use, and the output path to write to (`dags/custom/operators.py`).

Listing 9.21 Start of the custom operator

```
class MovielensFetchRatingsOperator(BaseOperator):
    """
    Operator that fetches ratings from the Movielens API.

    Parameters
    ----------
    conn_id : str
        ID of the connection to use to connect to the Movielens
        API. Connection is expected to include authentication
        details (login/password) and the host that is serving the API.
    output_path : str
        Path to write the fetched ratings to.
    start_date : str
        (Templated) start date to start fetching ratings from (inclusive).
```

```
        Expected format is YYYY-MM-DD (equal to Airflow's ds formats).
    end_date : str
        (Templated) end date to fetching ratings up to (exclusive).
        Expected format is YYYY-MM-DD (equal to Airflow's ds formats).
    """

    def __init__(
      self,
      conn_id:str,
      output_path:str,
      start_date:str,
      end_date:str,
      **kwargs,
    ):

        super(MovielensFetchRatingsOperator, self).__init__(**kwargs)

        self._conn_id = conn_id
        self._output_path = output_path
        self._start_date = start_date
        self._end_date = end_date
```

Next, we implement the body of the operator, which fetches the ratings and writes them to an output file. To do this, we fill in the operator's execute method with a modified version of our implementation for _fetch _ratings, as follows (dags/custom/operators.py).

Listing 9.22   Adding the `execute` **method**

```
class MovielensFetchRatingsOperator(BaseOperator):
    ...

    def execute(self, context:Context):
        hook = MovielensHook(self._conn_id)          ◀── Creates an instance of
        try:                                              the MovielensHook
            self.log.info(
                f"Fetching from {self._start_date} to {self._end_date}"
            )
            ratings = list(
                hook.get_ratings(
                    start_date=self._start_date,             Uses the hook to
                    end_date=self._end_date,                 fetch ratings
                )
            )
            self.log.info(f"Fetched {len(ratings)} ratings")
        finally:                                     Closes the hook to
            hook.close()                             release any resources

        self.log.info(f"Writing ratings to {self._output_path}")

        output_dir = os.path.dirname(self._output_path)      Creates the output
        os.makedirs(output_dir, exist_ok=True)               directory if it
                                                             doesn't exist
```

```
with open(self._output_path, "w") as file_:      ◀─────┐ Writes out the results
    json.dump(ratings, fp=file_)
```

Migrating the code to a custom operator required relatively few changes. Like the `_fetch_ratings` function, this `execute` method starts by creating an instance of the `MovielensHook` and using it to fetch ratings between the given start and end dates. One difference is that now the code takes its parameters from `self`, using the values passed when we instantiated the operator. We also switched our logging calls to use the logger provided by the `Base-Operator` class, which is available in the `self.log` property. Finally, we added some exception handling to make sure that our hook always closes properly, even if the call to `get_ratings` fails. This way, we don't waste resources by forgetting to close our API sessions, which is good practice when implementing code that uses hooks. Using this operator is relatively straightforward: we simply instantiate it and include it in our DAG.

Listing 9.23   Using the `MovielensFetchRatingsOperator`

```
fetch_ratings = MovielensFetchRatingsOperator(
    task_id="fetch_ratings",
    conn_id="movielens",
    start_date="2023-01-01",
    end_date="2023-01-02",
    output_path="/data/2023-01-01.json"
)
```

A drawback of this implementation is that it takes predefined dates for which the operator will fetch ratings. Therefore, the operator fetches ratings only for a single hard-coded time period without taking data-interval dates into account.

Fortunately, Airflow allows us to make certain operator variables *templatable*, meaning that they can refer to context variables such as `data_interval_start`. To allow specific instance variables to be templated, we tell Airflow to template them by using the `templates_field` class variable, as shown in the next listing (`dags/custom/operator.py`).

Listing 9.24   Adding template fields

```
class MovielensFetchRatingsOperator(BaseOperator):
    ...
    template_fields = (
        "_start_date",
        "_end_date",           Tells Airflow to template these
        "_output_path"         instance variables on the operator
    )  ...

    def __init__(
        self,
        conn_id:str,
```

```
        output_path:str,
        start_date:str="{{data_interval_start | ds}}",
        end_date:str="{{data_interval_end | ds}}",
        **kwargs,
    ):
        super(MovielensFetchRatingsOperator, self).__init__(**kwargs)

        self._conn_id = conn_id
        self._output_path = output_path
        self._start_date = start_date
        self._end_date = end_date
```

This code effectively tells Airflow that the variables _start_date, _end_date, and _output _path (created in __init__) are available for templating. If we use any Jinja templating in these string parameters, Airflow makes sure that these values are templated before our execute method is called. As a result, we can use our operator with templated arguments as follows (dags/03_operator.py).

```
from custom.operators import MovielensFetchRatingsOperator

fetch_ratings = MovielensFetchRatingsOperator(
    task_id="fetch_ratings",
    conn_id="movielens",
    start_date="{{data_interval_start | ds}}",
    end_date="{{data_interval_end | ds}}",
    output_path="/data/custom_operator/{{data_interval_start | ds}}
.json"
)
```

This way, Airflow fills in the values of the start of the execution window (data_interval_start) for the start date and the end of the execution window (data_interval_end) for the end date. It also makes sure that the output is written to a file tagged with the start of the execution window (data_interval_start).

9.4   *Building custom sensors*

With all this talk about operators, you may wonder how much effort it takes to build a custom sensor. In case you skipped previous chapters, a *sensor* is a special type of operator that can wait for a certain condition to be fulfilled before executing any downstream tasks in the DAG. You might want to use a sensor, for example, to check whether certain files or data are available in a source system before trying to use the data in any downstream analysis. Regarding their implementation, sensors are similar to operators except that they inherit from the BaseSensorOperator class instead of the BaseOperator. The next listing shows a bare-bones implementation of a custom sensor.

```
Listing 9.26    Skeleton for a custom sensor
```

```
from airflow.sdk import BaseSensorOperator

class MyCustomSensor(BaseSensorOperator):
    ...
```

As the name of the superclass (BaseSensorOperator) suggests, sensors are in fact special types of operators. The BaseSensorOperator class, for example, provides the basic functionality for a sensor and requires sensors to implement a special poke method rather than the execute method.

```
Listing 9.27    The sensor's poke method
```

```
class MyCustomSensor(BaseSensorOperator):

    def poke(self, context:Context):
        ...
```

The signature of the poke method is similar to execute in that it takes a single argument containing the Airflow context. Unlike the execute method, however, poke is expected to return a Boolean value that indicates whether the sensor condition is true. If the condition is true, the sensor finishes its execution, allowing downstream tasks to start executing. If the condition is false, the sensor sleeps several seconds before checking the condition again. This process repeats until the condition becomes true or the sensor hits its timeout.

Although Airflow has many built-in sensors, you can build your own to check any type of condition. For this example, you may want to implement a sensor that checks whether ratings data is available for a given date before continuing with the execution of the DAG.

To start building our MovielensRatingsSensor, first we define the __init__ of our custom sensor class, which should take a connection ID (which species the connection details to use for the API) and a range of start and end dates, specifying the date range we want to check for ratings. The code looks something like the following listing (dags/custom/sensors.py).

```
Listing 9.28    Start of the sensor class
```

```
from airflow.sdk import BaseSensorOperator

class MovielensRatingsSensor(BaseSensorOperator):

    template_fields = ("_start_date", "_end_date")     ◄──  Because sensors are
                                                            special types of operators,
    def __init__(                                           we can use the same basic
        self,                                               setup that we used to
        conn_id:str,                                        implement an operator.
```

```
        start_date:str="{{data_interval_start | ds}}",
        end_date:str="{{data_interval_end | ds}}",
        **kwargs
    ):
        super().__init__(**kwargs)
        self._conn_id = conn_id
        self._start_date = start_date
        self._end_date = end_date
```

> Because sensors are special types of operators, we can use the same basic setup that we used to implement an operator.

After specifying the constructor, we implement the poke method. In this method, we can check for ratings in a specific date range simply by requesting ratings between the given start and end dates that return true if any records exist. The method doesn't fetch all rating records; we need to demonstrate only that at least one record in the range exists.

When we use MovielensHook, implementing this algorithm is straightforward. First, we instantiate the hook and then call get_ratings to start fetching records. Because we're interested only in seeing whether at least one record exists, we can try calling next on the generator returned by get_ratings, which raises a StopIteration if the generator is empty. We can use try/except to test for the exception, returning True if no exception is raised and False if one is, indicating that no records existed (dags/custom/sensors.py).

Listing 9.29 Implementing the poke method

```
class MovielensRatingsSensor(BaseSensorOperator):
    def poke(self, context:Context):
        hook = MovielensHook(self._conn_id)

        try:
            next(
                hook.get_ratings(
                    start_date=self._start_date,
                    end_date=self._end_date,
                    batch_size=1
                )
            )
            self.log.info(
                f"Found ratings for {self._start_date} to {self._end_date}"
            )
            return True
        except StopIteration:
            self.log.info(
                f"Didn't find any ratings for {self._start_date} "
                f"to {self._end_date}, waiting..."
            )
            return False
        finally:
            hook.close()
```

> Tries to fetch one record from the hook (using next to fetch the first record)

> If this succeeds, we have at least one record, so return True.

> If this fails with a StopIteration, the collection of records is empty, so return False.

> Makes sure to close the hook to free resources

The reuse of our `MovielensHook` makes this code relatively short and clear, demonstrating the power of containing the details of interacting with the MovieLens API within the hook class. Now we can use the sensor class to make the DAG check and wait for new ratings to come in before executing the rest of the DAG, as follows (`dags/04_sensor.py`).

Listing 9.30 Using the sensor to wait for ratings

```
...

from custom.operators import MovielensFetchRatingsOperator
from custom.sensors import MovielensRatingsSensor

with DAG(
    dag_id="04_sensor",
    description="Fetches ratings with a custom sensor.",
    start_date=datetime(2023, 1, 1),
    end_date=datetime(2023, 1, 10),
    schedule=CronDataIntervalTimetable("@daily", "UTC"),
    catchup=True
):
    wait_for_ratings = MovielensRatingsSensor(          ◄──── Sensor that waits for
        task_id="wait_for_ratings",                           records to be available
        conn_id="movielens",
        start_date="{{data_interval_start | ds}}",
        end_date="{{data_interval_end | ds}}",
    )

    fetch_ratings = MovielensFetchRatingsOperator(      ◄──── Operator that fetches
        task_id="fetch_ratings",                              records when the
        conn_id="movielens",                                  sensor has completed
        start_date="{{data_interval_start | ds}}",
        end_date="{{data_interval_end | ds}}",
        output_path=
        "/data/custom_sensor/{{data_interval_start | ds}}.json"
    )

    ...

    wait_for_ratings >> fetch_ratings >> rank_movies
```

9.5 Building a custom deferrable operator

When we build pipelines, some tasks have to be executed on external systems, and these tasks can take several minutes or even hours to finish. You might run an Apache Spark job, download a large file from an FTP server, or wait for a new file to appear in an Amazon S3 bucket, for example.

In chapter 6, we discussed sensor deadlock, which happens when all the worker slots in Airflow are occupied by running sensors. We fixed this problem by changing the sensor settings to `reschedule` mode. This way, the workers aren't busy while the sensor is waiting. The same problem can arise with any operator, however. If many long-running tasks are expected to run in parallel, each will occupy a worker slot, therefore preventing other tasks from running. In this scenario, there's no way to free a worker while the task is in progress.

9.5.1   *Executing asynchronous tasks using the triggerer*

Wouldn't it be great to run multiple tasks at the same time without using a worker while we wait for external resources to complete? Fortunately, Airflow has a solution: *deferrable operators*, which are special operators that can be paused or put on hold. Instead of occupying a worker slot while waiting for an external task to finish, a deferrable operator can free that slot for other workers, allowing us to run multiple tasks in parallel without wasting worker resources.

To understand how a deferrable operator works, consider a hypothetical situation: running a compute-intensive job on a Spark cluster that on average takes an hour to complete. In a standard workflow, without a deferrable operator, a worker would be assigned to this task for the entire hour. During this waiting period, however, the worker isn't processing anything; all the computation happens within the Spark cluster. Now imagine that the workflow scaled up to 100 Spark jobs. Essentially, all the workers would be idling, waiting for the jobs to finish.

The issue escalates when we have a limited number of workers, which is often the case. Suppose that we have only 10 workers available in our system. We'd need at least 10 hours to complete all the jobs because we'd have to process them in batches of 10—a highly inefficient situation and certainly not an ideal one.

We can save worker resources by assigning these tasks to a part of Airflow that can handle many tasks at the same time. This is where the triggerer comes in. The triggerer is an Airflow component that's designed to handle tasks that are mostly waiting, and it can handle lots of these tasks at the same time. The triggerer can achieve this parallelism by using the asynchronous functionality of Python's asyncio library. In asynchronous execution, we can begin a task and proceed to the next without waiting for the first one to complete. This way, while one task is waiting (such as waiting for a response from our Spark job), the program can continue with other tasks.

That's precisely what we do when we implement deferrable tasks. Instead of managing these lengthy tasks with a worker, we shift (defer) them to the triggerer, which can handle a large number of deferred tasks simultaneously. We can assign a single Airflow component—the triggerer—to manage hundreds or thousands of tasks in parallel instead of handling them one at a time with a worker, resulting in significant savings of compute resources. Figure 9.6 shows this schematically, with the workers no longer directly involved.

How does the triggerer manage multiple tasks simultaneously within a single component? The triggerer doesn't perform the tasks itself. Rather, it's designed to delegate task execution to external systems and monitor their status in an asynchronous manner. Unlike a synchronous system in which a worker performs a task and waits for its completion before starting the next, the triggerer executes the next task immediately without

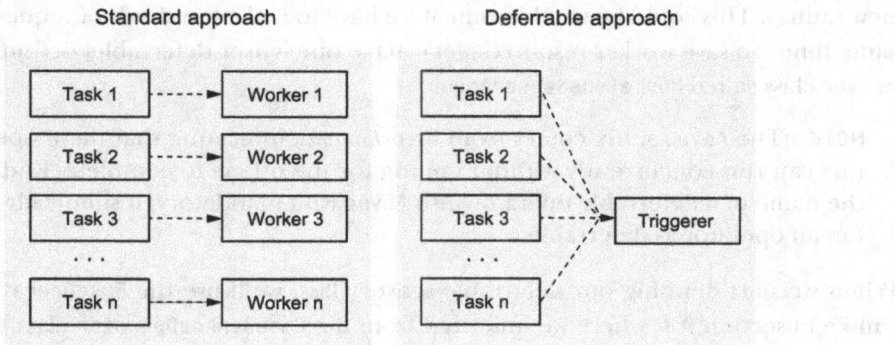

Figure 9.6 In the standard (nondeferrable) method of running tasks, each task must be assigned to a worker. The deferrable approach transfers all the tasks to the triggerer.

waiting for the completion of the previous one. Some restrictions apply, however. Notably, the processes we want to defer must be capable of running asynchronously using Python's `asyncio` package, which could be a implementation limitation. The popular Python library boto3, for example, which interacts with Amazon Web Services (AWS), doesn't natively support asynchronous requests.

Defining deferrable operators: Single vs. separate class

You usually implement a deferrable operator in one of two ways:

- *Adding a Boolean parameter named* `deferrable` *and implementing both deferrable and nondeferrable logic in a single class*—This approach can be cumbersome in certain situations, however, because it increases code complexity by defining both approaches in a single class. For a sensor, for example, you'd have to define a `poke` method to support rescheduling at the same time that you define the deferrable functionality in the same class.
- *Creating a separate class dedicated to the deferrable logic*—This approach is simpler because it allows you to separate the logic into a single class.

9.5.2   *Running the Movielens sensor asynchronously*

In section 9.4, we used a sensor with our custom logic to check whether MovieLens ratings were available for a certain date. We can make that sensor considerably more efficient by writing it as a deferrable operator. This allows us to avoid using a worker every time we check for available ratings.

To understand the point of deferrable operators, suppose that a sensor has to start checking for the ratings at a certain time of day and that it could take up to an hour for the ratings to become available. In the standard approach, even with rescheduling, we'd have to use a worker every time the sensor made a request to the API to check for new ratings. This could be troublesome if we have to make hundreds of requests at the same time. To save worker resources, let's make our sensor deferrable, defining a new sensor class called `MovielensSensorAsync`.

NOTE The `Async` suffix comes from *asynchronous*, indicating that these operators can run concurrently without waiting for the others to complete. Ending the name of a deferrable operator with `Async` isn't mandatory; it simply identifies an operator as deferrable.

When we start defining our deferrable sensor class, we'll use the `BaseOperator` class, unlike in section 9.4, where we inherited from the `BaseSensorOperator` class. We'll do this because (as previously discussed) we no longer require the poke functionality from the sensor base class.

One thing that doesn't change is the initialization of the `sensor` class. We define our initialization parameters using the `__init__` method as we did before.

Listing 9.31   Class definition of a custom deferrable sensor

```
class MovielensSensorAsync(BaseOperator):                    ◀─────┐
                                                                   │  The deferrable sensor also
    template_fields = ("_start_date", "_end_date")                 │  inherits from the BaseOperator.

    def __init__(
            self,
            conn_id:str,
            start_date:str=f"{{data_interval_start | ds}}",
            end_date:str=f"{{data_interval_end | ds}}",
            sleep_interval:int = 30,
            **kwargs
    ):                                               ◀──┐  Initializes all relevant parameters
        super().__init__(**kwargs)
        self._sleep_interval = sleep_interval
        self._conn_id = conn_id
        self._start_date = start_date
        self._end_date = end_date
        self._timeout = kwargs.get('execution_timeout')
```

Things start to change when we define the deferrable functionality. Rather than implement a `poke` method, we define the sensor functionality in the `execute` method as we did for a regular operator in chapter 8. But here, we do something new: instead of handling the execution logic directly, we call a `defer` method, which moves the execution of our task to the triggerer (figure 9.7).

As you see in figure 9.7, the `defer` method also takes a `method_name` parameter. This method (called `execution_complete` in the figure) defines what should happen when the task completes. Given the requirements of our example, the `execute_complete` method provides a log message when the triggerer finishes its job, informing us that it found ratings for the given interval. In addition, we define a `timeout` parameter to

```
DAG(...):
```

Scheduler

```
task = MovielensSensorAsync()
```

⏱ Run time < 1 sec

①

```
class MovielensSensorAsync(BaseOperator):
```

④

Worker

```
+ execute(self,...):
    self.defer(
      trigger=MovielensTrigger(...),
      method_name='execute_complete',
    )

+ execute_complete(self,...):
    # Executes post-task action
```

⏱ Run time < 1 sec

②

```
class MovielensTrigger(BaseTrigger):
```

Triggerer

```
+ serialize(self):

+ async run(self):
    # Runs workflow in external system
```

⏱ Run time ~ 1 hour

③

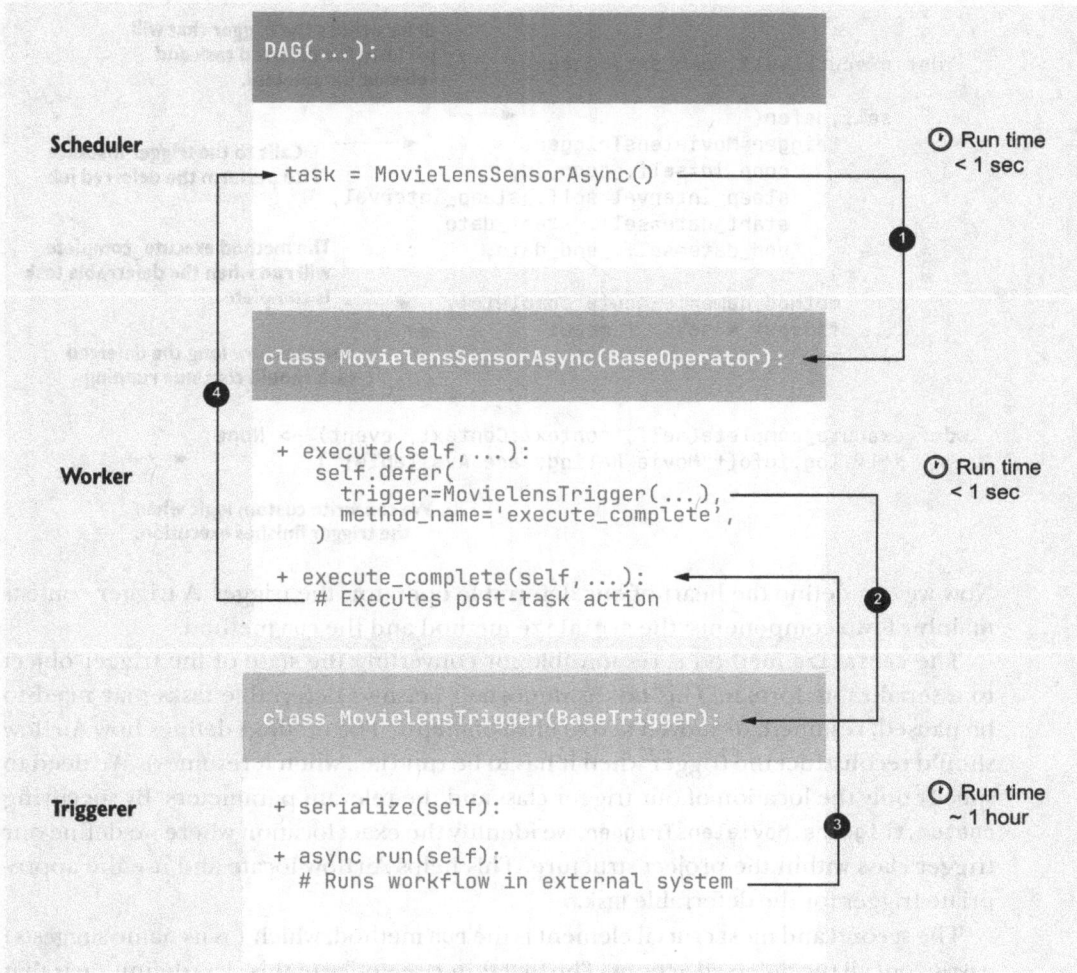

Figure 9.7 Deferrable sensor execution sequence. Task execution begins in the scheduler. When the task is ready to run, the execution of the sensor moves to a worker (1). The worker passes the execution of the deferred task to the triggerer (2), using the `defer` method. The triggerer spends most of the run time waiting for the external task to complete. When it finds new records, the triggerer returns the execution to the worker (3). The worker runs any remaining commands defined in the `execute_complete` method. Finally, the scheduler (4) marks the task as successful and proceeds with the execution of any downstream tasks.

control what happens if our sensor doesn't find data. If our deferred task runs for more than 60 minutes, a timeout exception occurs, and our task fails.

Listing 9.32 Custom deferrable sensor

```
class MovielensSensorAsync(BaseOperator):

    def __init__( self, ...):
```

```
...

def execute(self, context:Context):

    self.defer(
        trigger=MovielensTrigger(
            conn_id=self._conn_id,
            sleep_interval=self._sleep_interval,
            start_date=self._start_date,
            end_date=self._end_date,
        ),
        method_name='execute_complete',
        timeout = self._timeout
    )

def execute_complete(self, context:Context, event) -> None:
    self.log.info(f"Movie Ratings are Available!")
```

defer defines the trigger that will perform the deferred task and relevant parameters.

Calls to the trigger instance to perform the deferred job

The method execute_complete will run when the deferrable task is complete.

Specifies how long the deferred task should continue running

We can write custom logic when the trigger finishes execution.

Now we can define the heart of our deferrable operator: the trigger. A trigger consists mainly of two components: the serialize method and the run method.

The serialize method is responsible for converting the state of the trigger object to a serializable format. This task is important because deferrable tasks may need to be paused, resumed, or moved across environments. The method defines how Airflow should reconstruct the trigger when it has to be run (i.e., when it resumes). We need to specify only the location of our trigger class and the relevant parameters. By specifying custom.triggers.MovielensTrigger, we identify the exact location where we define our trigger class within the project structure. This helps Airflow locate and use the appropriate trigger for the deferrable task.

The second and most crucial element is the run method, which (as its name suggests) carries out all the deferred actions. The first thing we notice in this class definition is that we're dealing with an asynchronous method. This method is particularly useful when we need to wait for certain operations to finish without stopping the entire workflow.

In this case, the function uses await asyncio.sleep()to pause for a few seconds before retrying the request to check for movie ratings within the specified date range. If a StopIteration exception occurs, indicating that no ratings were found, it waits for a specified interval (in self.check_interval) before trying again. On the other hand, If the API call returns some data, it logs a message indicating success and sets found_records to True, breaking out of the loop and returning execution to the sensor.

The run method is where the asynchronous magic happens. By using the async/ await pattern, we're telling Python that the 30-second wait can be performed asynchronously. Note, however, that this part of the run function is the only one that runs asynchronously. Therefore, if we don't include async logic in our trigger, we won't benefit at all from the deferrable functionality. Also, it's important not to include any heavy logic in the non-asynchronous part of the run function to avoid disrupting the asynchronous flow of our function. The next listing shows the implementation of our trigger.

Listing 9.33 Defining a custom trigger class

```
class MovielensTrigger(BaseTrigger):
    def __init__(self,
                 conn_id,
                 start_date,
                 end_date,
                 sleep_interval,

    ):
        super().__init__()
        self._sleep_interval = sleep_interval
        self._conn_id = conn_id
        self._start_date = start_date
        self._end_date = end_date

    def serialize(self):
        return ("custom.triggers.MovielensTrigger", {     ◀── Points to the location
                "sleep_interval": self._sleep_interval,          in which the custom
                "conn_id": self._conn_id,                        trigger is defined
                "start_date": self._start_date,
                "end_date": self._end_date,
        }
    )

    async def run(self):                              ◀── The run method is defined
        with MovielensHook(self._conn_id) as hook:        asynchronously.
            found_records = True                 ◀── The hook allows us to connect
            while not found_records:                  to the Movielens DB.
                try:                         ◀── Loops if we find no new records
                    next(
                        hook.get_ratings(          ◀── Checks the DB for
                        start_date=self._start_date,    records for that day
                        end_date=self._end_date,
                        batch_size=1
                        )
                    )
                                              If we find at least one record,
                                                  we can stop the loop.
                    self.log.info(f"Found ratings for {self._start_date)")
                    found_records = True       ◀──

                except StopIteration:       ◀── If StopIteration is raised, we know
                    self.log.info(              that we didn't find any records.
               f"Didn't find ratings for {self._start_date}")
                    self.log.info("waiting...")        ◀── Waits and retries

                await asyncio.sleep(self.check_interval)   ◀── Generates a
                                                               unique identifier
        yield TriggerEvent(str(uuid.uuid4()))    ◀──          for the event
```

Now we can implement this deferrable sensor in our DAG, as shown in the following listing (dags/05_deferrable_sensor.py). The sensor will wait for new ratings without wasting a worker's resources while it's executing.

Listing 9.34 Using the sensor to wait for ratings

```python
from custom.operators import MovielensFetchRatingsOperator
from custom.sensors import MovielensSensorAsync

with DAG(
    dag_id="05_deferrable_sensor",
    start_date=datetime(2023, 1, 1),
    end_date=datetime(2023, 1, 10),
    schedule=CronDataIntervalTimetable("@daily", "UTC"),
    catchup=True
):
    wait_for_ratings = MovielensSensorAsync(
        task_id="wait_for_ratings",
        conn_id="movielens",
        start_date="{{data_interval_start | ds}}",
        end_date="{{data_interval_end | ds}}",
        execution_timeout= timedelta(minutes=60),
        )

    fetch_ratings = MovielensFetchRatingsOperator(
        task_id="fetch_ratings",
        conn_id="movielens",
        start_date="{{data_interval_start | ds}}",
        end_date="{{data_interval_end | ds}}",
        output_path=
        "/data/custom_sensor/{{data_interval_start | ds}}.json"
)

    wait_for_ratings >> fetch_ratings
```

Sensor that defers the waits for new records to be available to the triggerer

The deferrable sensor times out after 60 seconds.

The operator runs after the sensor detects new records in the database.

At run time, the Airflow UI marks the `wait_for_ratings` task as deferred while it waits for the trigger to detect new records (figure 9.8). Downstream tasks won't run until the sensor finds available data for the given interval, which is consistent with the sensor behavior that we expect.

Figure 9.8 Deferred task in the Airflow UI

9.6 *Packaging the components*

Up to now, we've relied on including our custom components in a subpackage within the dags directory to make them importable by our DAGs. This approach isn't necessarily ideal, however, if we want to use these components in other projects, share them with other people, or perform more rigorous testing on them.

A better approach to distributing components is putting your code in a Python package. Although this approach requires a bit of extra setup, it enables you to install your components in your Airflow environment the way you would any other package. Moreover, keeping the code separate from your DAGs allows you to set up a proper continuous integration/continuous delivery (CI/CD) process for your custom code and makes it easier to share and/or collaborate on the code.

9.6.1 *Bootstrapping a Python package*

Unfortunately, packaging can be complicated in Python. In this case, we'll focus on the most basic example of Python packaging, which involves using setuptools to create a simple Python package. Our aim is to create a small package called airflow_movielens that will contain the hook, operator, and sensor classes we wrote in previous sections.

NOTE In-depth discussions of Python packaging and packaging approaches are beyond the scope of this book and are explained more elaborately in many Python books and/or online articles.

To start building the package, create a directory:

```
$ mkdir -p airflow-movielens
$ cd airflow-movielens
```

Next, start including the code by creating the base of the package. To do this, create a src subdirectory in the airflow-movielens directory; then create a directory called airflow_movielens (the name of our package) inside the src directory. To make airflow_movielens a package, also create an __init__.py file inside the directory:

```
$ mkdir -p src/airflow_movielens
$ touch src/airflow_movielens/__init__.py
```

NOTE Technically, the __init__.py file is no longer necessary with PEP 420, but we like to be explicit.

Next, start including code by creating the hooks.py, sensors.py, and operators.py files in the airflow_movielens directory and copying the implementations of the custom hook, sensor, and operator classes to their respective files. When you're done, you should have a result something like this:

```
$ tree airflow-movielens/
airflow-movielens/
```

```
└── src
    └── airflow_movielens
        ├── __init__.py
        ├── hooks.py
        ├── operators.py
        └── sensors.py
```

Now all you have to do to turn this set of files into a package is include a `setup.py` file, which tells `setuptools` how to install it. A basic `setup.py` file typically looks something like the following listing (package/airflow-movielens/setup.py).

Listing 9.35 Example `setup.py` file

```python
#!/usr/bin/env python
import setuptools

requirements = ["apache-airflow", "requests"]          ◀── List of Python packages that
                                                            our package depends on

setuptools.setup(                                       ◀── Name, version, and
    name="airflow_movielens",                               description of our package
    version="0.1.0",
    description="Hooks, sensors and operators for the Movielens API.",
    author="Anonymous",
    author_email="anonymous@example.com",               ◀── Author details (metadata)
    install_requires=requirements,
    packages=setuptools.find_packages("src"),
    package_dir={"": "src"},
    url="https://github.com/example-repo/airflow_movielens",   ◀──
    license="MIT license",   ◀──                        Package home page
)                            License of the code
Informs setuptools                                      Tells setuptools where to look
about our dependencies                                  for our package's Python files
```

The most important part of this file is the call to `setuptools.setup`, which gives `setuptools` detailed metadata about our package. The most important fields in this call are as follows:

- `name`—Defines the name of the package (what it will be called when installed).
- `version`—Defines the version number of the package.
- `install_requires`—Defines a list of dependencies required by the package.
- `packages/package_dir`—Tells `setuptools` which packages to include during installation and where to look for them. In this case, we use a `src` directory layout for our Python package. (For more details on `src`- versus non-`src`-based layouts, see the blog post at https://mng.bz/4nx5.)

`setuptools` also allows you to include many optional fields to describe your package, including the following:

- `author`—The name of the package author (you).
- `author_email`—Contact details for the author.

- description—A short, readable description of the package (typically, one line). You can provide a longer description by using the long_description argument.
- url—Where to find your package online.
- license—The license under which your package code is released (if any).

TIP For a full list of parameters that you can pass to setuptools.setup, please refer to the setuptools documentation (https://setuptools.pypa.io/en/latest).

In the setup.py implementation, we tell setuptools that our dependencies include apache-airflow and requests, that our package should be called airflow_movielens with a version of 0.1, and that it should include files from the airflow_movielens package situated in the src directory while including some extra details about ourselves and the package description license. When we finish writing setup.py, our package should look like the following:

```
$ tree airflow-movielens
airflow-movielens
├── setup.py
└── src
    └── airflow_movielens
        ├── __init__.py
        ├── hooks.py
        ├── operators.py
        └── sensors.py
```

TIP More elaborate packages typically include tests, documentation, and so on, which we don't describe here. If you want to see extensive setups for Python packaging, we recommend checking out the many templates available online (e.g., https://github.com/audreyr/cookiecutter-pypackage), which provide excellent starting points for bootstrapping Python package development.

9.6.2 *Installing the package*

Now that you have your basic airflow_movielens Python package, you should be able to install airflow_movielens in your Python environment. You can try running pip to install the package in your active environment:

```
$ python -m pip install ./airflow-movielens
Looking in indexes: https://pypi.org/simple
Processing ./airflow-movielens
Collecting apache-airflow
...
Successfully installed ... airflow-movielens-0.1.0 ...
```

When pip is done installing the package and dependencies, you can check whether your package was installed by starting Python and trying to import one of the classes from the package:

```
$ python
Python 3.10.11 (main, Jul  4 2023, 11:24:19) [GCC 11.3.0] on linux
Type "help", "copyright", "credits" or "license" for more information.
>>> from airflow_movielens.hooks import MovielensHook
>>> MovielensHook
<class 'airflow_movielens.hooks.MovielensHook'>
```

NOTE Deploying your package to your Airflow environment shouldn't require much more effort than installing your package in Airflow's Python environment. Depending on your setup, however, make sure that your package and all its dependencies are installed in all the environments Airflow uses (that is, the scheduler, web server, and worker environments).

9.6.3   *Sharing the package with others*

To share your custom operators with others, you have a few options. If you want to share your package directly, you can distribute it by installing directly from a GitHub repository,

```
$ python -m pip install git+https://github.com/...
```

using a pip package feed such as PyPI (or a private feed),

```
$ python -m pip install airflow_movielens
```

or installing from a file-based location (as you initially did here). In the latter case, make sure that the Airflow environment can access the directory in which you want to install the package.

Another option is contributing your custom operators to an existing open source Airflow provider. This approach is preferred if your operator adds functionality to an existing integration. Contributing in this manner is the best way to give back to the community because more people will be able to find and use your operator.

The final option is creating a new provider. This approach, however, requires a lot more work and also means that the provider needs to distinguish itself from existing ones.

Summary

- You can extend Airflow's built-in functionality by building custom components that fit your specific use case. In our experience, custom operators are particularly powerful in two use cases:
  - Running tasks on systems that Airflow doesn't natively support (new cloud services, databases, and so on)
  - Providing operators, sensors, and/or hooks for common operations so that they're easy for members of your team to implement across DAGs

This list is by no means exhaustive; you may want to build your own components in many other situations.

- In Airflow, you can create components by defining Python classes and incorporating custom logic. These components can be imported and used in other DAGs to achieve any custom functionality that your Airflow pipeline requires.
- Custom hooks allow you to interact with systems that don't have built-in Airflow support.
- You can create custom operators to perform tasks that are specific to your workflows and aren't covered by built-in operators.
- Custom sensors allow you to build components for waiting on external events.
- Deferrable operators in Airflow can defer tasks, freeing Airflow workers during waiting periods. This approach is particularly useful when a task has to wait for an external system to complete a process.
- The triggerer is an Airflow component that's responsible for managing deferred tasks. Whereas a worker in Airflow handles one task at a time, a triggerer can manage multiple deferred tasks asynchronously, making the process of managing workers more efficient.
- Although many operators have a deferrable version, you can create your own custom deferrable operators if your workflow requires a unique logic implementation.
- To incorporate deferrable functionality, you could integrate both deferrable and nondeferrable logic into a single class or create separate classes in which each class implements either deferrable or nondeferrable logic. Both approaches are valid; the choice depends on the complexity and needs of the implementation.
- You can structure code containing custom operators, hooks, sensors, and so on by implementing them in a distributable Python library. Custom hooks, operators, and sensors must be installed with their dependencies on your Airflow cluster before they can be used, which can be tricky if you don't have permission to install software on the cluster or have software with conflicting dependencies.
- Some people prefer to rely on generic operators such as the built-in `Docker -Operator` and the `KubernetesPodOperator` to execute their tasks. An advantage of this approach is that you can keep your Airflow installation lean because Airflow is coordinating only containerized jobs; you can keep all dependencies of specific tasks with the container. We'll focus on this approach in chapter 11.

10
Testing

Up to now, we've focused on building data pipelines with Airflow. But how do you ensure that the code you've written is valid before deploying it into a production system? As in any software development process, testing your DAGs is a crucial step toward ensuring that they function correctly in both normal situations (the "happy" flow) and edge cases.

In this chapter, we explore testing in Airflow. This topic is often regarded as a tricky one due to the interconnectedness of data pipelines with external systems, which can make pipelines difficult to test. That's no excuse to skip writing tests, however. We'll show you how to write effective tests for your pipelines, resulting in more reliable systems.

10.1 Getting started with testing

Tests can be applied on various levels. Small individual units of work (i.e., single functions) can be tested with unit tests. Although unit tests may validate correct behavior, they don't validate the behavior of a system composed of multiple units. For this purpose, we write integration tests, which validate the behavior of multiple components together. In testing literature, the next level of testing is acceptance testing (evaluating fit with business requirements), which doesn't apply to this chapter. Here, we cover unit and integration testing.

Throughout this chapter, we demonstrate various code snippets written with `pytest` (https://pytest.org). Although Python has a built-in framework for testing named `unittest`, `pytest` is one of the most popular third-party frameworks for testing features such as fixtures, which we'll be using in this chapter. No previous knowledge of `pytest` is necessary.

Because the supporting code for this book lives on GitHub, we'll demonstrate a continuous integration/continuous delivery (CI/CD) pipeline running tests with GitHub Actions (https://github.com/features/actions), the CI/CD system that integrates with GitHub. With the ideas and code from the GitHub Actions examples, you should be able to get your CI/CD pipeline running in any system. All popular CI/CD systems—GitLab, Bitbucket, Microsoft Azure DevOps, Travis CI, and so on—work by defining the pipeline in YAML format in the root of the project directory, which we'll also do in the GitHub Actions examples.

10.1.1 Integrity testing all DAGs

In the context of Airflow, the first step in testing generally is a *DAG integrity test*, a term first made known by a blog post titled "Data's Inferno: 7 Circles of Data Testing Hell with Airflow" (http://mng.bz/1rOn). This test verifies all your DAGs for their *integrity* (i.e., validating the correctness of the DAG, confirming that the DAG doesn't cycle, the task IDs in the DAG are unique, and so on). A DAG integrity test often filters simple mistakes. A common mistake while generating tasks in a `for` loop, for example, is using a fixed task ID instead of a dynamically set task ID, which results in each generated task having the same ID. Upon loading DAGs, Airflow performs these checks itself and displays an error if it finds one (figure 10.1). To avoid going through a deployment

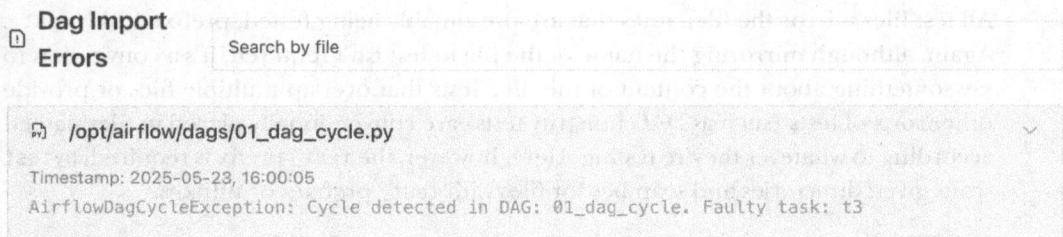

Dag Import Errors

Search by file

/opt/airflow/dags/01_dag_cycle.py

Timestamp: 2025-05-23, 16:00:05

AirflowDagCycleException: Cycle detected in DAG: 01_dag_cycle. Faulty task: t3

Figure 10.1 DAG cycle error displayed by Airflow

cycle only to discover in the end that your DAG contains a simple mistake, it's wise to perform DAG integrity tests in your test suite.

The DAG in the following listing (dags/01_dag_cycle.py) would display an error in the UI because there is a cycle from t1 > t2 > t3 > back to t1. This cycle violates the property that a DAG should have finite start and end nodes.

Listing 10.1   Example cycle in a DAG resulting in an error

```
t1 = EmptyOperator(task_id="t1")
t2 = EmptyOperator(task_id="t2")
t3 = EmptyOperator(task_id="t3")

t1 >> t2 >> t3 >> t1
```

Let's catch this error in a DAG integrity test. First, let's install pytest.

Listing 10.2   Installing pytest

```
pip install pytest

Collecting pytest
...............
Installing collected packages: pytest
Successfully installed pytest-8.3.2
```

This code creates a pytest command-line interface (CLI) utility. To see all available options, run pytest --help. For now, you don't need to know all the options; knowing that you can run tests with pytest [file/directory] (where the directory contains test files) is enough.

Let's create such a file. A convention is to create a tests/ folder at the root of the project that holds all the tests and mirrors the directory structure of the rest of the project. If your project structure is like the one shown in figure 10.2, the tests/ directory structure would look like figure 10.3.

> **NOTE** pytest calls this structure "tests outside application code." The other structure that pytest supports stores test files directly next to application code, which it calls "tests as part of your application code."

All test files mirror the filenames that are presumably being tested, prefixed with test_. Again, although mirroring the name of the file to test isn't required, it's a convention to say something about the content of the file. Tests that overlap multiple files or provide other sorts of tests (such as DAG integrity tests) are conventionally placed in files named according to whatever they're testing. Here, however, the test_ prefix is required; pytest scans given directories and searches for files with test_ prefixes or suffixes.

> **NOTE** You can configure test discovery settings in pytest if you want to support test files named check_* =, for example.

```
├── dags
│   ├── dag1.py
│   ├── dag2.py
│   └── dag3.py
├── mypackage
│   ├── airflow
│   │   ├── hooks
│   │   │   ├── __init__.py
│   │   │   └── movielens_hook.py
│   │   ├── operators
│   │   │   ├── __init__.py
│   │   │   └── movielens_operator.py
│   │   └── sensors
│   │       ├── __init__.py
│   │       └── movielens_sensors.py
│   └── movielens
│       ├── __init__.py
│       └── utils.py
```

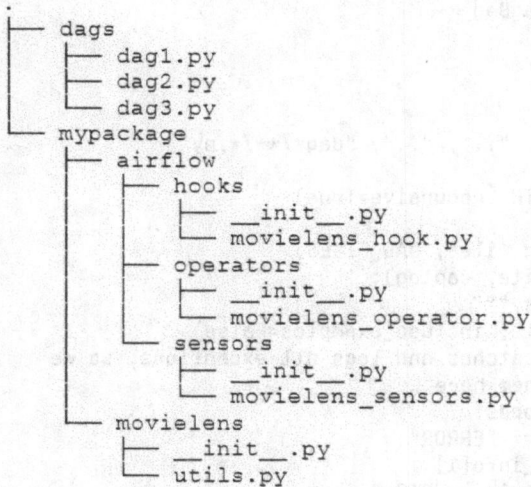

Figure 10.2 Example Python package structure

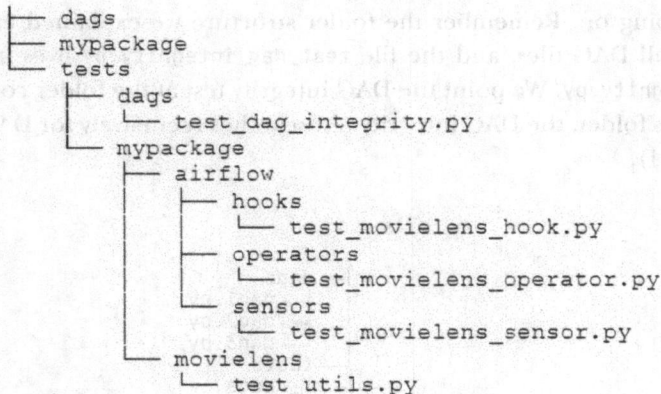

```
├── dags
├── mypackage
└── tests
    ├── dags
    │   └── test_dag_integrity.py
    └── mypackage
        ├── airflow
        │   ├── hooks
        │   │   └── test_movielens_hook.py
        │   ├── operators
        │   │   └── test_movielens_operator.py
        │   └── sensors
        │       └── test_movielens_sensor.py
        └── movielens
            └── test_utils.py
```

Figure 10.3 Test directory structure following the structure in figure 10.2

Also, there are no __init__.py files in the tests/ directory; the directories aren't modules, and tests should be able to run independently without importing one another. pytest scans directories and files and autodiscovers tests; you don't need to create modules with __init__.py files. Next, let's create a file named tests/dags/test_dag_integrity.py.

Listing 10.3 DAG integrity test

```
import glob
import os

import pytest
```

```
from airflow.models import DagBag


DAG_PATH = os.path.join(
    os.path.dirname(__file__), "..", "..", "dags/**/*.py"
)
DAG_FILES = glob.glob(DAG_PATH, recursive=True)

@pytest.mark.parametrize("dag_file", DAG_FILES)
def test_dag_integrity(dag_file, caplog):
    """Test integrity of DAGs."""
    DagBag(dag_folder=dag_file, include_examples=False)
    # The DagBag's function catches and logs all exceptions, so we
    parse the logs to raise them here
    for record in caplog.records:
        if record.levelname == "ERROR":
            raise record.exc_info[1]
        elif "assumed to contain no DAGs" in record.message:
            assert False, f"No DAGs found in {dag_file}"
```

The function named `test_dag_integrity` performs the test. We'll break down the code to explain what's going on. Remember the folder structure we explained earlier? A `dags/` folder holds all DAG files, and the file `test_dag_integrity.py` lives in `tests/dags/test_dag_integrity.py`. We point the DAG integrity test at the folder containing all DAGs. Within this folder, the DAG integrity test searches recursively for DAGs in all `*.py` files (figure 10.4).

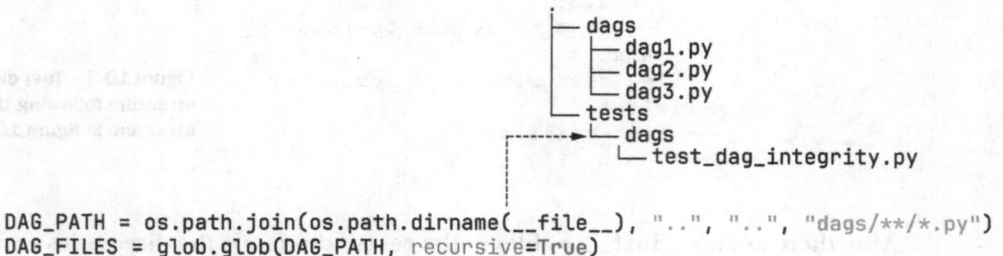

```
├── dags
│   ├── dag1.py
│   ├── dag2.py
│   └── dag3.py
└── tests
    └── dags
        └── test_dag_integrity.py

DAG_PATH = os.path.join(os.path.dirname(__file__), "..", "..", "dags/**/*.py")
DAG_FILES = glob.glob(DAG_PATH, recursive=True)
```

Figure 10.4   DAG_PATH points to the directory that contains all the DAG files.

`dirname()` returns the directory of `test_dag_integrity.py`. We browse two directories up, first to `tests/` and then to the root, and from there, we search for anything matching the pattern `dags/**/*.py`. "`**`" searches recursively, so DAG files in, say, `dags/dir1/dir2/dir3/mydag.py`, will also be found. Finally, the variable `DAG_FILES` holds a list of files in `dags/` that end in `.py`. Next, the decorator `@pytest.mark.parametrize` runs the test for every found Python file (figure 10.5).

```
@pytest.mark.parametrize("dag_file", DAG_FILES)
def test_dag_integrity(dag_file):
```

Run test for every element in DAG_FILES.

Figure 10.5   A parameterized test runs a test for every dag_file.

Now let's look at the content of the test, which uses an internal Airflow object called the DagBag. We won't go into the details of what this object does, but it has a useful function that allows us to load all DAGs from a file path (`tests/dags/01_test_dag_integrity`).

Listing 10.4   The DAG integrity test trying to instantiate every DAG object found

```
DagBag(dag_folder=dag_file, include_examples=False)

for record in caplog.records:
    if record.levelname == "ERROR"
        raise record.exc_info[1]
    elif "assumed to contain no DAGs" in record.message:
        assert False, f"No DAGs found in {dag_file}"
```

Loads all DAGs from a file; doesn't load the Airflow example DAGs

Checks for any errors that occurred while loading

Checks for any files that had no DAGs

After this function runs, we can perform some checks. If the function encounters any incorrect DAGs while parsing, it catches the exceptions thrown and prints certain log messages. First, using the `caplog` built-in fixture, we check whether any DAG errors were thrown. If so, we raise whatever error was initially caught within the DagBag's implementation. If no error occurred, we check for the files that did *not* contain DAGs. Adding this assertion validates all Python files found in /dags if they contain at least one DAG object. Therefore, script utility functions stored in /dags for which no DAG objects are instantiated fail. Whether this is desirable is up to you, but having one directory that holds only DAG files provides a clear separation of concerns.

You can add your own example checks, of course. If you want each DAG name to start with import or export, for example, you can check the dag_ids:

assert dag.dag_id.startswith(("import", "export"))

Now let's run the DAG integrity test. On the command line, run pytest, optionally telling pytest where to search with pytest tests/ to avoid scanning other directories.

Listing 10.5   Output of a pytest run for DAG integrity test

```
$
pytest tests
========================= test session starts =============================
...
```

```
collected 1 item
tests/dags/test_dag_integrity.py F
test_dag_integrity[…data-pipelines-with-airflow-2nd-ed/chapter10/
  tests/dags/../../dags/01_dag_cycle.py] _____

E                 airflow.exceptions.AirflowDagCycleException: Cycle
  detected in DAG: 01_dag_cycle. Faulty task: t3

Chapter10/lib/python3.12/site-packages/airflow/utils/
  dag_cycle_tester.py:50: AirflowDagCycleException
======================= short test summary info==========================
FAILED tests/dags/test_dag_integrity.py::test_dag_integrity
  [.../sources/data-pipelines-with-airflow-2nd-ed/chapter10/tests/
  dags/../../dags/01_dag_cycle.py] -
  airflow.exceptions.AirflowDagCycleException:
  Cycle detected in DAG: 01_dag_cycle. Faulty task: t3
===========================1 failed in 0.41s ============================
```

The result of the test is quite lengthy, but typically, you search for answers at the top and bottom. Near the top, you find the test that failed, and at the bottom, you see why the test failed.

The following listing shows, as expected, that a cycle was detected from t3 to t1. Upon instantiation of DAGs and operators, several other checks are performed out of the box.

Listing 10.6   Exception reason found in listing 10.5

```
airflow.exceptions.AirflowDagCycleException: Cycle detected in DAG:
  01_dag_cycle. Faulty task: t3
```

Suppose that you're using a `BashOperator` but forgot to add the required `bash_command` argument. The DAG integrity test will evaluate all statements in the script and fail when evaluating the `BashOperator`, as shown in the next listing (dags/02_bash_operator_no_command.py). The DAG integrity test encounters an exception and fails (listing 10.8).

Listing 10.7   Faulty instantiation of the `BashOperator`

```
BashOperator(task_id="this_should_fail", dag=dag)
```

Listing 10.8   Exception raised by the faulty instantiation in listing 10.7

```
airflow.exceptions.AirflowException:  missing keyword argument
  'bash_command'
```

10.1.2 *Setting up a CI/CD pipeline*

With the DAG integrity test in place, let's run it automatically in a CI/CD pipeline. As your Airflow deployment matures, it's best practice to move from manual deployment of DAGs to automated testing and deployment with CI/CD. Briefly, a *CI/CD pipeline* is a system that runs predefined scripts when you make a change to your code repository. *CI* denotes checking and validating the changed code to ensure that it complies with coding standards and a test suite. Upon pushing code, for example, you could check with Flake8 (http://flake8.pycqa.org), Pylint (https://www.pylint.org), and Black (https://github.com/psf/black) and then run a series of tests. *CD* indicates deploying the code into production systems automatically, without human interference. The goal is to maximize coding productivity without having to deal with validating and deploying it manually.

A wide range of CI/CD systems is available. Our discussion in this chapter covers GitHub Actions (https://github.com/features/actions); the general ideas should apply to any CI/CD system. Most CI/CD systems start with a YAML configuration file in which a pipeline is defined, a series of steps to execute upon changing code. Each step should complete successfully to make the pipeline successful. Then, in the Git repository, we can enforce rules such as "only merge to master with a successful pipeline."

The pipeline definitions typically live at the root of your project. GitHub Actions requires YAML files stored in a directory: `.github/workflows`. In GitHub Actions, the name of the YAML doesn't matter, so you could create a file named `airflow-tests.yaml` with the following content (`.github/workflows/ci.yaml`).

Listing 10.9 Example GitHub Actions pipeline for Airflow project

```yaml
name: Python static checks and tests

on: [push]

jobs:
  testing:
    runs-on: ubuntu-22.04
    steps:
      - uses: actions/checkout@v4
      - name: Setup Python
        uses: actions/setup-python@v4
        with:
          python-version: 3.12.4

      - name: Install Flake8
        run: pip install flake8
      - name: Run Flake8
        run: flake8

      - name: Install Pylint
        run: pip install pylint
      - name: Run Pylint
        run: find . -name "*.py" | xargs pylint --output-format=colorized

      - name: Install Black
        run: pip install black
      - name: Run Black
```

```
      run: find . -name "*.py" | xargs black --check

    - name: Install dependencies
      run: pip install apache-airflow pytest

    - name: Test DAG integrity
      run: pytest tests/
```

The keywords shown in this YAML file are unique to GitHub Actions, although the general ideas apply to other CI/CD systems. Important things to note are the tasks in GitHub Actions defined below steps. Each step runs a piece of code. Flake8, for example, performs static code analysis and fails if it encounters any issues, such as an unused import. Line 3 states on: [push], which tells GitHub to run the complete CI/CD pipeline every time it receives a push. In a completely automated CD system, the pipeline definition would contain filters for steps on specific branches, such as master, to run steps and deploy code only if the pipeline succeeds on that branch.

10.1.3 *Writing unit tests*

We have a CI/CD pipeline up and running to initially check the validity of all DAGs in the project. It's time to dive a bit deeper into the Airflow code and start unit testing individual bits and pieces.

Looking at the custom components demonstrated in chapter 9, we could test several things to validate correct behavior. There's a saying "Never trust user input," so we'd like to be certain that our code works correctly in both valid and invalid situations.

Take, for example, the MovielensHook from chapter 9, which holds a get_ratings() method. This method accepts several arguments; one argument is batch_size, which controls the size of batches requested from the API. You can imagine that valid input would be any positive number (maybe with some upper limit). But what if the user provides a negative number, such as –3? Maybe the API handles the invalid batch size correctly and returns an HTTP error, such as 400 or 422, but how does the MovielensHook respond to that error? Sensible options might be input-value handling before sending the request or proper error handling if the API returns an error. This behavior is what you want to check.

Let's continue the work of chapter 9 and implement a MovielensPopularity-Operator. This operators returning the top *N* popular movies between two given dates (custom/movielens_popularity_operator.py).

Listing 10.10 Example MovielensPopularityOperator

```python
class MovielensPopularityOperator(BaseOperator):
    def __init__(
        self,
        conn_id,
        start_date,
        end_date,
        min_ratings=4,
```

```
            top_n=5,
            **kwargs,
        ):
            super().__init__(**kwargs)
            self._conn_id = conn_id
            self._start_date = start_date
            self._end_date = end_date
            self._min_ratings = min_ratings
            self._top_n = top_n

        def execute(self, context):
            with MovielensHook(self._conn_id) as hook:
                ratings = hook.get_ratings(          ◁──────┐ Gets raw ratings
                    start_date=self._start_date,
                    end_date=self._end_date,
                )

                rating_sums = defaultdict(Counter)        ◁──  Sums up ratings per movie_id
                for rating in ratings:
                    rating_sums[rating["movieId"]].update(count=1,
                        ↪ rating=rating["rating"])
                                                           Filters min_ratings and calculates
                                                             mean rating per movie_id
                averages = {
                    movie_id: (rating_counter["rating"] /
                        ↪ rating_counter["count"], rating_counter["count"])
                    for movie_id, rating_counter in rating_sums.items()
                    if rating_counter["count"] >= self._min_ratings  ◁───
                }
                return sorted(averages.items(),
                    ↪ key=lambda x: x[1], reverse=True)[:self._top_n]  ◁────┐

                                                    Returns top_n ratings sorted by
                                                    mean ratings and number of ratings
```

How do we test the correctness of this MovielensPopularityOperator? First, we could test it as a whole by running the operator with given values and check whether the result is what we expected. To do this, we need a couple of pytest components to run the operator by itself, outside a live Airflow system and inside a unit test. This test allows us to run the operator under different circumstances and validate whether it behaves correctly.

10.1.4 *Creating the pytest project structure*

pytest requires a test script to be prefixed with test_. As in the directory structure, we also mimic the filenames, so a test for code in movielens_operator.py would be stored in a file named test_movielens_operator.py. Inside this file, we create a function to be called as a test (tests/dags/test_example.py).

Listing 10.11 Example test function testing the BashOperator

```
def test_example():
    task = BashOperator(
        task_id="test",
```

```
        bash_command="echo 'hello!'",
    )
    result = task.execute(context={})
    assert result == "hello!"
```

In this example, we instantiate the BashOperator and call the execute() function, given an empty context (empty dictionary, or *dict*). When Airflow runs the operator in a live setting, several things happen before and after—rendering templated variables, for example, and setting up the task instance context and providing it to the operator. In this test, we're not running in a live setting but calling the execute() method directly. This method is the lowest-level function we can call to run an operator and the one that every operator implements to perform its functionality. We don't need any task instance context to run the BashOperator, so we provide it an empty context. In case the test depends on processing something from the task instance context, we could fill it with the required keys and values. Let's run this test. Listing 10.12 shows the result.

NOTE The xcom_push=True argument returns stdout in the bash_command as a string, which we use in this test to fetch and validate the bash_command. In a live Airflow setup, any object returned by an operator is automatically pushed to XCom.

Listing 10.12 Output of running the test in listing 10.11

```
$ pytest tests/dags/test_example.py::test_example
=========================== test session starts ===========================
platform darwin -- Python 3.12.4, pytest-8.3.2, pluggy-1.5.0
rootdir: .../data-pipelines-with-apache-airflow
collected 1 item

tests/dags/test_example.py .
```

Now let's apply this test to the MovielensPopularityOperator, as shown in the following listing. The first thing that appears is red text telling us that the operator is missing a required argument (listing 10.14).

Listing 10.13 Example test function testing the MovielensPopularityOperator

```
def test_movielenspopularityoperator():
    task = MovielensPopularityOperator(
        task_id="test_id",
        start_date="2015-01-01",
        end_date="2015-01-03",
        top_n=5,
    )
    result = task.execute(context={})
    assert len(result) == 5
```

Listing 10.14 Output of the test in listing 10.13

```
$ pytest tests/dags/custom/test_movielens_popularity_operator.py::
  test_movielenspopularityoperator
========================= test session starts =========================
platform darwin -- Python 3.12.4, pytest-8.3.2, pluggy-1.5.0
rootdir: /.../data-pipelines-with-apache-airflow
collected 1 item

tests/dags /custom/test_movielens_popularity_operator.py F

============================== FAILURES ===============================
_____ test_movielenspopularityoperator _____

mocker = <pytest_mock.plugin.MockFixture object at 0x10fb2ea90>

    def test_movielenspopularityoperator(mocker: MockFixture):
        task = MovielensPopularityOperator(
>           task_id="test_id", start_date="2015-01-01",
    end_date="2015-01-03", top_n=5
        )
E           TypeError: missing keyword argument 'conn_id'

FAILED tests/dags/custom/test_movielens_popularity_operator.py
  ::test_movielenspopularityoperator
  - TypeError: missing keyword argument 'conn_id'
========================= 1 failed in 0.10s =========================
```

We see that the test failed because we're missing the required argument conn_id, which points to the connection ID in the metastore. But how do we provide this argument in a test? Tests should be isolated; they shouldn't be able to influence the results of other tests, so a database shared between tests isn't ideal. In this case, mocking comes to the rescue. *Mocking* is faking certain operations or objects. We could mock the call to a database that's expected to exist in a production setting but not during testing by telling Python to return a certain value instead of making the actual call to the database, which is nonexistent during testing. This allows us to develop and run tests without requiring a connection to external systems. It requires insight into the internals of whatever we're testing, so it sometimes requires us to dive into third-party code.

pytest has a set of supporting plug-ins (not officially by pytest) that ease the use of concepts such as mocking. For this purpose, we can install pytest-mock:

```
pip install pytest-mock
```

pytest-mock is a Python package that provides a tiny convenience wrapper around the built-in mock package. To use it, pass an argument named mocker to your test function as shown in listing 10.5. (tests/dags/custom/test_movielens_popularity_operator.py). This object is the main point of interaction for everything in the pytest-mock package.

NOTE   If you want to type your arguments, mocker is of type pytest_mock
.MockFixture.

Listing 10.15   Mocking an object in a test

```python
def test_movielenspopularityoperator(mocker):
    mocker.patch.object(
        MovielensHook,
        "get_connection",
        return_value=Connection(
            conn_id="test",
            login="airflow",
            password="airflow",
        ),
    )
    task = MovielensPopularityOperator(
        task_id="test_id",
        conn_id="test",
        start_date="2015-01-01",
        end_date="2015-01-03",
        top_n=5,
    )
    result = task.execute(context=None)
    assert len(result) == 3
```

With this code, the get_connection() call on the MovielensHook is *monkey patched* (it's
functionality is substituted at run time to return the given object instead of querying
the Airflow metastore). MovielensHook.get_connection() won't fail when we run the
test because no call to the nonexistent database is made during testing; instead, the
predefined, expected connection object is returned.

Listing 10.16   Substituting a call to an external system in a test

> The mocker object magically exists
> at run time; no import is required.

> Patches an attribute on an
> object with a mock object

```python
def test_movielenspopularityoperator(mocker):
    mock_get = mocker.patch.object(
        MovielensHook,
        "get_connection",
        return_value=Connection(conn_id="test", login="airflow",
password="airflow"),
    )
    task = MovielensPopularityOperator(...)
```

> The object to patch

> The function to patch

> The value to return

This example shows how to substitute a call to an external system (the Airflow metastore) at test time by returning a predefined Connection object. What if you want to
validate that the call is actually made in your test? You can assign the patched object
to a variable that holds several properties collected when calling the patched object.
Suppose that you want to ensure that the get_connection() method is called only once

and that the `conn_id` argument provided to `get_connection()` holds the same value provided to the `MovielensPopularityOperator`.

Listing 10.17 Validating the behavior of a mocked function

```
mock_get = mocker.patch.object(          ◄─────  Assigns mock to variable
    MovielensHook,                               to capture behaviors
    "get_connection",
    return_value=Connection(...),
)
task = MovielensPopularityOperator(..., conn_id="testconn")
task.execute(...)
                                         ◄─────  Asserts that it was
assert mock_get.call_count == 1                  called only once
mock_get.assert_called_with("testconn")  ◄─────  Asserts that it was called
                                                 with the expected conn_id
```

Assigning the return value of `mocker.patch.object` to a variable named `mock_get` captures all calls made to the mocked object and gives us the possibility of verifying the given input, number of calls, and more. In this example, we verify the `call_count` to ensure that the `MovielensPopularityOperator` doesn't unintentionally make multiple calls to the Airflow metastore in a real-world environment. If multiple calls were made, this test would fail because of this assertion. Also, because we provide the `conn_id` `"testconn"` to the `MovielensPopularityOperator`, we expect this `conn_id` to be requested from the Airflow metastore, which we validate with `assert_called_with()`. (A convenience method exists for these two asserts: `assert_called_once_with()`.) The `mock_get` object holds more properties to verify, such as a called property to assert whether the object was called any number of times (figure 10.6).

NOTE The screen shot in figure 10.6 was taken using the Python debugger in PyCharm.

```
∨ ⊟ mock_get = {MagicMock: 0} <MagicMock name='get_connection' id='4421569184'>
     ₀¹ call_args = {NoneType} None
   > ⊟ call_args_list = {_CallList: 0} []
     ₀¹ call_count = {int} 0
     ₀¹ called = {bool} False
   > ⊟ method_calls = {_CallList: 0} []
   > ⊟ mock_calls = {_CallList: 2} [call.__len__(), call.__len__(), call.shape.__len__()]
   > ⊟ return_value = {Connection} test
   > ⊟ shape = {MagicMock: 0} <MagicMock name='get_connection.shape' id='4414677616'>
     ₀¹ side_effect = {NoneType} None
   > ⚡ Protected Attributes
```

Figure 10.6 `mock_get` contains several properties that we can use to validate behavior.

One of the biggest pitfalls with mocking in Python is mocking the incorrect object. In the example code, we're mocking the get_connection() method. This method is called on the MovielensHook, which inherits from the BaseHook (airflow.hooks.base package. The get_connection() method is defined on the BaseHook. Intuitively, therefore, we'd probably mock BaseHook.get_connection(). This would be incorrect, however. The correct way to mock in Python is to mock the location where the method is being called, not where it's defined. Listing 10.18 shows the code.

> **NOTE** The Python documentation explains this approach (https://mng.bz/ Qwj1). It's also demonstrated at https://mng.bz/X7Bl.

Listing 10.18   Paying attention to the correct import location when mocking in Python

```
from chapter10.dags.custom.movielens_hook
  import MovielensHook                          ◀── We must import the
from chapter10.dags.custom.movielens_popularity_operator     method to mock from
  import MovielensPopularityOperator            where it's called.

def test_movielenspopularityoperator(mocker):
    mock_get = mocker.patch.object(
        MovielensHook,
        "get_connection",
        return_value=Connection(...),
    )                                     Inside the Movielens-PopularityOperator
    task = MovielensPopularityOperator(...)  ◀── code, MovielensHook.get_connection()
                                             is called.
```

10.1.5 *Testing with files on disk*

Consider an operator that reads one file holding a list of JSONs and writes them to CSV format (figure 10.7). The operator for this operation could look like listing 10.19 (custom/json_to_csv_operator.py).

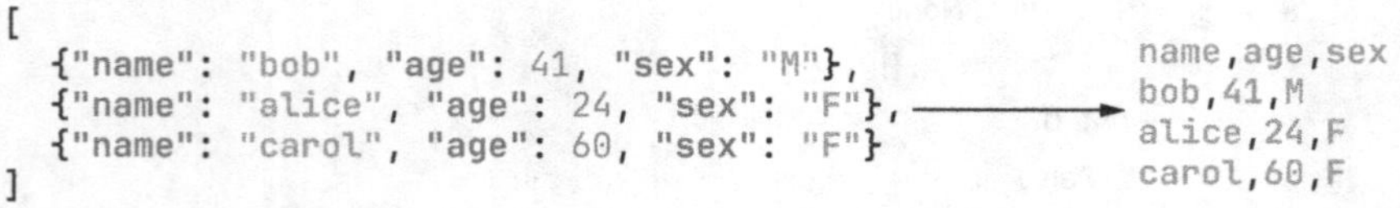

```
[
  {"name": "bob", "age": 41, "sex": "M"},                name,age,sex
  {"name": "alice", "age": 24, "sex": "F"},   ────────▶  bob,41,M
  {"name": "carol", "age": 60, "sex": "F"}               alice,24,F
]                                                         carol,60,F
```

Figure 10.7   Converting JSON to CSV format

Listing 10.19   Example operator using local disk

```
class JsonToCsvOperator(BaseOperator):
    def __init__(self, input_path, output_path, **kwargs):
        super().__init__(**kwargs)
```

```
        self._input_path = input_path
        self._output_path = output_path

    def execute(self, context):
        with open(self._input_path, "r") as json_file:
            data = json.load(json_file)

        columns = {key for row in data for key in row.keys()}

        with open(self._output_path, mode="w") as csv_file:
            writer = csv.DictWriter(csv_file, fieldnames=columns)
            writer.writeheader()
            writer.writerows(data)
```

This `JsonToCsvOperator` takes two input arguments: the input (JSON) path and the output (CSV) path. To test this operator, we could store a static file in our test directory to use as input for the test, but where do we store the output file?

In Python, we have the `tempfile` module for tasks involving temporary storage. It leaves no remainders on the filesystem because the directory and its contents are wiped after use. Once again, pytest provides a convenient access point to this module named `tmp_dir` (gives the `os.path` object) and `tmp_path` (gives the `pathlib` object). Let's view an example using `tmp_path`.

Listing 10.20   Testing using temporary paths

```
import csv
import json
from pathlib import Path

from custom.json_to_csv_operator import JsonToCsvOperator

def test_json_to_csv_operator(tmp_path: Path):          ◄─── Uses tmp_path fixture
    input_path = tmp_path / "input.json"
    output_path = tmp_path / "output.csv"               ◄─── Defines paths

    input_data = [
        {"name": "bob", "age": "41", "sex": "M"},
        {"name": "alice", "age": "24", "sex": "F"},
        {"name": "carol", "age": "60", "sex": "F"},       ◄─── Saves input file
    ]
    with open(input_path, "w") as f:
        f.write(json.dumps(input_data))

    operator = JsonToCsvOperator(
        task_id="test",
        input_path=input_path,
        output_path=output_path,
    )
    operator.execute(context={})                         ◄─── Executes JsonToCsvOperator
```

```
    with open(output_path, "r") as f:
        reader = csv.DictReader(f)              Reads output file
        result = [dict(row) for row in reader]

    assert result == input_data    ◄──────── Asserts content
                                              ◄─────
                                              After the test, the tmp_path
                                              and its contents are removed.
```

When the test starts, a temporary directory is created. The `tmp_path` argument refers to a function that's executed for each test in which it's called. In pytest, these kinds of functions are called *fixtures* (https://docs.pytest.org/en/stable/fixture.html). Although fixtures bear some resemblance to `unittest`'s `setUp()` and `tearDown()` methods, they provide greater flexibility because fixtures can be mixed and matched. One fixture could initialize a temporary directory for all tests in a class, for example, while another fixture initializes for a single test. (Search for *pytest scope* if you're interested in learning how to share fixtures across tests.)

The default scope of fixtures is every test function. We can see this by printing the path and running different tests or even the same test twice:

```
print(tmp_path.as_posix())
```

This test prints

- tests/custom/test_json_to_csv_operator.py /private/var/folders/y5/
  wjlkprcx3hnc32tvfych5hl40000gn

  /T/pytest-of-daniel/pytest-2/test_json_to_csv_operator0

- tests/custom/test_json_to_csv_operator.py /private/var/folders/y5/
  wjlkprcx3hnc32tvfych5hl40000gn

  /T/pytest-of-daniel/pytest-3/test_json_to_csv_operator0

We can use other fixtures; also, pytest fixtures have many features that we don't discuss in this book. If you're serious about all pytest features, see the documentation (https://docs.pytest.org/en/stable).

10.2   *Working with external systems*

Suppose that we're working with an operator that connects to a database, such as `Movielens-ToPostgresOperator`, which reads MovieLens ratings and writes the results to a PostgreSQL database. This use case is common: a source provides data as it is at the time of the request but can't provide historical data, and people want to build up the history of the source. Suppose that John gave *The Avengers* a four-star rating in Movie-Lens yesterday but changed his rating to five stars today. If you check the MovieLens API today, it returns only John's five-star rating.

Once a day, an Airflow job could fetch all data and store the daily export together with the time of writing. The operator for such an operation could look like the following listing (`custom/movielens_to_postgres_operator.py`).

Listing 10.21 Example operator connecting with a PostgreSQL database

```python
from airflow.models import BaseOperator
from airflow.providers.postgres.hooks.postgres
    import PostgresHook


from custom.movielens_hook import MovielensHook


class MovielensToPostgresOperator(BaseOperator):
    template_fields = ("_start_date", "_end_date", "_insert_query")

    def __init__(
        self,
        movielens_conn_id,
        start_date,
        end_date,
        postgres_conn_id,
        insert_query,
        **kwargs,
    ):
        super().__init__(**kwargs)
        self._movielens_conn_id = movielens_conn_id
        self._start_date = start_date
        self._end_date = end_date
        self._postgres_conn_id = postgres_conn_id
        self._insert_query = insert_query

    def execute(self, context):
        with MovielensHook(self._movielens_conn_id) as movielens_hook:
            ratings = list(movielens_hook.get_ratings(
                start_date=self._start_date,
                end_date=self._end_date),
        )

        postgres_hook = PostgresHook(
            postgres_conn_id=self._postgres_conn_id
        )
        insert_queries = [
            self._insert_query.format(",".join([str(_[1])
                for _ in sorted(rating.items())]))
            for rating in ratings
        ]
        postgres_hook.run(insert_queries)
```

Let's break down the execute() method. It connects the MovieLens API and PostgreSQL database by fetching data and transforming the results into queries for PostgreSQL (figure 10.8).

How do we test this, assuming that we can't access our production PostgreSQL database from our laptops? Luckily, it's easy to spin a local PostgreSQL database for testing with Docker. Several Python packages provide convenient functions for controlling

Get all ratings between given start_date and end_date using MovielensHook.

Create PostgresHook for communicating with PostgreSQL.

```
def execute(self, context):
    with MovielensHook(self._movielens_conn_id) as movielens_hook:
        ratings = list(movielens_hook.get_ratings(start_date=self._start_date, end_date=self._end_date))

    postgres_hook=PostgresHook(postgres_conn_id=self._postgres_conn_id)
    insert_queries=[
        self._insert_query.format(",".join([str(_[1]) for _ in sorted(rating.items())]))
        for rating in ratings
    ]
    postgres_hook.run(insert_queries)
```

Create list of insert queries. Ratings return as a list of dicts:
```
{'movieId': 51935, 'userId': 21127, 'rating': 4.5,  'timestamp': 1419984001}
```

For each rating, we

1. Sort by key for deterministic results:
```
sorted(ratings[0].items())
[('movieId', 51935), ('rating', 4.5), ('timestamp',  1419984001), ('userId', 21127)]
```

2. Create list of values, cast to string for .join():
```
[str(_[1]) for _ in sorted(ratings[0].items())]
['51935', '4.5', '1419984001', '21127']
```

3. Join all values to string with comma:
```
",".join([str(_[1]) for _ in sorted(rating.items())])
'51935,4.5,1419984001,21127'
```

4. Provide result to insert_query.format(...):
```
self._insert_query.format(",".join([str(_[1]) for _ in sorted(rating.items())]))
'INSERT INTO movielens (movieId,rating,ratingTimest amp,userId,...) VALUES (51935,4.5,1419984001,21127,  ...)'
```

Figure 10.8   Breakdown of converting JSON data to PostgreSQL queries

Docker containers within the scope of pytest tests. For the following example, we'll use pytest-docker-tools (https://github.com/Jc2k/pytest-docker-tools). This package provides a set of convenient helper functions with which we can create a Docker container for testing.

We won't go into all the details of the package but will demonstrate how to create a sample PostgreSQL container for writing MovieLens results. If the operator works correctly, we should have results written to the PostgreSQL database in the container at the end of the test. Testing with Docker containers allows us to use the real methods of hooks without having to mock calls, the aim being to test as realistically as possible.

First, we install pytest-docker-tools in our environment with pip install pytest_docker_tools. This gives us a few helper functions, such as fetch and container. Then we fetch the container.

Listing 10.22   Fetching a Docker image for testing with pytest_docker_tools

```
from pytest_docker_tools import fetch

postgres_image = fetch(repository="postgres:16-alpine")
```

The fetch function triggers docker pull on the machine on which it's running (and therefore requires Docker to be installed) and returns the pulled image. The fetch function itself is a pytest fixture, which means we can't use it directly but must provide it as a parameter to a test, as shown in the next listing (tests/custom/test_print_image_id.py). Then we can use this image ID to configure and start a PostgreSQL container (listing 10.24).

Listing 10.23 Using a Docker image in a test with `pytest_docker_tools` fixture

```python
from pytest_docker_tools import fetch

postgres_image = fetch(repository="postgres:16-alpine")

def test_call_fixture(postgres_image):
    print(postgres_image.id)
```

Running this test prints

```
Fetching postgres:16-alpine
PASSED                    [100%]
sha256:77e5c8fa46d86943578f5446e2b107d30b9749838be18cb3af69ee2c8abcbd08
```

> **NOTE** To run this code on your machine, make sure that your container environment allows other programs to use the Docker socket. In Docker Desktop, for example, this setting isn't enabled by default.

Listing 10.24 Starting a Docker container for a test with `pytest_docker_tools` fixture

```python
from pytest_docker_tools import container

postgres_container = container(
    image="{postgres_image.id}",
    ports={"5432/tcp": None},
)

def test_call_fixture(postgres_container):
    print(
        f"Running Postgres container named {postgres_container.name} "
        f"on port {postgres_container.ports['5432/tcp'][0]}."
    )
```

The container function in pytest_docker_tools is also a fixture, so we can call it only by providing it as an argument to a test. The function takes several arguments that configure the container to start—in this case, the image ID, which was returned from the fetch() fixture, and the ports to expose. As we do when running Docker containers on the command line, we could also configure environment variables, volumes, and so on.

The ports configuration requires a bit of explanation. Typically, we map a container port to the same port on the host system (i.e., docker run -p 5432:5432 postgres). A container for tests isn't meant to be a container running until infinity, however, and we don't want to conflict with any other ports in use on the host system.

Providing a dict to the `ports` keyword argument, in which keys are container ports and values map to the host system, and leaving the values set to `None` will map the host port to a random open port on the host (like running `docker run -P`). Providing the fixture to a test executes the fixture (i.e., runs the container). Then `pytest-docker -tools` then maps the assigned ports internally on the host system to a `ports` attribute on the fixture itself. `postgres_container.ports['5432/tcp'][0]` gives us the assigned port number on the host, which we can connect to in the test.

To mimic a real database as much as possible, we'll set a username and password and initialize the database with a schema and data to query. We can provide both the username and password to the container fixture, as shown in the following listing. Then we can initialize the database structure and data in `postgres-init.sql` (listing 10.26).

Listing 10.25   Initializing a PostgreSQL container for testing against a real database

```
postgres_image = fetch(repository="postgres:16-alpine")
postgres = container(
    image="{postgres_image.id}",
    environment={
        "POSTGRES_USER": "testuser",
        "POSTGRES_PASSWORD": "testpass",
    },
    ports={"5432/tcp": None},
    volumes={
        os.path.join(os.path.dirname(__file__), "postgres-init.sql"): {
            "bind": "/docker-entrypoint-initdb.d/postgres-init.sql"
        }
    },
)
```

Database structure and data can be initialized in `postgres-init.sql`.

Listing 10.26   Initializing a schema for the test database

```
SET SCHEMA 'public';
CREATE TABLE movielens (
    movieId integer,
    rating float,
    ratingTimestamp integer,
    userId integer,
    scrapeTime timestamp
);
```

In the container fixture, we provide a PostgreSQL username and password via environment variables. This feature of the PostgreSQL Docker image allows us to configure several settings via environment variables. See the PostgreSQL Docker image documentation (https://hub.docker.com/_/postgres) for a list of all environment variables.

Another feature of the Docker image enables us to initialize a container with a startup script by placing a file with the extension `*.sql`, `*.sql.gz`, or `*.sh` in the directory

/docker-entrypoint-initdb.d. These scripts are executed while booting the container, before starting the actual PostgreSQL service, and we can use them to initialize our test container with a table to query. In listing 10.25, we mount a file named postgres-init .sql to the container with the volumes keyword to the container fixture:

```
volumes={
    os.path.join(os.path.dirname(__file__), "postgres-init.sql"): {
        "bind": "/docker-entrypoint-initdb.d/postgres-init.sql"
    }
}
```

We provide a dict in which the keys show the absolute location on the host system. In this case, we saved a file named postgres-init.sql in the same directory as our test script, so os.path.join(os.path.dirname(__file__), "postgres-init.sql") will give us the absolute path to it. The values are also a dict in which the key indicates the mount type (bind) and the value of the location inside the container, which should be in /docker-entrypoint-initdb.d to run the *.sql script when the container boots. Put all this together in a script, and we can finally test against a real PostgreSQL database.

Listing 10.27 Completing the test using a Docker container to test external systems

```
import os

from airflow.models import Connection
from airflow.providers.postgres.hooks.postgres
    import PostgresHook
from pytest_docker_tools import fetch, container

from custom.movielens_hook import MovielensHook
from custom.movielens_to_postgres_operator import
    MovielensToPostgresOperator

postgres_image = fetch(repository="postgres:16-alpine")    ◄──┐ Sets up the
postgres = container(                                           PostgreSQL container

    image="{postgres_image.id}",
    environment={
        "POSTGRES_USER": "testuser",
        "POSTGRES_PASSWORD": "testpass",
    },
    ports={"5432/tcp": None},
    volumes={
        os.path.join(os.path.dirname(__file__), "postgres-init.sql"): {
            "bind": "/docker-entrypoint-initdb.d/postgres-init.sql"
        }
    },
)


def test_movielens_to_postgres_operator(mocker, postgres, test_dag):
```

```
mocker.patch.object(                          ◄────  Mocks some non-PostgreSQL-related
    MovielensHook,                                   things (e.g., the MovieLens API call)
    "get_connection",
    return_value=Connection(
        conn_id="test",
        login="airflow",
        password="airflow",
    ),
)
mocker.patch.object(
    MovielensHook,
    "get_ratings",
    return_value=[
    {"movieId": 1, "rating": 5, "userId": 123,
      "timestamp": 1725299750},
    {"movieId": 2, "rating": 4, "userId": 456,
      "timestamp": 1525299750 }]
)
mocker.patch.object(              ◄────  Hooks up the Postgreshook used in
                                         the DAG so it points to the test
    PostgresHook,                        PostgreSQL container set up above
    "get_connection",
    return_value=Connection(
        conn_id="postgres",
        conn_type="postgres",
        host="localhost",
        login="testuser",
        password="testpass",
        port=postgres.ports["5432/tcp"][0]
    ),
)
task = MovielensToPostgresOperator(
    task_id="test",
    movielens_conn_id="test",
    start_date="{{ data_interval_start | ds }}",
    end_date="{{ data_interval_end | ds}}",
    postgres_conn_id="postgres",
    insert_query=("INSERT INTO movielens
        (movieId,rating,ratingTimestamp,userId,scrapeTime) "
        "VALUES ({0}, '{{ macros.datetime.now() }}')"
    ),
    dag=test_dag,       │  Adds the operator with
)                       └─ insertion query to the test DAG    Validates before running
                                                              anything that the database is
                                                              empty (a precondition check)
pg_hook = PostgresHook()
row_count = pg_hook.get_first("SELECT COUNT(*) FROM movielens")[0]
assert row_count == 0                              ◄──────────────

                                                   Checks whether the task did
task.execute()   ◄────┐  Runs the task            what we wanted it to (inserted
                                                   rows into the database)

row_count = pg_hook.get_first("SELECT COUNT(*) FROM movielens")[0]
assert row_count > 0                               ◄──────────────
```

The full test turns out a bit lengthy because of the container initialization and the connection mocking we have to do. Next, we instantiate a PostgresHook, which uses the same mocked get_connection() as in the MovielensToPostgresOperator and thus connects to the Docker PostgreSQL container. First, we assert whether the number of rows is zero; then, we run the operator; finally, we test whether any data was inserted.

Outside the test logic itself, what happens? During test startup, pytest figures out which tests use a fixture and executes only if the given fixture is used (figure 10.9).

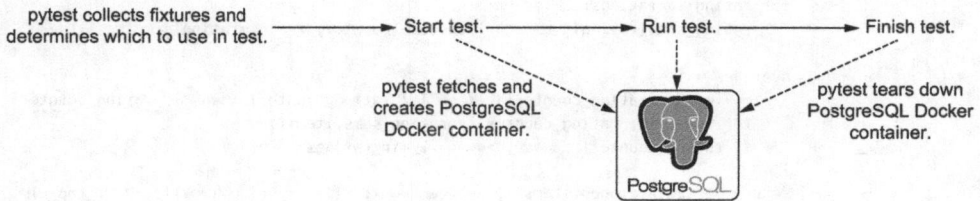

Figure 10.9   Running a test with pytest-docker-tools. Running Docker containers during tests enables testing against real systems. pytest-docker-tools manages the life cycle of the Docker container, and the user must implement the test.

When pytest decides to start the container fixture, it fetches, runs, and initializes the container. This process takes a couple of seconds, so there will be a small delay in the test suite. When the tests finish, the fixtures are terminated. pytest-docker-tools puts a small wrapper around the Python Docker client, providing a couple of convenient constructs and fixtures to use in tests.

10.3   *Using tests for development*

Tests are also helpful during development because they allow us to run a small snippet of code without using a live system. Let's see how they can help us develop workflows. We'll show a couple of screenshots of PyCharm, but any modern IDE allows us to set breakpoints and debug.

Let's go back to the MovielensPopularityOperator in section 10.1.3. In the execute() method, it runs a series of statements, and we want to know the state halfway through. With PyCharm, we can do this by placing a breakpoint and running a test that hits the line of code to which the breakpoint is set (figure 10.10).

Now run the test_movielenspopularityoperator test and start it in debug mode (figure 10.11). When the test reaches the line of code on which you've set a breakpoint, you can inspect the current state of variables but also execute code at that moment. Here, for example, you can inspect the ratings being processed halfway through the execute() method (figure 10.12).

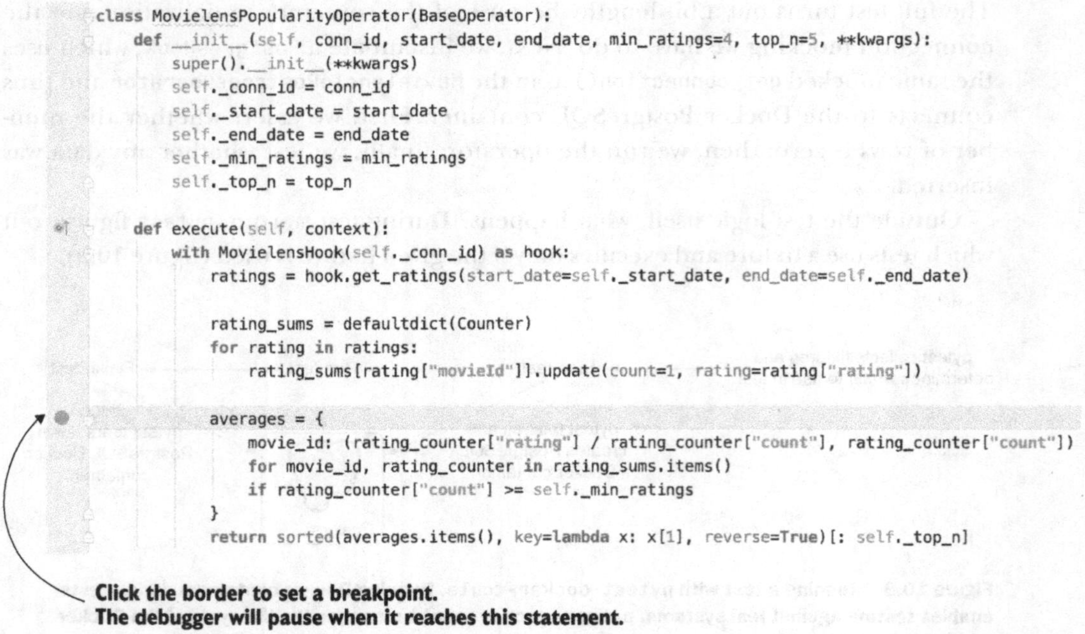

```python
class MovielensPopularityOperator(BaseOperator):
    def __init__(self, conn_id, start_date, end_date, min_ratings=4, top_n=5, **kwargs):
        super().__init__(**kwargs)
        self._conn_id = conn_id
        self._start_date = start_date
        self._end_date = end_date
        self._min_ratings = min_ratings
        self._top_n = top_n

    def execute(self, context):
        with MovielensHook(self._conn_id) as hook:
            ratings = hook.get_ratings(start_date=self._start_date, end_date=self._end_date)

            rating_sums = defaultdict(Counter)
            for rating in ratings:
                rating_sums[rating["movieId"]].update(count=1, rating=rating["rating"])

            averages = {
                movie_id: (rating_counter["rating"] / rating_counter["count"], rating_counter["count"])
                for movie_id, rating_counter in rating_sums.items()
                if rating_counter["count"] >= self._min_ratings
            }
            return sorted(averages.items(), key=lambda x: x[1], reverse=True)[: self._top_n]
```

Click the border to set a breakpoint.
The debugger will pause when it reaches this statement.

Figure 10.10   Setting a breakpoint in an IDE. This screenshot was taken in PyCharm, but any IDE allows you to set breakpoints and debug.

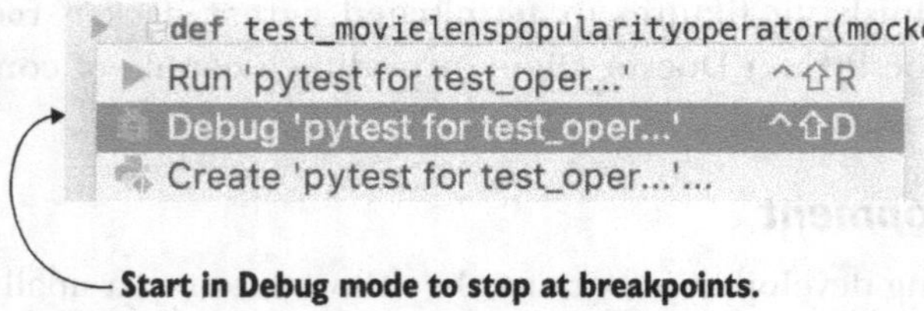

```python
    def test_movielenspopularityoperator(mocker):
```
▶ Run 'pytest for test_oper...'   ^⇧R
🐞 Debug 'pytest for test_oper...'   ^⇧D
🐍 Create 'pytest for test_oper...'...

Start in Debug mode to stop at breakpoints.

Figure 10.11   Starting a test in debug mode so that it stops at breakpoints

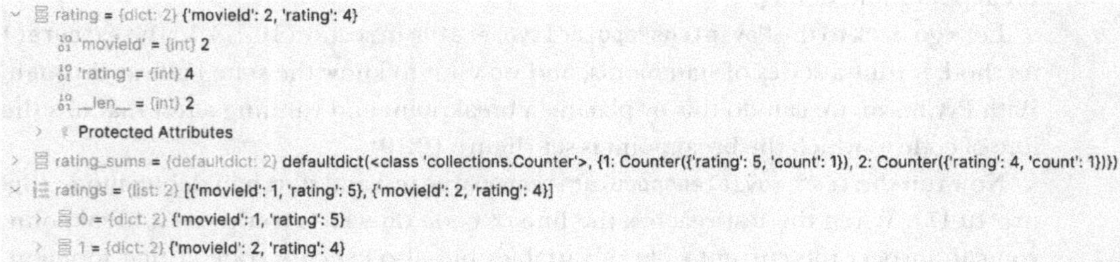

```
∨ ▤ rating = {dict: 2} {'movieId': 2, 'rating': 4}
     ₀¹ 'movieId' = {int} 2
     ₀¹ 'rating' = {int} 4
     ₀¹ __len__ = {int} 2
  >   Protected Attributes
> ▤ rating_sums = {defaultdict: 2} defaultdict(<class 'collections.Counter'>, {1: Counter({'rating': 5, 'count': 1}), 2: Counter({'rating': 4, 'count': 1})})
∨ ▤ ratings = {list: 2} [{'movieId': 1, 'rating': 5}, {'movieId': 2, 'rating': 4}]
  > ▤ 0 = {dict: 2} {'movieId': 1, 'rating': 5}
  > ▤ 1 = {dict: 2} {'movieId': 2, 'rating': 4}
```

Figure 10.12   Debugging allows you to inspect the state of the program at the set breakpoint. Here, you inspect the values of ratings.

Sometimes, your code works locally but returns an error on a production machine. How would you debug on a production machine? There's a way to debug remotely, but that approach is beyond the scope of this book; it allows you to connect your local PyCharm (or other IDE) debugger to a remote running Python process. (Search for *PyCharm remote debugging* for more information.)

Another alternative, if you can't use a real debugger, is a command-line debugger. (For this option, you need access to the command line on the remote machine.) Python has a built-in debugger named pdb (Python debugger). It works by adding a line of code in the location you want to debug, as shown in listing 10.28.

NOTE Python 3.7 and PEP 553 introduced a new way to set breakpoints: calling breakpoint().

Listing 10.28 Setting a breakpoint in code

```
import pdb; pdb.set_trace()
```

Now you can start your code from the command line by running a test with pytest or by starting an Airflow task in a DAG from the CLI by running

```
airflow tasks test [dagid] [taskid] [execution date]
```

Here's an example:

```
airflow tasks test movielens_download fetch_data 2024-01-01T12:00:00
```

airflow tasks test runs the task without registering any records in the metastore. It's useful for running and testing individual tasks in a production setting. When the pdb breakpoint is reached, you can execute code and control the debugger with certain keys, such as n for executing the statement and going to the next line and l for displaying the surrounding lines (figure 10.13). (To see the full list of commands, search for *pdb cheat sheet*.)

10.4 Testing complete DAGs

So far, we've focused on various aspects of testing individual operators: testing with and without task instance context, operators using the local filesystem, and operators using external systems with the help of Docker. But all these discussions focused on testing a single operator. A large, important aspect of workflow development is ensuring that all building blocks fit together nicely. Although one operator may run correctly from a logical point of view, it could transform data in an unexpected way, making the subsequent operator fail. How do you ensure that all operators in a DAG work together as expected?

Unfortunately, this question isn't easy to answer. Mimicking a real environment isn't always possible, for various reasons. With a DTAP (development, test, acceptance,

The statement where pdb pauses

"1" to inspect surrounding lines

-> shows next line to execute.

```
>>>>>>>>>>>>>>>>>>>>>>>>>>>>>>>>>>>>>>>>>>> PDB   set_trace >>>>>>>>>>>>>>>>>>>>>>>>>>>>>>>>>>>>>>>> >>>>>
> /src/airflowbook/operators/movielens_operator.py( 70)execute()
-> postgres_hook = PostgresHook(postgres_conn_id=se lf._postgres_conn_id)
(Pdb) l
 65 with MovielensHook(self._movielens_conn_id) as m ovielens_hook:
 66 ratings = list(movielens_hook.get_ratings(start_ date=self._start_date, end_date=self._end_date))
 67
 68 import pdb; pdb.set_trace()
 69
 70 -> postgres_hook = PostgresHook(postgres_conn_id =self._postgres_conn_id)
 71 insert_queries = [
 72 self._insert_query.format(",".join([str(_[1]) fo r _ in sorted(rating.items())]))
 73 for rating in ratings
 74 ]
 75 postgres_hook.run(insert_queries)
(Pdb) len(ratings)
3103
(Pdb) n
> /src/airflowbook/operators/movielens_operator.py( 72)execute()
-> self._insert_query.format(",".join([str(_[1]) fo r _ in sorted(rating.items())]))
```

Check whether the variable ratings hold any values by printing the length.

Evaluate line and go to the next.

Figure 10.13   Debugging on the command line with pdb

production) separated system, for example, we can't always create a perfect replica of production in the development environment because of privacy regulations or data size. Suppose that the production environment holds a petabyte of data; it would be impractical (to say the least) to keep the data in sync in all four environments. Therefore, people have created production environments that are as real as possible, and we can use these environments to develop and validate our software. When we're using Airflow, we encounter the same problems. In this section, we briefly describe three approaches to addressing these problems: using dag.test, using Whirl to emulate a production environment, and creating DTAP environments.

10.4.1   *Using dag.test() to test the whole DAG*

One way to test entire DAGs is to use the dag.test() method, introduced in Airflow 2.5.0; it allows you to do a DAG test run programmatically. The simplest way to use it is to add these two lines to the bottom of your DAG's code.

Listing 10.29   Adding dag.test()

```
if __name__ == "__main__":
    dag.test()
```

Broken in Airflow 3.1: Can't create DAG run for DAG

Unfortunately, this example doesn't work in Airflow 3.1 as of this writing because the DAG is no longer automatically serialized when `.test()` is called. This issue has been reported (https://github.com/apache/airflow/issues/56657). Because the example is still present in the Airflow documentation, we expect this issue to be fixed in the near future.

If you run your DAG file using the Python command, Python tries to execute the tasks in your DAG. Without these lines, it merely parses the file, creates the objects, and terminates.

One downside of this approach is that it mixes actual logic (i.e., the DAG) with testing logic. If you want to use mocks or assertions to verify the behavior, things could get messy quite quickly.

Instead, you can use `dag.test()` from a test. Consider a simple example. What if you create a DAG to use your `MovielensToPostgresOperator` (see section 10.2)? The code would look something like the following listing (`dags/dagtestdag.py`).

Listing 10.30 A DAG using the `MovielensToPostgresOperator`

```python
import datetime

from airflow import DAG

from custom.movielens_to_postgres_operator import MovielensToPostgresOperator

dagtestdag = DAG(

    "dagtestdag",
    default_args={
        "owner": "airflow",
        "start_date": datetime.datetime(2024, 1, 1),
    },
    schedule=None,
)


task = MovielensToPostgresOperator(
    task_id="retrieve_and_insert",
    movielens_conn_id="test",
    start_date="{{ data_interval_start | ds }}",
    end_date="{{ data_interval_end | ds}}",
    postgres_conn_id="postgres",
    insert_query=("INSERT INTO movielens
        (movieId,rating,ratingTimestamp,userId,scrapeTime) "
        "VALUES ({0}, '{{ macros.datetime.now() }}')"
    ),
    dag=dagtestdag
)
```

> ◄─ Uses the variable-style declaration, which allows us to import the DAG object from our test. The context manager notation we use elsewhere doesn't support this.

We saw in section 10.2 that we can test the behavior of only the task using the Movielens-ToPostgresOperator. Now we can do the same by running the entire DAG (tests/dags/custom/test_dagtestdag.py).

Listing 10.31   Testing an entire DAG

```python
import os

from airflow.models import Connection
from airflow.providers.postgres.hooks.postgres
    import PostgresHook
from pytest_docker_tools import fetch, container

from dagtestdag import dagtestdag
from custom.movielens_hook import MovielensHook
from custom.movielens_to_postgres_operator import MovielensToPostgresOperator

postgres_image = fetch(repository="postgres:16-alpine")
postgres = container(
    image="{postgres_image.id}",
    environment={
        "POSTGRES_USER": "testuser",
        "POSTGRES_PASSWORD": "testpass",
    },
    ports={"5432/tcp": None},
    volumes={
        os.path.join(os.path.dirname(__file__), "postgres-init.sql"): {
            "bind": "/docker-entrypoint-initdb.d/postgres-init.sql"
        }
    },
)


def test_movielens_to_postgres_operator(mocker, postgres):
    mocker.patch.object(
        MovielensHook,
        "get_connection",
        return_value=Connection(
            conn_id="test",
            login="airflow",
            password="airflow",
        ),
    )
    mocker.patch.object(
        MovielensHook,
        "get_ratings",
        return_value=[{"movieId": 1, "rating": 5, "userId": 123,
            "timestamp": 1725299750}, {"movieId": 2, "rating": 4, "userId": 456,
                "timestamp": 1525299750 }]
    )
    mocker.patch.object(
        PostgresHook,
        "get_connection",
```

```
        return_value=Connection(
            conn_id="postgres",
            conn_type="postgres",
            host="localhost",
            login="testuser",
            password="testpass",
            port=postgres.ports["5432/tcp"][0]
        ),
    )
    pg_hook = PostgresHook()
    row_count = pg_hook.get_first("SELECT COUNT(*) FROM movielens")[0]
    assert row_count == 0

    dagtestdag.test(logical_date=datetime.now(timezone.utc))   ◄──

    row_count = pg_hook.get_first("SELECT COUNT(*) FROM movielens")[0]
    assert row_count > 0
```

> Runs the DAG test, given a logical_date to make sure that the data_interval was set correctly

This test has a lot of similarities with the test in listing 10.27. The main difference is that we're testing the entire DAG, not just the outcome of the MovielensToOperator task. If any tasks were added to this DAG that affect the contents of PostgreSQL, our test might be affected and could alert us to issues.

Also, we don't use the ContextManager notation here to define the DAG. We need to import the DAG object in our test, and the ContextManager approach wouldn't allow us to do that. Instead, we define the DAG with the variable style (dagtestdag = DAG(..)).

As in the testing of single tasks, one main challenge in testing Airflow DAGs is dealing with external systems. At a high level, you have two options. The first option is to mock all external systems. In the example here, we mocked the call to the MovieLens API, which means having a single mock, but you can imagine having many more. Apart from having a lot of mocks, you'd need a clear idea and definition of what each of these external systems is expected to return. The up side is that this option will work, and you don't have any external requirements for running your tests.

The other option is to emulate the external systems to build a productionlike environment, similar to PostgreSQL in this example. That could lead to some complexity in your setup because coordinating multiple dependencies can be tricky. Luckily, there are tools to help.

10.4.2 *Emulating production environments with Whirl*

One approach to re-creating a production environment is using a project named Whirl (https://github.com/godatadriven/whirl). Whirl simulates all components of your production environment in Docker containers and manages them with Docker Compose. It comes with a CLI utility that makes controlling these environments easy. Although Docker is a great tool for development, one down side is that not everything is available as a Docker image. No Google Cloud Storage is available as a Docker image, for example.

10.4.3 *Creating DTAP environments*

Simulating your production environment locally with Docker or working with a tool like Whirl isn't always possible. One reason is security. Sometimes, you can't connect your local Docker setup to an FTP server used in your production DAGs because the FTP server is IP-allowlisted.

One approach that is often more negotiable with a security officer is setting up isolated DTAP environments. Four full-fledged environments can be cumbersome to set up and manage, so smaller projects with few people may use only two (development and production). Each environment can have specific requirements, such as dummy data in the development and test environments. The implementation of such a DTAP setup may be very specific to the project and infrastructure, so it's beyond the scope of this book.

In the context of an Airflow project, it's wise to create one dedicated branch in your GitHub repository per environment: development environment > development branch, production environment > production/main, and so on. This way, you can develop locally in branches. Then merge into the development branch and run DAGs on the development environment. When you're satisfied with the results, merge your changes into the next branch, such as main, and run the workflows in the corresponding environment.

Summary

- A DAG integrity test filters basic errors in your DAGs.
- Unit testing verifies the correctness of individual operators.
- `pytest` and plug-ins provide several useful constructs for testing, such as temporary directories and plug-ins for managing Docker containers during tests.
- You can run operators with `execute()`.
- You can simulate an entire DAG using `dag.test()`.
- For integration testing, you must simulate your production environment as closely as possible.
- Different tests catch different errors. Before implementing any test, consider what you aim to test. That information will guide you toward the test type.
- Run tests in your CI/CD pipeline if possible to ensure that you catch issues early.

Running tasks in containers

This chapter covers

- Identifying challenges in managing Airflow deployments
- Examining how containerized approaches can help simplify Airflow deployments
- Running containerized tasks in Airflow on Docker
- Establishing a high-level overview of workflows in developing containerized DAGs

Previously, we implemented several DAGs using different Airflow operators, each specialized to perform a specific type of task. Although operators are powerful tools, they can also pose challenges in deploying and maintaining your DAGs if you use a wide variety of operators across your pipelines. This chapter explores some of these challenges and examines how a containerized workflow using Docker and/or Kubernetes can simplify your workflow.

11.1   *Challenges of different operators*

Operators are arguably some of the strongest features of Airflow because they give you great flexibility in coordinating jobs across different types of systems. But creating and managing DAGs with many operators can be quite challenging due to the complexity involved.

To see why, consider the DAG in figure 11.1, which is based on our recommender use case from chapter 9. The DAG consists of three tasks: fetching movie recommendations from our movie API, ranking movies based on the fetched recommendations, and pushing some information about these movies to a MySQL database for further use downstream. This relatively simple DAG already uses three operators: an HttpOperator (or some other API operator) for accessing the API, a PythonOperator for executing the Python recommender function, and a MySQLOperator for storing the results.

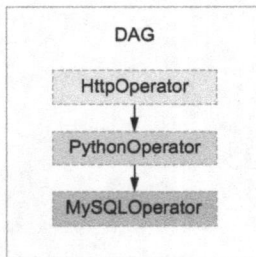

Figure 11.1   Illustration of our movie-recommender DAG. The DAG fetches movie recommendations, uses them to rank movies, and stores the result in a database. Each step involves a different operator, adding complexity to the development and maintenance of the DAG.

1. Fetch data from API.

2. Aggregate data to calculate stats.

3. Load into MySQL for analytics.

11.1.1   *Operator interfaces and implementations*

A drawback of using different operators for each task is the fact that we need to be familiar with the interfaces and inner workings of the operators to use them effectively. Also, if we encounter bugs in any of the operators, we must spend valuable time and resources tracking down and fixing the underlying issues. (This situation isn't unheard of, unfortunately, especially for more esoteric, less frequently used Airflow operators.) Although these efforts may seem tractable for this small example, imagine maintaining an Airflow deployment with many DAGs, which together use a multitude of operators. In such a scenario, working with all these operators may be more daunting.

11.1.2   *Complex and conflicting dependencies*

Another challenge in using many operators is that each one generally requires its own set of dependencies (Python or otherwise). The HttpOperator, for example, depends on the Python library requests for HTTP requests, whereas the MySQL-Operator depends on Python- and/or system-level dependencies for talking to MySQL. Similarly, the recommender code that the PythonOperator is calling is likely to have its own slew of dependencies (such as pandas or scikit-learn if machine learning is involved).

Because of the way Airflow is set up, all these dependencies must be installed in the environment that runs the Airflow scheduler, as well as the Airflow workers themselves. When we're using many operators, requiring the installation of many dependencies, we may face potential conflicts (figure 11.2) and a great deal of complexity in setting up and maintaining these environments—not to mention the potential security risks of installing so many software packages. (Look at Airflow's `pyproject.toml` file for an idea of the sheer number of dependencies involved in supporting all of Airflow's operators.) Conflicts are particularly problematic in Python environments because Python doesn't provide a mechanism for installing multiple versions of the same package in the same environment.

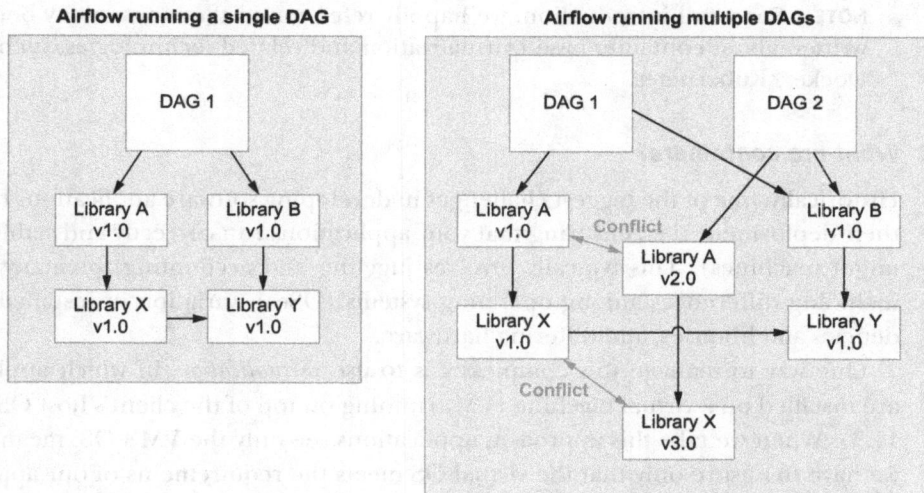

Figure 11.2   Complex and conflicting dependencies between Airflow tasks or DAGs. Running many DAGs in a single environment can lead to conflicts when DAGs depend on different versions of the same (or related) packages. Python in particular doesn't support installing different versions of the same package in the same environment. This means we have to resolve any conflicts in packages (right) by rewriting the DAGs or their dependencies to use the same package versions.

11.1.3 Moving toward a generic operator

Because of the challenges of using and maintaining many operators and dependencies, some people argue that it would be better to focus on using a single generic operator to run Airflow tasks. An upside of this approach is that we have to be familiar with only one kind of operator, which means that our many Airflow DAGs become much easier to understand because they consist of only one type of task. Moreover, if everyone uses the same operator to run their tasks, we're less likely to run into bugs in this heavily used operator. Finally, having only one operator means we have to worry about only one set of Airflow dependencies—those required for this single operator.

But where would we find a generic operator capable of running many tasks that doesn't require us to install and manage dependencies for each task? That's where containers come in.

11.2 Introducing containers

Containers have been touted as a major development, allowing applications to be easily packed with the required dependencies and easily (and uniformly) deployed in different environments. Before going into how to use containers within Airflow, we'll provide a short introduction to containers to make sure that we're all on the same page. (If you're familiar with Docker and the concepts behind containers, feel free to skip ahead to section 11.3.)

> **NOTE** For a full introduction, we happily refer you to the many, many books written about container-based virtualization and related technologies, such as Docker/Kubernetes.

11.2.1 What are containers?

Historically, one of the biggest challenges in developing software applications has been their deployment (i.e., ensuring that your applications run correctly and stably on the target machines). This typically involves juggling and accounting for many factors, including differences among operating systems (OSes), variation in installed dependencies and libraries, and differing hardware.

One way to manage this complexity is to use *virtualization*, in which applications are installed on a virtual machine (VM) running on top of the client's host OS (figure 11.3). When we take this approach, applications see only the VM's OS, meaning that we have to ensure only that the virtual OS meets the requirements of our application rather than modify the host OS. Therefore, to deploy our application, we can simply install it and any required dependencies in the virtual OS, which we ship to our clients.

VMs have a drawback: they're quite heavy because they require running an entire OS (virtual or guest) on top of the host OS. Moreover, every new VM runs its own guest OS, meaning that considerable resources are required to run multiple applications in VMs on a single machine.

This limitation led to the development of container-based virtualization, which is a much more lightweight approach than VMs (figure 11.3). Unlike VMs, container-based virtualization uses kernel-level functionality in the host OS to virtualize applications. This means containers can segregate applications and their dependencies in the same fashion as VMs without requiring each application to run its own OS; they can simply use this functionality from the host OS.

Interaction between containers and the host OS is often managed by a service called the *container engine*, which provides an API for managing and running the application containers and their images. Also, this service often provides command-line tools that help users build and interact with their containers. The best-known container engines

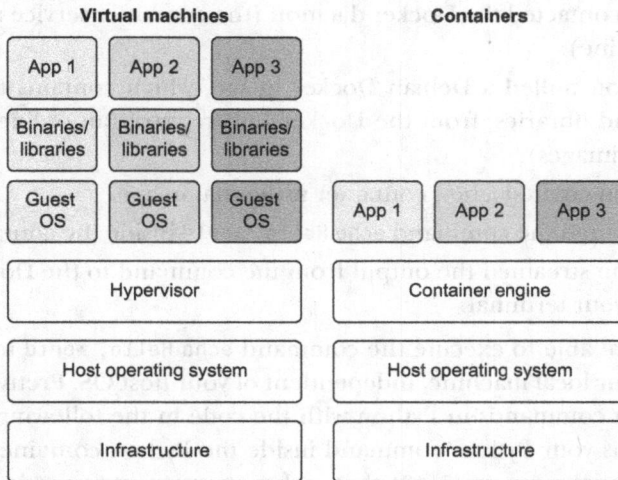

Figure 11.3 Comparison of VMs and containers. Containers are much more lightweight because they don't require running a full guest OS for each application.

are Docker and Podman, which have gained a lot of popularity over the years due to their relative ease of use and large communities.

11.2.2 Running a first Docker container

To explore the life cycle of building and running a container, let's try to build a small container using Docker. This exercise should give you a feel for working with containers and the development workflow involved. Before starting, make sure that you have Docker installed. You can find instructions for installing Docker Desktop at https://www.docker.com/get-started. When you have Docker installed and running, you can run your first container by using the following command in your terminal.

Listing 11.1 Running a Docker container

```
$ docker run debian:buster-slim echo Hello, world!
```

Running this command should give you something like the following output:

```
Unable to find image 'debian:buster-slim' locally
latest: Pulling from library/debian
...
Digest:
sha256:76c15066d7db315b42dc247b6d439779d2c6466f7dc2a47c2728220e288fc680
Status: Downloaded newer image for debian:buster-slim
Hello, world!
```

What happened when you ran this command? In short, Docker performed the following steps:

1 The Docker client contacted the Docker daemon (the container service running on your local machine).

2 The Docker daemon pulled a Debian Docker image, which contains the base Debian binaries and libraries, from the Docker hub registry (an online service for storing Docker images).

3 The Docker daemon created a new container using that image.

4 The container executed the command echo Hello, world inside the container.

5 The Docker daemon streamed the output from the command to the Docker client, showing it on your terminal.

This means that you were able to execute the command echo Hello, world inside an Ubuntu container on your local machine, independent of your host OS. Pretty cool!

Similarly, you can run commands in Python with the code in the following listing. This code effectively runs your Python command inside the Python container. Here, you're specifying a tag for the image (3.12) that makes sure you use a version of the Python image that contains Python 3.12.

Listing 11.2   Running a command inside a Python container

```
$ docker run python:3.12 python -c 'import sys; print(sys.version)'
```

11.2.3 Creating a Docker Image

Although running an existing image is fairly straightforward, what if we want to include our own application in an image so we can use Docker to run it? We'll illustrate the process with a small example. In this example, we have a small script (fetch_weather.py) that fetches weather predictions from the wttr.in API (https://wttr.in) and writes the output of this API to an output file. This script has a couple of dependencies (Python and the Python packages click and requests), and we want to package the whole thing as a Docker image so that it's easy for end users to run.

We can start building a Docker image by creating a Dockerfile, which is essentially a text-based file that tells Docker how to build the image. The basic structure of a Dockerfile is something like the following listing.

Listing 11.3   Dockerfile for fetching weather from the wttr.in API

Tells Docker which image to use as a base for building our image

Copies requirements file and runs pip to install the requirements

Copies our script and makes sure that it's executable

```
FROM python:3.12-slim

COPY requirements.txt /tmp/requirements.txt
RUN pip install -r /tmp/requirements.txt

COPY scripts/fetch_weather.py /usr/local/bin/fetch-weather
RUN chmod +x /usr/local/bin/fetch-weather
```

```
ENTRYPOINT [ "/usr/local/bin/fetch-weather" ]   ◄────┐  Tells Docker which command to
CMD [ "--help" ]                                      │  run when starting the container
                                        ◄─────────────┘
                                                         Tells Docker which default arguments
                                                         to include with the command
```

Each line of the Dockerfile is essentially an instruction that tells Docker to perform a specific task when building the image. Most Dockerfiles start with a FROM instruction that tells Docker which base image to use as a starting point. The remaining instructions (COPY, ADD, ENV, and so on) tell Docker how to add extra layers to the base image that contains our application and its dependencies. To build an image using this Dockerfile, use the following docker build command.

Listing 11.4 Building a Docker image using the Dockerfile

```
$ docker build --tag manning-airflow/wttr-example .
```

This command tells Docker to build a Docker image using the current directory (.) as a build context. Then Docker looks inside this directory for the Dockerfile and searches for any files included in ADD/COPY statements (such as our script and the requirements file). The --tag argument tells Docker which name to assign to the built image (in this case, manning-airflow/wttr-example). Running this build command produces something like the following output:

```
[+] Building 5.8s (10/10) FINISHED
=> [internal] load build definition from Dockerfile
=> => transferring dockerfile: 598B
=> [internal] load metadata for docker.io/library/python:3.12-slim
=> [internal] load .dockerignore
=> => transferring context: 2B
=> [1/5] FROM docker.io/library/python:3.12-slim@sha256:
   105e9d85a67db1602e70fa2bbb49c1e66bae7e3bdcb6259344fe8ca116434f74
=> [internal] load build context
=> [2/5] COPY requirements.txt /tmp/requirements.txt
=> [3/5] RUN pip install -r /tmp/requirements.txt
=> [4/5] COPY scripts/fetch_weather.py /usr/local/bin/fetch-weather
=> [5/5] RUN chmod +x /usr/local/bin/fetch-weather
=> exporting to image
=> => exporting layers
=> => writing image sha256:
   3c4b742a8f5df734f924ce5dcb4eb9200571e3c0b3173f4d6a29df26132c9674
=> => naming to docker.io/manning-airflow/wttr-example
```

This output shows the entire build process involved in creating our image, stating that Docker tagged the built image with the provided name. To do a test run of the built image, use the following command.

Listing 11.5 Running a Docker container using the wttr image

```
$ docker run manning-airflow/wttr-example:latest
```

This command should print the following help message from our script inside the container:

```
Usage: fetch-weather [OPTIONS] CITY

  CLI application for fetching weather forecasts from wttr.in.

Options:
  --output_path FILE  Optional file to write output to.
  --help              Show this message and exit.
```

11.2.4 *Persisting data using volumes*

Now we can run the wttr-example image we built in section 11.2.3 to fetch the weather for a city like Amsterdam using listing 11.6. Assuming that everything goes correctly, this command should print some weather forecasts for Amsterdam on the terminal, along with some fancy graphs (figure 11.4).

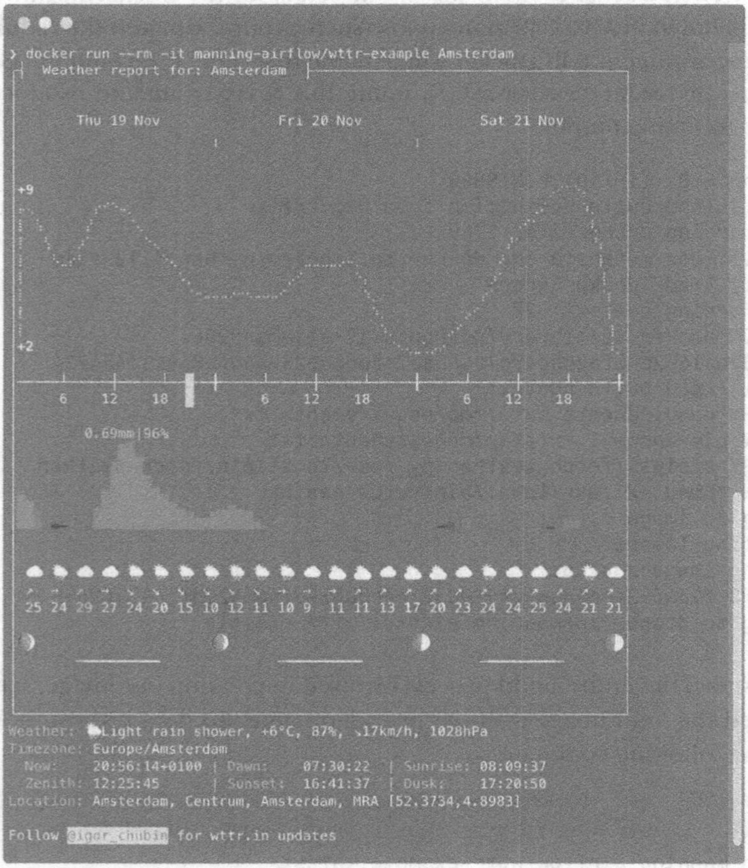

Figure 11.4
Example output
from the wttr
-example
container for
Amsterdam

Listing 11.6 Running the wttr container for a specific city

```
$ docker run wttr-example:latest Amsterdam
```

To build some history of weather forecasts, we may also want to write the forecasts to some output file(s) that we can use for future reference or analysis. Fortunately, our command-line-interface (CLI) script includes an extra argument: --output_path, which allows us to specify an output file path to write the forecasts to instead of writing them to the console. If we try to run this command with a local file path, however, we'll see that it doesn't create any output file on our local filesystem:

```
$ docker run manning-airflow/wttr-example:latest Amsterdam
 --output_path amsterdam.out
$ ls amsterdam.out
ls: amsterdam.out: No such file or directory
```

The reason is that your container environment is isolated from your host OS, meaning that it (among other things) has an isolated filesystem separated from the host filesystem.

To share files with your container, make sure that the files are available in a filesystem your container can access. One common option is to read/write files using storage that can be accessed via the internet (such as Amazon's S3 storage) or the local network. Alternatively, you can mount files or folders from your host system into the container to make them accessible from within the container. To mount a file or folder into your container, supply a --volume argument to docker run that specifies the file/folder to mount and the desired path inside the container.

Listing 11.7 Mounting a volume when running a container

```
$ docker run --volume `pwd`/data:/data wttr-example ...
```
> Mounts the local directory data (left) in the container under /data

This effectively tells Docker to mount the local folder data under the path /data within the container. Now you can write your weather output to the mounted data volume using the following command.

Listing 11.8 Persisting output from the wttr container

```
$ docker run --rm --volume `pwd`/data:/data \
manning-airflow/wttr-example Amsterdam \
--output_path /data/amsterdam.out
```
> Passes extra arguments from Amsterdam and --output_path to the container

You can verify that everything worked by checking whether the text file exists after your container finished running:

```
$ ls data/amsterdam.out
data/amsterdam.out
```

When you're done running containers, use the following command to check whether any containers are still secretly running:

```
$ docker ps
```

You can stop any running containers with Docker's `stop` command, using the container IDs obtained from the previous command to reference the running containers:

```
$ docker stop <container_id>
```

Stopped Docker containers hang around in the background in a suspended state in case you want to start them again later. If you don't need a container anymore, you can remove it fully by using Docker's `rm` command:

```
$ docker rm <container_id>
```

Stopped containers aren't visible by default when you use Docker's `ps` command to look for running containers. You can view stopped containers by including the `-a` flag when running the `ps` command:

```
$ docker ps -a
```

11.3 *Containers and Airflow*

Now that we have a basic understanding of what Docker containers are and how they can be used, let's turn back to Airflow. In this section, we'll dive into how containers can be used within Airflow and their potential benefits.

11.3.1 *Tasks in containers*

Airflow allows you to run tasks as containers. In practice, this means you can use container-based operators (such as the `DockerOperator` and the `Kubernetes-PodOperators`) to define tasks. These operators, when executed, start running a container and wait for it to finish running whatever it was supposed to run (similar to `docker run`).

The result of each task depends on the executed command and the software inside the container image. As an example, consider our recommender DAG (refer to figure 11.1). The original example uses three operators to perform three tasks: fetching ratings (using the `HttpOperator`), ranking movies (using the `PythonOperator`), and posting the results (using a MySQL-based operator). Using a Docker-based approach (figure 11.5), we could replace these tasks using the `DockerOperator` and execute commands in three Docker containers with the appropriate dependencies.

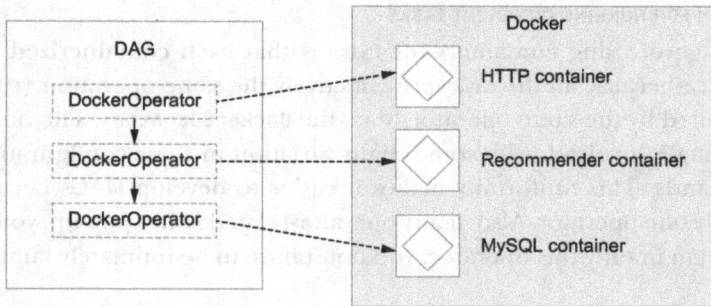

Figure 11.5 Docker version of the recommender DAG from figure 11.1

11.3.2 Why use containers?

This container-based approach requires building an image for each task, although sometimes, you may be able to share images between related or similar tasks. As a result, you may wonder why you'd go through the hassle of building and maintaining these Docker images instead of implementing everything in a few scripts or Python functions.

EASIER DEPENDENCY MANAGEMENT

One big advantage of using Docker containers is that they make managing dependencies easier. By creating different images for different tasks, you can install the exact dependencies that each task requires in its respective image. Because tasks run in isolation within these images, you no longer have to deal with conflicts in dependencies between tasks (figure 11.6). As an extra advantage, you don't have to install task dependencies in the Airflow worker environment (only in Docker) because the tasks are no longer run directly on the workers.

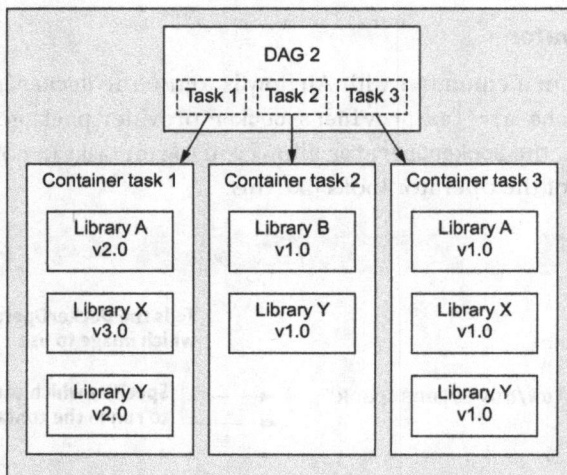

Figure 11.6 Managing dependencies across different tasks using containers

UNIFORM APPROACH FOR RUNNING DIFFERENT TASKS

Another advantage of using containers for tasks is that each containerized task has the same interface because all the tasks are effectively the same operation (running a container) executed by the same operator (e.g., the `DockerOperator`). The only differences are the images involved, with some slight variation in their configurations and executed commands. This uniformity makes it easier to develop DAGs because you have to learn only one operator. Also, if any operator-related issues pop up, you have to debug and fix them in only this operator; you don't have to be intimately familiar with many operators.

IMPROVED TESTABILITY

Another benefit of using container images is that they can be developed and maintained separately from the Airflow DAG in which they run. This means that each image can have its own development life cycle and can be subjected to a dedicated test suite (e.g., running on mock data), which verifies whether the software in the image does what we expect. Separation into containers makes this testing easier than, say, using the `PythonOperator`, which often involves tasks that are tightly coupled to the DAG itself, making it hard to test the functions separately from Airflow's orchestration layer.

IMPROVED SAFETY

Finally, improved safety is another benefit. You may want to add a dependency on open source tools for one part of your DAG (such as analytics or logging), but you want only dependencies in secure approved libraries for critical workflows. Separating the dependencies into containers allows for that.

11.4 *Running tasks in Docker*

It's time to implement part of our recommender DAG in containers. In this section, we'll show how to run the existing DAG in containers using Docker.

11.4.1 *Introducing the DockerOperator*

The easiest way to run a task in a container with Airflow is to use the `DockerOperator`, which is available in the `apache-airflow-providers-docker` provider package. As the name of the operator implies, the `DockerOperator` allows you to run tasks in containers using Docker. The basic API of the operator looks like this.

Listing 11.9   Example use of the `DockerOperator`

```
rank_movies = DockerOperator(
    task_id="rank_movies",
    image="manning-airflow/movielens-rank",     ◀—— Tells the DockerOperator
    command=[                                         which image to use
        "rank_movies.py",                        ◀—— Specifies which command
        "--input_path",                               to run in the container
```

```
            "/data/ratings/{{data_interval_start | ds}}.json",
            "--output_path",
            "/data/rankings/{{data_interval_start | ds}}.csv",
        ],
        volumes=["/tmp/airflow/data:/data"],        ◄──  Defines which volumes to mount
    )                                                     inside the container (format:
                                                          host_path: container_path)
```

The idea behind the `DockerOperator` is that it performs the equivalent of a `docker run` command to run a specified container image with specific arguments and wait for the container to finish doing its work. In this case, we're telling Airflow to run the `rank_movies.py` script inside the `manning-airflow/movielens-rank` Docker image, with some extra arguments indicating where the script should read/write its data. We also provide an extra `volumes` argument that mounts a data directory into the container so that we can provide input data to the container and keep the results after the task/container finishes.

What happens when this operator is executed? In essence, figure 11.7 shows what happens:

1 Airflow tells a worker to execute the task by scheduling it.
2 The `DockerOperator` executes a `docker run` command on the worker machine with the appropriate arguments.
3 If necessary, the Docker daemon fetches the required Docker image from the registry.
4 Docker creates a container running the image.
5 Docker mounts the local volume into the container. As soon as the command finishes, the container is terminated, and the `DockerOperator` retrieves the results in the Airflow worker.

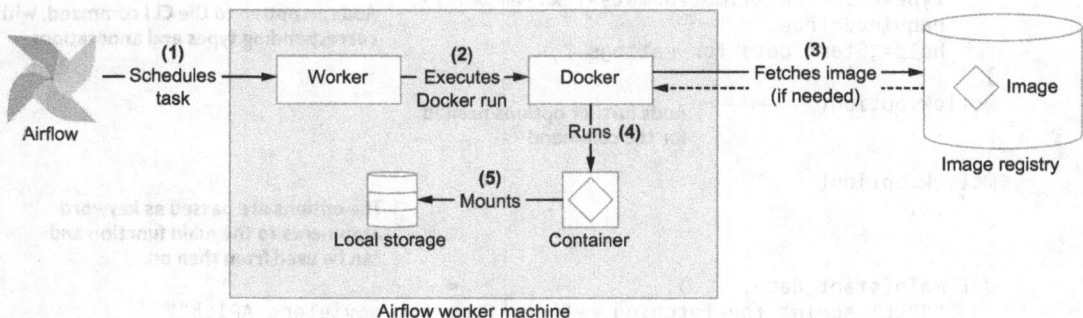

Figure 11.7 What happens when a task is executed using the `DockerOperator`. The image registry stores a collection of Docker images. This registry can be a private one containing our own images or a public registry like Docker Hub, which is used by default to fetch images. Images are cached locally when they're fetched so that you have to fetch them only once (barring any updates to the image).

11.4.2 Creating container images for tasks

Before we can run tasks using the DockerOperator, we have to build any required Docker images for the various tasks. To build an image for any given task, we must determine which software and corresponding dependencies we need to execute the task. When the requirements are clear, we can start creating a Dockerfile and any supporting files and then use docker build to create the required image.

As an example, let's look at the first task in our movie-recommender DAG: the task for fetching ratings (refer to figure 11.1). This task has to contact an external API to fetch movie ratings from users for a given range of dates so we can use these ratings as input for our recommender model in the next task.

To run this process within a container, first we have to convert the code we wrote for fetching ratings (chapter 9) to a script that's easy to run inside the container. The first step in building this script is using a small scaffold to create a CLI script in Python, which we can fill in with the required functionality. If we use the popular click Python library, the scaffold could look something like listing 11.10.

NOTE   We could also use the built-in argparse library, of course, but we quite like the brevity of the click library's API for building CLI applications.

Listing 11.10   Skeleton for a Python CLI script based on the click library

```
#!/usr/bin/env python          ◀─── The shebang tells Linux to
                                    execute this script using Python.
import logging
import click

logging.basicConfig(level=logging.INFO)   ◀─── Sets up logging to provide
                                               feedback to the user

@click.command()                   ◀─── Converts the main function
@click.option(                     ◀─── to a click CLI command
    "--start_date",
    type=click.DateTime(formats=["%Y-%m-%d"]),
    required=True,                      Adds an option to the CLI command, with
    help="Start date for ratings.",     corresponding types and annotations
)
@click.option(        ◀─── Adds further options needed
    ...                    for the command
)
@click.option(
    ...                             The options are passed as keyword
)                                   arguments to the main function and
...                                 can be used from then on.
def main(start_date, ...):    ◀───
    """CLI script for fetching ratings from the movielens API."""
    ...

if __name__ == "__main__":    ◀─── Python's way of ensuring that the
    main()                         main function/command is called
                                   when this script is executed
```

In this scaffold, we define one function, `main`, which is executed when our script runs and therefore should implement our rating-fetching functionality. We also use the `click.command` decorator to convert the main function to a `click` CLI command, which will parse any arguments from the command line and present useful feedback to the user. The `click.option` decorators tell the `click` library which arguments our CLI should accept and what types of values to expect. The nice thing about this approach is that `click` also parses and validates arguments for us, so we don't have to handle this type of logic ourselves. Using the scaffold, we can start filling in the main function with the same logic we started with in chapter 9 (`docker/images/movielens-fetch/scripts/fetch_ratings.py`). The code in the following listing is adapted from the `PythonOperator`-based example in that chapter.

Listing 11.11 Ratings script

```
...
from pathlib import Path                    ◀── Defines the different CLI arguments for click. The
                                                arguments for defining the click command-line
@click.command()                                options are omitted here for brevity; the full
@click.option(...)                              implementation is available in the code samples.
...
def main(start_date, end_date, output_path,
        host, user, password, batch_size):
    """CLI script for fetching ratings."""      ◀── Sets up the requests session for
                                                    performing HTTP requests, with
    session = requests.Session()                    the correct authentication details
    session.auth = (user, password)

    logging.info("Fetching ratings from %s (user: %s)"    ◀── Logging is used to provide
, host, user)                                                 feedback to the user.
    ratings = list(
        _get_ratings(              ◀── Uses the _get_ratings function
            session=session,           (omitted for brevity) to fetch
            host=host,                 ratings using the provided session
            start_date=start_date,
            end_date=end_date,
            batch_size=batch_size,
        )
    )
    logging.info("Retrieved %d ratings!", len(ratings))
    output_path = Path(output_path)
    output_dir = output_path.parent              ◀── Makes sure that the
    output_dir.mkdir(parents=True, exist_ok=True)    output directory exists
    logging.info("Writing to %s", output_path)       Writes the output as JSON
    with output_path.open("w") as file_:      ◀── to the output directory
        json.dump(ratings, file_)
```

In short, this code starts by setting up a requests session for performing HTTP requests and then uses the `_get_ratings` function to retrieve ratings for the defined time period from the API. (The `_get_ratings` function is omitted here for brevity but is available in the source code that accompanies this book.) The result from this function call is a list of records (as dicts), which is written to the output path in JSON format. We also use some logging statements in between to provide feedback to the user.

Now that we have our script, we can start building the Docker image. To do so, we create a Dockerfile that installs the dependencies for our script (`click` and `requests`), copies our script into the image, and makes sure that this script is in our PATH so we can run the script using the `fetch-ratings` command instead of specifying the full path to the script. The Dockerfile should look something like the following listing (docker/ images/movielens-fetch/Dockerfile).

Listing 11.12   Embedding the ratings script

Installs the required dependencies

Copies the fetch_ratings script and makes it executable

```
FROM python:3.12-slim
RUN pip install click==8.1.7 requests==2.32.3
COPY scripts/fetch_ratings.py /usr/bin/local/fetch-ratings
RUN chmod +x /usr/bin/local/fetch-ratings
ENV PATH="/usr/local/bin:${PATH}"
```

Ensures that the script is on the PATH so we can run it without specifying the full path to the script

This code assumes that we put our script `fetch_ratings.py` in a `scripts` directory next to our Dockerfile. We installed our dependencies by specifying them directly in the Dockerfile, although we could have used a `requirements.txt` file instead, copying it into the image before running pip, as shown in the next listing (docker/images/ movielens-fetch-reqs/Dockerfile).

Listing 11.13   Using `requirements.txt`

```
COPY requirements.txt /tmp/requirements.txt
RUN pip install -r /tmp/requirements.txt
```

With this Dockerfile, we can finally build our image for fetching ratings:

```
$ docker build -t manning-airflow/movielens-fetch .
```

To test the built image, we can try executing it with `docker run`:

```
$ docker run --rm manning-airflow/movielens-fetch fetch-ratings --help
```

This command should print the help message from our script, which looks something like this:

```
Usage: fetch-ratings [OPTIONS]

  CLI script for fetching movie ratings from the movielens API.
```

```
Options:
  --start_date [%Y-%m-%d]    Start date for ratings.  [required]
  --end_date [%Y-%m-%d]      End date for ratings.  [required]
  --output_path FILE         Output file path.  [required]
  --host TEXT                Movielens API URL.
  --user TEXT                Movielens API user.  [required]
  --password TEXT            Movielens API password.  [required]
  --batch_size INTEGER       Batch size for retrieving records.
  --help                     Show this message and exit.
```

Now we have a container image for our first task. We can use a similar approach to build different images for the other tasks.

> **NOTE** Depending on the amount of shared code, you may also want to create images that are shared between tasks but that can run with different arguments or even different scripts. How you organize this is up to you.

11.4.3 Building a DAG with Docker tasks

In this section, we start building the DAG to run the Docker tasks. Building such a Docker-based DAG is relatively simple: we need only replace our existing tasks with DockerOperators and make sure that each DockerOperator runs its task with the correct arguments. We also have to think about how to exchange data between tasks because the Docker containers' filesystems won't exist past the duration of the task. Starting with fetching the ratings, the first part of our DAG (docker/dags/01_docker.py) is a Docker-Operator that calls the fetch-ratings script inside the manning-airflow/movielens-fetch container, which we built in section 11.4.2.

Listing 11.14 Running the `fetch` container

```python
import os
from datetime import datetime

from airflow.sdk import DAG
from airflow.providers.docker.operators.docker
    import DockerOperator
from docker.types import Mount

with DAG(
    dag_id="01_docker",
    description="Fetches ratings using Docker.",
    start_date=datetime(2023, 1, 1),
    end_date=datetime(2023, 1, 3),
    schedule="@daily",
):
    fetch_ratings = DockerOperator(
        task_id="fetch_ratings",
        image="manning-airflow/movielens-fetch",    ◀── Tells the DockerOperator to use the movielens-fetch image
        command=[
            "fetch-ratings",    ◀── Runs the fetch-ratings script in the container with the required arguments
            "--start_date",
```

```
                "{{data_interval_start | ds}}",
                "--end_date",
                "{{data_interval_end | ds}}",
                "--output_path",
                "/data/ratings/{{logical_date | ds}}.json",
                "--user",
                os.environ["MOVIELENS_USER"],          ◀──────  Provides host and authentication
                "--password",                                    details for our API
                os.environ["MOVIELENS_PASSWORD"],
                "--host",
                os.environ["MOVIELENS_HOST"],
        ],
        mounts=[Mount(                              Mounts a volume to store data.
            source="docker_airflow-data-volume",    This host path is on the Docker
            target="/data", type="volume")          host, not the Airflow container.
        ],
        network_mode="docker_default",   ◀─────  Makes sure that the container is attached to the
)                                                 airflow Docker network so it can reach the API
                                                  (which is running on the same network)
```

When you're running the container from the operator, make sure to include arguments that tell the operator how to connect to the MovieLens API (host, user, password), which range of dates to fetch ratings for (start_date/end_date), and where to write the retrieved ratings to (output_path).

Also tell Docker to mount a host filesystem path in the container under /data so you can persist the fetched ratings outside the container. Further, tell Docker to run the container on a specific Docker network called Airflow, which is where the MovieLens API container is running if you're using the docker-compose templates to run Airflow.

NOTE We won't go any deeper into Docker networking here because it's a bit of an implementation detail; you won't need to configure networking if you're accessing an API on the internet. If you're interested, check out Docker networking in a good Docker book or in the online documentation.

For our second movie-ranking task, we can take a similar approach. We'll build a Docker container for the task (docker/dags/01_docker.py), which we'll run using the DockerOperator.

Listing 11.15   Adding the ranking task to the DAG

```
rank_movies = DockerOperator(
  task_id="rank_movies",
  image="manning-airflow/movielens-rank",   ◀───── Uses the movielens-ranking image
  command=[
      "rank-movies",        ◀────── Calls the rank-movies script with
      "--input_path",               the required input/output paths
      "/data/ratings/{{data_interval_start | ds}}.json",
      "--output_path",
      "/data/rankings/{{data_interval_start | ds}}.csv",
  ],
```

```
    mounts=[Mount(
            source="docker_airflow-data-volume",
            target="/data", type="volume")],
        network_mode="docker_default",                        )
fetch_ratings >> rank_movies
```

Here, you see one of the big advantages of using the DockerOperator: even though these tasks do different things, the interface for running the tasks is the same (except for the command arguments that are passed to the container). As a result, this task runs the rank-movies command inside the manning-airflow/movielens-rank image, reading and writing data to the same host-path mount as the previous task. This allows the ranking task to read the output from the fetch_ratings task and persist the ranked movies in the same directory structure.

Now that we have our first two tasks in the DAG, we can try running the DAG from within Airflow. (We'll leave the third task—loading recommendations into a database—to you as an exercise.)

To run the DAG, open the Airflow web UI, and activate the DAG. After it finishes running, you should see a couple of successful runs for the past few days (figure 11.8).

fetch_ratings
DockerOperator
✓ success

rank_movies
DockerOperator
✓ success

Figure 11.8 The Docker-based DAG in the Airflow UI

You can check the result of the run by clicking the task and then opening the logs by clicking View Logs. For the fetch_ratings task, you should see something like the log entries in listing 11.16, showing that the DockerOperator started your image and logged the output logs from the container. You can also check the output files from the DAG run by looking at the output files, which (in this example) were written to the /data directory on the Docker host.

Listing 11.16 Log output from the fetch_ratings task

```
[2024-08-09, 19:58:57 UTC] {local_task_job_runner.py:120} ▶
    Pre task execution logs
[2024-08-09, 19:58:57 UTC] {docker.py:366} INFO - Starting docker
    container from image manning-***/movielens-fetch
[2024-08-09, 19:58:58 UTC] {docker.py:436} INFO - INFO:root:Fetching
    ratings from http://movielens:8081 (user: ***)
[2024-08-09, 19:58:59 UTC] {docker.py:436} INFO - INFO:root:Retrieved
    471 ratings!
[2024-08-09, 19:58:59 UTC] {docker.py:436} INFO - INFO:root:Writing to
    /data/ratings/2023-01-01.json
```

```
movieId,avg_rating,num_ratings
912,4.833333333333333,6
38159,4.833333333333333,3
48516,4.833333333333333,3
4979,4.75,4
7153,4.75,4
```

11.4.4 Docker-based workflow

As we've seen, the workflow for building DAGs using Docker containers is a bit different from the approach we used for other DAGs. The biggest difference in the Docker-based approach is that, first, we have to create Docker containers for our different tasks. As a result, the overall workflow typically consists of several steps (illustrated in figure 11.9):

1. A developer creates a Dockerfile for the required image, which installs the required software and dependencies. Then the developer or a continuous integration/continuous delivery (CI/CD) process tells Docker to use the Dockerfile to build the image.

2. The Docker daemon builds the image on the development machine or a machine in the CI/CD environment.

3. The Docker daemon pushes the built image to a container registry to expose the image for further use downstream.

4. A developer creates the DAG using DockerOperators that reference the built images.

5. After the DAG is activated, Airflow starts running the DAG and scheduling Docker-Operator tasks for the respective runs.

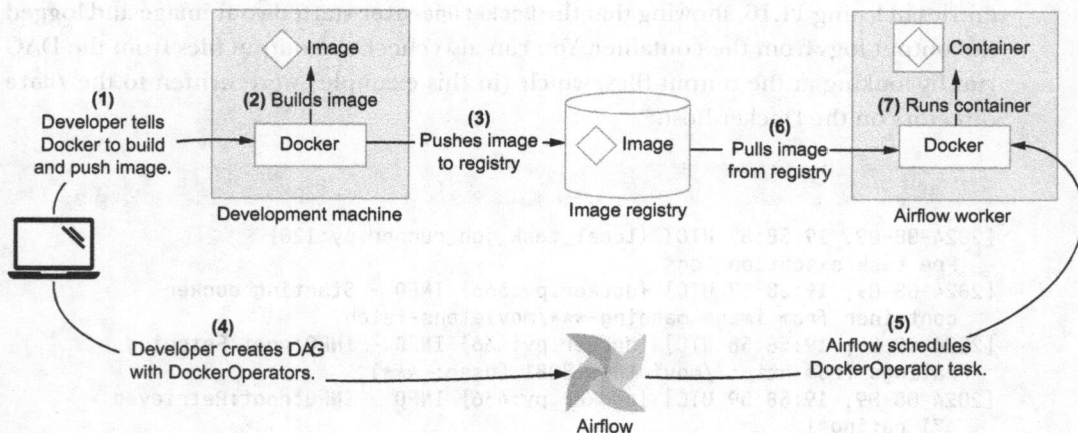

Figure 11.9   Common workflow for working with Docker images in Airflow

6 Airflow workers pick up the `DockerOperator` tasks and pull the required image from the container registry.

7 For each task, the Airflow worker runs a container with the corresponding image and arguments using the Docker daemon installed on the worker.

One benefit of this approach is that it effectively decouples the development of the software for running the task, which is now stored inside the Docker image, from the development of the overall DAG. This allows the development of the images to occur within their own life cycle and allows you to test the images separately from the DAG itself.

11.5 *Running tasks in Kubernetes*

Although Docker provides a convenient approach for running containerized tasks on a single machine, it doesn't help you orchestrate and distribute the work over multiple machines, thus limiting the scalability of the approach. This limitation of Docker led to the development of container orchestration systems such as Kubernetes, which help scale containerized applications across computer clusters. In this section, we'll show how to run containerized tasks on Kubernetes instead of Docker and illustrate some of the benefits and drawbacks of using Kubernetes on top of Docker.

11.5.1 *Introducing Kubernetes*

Because Kubernetes is a topic that could fill an entire book, we won't provide a full account of what it is; we simply aim to give you a high-level understanding of what it can do for you. For a full overview of Kubernetes, we recommend reading a comprehensive book on the subject, such as *Kubernetes in Action*, by Marko Lukša (Manning, 2017).

Kubernetes is an open source container orchestration platform that focuses on the deployment, scaling, and management of containerized applications. Compared with Docker, which is more vanilla, Kubernetes helps you scale your containers by managing their deployment across multiple worker nodes while taking into account things like required resources (CPU and/or memory), storage, and special hardware requirements (e.g., GPU access) when scheduling containers onto nodes.

Kubernetes is organized into two main components: the Kubernetes master (or control plane) and the nodes (figure 11.10). The Kubernetes master is responsible for running many components, including the API server, the scheduler, and other services responsible for managing deployments, storage, and so on. The Kubernetes API server is used by clients such as `kubectl` (Kubernetes's main CLI interface) or the Kubernetes Python SDK to query Kubernetes and run commands to initiate deployments. This makes the Kubernetes master the main contact point for managing your containerized applications on a Kubernetes cluster.

The Kubernetes worker nodes are responsible for running the container applications assigned to them by the scheduler. In Kubernetes, these applications are called *pods*, which can contain one or multiple containers that must run together on a single

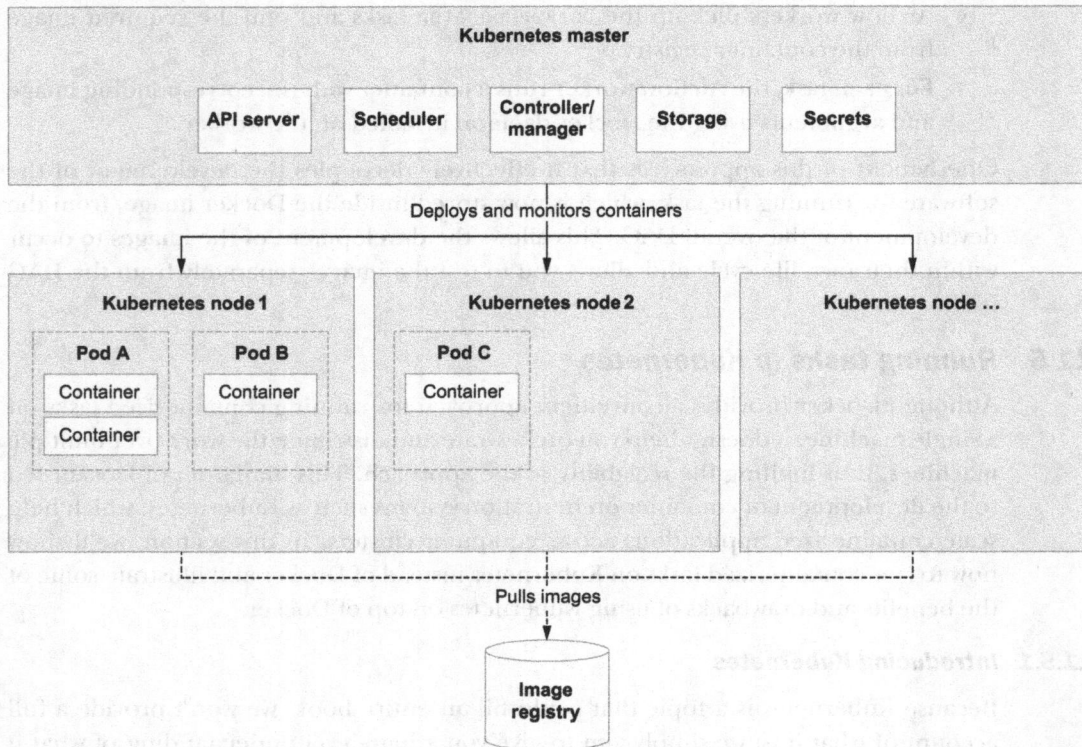

Figure 11.10   High-level overview of Kubernetes

machine. For now, all you need to know is that a pod is the smallest unit of work inside Kubernetes. In the context of Airflow, each task runs as a container inside a single pod.

Kubernetes also provides built-in functionality for managing secrets and storage. In essence, this means we can request a storage volume from the Kubernetes master and mount it as persistent storage inside the container. These storage volumes function similarly to the Docker-volume mounts discussed in section 11.2.4 but are managed by Kubernetes. We don't have to worry about where the storage comes from (unless we're responsible for operating the cluster, of course); we can simply request and use the volume provided.

11.5.2   *Setting up Kubernetes*

Before you adjust your DAG to run in Kubernetes, you must set up the resources you'll need in Kubernetes. First, make sure that you have access to a Kubernetes cluster and have the kubectl client installed locally. The easiest ways to get access are to install one locally (using, for example, Docker Desktop, minikube, or K3s within Docker Compose) or set one up in one of the cloud providers.

NOTE You can find installation guides for Kubernetes-related tools at https:// kubernetes.io/docs/tasks/tools.

When you have Kubernetes set up properly, you can verify that it's functioning by running this command:

```
$ kubectl cluster-info
```

If you're using Docker Desktop, the command should return something like the following output:

```
Kubernetes master is running at https:/ /kubernetes.docker.internal:6443
KubeDNS is running at https:/ /kubernetes.docker.internal:6443/api/v1/
 namespaces/kube-system/services/kube-dns:dns/proxy
```

If your Kubernetes cluster is up and running, you can continue creating resources. First, create a Kubernetes namespace to contain all your Airflow-related resources and task pods.

Listing 11.18 Creating a Kubernetes namespace

```
$ kubectl create namespace airflow
namespace/airflow created
```

Next, create some storage resources for your Airflow DAG, which will allow you to store the results of your tasks. These resources are defined as follows using Kubernetes's YAML syntax for specifying resources (`kubernetes/resources/data-volume.yml`).

Listing 11.19 YAML specification for storage

```
apiVersion: v1
kind: PersistentVolume      ◄──── Kubernetes specification for defining a
metadata:                          persistent volume, a virtual disk that
 name: data-volume          ◄──── provides space for pods to store data
 Labels:
   type: local              ──── Name to assign to the volume
Spec:
 storageClassName: manual
 capacity:                   ──── Size for the volume
   storage: 1Gi             ◄────
 accessModes:                     Allows read/write access
  - ReadWriteOnce           ◄──── one container at a time
 hostPath:                        Specifies the file path on the host
   path: "/tmp/data"        ◄──── where this storage will be kept
---
apiVersion: v1                    Kubernetes specification for a persistent
kind: PersistentVolumeClaim ◄──── volume claim, which represents a reservation
metadata:                         of some of the storage in the specified volume
 name: data-volume          ◄────
spec:                             The name of the volume to
                                  claim storage space on
```

```
storageClassName: manual
accessModes:                    ◄——  Allowed access modes
  - ReadWriteOnce                     for the storage claim
resources:
  requests:
    storage: 1Gi                ◄——  The amount of storage to claim
```

In essence, this specification defines two resources for storage: a Kubernetes volume and a storage claim, which essentially tells Kubernetes that you need some storage for your containers. Any of the Kubernetes pods run by Airflow can use this claim to store data (as you'll see in section 11.5.3). Using this YAML, you can create the required storage resources as follows.

Listing 11.20   Deploying the storage resources using `kubectl`

```
$ kubectl --namespace airflow apply -f resources/data-volume.yml
persistentvolumeclaim/data-volume created
persistentvolume/data-volume created
```

You also need to create a deployment of the MovieLens API, which you'll use your DAG to query. The YAML in listing 11.21 (`kubernetes/resources/api.yml`) allows you to create deployment and service resources for the MovieLens API, which tells Kubernetes how to start running the API service. You can create the service the same way you did the storage resources (listing 11.22).

Listing 11.21   YAML specification for the API

```
apiVersion: apps/v1
kind: Deployment                 ◄——  Kubernetes specification for creating
metadata:                              a deployment of a container
  name: movielens-deployment    ◄——
  labels:                              Name of the deployment
    app: movielens              ◄——
spec:                                  Labels for the deployment
  replicas: 1                          (which are matched in the service)
  selector:
    matchLabels:
      app: movielens
  template:
    metadata:
      Labels:
        app: movielens                 Specifies which containers to include in the
      spec:                            deployment, together with their respective
        containers:             ◄——    ports, environment variables, and so on
        - name: movielens
          image: manning-airflow/movielens-api  ◄——  Tells Kubernetes to use the latest
          ports:                                       version of the movielens-api image
          - containerPort: 8081                        (latest is the default image tag used
          env:                                         by Docker/Kubernetes if no specific
          - name: API_USER                             version tag is specified)
```

```
        value: airflow
     - name: API_PASSWORD
        value: airflow
---
apiVersion: v1
kind: Service
metadata:
 name: movielens
spec:
  selector:
    app: movielens
ports:
  - protocol: TCP
    port: 8081
    targetPort: 8081
```

Kubernetes specification for creating a service, which allows us to connect to a given deployment

Selector that matches the labels of the deployment, linking this service to the deployment

Maps the service port (8081) to the port exposed by the container in the deployment (8081)

Listing 11.22   Deploying the MovieLens API

```
$ kubectl --namespace airflow apply -f resources/api.yml
deployment.apps/movielens-deployment created
service/movielens created
```

After waiting a couple of seconds, you should see the pods for the API coming online:

```
$ kubectl --namespace airflow get pods

NAME                        READY   STATUS     RESTARTS    AGE
movielens-deployment-...    1/1     Running    0           11s
```

You can check if the API service is working by running

```
$ kubectl --namespace airflow port-forward --address 0.0.0.0 svc/movielens
8081:8081
```

and then opening http://localhost:8081 in a browser. If everything is working correctly, you should see the "hello world" message from the API displayed in your browser.

11.5.3 *Using the KubernetesPodOperator*

After creating the required Kubernetes resources, we can start adjusting our Docker-based recommender DAG to use the Kubernetes cluster instead of Docker. To start running our tasks on Kubernetes, we replace our DockerOperators with instances of the KubernetesPodOperator, which are available in the apache-airflow-providers-cncf-kubernetes providers package. As the name implies, the KubernetesPodOperator runs tasks within pods on a Kubernetes cluster. The following listing shows the basic API of the operator (kubernetes/dags/02_kubernetes.py).

Listing 11.23   Using the `KubernetesPodOperator`

```
fetch_ratings = KubernetesPodOperator(
    task_id="fetch_ratings",
    image="manning-airflow/movielens-fetch",
    cmds=["fetch-ratings"],
    arguments=[
        "--start_date",
        "{{ data_interval_start | ds}}",
        "--end_date",
        "{{ data_interval_end | ds}}",
        "--output_path",
        "/data/ratings/{{data_interval_start | ds}}.json",
        "--user",
        os.environ["MOVIELENS_USER"],
        "--password",
        os.environ["MOVIELENS_PASSWORD"],
        "--host",
        os.environ["MOVIELENS_HOST"],
    ],
    namespace="airflow",
    name="fetch-ratings",
    in_cluster=False,
    volumes=[volume],
    volume_mounts=[volume_mount],
    image_pull_policy="IfNotPresent",
    is_delete_operator_pod=True,
)
```

Which image to use

The executable to run inside the container

Arguments to pass to the executable (specified separately here, in contrast to the DockerOperator)

Kubernetes namespace to run the pod in

Name to use for the pod

Specifies that we're not running Airflow itself inside Kubernetes

Volumes and volume mounts to use in the pod

Specifies an image pull policy that requires Airflow to use our locally built images rather than trying to pull images from Docker Hub

Deletes pods automatically when they finish running

As with the `DockerOperator`, the first few arguments tell the `KubernetesPodOperator` how to run our task as a container. The `image` argument tells Kubernetes which Docker image to use, and the `cmds` and `arguments` parameters define which executable to run (`fetch-ratings`) and which arguments to pass to the executable. The remaining arguments tell Kubernetes the namespace in which to run the pod (`namespace`) and what name to use for the container (`name`).

We also supply two extra arguments, `volumes` and `volume_mounts`, to specify how the volumes we created in section 11.5.2 should be mounted into the tasks in the Kubernetes pod. We create these configuration values using two config classes from the Kubernetes Python SDK: `V1Volume` and `V1VolumeMount` (kubernetes/dags/02_kubernetes.py).

Listing 11.24   Volumes and volume mounts

```
from kubernetes.client import models as k8s

...

volume_claim = k8s.V1PersistentVolumeClaimVolumeSource(
    claim_name="data-volume"
```

References to the previously created claim

```
)
volume = k8s.V1Volume(                    ◄────  References to the previously
    name="data-volume",                          created storage volume
    persistent_volume_claim=volume_claim
)
volume_mount = k8s.V1VolumeMount(
    name="data-volume",
    mount_path="/data",          ◄────┘  Where to mount the volume
    sub_path=None,
    read_only=False,        ◄────┘  Mounts the volume as writable
)
```

First, we create a `V1Volume` configuration object that references the persistent volume claim `data-volume`, which we created as a Kubernetes resource earlier. Next, we create a `V1VolumeMount` configuration object, which refers to the volume configuration we just created (`data-volume`) and specifies where this volume should be mounted in the pod's container. Then we can pass these configuration objects to the `KubernetesPod-Operators` using the `volumes` and `volume_mounts` arguments. The only thing left to do is create a second task for the movie-ranking task, as shown in listing 11.25 (kubernetes/dags/02_kubernetes.py). Then we tie everything together into the final DAG (listing 11.26; kubernetes/dags/02_kubernetes.py).

Listing 11.25   Adding the movie-ranking task

```
rank_movies = KubernetesPodOperator(
    task_id="rank_movies",
    image="manning-airflow/movielens-rank",
    cmds=["rank-movies"],
    arguments=[
        "--input_path",
        "/data/ratings/{{data_interval_start | ds}}.json",
        "--output_path",
        "/data/rankings/{{ data_interval_start | ds}}.csv",
    ],
    namespace="airflow",
    name="fetch-ratings",
    in_cluster=False,
    volumes=[volume],
    volume_mounts=[volume_mount],
    image_pull_policy="IfNotPresent",
    is_delete_operator_pod=True,
)
```

Listing 11.26   Implementing the overall DAG

```
from datetime import datetime
import os

from kubernetes.client import models as k8s

from airflow.sdk import DAG
```

```
from airflow.timetables.interval import CronDataIntervalTimetable
from airflow.providers.cncf.kubernetes.operators. pod import (
    KubernetesPodOperator,
)

with DAG(
    dag_id="02_kubernetes",
    description="Fetches ratings from the Movielens API using kubernetes.",
    start_date=datetime(2023, 1, 1),
    end_date=datetime(2023, 1, 3),
    schedule= CronDataIntervalTimetable("@daily", "UTC"),
    catchup=True,
):
    volume_claim = k8s.V1PersistentVolumeClaimVolumeSource(...)
    volume = k8s.V1Volume(...)
    volume_mount = k8s.V1VolumeMount(...)

    fetch_ratings = KubernetesPodOperator(...)
    rank_movies = KubernetesPodOperator(...)

    fetch_ratings >> rank_movies
```

After finishing the DAG, you can start running it by enabling it from the Airflow web UI. After a few moments, Airflow starts to schedule and run your tasks (figure 11.11). For more details, open the log of an individual task instance by clicking the task and then clicking View Logs. Airflow displays the output of the task, which should look something like listing 11.27.

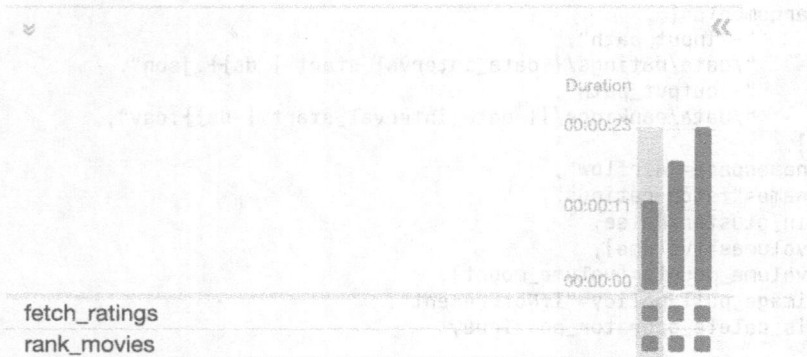

Duration

00:00:23

00:00:11

00:00:00

fetch_ratings
rank_movies

Figure 11.11   Several successful runs of the recommender DAG based on the `KubernetesPodOperator`

Listing 11.27   Logs from the Kubernetes-based `fetch_ratings` task

```
...
[2024-08-23, 11:14:39 UTC] {local_task_job_runner.py:120} ▶
Pre task execution logs
```

```
[2024-08-23, 11:14:40 UTC] {pod.py:1121} INFO - Building pod
  fetch-ratings-gwc037q3 with labels: {'dag_id': '02_kubernetes',
  'task_id': 'fetch_ratings',
  'run_id': 'scheduled__2023-01-01T0000000000-97b7fa9b0',
  'kubernetes_pod_operator': 'True',
{CA}'try_number': '2'}
[2024-08-23, 11:14:40 UTC] {pod.py:553} INFO - Found matching pod
  fetch-ratings-gwc037q3 with labels {'airflow_kpo_in_cluster': 'False',
  'airflow_version': '2.9.2',
  'dag_id': '02_kubernetes',
  'kubernetes_pod_operator': 'True',
  'run_id': 'scheduled__2023-01-01T0000000000-97b7fa9b0',
  'task_id': 'fetch_ratings', 'try_number': '2'}
[2024-08-23, 11:14:40 UTC] {pod.py:554} INFO - `try_number` of
  task_instance: 2
[2024-08-23, 11:14:40 UTC] {pod.py:555} INFO - `try_number` of pod: 2
[2024-08-23, 11:14:40 UTC] {pod_manager.py:378} WARNING - Pod not yet
  started: fetch-ratings-gwc037q3
[2024-08-23, 11:14:45 UTC] {pod_manager.py:472} INFO - [base]
  INFO:root:Fetching ratings from
  http://movielens.***.svc.cluster.local:8081
  (user: ***)
[2024-08-23, 11:14:45 UTC] {pod_manager.py:472} INFO - [base]
  INFO:root:Retrieved 471 ratings!
[2024-08-23, 11:14:45 UTC] {pod_manager.py:490} INFO - [base]
  INFO:root:Writing to /data/ratings/2023-01-01.json
[2024-08-23, 11:14:45 UTC] {pod.py:970} INFO - Deleting pod:
  fetch-ratings-gwc037q3
...
```

11.5.4 Diagnosing Kubernetes-related issues

If you're unlucky, your tasks may have gotten stuck in the running state instead of finishing correctly. When this happens, it is usually because Kubernetes is unable to schedule the tasks pod, which means that the pod will be stuck in the pending state rather than running on the cluster. To check whether this is indeed the case, look at the logs of the corresponding task(s), which can tell you more about the state of the pods on the cluster.

Listing 11.28 Log output showing a task stuck in a pending state

```
[2024-08-23, 11:12:06 UTC] {pod.py:554} INFO - `try_number` of
  task_instance: 1
[2024-08-23, 11:12:06 UTC] {pod.py:555} INFO - `try_number` of pod: 1
[2024-08-23, 11:12:06 UTC] {pod_manager.py:378} WARNING - Pod not yet
  started: fetch-ratings-pyvr373v
[2024-08-23, 11:12:11 UTC] {pod_manager.py:378} WARNING - Pod not yet
  started: fetch-ratings-pyvr373v
[2024-08-23, 11:12:16 UTC] {pod_manager.py:378} WARNING - Pod not yet
  started: fetch-ratings-pyvr373v
[2024-08-23, 11:12:21 UTC] {pod_manager.py:378} WARNING - Pod not yet
  started: fetch-ratings-pyvr373v
```

```
[2024-08-23, 11:12:26 UTC] {pod_manager.py:378} WARNING - Pod not yet
  started: fetch-ratings-pyvr373v
[2024-08-23, 11:12:31 UTC] {pod_manager.py:378} WARNING - Pod not yet
  started: fetch-ratings-pyvr373v
[2024-08-23, 11:12:36 UTC] {pod_manager.py:378} WARNING - Pod not yet
  started: fetch-ratings-pyvr373v
[2024-08-23, 11:12:41 UTC] {pod_manager.py:378} WARNING - Pod not yet
  started: fetch-ratings-pyvr373v
[2024-08-23, 11:12:46 UTC] {pod_manager.py:378} WARNING - Pod not yet
  started: fetch-ratings-pyvr373v
[2024-08-23, 11:12:51 UTC] {pod_manager.py:378} WARNING - Pod not yet
  started: fetch-ratings-pyvr373v
[2024-08-23, 11:12:56 UTC] {pod_manager.py:378} WARNING - Pod not yet
  started: fetch-ratings-pyvr373v
...
```

Here, you see that the pods are indeed still pending on the cluster. To diagnose the underlying issue, you can look up the task pods with this command:

```
$ kubectl --namespace airflow get pods
```

After you identify the name of the corresponding pod, you can ask Kubernetes for more details on the state of the pod by using the describe subcommand in kubectl.

Listing 11.29 Describing a specific pod to identify any issues

```
$ kubectl --namespace describe pod [NAME-OF-POD]
...
Events:
  Type      Reason            Age    From               Message
  ----      ------            ----   ----               -------
  Warning   FailedScheduling  82s    default-scheduler
  persistentvolumeclaim "data-volume" not found
```

This command produces a great amount of detail about the corresponding pod, including recent events (in the Events section). Here, the pod wasn't being scheduled because the required persistent volume claim wasn't created properly. To fix this problem, try fixing the resources by applying the resource specification properly (which you probably forgot to do) and then checking for new events, as shown in the next listing. This output shows that Kubernetes was able to schedule the pod after you created the required volume claim, fixing the issue.

Listing 11.30 Fixing the issue by creating the missing resources

```
$ kubectl --namespace airflow apply -f resources/data-volume.yml
persistentvolumeclaim/data-volume created
persistentvolume/data-volume created

$ kubectl --namespace describe pod [NAME-OF-POD]
...
```

```
Events:
    Type       Reason        Age    From              Message
    ----       ------        ----   ----              ------
    Warning FailedScheduling 33s    default-scheduler persistentvolumeclaim
      "data-volume" not found
    Warning FailedScheduling 6s     default-scheduler pod has unbound
      immediate PersistentVolumeClaims
    Normal    Scheduled     3s     default-scheduler Successfully assigned
      airflow/fetch-ratings-0a31c089 to docker-desktop
    Normal    Pulled        2s     kubelet, ...      Container image
      "manning-airflow/movielens-fetch" already present on machine
    Normal    Created       2s     kubelet, ...      Created container base
    Normal    Started       2s     kubelet, ...      Started container base
```

NOTE In general, we recommend that you start diagnosing any issues by checking the Airflow logs for any useful feedback. If you see anything that looks like a scheduling issue, kubectl is your best hope for identifying issues with your Kubernetes cluster or configuration.

Although this example is far from complete, we hope that it gives you some idea of the approaches you can use to debug Kubernetes-related issues when using the KubernetesPodOperator.

NOTE When you're developing DAGs, it's essential to remember that Kubernetes pods are assumed to be ephemeral resources. There can be many reasons why task pods fail to complete.

11.5.5 Differences between Kubernetes- and Docker-based workflows

The Kubernetes-based workflow (figure 11.12) is relatively similar to that of the Docker-based approach (refer to figure 11.9). In addition to setting up and maintaining a Kubernetes cluster (which is not necessarily trivial), there are other differences to keep in mind:

- The task containers are no longer executed on the Airflow worker node but on a separate (Kubernetes) node within the Kubernetes cluster. As a result, any resources used on the worker are fairly minimal, and you can use functionality in Kubernetes to make sure that your task is deployed to a node with the correct resources (CPU, memory, GPU, and so on).
- Any storage is no longer accessed from the Airflow worker but must be made available to the Kubernetes pod. Typically, this means using storage provided via Kubernetes (as we've shown with Kubernetes volumes and storage claims). But you can also use different types of network/cloud storage as long as the pod has the appropriate access to that storage.

Overall, Kubernetes provides considerable advantages over Docker, especially with regard to scalability, flexibility (e.g., providing different resources/nodes for different workloads) and managing other resources, such as storage and secrets. Also, Airflow

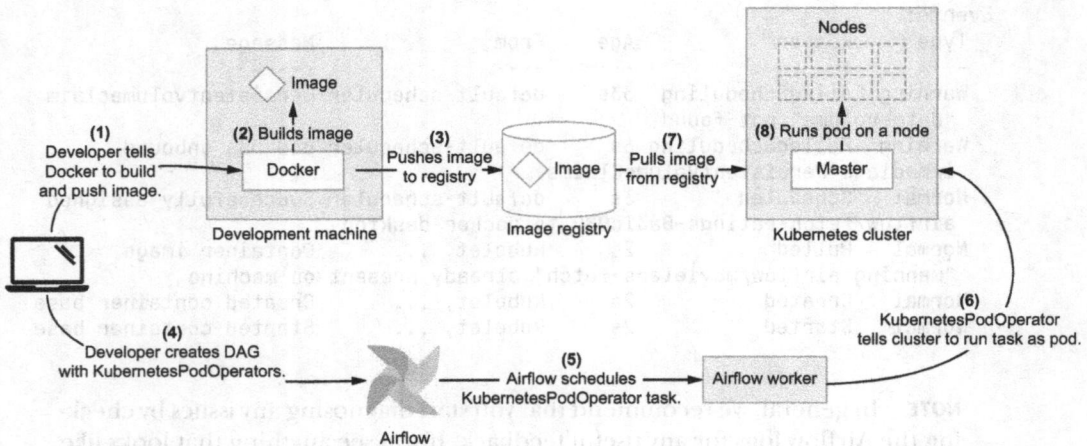

Figure 11.12   Workflow for building DAGs using the `KubernetesPodOperator`

itself can be run on top of Kubernetes, so you can have your entire Airflow setup running on a single, scalable, container-based infrastructure.

Summary

- Airflow deployments can be difficult to manage if they involve many operators, which requires knowledge of the different APIs and complicates debugging and dependency management.
- One way to tackle this issue is to use container technologies such as Docker to encapsulate your tasks inside container images and run the images from within Airflow.
- This containerized approach has several advantages, including easier dependency management, a more uniform interface for running tasks, and improved task testability.
- You can use volume mounts to share data between containers.
- With the `DockerOperator`, you can run tasks in container images directly using Docker, similar to the way you'd use the `docker run` CLI command.
- You can use the `KubernetesPodOperator` to run containerized tasks in pods on a Kubernetes cluster.
- Kubernetes allows you to scale your containerized tasks across a compute cluster, which provides (among other things) greater scalability and more flexibility in computing resources.

Part 3

Airflow in practice

Now that you've learned how to build complex pipelines, it's time to put your newfound skills in practice. To help you get started, part 3 discusses best practices for building pipelines in real-life situations and demonstrates these practices in two example use cases.

First, chapter 12 reviews some of the practices we've seen for implementing pipelines and highlights several best practices that should help you build efficient, maintainable pipelines. Chapters 13 and 14 tie all previous chapters together in two summary use cases. Chapter 13 focuses on the more generic use case of gathering different data sets into a combined result, and chapter 14 shows how to use Airflow in a generative AI context.

After completing part 3, you should be able to write efficient, maintainable pipelines in Airflow to solve actual business problems.

Best practices

This chapter covers

- Writing clean, understandable DAGs
- Generating DAGs and tasks with factory functions
- Designing idempotent and deterministic DAGs
- Handling data efficiently in your DAGs
- Managing concurrency with resource pools

By now, we've described most of the basic elements that go into building and designing data processes using Airflow DAGs. In this chapter, we'll dive a bit deeper into some best practices that can help you write well-architected DAGs that are both easy to understand and efficient in terms of how they handle your data and resources.

12.1 Writing clean DAGs

Writing DAGs can easily become a messy business. DAG code can quickly become overly complicated or difficult to read, for example, especially if the DAGs were written by team members who have different styles of programming. In this section, we touch on some tips to help you structure and style your DAG code. We hope we can provide some often-needed clarity for your intricate data processes.

12.1.1 *Using style conventions*

As in all programming exercises, one of the first steps in writing clean, consistent DAGs is adopting a common, clean programming style and applying it consistently across all your DAGs. Although a thorough exploration of clean coding practices is well beyond the scope of this book, we can provide several tips as starting points.

FOLLOWING STYLE GUIDES

The easiest way to make your code cleaner and easier to understand is to use a common style when writing your code. Multiple style guides are available in the community, including the widely known PEP 8 style guide (https://www.python.org/dev/peps/pep-0008) and the Google Python Style Guide (https://google.github.io/styleguide/pyguide.html). These guides generally include recommendations on indentation, maximum line lengths, naming styles for variables/classes/functions, and so on. When you follow these guides, other programmers will be better able to read your code. The following listing shows an example of code that isn't PEP 8 compliant, followed by the same code, now PEP 8 compliant (listing 12.2).

Listing 12.1   Examples of code that isn't PEP 8 compliant

```
spam( ham[ 1 ], { eggs: 2 } )

i=i+1
submitted +=1
my_list = [
    1, 2, 3,
    4, 5, 6,
    ]
```

Listing 12.2   Making the examples in listing 12.1 PEP 8 compliant

```
spam(ham[1], {eggs: 2})      ◄——— Less unnecessary whitespace

i = i + 1
submitted += 1              │ Consistent whitespace around operators

my_list = [                 ◄——— More readable indenting
    1, 2, 3,                  │ around list brackets
    4, 5, 6,
]
```

USING STATIC CHECKERS TO CHECK CODE QUALITY

The Python community has produced a plethora of software tools that you can use to check whether your code follows proper coding conventions and/or styles. Two popular tools are Pylint and Flake8, both of which function as static code checkers. You can run them over your code to get a report on how well your code adheres to their envisioned standards. To run Flake8 over your code, for example, install it using `pip` and run it by pointing it at your codebase.

Listing 12.3 Installing and running Flake8

```
python -m pip install flake8
python -m flake8 dags/*.py
```

This command runs Flake8 on all the Python files in the `dags` folder, giving you a report on the perceived code quality of these files. The report typically looks something like the following listing.

Listing 12.4 Example Flake8 output

```
$ python -m flake8 chapter09/dags/
chapter09/dags/04_sensor.py:2:1: F401
 'airflow.operators.python.PythonOperator' imported but unused
chapter09/dags/03_operator.py:2:1: F401
 'airflow.operators.python.PythonOperator' imported but unused
```

Both Flake8 and Pylint are used widely within the community, although Pylint is generally considered to have a more extensive set of checks in its default configuration. (This can be considered a strength or weakness, depending on your preferences; some people consider it overly pedantic.) You can configure both tools to enable or disable certain checks and combine them to provide comprehensive feedback. For more details, we refer you to https://www.pylint.org and https://flake8.pycqa.org.

USING CODE FORMATTERS TO ENFORCE COMMON FORMATTING

Although static checkers give you feedback on the quality of your code, tools such as Pylint and Flake8 don't impose overly strict requirements on how to format code (when to start a new line, how to indent function headers, and so on). As a result, Python code written by different people can follow different formatting styles, depending on the writers' preferences.

One way to reduce the heterogeneity of code formatting within teams is to use a code formatter to surrender control (and worry) to the formatting tool, which will ensure that your code is reformatted according to its guidelines. Applying a formatter consistently across your project ensures that all code follows one consistent formatting style: the style implemented by the formatter.

Two commonly used code Python formatters are YAPF (https://github.com/google/yapf) and Black (https://github.com/psf/black). Both tools reformat Python code according to their styles, which have slight differences, so the choice between Black and YAPF may depend on personal preference, although Black has gained great popularity within the Python community over the past few years.

To see how a formatter works, consider the following contrived example of an ugly function. Applying Black to this function gives you the cleaner result shown in listing 12.6.

Listing 12.5   Code example before Black formatting

```
def my_function(
    arg1, arg2,
    arg3):
    """Function to demonstrate black."""
    str_a = 'abc'
    str_b = "def"
    return str_a + \
        str_b
```

Listing 12.6   The same code example after Black formatting

```
def my_function(arg1, arg2, arg3):
    """Function to demonstrate black."""
    str_a = "abc"
    str_b = "def"
    return str_a + str_b
```

More consistent indenting for arguments

Consistent use of double quotes

Unnecessary line break removed

To run Black, install it using `pip` and apply it to your Python code as shown in the next listing. You should get something like the output in listing 12.8, indicating whether Black reformatted any Python files for you.

Listing 12.7   Installing and running Black

```
python -m pip install black
python -m black dags/
```

Listing 12.8   Example output from Black

```
reformatted dags/example_dag.py
All done!
1 file reformatted.
```

You can also perform a dry run of Black using the `--check` flag. This flag causes Black to indicate only whether it would reformat any files—not do any actual reformatting.

Recently, a new tool has gained considerable traction within the Python community. Ruff (https://astral.sh/ruff) aims to combine the functionality of linters such as Flake8 with that of code formatters such as Black in a single tool. In addition to simplifying your setup by removing dependencies, Ruff is considerably faster than the tools it replaces because its underlying implementation is in the Rust programming language.

You can configure Ruff via `pyproject.toml` (among others). It has a large overlap with the configuration you use for Flake8 and Black, so changes should be minimal. To run Ruff in check mode (checking only for violations of the standards), use the following code.

Listing 12.9 Installing and running Ruff in check mode

```
$ python -m pip install ruff
$ python -m ruff check dags/
```

> **NOTE** Many editors, such as Visual Studio Code and PyCharm, support integration with these tools, allowing you to reformat your code within your editor. For details on how to configure this type of integration, see the editor's documentation.

Airflow Ruff rules

Several Airflow-specific Ruff rules can alert you to issues with your DAG code, such as task variable names that don't match the `task_id`. Also, several Airflow rules can help you migrate from Airflow 2 to 3. These rules highlight anything you need to change to keep your DAGs working in Airflow 3 when moving from Airflow 2. To use these rules, run `ruff check dags/ --select AIR3 --preview --show-fixes`. More info is available at https://docs.astral.sh/ruff/rules.

FOLLOWING AIRFLOW-SPECIFIC STYLE CONVENTIONS

It's a good idea to agree on style conventions for your Airflow code, particularly when Airflow provides multiple ways to achieve the same result. Airflow provides multiple styles for defining DAGs, for example.

Listing 12.10 Multiple styles for defining DAGs

```
with DAG(...) as dag:                          ◀──┐ With a context manager
    task1 = PythonOperator(...)
    task2 = PythonOperator(...)


dag = DAG(...)                                 ◀──┐ Without a context manager
task1 = PythonOperator(..., dag=dag)
task2 = PythonOperator(..., dag=dag)


@dag(...)                    ◀── With the Taskflow API
def my_dag():
    @task()
    def task1():
        ...
    @task()
    def task2():
```

In principle, all these DAG definitions do the same thing, so you have no real reason to choose one over the other beyond style preferences. Within your team, however, it may be a good idea to choose one style and follow it throughout your codebase to keep things more consistent and understandable. Consistency is even more important when you're defining dependencies between tasks because Airflow provides several ways to define the same task dependency (listing 12.11).

> **NOTE**   We deliberately exclude the Taskflow API here because it dictates a specific mechanism for defining task dependencies that's different from the other mechanisms. If you're using Taskflow, this difference automatically determines your dependency-setting mechanism.

Listing 12.11   Different styles for defining task dependencies

```
task1 >> task2
task1 << task2
[task1] >> task2
task1.set_downstream(task2)
task2.set_upstream(task1)
```

Although each definition has its own merits, combining different styles of dependency definitions within a single DAG, as in listing 12.12, can be confusing. Your code will generally be more readable if you stick to a single style for defining dependencies across tasks (listing 12.13).

Listing 12.12   Mixing different task-dependency notations

```
task1 >> task2
task2 << task3
task5.set_upstream(task3)
task3.set_downstream(task4)
```

Listing 12.13   Using a consistent style to define task dependencies

```
task1 >> task2 >> task3 >> [task4, task5]
```

> **NOTE**   We don't have a clear preference for any style. Make sure to pick one that you and your team members like, and apply it consistently.

12.1.2 *Managing credentials centrally*

In DAGs that interact with many systems, you may juggle many different of credentials—databases, compute clusters, cloud storage, and so on. As you've seen, Airflow allows you to maintain these credentials in its metastore, which ensures that your credentials are maintained securely in a central location, assuming that Airflow has been configured securely. (See chapters 15 and 16 for information on configuring Airflow deployments and security.)

Although the metastore is the easiest place to store credentials for built-in operators, it can be tempting to store secrets for your custom `PythonOperator` functions (and other functions) in less secure places for ease of accessibility. We've seen quite a few DAG implementations with security keys hardcoded into the DAG itself or in external configuration files.

Fortunately, it's relatively easy to use the Airflow connections store to maintain credentials for your custom code too. Retrieve the connection details from the store in your custom code, and then use the obtained credentials to do your work.

Listing 12.14 Fetching credentials from the Airflow metastore

```
from airflow.hooks.base import BaseHook

def _fetch_data(conn_id, **context)
    credentials = BaseHook.get_connection(conn_id)        ◀── Fetching credentials
    ...                                                        using the given ID

fetch_data = PythonOperator(
    task_id="fetch_data",
    op_kwargs={"conn_id": "my_conn_id"},
    dag=dag
)
```

An advantage of this approach is that it uses the same method of storing credentials as all other Airflow operators, so credentials are managed in one single place. As a consequence, you have to worry only about securing and maintaining credentials in this central database.

Depending on your deployment, of course, you may want to maintain your secrets in other external systems (such as Kubernetes secrets or cloud secrets stores) before passing them into Airflow. In this case, it's still a good idea to make sure that these credentials are passed into Airflow (via environment variables, for example) and that your code accesses them via the Airflow metastore.

If you use some external secrets-management system, it's worthwhile to look into Airflow's support for secrets backends (https://mng.bz/yNP7). These backends offer native integration with several secrets-management solutions. When you use such a backend, secrets are kept in the secrets manager and made available in Airflow for use by DAGs.

12.1.3 *Specifying configuration details consistently*

You may have to pass other configuration parameters to your DAG, such as file paths and table names. Because these parameters are written in Python, Airflow DAGs provide many configuration options, including global variables (within the DAG), configuration files (e.g., YAML, INI, and JSON), environment variables, and Python-based configuration modules. Airflow also allows you to store configurations in the metastore using Airflow

Variables (https://mng.bz/MwzE). To load some configuration options from an example YAML file (listing 12.15), for example, you might use something like listing 12.16.

Listing 12.15   Example YAML configuration file

```
input_path: /data
output_path: /output
```

Listing 12.16   Loading configuration options from a YAML file

```
import yaml
with open("config.yaml") as config_file:
    config = yaml.load(config_file)          ◀─── Reads config file using PyYAML
...
fetch_data = PythonOperator(
    task_id="fetch_data",
    op_kwargs={
        "input_path": config["input_path"],
        "output_path": config["output_path"],
    },
    ...
)
```

WARNING Be careful to not store any sensitive secrets in configuration files, which are typically stored in plain text. If you do store sensitive secrets in configuration files, make sure that only the correct people have permission to access the files. Otherwise, consider storing secrets in more secure locations, such as the Airflow metastore.

Similarly, you could load the config using Variables, as shown in the following listing. Variables is an Airflow feature for storing global variables in the metastore.

Listing 12.17   Storing configuration options in Airflow Variables

```
from airflow.sdk import Variable

input_path = Variable.get("dag1_input_path")        ◀─── Fetching global variables using
output_path = Variable.get("dag1_output_path")           the Variables mechanism

fetch_data = PythonOperator(
    task_id="fetch_data",
    op_kwargs={
        "input_path": input_path,
        "output_path": output_path,
    },
    ...
)
```

NOTE Fetching Variables this way in the global scope of your DAG is generally bad for the performance of your DAG. See section 12.1.4 to find out why.

You can set Variables via the Airflow UI (choose Admin > Variables), environment variables, or the Airflow command-line interface (CLI). For more info, see https://mn.bz/a9Xx.

NOTE Fetching Variables in the global scope this way can be a bad idea because Airflow will refetch them from the database every time the DAG processor (part of the scheduler) reads your DAG definition.

In general, we don't have any real preference for configuration storage as long as it's consistent. If you store your configuration for one DAG as a YAML file, for example, it makes sense to follow the same convention for other DAGs as well.

For configuration that's shared across DAGs, we highly recommend specifying the configuration values in a single location, such as a shared YAML file, following the DRY (Don't Repeat Yourself) principle. That way, you'll be less likely to run into issues when you change a configuration parameter in one place and forget to change it in another.

Finally, it's good to realize that configuration options can be loaded in different contexts depending on where they're referenced within your DAG. Suppose that you load a config file in the main part of your DAG as follows.

Listing 12.18 Loading configuration options in the DAG definition (inefficient)

```
import yaml

with open("config.yaml") as config_file:
    config = yaml.load(config_file)          ◀── In the global scope, this config
                                                 is loaded on the scheduler.
fetch_data = PythonOperator(...)
```

The config.yaml file is loaded from the local filesystem of the machine(s) running the Airflow API server and/or scheduler, which means that both machines should have access to the config file path. By contrast, you can load the config file as part of a Python task.

Listing 12.19 Loading configuration options within a task (more efficient)

```
import yaml

def _fetch_data(config_path, **context):
    with open(config_path) as config_file:
        config = yaml.load(config_file)       ◀── In task scope, this config
    ...                                           is loaded on the worker.

fetch_data = PythonOperator(
    op_kwargs={"config_path": "config.yaml"},
    ...
)
```

In this case, the config file won't be loaded until an Airflow worker executes your function, so the config is loaded in the context of the Airflow worker. Depending on how you set up your Airflow deployment, this may be an entirely different environment (access to different filesystems and so on), leading to erroneous results or failures. Similar situations may occur with other configuration approaches.

You can avoid these situations by choosing one configuration approach that works well and sticking with it across DAGs. Also, be mindful of where different parts of your DAG are executed when configuration options are loaded, and, wherever possible, use approaches that are accessible to all Airflow components, such as nonlocal filesystems.

12.1.4 *Avoiding computation in your DAG definition*

Airflow DAGs are written in Python, which gives you a great deal of flexibility in writing them. A drawback of this approach, however, is that Airflow has to execute your Python DAG file to derive the corresponding DAG. Moreover, to pick up any changes you may have made to your DAG, Airflow has to reread the file at regular intervals and sync any changes to its internal state.

As you can imagine, repeated parsing of your DAG files can lead to problems if any file takes a long time to load. This can happen, for example, if you do any long-running or heavy computations when defining your DAG. The following implementation causes Airflow to execute `do_some_long_computation` every time the DAG file is loaded, blocking the entire DAG-parsing process until the computation finishes.

Listing 12.20 Performing computations in the DAG definition (inefficient)

```
...
task1 = PythonOperator(...)
my_value = do_some_long_computation()         This long computation will be computed
task2 = PythonOperator(op_kwargs={"my_value": my_value})   every time the DAG is parsed.
...
```

This type of *computation creep*, in which you accidentally include computations in your DAG definitions, can be subtle and requires some vigilance to avoid. Some cases may be worse than others. You may not mind loading a configuration file from a local filesystem repeatedly, but repeated loading from cloud storage or a database may be less desirable. One way to avoid this issue is to postpone the computation to the execution of the task that requires the computed value.

Listing 12.21 Performing computations within tasks (more efficient)

```
def _my_not_so_efficient_task(value, ...):
    ...

PythonOperator(
    task_id="my_not_so_efficient_task",
    ...
    op_kwargs={
```

```
        "value": calc_expensive_value()  ◄─────  Here, the value is computed
    }                                            every time the DAG is parsed.
)

def _my_more_efficient_task(...):
    value = calc_expensive_value()
    ...                                    ◄─    When you move the
                                                 computation into the task,
                                                 the value is calculated only
PythonOperator(                                  when the task is executed.
    task_id="my_more_efficient_task",
    python_callable=_my_more_efficient_task,  ◄
    ...
)
```

Something similar may occur in more subtle cases, in which a configuration is loaded from an external data source or filesystem in your main DAG file. You may want to load credentials from the Airflow metastore and share them across a few tasks by doing something like the following.

Listing 12.22   Fetching credentials from the metastore in the DAG definition (inefficient)

```
from airflow.hooks.base_hook import BaseHook

api_config = BaseHook.get_connection("my_api_conn")  ◄──   This call hits the
api_key = api_config.login                                 database every time
api_secret = api_config.password                           the DAG is parsed.

task1 = PythonOperator(
    op_kwargs={"api_key": api_key, "api_secret": api_secret},
    ...
)
...
```

A drawback of this approach is that it fetches credentials from the database every time your DAG is parsed instead of only when the DAG is executed. As a result, you see queries repeated every 30 seconds or so (depending on the Airflow config) against your database simply to retrieve these credentials. Generally, you can avoid these performance issues by postponing the fetching of credentials to the execution of the task function, as shown in listing 12.23. This way, credentials are fetched only when the task is executed, making your DAG much more efficient. Another approach would be to write your own hook/operator, which fetches credentials only when necessary for execution, but this may require a bit more work.

Listing 12.23   Fetching credentials within a task (more efficient)

```
from airflow.hooks.base import BaseHook
                                                    This call hits the
def _task1(conn_id, **context):                     database only when
    api_config = BaseHook.get_connection(conn_id)  ◄──  the task is executed.
    api_key = api_config.login
```

```
        api_secret = api_config.password
    ...

task1 = PythonOperator(op_kwargs={"conn_id": "my_api_conn"})
```

12.1.5 Using factories to generate common patterns

In some cases, you may find yourself writing variations of the same DAG over and over again. This often occurs when you're ingesting data from related data sources, with only small variations in source paths and transformations applied to the data. Or common data processes within your company may require many of the same steps and transformations, and as a result, they're repeated across many DAGs.

One effective way to speed the process of generating these common DAG structures is to write a factory function. This type of function takes any required configuration for the steps and generates the corresponding DAG or set of tasks, thus producing it (like a factory). If you have a common process that involves fetching some data from an external API and preprocessing it with a script, you could write a factory function that looks a bit like the following listing (dags/01_task_factory.py). Then you could use this factory function to ingest multiple data sets, as shown in listing 12.25.

Listing 12.24   Generating sets of tasks with a factory function

Parameters that configure the tasks that the factory function will create →   File paths used by the different tasks

```
def generate_tasks(dataset_name, raw_dir, processed_dir,
                   preprocess_script, output_dir, dag):  ◄
    raw_path = os.path.join(raw_dir, dataset_name, "{ds_nodash}.json")  ◄
    processed_path = os.path.join(
        processed_dir, dataset_name, "{ds_nodash}.json"
    )
    output_path = os.path.join(output_dir, dataset_name, "{ds_nodash}.json")
    fetch_task = BashOperator(  ◄
        task_id=f"fetch_{dataset_name}",
        bash_command=f"echo 'curl http://example.com/{dataset_name}.json
        > {raw_path}.json'",
        dag=dag,                                    Creates the individual tasks
    )

    preprocess_task = BashOperator(
        task_id=f"preprocess_{dataset_name}",
        bash_command=f"echo '{preprocess_script} {raw_path}
        {processed_path}'",
        dag=dag,
    )

    export_task = BashOperator(
        task_id=f"export_{dataset_name}",
        bash_command=f"echo 'cp {processed_path} {output_path}'",
        dag=dag,
    )
```

```
    fetch_task >> preprocess_task >> export_task          Defines task dependencies

    return fetch_task, export_task          Returns the first and last tasks in the
                                            chain so you can connect them to other
                                            tasks in the larger graph (if necessary)
```

Listing 12.25   Applying the task factory function

```python
import pendulum
from airflow.sdk import DAG

with DAG(
    dag_id="01_task_factory",
    start_date=pendulum.today("UTC").add(days=-5),
    schedule=CronTriggerTimetable("0 16 * * *", timezone="UTC"),
) as dag:
    for dataset in ["sales", "customers"]:          Creates sets of tasks with
        generate_tasks(                             different configuration values
            dataset_name=dataset,
            raw_dir="/data/raw",
            processed_dir="/data/processed",
            output_dir="/data/output",              Passes the DAG
            preprocess_script=f"preprocess_{dataset}.py",    instance to
            dag=dag,                                connect the tasks
        )                                           to the DAG
```

This code should give you a DAG similar to the one in figure 12.1. For independent data sets, of course, it might not make sense to ingest the two in a single DAG, but you can easily split the tasks across multiple DAGs by calling the generate_tasks factory function from different DAG files. You can also write factory functions to generate entire DAGs, as shown in listing 12.26 (dags/02_dag_factory.py).

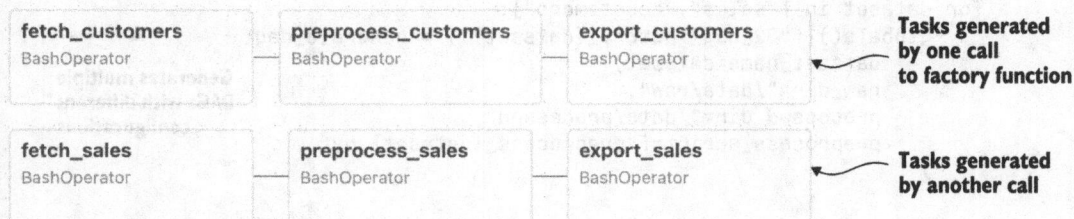

Figure 12.1   Generating repeated patterns of tasks using factory functions. This example DAG contains multiple sets of almost-identical tasks, which were generated from a configuration object using a task factory function.

Listing 12.26   Generating DAGs with a factory function

```python
def generate_dag(dataset_name, raw_dir, processed_dir, preprocess_script):
    with DAG(
```

```
            dag_id=f"02_dag_factory_{dataset_name}",
            start_date=pendulum.today("UTC").add(days=-5),
            schedule=CronTriggerTimetable("0 16 * * *", timezone="UTC")
    ) as dag:
            raw_file_path = ...
            processed_file_path = ...

            fetch_task = BashOperator(...)
            preprocess_task = BashOperator(...)

            fetch_task >> preprocess_task

    return dag
```

Generates the DAG instance within the factory function (annotation pointing to `) as dag:` line)

This code allows you to generate a DAG using the following minimalistic DAG file (dags/02_dag_factory.py). You can also use this approach to generate multiple DAGs using a DAG file (listing 12.28).

Listing 12.27   Applying the DAG factory function

```
...

dag = generate_dag(
    dataset_name="sales",
        raw_dir="/data/raw",
        processed_dir="/data/processed",
        preprocess_script="preprocess_sales.py",
)
```

Creates the DAG using the factory function (annotation pointing to `dag = generate_dag(`)

Listing 12.28   Generating multiple DAGs with a factory function

```
...

for dataset in ["sales", "customers"]:
    globals()[f"02_dag_factory_{dataset}"] = generate_dag(
        dataset_name=dataset,
        raw_dir="/data/raw",
        processed_dir="/data/processed",
        preprocess_script=f"preprocess_{dataset}.py",
)
```

Generates multiple DAGs with different configurations (annotation)

NOTE You have to assign each DAG a unique name in the global namespace (using the globals trick) to make sure that the names don't overwrite one another.

This loop effectively generates multiple DAG objects in the global scope of your DAG file, which Airflow picks up as separate DAGs (figure 12.2). The objects must have different variable names to prevent them from overwriting one another. Otherwise, Airflow will see only a single DAG instance: the last one generated by the loop. The screenshot in figure 12.2 was taken from the Airflow UI, showing multiple DAGs that were generated from a single DAG file using a DAG factory function.

WARNING We recommend some caution when generating multiple DAGs from a single DAG file, because the process can be confusing. A more general pattern is to have one file for each DAG. As a result, this pattern is best used sparingly and only when it provides significant benefits.

Dag ⬍	Schedule	Next Dag Run ⬍	Last Dag Run ⬍	Tags ⚊
01_task_factory	🗓 0 16 * * *	2025-06-27, 18:00:00	2025-06-26, 18:00:00 ✓	▷
02_dag_factory_customers	🗓 0 16 * * *	2025-06-27, 18:00:00	2025-06-26, 18:00:00 ✓	▷
02_dag_factory_sales	🗓 0 16 * * *	2025-06-27, 18:00:00	2025-06-26, 18:00:00 ✓	▷

DAGs generated by the DAG factory

Figure 12.2 Multiple DAGs generated from a single file using a DAG factory function

Task or DAG factory functions can be particularly powerful when combined with configuration files or other forms of external configuration. This approach allows you to build a factory function that takes a YAML file as input and generates a DAG based on the configuration defined in that file. This way, you can configure repetitive extract, transform, load (ETL) processes using a bunch of relatively simple configuration files, which can be edited by users who have little knowledge of Airflow.

12.1.6 Grouping related tasks with task groups

Complex Airflow DAGs, particularly those generated with factory functions, can be difficult to understand due to complex DAG structures or the sheer number of tasks involved. To organize these complex structures, you can structure your tasks into task groups. Task groups allow you to visually group sets of tasks into smaller groups, making your DAG structure easier to oversee and comprehend.

You can create task groups using the `TaskGroup` context manager. Building on the earlier task factory example, you can group the tasks generated for each data set, as shown in the next listing (`dags/03_task_groups.py`).

Listing 12.29 Using `TaskGroups` to group tasks visually

```
from airflow.sdk import DAG, TaskGroup
...
```

```
for dataset in ["sales", "customers"]:
    with TaskGroup(dataset, tooltip=f"Tasks for processing {dataset}"):
        generate_tasks(
            dataset_name=dataset,
            raw_dir="/data/raw",
            processed_dir="/data/processed",
            output_dir="/data/output",
            preprocess_script=f"preprocess_{dataset}.py",
            dag=dag,
        )
```

This code organizes the set of tasks generated for the `sales` and `customers` data sets into two task groups—one for each data set. As a result, the grouped tasks are shown as a single condensed task group in the web interface, which you can expand by clicking a group (figure 12.3).

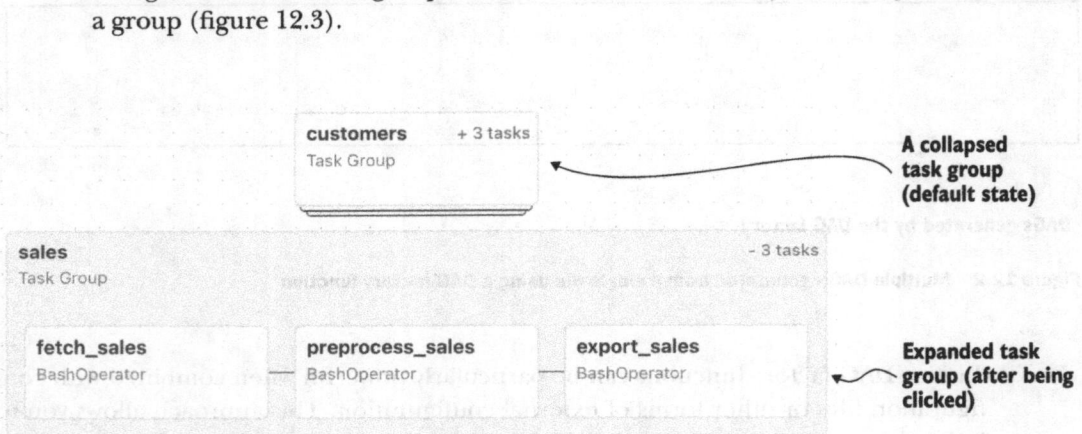

Figure 12.3   Task groups can help you organize DAGs by grouping related tasks. Initially, task groups are depicted as single nodes in the DAG, as shown for the `customers` task group in this figure. By clicking a task group, you can expand it and view the tasks within the group, as shown here for the `sales` task group. Task groups can be nested, meaning that you can have task groups within task groups.

Although this example is relatively simple, the task group feature can be quite effective in reducing the amount of visual noise in complex cases. In our DAG for training machine learning models in chapter 6, for example, we created a considerable number of tasks for fetching and cleaning weather and sales data from different systems. Task groups allow us to reduce the apparent complexity of this DAG by grouping the sales- and weather-related tasks into task groups. This allows us to hide the complexity of fetching tasks by default but still zoom in on the individual tasks when necessary (figure 12.4; you can find the code in `dags/04_task_groups_umbrella.py`.)

12.1.7   *Being explicit when specifying your DAG schedule*

As discussed at length in chapters 3 and 4, you have multiple ways to define your DAG's schedule in Airflow. You can use specific points in time (`CronTriggerTimetable`),

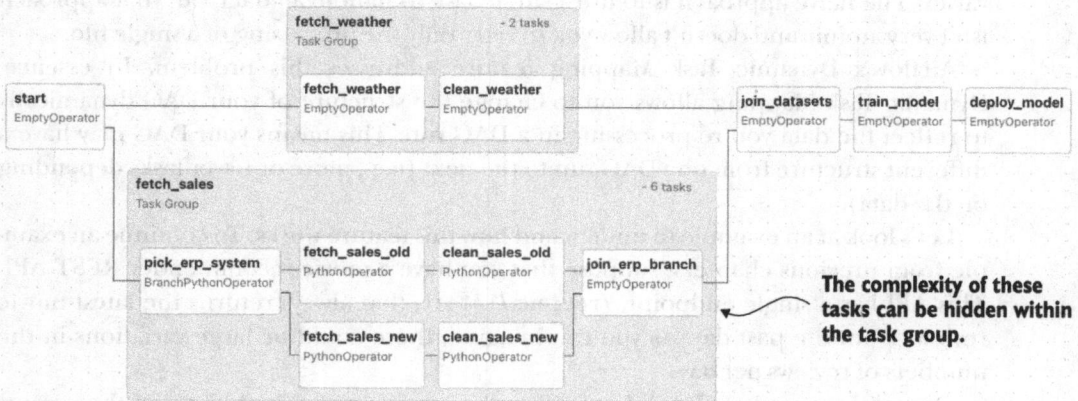

Figure 12.4 Using task groups to organize the umbrella DAG from chapter 6. Here, grouping the tasks for fetching and cleaning the weather and sales data sets greatly simplifies the complex task structures involved in these processes.

intervals (`CronDataIntervalTimetable`), time deltas (`DeltaDataIntervalTimetable`), and so on. All these options are valid. Airflow also allows you to use shorthand or cron expressions directly as the value for the schedule of a DAG. But this approach can be confusing for a couple of reasons:

- You can configure the way that Airflow applies these expressions at the instance level using the settings `AIRFLOW__SCHEDULER__CREATE_CRON_DATA_INTERVALS` and `AIRFLOW__SCHEDULER__CREATE_DELTA_DATA_INTERVALS`. This means that setting a schedule to `@daily` in one instance may give you a different result in the other.
- The default behavior changed between Airflow 2 and 3. In Airflow 2, the default behavior is to use intervals, whereas in Airflow 3, the default is to use points in time.

NOTE To avoid confusion and provide clarity, we strongly recommend always using one of the timetable classes explicitly, as we've done throughout this book.

12.1.8 Using Dynamic Task Mapping to generate tasks dynamically

Section 12.1.5 discussed generating tasks and DAGs using a factory function. This approach works well in many cases, but the implicit assumption is that your DAG structure is known beforehand and doesn't change in any dynamic way. It's impossible to adapt your DAG structure on the fly based on the data that's being processed in a specific DAG run.

A good example of a situation in which it's impossible to know the DAG structure beforehand is one in which you receive new data files every day, but the number of files varies. The naive approach is to use a single task to handle all data, but that approach isn't very atomic and doesn't allow you to retry only the processing of a single file.

Airflow's Dynamic Task Mapping feature addresses this problem. In essence, Dynamic Task Mapping allows you to change the structure of your DAG dynamically to reflect the data you're processing in a DAG run. This means your DAG may have a different structure from one DAG run to the next (e.g., more or fewer tasks depending on the data).

Let's look at an example to understand how this feature works. To continue an example from previous chapters, suppose that you have a movie-recommender REST API. This API has a single endpoint, /reviews/latest, that always returns the latest movie reviews from the past day. As you can imagine, there could be large variations in the numbers of reviews per day.

Our goal is to write a DAG that fetches the movie reviews each day and then prints the result in a specific format. Although we could do this with two tasks (one to fetch the ratings and one to print), we don't have much scope to handle ratings individually (atomically; see chapter 3 for a discussion of atomicity). Moreover, if the set is large or the processing is complex, we won't be able to parallelize this DAG in any way. The DAG would look something like the following listing (dags/08_no_dynamic_task_mapping.py).

Listing 12.30　Processing movie reviews without Dynamic Task Mapping

```python
def _fetch_ratings(ti):
    data = requests.get(                              # Retrieves the data
    "http://movie-reviews:8081/reviews/latest")       # from the API
    ti.xcom_push(key="movie_ratings",
    value=[[x] for x in data.json()])                 # Pushes the data retrieved into XCom
                                                       # so downstream tasks can use it

def _print_rating(ti):
    data = ti.xcom_pull(key="movie_ratings",
    task_ids="fetch_ratings")                          # Retrieves the data from XCom
    for rating in data:
        print(f"New rating for Movie: {rating[0]["movie"]}.
    Rating: {rating[0]["rating"]}")                    # Outputs the data in
                                                       # the desired form

with DAG(
    dag_id="08_no_dynamic_task_mapping",
    start_date=pendulum.today("UTC").add(days=-5),
    schedule=CronTriggerTimetable("0 16 * * *", timezone="UTC")
):
    fetch_ratings = PythonOperator(
        task_id="fetch_ratings",
        python_callable=_fetch_ratings
    )

    print_rating = PythonOperator(
        task_id="print_rating",
```

```
        python_callable=_print_rating
)

    fetch_ratings >> print_rating
```

We're using XCom here to pass data between the two tasks. We could also do this by writing to and reading from a file (or some other external storage system). We chose to use XCom here because Dynamic Task Mapping also makes heavy use of XCom under the hood, so it's the best equivalent.

Because we don't know the number of movie reviews per day beforehand, we also can't use the factory pattern we used earlier. But we can use Dynamic Task Mapping to tell Airflow to generate the print tasks dynamically based on the output of the `fetch_ratings` task. To do this, we're going to map over each rating output by `fetch_ratings` and apply another task on each mapped value.

Before looking at how this approach works for this example, let's look at the syntax of Dynamic Task Mapping. At a high level, each operator in Airflow can use two methods with Dynamic Task Mapping:

- `expand()`—This function is the one into which we pass the values we want to map over. For each element of the input, a separate task is created and rendered in the Airflow UI.
- `partial()`—Any parameters that should remain constant for all mapped values passed into expand should be passed into `partial`, including the base operator parameters such as `task_id`.

In practice, this approach gives us something like the following setup. This code results in three mapped task instances—one for each value of the list passed into the expand function. Figure 12.5 provides a schematic representation.

```
...
def add_function(x: int, y: int):
    return x + y

added_values = PythonOperator.partial(
    task_id="add",
    python_callable=add_function,
    op_kwargs={"y": 10}
).expand(op_args=[[1], [2], [3]])
```

Adds static arguments such as task_id to the partial function

In this case, the value of y is static. We want to map over input elements and add 10 to them.

In the expand function, we pass the parameters we want to map over. We have to wrap each value in a list due to the use of XCom.

Now let's return to our movie-recommender example. If we want to map over the reviews obtained from the API, we could chain the two tasks together and put the output of the `fetch_ratings` task in the expand function of the `print_rating` task, as shown in the next listing (dags/05_dynamic_task_mapping.py).

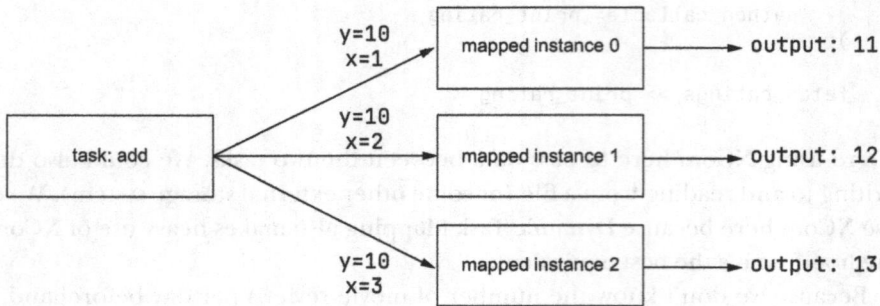

Figure 12.5   A schematic overview of the example code in listing 12.31

Listing 12.32   Using Dynamic Task Mapping to generate tasks

```
def _fetch_ratings():
    data = requests.get("http://movie-reviews:8081/reviews/latest")
    return [[x] for x in data.json()]

def _print_rating(rating):
    print(f"New rating for Movie:
        {rating["movie"]}. Rating: {rating["rating"]}")

with DAG(
    dag_id="05_dynamic_task_mapping",
    start_date=pendulum.today("UTC").add(days=-5),
    schedule=CronTriggerTimetable("0 16 * * *", timezone="UTC")
):
    fetch_ratings = PythonOperator(
        task_id="fetch_ratings",
        python_callable=_fetch_ratings
    )

    print_rating = PythonOperator.partial(
        task_id="print_rating",
        python_callable=_print_rating
    ).expand(op_args=fetch_ratings.output)

    fetch_ratings >> print_rating
```

We have to wrap each element in a list when using traditional syntax with Dynamic Task Mapping due to XCom.

Puts all static attributes for the mapped task in the partial method

Passes the argument to map over to the expand method

Now, regardless of how many reviews have been left, each time the DAG runs, a separate task is created for each review, allowing for parallel and independent processing of each review. This approach could make our DAG considerably more efficient. The Airflow UI's grid view also shows this Dynamic Task Mapping (figure 12.6); it's visible in the graph view as well (figure 12.7). Because each DAG run may have a different number of mapped task instances, Airflow renders dynamically mapped tasks with a [] behind their name in the grid view to provide some visual indication that multiple instances may exist.

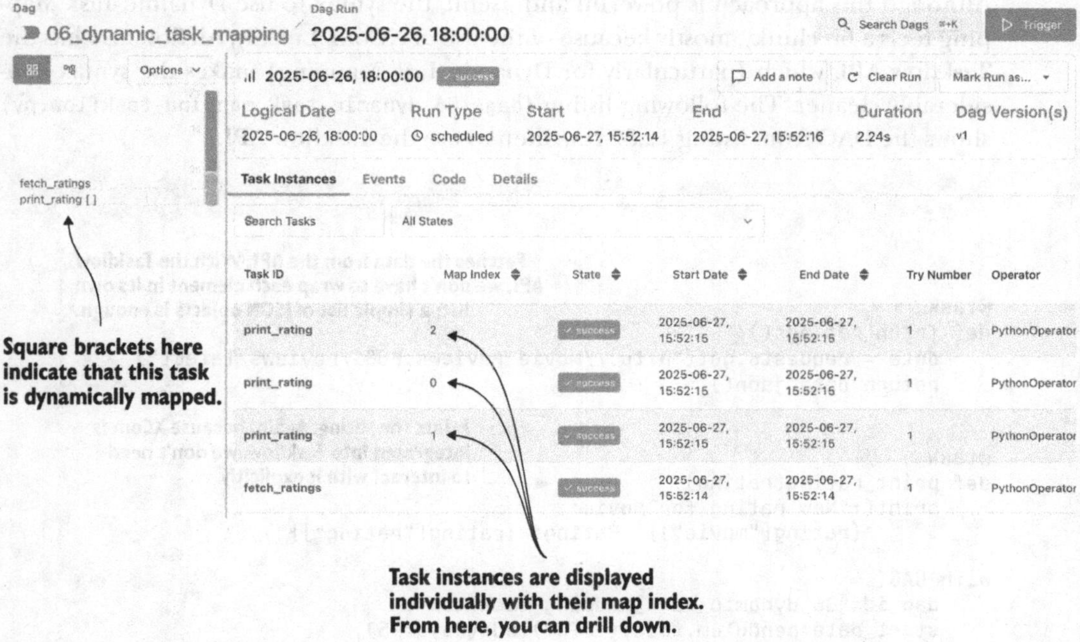

Square brackets here indicate that this task is dynamically mapped.

Task instances are displayed individually with their map index. From here, you can drill down.

Figure 12.6 The Airflow UI's grid view provides insight into Dynamic Task Mapping in several places, most notably with the [ ] notation at the top level, showing that the specific task has dynamically mapped instances below it.

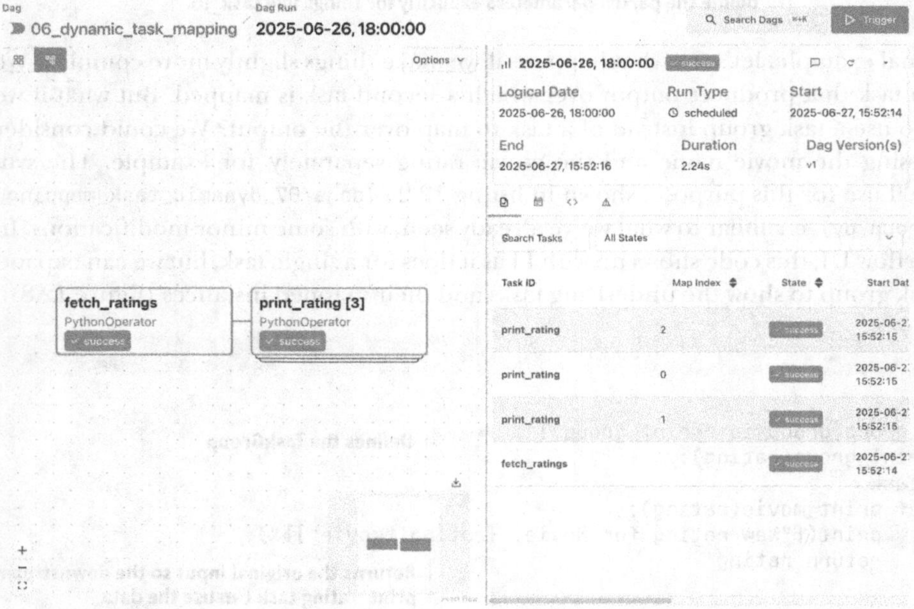

Figure 12.7 In the graph view, the mapped task is displayed visually (with additional tasks behind the top one). The mapped instances are also visible and show the individual instances.

Although this approach is powerful and useful, the syntax to use Dynamic Task Mapping feels a bit clunky, mostly because of the use of XCom. Luckily, Airflow also has the Taskflow API, which (particularly for Dynamic Task Mapping) makes the syntax considerably cleaner. The following listing (dags/06_dynamic_task_mapping_taskflow.py) shows the DAG from listing 12.32 rewritten to use the Taskflow API.

Listing 12.33 Using the Taskflow API with Dynamic Task Mapping

Fetches the data from the API. With the Taskflow API, we don't have to wrap each element in its own list; a simple list of JSON objects is enough.

```
@task
def fetch_ratings():
    data = requests.get("http://movie-reviews:8081/reviews/latest")
    return data.json()
```

Prints the rating. Again, because XCom is integrated into Taskflow, we don't need to interact with it explicitly.

```
@task
def print_rating(rating):
    print(f"New rating for Movie:
        {rating["movie"]}. Rating: {rating["rating"]}")

with DAG(
    dag_id="06_dynamic_task_mapping_taskflow",
    start_date=pendulum.today("UTC").add(days=-5),
    schedule=CronTriggerTimetable("0 16 * * *", timezone="UTC")
) as dag:
    print_rating.expand(rating=fetch_ratings())
```

We still pass the output of the fetch_ratings task into the expand method of the print_ratings operator. With Taskflow, however, we don't need to define the partial parameters explicitly for things like task_id.

As a final example, let's see what happens if we make things slightly more complex. We have a task that produces output over which a second task is mapped. But what if we want to use a task group instead of a task to map over the output? We could consider processing the movie name and the movie rating separately, for example. The syntax we'll use for this purpose, shown in listing 12.24 (dags/07_dynamic_task_mapping_taskgroup.py), is similar to what we've already seen, with some minor modifications. In the Airflow UI, this code shows up with [ ] as it does for a single task, but we can expand the task group to show the underlying tasks and their mapped instances (figure 12.8).

Listing 12.34 Using TaskGroups with Dynamic Task Mapping

```
...
@task_group(group_id="print_group")          Defines the TaskGroup
def print_group(rating):
    @task
    def print_movie(rating):
        print(f"New rating for Movie: {rating["movie"]}")
        return rating
```

Returns the original input so the downstream print_rating task can use the data

```
@task
def print_rating(rating):
    print(f"Rating: {rating["rating"]}")

print_movie(rating) >> print_rating(rating)

with DAG(
    dag_id="07_dynamic_task_mapping_taskgroup",
    start_date=pendulum.today("UTC").add(days=-5),
    schedule=CronTriggerTimetable("0 16 * * *", timezone="UTC")
) as dag:
    print_group.expand(rating=fetch_ratings())   ◄──  Uses the expand function as
                                                       before, but now on the
                                                       TaskGroup instead of the task
```

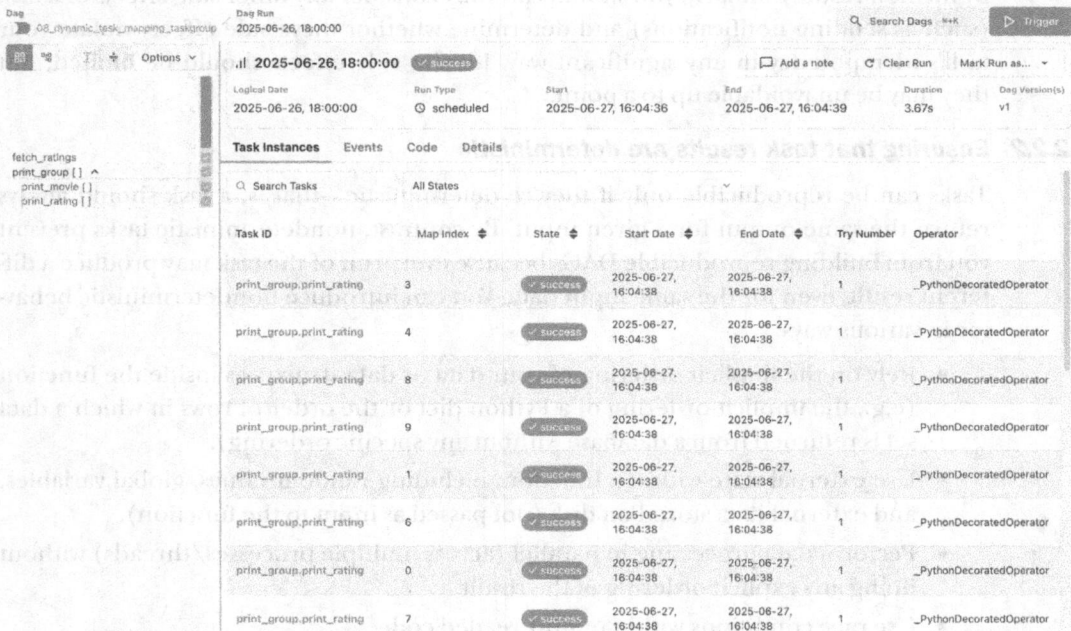

Figure 12.8 For task groups, the UI provides a similar representation, with [ ] indicating at both the task and task-group levels that this task is mapped. For all mapped tasks, the individual instances are visible in the right panel, as before.

12.2 Designing reproducible tasks

Aside from DAG code, one of the biggest challenges in writing a good Airflow DAG is designing your tasks to be reproducible, meaning that you can easily rerun a task and expect the same result even if the task is run at different times. In this section, we revisit some key ideas and offer some advice on ensuring that your tasks fit this paradigm.

12.2.1   *Requiring tasks to be idempotent*

As briefly discussed in chapter 3, one of the key requirements for a good Airflow task is *idempotency*, which means that rerunning the same task multiple times produces the same overall result (assuming that the task itself hasn't changed). Idempotency is important because you or Airflow may rerun a task in many situations. You may want to rerun some DAG runs after changing some code, for example, leading to the re-execution of a given task. In other cases, Airflow may rerun a failed task using its retry mechanism, even though the given task managed to write some results before failing. In both cases, you want to avoid introducing multiple copies of the same data into your environment or running into other undesirable side effects.

Typically, you can enforce idempotency by requiring any output data to be overwritten when a task is rerun, ensuring that any data written by a previous run is overwritten by the new result. Similarly, you should carefully consider any other side effects of a task (such as sending notifications) and determine whether these side effects violate your task's idempotency in any significant way. Ideally, side effects should be limited, but they may be unavoidable up to a point.

12.2.2   *Ensuring that task results are deterministic*

Tasks can be reproducible only if they're deterministic—that is, a task should always return the same output for a given input. By contrast, nondeterministic tasks prevent you from building reproducible DAGs because every run of the task may produce a different result, even for the same input data. You can introduce nondeterministic behavior in various ways:

- Rely on the implicit ordering of your data or data structures inside the function (e.g., the implicit ordering of a Python dict or the order of rows in which a data set is returned from a database without any specific ordering).
- Use external state within a function, including random values, global variables, and external data stored on disk (not passed as input to the function).
- Perform data processing in parallel (across multiple processes/threads) without doing any explicit ordering of the result.
- Use race conditions within multithreaded code.
- Perform improper exception handling.

In general, you can avoid issues with nondeterministic functions by thinking carefully about sources of nondeterminism that may occur within your function. You can avoid nondeterminism in the ordering of your data set by applying an explicit sort to it, for example. Similarly, you can avoid issues with algorithms that include randomness by setting the random seed before performing the corresponding operation.

12.2.3   *Designing tasks using functional paradigms*

One approach that may help with creating tasks is designing them according to the paradigm of functional programming. Functional programming is an approach to building computer programs that treats computation as the application of mathematical functions while avoiding changing state and mutable data. Also, functions in functional programming languages are typically required to be pure, meaning that they return a result but otherwise have no side effects.

One advantage of this approach is that the result of a pure function in a functional programming language should always be the same for a given input. Therefore, pure functions are generally both idempotent and deterministic—exactly what we're trying to achieve for our tasks in Airflow functions. Proponents of the functional paradigm argue that similar approaches can be applied to data processing applications, introducing the functional data engineering paradigm.

Functional data engineering approaches aim to apply the concepts of functional programming languages to data engineering tasks, including requiring tasks to have no side effects and always return the same result when applied to the same input data set. The main advantage of enforcing these constraints is that they go a long way toward achieving our ideals of idempotent and deterministic tasks, making our DAGs and tasks reproducible.

NOTE For more details, see this blog post by Maxime Beauchemin (one of the key people behind Airflow), which provides an excellent introduction to the concept of functional data engineering for data pipelines in Airflow (http://mng.bz/2eqm).

12.3 Handling data efficiently

DAGs that are meant to handle large amounts of data should be carefully designed to do so in the most efficient manner possible. In this section, we'll discuss a couple of tips on handling large data volumes efficiently.

12.3.1 Limiting the amount of data being processed

Although it may sound a bit trivial, the best way to handle data efficiently is to limit your processing to the minimal data required to obtain the desired result. After all, processing data that's going to be discarded anyway is a waste of time and resources.

In practice, this means thinking carefully about your data sources and determining whether all of them are required. For the data sets that are needed, you can try to reduce their size by discarding rows and columns that aren't used. Also, performing aggregations early can increase performance substantially: the right aggregation can greatly reduce the size of an intermediate data set, thereby decreasing the amount of work to be done downstream.

As an example, imagine a data process in which we're interested in calculating the monthly sales volumes of our products among a particular customer base (figure 12.9). We can calculate the aggregate sales by joining the sales and customer data sets, then aggregating our sales to the required granularity and filtering for the required customers. A drawback of this approach is that we're joining two potentially large data sets to get our result, which may take considerable time and resources.

A. Inefficient processing using the full data set

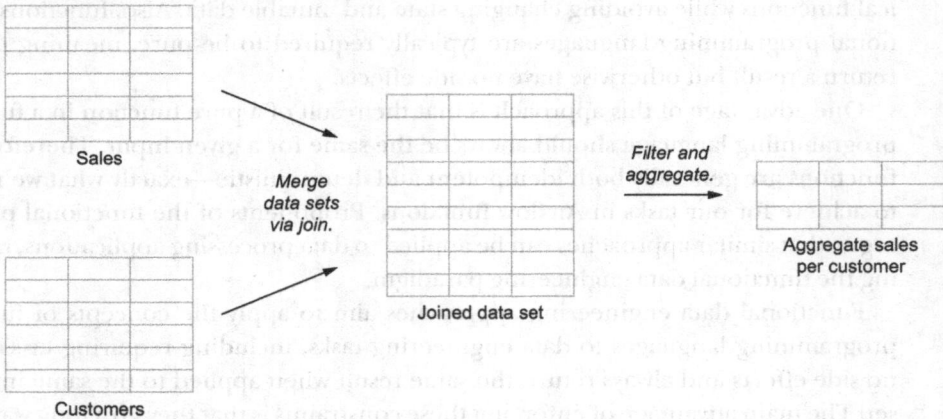

B. More efficient processing via early filtering

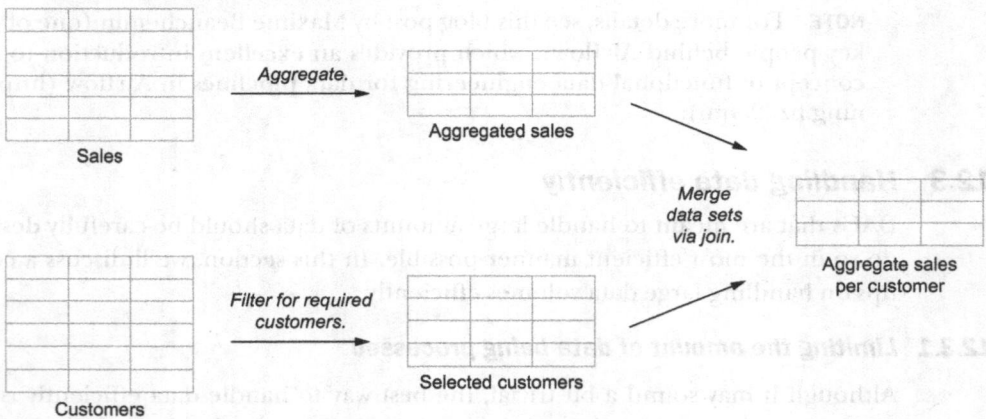

Figure 12.9 Example of an inefficient data process compared with a more efficient one. (A) One way to calculate the aggregate sales per customer is to fully join both data sets and then aggregate sales to the required granularity and filter for customers of interest. Although this approach may give us the desired result, it's not efficient due to the potentially large size of the joined table. (B) A more efficient approach is to filter/aggregate the sales and customer tables down to the minimum required granularity, allowing us to join the two smaller data sets.

A more efficient approach is to push the filtering/aggregation steps forward, reducing the sizes of the customer and sales data sets before joining them. This potentially greatly reduces the size of the joined data set, making our computation much more efficient.

Although this example may be a bit abstract, we've encountered many cases in which smart aggregation or the filtering of data sets (in terms of rows and columns) greatly increased the performance of the data processes involved. It may be beneficial to look carefully at DAGs to see whether they're processing more data than needed.

Many modern data processing tools do this kind of optimization internally. But it can still be beneficial to consider whether performing this kind of split in your Airflow DAG structure will help you optimize overall performance.

12.3.2 Loading/processing data incrementally

In many cases, you may not be able to reduce the size of your data set by using clever aggregation or filtering. But especially for time-series data sets, you may be able to limit the amount of processing in each run by using incremental data processing.

The main idea behind incremental processing (which we touched on in chapter 3) is to split data into time-based partitions and process them individually in each DAG run. This way, you limit the amount of data being processed in each run to the size of the corresponding partition, which usually is much smaller than the entire data set. By adding each run's results as increments to the output data set, however, you'll still build up the entire data set over time (figure 12.10).

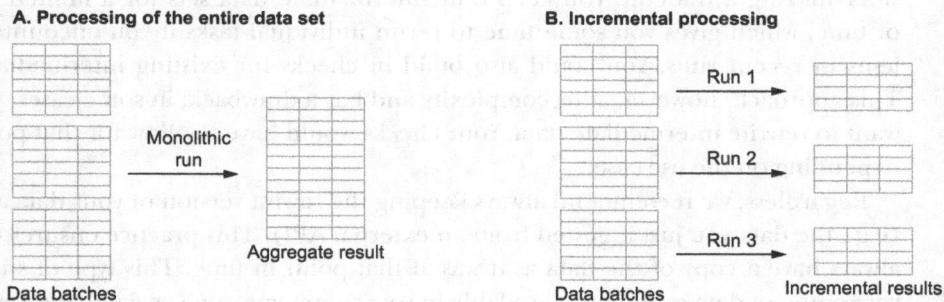

Figure 12.10   Illustration of monolithic processing (A), in which the entire data set is processed on every run, compared with incremental processing (B), in which the data set is analyzed in incremental batches as data comes in

An advantage of designing your process to be incremental is that any error in a run won't require you to redo your analysis for the entire data set; you can simply restart the run that failed. In some cases, you may still have to do analyses on the entire data set. But you can still benefit from incremental processing by performing filtering/ aggregation steps in the incremental part of your process and doing the large-scale analysis on the reduced result.

12.3.3 Caching intermediate data

In most data processing workflows, DAGs consist of multiple steps, each of which performs additional operations on data from preceding steps. An advantage of this approach is that it breaks our DAG into clear, atomic steps, which are easy to rerun if we encounter any errors.

To rerun any steps in such a DAG efficiently, however, we must make sure that the data required for those steps is readily available (figure 12.11). Otherwise, we won't be able to rerun any individual step without also rerunning all its dependencies, which defeats part of the purpose of splitting our workflow into tasks in the first place.

Figure 12.11   Storing intermediate data from tasks ensures that we can easily run each task independently. In this case, cloud storage (indicated by the bucket) is used to store intermediate results of the fetch/preprocess tasks.

A drawback of caching intermediate data is that it may require excessive storage if you have several intermediate versions of large data sets. In this case, you might consider making a tradeoff: you keep only intermediate data sets for a limited amount of time, which gives you some time to rerun individual tasks if you encounter problems in recent runs. You could also build in checks for existing intermediate data. This approach, however, adds complexity and has a drawback: in some cases, you may want to rewrite intermediate data. Your checks would have to allow for that possibility, depending on the use case.

Regardless, we recommend always keeping the rawest version of your data available (e.g., the data you just ingested from an external API). This practice ensures that you always have a copy of the data as it was at that point in time. This type of snapshot/ versioning of data is often not available in source systems, such as databases (assuming that no snapshots are made) and APIs. Keeping this raw copy of your data around ensures that you can always reprocess it as necessary, such as when you make changes to your code or problems occur during initial processing.

12.3.4   Avoiding storing data on local filesystems

When you're handling data within an Airflow job, it can be tempting to write intermediate data to a local filesystem. This is especially true when you use operators that run locally on the Airflow worker, such as the Bash and Python operators, because the local filesystem is easily accessible from within them.

A drawback of writing files to local systems is that downstream tasks may not be able to access them. Airflow runs its tasks across multiple workers, which allows it to run multiple tasks in parallel. Depending on your Airflow deployment, this can mean that two dependent tasks (i.e., one task expects data from the other) can run on two workers, which don't have access to each other's filesystems and therefore can't access each other's files.

The easiest way to prevent this issue is to use shared storage that can be accessed in the same manner from every Airflow worker. One common approach is to write intermediate files to a shared cloud storage bucket, which can be accessed from each worker using the same file URLs and credentials. Similarly, you can use shared databases or other storage systems to store data, depending on the type of data involved.

NOTE Wherever you store your intermediate data, don't forget to clean it up when you're done with it.

12.3.5 *Offloading work to external/source systems*

In general, Airflow shines when you use it as an orchestration tool rather than using the Airflow workers themselves to perform data processing. With small data sets, for example, you can typically get away with loading data directly on the workers using the PythonOperator. For larger data sets, this approach can be problematic because it requires you to run Airflow workers on increasingly large machines.

In such cases, you can get much more performance out of a small Airflow cluster by offloading your computations or queries to external systems that are better suited to that type of work. When you're querying data from a database, for example, you can make your work more efficient by pushing any required filtering/aggregation to the database system rather than fetching data locally and performing the computations in Python on your worker. Similarly, for big data applications, you typically get better performance by using Airflow to run your computation on an external Apache Spark cluster.

The key message here is that Airflow was designed primarily as an orchestration tool, so you'll get the best results if you use it that way. Other tools are generally better suited to performing data processing, so be sure to use them for that purpose, allowing the different tools to play to their strengths.

12.4 *Managing concurrency using pools*

When you work with large volumes of data, it can be easy to overwhelm your Airflow cluster or the other systems you use to process the data. In this section, we'll show how to approach this problem.

When running many tasks in parallel, you may find that multiple tasks need access to the same resource, which can overwhelm the resource if it isn't designed to handle that kind of concurrency. Examples include shared resources such as databases and graphics processing unit (GPU) systems, as well as Spark clusters if you want to limit the number of jobs running on a given cluster.

Airflow allows you to control how many tasks have access to a given resource by using resource pools. Each pool contains a fixed number of slots, which grant access to the corresponding resource. Individual tasks that need access to the resource can be assigned to the resource pool, telling the Airflow scheduler that it needs to obtain a slot from the pool before it schedules the corresponding task.

You can create a resource pool by choosing Admin > Pools in the Airflow UI. The resulting view shows an overview of the pools defined within Airflow. To create a new resource pool, click Add Pool (the blue plus-sign button at the top). In the next screen (figure 12.12), you can enter a name and description for the new resource pool, along with the number of slots you want to assign to it. The number of slots defines the degree of concurrency for the resource pool. A resource pool with 10 slots, for example, allows 10 tasks to access the corresponding resource simultaneously.

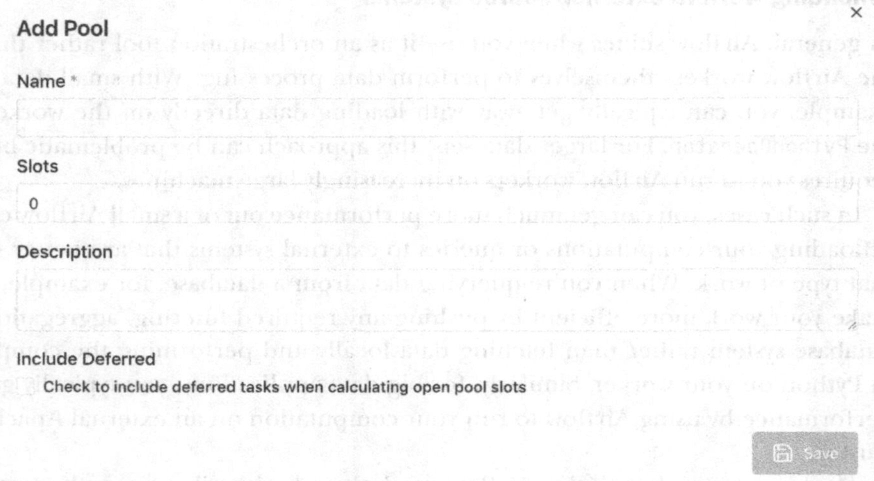

Add Pool   ✕

Name *

Slots

0

Description

Include Deferred
Check to include deferred tasks when calculating open pool slots

💾 Save

Figure 12.12   Creating a new resource pool in the Airflow web UI. The final check box lets you control whether deferrable tasks count toward pool-slot consumption.

To make your tasks use the new resource pool, assign the resource pool when you create the task, as shown in listing 12.35. This way, Airflow will check to see whether any slots are still available in `my_resource_pool` before scheduling the task in a given run. If the pool still contains free slots, the scheduler will claim an empty slot (decreasing the number of available slots by one) and schedule the task for execution. If the pool doesn't contain any free slots, the scheduler will postpone scheduling the task until a slot becomes available. The size of your pool depends on what concurrency you want or can support for your use case.

Listing 12.35   Assigning a specific resource pool to a task

```
PythonOperator(
    task_id="my_task",
    ...
    pool="my_resource_pool"
)
```

Summary

- Adopting common style conventions and supporting linting/formatting tools can greatly increase the readability of your DAG code.

- Credentials should always be managed centrally. Airflow offers multiple secret backend interfaces with external secrets-management systems, allowing you to reuse existing infrastructure if available.

- Be consistent in how you specify configuration to prevent confusion.

- Avoid doing computations in your DAG definition, which can greatly slow Airflow.

- Factory functions allow you to generate recurring DAGs or task structures efficiently while capturing differences between instances in small configuration objects or files.

- Dynamic Task Mapping enables you to make your DAG structure dynamic, depending on the data at hand. This can enhance parallelism and atomicity in your tasks.

- Task groups allow you to structure your DAGs visually, especially when the DAGs have many tasks.

- Idempotent and deterministic tasks are key to building reproducible tasks and DAGs that are easy to rerun and backfill from within Airflow. Concepts from functional programming can help you design tasks with these characteristics.

- You can implement data processes efficiently by carefully considering how data is handled (i.e., processing in the appropriate systems, limiting the amount of data that is loaded, and using incremental loading) and by caching intermediate data sets in filesystems that are available across workers.

- You can manage or limit access to your resources in Airflow by using resource pools.

Project: Finding the
fastest way to get
around NYC

This chapter covers

- Setting up an Airflow pipeline from scratch
- Structuring intermediate output data
- Developing idempotent tasks
- Implementing one operator to handle multiple similar transformations

By now, we've discussed most of the ins and outs of using Airflow, and you're well on your way to becoming an Airflow expert. It's time for you to make good use of all that knowledge and see how to apply your new skills to a real-life use case.

13.1 Use case: Investigating traffic in New York City

Transportation in New York City (NYC) can be hectic. It's always rush hour. Fortunately, more alternative ways of transportation are available than ever. In May 2013, Citi Bike started operating in New York City with 6,000 bikes. Over the years, Citi Bike has grown and expanded, becoming a popular method of transportation in the city.

Another iconic method of transportation is the Yellow Cab taxi. Taxis were introduced in NYC in the late 1890s and have always been popular. In recent years, however, the number of taxi drivers has plummeted, and many drivers have started driving for ride-sharing services such as Uber and Lyft.

Regardless of the type of transportation you choose in NYC, your typical goal is to go from point A to point B as fast as possible. Luckily, the city of New York is active about publishing data, including rides from Citi Bike and Yellow Cab taxis.

In this section, we try to answer this question: "If I were to go from A to B in NYC right now, which method of transportation would be fastest?" We've created an Airflow mini project to extract and load data, transform it into a usable format, and ask the data which method of transportation is faster depending on the neighborhoods we're traveling between and the time of day.

NOTE Some ideas in this chapter are based on a blog post by Todd Schneider (https://mng.bz/gmpZ) in which he analyzes the fastest transportation method by applying a Monte Carlo simulation.

To make this mini project reproducible, we created a Docker Compose file running several services in Docker containers. These services give us the building blocks shown in figure 13.1:

- One REST API serving Citi Bike data
- One file share serving Yellow Cab taxi data
- MinIO, an object store that supports the Amazon Web Service (AWS) S3 protocol
- A PostgreSQL database for querying and storing data
- An Apache Flask application for displaying results

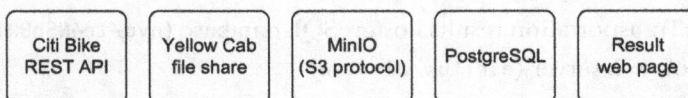

Citi Bike REST API	Yellow Cab file share	MinIO (S3 protocol)	PostgreSQL	Result web page

Figure 13.1 Our Docker Compose file creates several services. Our task is to load data from the REST API and file share and then transform it so we can eventually view the fastest method of transportation on the resulting web page.

Our goal throughout this chapter is to use these building blocks to extract data from the REST API and file share and then develop a data pipeline connecting these dots. We chose MinIO because AWS S3 is often used for data storage and MinIO supports the S3 protocol. The results of the analysis will be written to a PostgreSQL database, and the web page will display the results. To get started, ensure that your current directory holds the `compose.yaml` file, and create all containers, as shown in the following listing.

Listing 13.1 Running use-case building blocks in Docker containers

```
$ docker compose up --build -d
[+] Running 27/27
✓ citibike_api-1                                   Built
✓ citibike_db                                      Built
✓ nyc_transportation_api                           Built
✓ taxi_db                                          Built
✓ taxi_fileserver                                  Built
✓ Container chapter13-taxi_db-1                     Created
✓ Container chapter13-citibike_db-1                 Created
✓ Container chapter13-minio-1                       Created
✓ Container chapter13-postgres-1                    Created
✓ Container chapter13-result_db-1                   Created
✓ Container chapter13-redis-1                       Created
✓ Container chapter13-airflow-python-build-1        Created
✓ Container chapter13-nyc_transportation_api-1      Created
✓ Container chapter13-minio_init-1                  Created
✓ Container chapter13-airflow-init-1                Created
✓ Container chapter13-airflow-scheduler-1           Created
✓ Container chapter13-airflow-triggerer-1           Created
✓ Container chapter13-airflow-apiserver-1           Created
✓ Container chapter13-airflow-dag-processor-1       Created
✓ Container chapter13-airflow-worker-1              Created
✓ Container chapter13-taxi_fileserver-1             Created
✓ Container chapter13-citibike_api-1                Created
```

This code exposes the following services on localhost:[port], with [username]/[password] given between parentheses:

- 5432—Airflow PostgreSQL metastore (airflow/airflow)
- 5433—NYC Taxi PostgreSQL database (taxi/ridetlc)
- 5434—Citi Bike PostgreSQL database (citi/cycling)
- 5435—NYC Transportation results PostgreSQL database (nyc/tr4N5p0RT4TI0N)
- 8080—Airflow web server (airflow/airflow)
- 8081—NYC taxi static file server
- 8082—Citi Bike API (citibike/cycling)
- 8083—NYC transportation web page
- 9001—MinIO (AKIAIOSFODNN7EXAMPLE/wJalrXUtnFEMI/K7MDENG/bPxRfiCYEXAMPLE KEY)

Data for both Yellow Cab and Citi Bike rides has been made available in monthly batches:

- *NYC Yellow Taxi*—https://mng.bz/eBOw
- *NYC Citi Bike*—https://www.citibikenyc.com/system-data

The goal of this project is to demonstrate a real environment with several real challenges you might encounter and show how to deal with them in Airflow. The data sets are released once a month. One-month intervals are quite long, so we've created two APIs in the Docker Compose setup that provide the same data at intervals configurable to a single minute. Also, the APIs mimic several characteristics of production systems, such as authentication. Let's look at a map of NYC to develop an idea for determining the fastest method of transportation (figure 13.2).

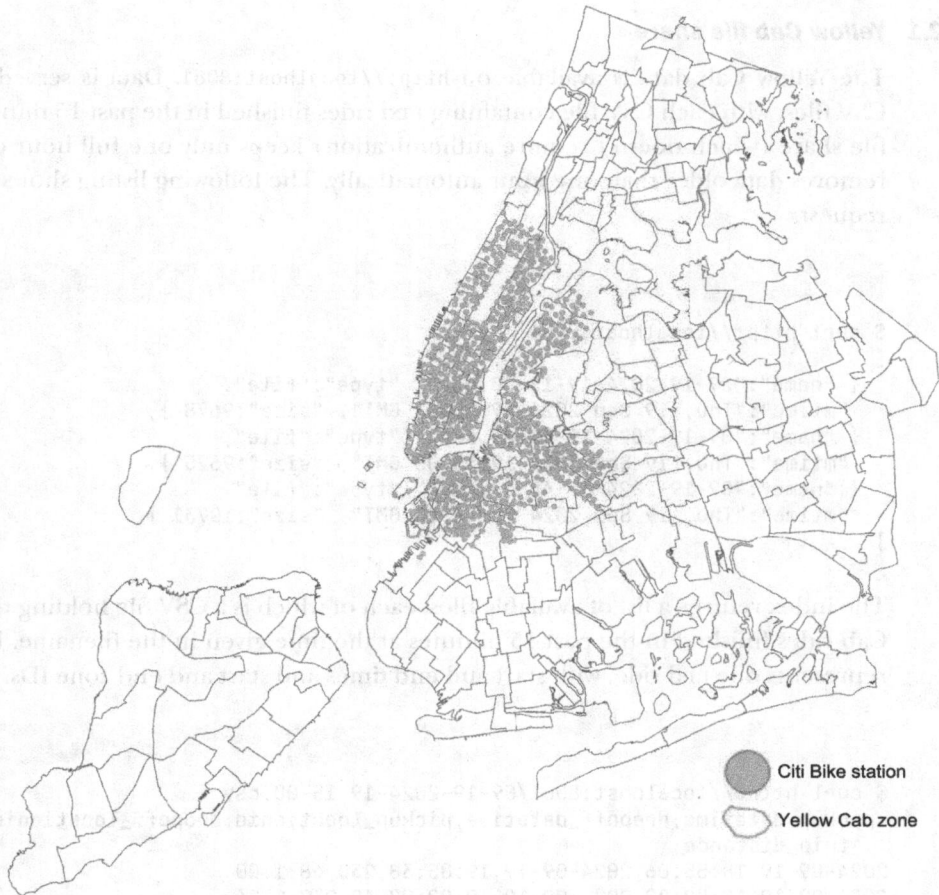

Figure 13.2 NYC Yellow Cab zones plotted with Citi Bike station locations

We clearly see that Citi Bike stations are based only in the center of New York City. Therefore, to produce any meaningful advice about the fastest method of transportation, we're limited to zones in which both Citi Bike and Yellow Cab are present. In section 13.2, we'll inspect the data and develop a plan of approach.

13.2   Understanding the data

The Docker Compose file provides two endpoints with the Yellow Cab and Citi Bike data:

- Yellow Cab data on `http://localhost:8081`
- Citi Bike data on `http://localhost:8082`

Let's see how to query these endpoints and what data they return.

13.2.1   Yellow Cab file share

The Yellow Cab data is available on `http://localhost:8081`. Data is served as static CSV files, with each CSV file containing taxi rides finished in the past 15 minutes. The file share (which doesn't require authentication) keeps only one full hour of data; it removes data older than one hour automatically. The following listing shows a sample request.

Listing 13.2   Sample request to the Yellow Cab file share

```
$ curl http://localhost:8081
[
  { "name":"09-19-2024-19-15-00.csv", "type":"file",
  "mtime":"Thu, 19 Sep 2024 19:15:01 GMT", "size":9678 },
  { "name":"09-19-2024-19-30-00.csv", "type":"file",
  "mtime":"Thu, 19 Sep 2024 19:30:00 GMT", "size":9625 },
  { "name":"09-19-2024-19-45-00.csv", "type":"file",
  "mtime":"Thu, 19 Sep 2024 19:45:00 GMT", "size":10731 }
]
```

The index returns a list of available files, each of which is a CSV file holding the Yellow Cab rides finished in the past 15 minutes at the time given in the filename. Each line represents one taxi ride, with start and end times and start and end zone IDs.

Listing 13.3   Sample snippet of Yellow Cab file

```
$ curl http://localhost:8081/09-19-2024-19-15-00.csv
 pickup_datetime,dropoff_datetime,pickup_locationid,dropoff_locationid,
 trip_distance
2024-09-19 18:55:06,2024-09-19 19:05:38,230,68,1.00
2024-09-19 18:50:29,2024-09-19 19:02:07,48,239,1.86
2024-09-19 18:53:02,2024-09-19 19:11:13,100,161,1.57
2024-09-19 18:27:28,2024-09-19 19:03:36,249,237,3.73
2024-09-19 18:50:48,2024-09-19 19:13:04,74,239,3.20
...
```

13.2.2   Citi Bike REST API

The Citi Bike data is available on `http://localhost:8082`, which serves data via a REST API. This API enforces basic authentication, meaning that we have to supply a username and password. The API returns Citi Bike rides finished within a configurable period of time. A sample request follows.

```
$ date
Thu 19 Sep 2024 20:31:07 CEST

$ curl --user citibike:cycling              Request data from
⮑  http://localhost:8082/recent/hour/1  ◄───┤ the past hour
[
{
  "end_station_id": "5746.02",
  "end_station_latitude": 40.7667405590595,
  "end_station_longitude": -73.9790689945221,
  "end_station_name": "7 Ave & Central Park South",
  "start_station_id": "6046.02",                    Each JSON object represents
  "start_station_latitude": 40.77492513,            one Citi Bike ride.
  "start_station_longitude": -73.98266566,
  "start_station_name": "W 67 St & Broadway",
  "starttime": "Thu, 19 Sep 2024 19:21:35 GMT",
  "stoptime": "Thu, 19 Sep 2024 19:27:08 GMT",
  "tripduration": 333
},
{
  "end_station_id": "5414.06",
  "end_station_latitude": 40.711066,
  "end_station_longitude": -74.009447,
  "end_station_name": "Fulton St & Broadway",
  "start_station_id": "6046.02",
  "start_station_latitude": 40.692418292578466,
  "start_station_longitude": -73.98949474096298,
  "start_station_name": "Fulton St & Adams St",
  "starttime": "Thu, 19 Sep 2024 19:18:10 GMT",
  "stoptime": "Thu, 19 Sep 2024 19:30:33 GMT",
  "tripduration": 744
},
...
]
```

This query requests the Citi Bike rides finished in the past hour. Each record in the response represents one ride with Citi Bike and provides latitude/longitude coordinates of the start and end locations as well as the start and end times. We can configure the endpoint as follows to return rides at smaller or larger intervals,

```
http://localhost:8082/recent/<period>/<amount>
```

where <period> can be a minute, hour, or day. <amount> is an integer representing the number of periods. Querying `http://localhost:8082/recent/` day/3, for example, would return all Citi Bike rides finished in the past three days.

The API knows no limitations in terms of request size. In theory, we could request data for an infinite number of days. In practice, APIs often limit compute power and data-transfer size; an API might limit the number of results to 1,000, for example. With such a limitation, we'd have to know how many bike rides (approximately) are made within a certain period and make requests often enough to fetch all data while staying below the maximum 1,000 results.

13.2.3 Deciding on a plan of approach

Now that we've seen samples of the data in listings 13.3 and 13.4, let's lay out the facts and decide on how to continue. To compare apples with apples, we must map the locations in both data sets to overlapping geographical areas. The Yellow Cab ride data provides taxi-zone IDs, and the Citi Bike data provides the latitude/longitude coordinates of the bike stations. To simplify our use case but sacrifice a little accuracy, we'll map the latitude and longitude of Citi Bike stations to taxi zones (figure 13.3).

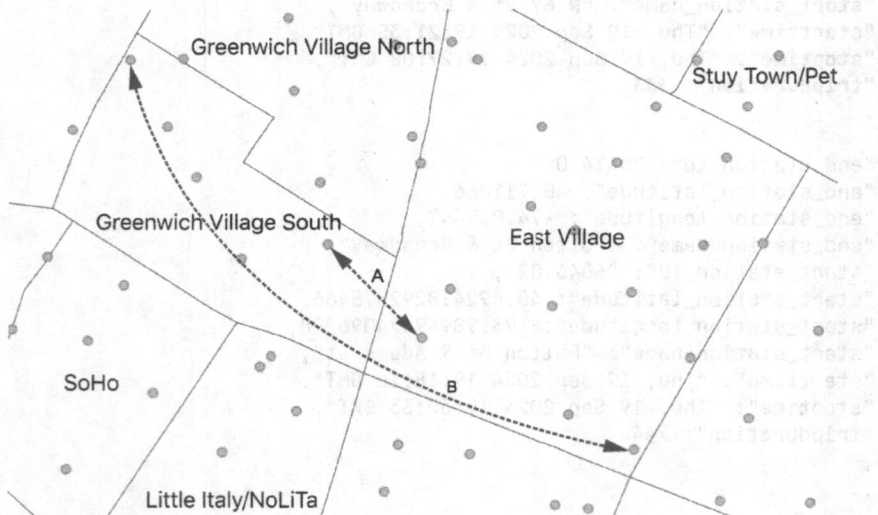

Figure 13.3 Mapping Citi Bike stations (dots) to Yellow Cab zones enables accurate comparison but ignores the fact that rides within one zone can vary in distance. Ride A is obviously shorter than ride B. By averaging all ride times from Greenwich Village South to the East Village, for example, we lose such information.

Because the Yellow Cab data is provided in the file share for only one hour, we must download and save it in our own systems. This way, we'll build a collection of historical taxi data over time, and we can always go back to the downloaded data if we change our processing. As mentioned earlier, the Docker Compose file creates a MinIO service, which is an object storage service, so we'll use it to store the data.

13.3 Extracting the data

When we're extracting multiple data sources, it's important to note the time intervals of the data. The Yellow Cab data is available at 15-minute intervals, and the Citi Bike data interval is configurable. To make things easy, let's also request Citi Bike data at 15-minute intervals. This configuration allows us to make two requests at the same interval, in the same DAG, and process all data in parallel. If we choose a different interval, we have to align the processing of both data sets differently. The following listing shows the configuration of the DAG running every 15 minutes.

Listing 13.5 DAG running every 15 minutes

```
import pendulum
from airflow.models import DAG
dag = DAG(
    dag_id="nyc_dag",
    schedule="*/15 * * * *",          ◄─────┐ Runs every 15 minutes
    start_date=pendulum.today("UTC").add(days=-1),
    catchup=False,
)
```

13.3.1 Downloading Citi Bike data

Within Airflow, we have the SimpleHttpOperator to make HTTP calls. In short order, however, it turns out to be unsuitable for our use case: the SimpleHttpOperator simply makes an HTTP request but provides no functionality for storing the response anywhere. In such a situation, we're forced to implement our own functionality and call it with a PythonOperator. Let's see how to query the Citi Bike API and store the output on the MinIO object storage.

Listing 13.6 Downloading data from the Citi Bike REST API to MinIO

Loads Citi Bike credentials
from the Airflow connection

Uses the timestamp of the Airflow
task in the resulting filename

```
import json
import requests
from airflow.hooks.base import BaseHook
from airflow.sdk import DAG
from airflow.timetables.interval import CronDataIntervalTimetable
from airflow.operators.standard.operators.python import PythonOperator
from airflow.providers.amazon.aws.hooks.s3 import S3Hook
from requests.auth import HTTPBasicAuth

def _download_citi_bike_data(data_interval_start, **_):     ◄───┐
    citibike_conn = BaseHook.get_connection(conn_id="citibike")   ◄───

    url = f"http://{citibike_conn.host}:{citibike_conn.port}/recent/minute/15"
    response = requests.get(url, auth=HTTPBasicAuth(citibike_conn.login,
    citibike_conn.password))
    data = response.json()
```

```
    s3_hook = S3Hook(aws_conn_id="s3")           ◀——  Uses S3Hook to
    s3_hook.load_string(                               communicate with MinIO
        string_data=json.dumps(data),
        key=f"raw/citibike/{{data_interval_start.
    strftime("%Y%m%dT%H%M%S")} }.json",          ◀——  Uses the timestamp of the Airflow
        bucket_name="datalake"                         task in the resulting filename
)


download_citi_bike_data = PythonOperator(
    task_id="download_citi_bike_data",
    python_callable=_download_citi_bike_data,
)
```

We have no Airflow operator to use for this specific HTTP-to-S3 operation, but we can apply Airflow hooks and connections. First, we must connect to the Citi Bike API (using the Python `requests` library) and MinIO storage (using the `S3Hook`). Because both require credentials to authenticate, we'll store them in Airflow to be loaded at run time.

Listing 13.7   Setting connection details via environment variables

```
export AIRFLOW_CONN_CITIBIKE=http://citibike:cycling@citibike_api:5000
export AIRFLOW_CONN_S3="aws://AKIAIOSFODNN7EXAMPLE:wJalrXUtnFEMI%2
    FK7MDENG%2FbPxRfiCYEXAMPLEKEY@/?endpoint_url=http%3A%2F%2F
    minio%3A 9000"                                   ◀——  Custom S3 host must
                                                           be given via extras.
```

By default, the S3 hook communicates with AWS S3 on http://s3.amazonaws.com. Because we're running MinIO on a different address, we must provide this address in the connection details. Unfortunately, this task isn't straightforward. Sometimes, such oddities mean we have to read a hook's implementation to understand its inner workings. In the case of the `S3Hook`, we can provide the hostname via a key `endpoint_url` in the extras (figure 13.4).

```
AIRFLOW_CONN_S3=aws://EXAMPLE:EXAMPLEKEY@/?endpoint_url=http%3A%2F%2Fminio%3A9000
```

**Where you expect to
set the hostname**

**Hostname provided
via endpoint_url in extras**

Figure 13.4   You can set a custom S3 hostname, but not where you expect it.

Now that we have the connections set up, let's transfer some data. If everything succeeds, we can log in on the MinIO interface at http://localhost:9001 and view the first downloaded file (figure 13.5).

Listing 13.8 Uploading a piece of data to MinIO using the S3Hook

```
s3_hook = S3Hook(aws_conn_id="s3")
s3_hook.load_string(
    string_data=json.dumps(data),
    key=f"raw/citibike/
    {data_interval_start.strftime("%Y%m%dT%H%M%S")}.json",
    bucket_name="datalake"
)
```

Writes to object with the task timestamp templated in the key name

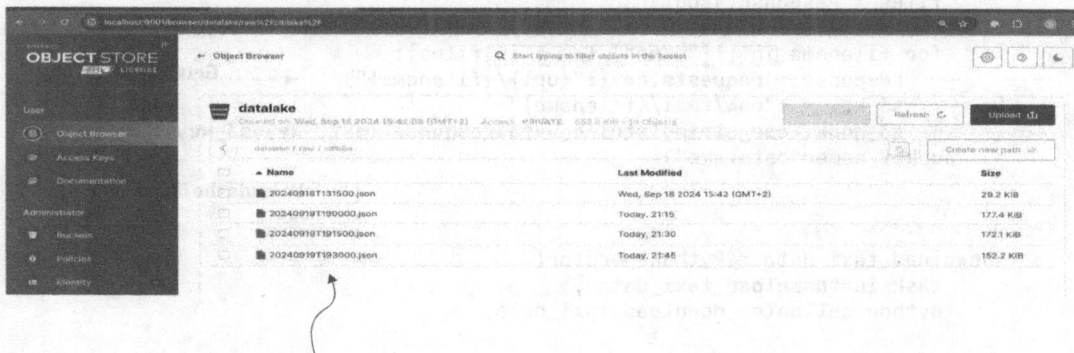

Timestamp set by data_interval_start

Figure 13.5 Screenshot of the MinIO interface showing a file written to /datalake/raw/citibike and the filename templated with data_interval_start

TIP If you perform this HTTP-to-S3 operation more often with different parameters, you'll probably want to write an operator for this task to avoid code duplication.

13.3.2 Downloading Yellow Cab data

We also want to download taxi data to the MinIO object storage. This operation is also HTTP to S3, but it has a few different characteristics:

- The file share serves files, whereas we had to create new files on MinIO for the Citi Bike data.
- These files are CSV files, whereas the Citi Bike API returns data in JSON format.
- We don't know the filenames up front; we have to list the index to receive a file list.

When you encounter such specific features, you usually have to implement your own behavior instead of applying one of Airflow's built-in operators. Some Airflow operators are highly configurable, and others are not, but for such specific features, you usually have to resort to implementing your own functionality. That said, let's see a possible implementation.

Listing 13.9   Downloading data from the Yellow Cab file share to MinIO storage

```python
def _download_taxi_data():
    taxi_conn = BaseHook.get_connection(conn_id="taxi")
    s3_hook = S3Hook(aws_conn_id="s3")

    url = f"http://{taxi_conn.host}"
    response = requests.get(url)              ◄─── Gets a list of files
    files = response.json()

    for filename in [f["name"] for f in files]:
        response = requests.get(f"{url}/{filename}")   ◄─── Gets one single file
        s3_key = f"raw/taxi/{filename}"
        s3_hook.load_string(string_data=response.text, key=s3_key,
    bucket_name="datalake")                   ◄───┐
                                                   │  Uploads the file to MinIO
)

download_taxi_data = PythonOperator(
    task_id="download_taxi_data",
    python_callable=_download_taxi_data,

)
```

This code downloads data from the file server and uploads it to MinIO. But there's a problem. Can you spot it?

s3_hook.load_string() isn't an idempotent operation. It doesn't override files and uploads only one file (or string, in this case) if it doesn't exist yet. If a file with the same name already exists, the operation fails:

```
[2024-09-19 19:24:03,053] {taskinstance.py:1145} ERROR - The key
    raw/taxi/09-19-2024-19-15-00.csv already exists.
...
    raise ValueError("The key {key} already exists.".format(key=key))
ValueError: The key raw/taxi/09-19-2020-14-30-00.csv already exists.
```

To avoid failing on existing objects, we could apply Python's EAFP (easier to ask for forgiveness than permission) idiom, trying first and catching exceptions instead of checking every possible condition to skip when encountering a ValueError.

Listing 13.10   Downloading data from the Yellow Cab file share to MinIO storage

```python
def _download_taxi_data():
    taxi_conn = BaseHook.get_connection(conn_id="taxi")
    s3_hook = S3Hook(aws_conn_id="s3")

    url = f"http://{taxi_conn.host}"
    response = requests.get(url)
```

```
files = response.json()

for filename in [f["name"] for f in files]:
    response = requests.get(f"{url}/{filename}")
    s3_key = f"raw/taxi/{filename}"
    try:
        s3_hook.load_string(
            string_data=response.text,
            key=s3_key,
            bucket_name="datalake",
        )
        print(f"Uploaded {s3_key} to MinIO.")
    except ValueError:
        print(f"File {s3_key} already exists.")
```

> **Catches ValueError exceptions raised when the file already exists**

With the addition of this check for existing files, our pipeline won't fail anymore. Now we have two download tasks, both of which download data to store on the MinIO object storage (figure 13.6). The data from both the Citi Bike API and Yellow Cab file share is available in the Mino object storage (figure 13.7).

Figure 13.6   First two tasks of the NYC transportation DAG downloading data

13.4   *Applying similar transformations to data*

After we download the Citi Bike and Yellow Cab data, we apply several transformations to map the Citi Bike station coordinates to Yellow Cab zones and start comparing them accurately. We have various ways to do this, depending on the size of the data.

In a big data scenario, we'd want to apply Apache Spark to process the data using a cluster of machines. A Spark job can be triggered with the SparkSubmitOperator or

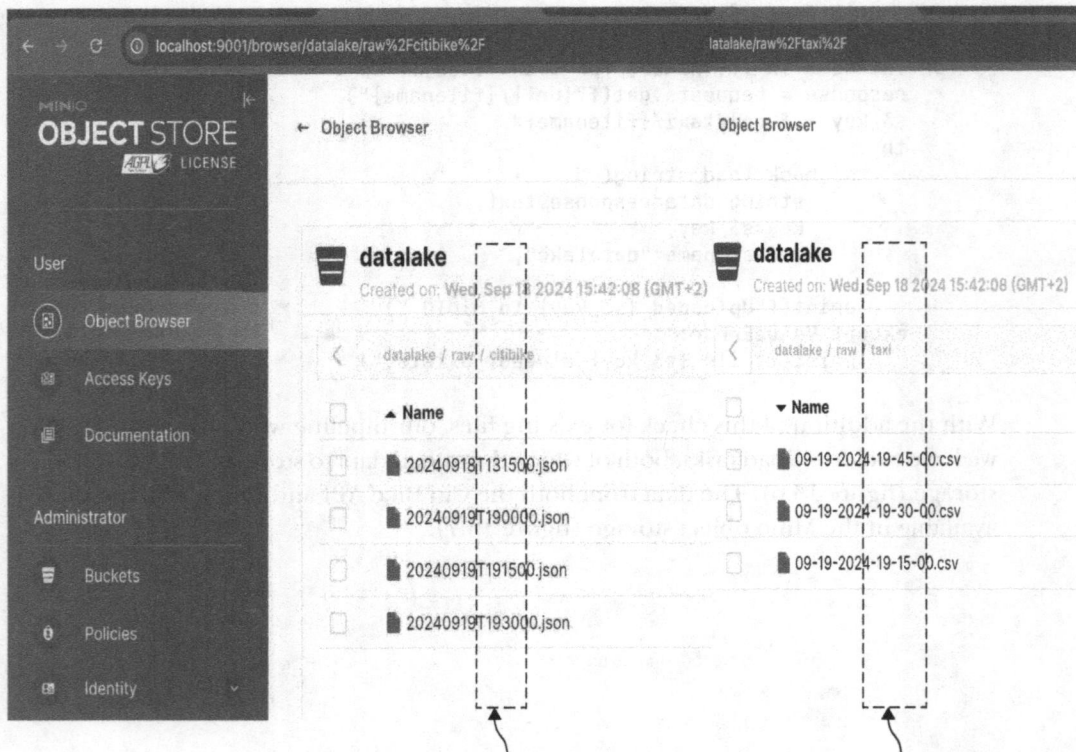

Every 15 minutes, a new export is saved in the datalake for both data sets.

Figure 13.7   Data exported to the MinIO storage. We have MinIO under our control and can always refer to these files later.

another Airflow operator that could trigger a Spark job, such as a `spark-submit` command in a `BashOperator`. Then the Spark job would read from S3, apply transformations to the data, and write back to S3.

On a smaller scale (i.e., with data processable on a single machine), we can apply pandas for this task, but no `PandasOperator` is available at the time of writing, so pandas code is typically executed using the `PythonOperator`. Python code is run on the same machine as Airflow, whereas a Spark job is typically executed on other machines dedicated to that task, so it won't affect the Airflow machine's resources. In the latter case, Airflow is responsible only for starting and monitoring the Spark job. If a pandas job is hitting the limits of the machine's resources, it could theoretically take down the machine and Airflow with it.

Another way to avoid claiming the Airflow machine's resources is to offload the job to Kubernetes using the `KubernetesPodOperator` or a similar containerized system, such as AWS ECS, using the `ECSOperator`.

Let's assume that we can apply pandas for processing small data. Instead of demonstrating how to use yet another `PythonOperator`, let's look at how we can generalize some components for reusability and code deduplication. We have two data sets stored in /raw:

- /raw/citibike/*.json
- /raw/taxi/*.csv

Both data sets will be read using pandas, a few transformations will be applied, and the result will eventually be written to the following:

- /processed/citibike/{datetime }.parquet
- /processed/taxi/{datetime }.parquet

There are a few small differences between our transformations, such as the input data sets and output file locations. Although the input formats differ, the object type into which they're loaded and the output formats do not. The core abstraction to which operations are applied in pandas is the pandas DataFrame (similar to a Spark Data-Frame), so we could implement a single operator to deal with both transformations.

> **Listing 13.11 Using a single operator for all pandas DataFrame operations**

```
import logging

from airflow.models import BaseOperator
from airflow.utils.decorators import apply_defaults


class PandasOperator(BaseOperator):
    template_fields = (
        "_input_callable_kwargs",
        "_transform_callable_kwargs",       ◁──  All kwargs arguments can
        "_output_callable_kwargs",               hold templated values.
    )


    def __init__(
        self,
        input_callable,
        output_callable,
        transform_callable=None,
        input_callable_kwargs=None,
        transform_callable_kwargs=None,
        output_callable_kwargs=None,
        **kwargs,
    ):
        super().__init__(**kwargs)

        # Attributes for reading data
        self._input_callable = input_callable
        self._input_callable_kwargs = input_callable_kwargs or {}
```

```
# Attributes for transformations
self._transform_callable = transform_callable
self._transform_callable_kwargs = transform_callable_kwargs or {}

# Attributes for writing data
self._output_callable = output_callable
self._output_callable_kwargs = output_callable_kwargs or {}

def execute(self, context:Context):
    df = self._input_callable(**self._input_callable_kwargs)
    logging.info("Read DataFrame with shape: %s.", df.shape)

    if self._transform_callable:
        df = self._transform_callable(
            df,
            **self._transform_callable_kwargs,
        )
        logging.info("DataFrame shape after transform: %s.", df.shape)

    self._output_callable(df, **self._output_callable_kwargs)
```

> Calls the input callable to return a pandas DataFrame

> Applies transformations on the DataFrame

> Writes the DataFrame

Let's break down how to use this `PandasOperator`. As mentioned earlier, the commonality among various transformations is the pandas DataFrame. We use this commonality to compose operations on the DataFrame given three functions:

- `input_callable`
- `transform_callable` (optional)
- `output_callable`

The `input_callable` reads data into a pandas DataFrame, the `transform_callable` applies transformations to this DataFrame, and the `output_callable` writes the Data-Frame. As long as the input/output of all three functions is a pandas DataFrame, we can mix and match callables to process the data using this `PandasOperator`. Let's look at an example.

Listing 13.12   Applying the `PandasOperator` from listing 13.11

```
process_taxi_data = PandasOperator(
    task_id="process_taxi_data",
    input_callable=get_minio_object,
    input_callable_kwargs={
        "pandas_read_callable": pd.read_csv,
        "bucket": "datalake",
        "paths": "{{ ti.xcom_pull(task_ids='download_taxi_data') }}",
    },
    transform_callable=transform_taxi_data,
    output_callable=write_minio_object,
    output_callable_kwargs={
        "bucket": "datalake",
        "path": "processed/taxi/{{ data_interval_start | ts_nodash }}.parquet",
```

> Reads CSV from MinIO storage

> Applies transformations on DataFrame

> Writes Parquet to MinIO storage

```
        "pandas_write_callable": pd.DataFrame.to_parquet,      ◄───  Converts data
        "pandas_write_callable_kwargs": {"engine": "auto"},          to the Parquet
    },                                                               format
)
```

The goal of the PandasOperator is to provide a single operator that allows mixing and matching various input, transformation, and output functions. As a result, defining an Airflow task glues these functions together by pointing to them and providing their arguments. We start with the input function, which returns a pandas DataFrame, as shown in listing 13.13. Listing 13.14 shows the transformation function, which adheres to "DataFrame in, DataFrame out."

Listing 13.13   Example function reading MinIO objects and returning pandas DataFrames

```
def get_minio_object(
    pandas_read_callable,
    bucket,
    paths,
    pandas_read_callable_kwargs=None,
):
    s3_conn = BaseHook.get_connection(conn_id="s3")           ◄───  Initializes a
    minio_client = Minio(                                            MinIO client
        s3_conn.extra_dejson["endpoint_url"].split("://")[1],
        access_key=s3_conn.login,
        secret_key=s3_conn.password,
        secure=False,
    )

    if isinstance(paths, str):
        paths = [paths]

    if pandas_read_callable_kwargs is None:
        pandas_read_callable_kwargs = {}

    dfs = []
    for path in paths:
        minio_object = minio_client.get_object(
            bucket_name=bucket,
            object_name=path,
        )
        df = pandas_read_callable(          ◄───  Reads the file from MinIO
            minio_object,
            **pandas_read_callable_kwargs,
        )
        dfs.append(df)                           Returns the
    return pd.concat(dfs)          ◄───────────  pandas DataFrame
```

Listing 13.14   Example function transforming taxi data

```
def transform_taxi_data(df):          ◄───
    return (                                  DataFrame in
```

```
        df
            .assign(
                starttime=lambda df: pd.to_datetime(df.pickup_datetime),
                stoptime=lambda df: pd.to_datetime(df.dropoff_datetime),
                tripduration=lambda df: (df.stoptime -
    df.starttime).dt.total_seconds().astype(int),
            )
            .rename(columns={"pickup_locationid":
    "start_location_id","dropoff_locationid": "end_location_id"})
                .drop(columns=["trip_distance", "pickup_datetime",
    "dropoff_datetime"])
        )                          ◀───┃ DataFrame out
```

Listing 13.15 shows the output function, which takes a pandas DataFrame. Passing pandas DataFrames among the input, transform, and output functions gives us the option to change the input format of a data set simply by changing the argument `"pandas_read_ callable": pd.read_csv` to, say, `"pandas_read_ callable": pd.read_parquet`. As a result, we don't have to reimplement logic with every change or every new data set, so we have no code duplication and more flexibility.

TIP Whenever you find yourself repeating logic and wanting to develop a single piece of logic to cover multiple cases, think of something your operations have in common, such as a pandas DataFrame or a Python file-like object.

Listing 13.15   Example function writing transformed DataFrame back to MinIO storage

```
def write_minio_object(
    df,
    pandas_write_callable,
    bucket,
    path,
    pandas_write_callable_kwargs=None
):
    s3_conn = BaseHook.get_connection(conn_id="s3")
    minio_client = Minio(
        s3_conn.extra_dejson["endpoint_url"].split("://")[1],
        access_key=s3_conn.login,
        secret_key=s3_conn.password,
        secure=False,
    )
    bytes_buffer = io.BytesIO()
    pandas_write_method = getattr(df,
    pandas_write_callable.__name__)
    pandas_write_method(bytes_buffer,
    **pandas_write_callable_kwargs)
    nbytes = bytes_buffer.tell()
    bytes_buffer.seek(0)
    minio_client.put_object(
        bucket_name=bucket,
        object_name=path,
```

Fetches the reference to the DataFrame writing method (e.g., pd.DataFrame.to_parquet)

Calls the DataFrame writing method to write the DataFrame to a bytes buffer, which can be stored in MinIO

Stores the bytes buffer in MinIO

```
        length=nbytes,
        data=bytes_buffer,
)
```

13.5 Structuring a data pipeline

In section 13.4, we created the folders raw and processed in a bucket named datalake. How did we get to those folders, and why? In terms of efficiency and in principle, we could write a single Python function that extracts data, transforms it, and writes the results to a database, all while keeping the data in memory and never touching the filesystem. This approach would be much faster, so why don't we take it? There are several reasons:

- Data is often used by more than one person or data pipeline. So that it can be distributed and reused it, the data is stored in a location where other people and processes can read it.
- More important, we want to make our pipeline reproducible.

What does *reproducibility* imply in terms of a data pipeline? Data is never perfect, and software is always in progress, which means that we want to be able to go back to previous DAG runs and rerun a pipeline with the data that was processed. If we're extracting data from a web service such as a REST API, which returns a result only for the state at that given point in time, we can't go back to the API and ask for the same result from two months ago. In that situation, it's best to keep an unedited copy of the result. For privacy reasons, sometimes certain parts of the data are redacted, which is inevitable, but the starting point of a reproducible data pipeline should be to store a copy of the input data (edited as little as possible). This data is typically stored in a raw folder, as shown in figure 13.8.

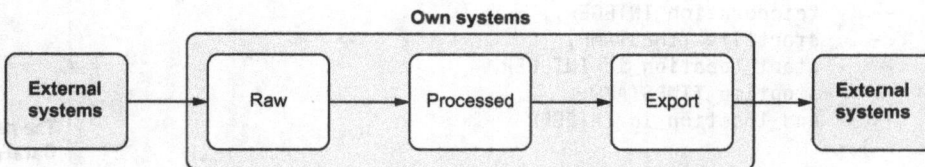

Figure 13.8 We can't control the structure of data in external systems. In our own systems, it's logical to store data according to the life cycle of data. Unedited data, for example, is stored in raw, derived and transformed data is stored in processed, and data sets ready for transfer are stored in export.

Starting with this raw data, we (and others) can alter, enrich, refine, transform, and mingle with it as much as we like, and the result is written back to a processed folder. Transformations are often compute and time intensive, so we try to avoid rerunning a task by saving the results so that processed results can easily be read over and over.

> **NOTE** In practice, many organizations apply more fine-grained separations between the stages of data, such as Raw > Preprocessed > Enriched > Processed > Export. No one structure suits all; your project and the project's requirements determine the best way to structure the movement of data.

13.6 *Developing idempotent data pipelines*

Now that we have data in the raw folder, we can process it and insert the results into a PostgreSQL database. Because this chapter isn't about the best way to process data with pandas or Spark, we won't discuss the details of this transformation job. Instead, we'll reiterate an important aspect of data pipelines in general: ensuring that a data pipeline can be executed multiple times without our having to reset state manually or introduce a change in the results (idempotency).

We could introduce idempotency at two points in this data pipeline. The first point is is easy: when we transform the raw data to a processed state and store it in a processed folder, we should set a flag to overwrite destination files. This ensures that rerunning a task won't fail due to an existing output path.

The second stage, where we write results into the database, is less evident. Rerunning a task that writes results to a database may not fail, but it could result in duplicate rows that might pollute the results. How can we ensure that results are being written to a database in idempotent fashion so that we can rerun pipelines without duplicating results?

One way is to add a column to the table that identifies something unique about the job writing to the database, such as the execution date of the Airflow job. Suppose that we're using pandas to write a DataFrame to a database.

Listing 13.16   Writing a pandas DataFrame to a SQL database

```
--CREATE TABLE citi_bike_rides(
--     tripduration INTEGER,
--     starttime TIMESTAMP,
--     start_location_id INTEGER,
--     stoptime TIMESTAMP,
--     end_location_id INTEGER
--);

df = pd.read_csv(... citi bike data ...)
engine = sqlalchemy.create_engine(
    BaseHook.get_connection(self._postgres_conn_id).get_uri()
)
df.to_sql("citi_bike_rides", con=engine,
    index=False, if_exists="append")
```

The pandas DataFrame and table structure must match.

When executing df.to_sql(), we have no way to tell if we're going to insert existing rows into the table. In this situation, we could alter the database table to add a column for Airflow's execution date, as follows.

Listing 13.17 Writing a pandas DataFrame to a SQL database in one operation

```
--CREATE TABLE citi_bike_rides(
--    tripduration INTEGER,
--    starttime TIMESTAMP,
--    start_location_id INTEGER,
--    stoptime TIMESTAMP,
--    end_location_id INTEGER,
--    airflow_execution_date TIMESTAMP
--);

df = pd.read_csv(... citi bike data ...)
df["airflow_execution_date"] = pd.Timestamp(
    context["data_interval_start"].timestamp(),      Adds execution_date as a column
    unit='s',                                          to the pandas DataFrame
)
engine = sqlalchemy.create_engine(
    BaseHook.get_connection(self._postgres_conn_id).get_uri()
)
with engine.begin() as conn:      ◄─── Begins a transaction
    conn.execute(
        "DELETE FROM citi_bike_rides"
        f"WHERE airflow_execution_date=            First deletes any existing
'{context['data_interval_start']}';"               records with the current
    )                                               execution_date
    df.to_sql("citi_bike_rides", con=conn, index=False,
if_exists="append")
```

In this example, we start a database transaction because the interaction with the database is twofold: we delete any existing rows with a given execution date and then insert the new rows. If there are no existing rows with a given execution date, nothing is deleted. The two SQL statements (df.to_sql() executes SQL under the hood) are wrapped in a transaction, which is an atomic operation, meaning that either both queries complete successfully or neither does. This ensures that no remainders are left over in case of failure.

When the data is processed and stored successfully in the database, we can start a web application on http://localhost:8083 to query the results in the database (figure 13.9). The results display which method of transportation is faster between two neighborhoods at a given time. In row 1, for example on Thursday between 19:00 and 22:00, traveling from Astoria to Old Astoria is on average faster by taxi: 996 seconds (16.6 minutes) versus 1465.0 seconds (24.42 minutes) by Citi Bike.

Airflow triggers jobs downloading, transforming, and storing data in the PostgreSQL database at 15-minute intervals. For a real user-facing application, you'd probably want a better-looking, more searchable frontend. But from the backend perspective, we have an automated data pipeline running automatically at 15-minute intervals and showing whether a taxi or Citi Bike is faster between given neighborhoods at given times, as shown in figure 13.9.

Start location	End location	Weekday	Time group	Avg time Citi Bike	Avg time Taxi
Astoria	Old Astoria	Thursday	7 PM – 10 PM	1465.0	996.0
Battery Park City	East Chelsea	Thursday	7 PM – 10 PM	878.0	4208.0
Battery Park City	Flatiron	Thursday	7 PM – 10 PM	1266.0	580.0
Battery Park City	TriBeCa/Civic Center	Thursday	7 PM – 10 PM	284.0	616.0
Central Park	Central Harlem North	Thursday	7 PM – 10 PM	1822.0	1577.0
Central Park	Greenwich Village North	Thursday	7 PM – 10 PM	2591.0	1251.0
Central Park	Lincoln Square West	Thursday	7 PM – 10 PM	323.0	494.0
Chinatown	Financial District North	Thursday	7 PM – 10 PM	375.0	346.0
Clinton East	Lincoln Square East	Thursday	7 PM – 10 PM	815.0	475.0
Clinton East	Midtown Center	Thursday	7 PM – 10 PM	374.0	700.0
Clinton East	Upper West Side South	Thursday	7 PM – 10 PM	704.0	679.25
East Chelsea	Garment District	Wednesday	11 AM – 4 PM	426.0	618.0
East Chelsea	Gramercy	Thursday	7 PM – 10 PM	558.0	576.0
East Chelsea	Greenwich Village North	Thursday	7 PM – 10 PM	312.0	625.0
East Chelsea	Midtown South	Thursday	7 PM – 10 PM	385.0	709.0
East Chelsea	Penn Station/Madison Sq West	Thursday	7 PM – 10 PM	451.0	266.5
East Chelsea	TriBeCa/Civic Center	Thursday	7 PM – 10 PM	908.0	774.0

Figure 13.9   Web application displaying results stored in the PostgreSQL database, continuously updated by the Airflow DAG

Summary

- You can't control the structure of data in external systems. In your own systems, it's logical to store data according to the life cycle of data.
- Many organizations apply fine-grained separations between the stages of data. No one structure fits all. Your project and the project's requirements determine the best way to structure the movement of data.
- When an operator's functionality doesn't fulfill a need, you must resort to calling a function with a PythonOperator or implement your own operator.
- We generalized the execution of pandas transformations in a custom-written PandasOperator for reusability and code deduplication.
- The tasks that use the PandasOperator can provide a specific callable for reading into a pandas DataFrame and writing that DataFrame to a specific output format.

Project: Keeping family traditions alive with Airflow and generative AI

This chapter covers

- Understanding retrieval-augmented generation (RAG)
- Implementing Airflow tasks to populate a vector database with your content
- Retrieving relevant documents from a vector database using vector similarity search
- Using a large language model to generate content based on your own knowledge base

In recent years, the generative AI (GenAI) revolution has reshaped the way we create text, audio, and image-related content. GenAI systems have emerged as powerful tools capable of generating coherent, contextually relevant text that closely mimics human writing, opening new possibilities across various sectors, from marketing and copywriting to education and customer service.

Having high-quality data is paramount to building a good GenAI system or product because poor input data inevitably leads to poor results. Fortunately, Airflow can play an important role in ensuring high-quality input data by automating the processes involved in data preparation. In this chapter, we'll explore Airflow's role in building robust GenAI solutions with an example use case involving family recipes.

As we navigate this new era, the demand for high-quality, curated data has never been greater. Organizations and individuals alike are recognizing the importance of preparing, organizing, and providing access to their data pipelines to fuel GenAI applications.

14.1   Use case: Bringing family recipes to life

As we embark on this journey, we'll introduce a compelling use case that highlights the intersection of GenAI and culinary treasures. Food from our childhood always holds a special place in our hearts. Each meal has memories that remain with us as we grow up. But often, these recipes vanish with time. They may fade from memory, or the people who made those meals are no longer here to enjoy them with us.

Each recipe is a story that enriches the cultural fabric we all share. As time passes, however, the recipes we hold dear can disappear, often because we neglected to write them down. This is where GenAI can make a real difference. By turning recipes into structured, searchable knowledge, GenAI allows us not only to preserve them but also adapt and personalize them for different ingredients, diets, and contexts and even make the recipes available in multiple languages.

Fortunately, the rise in GenAI opens exciting new possibilities. Specifically, large language models (LLMs), which are components of GenAI, have paved the way for numerous applications in areas including content creation, customer support, code generation, and education. Many other applications are continually emerging and improving.

One area in which LLMs are particularly good is providing recipes for nearly every dish you can think of because they've been trained on a vast sea of public data. LLMs can suggest substitutes for ingredients that are hard to find in local stores, translate recipes from foreign languages, and even suggest dishes inspired by a list of ingredients.

> **DEFINITION**   A *text corpus* is a large, structured collection of written texts that serves as a data set for the LLM to be trained on. ChatGPT-2, released in 2019, used Reddit posts as a corpus. On the other hand, GPT-3, released in 2022, used a combination of data derived from web crawls, books, and Wikipedia.

Suppose that you have a family recipe you want to share with everyone. This recipe is very particular, and you want to add it to the knowledge of an LLM so that others can not only access it but also ask questions about it, translate it, or ask for alternatives in case they're missing an ingredient. We can tackle this project in different ways, so first, let's examine how we can bring this idea to life.

14.2   Fine-tuning an existing LLM

The first option for incorporating our recipes into the training workflow is retraining our language model, a method commonly known as *fine-tuning*. In our case, fine-tuning involves using a commercial language model and carrying out an additional training cycle that incorporates the recipe we want to add. In this way, the LLM will become familiar with the recipe while maintaining its existing capabilities, such as providing the ingredients of a recipe (*summarization*), providing the instructions for a recipe (*explanation*), and providing the recipe in multiple languages (*translation*).

Although fine-tuning may seem to be a good way to incorporate our recipe knowledge base, this solution has drawbacks:

- *Cost*—The main issue is cost. LLMs are made up of billions (sometimes trillions) of parameters that control how the model generates content. During fine-tuning, many of these parameters must be adjusted, which takes a lot of computing power and specialized hardware.

- *Retraining*—Moreover, whenever we add a new batch of recipes, we have to retrain the LLM to keep it updated with the latest content, which means we have to develop and maintain a retraining pipeline.

- *Hosting*—On top of that, we face the challenge of hosting the language model, which requires additional computing resources to keep our custom model available for users and adds further costs.

- *Source clarity*—Source clarity is another challenging aspect of working with LLMs. When we pose a question to an LLM, it's challenging to determine which recipes the LLM knew before we retrained it and which ones are our recipes. This is because the LLM's knowledge before and after training blends together, making it difficult to distinguish between what is new and what was there before retraining. It's impossible to be certain whether the content that the LLM provides is entirely from our own recipe or whether it includes elements from similar recipes.

14.3 RAG to the rescue

Retrieval-augmented generation (RAG) solves many of the challenges of fine-tuning because it gives LLMs the power to read efficiently from an external library. This way, we don't have to retrain the LLM every time we add a recipe collection.

RAG systems can involve several moving parts and may seem complex at first. To make things easier to understand, let's create a simple example.

Suppose that we can transform each recipe into an arbitrary representation within a 2D space (figure 14.1). The first dimension in this space rates a recipe on a scale from mild (-1) to spicy (1). The second dimension determines whether a dish is sweet (1) or savory (-1).

In this case, we're converting our recipes to *vectors*, which are numerical representations structured in a way that computers can easily understand and process. This transformation allows us to compare different texts based on meaning rather than exact wording. In the context of LLMs, these vector representations make it possible to find and retrieve relevant information quickly and with high accuracy. This becomes

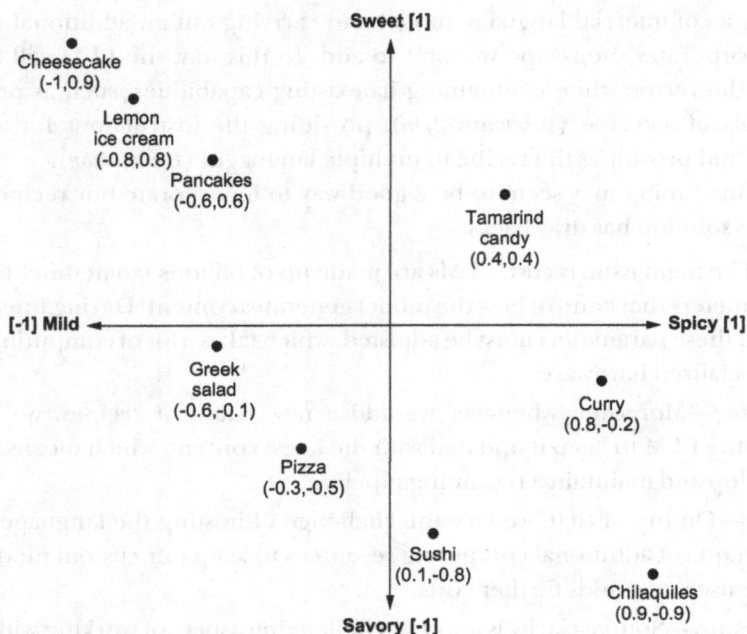

Figure 14.1   Flavor vector space representation of mildness/spiciness and sweet/savory taste for our recipe collection

especially important when we're scaling up from a small number of recipes to managing billions.

After we have enough recipes classified in this flavor space, we train a machine-learning model to determine where a new recipe would fall within the vector space based on its ingredients and instructions. A model that translates text into a vector representation is called an *embedding model*. The specific training details of this model aren't important for this example; in a real-world scenario, we wouldn't train the embedding model based on flavors. What's important is the concept that we can change text to a form that's represented by numbers.

Based on this powerful embedding model, we can classify any new recipe and create a database of recipes represented by 2D vectors. But what's the point of converting our recipes to vector representations? Suppose that want to add a new poke-bowl recipe to our vector database. We can determine the vector representation of the recipe and check which other recipes are closest to it in the flavor space. Two recipes with similar ingredients in similar proportions would be close to each other in the flavor vector space. In this case, we see that the sushi recipe is close to the poke-bowl recipe, which makes a lot of sense (figure 14.2).

In real-world situations, we won't judge how similar two recipes are based on their taste; instead, we'll look at how similar the text in the recipes is. An embedding model

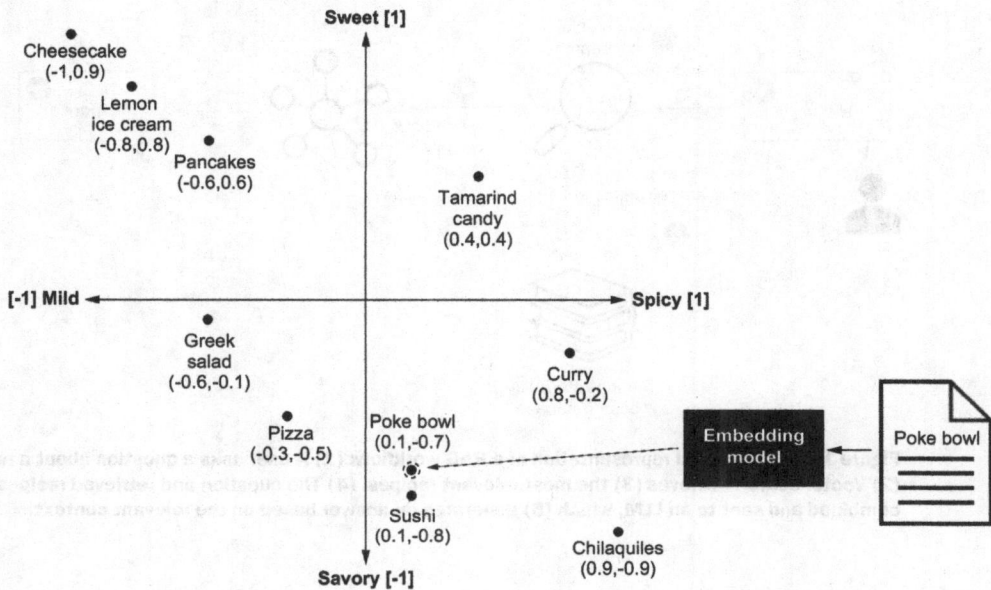

Figure 14.2   A user could input a poke-bowl recipe into the embedding model and discover that sushi is the most similar recipe in the vector database.

will convert the recipes to numerical representations. The model has been trained on a broad range of topics, much the way LLMs are trained. As a result, it can encode intricate language relationships using thousands of dimensions, not just the two we used in our taste-vector space. Therefore, the embedding model can capture complex relationships over general language concepts the way that LLMs do.

By combining the generative capabilities of LLMs with a vector database built on recipe embeddings, you can efficiently identify the similar recipes in the database. You can save your mother-in-law's pizza recipe in the database, for example. Later, if you ask a question like "Does my mother-in-law's pizza recipe use yeast?" the LLM can search the database and give you the right answer based on what it finds, including suggestions for alternative ingredients, or translate the instructions into another language.

This example is exactly what RAG is all about. The first step is identifying the most relevant content in our knowledge base based on a user question so that an LLM can provide an answer based on the retrieved relevant documents (figure 14.3).

In this chapter, we'll build our own recipe library for storing personal recipes: a recipe vault. At the same time, we'll use the capabilities of LLMs, such as suggesting alternative ingredients and providing instructions in different languages—all while preserving the original flavors because the recipes come directly from our recipe collection.

The Recipe Vault project, managed by Airflow, includes a user interface for uploading our recipes, preprocessing them, and storing them in a vectorized database. This

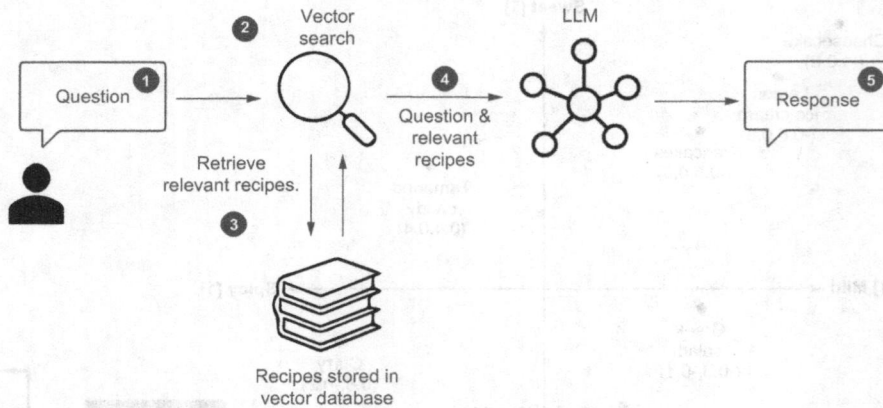

Figure 14.3   Simplified representation of a RAG workflow: (1) A user asks a question about a recipe. (2) Vector search retrieves (3) the most relevant recipes. (4) The question and retrieved recipes are combined and sent to an LLM, which (5) generates an answer based on the relevant context.

process will transform our recipes into vectors, which the LLM can understand and process at speed. On top of that, we've integrated a chat interface. This feature acts like a chatbot, allowing users to ask questions in natural language and receive relevant answers based on the recipe collection. When the recipes are uploaded, the chatbot uses the LLM to search, retrieve, and present the most relevant content, making the experience interactive, intuitive, and user friendly.

This project integrates many services into our RAG system (figure 14.4). Primarily, we need a vector database. We'll use Weaviate (https://github.com/weaviate/weaviate and https://weaviate.io), an open source vector database, to store the vector versions of our recipes. We'll also create a few custom and third-party services to perform all the steps necessary to prepare our recipes for vectorization. As we did in chapter 13, we'll build our project using a Docker Compose file to ensure that all our services run in Docker containers. In addition to the standard Airflow components, we'll have the services listed in table 14.1 running.

Table 14.1   Services installed with the `docker-compose` service

Service	Description
MinIO	An object-storage service, comparable to a cloud-based object-storage service like Amazon's S3; used to store text files as blob storage
Weaviate	A vector database to store our recipes in vector format
`vectorflow`	A custom Python package to handle the processing of the recipes and convert them to vectors for storage
`recipe_vault`	A containerized app that provides a chat interface for interaction with an LLM and assists in uploading new recipes

To run these services, navigate into the chapter 14 project folder (https://mng
.bz/vZBm), and run `docker-compose up`. The following services are exposed on
`localhost:[port]`, with `[username]`/`[password]` provided in parentheses (if applicable):

- 8080—Airflow web server (`airflow`/`airflow`)
- 8082—MinIO (`airflow`/`apacheairflow`)
- 8083—Weaviate vector database
- 8084—Recipe Vault UI

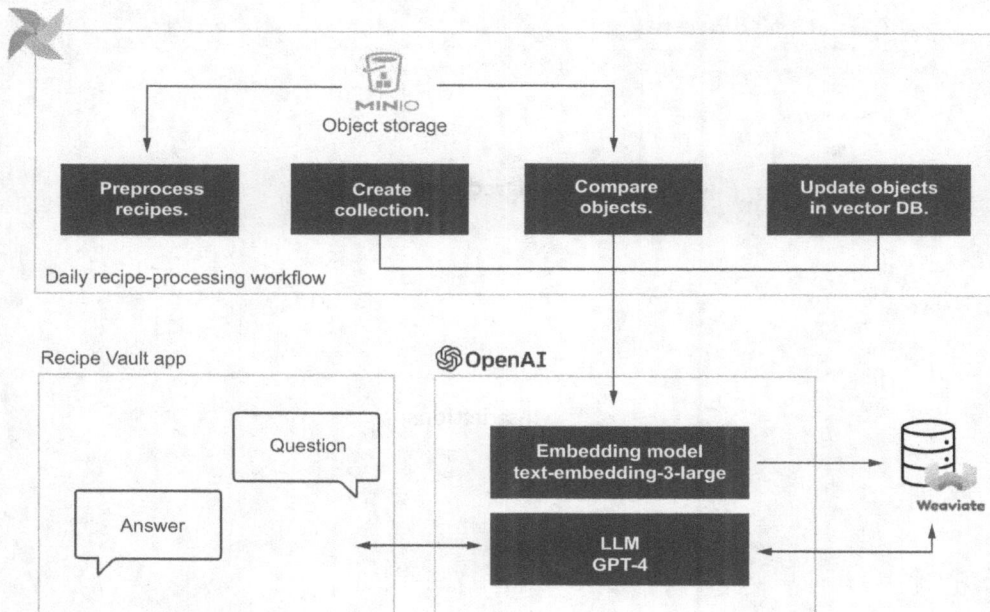

Figure 14.4   **This project implements a RAG workflow in which Airflow manages recipe processing and communication with the vector database. Via the Recipe Vault app, users can interact with an LLM to retrieve recipes stored in the vector database and generate an answer based on the most relevant recipes.**

The whole setup may seem to have a lot of components running at the same time. But we'll go step by step to understand how our data is ingested, processed, and stored in vectors.

14.4 *Uploading recipes to the Recipe Vault UI*

Cooking recipes consist of various elements, such as ingredients, quantities, preparation steps, cooking times, and notes. Recipes are often written in free-form text. Sometimes, instructions are written as bullet points; at other times, they consist of numbered steps; often, they also have a backstory that describes the origin of the recipe.

Getting this project off the ground begins with collecting new recipes. For this reason, we've created a Recipe Vault UI (`http://localhost:8084/Upload`). This UI (figure 14.5) is based on a Streamlit application to which we can start uploading our recipes. Then the recipes will be stored in MinIO in JSON format for further processing.

NOTE Streamlit is a popular Python framework used to build frontend applications. You can find more info at https://streamlit.io.

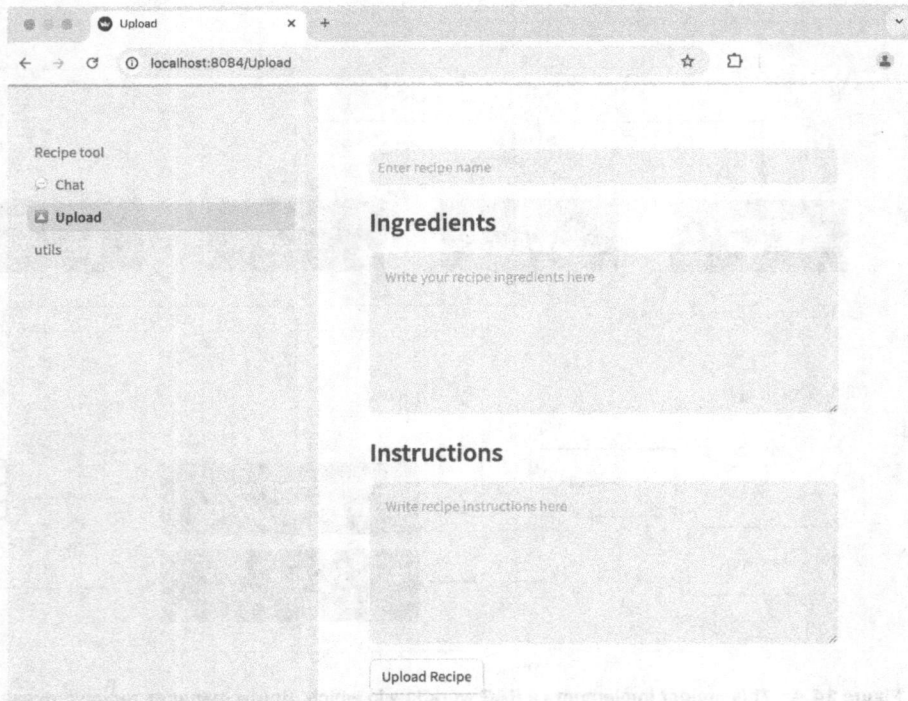

Figure 14.5   The Recipe Vault UI is available at `http://localhost:8084/Upload` for you to start uploading recipes.

We understand that coming up with new recipes for this project could be a time-consuming process that you might like to skip. For this reason, we've created a directed acyclic graph (DAG) to upload a set of starter recipes to MinIO. You can trigger the `01_preload_recipes` DAG and manually run a backfill from `2024-10-01 00:00` to `2024-10-07 00:00` because we've provided recipes for these days.

After running the DAG, check whether the recipes were successfully uploaded to MinIO. To do this, go to the data bucket at `http://localhost:8082` using MinIO's Object Browser. There, you should see all the recipes uploaded in JSON format, organized in the `raw` folder for each date (figure 14.6).

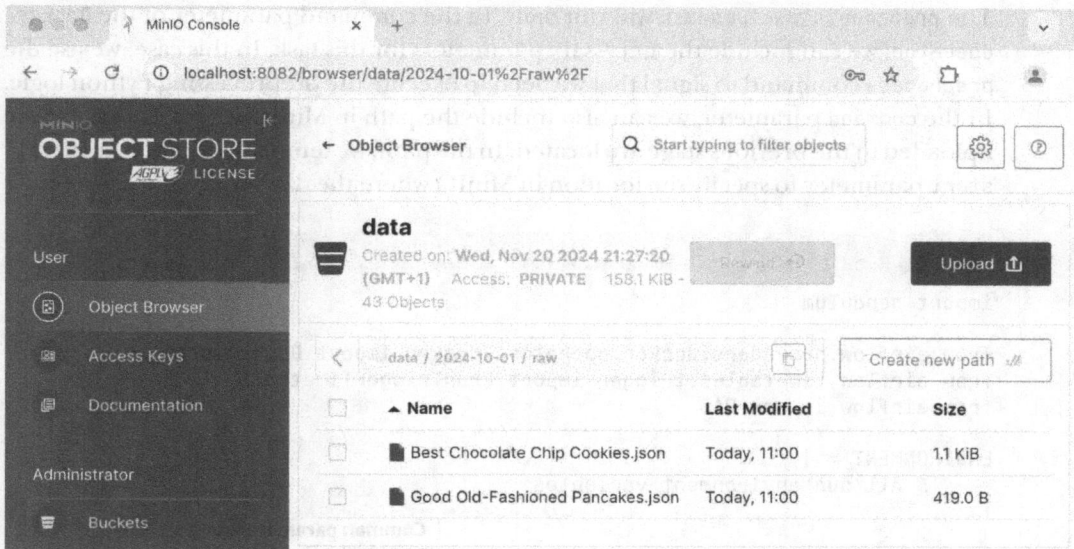

Figure 14.6 Recipes uploaded to MinIO in JSON format

14.5 *Preprocessing the recipes with DockerOperator*

In section 14.4, we compiled a starter set of recipes to provide initial text for the vectorization process, but we didn't go into the specifics of how we did it. This omission was intentional; we wanted to keep your focus on making the recipes available. Now is the time to go deeper into how to use Docker containers to execute our custom code.

In chapter 11, we used the DockerOperator to fetch data from an API. We can use this same pattern to develop GenAI applications. By containerizing our code with Docker, we can run heavy processes on compute instances separate from the Airflow cluster, allowing Airflow to focus on orchestrating, which is its strength.

Going back to our Recipe Vault project, the next step involves getting our recipes ready to be transformed into vectors. To streamline the ingestion process, we'll merge all the individual files collected over a day into a single pandas DataFrame, which will make the subsequent processing steps in our pipeline more efficient.

The pipeline is configured to start from today's date and run daily going forward, processing the recipes collected each day. To load the recipes uploaded to MinIO in section 14.4, you have to trigger the pipeline manually and run a backfill from 2024-10 -01 00:00 to 2024-10-07 00:00, as we provided recipes for those dates. The initial step in getting the recipes ready for vectorization is done by the preprocess_recipes task, as shown in listing 14.1.

It's important to note that all tasks in our DAG will use the vectorflow Docker image for all the steps in the pipeline. Inside the Docker image, we'll run a Python package with a command-line interface (CLI) to handle the logic each task requires.

The preprocess_recipes task will run daily. In the command parameter of the Docker-Operator, we can include the necessary parameters for this task. In this case, we use the preprocess command to signal that we need to execute the preprocessing Python logic. In the command parameter, we can also include the path in MinIO where the recipes we uploaded in the previous stage are located. In the path, we template the data_interval_start parameter to specify the location in MinIO where the day's recipes are stored.

Listing 14.1   Calling the CLI command to preprocess the recipe from our task

```python
import pendulum

from airflow.providers.docker.operators.docker import DockerOperator
from airflow.timetables.trigger import CronTriggerTimetable
from airflow import DAG

ENVIRONMENT = {
    # All our environment variables
}

docker_kwargs= {
    "image":" vectorvault_cli:latest",
    "environment":ENVIRONMENT,
    "docker_url":"tcp://docker-socket-proxy:2375",
    "network_mode":"chapter14_default",
    "environment":ENVIRONMENT,
    "auto_remove":"success",
    "tty":True,
}

with DAG(
    dag_id=" 01_ingestion",
    schedule=CronTriggerTimetable("@daily", timezone="UTC"),
    start_date=pendulum.today("UTC"),
):
    ...

    preprocess_recipes = DockerOperator(
        task_id="preprocess_recipes",
        command=[
            "preprocess",
            "s3://data/{{data_interval_start | ds}}",
        ],
        **docker_kwargs
    )
```

Common parameters to be used in the DockerOperator

Call to the CLI command in our Docker image

MinIO path is aliased as s3.

All DockerOperators in the DAG receive the same parameters.

You're probably wondering why we're passing the **docker_kwargs parameter to the preprocess_recipes task. The reason is simple: all the tasks in our DAG are executed using the DockerOperator, and many of the parameters that have to be declared for each task are repeated. To keep our code DRY (Don't Repeat Yourself) and avoid code duplication, we group all the common parameters in a dictionary (*dict*) and unpack them using the "**" syntax within the DockerOperator. Because we're going to reuse these parameters for every task in this DAG, let's take a moment to understand them better before moving along:

- image—Specifies the name of the Docker image used to run the task. The image is a containerized environment containing all necessary dependencies and configurations to run a task. When the operator runs, it pulls the image we specified and creates a container. The definition of this Docker service is available in the docker-compose file of this project.

- environment—Specifies a set of environment variables that will be passed to the Docker container when it runs, including port and connection configurations for all our services, such as MinIO, Weaviate, and OpenAI.

- docker_url—Specifies the URL of the Docker daemon that the operator will communicate with to manage containers. In this project, we implemented a Docker socket proxy setup, defined in the docker-compose file. This setup is also important for security reasons because it allows us to expose the Docker daemon over a network safely.

- network_mode—Specifies the network on which the Docker container is running. This setting allows the container to communicate with all the services and containers within the same network and at the same time provide necessary isolation for the services running on the network.

- auto_remove—Controls whether the Docker container is removed automatically when the task is complete. Because we're specifying this parameter as success, the container will be removed automatically after successful task completion. This helps with cleaning up resources and preventing the accumulation of stopped containers.

- yty—Allocates a pseudo-teletypewriter terminal to the Docker container. This is particularly useful for improving the readability of the logs that the container generates.

Now that we understand how our preprocess_recipes task is configured, we can focus on the Python code the CLI command will execute when we run our task, as shown in the next listing. This is where the date-templated file path from the command in the DockerOperator comes in handy: it allows the list_files_from_fs function to find the recipes available for a given day. This function provides a list of the recipes stored in the specified path so we can start working on them.

Listing 14.2 Preparing our recipes to be stored in the vector database

```
from vectorflow.utils import list_files_from_fs, save_df_in_minio
from vectorflow.etl import create_chunks, assign_uuids

import logging
import typer
```

```
app = typer.Typer()
log = logging.getLogger(__name__)

...

@app.command()
def preprocess(path:str) -> None:

    files_to_process = list_files_from_fs(          Creates a list of files
      path=f"{path}/raw",                           uploaded by users
      extension=".json".        ◄───── Lists only JSON files
    )

    df = (
      create_chunks(files_to_process, f"{path}/raw")
      .pipe(assign_uuids)                           Splits recipes into chunks
    )                                               and creates universally
                                                    unique identifiers (UUIDs)
    save_df_in_minio(df, path, "preprocessed")  ◄──── Stores pandas back to MinIO
```

When we have a list of the day's available recipes, we can begin processing them. In a RAG system, text needs to be broken into smaller pieces to make retrieval more efficient. We call these pieces *chunks*. RAG systems are designed to provide answers based on the content stored in the database in vector format. One of the most powerful features of RAG systems, however, is their capability to reference the original source, which implies that even as we convert recipes to vectors, we can still trace back to the original recipe from which the content was derived.

This feature is precisely why determining the correct chunking size is so important. Suppose that we have a collection of thousands of recipes and put them all in a single chunk. Apart from the fact that it would be difficult for our systems to handle all the data in a single chunk, it would be challenging to determine which recipe is the source—like asking for a recipe and getting a big stack of cookbooks in return. We'd struggle to identify precisely which book and page contains the recipe we're searching for. The other extreme isn't ideal either. Suppose that we split our recipes by sentences, ending up with 30 to 50 chunks per recipe. This approach would also be inefficient because we'll get many chunks from the same recipe as the source for a single query.

To strike the right balance in this project, we'll divide each recipe in two. The first chunk contains the ingredients, and the second contains the instructions to make the recipe. This approach will be advantageous later when we have to identify the source document in the vector database that aligns most closely with our content. For now, we'll implement the division of our recipes into chunks as follows.

Listing 14.3   Splitting recipes into chunks

```
from typing import List
import pandas as pd
```

```
def create_chunks(files_to_process: List[str], path:str) -> pd.DataFrame:

    chunks = []
    for file in files_to_process:

        recipe_name = file.replace(".json","").split("/")[-1]
        data = load_json_from_minio(recipe_name, path)

        ingredients = data.get('ingredients', 'No ingredients found')
        instructions = data.get('instructions', 'No instructions found')

        chunks.append({
            "recipe_name": recipe_name,
            "chunk": f"{recipe_name} \n Ingredients: {ingredients}"
        })

        chunks.append({
            "recipe_name": recipe_name,
            "chunk": f"{recipe_name} \n Instructions: {instructions}"
        })

    return pd.DataFrame(chunks)
```

Links the ingredients to the recipe name

Links the Instructions to the recipe name

When we upload our recipes via the Recipe Vault UI, they're already split into ingredients and instructions in the JSON file that gets uploaded to MinIO. The goal of the `preprocess_recipes` task is to consolidate all the recipes uploaded in a day into a single pandas DataFrame. We'll store the content of the recipe in a column named `chunk`, whether it's related to the ingredients or the instructions, to ensure that we link the recipes with the corresponding instructions and ingredients. Furthermore, the name of the recipe goes in the `recipe_name` column, acting as a unique identifier for each recipe (figure 14.7).

The next step of the preprocessing pipeline is creating a UUID for every `recipe_name` and `chunk` in our DataFrame. We use the `generate_uuid5` function from Weaviate utils, which uses a special process to create a unique 32-character key for each string combination (figure 14.8).

The unique keys we create are important because Weaviate uses them to identify and retrieve objects efficiently. These UUIDs are generated based on the content of each recipe, meaning that exactly the same text (including punctuation and spacing) always produces the same UUID.

Suppose that we want to check whether a recipe has already been added to the database. Without UUIDs, we'd have to compare the new recipe with every existing one word by word, which is slow and inefficient. With UUIDs, each recipe is assigned a fixed-length key based on its content. Instead of comparing texts, we simply check whether the UUID already exists. This approach makes the process much faster and easier to scale as the number of recipes increases.

Recipes (json)

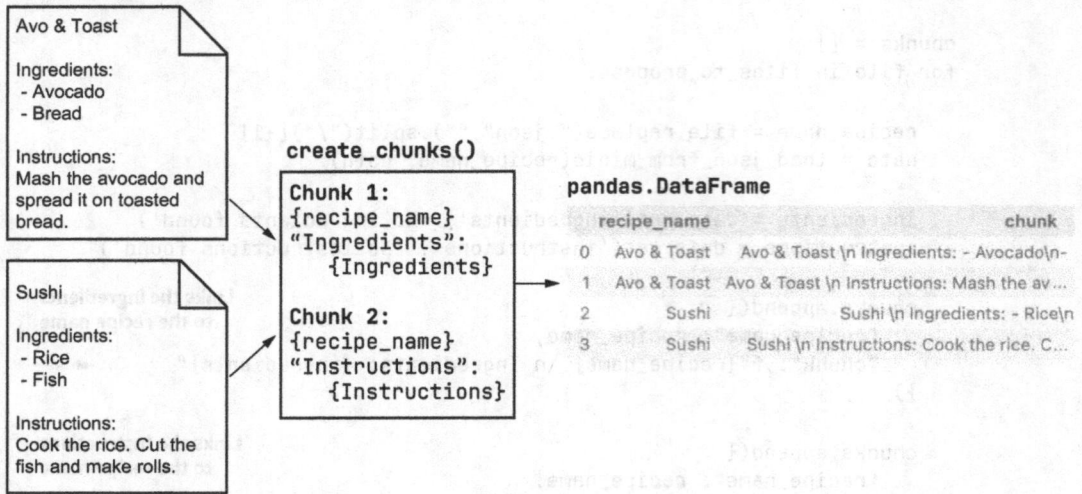

Figure 14.7   Each recipe is divided into two parts (chunks). The first chunk includes the recipe's name and the ingredients. The second chunk includes the recipe's name and instructions. All these parts are combined into one pandas DataFrame for the date when the recipes are processed.

UUIDs will play a special role in our project in section 14.7, where we'll use them to determine whether the content of our recipes needs to be updated. At the moment, our primary focus is on creating the UUIDs, which we can accomplished using the assign_uuids function as shown in listing 14.4.

```
from weviate.util import generate_uuid5

text1 = """
Cheese Cake Recipe
Ingredients:
- 2 cups of cream cheese
- 1 cup of sugar
- 2 eggs
- 1 cup of vanilla extract
Instructions:
1. Mix all ingredients in a bowl
2. Pour mixture into a baking pan
3. Bake at 350 degrees for 30 minutes
"""

print(generate_uuid5(text1))

> '1a24c80d-187b-5232-b1f4-f3205b2e87c8'
```

```
from weviate.util import generate_uuid5

text2 = """
Cheese Cake Recipe
Ingredients:
- 2 cups of cream cheese
- 1 cup of sugar
- 3 eggs
- 1 cup of vanilla extract
Instructions:
1. Mix all ingredients in a bowl
2. Pour mixture into a baking pan
3. Bake at 350 degrees for 30 minutes
"""

print(generate_uuid5(text2))

> 'dc2a77c9-9810-596c-8b53-fa01000fdf01'
```

Figure 14.8   The string on the left differs from the one on the right only in the number of eggs. Two nearly identical strings generate a completely different UUID.

Listing 14.4 Creating UUIDs for the recipe name and chunks

```
import pandas as pd
from weaviate.util import generate_uuid5

def assign_uuids(df: pd.DataFrame) -> pd.DataFrame:
  return (
  df
  .assign(
    chunk = lambda df: df.chunk.astype(str).str.strip(),          ──── Removes trailing characters
    recipe_name=lambda df: df.recipe_name.astype(str).str.strip(),
    recipe_uuid=lambda df:[generate_uuid5(n) for n in df.recipe_name],
    chunk_uuid=lambda df:[generate_uuid5(c) for c in df.chunk],    ──── Creates a UUID key for every text element
  )
  .reset_index(drop=True)
)
```

After we've created the chunks for our recipes and assigned the UUIDs, we can save the DataFrame we created in MinIO as `preprocessed.parquet` (figure 14.9). We'll use this file in future tasks for executing all operations required to upload the recipes to the vector database.

	recipe_uuid	recipe_name	chunk_uuid	chunk
0	1a505362-5d60-58f7-a952-34d5ec8cdc7e	Best Chocolate Chip Cookies	094acc40-03ec-5f72-b273-54763544ba3b	Best Chocolate Chip Cookies \n Ingredients: 1 ...
1	1a505362-5d60-58f7-a952-34d5ec8cdc7e	Best Chocolate Chip Cookies	2671fc7f-e803-5d8d-b837-6bb4107fefc9	Best Chocolate Chip Cookies \n Instructions: G...
2	8f697fc5-07e8-524e-b145-c6e20d6186b6	Good Old-Fashioned Pancakes	4ab3cb54-2162-5041-88fd-f733b8b88968	Good Old-Fashioned Pancakes \n Ingredients: 1 ...
3	8f697fc5-07e8-524e-b145-c6e20d6186b6	Good Old-Fashioned Pancakes	e0f04d73-fff0-588f-ba42-d80f59c0d52c	Good Old-Fashioned Pancakes \n Instructions: S...

Figure 14.9 Processed recipes are incorporated into a single pandas DataFrame.

14.6 Creating a collection to store our recipes

Now that we have our recipes ready to be uploaded, it's time to start figuring out how we're going to store the data in the vector database. Weaviate organizes data in collections. A *collection* is similar to a table in a traditional database, in which each table contains fields associated with entities of our business logic, such as users, products, and suppliers. Weaviate uses a collection to put together objects that fit with one another, much like the recipes we're trying to vectorize. The next task in DAG, as shown in the following listing, is making sure that, each time we run our pipeline, a collection where we can store our recipes is available.

Listing 14.5   Defining the task to create a Weaviate collection

```
from airflow.providers.docker.operators.docker import DockerOperator
from airflow import DAG

COLLECTION_NAME = "recipes"          ◄──── We use the collection name,
                                            which we declared as a global
with DAG(                                   variable, in multiple tasks.
    dag_id="01_ingestion",
    ...
):

    ...

    create_collection = DockerOperator(
        task_id="create_collection",
        command=f"create {COLLECTION_NAME} text-embedding-3-large",
        **docker_kwargs
    )
```

In the `create_collection` task, we call the `create` command on the CLI of our Python package, which (as its name indicates) creates the Weaviate collection for us. When we call the `create` command, we specify three parameters (listing 14.6):

- A *collection name* so we can logically group the records in our collection by a common identifier
- A list of *properties* to define the fields in our collection
- A *vectorizer configuration* to define the embedding model and how to connect with the embedding service

Listing 14.6   Parameters required to create a collection

```
...

@app.command()
def create(collection_name:str, embedding_model:str) -> None:

    ...

with get_weaviate_client() as client:

    collection = client.collections.create(
        name = collection_name,
        vectorizer_config= ...,
        properties = ...
    )
```

The first parameter we need to define is the name of our collection. Choosing the collection name is straightforward; it's simply a text string that identifies our collection. Because we're creating a collection to store recipes in vectors, we'll name the collection recipes. In listing 14.5, we passed the COLLECTION_NAME as the first parameter of our CLI when we called the create command in the DockerOperator.

On the other hand, defining the properties and vectorizer_config parameters is a bit more complex. Let's go deeper into how each step should be defined.

14.6.1　*Defining how to vectorize our text*

When we define our collection, one important aspect is how we're going to turn the text of the recipe into numerical vectors. Specifically, we must decide which algorithm to use to generate those numbers. Every recipe we upload must be converted to a numerical representation. But we need a way to decode the numerical representations into text.

This is why we need an embedding model that allows us to transform words, sentences, and even entire sections of our recipes into a numerical vector representation, which is the format a vector database can store. Remember when we talked about embedding models at the beginning of the chapter? Here is where they come into play. In this project, we'll use the text-embedding-3-large embedding model from OpenAI to embed our recipes. In listing 14.5, we passed the embedding model text-embedding -3-large as the second parameter of our CLI when we called the create command in the DockerOperator.

> **The current embedding model landscape**
>
> text-embedding-3-large isn't the only option for text embedding; many other embedding models are on the market. Notable ones include Word2vec (Google), text-embedding-ada-002 (OpenAI), Embed v3 (Cohere), and Llama 3 (Meta). In fact, most major players in the GenAI field, including all the big cloud providers, have their own embedding models. This is important because the choice of embedding model often depends on the ecosystem or provider you plan to work with.

Now that we understand why the embedding model is so important, we can start defining in our collection how we're going to implement it in our project. We do this by using the vectorizer_config parameter. When we define the configuration, we use a function instead of declaring the parameters directly.

Listing 14.7　Getting the vectorized configuration with a function

```
...

@app.command()
def create(collection_name:str, embedding_model:str) -> None:

...

    with get_weaviate_client() as client:

    collection = client.collections.create(
```

```
    name = collection_name,
    vectorizer_config = [get_vectorizer_config(embedding_model)],    ◀─┐
    properties = ...                                                   │
)                                                    We call a function instead of
                                                   defining the parameters directly.
```

When working with OpenAI clients, we can connect to the service by using the OpenAI API service or deploying a model endpoint in Microsoft Azure. These options require different configuration parameters. For this reason, we implement the selection logic using the `get_vectorizer_config` function so we'll have the flexibility to work with both approaches:

- With the OpenAI API route, we need to provide a name for the configuration in the `name` parameter and the embedding model name.
- When we work with a model deployed in Azure, we need two additional parameters, `base_url` and `resource_name`, to specify how the endpoint is defined in our Azure OpenAI instance.

> **Defining Azure OpenAI parameters**
>
> The variable `AZURE_OPENAI_ENDPOINT` typically follows this format:
>
> `https://projectname-openai-us.openai.azure.com/`
>
> The variable `AZURE_OPENAI_RESOURCE_NAME` refers to the name of the Azure OpenAI resource in the Azure portal.

We can declare the connection type (`OPENAI_CONN_TYPE`) shown in the following listing and all the relevant `OPEN_AI` variables in the `.env` file at the root of the project. Any variable we pass there can be used as an environment variable in the Airflow operators and additional services such as third-party (MinIO) and custom services included in the Docker Compose file.

Listing 14.8   Defining the vectorized configuration

```
import os
from weaviate.classes.config import Configure

def get_vectorizer_config(embedding_model: str) -> Configure:

    connection_type = os.getenv("OPENAI_CONN_TYPE")    ◀─┐ Defined as an
                                                         │ environmental variable
    if connection_type == "azure":

        config = Configure.NamedVectors.text2vec_azure_openai(
            name=embedding_model.replace("-", "_"),
            deployment_id=embedding_model,
```

```
            base_url= os.getenv("AZURE_OPENAI_ENDPOINT"),
            resource_name=os.getenv("AZURE_OPENAI_RESOURCE_NAME"),
        )

    elif connection_type == "openai_api":

        config = Configure.NamedVectors.text2vec_openai(
            name=embedding_model.replace("-", "_"),
            model=embedding_model,
        )

    else:
        raise ValueError(
            "Set the env var OPENAI_CONN_TYPE to 'azure' or 'openai_api'"
            )

    return config
```

At this point, it may be important to highlight a small detail that may have gone unnoticed when we declared the configuration for our vectorizer: the `vectorizer_config` parameter can accept multiple sets of embedding configurations. This is why we put the `get_vectorizer_config` inside square brackets (`[]`).

If we define more than one configuration, Weaviate can use multiple embedding services during the embedding process. We could embed content using the `text-embedding-3-large` model from OpenAI and at the same time embed the text content with the `snowflake-arctic-embed` model from Meta, which might be useful when we're working with LLMs from different vendors. To keep things simple, in this project, we'll use only one embedding model.

14.6.2 *Creating a schema for the collection*

Earlier, we discussed how collections are similar to tables in a traditional database. Continuing with the analogy, tables use schemas to define the fields in the table, but a Weaviate collection has properties to specify which fields will be included in the vectorization process. Our recipe collection comprises four fields:

- `recipe_uuid`—A unique key that we create based on the name of our recipe
- `recipe_name`—Text field where we put the name of the recipe
- `chunk_uuid`—A unique key based on the content of the recipe
- `chunk`—The section of the content of the recipe to vectorize

At this stage, we can begin by outlining the fields our collection will include in the `properties` parameter of the `create` method. This requires us to define a list of fields in our collection using Weaviate's `Property` objects, where we specify each field's name and data type. Weaviate provides predefined data type objects to ensure consistency and simplify schema creation, using the `UUID` type for IDs and the `TEXT` type for text fields, for example. That's what we'll do. We can set up the properties of our collection as follows.

```
from weaviate.classes.config Property
from weaviate.classes.config import DataType

...

with get_weaviate_client() as client:

    collection = client.collections.create(
       name = ...,
    vectorizer_config = [...]
    properties=[
       Property(
          name="recipe_uuid",
          data_type= DataType.UUID,
          skip_vectorization=True
       ),
          Property(name="recipe_name", data_type= DataType.TEXT),
          Property(
             name="chunk_uuid",
             data_type= DataType.UUID,
             skip_vectorization=True
          ),
          Property(name="chunk", data_type=DataType.TEXT),
    ]
    )
```

UUIDs don't need to be vectorized because we're creating them only for indexing purposes.

14.6.3 *Preparing our collection of recipes*

Now that we have a clear understanding of all the properties we need to define to create a collection, let's take a look at the complete code.

```
from weaviate.classes.config Property
from weaviate.classes.config.DataType import UUID, TEXT
from .utils import get_weaviate_client, get_vectorizer_config

import logging
import typer

app = typer.Typer()
log = logging.getLogger(__name__)

...

@app.command()
def create(collection_name:str, embedding_model:str) -> None:

    with get_weaviate_client() as client:
        collections = list(client.collections.list_all().keys())
```

```
existing_collections = [item.lower() for item in collections]

if collection_name.lower()in existing_collections:
    log.info(f"Collection {collection_name} exists.")
    return

with get_weaviate_client() as client:

    collection = client.collections.create(
        name = ...,
        vectorizer_config = =[get_vectorizer_config(embedding_model)],
    properties=[
        Property(
        name="recipe_uuid",
        data_type= DataType.UUID,
        skip_vectorization=True
        ),
        Property(name="recipe_name", data_type= DataType.TEXT),
        Property(
            name="chunk_uuid",
            data_type= DataType.UUID,
            skip_vectorization=True
            ),
        Property(name="chunk", data_type=DataType.TEXT),
    ]
    )


    log.info(f"Collection {collection_name} created.")
```

Ends execution if the collection is already defined ◀

Collection creation starts. ◀

At the beginning of the create function, we check whether the collection already exists in the Weaviate instance. If the collection was created in an earlier run, we log a message and skip the creation process. This means the function will execute the creation process only during the first run; during subsequent runs, it simply performs a check and moves on. This approach may seem inefficient, but it guarantees that we'll always verify whether the collection exists before attempting to store our recipes. If we have to change or fix the collection, we must delete the existing one in Weaviate first. Then we can define a new schema and run the create_collection task again. In addition, having a dedicated task for this process makes it easy to review the Airflow UI to ensure that everything is in order.

14.7 Updating and creating new records in the vector database

So far, we've prepared our recipes and made them ready to be added to the vector database. We have to do one more thing before we can move forward: check whether our recipe is already there!

As we add new objects to the vector database, we may have to update an existing recipe. We could also attempt to upload a duplicate of an existing recipe. How can we handle these scenarios?

The UUIDs we defined in the `preprocess_recipes` task come in handy here. They provide a unique key for each text combination, so we can use this feature to check whether a recipe with the same content title exists in the database.

The `compare_objects` task in our DAG is trying to determine whether the recipes we're trying to upload already exist in the database. To do this, we retrieve the DataFrame we saved in MinIO in the `preprocess_recipes` step and query the vector database to check the UUIDs of the recipes that are already present in the vector database, which is done by the `compare` CLI command defined in listing 14.11. During this comparison process, we encounter three scenarios:

- The recipe is not in the vector database, which means it has to be added for the first time. In this situation, we keep all the records in the DataFrame and mark these records as `"create"` in a new column (figure 14.10).

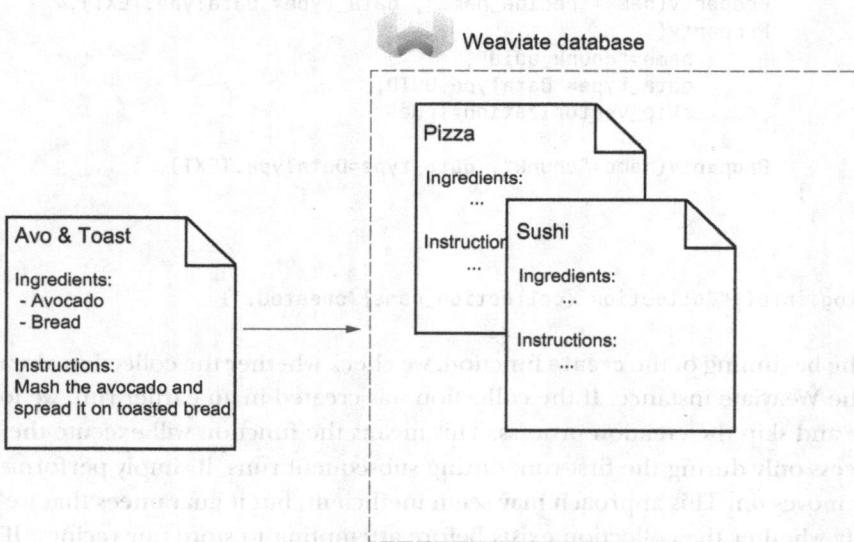

Figure 14.10   The recipe we're trying to upload isn't in the vector database, so we mark it as "create" in the tracking DataFrame, indicating that we're trying to add a new recipe.

- The recipe already exists in the database, but after comparing the chunk UUIDs of the recipe, we find that the content is different. In this case, we mark the recipe as `"update"` (figure 14.11).
- In the last scenario, the recipe we're trying to upload is exactly the same as the one already present in the vector database. This means the recipe name and all chunk UUIDs are the same as the ones in the vector database. We can save resources by deleting these records from the tracking DataFrame because they're already in the vector database (figure 14.12).

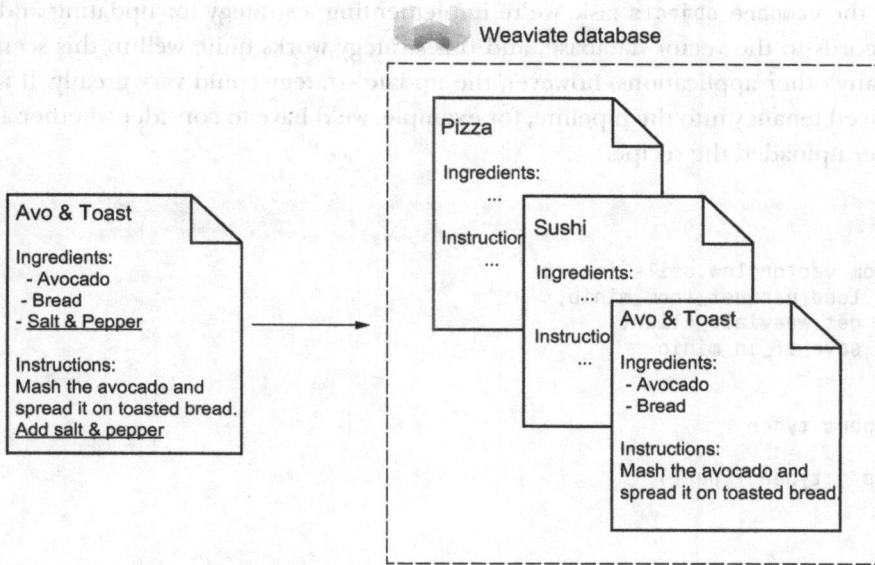

Figure 14.11 The recipe we're trying to upload is already in the vector database, but we have a different version. In this case, the version in the vector database didn't include `Salt & Pepper`, and the new recipe does. We mark it as `"update"` in the tracking DataFrame.

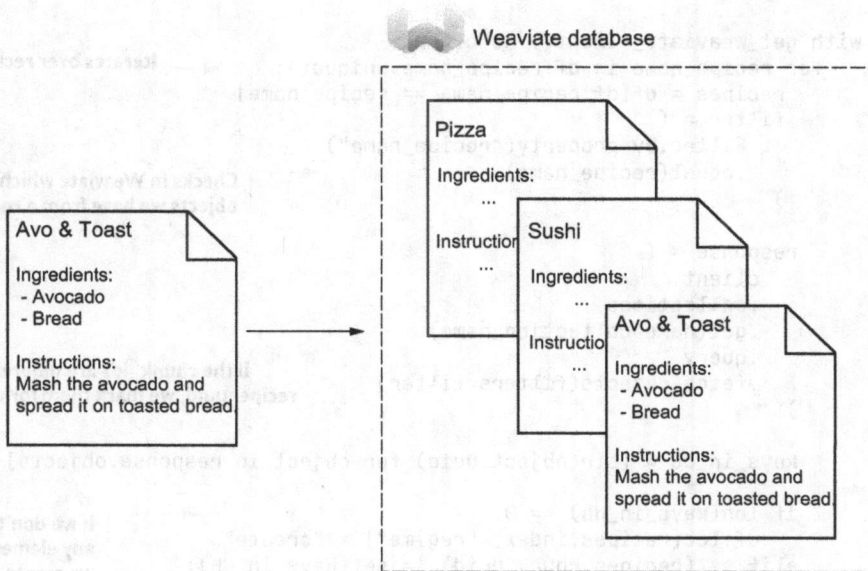

Figure 14.12 The recipe we're trying to upload is already in the vector database, and both records are the same version. Because the recipe is already in the data set, we don't need to process it. For this reason, we delete these records from the tracking DataFrame.

In the `compare_objects` task, we're implementing a strategy for updating and adding records to the vector database, and this strategy works quite well in this scenario. In many other applications, however, the update strategy could vary greatly. If we introduced tenancy into the pipeline, for example, we'd have to consider whether a specific user uploaded the recipe.

Listing 14.11   Checking whether recipes are already in the vector database

```python
from vectorflow.utils import (
    load_parquet_from_minio,
    get_weaviate_client,
    save_df_in_minio
)

import typer

app = typer.Typer()

...


@app.command()
def compare(path: str, collection_name:str) -> None:
    df = (
        load_parquet_from_minio("preprocessed", path)
        .assign(regime=None)
        .reset_index(drop=True)
    )

    with get_weaviate_client() as client:
        for recipe_name in df.recipe_name.unique():          # Iterates over recipe_uuid
            recipes = df[df.recipe_name == recipe_name]
            filter = (
                Filter.by_property("recipe_name")
                .equal(recipe_name)                          # Checks in Weaviate which
            )                                                #  objects we have from a recipe

            response = (
                client
                .collections
                .get(name=collection_name)
                .query
                .fetch_objects(filters=filter)               # If the chunk_ids are different for a
            )                                                # recipe_uuid, we mark them for update.

            keys_in_db = [str(object.uuid) for object in response.objects]

            if len(keys_in_db) == 0:                         # If we don't have
                df.loc[recipes.index, "regime"] = "create"   # any elements,
            elif set(recipes.chunk_uuid) != set(keys_in_db): # we create them.
                log.info(f"Recipe {recipe_name} will be updated")
                df.loc[recipes.index, "regime"] = "update"

        save_df_in_minio(df.dropna(subset="regime"), path, "compared")
```

After we complete the comparison process, we store the DataFrame back in MinIO, saving it as a file named `compared.parquet`. This file is used in the next two tasks to update and add records to the vector database.

14.8 *Deleting outdated records from the vector database*

In section 14.7, we marked the recipes for an update in a DataFrame but didn't perform any operation in the vector database. We'll address this in the `delete_outdated_objects` task.

The first thing to do is load the `compared.parquet` file from MinIO to get a list of the recipe UUIDs to be updated. The `delete_outdated_objects` task removes all the recipes labeled as "update" from the vector database. The next task in our DAG is uploading the most recent recipe version to the vector database.

Deleting the records is quite straightforward. Weaviate offers the `delete_many` method, which can delete multiple records in the vector database simultaneously. All we have to do is pass the list of `chunk_uuids` to the `delete` method. The Weaviate client will get rid of those records for us.

Listing 14.12 Deleting outdated records from the vector database

```
from vectorflow.utils import (
    load_json_from_minio,
    get_weaviate_client,
)

import logging
import typer

app = typer.Typer()
log = logging.getLogger(__name__)

@app.command()
def delete(path: str, collection_name:str) -> None:

    delete_recipes = (
        load_parquet_from_minio( "compared", path)        ⟵ Gets the compared.parquet
        .loc[lambda df:    df.regime == "update"]            file from MinIO and filters
        .recipe_name.unique().tolist()                       the objects to update
    )

    if len(recipes_to_delete) == 0:
        log.info("No records to delete")
        return

    filter = (
        Filter.by_property("recipe_name")
        .contains_any(delete_recipes)        ⟵ Deletes all the
    )                                            recipes to update

    with get_weaviate_client() as client:
```

```
(
    client
    .collections.get(name=collection_name)
    .data.delete_many(where=filter)
)
```

The first time we run the DAG on an empty vector database, there won't be any recipes to delete, and we'll have an empty DataFrame. This also happens when all the recipes we're trying to upload are new. This situation isn't an issue in our workflow because we use a conditional statement to skip the deletion process when there are no records to delete (`len(df) == 0`).

14.9 *Adding recipes to the vector database*

Until now, we've prepared everything required to get our recipes ready. We've uploaded them to MinIO, preprocessed them to ensure that they're in a workable format, created a Weaviate collection to store our content, and organized our records to handle new and existing recipes. With all these steps taken care of, we can start the most crucial operation in our pipeline: adding our recipes to the vector database.

Before we move forward, let's take a quick look at the structure of our data. Each row in the compared.parquet DataFrame is a section of a recipe (or chunk) that we want to upload to the vector database. In Weaviate, every record we upload is called an *object*; it includes the text we want to turn into vectors, UUIDs, and any other properties or attributes that help describe each recipe. But Weaviate isn't expecting a Parquet file format. To streamline the process, we convert each object to a dict and place the dicts inside a list (figure 14.13). This makes iteration easier and speeds the uploading process.

Now we have the records in the format we want, so we can store them in the vector database as implemented in the next listing. Weaviate recommends processing the objects in batches, and it conveniently provides a batch-oriented approach to create the batches dynamically without user intervention. Weaviate generates these batches under the hood based on the sizes of the chunks, which relieves us of the complexity of determining the batch size.

Listing 14.13   Saving the recipes to the vector database

```
from vectorflow.utils import (
    load_json_from_minio,
    get_weaviate_client,
)

import typer

app = typer.Typer()

@app.command()
def save(collection_name:str, path: str) -> None:

    source_objects = (
    load_parquet_from_minio( "compared", path).drop(columns=["regime"])
```

```
    .to_dict(orient="records")          ◄─────  We convert the DataFrame to JSON.
)

if len(source_objects) == 0:
    log.info("No objects to save")      ◄─────  There are no records to upload,
    return                                       so we end the execution.

with get_weaviate_client() as client:
    collection = client.collections.get(collection_name)

    failed_objects = []
    with collection.batch.dynamic() as batch:   ◄─────  Weaviate creates batches for us.
        for object in source_objects:
            batch.add_object(properties=object)  ◄─────  Dicts get uploaded into objects.

        if failed_objects:
            failed_objects =failed_objects.append(
                collection.batch.failed_objects
            )
                                              If there are failed objects,
        if len(failed_objects) > 0:   ◄───── we raise an error.
            raise ValueError(
                "Failed to save {len(failed_objects)} objects."
            )
```

```
[
    {
        "recipe_uuid": "1a505362-5d60-58f7-a952-34d5ec8cdc7e",
        "recipe_name": "Best Chocolate Chip Cookies",
        "chunk_uuid": "094acc40-03ec-5f72-b273-54763544ba3b",
        "chunk": "Best Chocolate Chip Cookies \n Ingredients: 1 ..."
    },
    {
        "recipe_uuid": "1a505362-5d60-58f7-a952-34d5ec8cdc7e",
        "recipe_name": "Best Chocolate Chip Cookies",
        "chunk_uuid": "2671fc7f-e803-5d8d-b837-6bb4107fefc9",
        "chunk": "Best Chocolate Chip Cookies \n Instructions: G..."
    },
    {
        "recipe_uuid": "8f697fc5-07e8-524e-b145-c6e20d6186b6",
        "recipe_name": "Good Old-Fashioned Pancakes",
        "chunk_uuid": "4ab3cb54-2162-5041-88fd-f733b8b88968",
        "chunk": "Good Old-Fashioned Pancakes \n Ingredients: 1 ..."
    },
    {
        "recipe_uuid": "8f697fc5-07e8-524e-b145-c6e20d6186b6",
        "recipe_name": "Good Old-Fashioned Pancakes",
        "chunk_uuid": "e0f04d73-fff0-588f-ba42-d80f59c0d52c",
        "chunk": "Good Old-Fashioned Pancakes \n Instructions: S..."
    }
]
```

	recipe_uuid	recipe_name	chunk_uuid	chunk
0	1a505362-5d60-58f7-a952-34d5ec8cdc7e	Best Chocolate Chip Cookies	094acc40-03ec-5f72-b273-54763544ba3b	Best Chocolate Chip Cookies \n Ingredients: 1 ...
1	1a505362-5d60-58f7-a952-34d5ec8cdc7e	Best Chocolate Chip Cookies	2671fc7f-e803-5d8d-b837-6bb4107fefc9	Best Chocolate Chip Cookies \n Instructions: G...
2	8f697fc5-07e8-524e-b145-c6e20d6186b6	Good Old-Fashioned Pancakes	4ab3cb54-2162-5041-88fd-f733b8b88968	Good Old-Fashioned Pancakes \n Ingredients: 1 ...
3	8f697fc5-07e8-524e-b145-c6e20d6186b6	Good Old-Fashioned Pancakes	e0f04d73-fff0-588f-ba42-d80f59c0d52c	Good Old-Fashioned Pancakes \n Instructions: S...

Figure 14.13
Each row in the
DataFrame is
converted to a
dictionary.

You may have noticed something interesting in this part of the code: you're not defining in any way how you're going to vectorize the data or the data types of the fields. But remember—you already defined this when you created the recipe collection (in the `create_collection` task). When you have a good understanding of the process of creating objects in Airflow, you can run the `save_in_vectordb` task to start vectorizing the recipes, as follows.

Listing 14.14   Defining the task to create a Weaviate collection

```
from airflow.providers.docker.operators.docker import DockerOperator
from airflow import DAG

COLLECTION_NAME = "recipes"

with DAG(
    dag_id="01_ingestion",
    ...
):

    ...
    save_in_vectordb = DockerOperator(
        task_id="save_recipes_to_weaviate",
        command=[
          "save",
          COLLECTION_NAME,
          "s3://data/{{data_interval_start | ds}}",
        ],
        **docker_kwargs
    )
```

All you need to do is pass the collection name and the path where you can get the Parquet file for the day. If there's an issue with updating any object, a value error is raised, and the task is flagged as a failure. In this case, the objects aren't added to the vector database. You can fix the problem, whether it's a connection or data issue, and rerun the task in Airflow to complete the ingestion process. On the other hand, if you can successfully upload the recipes, you can review them by visiting the Weaviate service at `http://localhost:8083/v1/objects` (figure 14.14).

14.10 RAG in action

So far, we've implemented all the steps required to add our recipes to the vector database. Let's take a moment to review those steps (illustrated in figure 14.15):

- With the `upload_recipes_to_minio` task, we made some recipes available to us in JSON format.
- In the `proprocess_recipes` task, we loaded the JSON files from MinIO; added UUIDs to the names and content of the recipes and converted them to a single pandas DataFrame for each day, which was uploaded back to MinIO.

```
{
  "deprecations": null,
  "objects": [
    {
      "class": "Recipes",
      "creationTimeUnix": 1734955760423,
      "id": "052d66e1-5adc-5112-9ca6-51470a30de0b",
      "lastUpdateTimeUnix": 1734955760423,
      "properties": {
        "chunk": "rollitos-de-pollo-con-salsa-de-champinones \n Instructions: Precalienta el horno a
180°C\nEn una ollita con agua hirviendo y sal, cocina la pasta para lasaña según las instrucciones del
paquete. Escurre y agrega una cucharada de aceite para evitar que se peguen y reserva.\nEn un sartén a fuego
medio, saltea la cebolla en aceite de oliva con mantequilla hasta que esté transparente y enseguida agrega
el ajo, cocina un minuto. Añade el pollo y cocina unos minutos.\nIncorpora los champiñones y el tomillo y
cocina por 5 minutos. Sazona con sal y pimienta. Reserva.\nPara la salsa, en una ollita derrite la
mantequilla y agrega la crema de champiñones Campbell's® y la leche. Deja que suelte el hervor y sazona con
sal. Reserva.\nPara el armado, sobre una lámina de pasta coloca un poco del relleno de pollo y una
cucharadita de la salsa de champiñones, enrolla y coloca en un refractario para horno. Repite.\nSalsea todos
los rollos con el resto de la salsa y cubre con el queso. Hornea por 15 minutos o hasta que el queso se
derrita. Sirve de inmediato.",
        "chunk_uuid": "052d66e1-5adc-5112-9ca6-51470a30de0b",
        "recipe_name": "rollitos-de-pollo-con-salsa-de-champinones",
        "recipe_uuid": "e81761b8-551d-5387-90a4-8d4e17fab450"
      },
      "vectorWeights": null
    },
    {
      "class": "Recipes",
      "creationTimeUnix": 1734958241085,
      "id": "061ba289-4ff3-56ff-bbc7-b449da85c17c",
      "lastUpdateTimeUnix": 1734958241085,
      "properties": {
        "chunk": "empanadas-argentinas \n Instructions: En un bowl, mezcla la harina, la sal, polvo para
hornear, la mantequilla y el vinagre hasta integrar muy bien la mantequilla, después vierte el agua poco a
poco y mezcla hasta formar una masa. Cuando la masa tenga una consistencia homogénea, tapa con un trapo y
deja reposar por 20 minutos.\nPara el relleno de carne: calienta el aceite de oliva en un sartén y agrega la
cebolla, el ajo y el pimiento rojo y cocina por 5 minutos. Incorpora la carne molida, la sal, la pimienta,
el orégano y el comino y cocina por 10 minutos o hasta que la carne esté muy bien cocida. Retira del fuego y
mezcla con el huevo y las aceitunas. Deja enfriar.\nPara el relleno de elote: derrite la mantequilla en un
sartén a fuego medio, agrega la cebolla y cocina por 5 minutos. Añade el elote, cocina por 2 minutos y
retira del fuego.\nEspolvorea un poco de harina sobre una superficie plana, extiende la masa y corta en
círculos de 5 cm de ancho. Coloca la mitad de los discos de masa en una charola, rellena con la carne y
```

Figure 14.14 At `http://localhost:8083/v1/objects`, you can review the objects uploaded to the vector database.

preprocess_recipes	create_collection	compare_objects	delete_outdated_objects	save_recipes_to_weaviate
DockerOperator	DockerOperator	DockerOperator	DockerOperator	DockerOperator

Figure 14.15 Upload our recipes to the vector database using the `01_ingestion` DAG.

- The `create_collection` task created a logical entity to store our recipes in Weaviate. In this step, we named our collection, defined the properties (or *schema*) of our fields, and defined how we'll embed the content of our recipes.
- By running the `compare_objects task`, we can determine whether any recipes we try to upload are already in the vector database. If we try to upload a new version of an existing recipe, we mark those records as `"update"`.

- The `delete_outdated_objects` tasks delete all the records in the vector database that have to be updated.

Finally, the `save_recipes_to_weaviate` task uploads all the new and updated recipes to the vector database.At this point, we've successfully stored all the recipes as vectors in the Weaviate database. But what can we do with the stored vectors?

This is where the RAG workflow comes into play, allowing us to transform vectors back into meaningful recipe recommendations. Let's take a moment to explore the key processes involved in a RAG workflow.

14.10.1 *The R is for retrieving*

Suppose that a user has a craving for lasagna but doesn't have a clear idea of how to prepare it. We have the lasagna recipe stored in the vector database among thousands of other recipes. The user asks the RAG system, "How can I make lasagna?"

The first step is converting the user's question to a vector, using the same embedding model (`text-embedding-3-large`) we used to store our recipes in the vector database. With this vector representation of the question, we can conduct a vector similarity search in our database to find the most relevant documents.

Earlier, we assessed the similarity of sushi and poke bowl by determining their proximity. In simple terms, we were evaluating the Euclidean distance between the two recipes in the flavor space to judge their similarity.

We don't embed the text of two recipes based on their flavor in real-world applications, however. Embeddings are created based on the words used in each recipe, which poses an interesting challenge. Two recipes may use very different words to describe their preparation, but they can refer to a similar recipe. For this reason, our focus should not be on the similarity of the words themselves; it should be on the meaning of the recipes. In this context, we care more about the direction of the vectors we're comparing than their exact values.

To go back to the flavor space discussed in section 14.3, two recipes in the mild/sweet quadrant will be more similar to each other than to recipes in the savory/spicy quadrant. What matters isn't how similar the values of the two recipes are, but whether they point in the same direction in the flavor space (figure 14.16). We can measure this by calculating the recipes' cosine similarity.

Two vectors that point in the same direction have a cosine similarity of 1. This concept is particularly useful in text analysis, in which the specific words in a recipe can vary widely, but the overall direction, which reflects the context or meaning, is what truly matters.

The example in figure 14.16 illustrates a simplified scenario in two dimensions. If we add more dimensions, such as a third dimension for acidity, we can classify our recipes on the flavor spectrum more effectively. In practice, the vector embedding from `text-embedding-3-large` consists of 3,072 dimensions. Even though not all these dimensions relate directly to the flavor spectrum, having so many dimensions allows embedding models to capture intricate semantic relationships, enabling us to capture complex, nonlinear relationships in text.

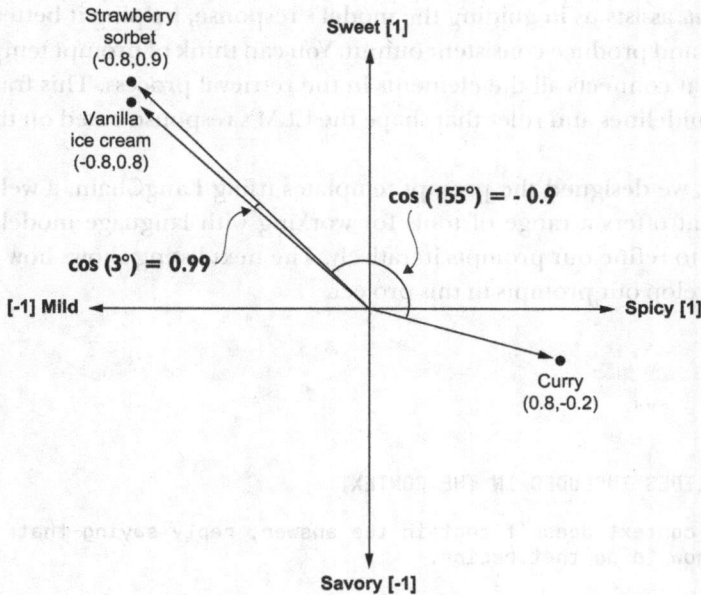

cos (155°) = - 0.9

cos (3°) = 0.99

Sweet [1]

Strawberry sorbet (-0.8,0.9)

Vanilla ice cream (-0.8,0.8)

[-1] Mild

Spicy [1]

Curry (0.8,-0.2)

Savory [-1]

Figure 14.16 Similar recipes, such as ice cream and sorbet, point in the same direction and have a cosine similarity close to 1. As the two recipes become more dissimilar, their similarity decreases. It's possible to have negative similarity, which indicates that the two recipes are very different.

Fortunately, most modern vector databases can calculate cosine similarity for us and quickly determine the similarity between two text segments. If we ask how to make lasagna, for example, the vector database handles the vectorization using the specified embedding model and retrieves the most relevant documents (figure 14.17).

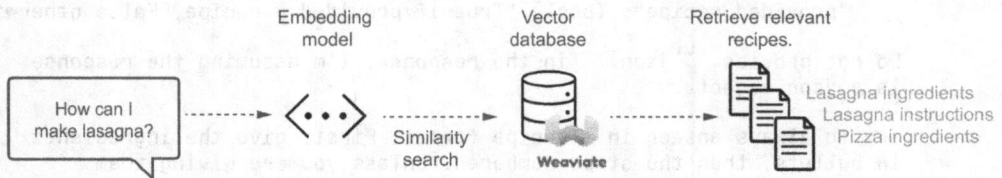

Embedding model

Vector database

Retrieve relevant recipes.

How can I make lasagna?

⟨ · · · ⟩

Similarity search

Weaviate

Lasagna ingredients
Lasagna instructions
Pizza ingredients

Figure 14.17 In the retrieval workflow, we can embed a user's question and perform a similarity search in the database using cosine similarity. The vector database returns the documents that are most relevant to the question.

14.10.2 Structuring our questions with prompt templates

Now that we have the most relevant documents for the lasagna recipe, we can feed them to the LLM to tell us how to make lasagna based on these recipes. Before passing these documents to a language model, however, it would be good to provide some structure to all the elements we have. We can do this by creating a prompt template.

A *prompt template* assists us in guiding the model's response, helping it better understand the context and produce consistent output. You can think of prompt templates as the framework that connects all the elements in the retrieval process. This framework aims to provide guidelines and rules that shape the LLM's response based on the documents retrieved.

In this project, we designed the prompt templates using LangChain, a well-known Python library that offers a range of tools for working with language models. LangChain enables us to refine our prompts iteratively. The next listing shows how we used LangChain to develop our prompts in this project.

Listing 14.15   Providing structure for asking questions to an LLM

```
prompt_template = """


ONLY PROVIDE RECIPES INCLUDED IN THE CONTEXT
However, If the context doesn't contain the answer, reply saying that
you don't know how to do that recipe.

You can respond politely to greetings if the user isn't specifically
asking for a recipe.

If you know the recipe, provide the whole recipe. If they ask you
for a recipe that is not in the context give them three options
based on recipes you do know from the context. The recipes should be
as similar as possible to the one they're asking for.

Return a json object with the following format:

    "answer": (str) "The answer to the question",
    "provided_recipe": (bool) "True if provided a recipe, False otherwise",

Do not provide ```json``` in the response. I'm assuming the response
is a json object.

Try to always answer in a recipe format. First, give the ingredients
in bullets, then the steps numbered. Unless you are giving them
options.

Question:
{input}          ◄──────┤ Question asked by the user

Message history:              Provides previous
{chat_history}   ◄────────    messages with the LLM

Context:             Relevant documents
{context}    ◄───────│ from the retrieval step

"""


PROMPT = PromptTemplate(
```

```
    template=prompt_template,
    input_variables=["context", "input" ,"chat_history"]
)
```

The first aspect of our prompt template specifies how the language model should respond to the user's question. Essentially, it instructs the LLM to act as a cooking assistant, establishing the tone for interactions with the user. These instructions can also determine the language used in responses and the actions to take in specific scenarios, such as when the user asks for something unrelated to cooking.

By defining a common prompt template, we guarantee that the instructions remain consistent for every question posed to the model. One valuable feature of LangChain is its capability to pass parameters that are essential for the RAG process. In our example, three parameters go into the prompt template:

- *Question*—This parameter refers to the specific question that the user is asking the language model.
- *Message history*—Because we'll use this prompt in a chat application, it's beneficial for the model to access not only the most recent question but also any previous messages between the user and the LLM.
- *Context*—This parameter includes the recipes retrieved from the vector database earlier, which are the recipes most relevant to the user's question.

In our instructions, we can also define how to handle situations in which the user's question doesn't correspond to any available recipe. If a user asks for a chocolate cake recipe that isn't included in the recipes retrieved by the vector database, the language model should respond by stating that it doesn't have that recipe.

Another aspect we can control in the context is the format of the LLM output. This feature is particularly useful because we can instruct the language model to provide answers in a JSON-like string format, ensuring that we have consistent output every time we make a call to the LLM service.

14.10.3 Searching for recipes

At this point, we have everything we need for the RAG process. Our favorite recipes are saved in the vector database. We can pull up important documents when a user asks a question, and we've made a prompt that helps us put the whole process together. The final step is using a language model to generate the recipes (figure 14.18).

At this point, we can begin using the Recipe Vault UI, accessible at `http://localhost:8084/Chat`. With this chat assistant (shown in figure 14.19), a user can request a recipe from the collection saved in the vector database. If the recipe is part of the vector database, the assistant provides the recipe's ingredients and steps. If a user asks for a recipe that's not in the vector database, however, the assistant replies that it doesn't know how to make that specific recipe. The virtual assistant uses the LLM's capabilities to share recipes in different languages or offer recipe suggestions from the vector database based on a list of ingredients we provide (figure 14.20).

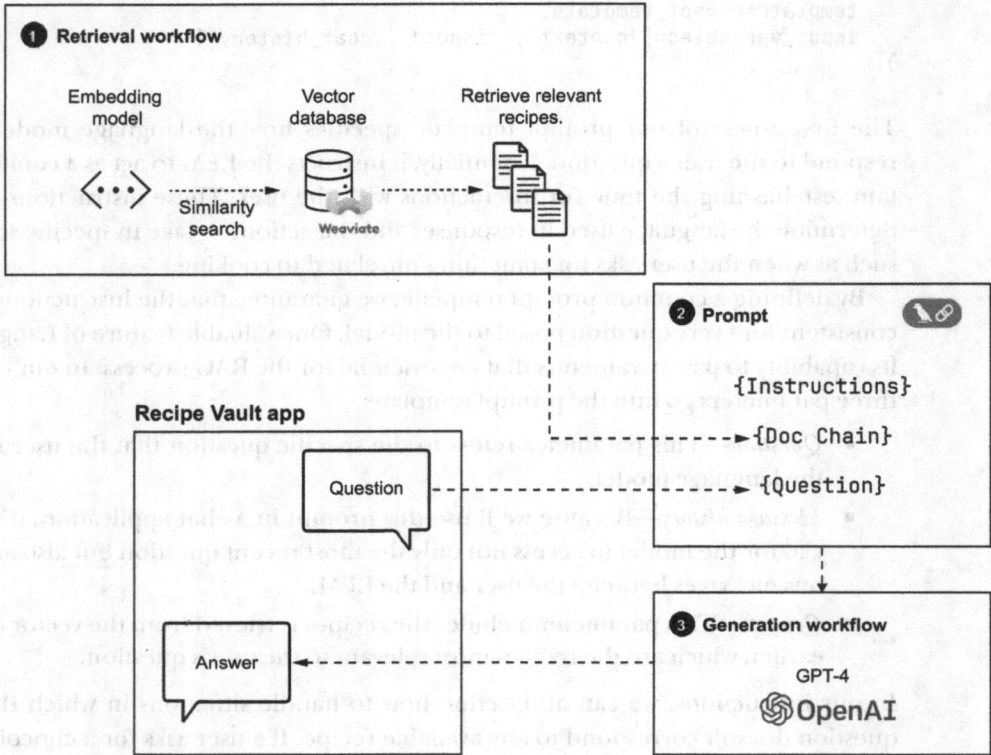

Figure 14.18 Complete RAG process

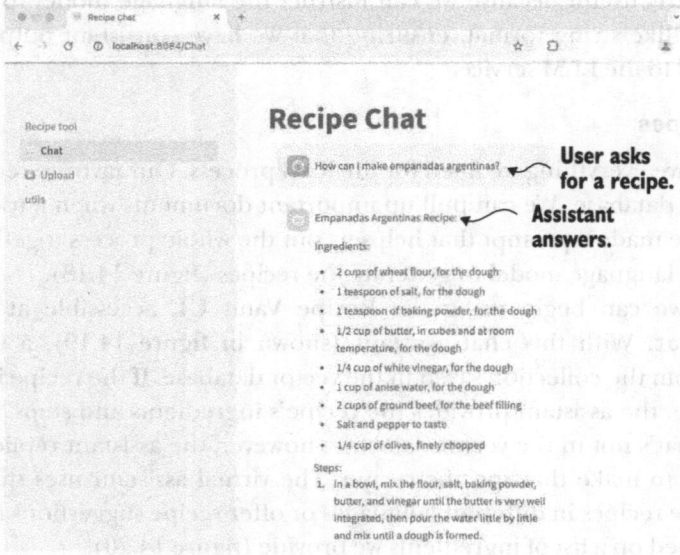

Figure 14.19 In Recipe Chat, users can interact with an LLM to retrieve or generate new recipe suggestions, using recipes they've previously stored in the vector database.

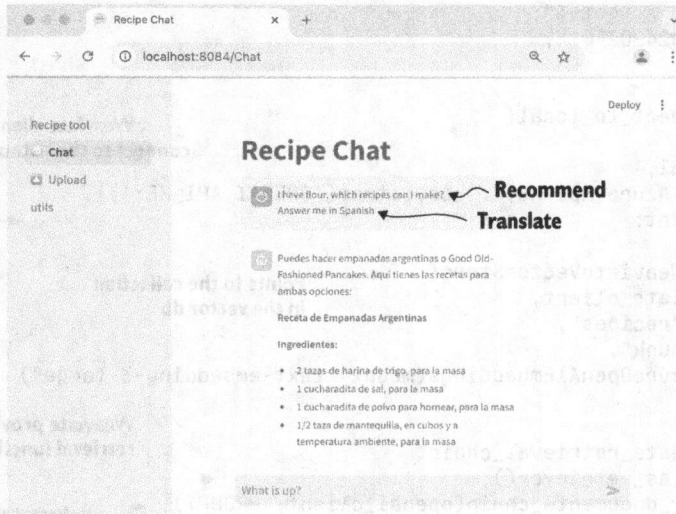

Figure 14.20 Recipe Chat can translate user-stored recipes and provide tailored recommendations. This functionality is achieved through the RAG framework, which integrates the language understanding and generation abilities of LLMs with efficient recipe storage and retrieval using a vector database.

The RAG code execution in the Recipe Vault chat (data-pipelines-with-airflow-2nd-ed/chapter14/vectorvault/src/vectorvault/chat/pages/1_☺_Chat.py) in this chapter's codebase might be tricky to get hold of at first glance because the RAG and frontend code are in the same file. For this reason, we've prepared the following working code snippet, which focuses only on the RAG workflow and uses an LLM to generate an answer to a specific question.

Listing 14.16 Interacting with the vector database via Python

```python
#  IMPORTANT!! To run this implementation, Don't forget to make sure
#  the environment variables we declared in the .env files
#  are accessible in the Python environment.

from langchain_openai.chat_models import AzureChatOpenAI
from langchain_openai import AzureOpenAIEmbeddings
from langchain_weaviate.vectorstores import WeaviateVectorStore

from langchain.chains import create_retrieval_chain
from langchain.chains.combine_documents import create_stuff_documents_chain

from vectorvault.chat.pages.utils import PROMPT

import weaviate
import os
import json

question = "Whats the recipe for chocolate cookies?"

openai_client = AzureChatOpenAI(          ◄── Can also be ChatOpenAI if not
    model_name="gpt-4",                       hosted in Microsoft Azure
```

```
    deployment_name = "gpt-4",
    api_version="2024-02-01",
)

with weaviate.connect_to_local(              ◄── Weaviate client to
    port=8083,                                    connect to the database
    grpc_port=50051,
    headers = {"X-Azure-Api-Key":  os.getenv('OPENAI_API_KEY')},
) as weaviate_client:

    weaviate_db = WeaviateVectorStore(    ◄── Points to the collection
        client=weaviate_client,               in the vector db
        index_name="recipes",
        text_key="chunk",
        embedding=AzureOpenAIEmbeddings(model="text-embedding-3-large")
    )
                                                  Weaviate provides the
                                                  retrieval function.
    rag_chain = create_retrieval_chain(
        weaviate_db.as_retriever(),       ◄──
        create_stuff_documents_chain(openai_client, PROMPT),  ◄──  Relevant documents
    )                                                              included in the
                                                                   Prompt as <context>
                                          We invoke the RAG         (see listing 14.15)
    output = rag_chain.invoke({       ◄── with the user question.
        "input": question,
        "chat_history": None          ◄──
    }                                     No chat history exists because
    )                                     we're not using the Chat UI.

    print(json.loads(output["answer"]))  ◄──  LLM returns a JSON-like string
                                              as specified in Prompt.

{
    'answer': 'Here is the recipe for the Best Chocolate Chip Cookies:\n\n
               Ingredients:\n- 1 cup butter, softened\n- 1 cup white sugar\n
               - 1 cup packed brown sugar\n- 2 large eggs\n- 2 teaspoo...',
    'provided_recipe': True
}
```

Just like that, we can pull up all the recipes we've stored in the vector database, including our family recipes. This way, all our family recipes are kept safe in the vector database, ensuring that we won't lose them as time goes by. Also, if we make Recipe Chat available online, we can easily share these beloved recipes with others.

Summary

- The rise in generative artificial intelligence, particularly LLMs, has revolutionized various fields. LLMs, trained on vast public data, excel in natural-language tasks, making them increasingly popular in today's tech landscape.
- RAG empowers language models to access an external library, eliminating the need for constant retraining with new data additions. RAG operates in a vector space, making it efficient compared with storing data as text, which can be unworkable with large data volumes.

- In a RAG system, text is broken into smaller pieces (chunks) to enhance retrieval efficiency. Despite converting data to vectors, RAG systems can reference the source. Incorrect chunk sizes in a RAG system can lead to inefficiencies. Too large a chunk can make it challenging to pinpoint the source; too small a chunk can lead to inefficient querying and source redundancy.

- An embedding model translates text into a numerical vector representation, facilitating the efficient processing of text data on natural-language tasks.

- Weaviate is an open source vector database that offers robust vector search capabilities, making it highly effective for language processing tasks. Weaviate organizes data in collections, similar to tables in traditional databases, containing fields associated with business entities. Collections group related objects, like the data we aim to vectorize.

- UUIDs, created via an algorithm, generate a unique 32-length key for every text combination, accelerating the search process in Weaviate. Regardless of text length, UUIDs maintain consistent length, enabling similarity comparison.

- Airflow is an effective tool for building RAG systems by automating tasks such as data ingestion, chunking, embedding generation, and updating a vector database. It schedules and monitors the entire workflow, ensuring scalability, reliability, and efficient handling of new data, making the RAG system easier to maintain.

Part 4

Airflow in production

At this point, you should be well on your way to mastering Airflow—able to write complex pipelines. So far, we've focused on using Airflow on a local system, either natively or using container technologies such as Docker. A common question is how to run and use Airflow in production settings. Part 4 focuses entirely on running Airflow in production, including topics such as designing architectures for Airflow deployments, securing Airflow, and choosing deployment options.

First, in chapter 15, we describe how to operate Airflow in production, touching on topics such as architectures for scaling Airflow, monitoring, logging, and alerting. Next, chapter 16 focuses specifically on securing Airflow to avoid unwanted access and minimizing the impact of security breaches. Finally, chapter 17 runs through options for deploying Airflow using managed services or deploying on your own Kubernetes cluster.

After completing part 4, you should have a good idea of how to operate and deploy Airflow and which implementation details to consider for a robust, secure deployment.

Operating Airflow
in production

This chapter covers

- Dissecting the Airflow components
- Configuring Airflow to scale horizontally using different executors
- Monitoring the status and performance of Airflow visually
- Sending out alerts in case of task failures

Up to now, we've focused mainly on the user side of Airflow: building data pipelines. Going forward, we'll switch gears and discuss what it takes to run and deploy Airflow from an operations perspective. A general understanding of concepts such as distributed software architecture, logging, monitoring, and alerting is assumed, but no specific technology knowledge is required.

15.1 Revisiting the Airflow architecture

Back in chapter 1, we showed the Airflow architecture displayed in figure 15.1. At minimum, Airflow consists of a number of components:

- API server
- Scheduler
- Directed acyclic graph (DAG) processor
- Metastore (also known as the database)
- Workers
- Triggerer (optional component, required for working with deferrable operators)
- Executor (not shown in the figure)

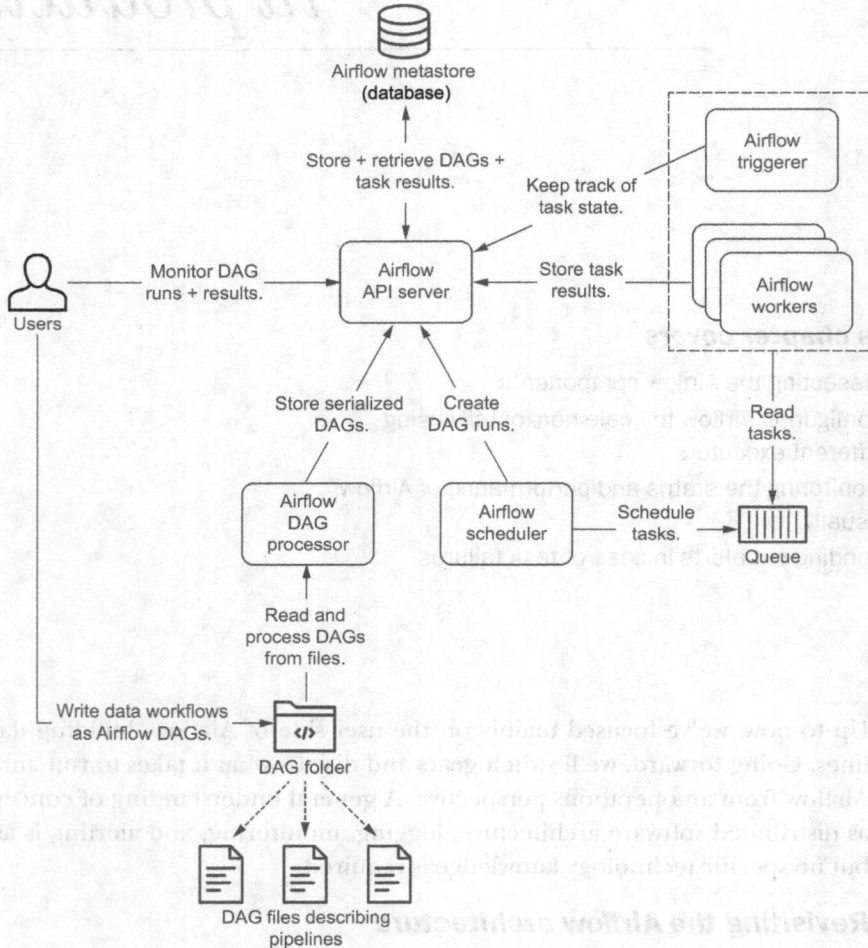

Figure 15.1   High-level Airflow architecture

Both the API server and scheduler are Airflow processes. The database is a separate service you must provide to Airflow for storing metadata from the API server and scheduler. The DAG processor must be able to access the folder containing DAG definitions. We briefly describe each component in the following list:

- The API server's responsibility is to visually display information about the status of the pipelines and allow the user to perform certain actions, such as triggering a DAG. In addition, the API server functions as the main communication portal for other Airflow components. In the past, it was possible to interact directly with the Airflow metastore from within a DAG. Although this interaction might have been useful for some specific use cases, it also opened the possibility of causing problems for the whole Airflow instance. For this reason, Airflow 3 introduced the API server as the intermediary between components.

- The DAG processor parses DAG files (i.e., reads DAG files, extracts bits and pieces, and stores these bits in the metastore) and makes them available to Airflow in general.

- The scheduler's responsibility is to determine which tasks to run and place these tasks in a queue.

- The triggerer is responsible for executing deferred tasks asynchronously. The triggerer is used only to work with deferrable operators.

- The workers pick up tasks to be executed and perform the required work. The workers are part of the execution framework defined by the executor. If you're using the CeleryExecutor, for example, the workers are Celery worker processes that do the actual work.

- The metastore stores all metadata related to Airflow-native entities (DAG runs, triggers, data set, and so on) as well as serialized versions of your DAGs. These serialized versions are accessible to all Airflow components so they don't need to parse the DAG files themselves.

NOTE Airflow 3 introduced the API server as a gateway to the metastore for all components. At the time of writing, this gateway wasn't yet fully implemented for all components. Because the target state is that all interaction with the metastore goes through the API server, all figures in this chapter (and in other places in this book) assume that this target state is in place. You may encounter slightly different behavior depending on when you work with Airflow in practice.

15.2 Choosing the executor

Now that you've refreshed your knowledge of the components, we're going to look at how you can configure these components in a productionlike environment and what choices you need to make. One such choice is how to install and run Airflow. You can install Airflow in various ways: from a single machine (which requires minimal effort to set up but isn't scalable) to multiple machines (which requires more initial work but has horizontal scalability).

In Airflow, an executor configures the execution modes. This section looks at executor types and tradeoffs and how to configure them.

15.2.1 Overview of executor types

At the time of writing, Airflow has six types of executors:

- `LocalExecutor`
- `CeleryExecutor`
- `BatchExecutor` (marked alpha/experimental at the time of writing)
- `KubernetesExecutor`
- `EcsExecutor`
- `EdgeExecutor` (marked as experimental prerelease at the time of writing)

The `BatchExecutor` and `EcsExecutor` are specific to Amazon Web Services (AWS); they use native AWS services as a platform for their Airflow executors. We'll focus on the other four executor types, which can be used regardless of underlying infrastructure.

Broadly speaking, the `BatchExecutor` can be considered an AWS-native alternative to the `CeleryExecutor`, and the `EcsExecutor` is most similar to the `KubernetesExecutor`. You configure the executor type by setting `AIRFLOW__CORE__EXECUTOR` to one of the executor types in the preceding list.

Configuring Airflow

Throughout this chapter, we often refer to the Airflow configuration. Configuration in Airflow is interpreted in this order of preference:

1. Environment variable (`AIRFLOW__[SECTION]__[KEY]`)
2. Command environment variable (`AIRFLOW__[SECTION]__[KEY]_CMD`)
3. A configuration value in `airflow.cfg`
4. Command in `airflow.cfg`
5. Default value

Whenever we refer to configuration options, we'll be using option 1. As an example, we'll show the configuration item `web_server_port` in the `webserver` section as `AIRFLOW__WEBSERVER__WEB_SERVER_PORT`.

To find the current value of any configuration item, scroll down the Configurations page of the Airflow UI to the table titled Running Configuration. This table shows all configuration options, their current values, and which of the five options was used to set the configuration.

You may also encounter a hybrid executor. As the name suggests, this type of executor combines two or more executor types. Combining the `CeleryExecutor` with the `KubernetesExecutor`, for example, gives you the `CeleryKubernetesExecutor`. The underlying idea is that by combining executors, you get the benefits of both and can run some tasks on one executor type while other tasks run on the other executor. If you want to run a lot of large tasks that require full isolation but also have a few small tasks that don't, it may make sense to use the KubernetesExecutor for the large tasks and the CeleryExecutor for the small ones. This approach would ensure that you play to each executor type's strengths.

That said about HybridExecutors, be careful about their practical application. At the time of writing, Airflow had two statically coded HybridExecutors:

- CeleryKubernetesExecutor
- LocalKubernetesExecutor

Because of the way they've been implemented (they abuse the queue attribute of tasks), we currently recommend *not* using these executors. In addition to the concerns about the implementation, many statically coded HybridExecutors aren't easy to maintain.

Instead, Airflow created a full-fledged implementation that allows you to use multiple executor types concurrently. As you'll see in chapter 17, the official Helm Airflow chart already uses it. In a nutshell, you can configure this implementation by adding the following configuration to your airflow.cfg file:

```
[core]
executor = 'LocalExecutor,CeleryExecutor'
```

In this case, a hybrid setup with a LocalExecutor and a CeleryExecutor would be used. To specify which executor to use, you can use the executor parameter as follows.

Listing 15.1   Using a specific executor

```
BashOperator(
    task_id="hello_world",
    executor="LocalExecutor",
    bash_command="echo 'hello world!'",
)
```

15.2.2 Which executor is right for you?

Given the variety in the executors that Airflow offers, it can be confusing and difficult to decide which executor to choose. This section looks at some of the characteristics of the executors so you can weigh them against one another. Table 15.1 provides a brief overview.

Table 15.1   Overview of Airflow executors

Executor	Distributed	Ease of installation	Good fit when
LocalExecutor	No	Easy	Running on a single machine is good enough.
CeleryExecutor	Yes	Moderate	You need to scale out over multiple machines.

Table 15.1   Overview of Airflow executors (*continued*)

Executor	Distributed	Ease of installation	Good fit when
KubernetesExecutor	Yes	Complex	You need to scale out over multiple machines, are familiar with Kubernetes, and prefer a containerized setup.
EdgeExecutor	Yes	Moderate	You need an executor to run outside the Airflow's instance environment (e.g., on premises while Airflow is in the cloud).

The LocalExecutor is the simplest executor option available. As the name suggests, it runs locally but can run multiple tasks in parallel. Internally, it registers tasks to execute in a Python *FIFO* (first in, first out) queue, which worker processes read and execute. By default, the LocalExecutor can run up to 32 parallel processes; this number is configurable.

If you want to distribute your workloads over multiple machines, you have two options: the CeleryExecutor and the KubernetesExecutor. You might choose to distribute work over multiple machines for various reasons: you've hit the resource limits of a single machine, want redundancy by running jobs on multiple machines, or want to run workloads faster by distributing the work across multiple machines.

The CeleryExecutor internally applies Celery (https://docs.celeryq.dev/en/stable) as the mechanism for queueing tasks to run, and workers read and process tasks from the queue. From a user's perspective, the CeleryExecutor works the same way as the LocaExecutor; it sends tasks to a queue, and workers read tasks to process from the queue. The main difference is that all components can run on different virtual machines, spreading the workload. Currently, Celery supports RabbitMQ, Redis, and AWS Simple Queue Service (SQS) as a stable queuing mechanism. There are also experimental queues, but as the name suggests, those queues are still in development.

Celery also comes with a monitoring tool named Flower for inspecting the state of the Celery system. Celery is a Python library, so it integrates nicely with Airflow. The command-line interface (CLI) command airflow celery worker, for example, will start a Celery worker. The only real external dependency for this setup is the queuing mechanism.

Next, the KubernetesExecutor runs workloads on Kubernetes (https://kubernetes .io). It requires you to set up and configure a Kubernetes cluster on which to run Airflow; the executor integrates with the Kubernetes APIs to distribute Airflow tasks. Kubernetes is the de facto solution for running containerized workloads, which implies that every task in an Airflow DAG is run in a Kubernetes pod. Kubernetes is highly configurable and scalable and is used in many organizations, which happily use Kubernetes in combination with Airflow.

Finally, the EdgeExecutor is a relatively new executor type that enables you to run an Airflow executor in a location different from the other Airflow components. You give this executor the API token it needs to communicate with the API server and the URL. A good use case is when you need to run some task in your DAG in a specific environment where you can't (or don't want to) run the other Airflow components. There are some limitations on the EdgeExecutor at the time of writing (particularly with respect to logging), and its performance is untested, but it's an interesting alternative to the other executors.

15.2.3 Installing each executor

There are many ways to install and configure Airflow, so it's impractical to elaborate on all of them in this book. Instead, we'll discuss the main items required to get each executor up and running.

As section 15.1 mentioned, the executor is part of Airflow's scheduler. You can start the DAG processor and task scheduler separately by running `airflow scheduler` or `airflow dag-processor`. In Airflow 2, you don't have to run the DAG processor separately; the default setup is to include it in the scheduler. You can choose to run it as a separate component by setting `AIRFLOW__SCHEDULER__STANDALONE_DAG_PROCESSOR` to `True`. From Airflow 3 onward, however, running a standalone DAG processor is required. The task executor can be installed in different ways, from a single process on a single machine to multiple processes on multiple machines, for performance and/or redundancy.

The executor type is set in Airflow with `AIRFLOW__CORE__EXECUTOR`, the value of which is one of the following:

- `LocalExecutor` (default)
- `CeleryExecutor`
- `KubernetesExecutor`
- `EdgeExecutor`

NOTE Again, we deliberately leave out the `BatchExecutor` and `EcsExecutor` because they're AWS specific and because the `BatchExecutor` is experimental.

You can validate the correct installation of any executor by running a DAG. If any task makes it to running state, it went through the cycle of being scheduled, queued, and running, which means that it was picked up by the executor.

SETTING UP THE LOCALEXECUTOR

From Airflow 3 on, the `LocalExecutor` is the default executor (figure 15.2). The executor itself can't be parallelized, but it can run multiple subprocesses, so tasks can be executed in parallel; thus, it performs faster. Each subprocess executes one task, and subprocesses can run in parallel.

To configure the `LocalExecutor`, set `AIRFLOW__CORE__EXECUTOR` to `LocalExecutor`. You can configure the amount of parallelism for the `LocalExecutor`. The scheduler can spawn a maximum number of subprocesses configured by `AIRFLOW__CORE__PARALLELISM` (default 32; minimum value 1). Technically, these processes aren't new; they're forked

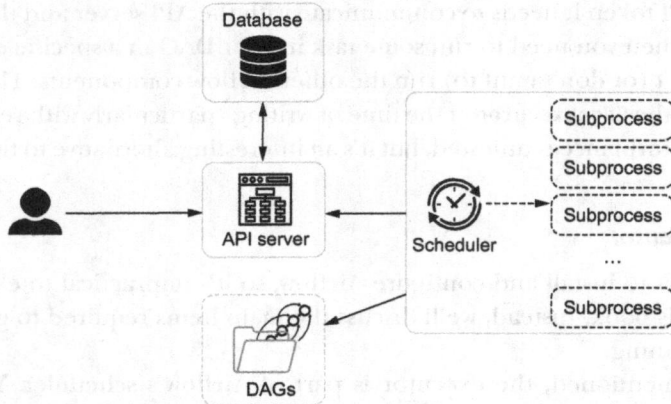

Figure 15.2 With the
`LocalExecutor`, all
components can run on
a separate machine. All
subprocesses created by
the scheduler, however,
run on a single machine.

from the parent (scheduler) process. You have other ways to limit the number of parallel tasks (e.g., by lowering the default pool size, `AIRFLOW__CORE__MAX_ACTIVE_TASKS_PER_DAG`, or `AIRFLOW__CORE__MAX_ACTIVE _RUNS_PER_DAG`).

To use the `LocalExecutor`, you have to set up a database that the executor can use, either MySQL or PostgreSQL. In addition to setting up the database itself, you have to install Airflow with the extra dependencies for the corresponding database system:

- *MySQL*—`pip install 'apache-airflow[mysql]'`
- *PostgreSQL*—`pip install 'apache-airflow[postgres]'`

The `LocalExecutor` is easy to set up and gives you decent performance. The system is limited by the resources of the scheduler's machine. When the `LocalExecutor` is no longer sufficient in terms of performance or redundancy, the `CeleryExecutor` and `KubernetesExecutor` (which we address later in this section) are the logical next steps.

SETTING UP THE CELERYEXECUTOR

The `CeleryExecutor` is built on top of the Celery project. Celery provides a framework for distributing messages to workers via a queuing system (figure 15.3).

As you see in figure 15.3, both the scheduler and Celery workers require access to both the DAGs. For the database, connectivity is arranged via the API server. This connectivity can be challenging to set up for the DAGs folder. You make the DAGs available to all machines either via a shared filesystem or by building a containerized setup in which the DAGs are built into an image with Airflow. In the containerized setup, any change to the DAG code results in redeployment of the Airflow components, which would be the user's responsibility.

To get started with Celery, install Airflow with the Celery extra dependencies and then configure the executor as follows:

- `pip install 'apache-airflow[celery]'`
- `AIRFLOW__CORE__EXECUTOR=CeleryExecutor`

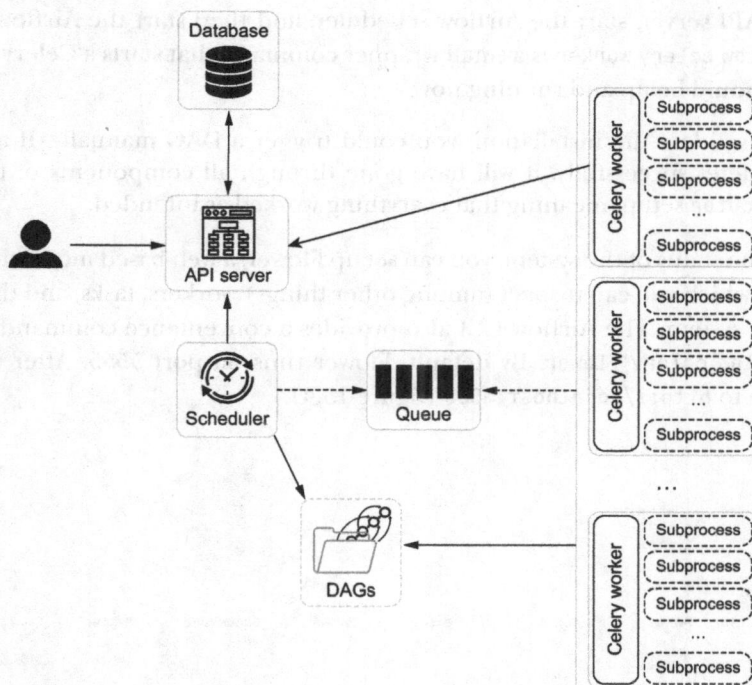

Figure 15.3 In the `CeleryExecutor`, tasks are divided among multiple machines running Celery workers. The workers wait for tasks to arrive in a queue.

The queueing system can be anything Celery supports (Redis, RabbitMQ, and AWS SQS at the time of writing). In Celery, the queue is called a *broker*. Installing a broker is not in the scope of this book, but after installation you must configure Airflow to use the broker by setting `AIRFLOW__CELERY__BROKER_URL`:

- *Redis*—`AIRFLOW__CELERY__BROKER_URL=redis://localhost:6379/0`
- *RabbitMQ*—`AIRFLOW__CELERY__BROKER_URL=amqp://user:pass@localhost:5672//`

Check the documentation for your queueing system for the corresponding Uniform Resource Identifier (URI) format. The `BROKER_URL` allows the scheduler to send messages to the queue. To enable the Celery workers to communicate with the Airflow metastore, you must also configure `AIRFLOW__CELERY__RESULT_BACKEND`. In Celery, the prefix `db+` indicates a database connection:

- *MySQL*—`AIRFLOW__CELERY__RESULT_BACKEND=db+mysql://user:pass@localhost/airflow`
- *PostgreSQL*—`AIRFLOW__CELERY__RESULT_BACKEND=db+postgresql://user:pass@local-host/airflow`

Ensure that the `DAGs` folder is accessible on the worker machines on the same path, as configured by `AIRFLOW__CORE__DAGS_FOLDER`. Then you should be good to go. Start the Airflow API server, start the Airflow scheduler, and then start the Airflow Celery worker. `airflow celery worker` is a small wrapper command that starts a Celery worker. Everything should be up and running now.

> **NOTE**   To validate the installation, you could trigger a DAG manually. If any task completes successfully, it will have gone through all components of the `CeleryExecutor` setup, meaning that everything worked as intended.

To monitor the status of the system, you can set up Flower, a web-based monitoring tool for Celery in which you can inspect (among other things) workers, tasks, and the status of the Celery system. The Airflow CLI also provides a convenience command to start Flower: `airflow celery flower`. By default, Flower runs on port 5555. After the tool starts, browse to `http://localhost:5555` (figure 15.4).

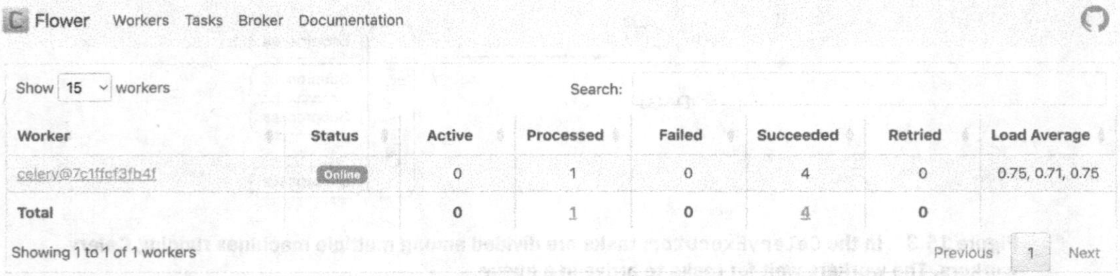

| Flower | Workers | Tasks | Broker | Documentation | | | | | |

Show 15 ∨ workers   Search:

Worker	Status	Active	Processed	Failed	Succeeded	Retried	Load Average
celery@7c1ffcf3fb4f	Online	0	1	0	4	0	0.75, 0.71, 0.75
Total		0	1	0	4	0	

Showing 1 to 1 of 1 workers   Previous 1 Next

Figure 15.4   The Flower dashboard shows the status of all Celery workers.

In the first view of Flower, you see the number of registered Celery workers, their status, and some high-level information on the number of tasks each worker has processed. From here, you can drill down into individual workers and their tasks. In the past (up to version 0.9.7), Flower contained a Monitor page that displayed useful graphics. This functionality has been deprecated in favor of Prometheus integration, however. Section 15.7.3 describes how to set up Prometheus in general and specifically how to set up the Prometheus metrics for Flower/Celery.

Of the two distributed executor modes Airflow offers (Celery and Kubernetes), the `CeleryExecutor` is easier to set up from scratch because you don't need to set up infrastructure in the form of Kubernetes.

SETTING UP THE KUBERNETESEXECUTOR

Another option is the `KubernetesExecutor`. Set `AIRFLOW__CORE__EXECUTOR=` `Kubernetes-Executor` to use it. As the name implies, this executor type is coupled with Kubernetes, which is the most-used system for running and managing software in containers. Many companies run their software on Kubernetes because containers provide an isolated environment that ensures what you develop on your computer runs the same on the production system. Thus, the Airflow community expressed a strong desire to run Airflow on Kubernetes. Architecturally, the KubernetesExecutor looks like figure 15.5.

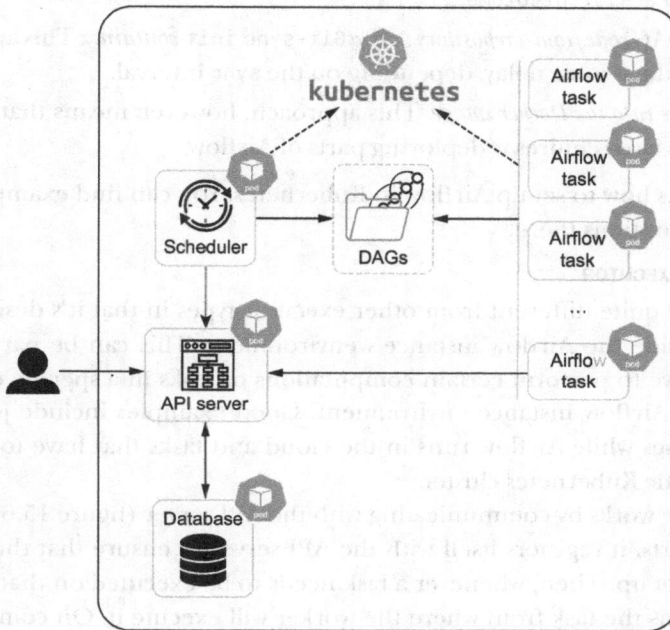

Figure 15.5 With the KubernetesExecutor, all tasks run in a pod in Kubernetes. Although it isn't necessary to run the API server, scheduler, and database in Kubernetes, it's sensible to run it there when using the KubernetesExecutor to reduce the complexity of the setup.

When you're working with the KubernetesExecutor, it helps to have existing knowledge of Kubernetes, which can be large and complex. But the Airflow Kubernetes-Executor uses only a small part of the components available on the Kubernetes platform. For now, it's good to know that a *pod* is the smallest unit of work in Kubernetes and can run one or more containers. In the context of Airflow, one task runs in one pod.

A pod is created every time a task is executed. When the scheduler decides to run a task, it sends a pod-creation request to the Kubernetes API, which creates a pod running an Airflow container with the command airflow tasks run .... Kubernetes itself monitors the status of the pod.

With the other executor setups, there is clear separation between physical machines. With Kubernetes, all processes run in pods, where they can be distributed over multiple machines, although they may also be running on the same machine. From a user's perspective, processes run in pods, and the user doesn't know about underlying machines.

The most common way to deploy software on Kubernetes is to use Helm, a package manager for Kubernetes. Chapter 17 describes the process of installing, configuring, and managing Airflow with Helm.

One of the trickiest parts of setting up the `KubernetesExecutor` is determining how to distribute DAG files between Airflow processes. You can use any of three methods:

- *Share DAGs between pods with a* `PersistentVolume`. The tricky part is how to get the code into the `PersistentVolume`.
- *Pull the latest DAG code from a repository with a* `Git-sync init` *container*. This approach tends to introduce some delay, depending on the `sync` interval.
- *Build the DAGs into the Docker image*. This approach, however, means that deploying new DAGs also requires redeploying parts of Airflow.

Chapter 17 describes how to set up Airflow in Kubernetes. You can find examples and discussions of these options there.

SETTING UP THE EDGEEXECUTOR

The `EdgeExecutor` is quite different from other executor types in that it's designed to work remotely, outside the Airflow instance's environment. This can be particularly useful when you have to perform certain computations or tasks in a specific environment that isn't the Airflow instance environment. Good examples include jobs that must run on premises while Airflow runs in the cloud and tasks that have to be executed within a specific Kubernetes cluster.

The `EdgeExecutor` works by communicating with the API server (figure 15.6). When an Edge Worker starts, it registers itself with the API server to ensure that the line of communication is set up. Then, whenever a task needs to be executed on that worker, the API server assigns the task from where the worker will execute it. On completion, the API server is notified again.

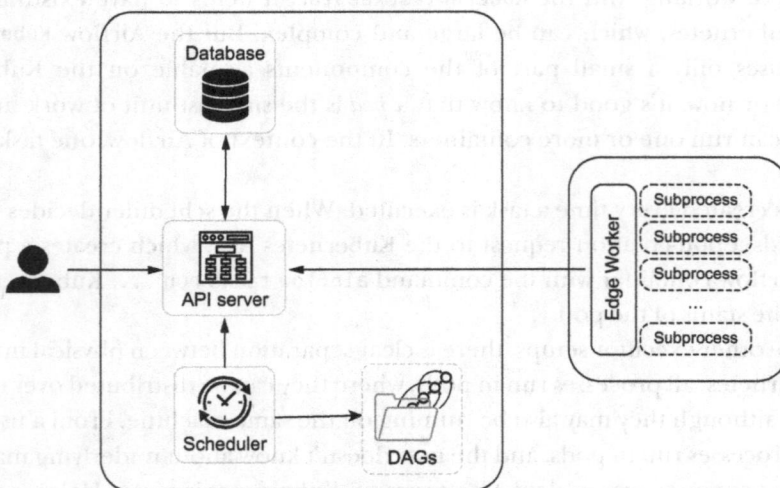

Figure 15.6   With the `EdgeExecutor`, the worker runs in a separate environment, outside the environment in which Airflow runs.

To use the EdgeExecutor, first make sure that the edge3 provider is installed:

```
pip install apache-airflow-providers-edge3
```

You should do this across your Airflow environment. Then you can start configuring the executor by setting the following parameters:

- AIRFLOW__CORE__EXECUTOR must include airflow.providers.edge3.executors.EdgeExecutor. This path is a full path, not just the top-level name, for reasons having to do with the current experimental state of the executor.

- AIRFLOW__CORE__INTERNAL_API_SECRET_KEY must be set because the EdgeExecutor and the API server will use this key to authenticate traffic. Currently, this key is still shared (i.e., all EdgeExecutors will use the same key to authenticate, regardless of where they run).

- AIRFLOW__EDGE__API_ENABLED must be set to True. This setting tells the API server that it must expose the Edge Worker endpoint.

- AIRFLOW__EDGE__API_URL must be set to the API server URL, usually http://<api_server_host>:<api_server_port>/edge_worker/v1/rpcapi.

When your Edge Worker has started, you can get some insight into its status using the Airflow CLI:

```
airflow edge list-workers
```

You can also put the Edge Worker in maintenance mode from within the environment running the worker or by sending a request to a remote Edge Worker:

- airflow edge maintenance on sets the worker running in the current environment to maintenance mode. To start the worker again, use airflow edge maintenance off.

- airflow edge remote-edge-worker-request-maintenance requests that a remote Edge Worker be put into maintenance mode. To request that the worker exits maintenance mode, run airflow edge remote-edge-worker-exit-maintenance.

These commands allow you to perform maintenance on the worker, such as installing specific packages in the environment or upgrading existing ones. In maintenance mode, the scheduler won't schedule any tasks to run on this specific worker. Airflow 2 offered a visual representation of the Edge Workers in the Airflow UI. This representation will be ported to Airflow 3 in the future but currently isn't available.

To use the Edge Worker alongside another worker, specify the full path of the Edge-Executor provider. The following listing shows the code (dags/05_hello_world_on_edge.py).

Listing 15.2 Using the EdgeExecutor

```
hello = BashOperator(
        task_id="hello",
```

```
        bash_command="echo 'hello'",
        executor='airflow.providers.edge3
                    .executors.EdgeExecutor'
)
world = PythonOperator(
        task_id="world",
        python_callable=lambda: print("airflow")
)
```

In this Airflow instance, the executor is configured to be `CeleryExecutor`, `airflow`
`.providers.edge3.executors.EdgeExecutor`. If no executor is explicitly provided, the
first one in the list is used. In this case, task `'hello'` runs on the `EdgeExecutor`, and task
`'world'` runs on the `CeleryExecutor`.

15.3   *Configuring the metastore*

Everything that happens in Airflow is registered in a database, referred to as the
metastore. When a DAG is parsed, for example, the metastore stores a serialized version
of it. Airflow performs all database operations with the help of SQLAlchemy, a Python
object-relational mapper (ORM) framework. This framework makes it convenient
to write Python objects directly to a database without manually writing SQL queries.
Because Airflow uses SQLAlchemy internally, only databases supported by SQLAlchemy
are supported by Airflow. Of the supported databases, Airflow recommends using
PostgreSQL or MySQL.

Without any configuration, running `airflow db migrate` creates a SQLite database
in `$AIRFLOW_HOME/airflow.db`. If you want to set up a production system and go with
MySQL or PostgreSQL, first create the database separately; then point Airflow to the
database by setting `AIRFLOW__CORE__SQL_ALCHEMY_CONN`.

You should provide the value of this configuration item in URI format (`protocol: //`
`[username:password@]host[:port]/path`). See the following examples:

- *MySQL*—`mysql://username:password@localhost:3306/airflow`
- *PostgreSQL*—`postgres://username:password@localhost:5432/airflow`

The Airflow CLI provides several commands for interacting with the database. A few of
the most important ones are

- `airflow db migrate`—Creates the Airflow database schema if it doesn't exist or
  migrates the existing schema to the latest version.
- `airflow db reset`—Wipes any existing database and creates a new, empty database. (This operation is destructive.)
- `airflow db check`—Checks whether the database is reachable. This command is
  useful for debugging database issues.
- `airflow db clean`—Deletes any old records from metastore tables. This command
  requires passing a timestamp indicating what records should be cleaned.

- airflow db downgrade—Downgrades the schema to an older version. You have to specify the revision or version to downgrade to.
- airflow db shell—Opens a direct shell connection to the database so you can look at the raw data. Be careful: editing the data in the metastore can lead to unexpected results.

To upgrade an existing metastore or initialize one, run the airflow db migrate command, which provides the output in listing 15.3. The output of this command contains logs from Alembic, a Python-based database framework that Airflow uses for scripting database migrations. If you upgrade to a newer Airflow version that contains database migrations (whether or not a new version containing database upgrades is listed in the release notes), you must also upgrade the corresponding database. Running airflow db migrate checks the migration step where your current database lives and applies the migration steps that were added in the new release. At this stage, you have a fully functional Airflow database and can run airflow webserver and airflow scheduler.

Listing 15.3   Initializing the Airflow metastore

```
$ airflow db migrate
DB: sqlite:////root/airflow/airflow.db
Performing upgrade to the metadata database sqlite:////root/airflow/airflow.db
[2025-07-11T17:12:23.701+0000] {migration.py:211} INFO - Context impl
  SQLiteImpl.
[2025-07-11T17:12:23.701+0000] {migration.py:214} INFO - Will assume non-
  transactional DDL.
[2025-07-11T17:12:23.702+0000] {migration.py:211} INFO - Context impl
  SQLiteImpl.
[2025-07-11T17:12:23.702+0000] {migration.py:214} INFO - Will assume non-
  transactional DDL.
[2025-07-11T17:12:23.702+0000] {db.py:729} INFO - Creating Airflow database
  tables from the ORM
[2025-07-11T17:12:23.777+0000] {migration.py:211} INFO - Context impl
  SQLiteImpl.
[2025-07-11T17:12:23.777+0000] {migration.py:214} INFO - Will assume non-
  transactional DDL.
[2025-07-11T17:12:23.783+0000] {migration.py:622} INFO - Running
  stamp_revision  -> 29ce7909c52b
[2025-07-11T17:12:23.784+0000] {db.py:740} INFO - Airflow database tables
  created
Database migrating done!
```

When you open the web page on http://localhost:8080, you'll see many example DAGs and connections (figure 15.7). These examples may come in handy during development but are likely not desirable for a production system. You can exclude example DAGs by setting AIRFLOW__ CORE__LOAD_EXAMPLES=False. Upon restarting the scheduler and web server, however, you'll probably be surprised to still see the DAGs and connections. The reason is that setting load_examples to False tells Airflow not to load example DAGs (doesn't apply to connections!), and Airflow won't reload them.

But DAGs that are already loaded remain in the database and are not deleted. The same behavior applies to default connections, which you can exclude by setting AIR-FLOW__CORE__LOAD_DEFAULT_CONNECTIONS=False. To plot this behavior to Airflow components, the DAGs and connections have already been serialized and stored in the metastore, but now they're disabled with these settings; they won't be parsed and processed again. As a result, any changes in the files themselves won't be visible in Airflow.

Figure 15.7   By default, Airflow loads example DAGs (and connections, not displayed here).

You can achieve a clean (no-examples) database by completing the following steps:

1 Install Airflow.
2 Set AIRFLOW__CORE__LOAD_EXAMPLES=False.
3 Set AIRFLOW__CORE__LOAD_DEFAULT_CONNECTIONS=False.
4 Run airflow db migrate.

NOTE If you forget to disable the examples and want to do so later, you must ensure that the example DAGs and connections are also removed from the metastore.

15.4 *Configuring the scheduler*

To understand how and when tasks are executed, let's take a closer look at the scheduler. The scheduler has two main responsibilities:

- Determining which tasks are ready to execute and placing them in the queued state, also known as the task *scheduler*
- Fetching and executing tasks in the queued state, also known as the *task executor*

In versions before Airflow 3, the scheduler could also parse and serialize DAGs from files. Airflow 3 made it mandatory to run this parsing and serialization process as a separate component. For more details on this component (the DAG processor), see section 15.5.

15.4.1 *Configuring scheduler components*

To configure the scheduler as a whole, it's best to look at the two main parts of the scheduler: the task scheduler and the task executor. In this section, we examine both.

THE TASK SCHEDULER

First, the scheduler is responsible for determining which task instances can be executed. A while True loop checks for each task instance periodically if a set of conditions is met, such as whether all upstream dependencies are satisfied, the end of an interval is reached, the task instance in the previous DAG ran successfully if depends_on_past=True, and so on. Whenever a task instance meets all conditions, it's set to a scheduled state, which means that the scheduler decided that it meets all conditions and is OK to execute.

Another loop in the scheduler determines another set of conditions in which tasks go from scheduled to queued state. Here, conditions include whether there are enough open slots and certain tasks have priority over others (given the priority_weight argument). When all these conditions have been met, the scheduler pushes a command to a queue to run the task and set the state of the task instance to queued.

When the task instance has been placed in a queue, it's no longer the scheduler's responsibility. At that point, tasks are the responsibility of the executor that will read the task instance from the queue and start the task on a worker.

The type of queue and how a task instance is processed when it's been placed in a queue is contained in the process named executor. You can configure the executor part of the scheduler in various ways, from a single process on a single machine to multiple processes distributed over multiple machines, as explained in section 15.1.

THE TASK EXECUTOR

In general, the task-executor process waits for the task-scheduler process to place task instances to be executed in a queue. When those task instances are placed in the queue, the executor fetches the task instances from the queue and executes them.

Airflow registers each state change in the metastore. The message placed in the queue contains several details on the task instance. In the executor, *executing* tasks means creating a new process for the task to run in so it doesn't bring Airflow down if something fails. In the new process, it executes the CLI command `airflow tasks run` to run a single task instance, as in the following example (using the `LocalExecutor`).

```
airflow tasks run [dag_id] [task_id] [execution date]

For example:
airflow tasks run chapter15_task_sla
sleeptask scheduled__2025-01-21T00:00:00+00:00
```

Right before executing the command, Airflow registers the state of the task instance as running in the metastore. Then it executes the task and checks in periodically by sending a heartbeat to the metastore. The heartbeat is yet another `while True` loop in which Airflow checks whether the task has finished:

- If the task has finished and the exit code is 0, the task is successful.
- If the task has finished and the exit code doesn't equal 0, the task fails.

If the task hasn't finished, Airflow does the following:

- Registers the heartbeat and waits X seconds, configured with `AIRFLOW__ SCHEDULER__JOB_HEARTBEAT_SEC` (default: 5).
- Repeats all the preceding steps (goes back to step 1 and starts over).

For a successful task, this process repeats a certain number of times until the task is complete. If no error occurred, the state of the task is changed to success. Figure 15.8 depicts the ideal flow of a task.

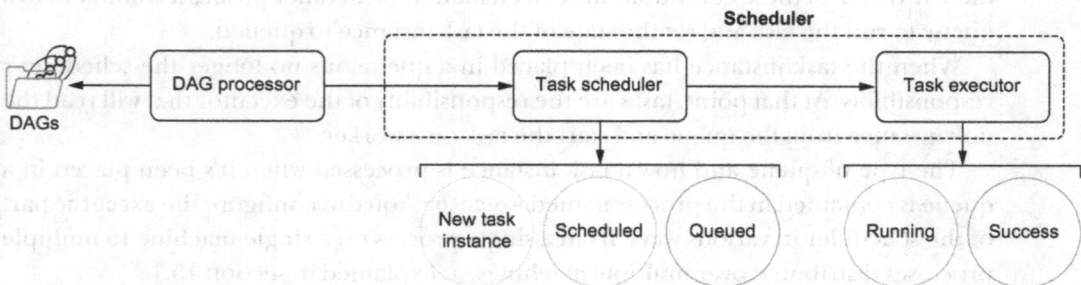

Figure 15.8   The ideal flow of a task and the task state for which the components of the scheduler are responsible. The dotted line represents the full scheduler responsibility.

When you're running in `LocalExecutor` mode, this process is a single process. The `CeleryExecutor` and the `KubernetesExecutor` run the task executor in separate processes designed to scale over multiple machines. The triggerer component is excluded, as mentioned earlier. Also, if something goes wrong (during task execution, scheduling, and so on), your task may end up in another state. This figure shows the ideal flow.

15.4.2 Running multiple schedulers

Because the scheduler is the heart and brains of Airflow, being able to run multiple instances of the scheduler can be useful for scalability and redundancy purposes. Distributed systems are complex, and most systems require the addition of a consensus algorithm to determine which process is the leader. In Airflow, the aim was to make system operations as simple as possible, so leadership was implemented by row-level locking (SELECT ... FOR UPDATE) on the database level. As a result, multiple schedulers can run independently without requiring additional tools for consensus. The only implication is that the database must support certain locking concepts. At the time of writing, the following databases and versions have been tested and supported:

- PostgreSQL 9.6+
- MySQL 8+

Airflow allows you to disable row-level locking. If you do this, however, you can't run multiple schedulers because of the risk that multiple schedulers would interact with the same rows in the database. To scale the scheduler, start another scheduler process:

```
airflow scheduler
```

Each scheduler instance figures out which tasks, represented by rows in the database, are available for processing (on a first-come, first-served basis) and whether additional configuration is required. When you're running multiple instances, if one of the machines on which one of the schedulers is running fails, it will no longer take down your Airflow, because the other scheduler instances will remain running.

15.4.3 Configuring system performance

When you're running a considerable number of tasks, you may notice a rising load on the metastore. Airflow relies heavily on the metastore to store all state. Every new Airflow version generally includes several performance-related improvements, so it helps to update regularly.

You can also tune the number of queries performed on the metastore. Raising the value of AIRFLOW__SCHEDULER__SCHEDULER_HEARTBEAT_SEC (default: 5) can lower the number of check-ins Airflow performs on the scheduler job, resulting in fewer database queries. A setting of 60 (seconds) is a reasonable value. By default, the Airflow UI displays a warning 30 seconds after the last scheduler heartbeat was received, but you can configure this setting with AIRFLOW__SCHEDULER__SCHEDULER_HEALTH_CHECK_THRESHOLD.

If you're running multiple schedulers and have complicated DAGs (with more than 10,000 tasks per DAG, for example), it can be good to experiment with

AIRFLOW__SCHEDULER__MAX_DAGRUNS_TO_CREATE_PER_LOOP. This setting allows you to configure how many DAGs a scheduler can create DAG runs for in each scheduler loop. By lowering this number, you can avoid skew among multiple schedulers. You may not want one scheduler to parse all the huge DAGs while the other sits idle, for example. Similarly, you can limit the number of DAG runs to examine during each loop with AIRFLOW__SCHEDULER__MAX_DAGRUNS_PER_LOOP_TO_SCHEDULE.

Finally, tweaking the value of AIRFLOW__SCHEDULER__IDLE_SLEEP_TIME can be useful. This configures the time to wait after a scheduler loop if there is nothing to do in the loop (i.e., no DAG runs or tasks require scheduling). If there is work, the next scheduler loop is scheduled immediately.

15.4.4 Controlling the maximum number of running tasks

Table 15.2 lists the Airflow configurations that control the number of tasks you can run in parallel. The configuration items are somewhat oddly named, so read their descriptions carefully.

Table 15.2   Overview of Airflow configurations related to running number of tasks

Configuration item	Default value	Description
AIRFLOW__CORE__ MAX_ACTIVE_TASKS_PER_DAG	16	The maximum number of tasks to be in the queued or running state per DAG
AIRFLOW__CORE__ MAX_ACTIVE_RUNS_PER_DAG	16	The maximum number of parallel DAG runs per DAG
AIRFLOW__CORE__ PARALLELISM	32	The maximum number of task instances to run in parallel globally
AIRFLOW__CELERY__ WORKER_CONCURRENCY	16	The maximum number of tasks per Celery worker

If you're running a DAG with a large number of tasks, your DAG is limited to 16 parallel tasks because max_active_tasks_per_dag is set to 16, even though parallelism is set to 32. A second DAG with a large number of tasks is also limited to 16 parallel tasks, but together, the DAGs will reach the global limit, 32, set by parallelism.

The global number of parallel tasks has one more limiting factor: by default, all tasks run in a pool named default_pool, with 128 slots. You have to increase max_active_tasks_per_dag and parallelism before reaching the default_ pool limit, though.

Specifically for the CeleryExecutor, the setting AIRFLOW__CELERY__WORKER_CONCURRENCY controls the number of processes per worker that Celery can handle. In our experience, Airflow can be quite resource consuming. Therefore, you should account for at least 200 MB of RAM per process as a baseline for getting a worker with the configured concurrency number up and running. Also estimate a worst-case scenario in which your most resource-consuming tasks are running in parallel to estimate how many parallel tasks your Celery worker can handle. For specific DAGs, you can override the default value `max_active_runs_per_dag` with the `concurrency` argument on the DAG class.

On an individual task level, you can set the `pool` argument to run a specific task in a pool, which limits the number of tasks it can run. Pools can be applied to specific groups of tasks. Although it may be fine for your Airflow system to run 20 tasks that query a database and wait for the result to return, for example, it may be troublesome when 5 CPU-intensive tasks have started. To limit such high-resource tasks, you could assign them to a dedicated `high_resource` pool with a low maximum number of tasks.

15.5 Configuring the DAG processor manager

The DAG processor manager's responsibility is to process Python files periodically in the dags directory (the directory set by `AIRFLOW__CORE__DAGS_FOLDER`). This means that even if no change was made to a DAG file, it evaluates each DAG file periodically and persists the found DAGs in the Airflow metastore because you can create dynamic DAGs (which change structure based on an external source in Airflow) while the code stays the same. An example is a DAG in which a YAML file is read, and tasks are generated based on its content. To pick up changes in dynamic DAGs, the scheduler reprocesses DAG files periodically.

> **NOTE** There are ongoing discussions in the Airflow community to make DAG parsing event based by listening for file changes in DAG files and explicitly configuring DAGs for reprocessing if necessary, which could reduce CPU use. This potential feature (event-based parsing) doesn't exist at the time of writing, however.

Processing DAGs takes processing power. The more you reprocess your DAG files, the faster changes will be picked up, but at the cost of requiring more CPU power. If you know that your DAGs don't change frequently, it's safe to raise default intervals to relieve the CPU. But if you use complex code to generate DAGs or do other work, it can affect the DAG processor manager's performance. The interval of DAG processing is related to the four configurations shown in table 15.3.

Table 15.3 Airflow configuration options related to DAG processing

Configuration item	Description
`AIRFLOW__DAG_PROCESSOR__MIN_FILE_PROCESS_INTERVAL`	The minimum interval for files to be processed (default: 0). There's no guarantee that files will be processed at this interval; it's a lower boundary, not the actual interval.
`AIRFLOW__DAG_PROCESSOR__REFRESH_INTERVAL`	The minimum time to refresh the list of files in the dags folder (default: 300). Already-listed files are kept in memory and processed at a different interval. This setting is a lower boundary, not the actual interval.

Table 15.3   Airflow configuration options related to DAG processing (*continued*)

Configuration item	Description
`AIRFLOW__DAG_PROCESSOR__` `PARSING_PROCESSES`	The maximum number of processes (not threads) to use for parsing all DAG files. This setting is an upper boundary, not the actual number of processes.

The optimal configuration for your system depends on the number of DAGs, the sizes of your DAGs (i.e., how long it takes for the DAG processor to evaluate them), and the available resources on the machine on which the scheduler is running. All intervals define a boundary for how often to perform a process. At times, the interval value is compared, but it's possible, for example, that the REFRESH_INTERVAL is checked after 305 seconds while the value is set to 300 seconds.

It's particularly useful to lower `AIRFLOW__DAG_PROCESSOR__REFRESH_INTERVAL`. If you often add new DAGs and wait for them to appear, you can address the issue by lowering this value.

WARNING   Take care when changing this number. Setting a very low value may give you the best experience in terms of getting DAG changes reflected quickly, but it can also lead to a significant increase in CPU use because the DAGs are being parsed constantly.

All DAG processing happens within a `while True` loop, in which Airflow loops over a series of steps for processing DAG files over and over. In the log files, you see the output of DAG processing in `/logs/dag_processor_manager/dag_processor_manager.log`.

Listing 15.5   Example output of DAG processor manager

```
===========================================================================
[2025-01-24T10:02:53.933+0000] {manager.py:821} INFO - Searching for files
  in /opt/airflow/dags
[2025-01-24T10:02:53.946+0000] {manager.py:824} INFO - There are 5 files in
  /opt/airflow/dags
[2025-01-24T10:02:55.984+0000] {manager.py:997} INFO -
  ================================================================
DAG File Processing Stats

File Path     PID  Runtime   # DAGs   # Errors  Last Runtime   Last Run
---------     ---  -------   ------   --------  ------------   --------
.../dag1.py   159  0.01s     1        0         0.06s          ... 10:02:25
.../dag2.py   160  0.00s     1        0         0.06s          ... 10:02:25
.../dag3.py        0.04s     1        0         0.04s          ... 10:02:25
.../dag4.py                  1        0         0.04s          ... 10:02:25
.../dag5.py                  1        0         0.04s          ... 10:02:25
```

These file processing stats aren't printed with every iteration; they're printed every *X* number of seconds, depending on how `AIRFLOW__DAG_PROCESSOR__PRINT_STATS_INTERVAL` is set (default: 30). Also, the displayed statistics represent the information from the last run, not the results of the last number of PRINT_STATS_INTERVAL seconds.

The value of AIRFLOW__DAG_PROCESSOR__PARSING_PROCESSES (default: 2; fixed to 1 if you're using SQLite) controls how many processes are run simultaneously to process a DAG's state. The higher this number is, the more DAGs will be checked simultaneously and the lower latency will exist between tasks. Raising this value comes at the cost of more CPU use, so increase and measure changes gently.

15.6 *Capturing logs*

All systems produce some sort of output, and at times, we want to know what's going on. Airflow has three types of logs:

- *API server web logs*—Hold information on web activity (i.e., which requests are sent to the web server)
- *Scheduler logs*—Hold information on all scheduler activity, such as scheduling tasks
- *Task logs*—Hold the logs of one single task instance in each log file

By default, logs are written in $AIRFLOW_HOME/logs on the local filesystem. You can configure logging in various ways. In this section, we demonstrate the default logging behavior and show how to write logs to a remote storage system.

15.6.1 *Capturing API server output*

The API server serves API endpoints that the Airflow UI uses. See the following example:

- INFO: 127.0.0.1:51342 - "GET /api/v2/version HTTP/1.1" 200 OK
- INFO: 172.18.0.13:47952 - "POST /edge_worker/v1/worker/e04919c38678 HTTP/1.1" 200 OK

When you're starting the web server on the command line, you see this output printed to stdout or stderr. What if you want to preserve logs after the API server shuts down? The API server has two types of logs: access logs, as shown here, and error logs to which errors are sent. If they're not configured otherwise, both logs are printed on stdout or stderr. Airflow's API server uses Gunicorn to serve its API and follows the same configuration logic. You can write both types of logs to a file by providing a flag when starting the Airflow web server:

```
airflow api-server --log_config [filename]
```

The file at the provided path (filename, in this case) should contain log config for Gunicorn with the following options set:

- accesslog—The path to write the access logs to
- errorlog—The path to write the error logs to

NOTE You can find full logging configuration for Gunicorn at https://docs
.gunicorn.org/en/stable/settings.html.

15.6.2 *Capturing scheduler output*

Unlike the web server, the scheduler writes logs to files by default. Looking at the
$AIRFLOW_HOME/logs directory again, we see various files related to scheduler logs. This
directory tree is the result of processing two DAGs: hello_world and second_dag.

Listing 15.6   Log files generated by the scheduler

```
├── dag_processor_manager
│   └── dag_processor_manager.log
└── scheduler
    └── 2025-01-24
        ├── hello_world.py.log
        └── second_dag.py.log
```

Every time the scheduler processes a DAG file to check whether anything needs to be
scheduled, several lines are written to the respective scheduler log file. These lines
are key to understanding how the scheduler operates. Next, let's look at hello_world
.py.log.

Listing 15.7   Scheduler reading DAG files and creating corresponding DAGs/tasks

Checks whether the DAG runs and corresponding task
instances can be created given their schedule and
whether any service-level agreements (SLAs) were missed

```
… Started process (PID=2600) to work on
➥ /opt/airflow/dags/hello_world.py
Processing file /opt/airflow/dags/hello_world.py
➥ for tasks to queue
Filling up the DagBag from /opt/airflow/dags/hello_world.py
'hello_world' retrieved from /opt/airflow/dags/hello_world.py
Sync 1 DAGs
Setting next_dagrun for hello_world to 2025-01-21 00:00:00+00:00,
➥ run_after=2025-01-22 00:00:00+00:00 #C Set next DAGRun
Processing /opt/airflow/dags/hello_world.py took 0.041 seconds

Started process (PID=46) to work on
➥ /opt/airflow/dags/hello_world.py
Processing file /opt/airflow/dags/hello_world.py
➥ for tasks to queue
Filling up the DagBag from /opt/airflow/dags/hello_world.py
DAG(s) dict_keys(['hello_world']) retrieved from
➥ /opt/airflow/dags/hello_world.py
Processing hello_world
Created <DagRun hello_world @ 2020-04-11 00:00:00 ...
```

Starts
processing
this file

The DAG
hello_world
was retrieved
from the file.

Creates DagRun because
the end of the interval
has been reached

Checks whether any existing task
instances should be set to running

```
Examining DAG run <DagRun hello_world @ 2020-04-11 00:00:00 ...>
Creating / updating <TaskInstance: hello_world.hello 2020-04-11 in ORM
Creating / updating <TaskInstance: hello_world.world 2020-04-11 in ORM
Processing /opt/airflow/dags/hello_world.py took 0.327 seconds
```

Processing of this file is complete.

Checks for tasks to create
and set to scheduled state

These steps of processing a DAG file, loading the DAG object from the file, and checking whether many conditions are met, such as DAG schedules, are executed many times and are part of the core functionality of the scheduler. From these logs, we can derive whether the scheduler is working as intended. The file dag_processor_manager .log contains an aggregated view of the files the DAG processor manager has parsed. By default, this happens every 30 seconds. Log rotation of this file is performed automatically when the file size reaches 100 MB.

15.6.3 Capturing task logs

Last, we have task logs, in which each file represents one attempt of one task. The contents of these files reflect what we see when we open a task in the web server UI, as shown in the following listing.

Listing 15.8 Log files generated upon task execution

```
.
├── dag_id=hello_world                              ◄── DAG name
│   ├── task_id=hello                               ◄── Task name
│   │   └── scheduled__2025-01-21T16:00:00+00:00    ◄──
│   │       ├── attempt=1.log                       ◄── DAG run
│   │       └── attempt=2.log                          Attempt number
│   ├── task_id=world
│   │   └── scheduled__2025-01-121T16:00:00+00:00
│   │       ├── attempt=1.log
│   │       └── attempt=2.log
├── dag_id=second_dag
│   └── task_id=print_context
│       ├── scheduled__2025-01-25T00:00:00+00:00
│       │   └── attempt=1.log
│       └── scheduled__2025-01-25T00:00:00+00:00
│           └── attempt=1.log
```

15.6.4 Sending logs to remote storage

Depending on your Airflow setup, you may want to send logs elsewhere, such as when you're running Airflow in ephemeral containers in which logs are gone when the container stops or for archival purposes. Airflow has a remote-logging feature that allows you to ship logs to a remote system. At the time of writing, that feature supports the following remote systems:

- Alibaba OSS (requires `pip install 'apache-airflow[alibaba]'`)
- AWS S3 (requires `pip install apache-airflow[amazon]`)
- Azure Blob Storage (requires `pip install apache-airflow[microsoft.azure]`)
- Elasticsearch (requires `pip install apache-airflow[elasticsearch]`)
- Google Cloud Storage (requires `pip install apache-airflow[google]`)
- OpenSearch (requires `pip install apache-airflow[opensearch]`)
- Redis (requires `pip install apache-airflow[redis]`)

To configure Airflow for remote logging, set the following configurations:

- `AIRFLOW__LOGGING__REMOTE_LOGGING=True`
- `AIRFLOW__LOGGING__REMOTE_LOG_CONN_ID=...`

The `REMOTE_LOG_CONN_ID` points to the ID of the connection holding the credentials to your remote system. Then each remote logging system can read configuration specific to that system. You can configure the path to which logs should be written in Google Cloud Storage, for example, as `AIRFLOW__LOGGING__REMOTE_BASE_LOG_FOLDER=gs://my-bucket/path/to/logs`. See the Airflow documentation for details on each system.

15.7 Visualizing and monitoring Airflow metrics

When you're running Airflow in production, it's important to keep track of the performance of your Airflow setup. In this section, we focus on numerical data on the status of the system, called *metrics*, such as the number of seconds' delay between queueing a task and executing the task. In monitoring literature, observability and full understanding of a system are achieved with a combination of three items: logs, metrics, and traces. Logs (textual data) are covered in section 15.6; this section covers metrics. Tracing is beyond the scope of this book because it's considerably more complex and domain dependent, requiring additional setup for environment specifics.

Each Airflow setup has its own characteristics. Some installations are big; others are small. Some have few DAGs and many tasks; others have many DAGs with only a few tasks. It's impractical to cover every possible situation in a book, so we'll demonstrate the main ideas for monitoring Airflow, which should apply to any installation. The goal is to show you how to start collecting metrics about your setup and actively use the metrics to your advantage, such as in a dashboard (figure 15.9).

15.7.1 Collecting metrics from Airflow

To capture metrics, you can configure Airflow to use StatsD (https://github.com/statsd/statsd) or OpenTelemetry (https://opentelemetry.io). Both tools provide the same metrics via different systems. In this chapter, we focus on StatsD, but the

Figure 15.9   An example visualization of the number of running tasks. Here, `parallelism` had the default value 32, to which the number of tasks sometimes spikes.

OpenTelemetry setup is more or less the same. (See the Airflow docs at https://mng .bz/0zqm.) Broadly speaking, the two tools are interchangeable in the context of Airflow monitoring.

It's common to say that you *instrument* a system (Airflow, in this case). What does it mean to be instrumented? In the context of StatsD and Airflow, being *instrumented* means that certain events in Airflow result in sending information about the event so that it can be collected, aggregated, and visualized or reported. Whenever a task fails, for example, an event named `ti_failures` is sent with a value of 1, meaning that one task failure occurred.

PUSHING VS. PULLING

When developers compare metrics systems, a common discussion is about pushing versus pulling—the *push-versus-pull model*. With the push model, metrics are pushed (sent) to a metrics-collection system. With the pull model, metrics are exposed by the system to monitor a certain endpoint, and a metrics-collection system must pull (fetch) metrics from the system to monitor from the given endpoint. Pushing may cause the metrics-collection system to overflow when many systems start pushing many metrics simultaneously.

StatsD works with the push model. When you start monitoring in Airflow, you must set up a collection system to which StatsD can push its metrics.

WHICH METRICS-COLLECTION SYSTEM?

StatsD is one of many metrics-collection systems; others include Prometheus and Graphite. A StatsD client is installed with Airflow, but you have to set up the server that will collect the metrics. The StatsD client communicates metrics to the server in a certain format; many metrics-collection systems can interchange components by reading one another's formats.

You can use Prometheus's server, for example, to store metrics from Airflow, but the metrics are sent in StatsD format, so you must provide a translation so Prometheus will understand the metrics. Also, Prometheus applies the pull model, whereas StatsD applies the push model, so you must install some intermediary system to which StatsD can push and from which Prometheus can pull. Airflow doesn't expose Prometheus's metrics format, so Prometheus can't pull metrics directly from Airflow.

The mixing and matching occurs mainly because Prometheus is the tool of choice for metrics collection among developers and sysadmins at many companies. It prevails over StatsD in many ways, such as data-model flexibility, ease of operation, and capability to integrate with virtually any other system. Therefore, we also prefer Prometheus for dealing with metrics. In the following sections, we demonstrate how to transform StatsD metrics into Prometheus metrics and then visualize the collected metrics with Grafana. Grafana is a dashboarding tool for visualizing time-series data for monitoring purposes. Let's set up this system from left (Airflow) to right (Grafana) to create a dashboard for visualizing metrics from Airflow. Figure 15.10 illustrates the steps.

NOTE   In the example setup we'll work on in the next few sections, we assume that Airflow is running on your local machine, which leads us to use `localhost` throughout in all host fields. If you're running in any other type of environment, such as Docker or Kubernetes, the value for this field will likely have to be different.

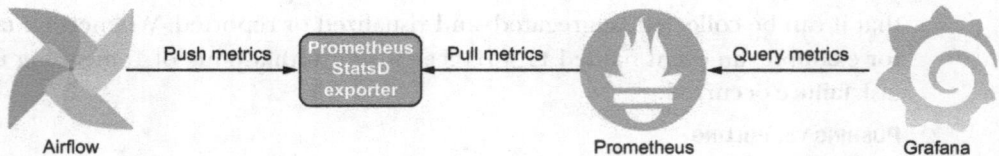

Figure 15.10   Software and steps required for collecting and visualizing metrics from Airflow. Prometheus collects metrics, and Grafana visualizes metrics in dashboards. The Prometheus StatsD exporter translates StatsD metrics to Prometheus's metrics format and exposes them for Prometheus to scrape.

15.7.2   *Configuring Airflow to send metrics*

To have Airflow push its StatsD metrics, we must install Airflow with the `statsd` extra dependency:

```
pip install apache-airflow[statsd]
```

Next, we configure the location to which Airflow should push its metrics. Currently, there is no system to collect the metrics, but we'll configure that system in section 15.7.3:

- `AIRFLOW__METRICS__STATSD_ON=True`
- `AIRFLOW__METRICS__STATSD_HOST=localhost` (default value)

- AIRFLOW__METRICS__STATSD_PORT=9125
- AIRFLOW__METRICS__STATSD_PREFIX=airflow (default value)

On the Airflow side, we're done. With this configuration, Airflow pushes events to port 9125 over User Datagram Protocol (UDP).

15.7.3 Configuring Prometheus to collect metrics

Prometheus is software for systems monitoring. It features a wide array of features, but at its core, it's a time-series database, which you can query with a language named PromQL. You can't manually insert data like an INSERT INTO ... query into a relational database, but Prometheus works by pulling metrics into the database. Every *X* seconds, it pulls the latest metrics from targets you configure. If Prometheus gets too busy, it automatically slows scraping the targets. This happens only when there are a large number of metrics to process.

First, you must install the Prometheus StatsD exporter, which translates Airflow's StatsD metrics into Prometheus metrics. The easiest way is to use Docker, as shown in listing 15.9.

NOTE Without Docker, you can download and run the Prometheus StatsD exporter from https://mng.bz/KwK4. Make sure that this port number aligns with the port set by AIRFLOW__SCHEDULER__STATSD_PORT.

Listing 15.9 Running a StatsD exporter with Docker

```
docker run -d -p 9102:9102 -p 9125:9125/udp prom/statsd-exporter
```
Prometheus metrics will be
shown on http://localhost:9102.

To start, run the StatsD exporter without configuration. Go to http://localhost:9102/metrics, and you should see the first Airflow metrics.

Listing 15.10 Sample Prometheus metrics, exposed using the StatsD exporter

Each metric comes with a
default HELP message.

Each metric
has a type,
such as a
gauge.

```
# HELP The number of errors encountered when processing DAGs
# TYPE airflow_dag_errors gauge
airflow_dag_errors 0
# HELP  Metric autogenerated by statsd_exporter.
# TYPE airflow_dag_processing_file_path_queue_size gauge
airflow_dag_processing_file_path_queue_size 0
# HELP  Metric autogenerated by statsd_exporter.
# TYPE airflow_dag_processing_file_path_queue_update_count counter
airflow_dag_processing_file_path_queue_update_count 33990
```

The metric airflow_dag_processing_file_path_queue_
update_count currently has a value of 33990. Prometheus
registers the scrape timestamp together with this value.

Now that we've made the metrics available on `http://localhost:9102`, we can install and configure Prometheus to scrape this endpoint. The easiest way to do this is use Docker to run a Prometheus container. First, we configure the StatsD exporter as a target in Prometheus so that it knows where to get the metrics.

Listing 15.11   Minimal Prometheus configuration

```
scrape_configs:
  - job_name: 'airflow'          ◄────┤ Defines a Prometheus metrics scraping job
    static_configs:
      - targets: ['localhost:9102']    ◄────┤ The target URL of the scraping job
```

Save the content of listing 15.11 in a file, such as `/tmp/prometheus.yml`. Then start Prometheus and mount the file as follows.

Listing 15.12   Running Prometheus with Docker to collect metrics

```
docker run -d -p 9090:9090 -v
  /tmp/prometheus.yml:/etc/prometheus/prometheus.yml prom/prometheus
```

Prometheus is up and running on `http://localhost:9090`. To verify, go to `http://localhost:9090/targets` and ensure that the Airflow target is up (figure 15.11). An up-and-running target means that Prometheus is scraping metrics and you can start visualizing the metrics in Grafana.

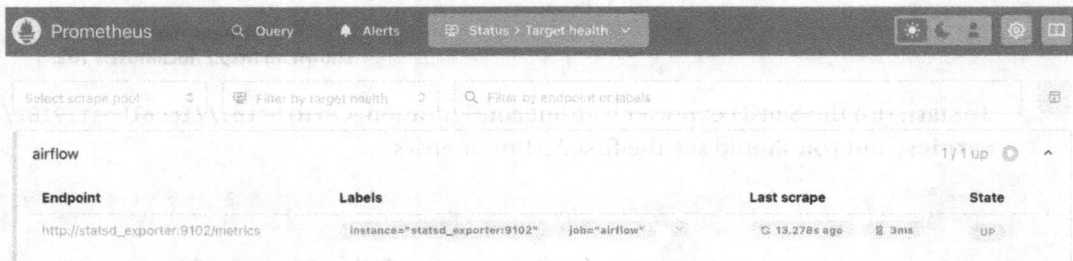

Figure 15.11   If everything is configured correctly, the targets page in Prometheus should display the state of the Airflow target as UP. If the target can't be reached, Airflow is considered unhealthy.

Metrics data models

The data model of Prometheus identifies unique metrics by a name (such as `task_duration`) and a set of key-value labels (such as `dag_id=mydag` and `task_id=first_task`). This allows great flexibility because you can select metrics with any desired combination of labels, such as `task_duration{task_id="first_task"}` for selecting only the `task_duration` of tasks named `"first_task"`. An alternative data model used in many other metrics systems, such as StatsD, is hierarchy based, with labels defined in dot-separated metric names like these:

- `task_duration.my_dag.first_task -> 123`
- `task_duration.my_other_dag.first_task -> 4`

This is problematic when you want to select the metric `task_duration` of all tasks named `first_task`, which is one reason why Prometheus gained popularity. Prometheus's StatsD exporter applies generic rules to the supplied metrics to convert them from StatsD's hierarchical model to Prometheus's label model. Sometimes, the default conversion rules work nicely, but they don't always, and a StatsD metric results in a unique metric name in Prometheus. In the metric `dag.<dag_id>.<task_id>.duration`, for example, `dag_id` and `task_id` aren't converted automatically to labels in Prometheus.

Although it's technically workable in Prometheus, this approach isn't optimal. Therefore, you can configure the StatsD exporter to convert specific dot-separated metrics to Prometheus metrics. For more information, read the StatsD exporter documentation (https://mng.bz/xZoY).

15.7.4 Creating dashboards with Grafana

After you collect metrics with Prometheus, the last piece of the puzzle is visualizing these metrics in a dashboard, which should give you a quick understanding of how the system is functioning. Grafana is the main tool for visualizing metrics. Docker is the easiest way to get Grafana up and running, as shown in the following listing. Figure 15.12 shows the first view of Grafana you'll see at `http://localhost:3000`.

Listing 15.13 Running Grafana with Docker to visualize metrics

```
docker run -d -p 3000:3000 grafana/grafana
```

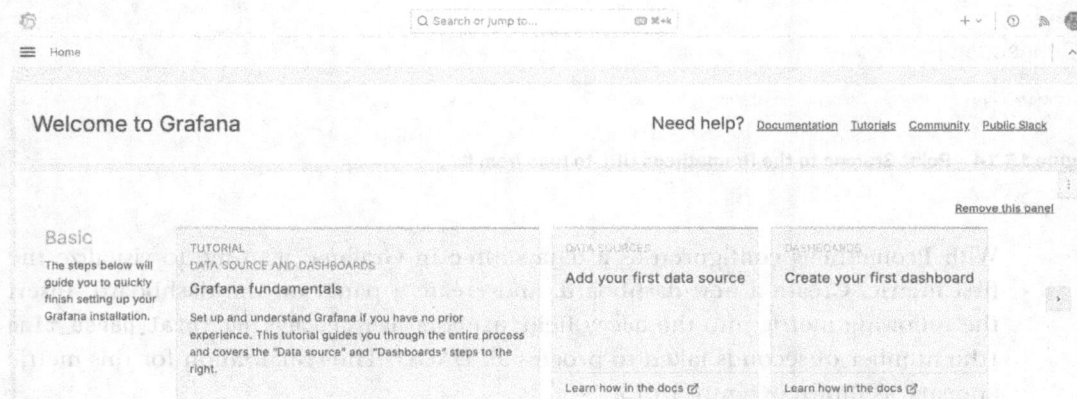

Figure 15.12 Grafana welcome screen

Click Add Your First Data Source to add Prometheus as a data source. You see a list of available data sources. Click Prometheus to configure it (figure 15.13). On the next screen, provide the URL, which will be `http://localhost:9090` (figure 15.14).

Add data source

Choose a data source type

🔍 Filter by name or type	← Cancel

Time series databases

Prometheus
Open source time series database & alerting
`Core`

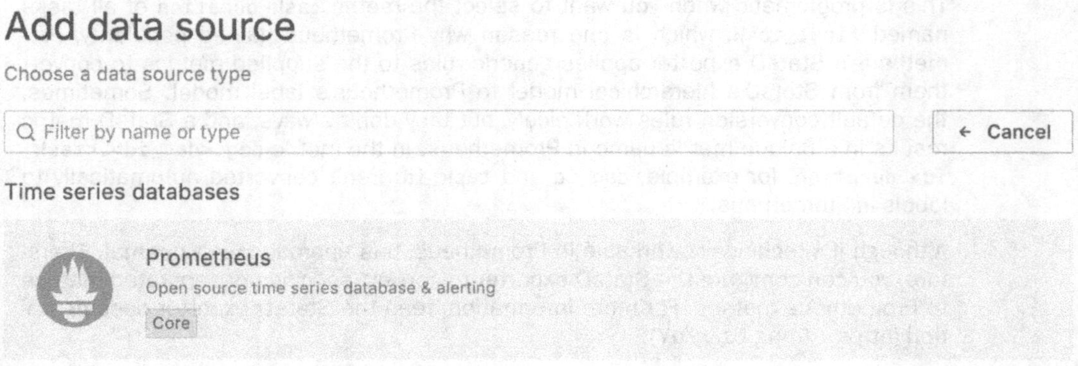

Figure 15.13   On the Add Data Source page, click Prometheus to configure it as a source to read metrics from.

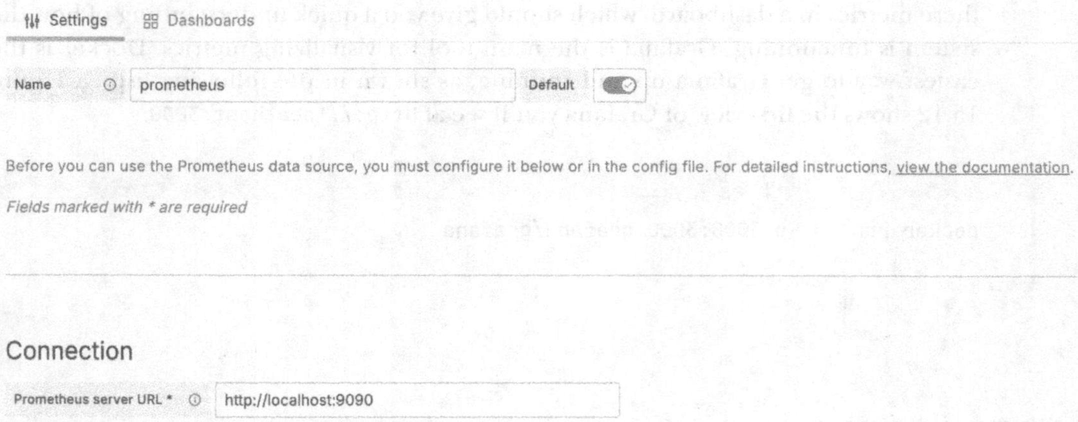

⚙ Settings	🔲 Dashboards

Name	ⓘ	prometheus	Default	🔘

Before you can use the Prometheus data source, you must configure it below or in the config file. For detailed instructions, view the documentation.

*Fields marked with * are required*

Connection

Prometheus server URL * ⓘ   `http://localhost:9090`

Figure 15.14   Point Grafana to the Prometheus URL to read from it.

With Prometheus configured as a data source in Grafana, it's time to visualize the first metric. Create a new dashboard, and create a panel on the dashboard. Insert the following metric into the query field: `airflow_dag_processing_total_parse_time` (the number of seconds taken to process all DAGs). The visualization for this metric appears, as shown in figure 15.15.

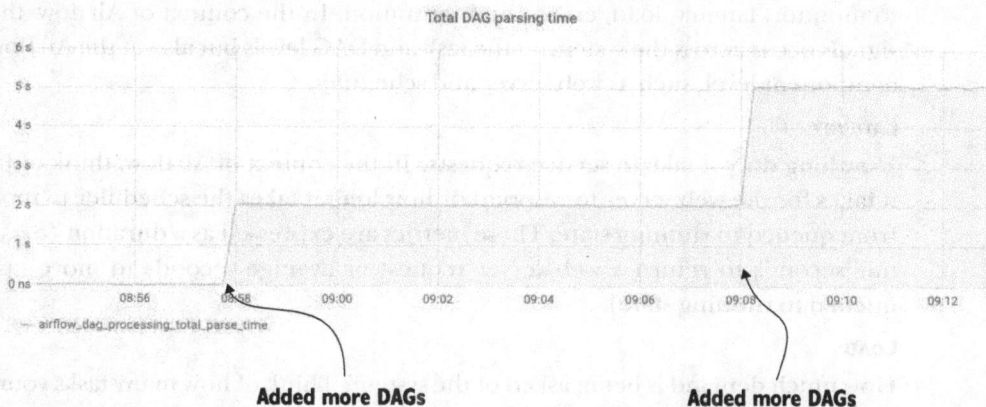

Figure 15.15   Plot of the number of seconds to process all DAG files. We see two change points at which more DAG files were added. A large spike in this graph could indicate a problem with the Airflow scheduler or a DAG file.

With Prometheus and Grafana in place, Airflow pushes metrics to Prometheus's StatsD exporter, and these metrics are eventually plotted in Grafana. Take note of three things in this setup:

- *The metrics in Grafana are close to real time but not millisecond real time.* Prometheus scrapes metrics in intervals (default: 1 minute, which can be lowered), which causes a one-minute delay in the worst case. Also, Grafana periodically queries Prometheus (query refresh is off by default), so in Grafana, we also have a slight delay. All in all, the delay between an event in Airflow and the graph in Grafana is at the minute level at most, which typically is more than good enough.

- *This setup uses Prometheus, which is great for monitoring and alerting metrics but isn't a reporting system and doesn't store individual events.* If you plan to report on individual events in Airflow, you might consider using InfluxDB as a time-series database because it's more geared toward event logging.

- *This setup focuses on monitoring metrics, not alerting.* Grafana offers support for alerting, but many other tools offer this functionality, such as PagerDuty. Along with monitoring metrics in dashboards and graphs, it can be useful to add alerting to warn you when critical values have been reached or exceeded. This approach is a double-edged sword, however: too many alerts can lead to *alert fatigue*, a situation in which people ignore alerts when they're too common. It's important to consider what to monitor and what to alert on. Section 15.7.5 discusses alerting from Airflow itself, such as when DAGs or tasks fail.

15.7.5 What should you monitor?

Now that we have a monitoring setup, what should we monitor to understand the functioning of Airflow? Generally, when monitoring anything, you have four basic signals to monitor: latency, load, errors, and saturation. In the context of Airflow, these four signals occur across the system, at the task and DAG levels but also at the Airflow system component level, such as web server and scheduler.

LATENCY

How long does it take to service requests? In the context of Airflow, think of how long it takes for the web server to respond or how long it takes the scheduler to move a task from queued to running state. These metrics are expressed as a duration (e.g., average milliseconds to return a web server request or average seconds to move tasks from queued to running state).

LOAD

How much demand is being asked of the system? Think of how many tasks your Airflow system must process or how many open pool slots Airflow has available. These metrics are typically expressed as an average per duration (e.g., number of tasks running per minute or open pool slots per second).

ERRORS

Which errors were raised? In the context of Airflow, the errors being raised can vary from the number of zombie tasks (running tasks where the underlying process has disappeared) to the number of non-HTTP 200 responses in the web server or the number of timed-out tasks.

SATURATION

What part of the capacity of your system is used? Measuring the machine metrics that Airflow is running on can be a good indicator of the current CPU load or the number of currently running tasks. To determine how full a system is, you must know its upper boundary, which isn't always trivial to determine.

Prometheus features a wide range of exporters that expose all sorts of metrics about a system. Therefore, start by installing several Prometheus exporters to learn more about all systems involved in running Airflow:

- *The node exporter*—For monitoring the machines on which Airflow is running (CPU, memory, disk I/O, network traffic, and so on)
- *The PostgreSQL/MySQL server exporter*—For monitoring the metastore
- *One of the several (unofficial) Celery exporters*—For monitoring Celery when you're using the `CeleryExecutor`
- *The Black Box exporter*—For polling a given endpoint to check whether a predefined HTTP code is returned
- *The Redis exporter*—For monitoring Redis's performance if you're using it as a queue for Celery
- *If you're using Kubernetes, one of the many Kubernetes exporters*—For monitoring Kubernetes resources (see the Kubernetes monitoring documentation at (https://mng.bz/AGM7).

The Airflow documentation includes an overview of all available metrics (https://mng.bz/Z9na); check it for your Airflow version. Following are some good metrics for understanding the status of Airflow:

- To know the correct functioning of your DAGs, see the following:
  - dag_processing.import_errors—The number of errors encountered while processing DAGs. Anything above 0 isn't good.
  - dag_processing.total_parse_time—Sudden large increases after adding/changing DAGs aren't good.
  - ti_failures—The number of failed task instances.
- To understand Airflow's performance, see the following:
  - dag_processing.last_duration.[filename—Time taken to process a DAG file. High values indicate something bad.
  - dag_processing.last_run.seconds_ago.[filename]—The number of seconds since the scheduler last checked on the file containing DAGs. The higher the value, the worse it is; the scheduler is too busy. Values should be on the order of a few seconds at most.
  - dagrun.[dag_id].first_task_scheduling_delay—The delay between the scheduled and actual execution dates of a DAG run.
  - executor.open_slots—The number of free executor slots.
  - executor.queued_tasks—The number of tasks with queued state.
  - executor.running_tasks—The number of tasks with running state.

15.8 Setting up alerts

When running any business-critical pipeline, we want to be notified of an incident the moment something goes wrong. Think of a failing task or a task that didn't finish within an expected time frame and delayed other processes. This section looks at Airflow options for detecting conditions that warrant alerts and sending the alerts.

Within Airflow, we can configure alerts at several levels. First, within the definition of DAGs and operators, we can configure *callbacks*—functions that call on certain events—as shown in the next listing (dags/02_dag_failure_callback.py).

Listing 15.14   Defining a failure callback function to execute on DAG failure

```
def send_error():
    print("ERROR!")



dag = DAG(
    dag_id="02_dag_failure_callback",
    on_failure_callback=send_error,
    ...
)
```

send_error is executed when a DAG run fails.

The `on_failure_callback` is an argument on the DAG, which is executed whenever a DAG run fails. Think of sending a Slack message to an errors channel, a notification to an incident reporting system such as PagerDuty, or a plain old email. The function to execute is something you have to implement yourself, though. Fortunately, some of the most common alerting systems have providers that make this task easy.

On a task level, you have more options to configure. You likely don't want to configure every task individually, so you can propagate configuration with the DAG's `default_args` down to all tasks, as follows (dags/03_task_failure_callback.py).

Listing 15.15 Defining a failure callback function to execute on task failure

```python
def send_error():
    print("ERROR!")


dag = DAG(
    dag_id="03_task_failure_callback",
    default_args={"on_failure_callback": send_error},
    on_failure_callback=send_error,
    ...
)

failing_task = BashOperator(
    task_id="failing_task",
    bash_command="exit 1",
    dag=dag,
)
```

default_args propagates arguments down to tasks.

Two notifications will be sent here: one for task failure and one for DAG failure.

This task won't return exit code 0; therefore, it fails.

The parent class of all operators (`BaseOperator`) holds an argument `on_failure_callback`; therefore, all operators hold this argument. Setting `on_failure_callback` in the `default_args` sets the configured arguments on all tasks in the DAG, so all tasks will call `send_error` whenever an error occurs. It's also possible to set `on_success_callback` (in case of success) and `on_retry_callback` (in case a task is retried).

Although you could send an email yourself inside the function called by `on_failure_callback`, Airflow provides a convenience argument, `email_on_failure`, that sends an email without requiring you to configure the message. But you must configure Simple Mail transfer Protocol (SMTP) in the Airflow configuration; otherwise, no emails can be sent. The next listing shows an example configuration specific to Gmail.

Listing 15.16 Sample SMTP configuration for sending automated emails

```
AIRFLOW__SMTP__SMTP_HOST=smtp.gmail.com
AIRFLOW__SMTP__SMTP_MAIL_FROM=myname@gmail.com
AIRFLOW__SMTP__SMTP_PORT=587
AIRFLOW__SMTP__SMTP_SSL=False
AIRFLOW__SMTP__SMTP_STARTTLS=True
```

You can't set two configuration values via the Airflow configuration: SMTP_USER and SMTP_PASSWORD. Instead, you should set these values via an Airflow connection. You're free to choose a name for this connection, but if you deviate from the default one (smtp_default), you have to configure it explicitly too. You can't set the other configuration (e.g., SMTP_PORT or SMTP_HOST) via the connection even though the fields are available in the UI. The underlying implementation ignores these fields in the connection; it uses only the configuration variables.

In fact, Airflow is configured to send emails by default, meaning that there is an argument email_on_failure on the BaseOperator that holds a default value of True. Without the proper SMTP configuration, however, Airflow won't email. You must also set a destination email address on the email argument of an operator, as shown in the next listing (dags/04_task_failure_email.py). When you have the correct SMTP configuration and a destination email address, Airflow sends an email notifying you of a failed task (figure 15.16). The task logs also tell you that an email was sent:

```
INFO - Sent an alert email to ['daniel@vdende.com']
```

Listing 15.17 Configuring email address to send alerts to

```
dag = DAG(
    dag_id="05_task_failure_email",
    default_args={"email": "daniel@vdende.com"},
    ...
)
```

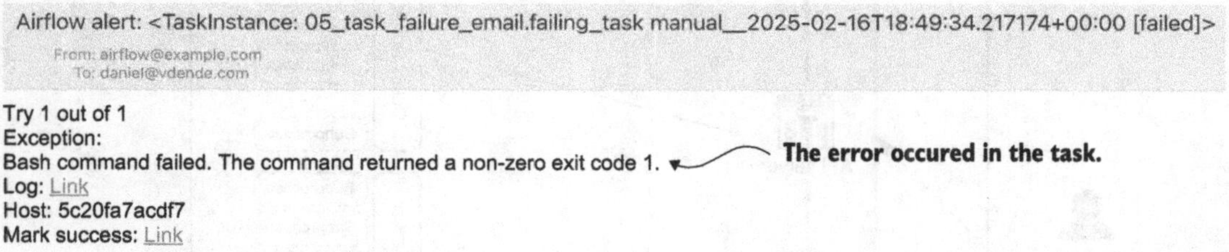

Airflow alert: <TaskInstance: 05_task_failure_email.failing_task manual__2025-02-16T18:49:34.217174+00:00 [failed]>

From: airflow@example.com
To: daniel@vdende.com

Try 1 out of 1
Exception:
Bash command failed. The command returned a non-zero exit code 1. ◄——— **The error occured in the task.**
Log: Link
Host: 5c20fa7acdf7
Mark success: Link

Figure 15.16 Example email alert notification

15.9 Scaling Airflow beyond a single instance

In the preceding sections, we discussed many parameters and configuration settings you can use to ensure that your Airflow environment continues running smoothly. When you reach a certain size (in terms of number of DAGs, complexity of DAGS, or size of the organization), however, it may be worthwhile to consider scaling up to multiple Airflow instances. In this section, we'll briefly explore the options and the considerations.

In the situation we're exploring here, the context in which Airflow is being used is so large that multiple teams are involved. Each team has its own set of DAGs and its own use cases for Airflow. In such a situation, it's good to consider options for scaling the use of Airflow. The two extremes can be succinctly described as follows:

- A single Airflow instance in which multiple teams build, run, and operate their DAGs
- A separate Airflow instance for each team to build, run, and operate its own DAGs

We'll briefly explore the consequences of both options. In the case of a single Airflow instance for multiple teams, all resources are shared by all teams using the Airflow instance (figure 15.17). This option can be cost efficient, especially if the teams' scheduling logic doesn't overlap much or at all; essentially, it maximizes resource use and, therefore, cost. But this option can be challenging if resource consumption overlaps considerably. It also raises challenges related to DAG ownership and permissions. Airflow offers some role-based access controls (RBACs) on who can see certain DAGs, but it's possible to overwrite DAGs without having proper checks in place. Finally, a setup like this makes Airflow the single point of failure for multiple teams. If a problem occurs with an Airflow component, multiple teams will be affected. Also, upgrades to Airflow itself can be cumbersome because alignment has to occur across all teams.

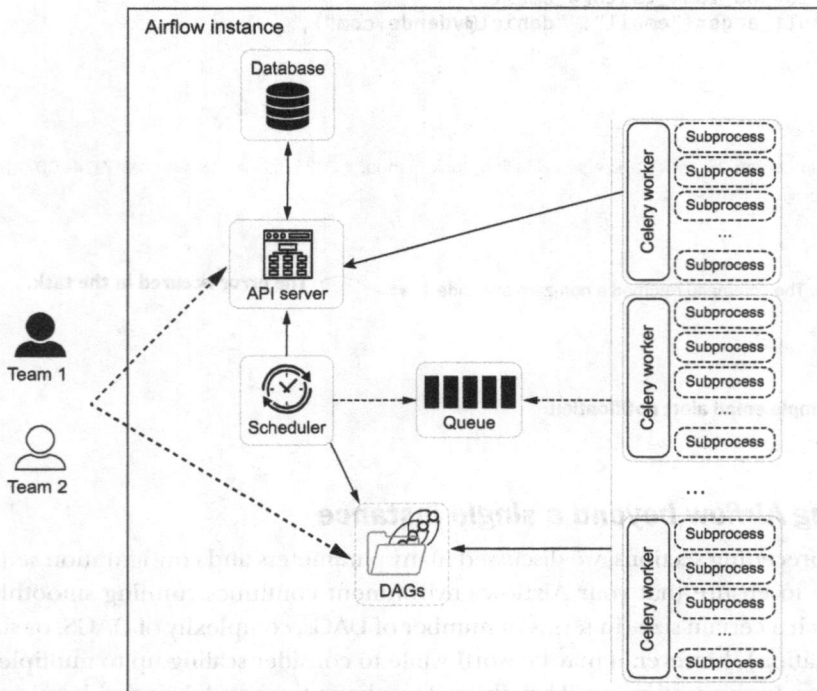

Figure 15.17   Two teams sharing an Airflow instance. In this case, the environment uses the `CeleryExecutor`, but it's is interchangeable with other executors.

The alternative is to set up an Airflow instance for each team (figure 15.18). This option offers complete isolation between teams and allows each team to configure its

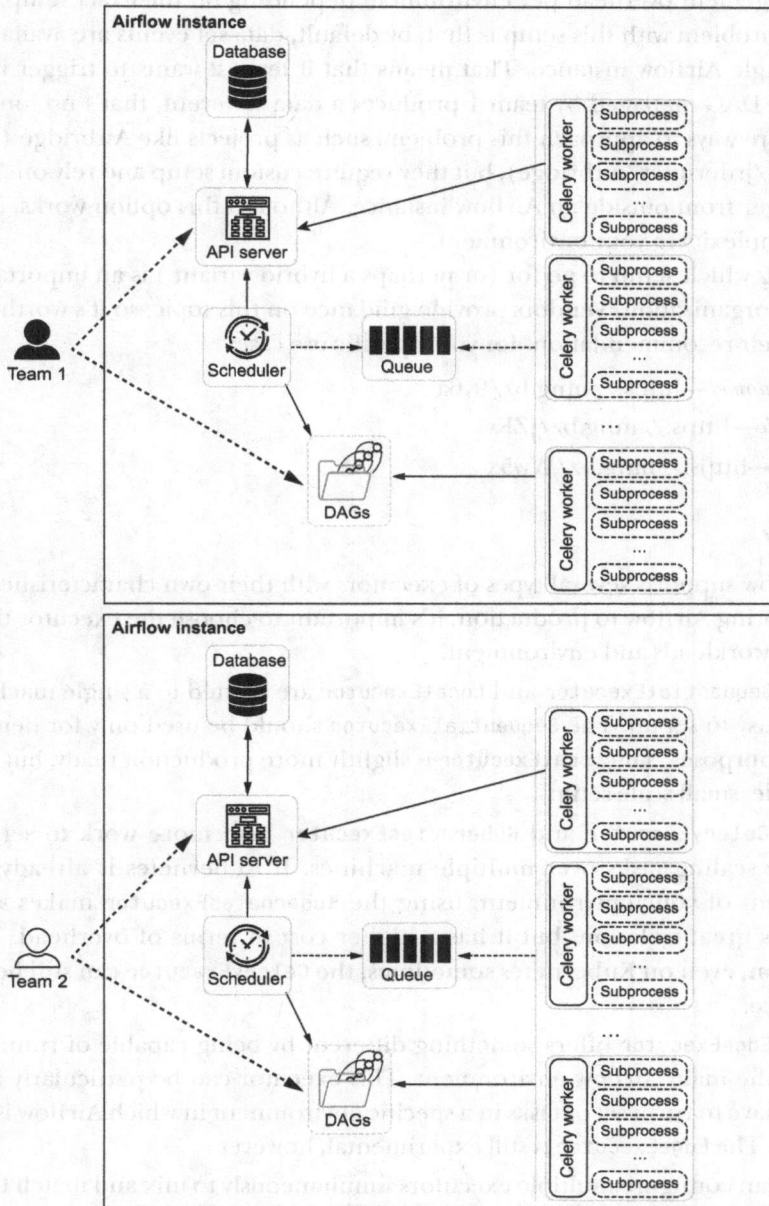

Figure 15.18   Two teams with their own Airflow instances. Each team could configure its own Airflow instance. Team 1 could use the `KubernetesExecutor` instead of the `CeleryExecutor` without affecting team 2, for example.

environment for its own use. It also enables teams to control upgrades (somewhat) without affecting other users. But having multiple instances will most likely be more costly because each Airflow component will be duplicated. In addition, there may be some management overhead per environment depending on the exact setup. A third important problem with this setup is that, by default, data set events are available only within a single Airflow instance. That means that if team 2 wants to trigger its DAGs whenever a DAG managed by team 1 produces a data set event, that's no longer trivial. There are ways to approach this problem, such as projects like Airbridge (https://github.com/jrderuiter/airbridge), but they require custom setup and rely on Airflow's API to trigger from outside an Airflow instance. Although this option works, it adds a layer of complexity to your environment.

Choosing which setup to go for (or perhaps a hybrid variant) is an important decision for an organization. Vendors provide guidance on this topic, so it's worthwhile to consider their recommendations for your specific use case:

- *Astronomer*—https://mng.bz/9y6a
- *Google*—https://mng.bz/jZKy
- *AWS*—https://mng.bz/Ww5x

Summary

- Airflow supports several types of executors with their own characteristics. When you bring Airflow to production, it's important to choose the executor that suits your workloads and environment.
- The SequentialExecutor and LocalExecutor are limited to a single machine but are easy to set up. The SequentialExecutor should be used only for demonstration purposes. The LocalExecutor is slightly more production ready, but only for simple, small-scale setups.
- The CeleryExecutor and KubernetesExecutor take more work to set up but allow scaling tasks over multiple machines. If Kubernetes is already a component of your environment, using the KubernetesExecutor makes sense. It offers great isolation, but it has a higher cost in terms of overhead. For this reason, even on Kubernetes sometimes, the CeleryExecutor can still be a great choice.
- The EdgeExecutor offers something different by being capable of running outside the main Airflow environment. This executor can be particularly useful if you have to run a set of tasks in a specific environment in which Airflow isn't running. The EdgeExecutor is still experimental, however.
- You can configure multiple executors simultaneously to mix and match the characteristics of multiple executor types.
- Airflow offers multiple ways to configure parallelism and performance. You can configure these settings via environment variables or directly in airflow.cfg.

- You can use Prometheus and Grafana for storing and visualizing metrics from Airflow. The data for these tools can be provided by StatsD or OpenTelemetry to instrument Airflow.
- Failure callbacks can send emails or custom notifications in case of certain events.
- You can configure Airflow to scale by setting parameters to increase parallelization. It's important to consider when multiple instances of Airflow make more sense as your organization and its use of Airflow grow.

Securing Airflow

As an orchestrator with access to many other systems, Airflow is a desirable target for hackers. To keep unwanted intruders at bay, Airflow offers several layers of security to help prevent unauthorized access.

In this chapter, we dive deeper into Airflow's security layers and show some practical examples of how to use them. This should give you a good starting point for implementing strategies to secure your own Airflow installation.

We assume that you have some knowledge of basic security principles. But the chapter was written for readers who have little knowledge of the topic, so it should be suitable for most readers.

16.1 Role-based access in the Airflow UI

Start Airflow, and then go to `http://localhost:8080`, where you'll see a login screen (figure 16.1). This is the first view of the role-based access control (RBAC) interface. At this point, the UI is asking for a username and password, but depending on your type of deployment, you may not have any users yet.

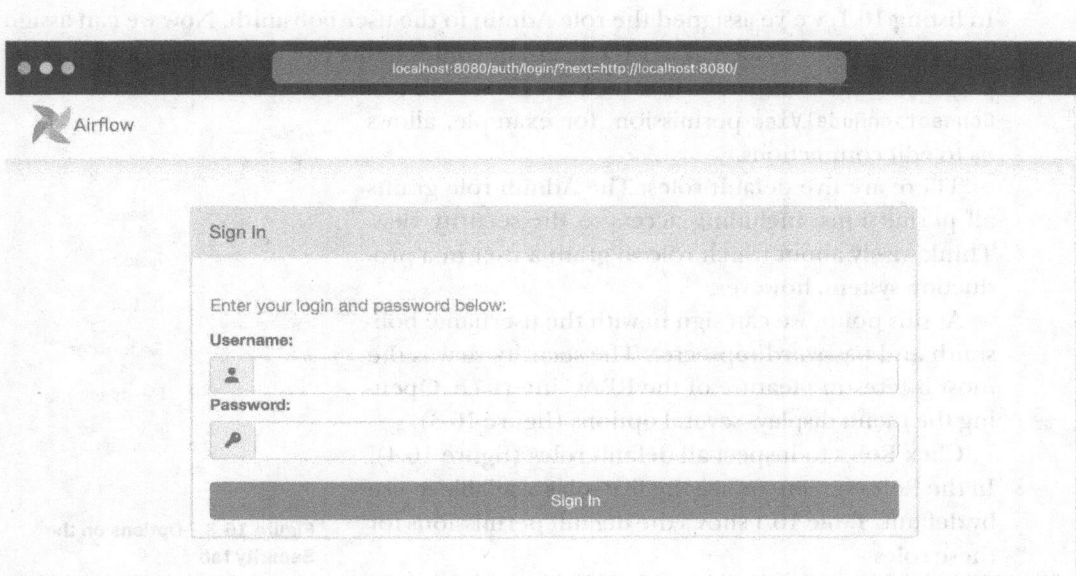

Figure 16.1 Home screen of the RBAC interface. Password authentication is enabled by default. The existence of a default user depends on the way Airflow is deployed.

16.1.1 Adding users

Next, create an account for a user named Bob Smith with a role named Admin, as shown in the following listing. The RBAC model consists of users, each of which is assigned to a single role. Permissions (certain operations) are assigned to those roles, which apply to certain components of the UI (figure 16.2).

Listing 16.1 Registering a user

```
airflow users create \
--role Admin \                    ◄─── Admin role grants all
--username bobsmith \                  permissions to this user.
```

```
--password topsecret \
--email bobsmith@company.com \
--firstname Bob \
--lastname Smith
```

Leave out the --password flag to
prompt for a password.

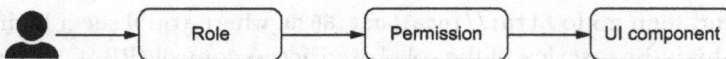

Figure 16.2   RBAC permissions model

In listing 16.1, we've assigned the role Admin to the user bobsmith. Now we can assign certain operations (such as `edit`) on certain components (such as menus) and specific pages (such as Connections) to a role. The `can edit` on `ConnectionModelView` permission, for example, allows us to edit connections.

There are five default roles. The Admin role grants all permissions, including access to the security view. Think wisely about which role to grant a user in a production system, however.

At this point, we can sign in with the username bobsmith and password topsecret. The security view is the most interesting feature of the RBAC interface. Opening the menu displays several options (figure 16.3).

Click Roles to inspect all default roles (figure 16.4). In the Roles screen, we see the five roles available to use by default. Table 16.1 shows the default permissions for these roles.

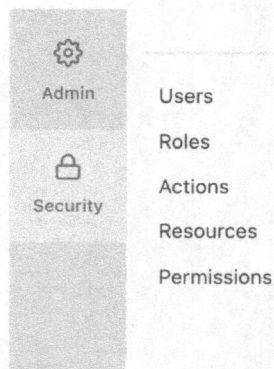

Figure 16.3   Options on the Security tab

Table 16.1   Airflow RBAC interface default role permissions

Role name	Intended users/use	Default permissions
Admin	Necessary only when managing security permissions	All
Public	Unauthenticated users	None
Viewer	Read-only view of Airflow	Read access to directed acyclic graphs (DAGs)
User	Grants permissions only to create DAGs, not secrets; useful if you want strict separation in your team between developers who can and can't edit secrets (connections, variables, and so on)	Same as Viewer but with edit permissions (clear, trigger, pause, and so on) on DAGs
Op	All permissions required for developing Airflow DAGs	Same as User but with additional permissions to view and edit connections, pools, variables, XComs, and configuration

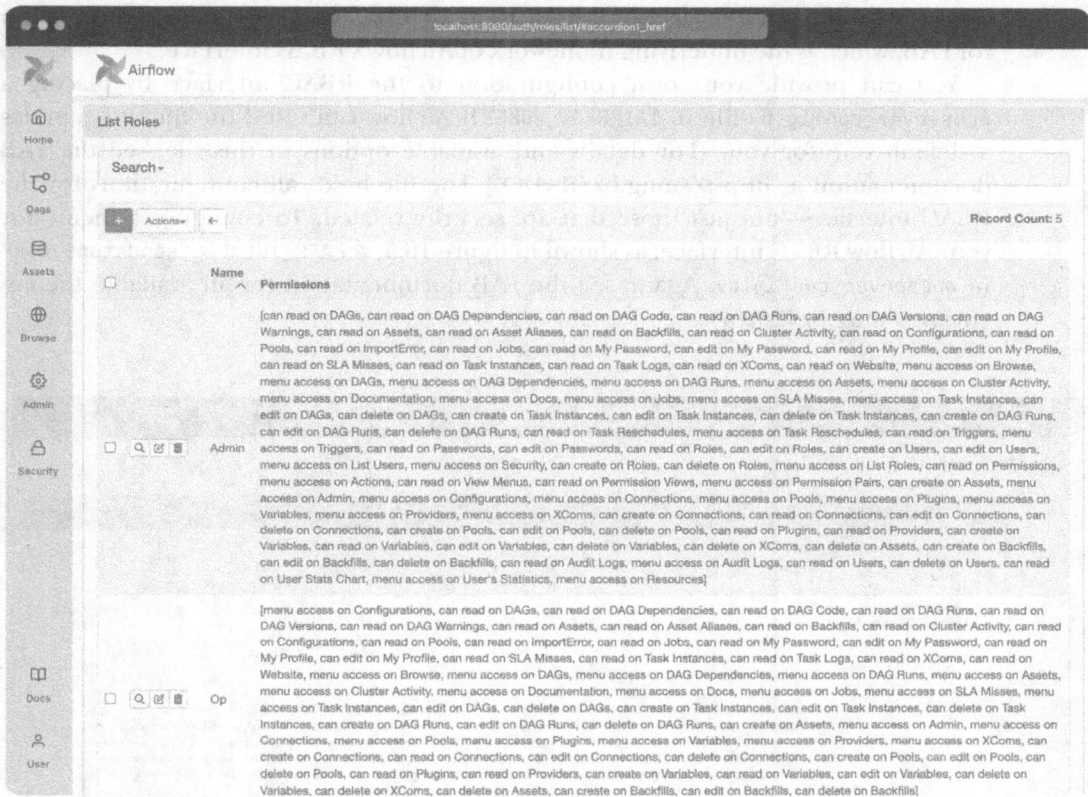

Figure 16.4 Default roles and corresponding permissions in Airflow

The new bobsmith user was assigned the Admin role, which grants all permissions. You may note that the Public role has no permissions. As the role name implies, all permissions attached to it are public (i.e., you don't have to be logged in).

The permissions are quite fine-grained; access to every menu and menu item is controlled by a permission. To make the Docs menu visible, for example, we must add the `menu access on Docs` permission, and to make the Documentation item on the Docs menu visible, we must add the `menu access on Documentation` permission. Finding the correct permissions can be cumbersome. It's easiest to inspect the other roles to learn which permissions are available. A permission is reflected by a string, which in most cases should explain the access it provides.

16.1.2 Configuring the RBAC Interface

Airflow's RBAC interface is developed on top of the Flask-AppBuilder (FAB) framework. When you first run the RBAC web server, you'll find a file named `webserver_config.py` in `$AIRFLOW_HOME`. FAB can be configured with a file named `config.py`, but for clarity, the same file is named `webserver_config.py` in Airflow. This file contains configuration for FAB, which is the underlying framework of Airflow's RBAC interface.

You can provide your own configuration to the RBAC interface by placing a `webserver_config.py` file in `$AIRFLOW_HOME`. If Airflow can't find the file, it generates a default one for you. (For details and available options in this file, see the FAB documentation at https://mng.bz/RwDO.) The file holds all configurations for the RBAC interface—not just those that are security related. To configure a theme for your Airflow RBAC interface, as shown in figure 16.5, set `APP_THEME = "sandstone.css"` in `webserver_config.py`. Again, see the FAB documentation for all available themes (https://mng.bz/262m).

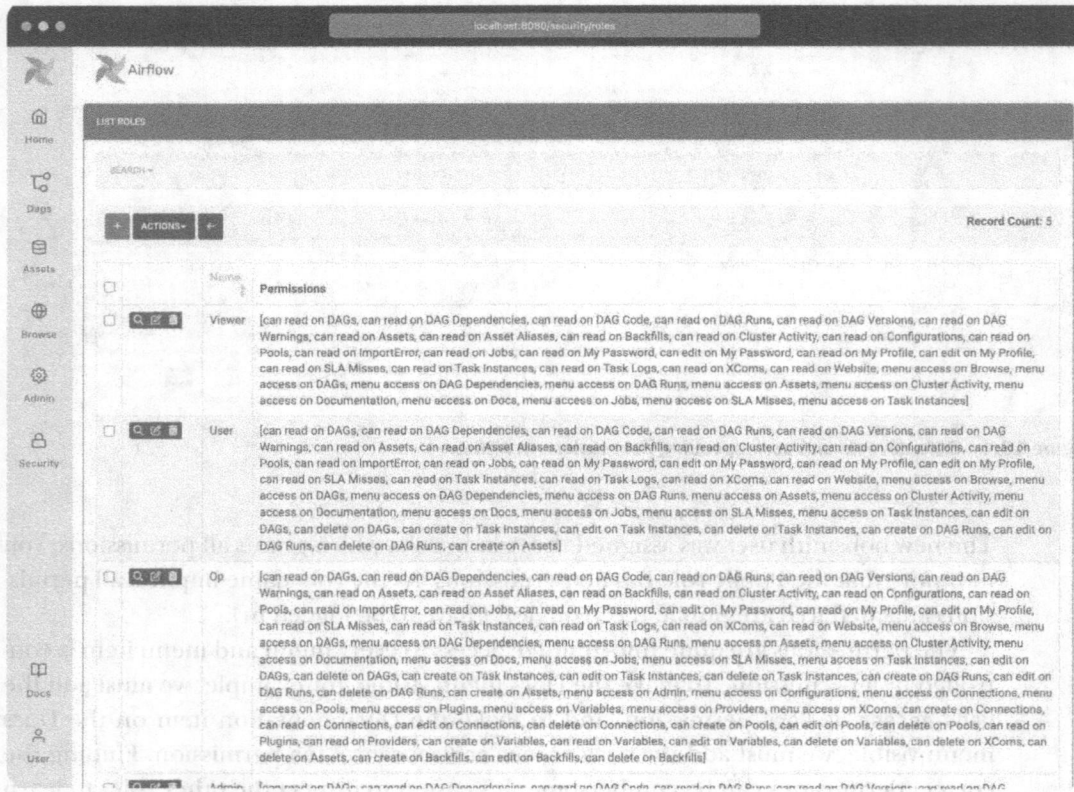

Figure 16.5   List Roles screen in the RBAC interface configured with the sandstone theme

16.2   *Encrypting data at rest*

The RBAC interface requires users to exist in the database with a username and password. This requirement prevents random strangers from accessing Airflow but is far from perfect. Before diving into encryption, let's review Airflow's basic architecture.

Airflow consists of several components. Every piece of software is a potential threat because it serves as a path through which uninvited guests can gain access to your systems (figure 16.6). Therefore, lowering the number of exposed entrance points (i.e., narrowing the attack surface) is always a good idea. If you must expose a service (such as the Airflow UI) for practical reasons, ensure that it's not accessible publicly.

TIP In any cloud, it's easy to expose a service to the internet. Simple measures you can take to avoid exposure include not using an external IP address and/or blocking all traffic and allowlisting only your IP range.

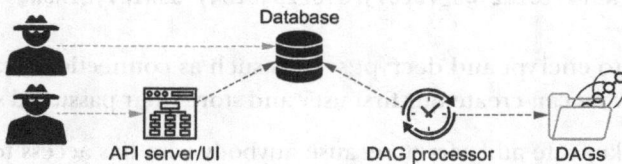

Figure 16.6 The UI and database expose a service and could offer uninvited guests access to Airflow. Protecting these entrance points reduces the attack surface.

You also want your data to be secure after an intruder manages to gain access. Before creating any users and passwords, ensure that you've enabled encryption in Airflow. Without encryption, passwords and other secrets, such as connections, are stored unencrypted in the database. Then anybody who has access to the database can read the passwords. When encrypted, passwords are stored as a sequence of seemingly random characters—essentially making them useless to an attacker. Airflow can encrypt and decrypt secrets using a Fernet key. Using one key for both encryption and decryption is called *symmetric encryption* (figure 16.7).

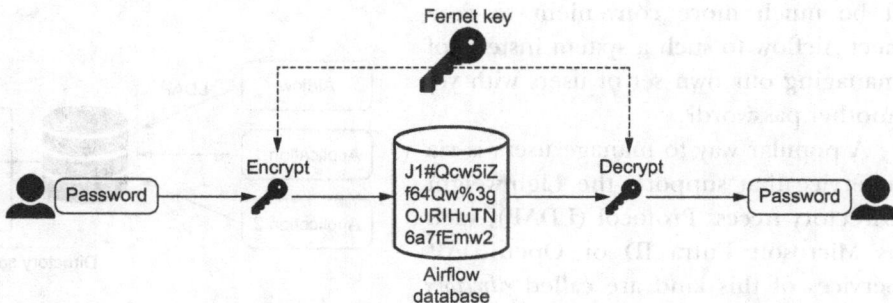

Figure 16.7 A Fernet key encrypts data before storing it in the database and decrypts data before reading it from the database. Without access to the Fernet key, passwords are useless to an intruder.

A *Fernet key* is a secret string used for encryption and decryption. If this key is lost, encrypted messages can no longer be decrypted. To give Airflow a Fernet key, we can generate it as follows.

Listing 16.2   Creating a Fernet key

```
from cryptography.fernet import Fernet

fernet_key = Fernet.generate_key()
print(fernet_key.decode())
# YlCImzjge_TeZc7jPJ7Jz2pgOtb4yTssA1pVyqIADWg=
```

Then we can provide the key to Airflow by setting the `AIRFLOW__CORE__FERNET_KEY` configuration item:

```
AIRFLOW__CORE__FERNET_KEY=YlCImzjge_TeZc7jPJ7Jz2pgOtb4yTssA1pVyqIADWg=
```

Airflow will use the key to encrypt and decrypt secrets such as connections, variables, and user passwords. Now we can create our first user and store their password safely.

> **WARNING**   Keep this key safe and secret because anybody who has access to it will be able to decrypt secrets. Also, you won't be able to decrypt secrets if you lose it!

To avoid storing the Fernet key in plain text in an environment variable, you can configure Airflow to read the value from a Bash command (e.g., `cat /path/to/secret`) instead. You can set the command itself in an environment variable: `AIRFLOW__CORE__FERNET_KEY_CMD=cat /path/to/secret`. Then the file that holds the secret value can be made read-only for specific users or groups.

16.3   *Connecting with a directory service*

As discussed in section 16.1, we can create and store users in Airflow itself. Most companies, however, typically have existing user-management systems in place. Wouldn't it be much more convenient to connect Airflow to such a system instead of managing our own set of users with yet another password?

A popular way to manage users is via a service that supports the Lightweight Directory Access Protocol (LDAP), such as Microsoft Entra ID or OpenLDAP. Services of this kind are called *directory services*. When Airflow is connected to an LDAP service, user information is fetched from the LDAP service in the background upon login (figure 16.8).

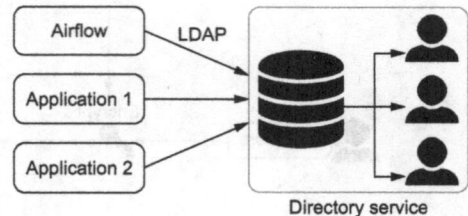

Figure 16.8   Users are stored in a directory service such as Entra ID or OpenLDAP, which can be accessed with LDAP. This way, a user is created only once and can connect to all applications.

> **NOTE**   Throughout this section, we'll use the term *LDAP service* to indicate a directory service that supports queries via the LDAP protocol. A *directory service* is a storage system typically used to store information about resources

such as users and services. LDAP is the protocol used to query most of these directory services.

16.3.1 Understanding LDAP

In this section, we provide a small introduction to LDAP and its corresponding technologies. Section 16.3.2 demonstrates how to connect Airflow to an LDAP service.

The relationship between SQL and a relational database (such as PostgreSQL or MySQL) is similar to the relationship between LDAP and a directory service (such as Entra ID or OpenLDAP). Just as a relational database stores data and SQL queries the data, a directory service stores data (albeit in a different structure), and LDAP queries the directory service.

Relational databases and directory services, however, are built for different purposes. relational databases are designed for transactional use of any data you want to store, whereas directory services are designed for high volumes of read operations in which the data follows a structure much like a phone book (e.g., employees in a company or devices within a building). A relational database is more suitable for supporting a payment system, for example, because payments are made often and payment analysis involves different types of aggregation. A directory service, on the other hand, is more suitable for storing user accounts because these accounts are requested often but usually don't change.

In a directory service, entities (e.g., users, printers, and network shares) are stored in a hierarchical structure named a *directory information tree* (DIT). Each entity is called an *entry*, where information is stored as key-value pairs of attributes and values. Also, each entry is uniquely identified by a *distinguished name* (DN). Visually, data in a directory service is represented as shown in figure 16.9.

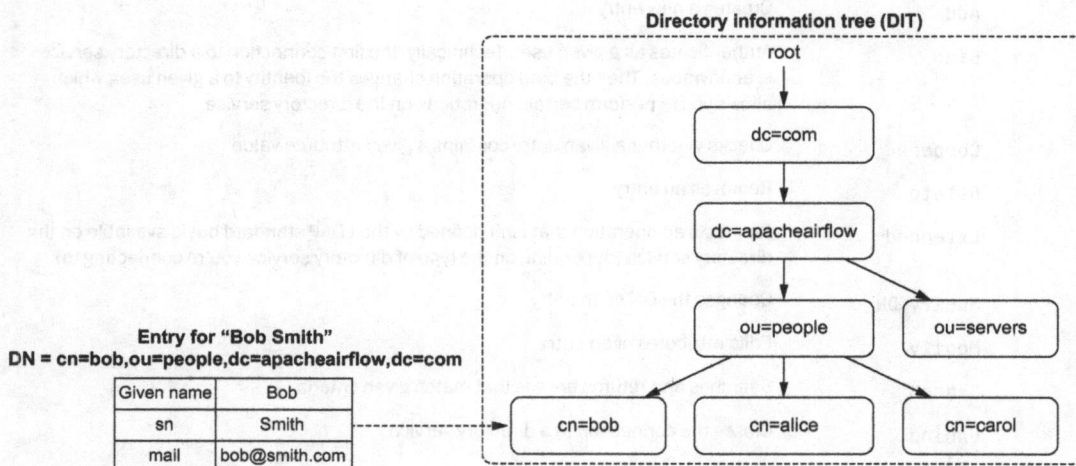

Figure 16.9 Information in a directory service is stored in a hierarchical structure named DIT. Entries represent an entity such as a person and hold key-value attributes about the entity.

You may wonder why we're showing you this hierarchy and what its abbreviations—dc, ou, and cn—stand for. Although a directory service is a database in which you can theoretically store any data, there are set LDAP requirements for storing and structuring data. (The standards are defined in RFC 4510-4519.) One convention is to start the tree with a *domain component* (dc), represented in figure 16.9 as dc=com and dc=apacheairflow. As the name suggests, these are domain components, so your company domain is split by the dots, as in apacheairflow and com.

Next, we have ou=people and cn=bob. ou is short for *organizational unit,* and cn is short for *common name.* Although nothing tells you how to structure your DIT, these components are commonly used.

The LDAP standard defines various ObjectClasses, which define a certain entity together with certain keys. The ObjectClass person, for example, defines a human being with keys such as sn (*surname*; required) and initials (optional). Because the LDAP standard defines such ObjectClasses, applications reading the LDAP service always find the surname of a person in the field named sn, so any application that can query an LDAP service knows where to find the desired information.

Now we know the main components of a directory service and how information is stored inside. But what is LDAP, exactly, and how does it connect with a directory service? Just as SQL provides certain statements, such as SELECT, INSERT, UPDATE, and DELETE, LDAP provides a set of operations on a directory service (table 16.2).

Table 16.2 Overview of LDAP operations

LDAP operation	Description
Abandon	Aborts a previously requested operation
Add	Creates a new entry
Bind	Authenticates as a given user. Technically, the first connection to a directory service is anonymous. Then the bind operation changes the identity to a given user, which allows you to perform certain operations on the directory service.
Compare	Checks whether a given entry contains a given attribute value
Delete	Removes an entry
Extended	Requests an operation that isn't defined by the LDAP standard but is available on the directory service (depending on the type of directory service you're connecting to)
Modify DN	Changes the DN of an entry
Modify	Edits attributes of an entry
Search	Searches and returns entries that match given criteria
Unbind	Closes the connection to a directory service

To fetch user information only, we need the operations bind (to authenticate as a user with permissions to read users in the directory service), search (to search for a given

DN), and `unbind` to close the connection. A search query contains a set of filters—typically, a DN selecting part of the DIT—plus several conditions the entries must meet, such as `uid=bsmith`. This is what any application that queries an LDAP service does under the hood. (`ldapsearch` requires installation of the `ldap-utils` package.) Applications that communicate with an LDAP service perform such searches to fetch and validate user information for authentication to the application. The following listing shows a few examples.

Listing 16.3 Example LDAP searches

```
ldapsearch -b "dc=apacheairflow,dc=com"                              Lists all entries under
ldapsearch -b "dc=apacheairflow,dc=com" "(uid=bsmith)"               dc=apacheairflow,dc=com
```

Lists all entries under dc=apacheairflow,dc=com
where uid=bsmith

16.3.2 Fetching users from an LDAP service

LDAP authentication is supported via FAB. Authentication in Airflow is a pluggable feature, and to configure an Airflow instance to use FAB, we have to set `AIRFLOW__CORE__AUTH_MANAGER` to `airflow.providers.fab.auth_manager.fab_auth_manager.FabAuthManager`. Then we can configure the authentication in `webserver_config.py` (in `$AIRFLOW_HOME`). When we've configured everything correctly and after we log in, FAB searches the LDAP service for the given username and password.

Listing 16.4 Configuring LDAP synchronization

```
from flask_appbuilder.const import AUTH_LDAP

AUTH_TYPE = AUTH_LDAP
AUTH_USER_REGISTRATION = True                           The default role assigned
AUTH_USER_REGISTRATION_ROLE = "User"                    to any user logging in

AUTH_LDAP_SERVER = "ldap://openldap:389"
AUTH_LDAP_USE_TLS = False                                          Section of the DIT
AUTH_LDAP_SEARCH = "dc=apacheairflow,dc=com"                       to search for users
AUTH_LDAP_BIND_USER = "cn=admin,dc=apacheairflow,dc=com"
AUTH_LDAP_BIND_PASSWORD = "admin"
AUTH_LDAP_UID_FIELD = "uid"
```

Name of the field in LDAP
service to search for username

User on the LDAP service to
connect (bind) with and search

If the username and password are found, FAB allows the found user access to the role configured by `AUTH_USER_REGISTRATION_ROLE`. At the time of writing, no feature exists for mapping LDAP groups to Airflow RBAC roles, but you can manually edit the table `ab_user_role` in the metastore to assign a different role after the first login.

With LDAP set up, you no longer have to manually create and maintain users in Airflow. All users are stored in the LDAP service, which is the only system in which user information will be stored, and all applications (including Airflow) will be able to verify user credentials in the LDAP service without having to maintain their own.

16.4 *Encrypting traffic to the web server*

An intruder can obtain data at various places in your system. One place is where data is transferred between two systems, known as *data in transit*. A *man-in-the-middle* (MITM) *attack* is one in which two systems or people communicate while another person intercepts the communication, reading the message (which potentially contains passwords and the like), and forwarding it so that nobody notices the interception (figure 16.10).

Figure 16.10   An MITM attack intercepts traffic between a user and the Airflow web server. Traffic is read and forwarded so that the user doesn't notice the interception while the attacker reads all traffic.

16.4.1 *Understanding HTTPS*

Having secrets intercepted by an unknown person is undesirable. How do we secure Airflow so that data in transit is safe? The details on how an MITM attack is performed are beyond the scope of this book, but we'll discuss how to mitigate the effects of such an attack.

We can work with the Airflow UI via a browser, which communicates with Airflow through the HTTP protocol (figure 16.11). To communicate with the Airflow UI securely, we must do so over HTTPS (HTTP Secure). Before securing traffic to

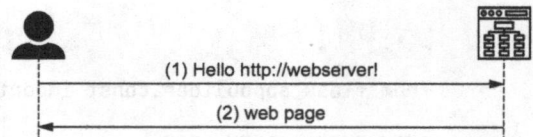

Figure 16.11   With HTTP, the validity of the caller isn't checked, and data is transmitted in plain text.

the web server, let's understand the difference between HTTP and HTTPS. (If you already know this material, you can skip to section 16.4.2.)

What's different about HTTPS? To understand how HTTPS works and what the private key and certificate are for, let's establish how HTTP works.

When a user browses to an HTTP website, no checks are performed on either side (the user's browser or the web server) to verify the identity of the request. All modern browsers display a warning about the insecure connection (figure 16.12).

Now that we know HTTP traffic isn't secure, how does HTTPS traffic help? First, from a user's perspective, modern browsers display a lock or something green to indicate a valid certificate (figure 16.13).

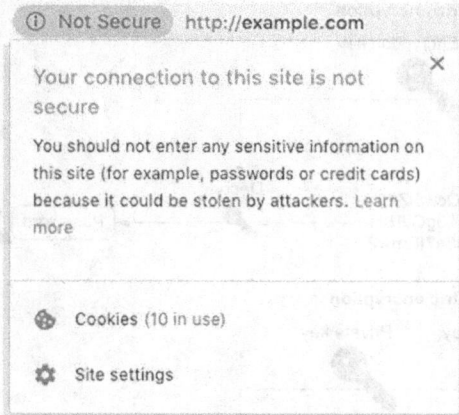

Figure 16.12 Navigating to `http://example.com` **in Google Chrome displays** `Not Secure` **because HTTP traffic is unsecured.**

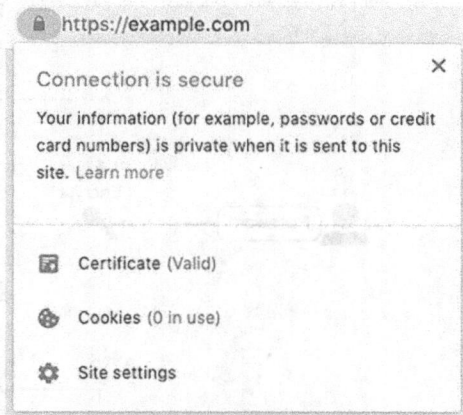

Figure 16.13 Navigating to an HTTPS website in Chrome displays a lock (if the certificate is valid) to indicate a secure connection.

When your browser and a web server communicate over HTTPS, the initial handshake involves more steps to verify the validity of the remote side (figure 16.14). The encryption used in HTTPS is Transport Layer Security (TLS), which uses both asymmetric encryption and symmetric encryption. Whereas symmetric encryption applies a single key for both encryption and decryption, asymmetric encryption consists of two keys: public and private. The magic of asymmetric encryption is that data encrypted with the public

Figure 16.14 At the start of an HTTPS session, the browser and web server agree on a mutual session key to encrypt and decrypt traffic between the two.

key can be decrypted only with the private key (which only the web server knows), and data encrypted with the private key can be decrypted only with the public key (figure 16.15).

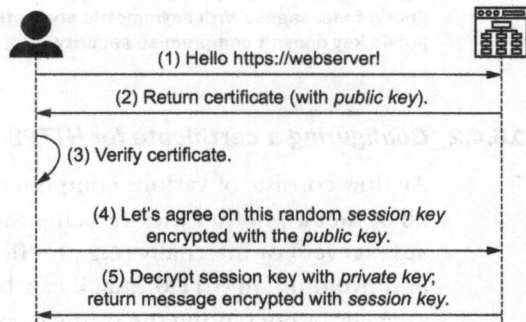

At the start of an HTTPS session, the web server returns the certificate, which is a file with a publicly sharable key. The browser returns a randomly generated session key to the web server, encrypted with the public key. Only the private key can decrypt this message, which only the web server should have access to. For this reason, it's important that you never share the private key; anybody who has this key can decrypt the traffic.

Symmetric encryption

(Single) Encryption key

Asymmetric encryption

Public key   Private key

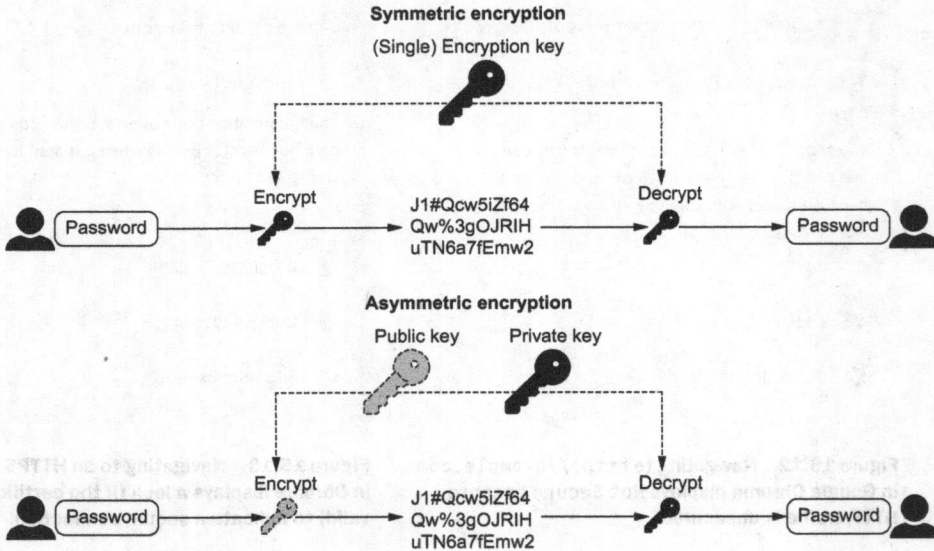

Figure 16.15   With symmetric encryption, the loss of the encryption key allows others to encrypt and decrypt messages. With asymmetric encryption, a public key is shared with others, but the loss of the public key doesn't compromise security.

16.4.2   *Configuring a certificate for HTTPS*

Airflow consists of various components, and you want to avoid attacks on and among all of them, whether they're being used externally (e.g., exposed in a URL such as the api-server) or internally (e.g., traffic between the scheduler and database). Detecting and avoiding an MITM attack can be difficult, but rendering the data useless to an attacker by encrypting the traffic is a straightforward process.

By default, we communicate with Airflow over HTTP. When browsing to Airflow, we can tell whether the traffic is encrypted by the URL: http(s)://localhost:8080. All HTTP traffic is transferred in plain text; an attacker reading the traffic could intercept and read passwords as they're transmitted. In HTTPS traffic, data is encrypted at one end and decrypted at the other. An attacker reading HTTPS traffic will be unable to interpret the data because it's encrypted.

Let's see how to secure the one public endpoint in Airflow: the api-server. You need two items:

- A private key (keep it secret)
- A certificate (safe to share)

We'll elaborate on these items later. For now, it's important to know that the private key and certificate are files provided by a certificate authority or a self-signed certificate (a certificate you generate yourself that isn't signed by an official certificate authority). The following listing shows how to create a self-signed certificate.

Listing 16.5 Creating a self-signed certificate

```
openssl req \
-x509 \
-newkey rsa:4096 \
-sha256 \
-nodes \
-days 365 \
-keyout privatekey.pem \
-out certificate.pem \
-extensions san \
-config \
 <(echo "[req]";
   echo distinguished_name=req;
   echo "[san]";
   echo subjectAltName=DNS:localhost,IP:127.0.0.1
   ) \
-subj "/CN=localhost"
```

- Generates a key that's valid for one year
- Filename of private key
- Filename of certificate
- Most browsers require the SAN extension for security reasons.

Both the private key and certificate must be stored on a path that's available to Airflow, and Airflow must be run with the following configuration:

- `AIRFLOW__API__SSL_CERT=/path/to/certificate.pem`
- `AIRFLOW__API__SSL_KEY=/path/to/privatekey.pem`

Start Airflow, and you'll see that `http://localhost:8080` doesn't serve the web server anymore. Instead, the web server is served on `https://localhost:8080` (figure 16.16).

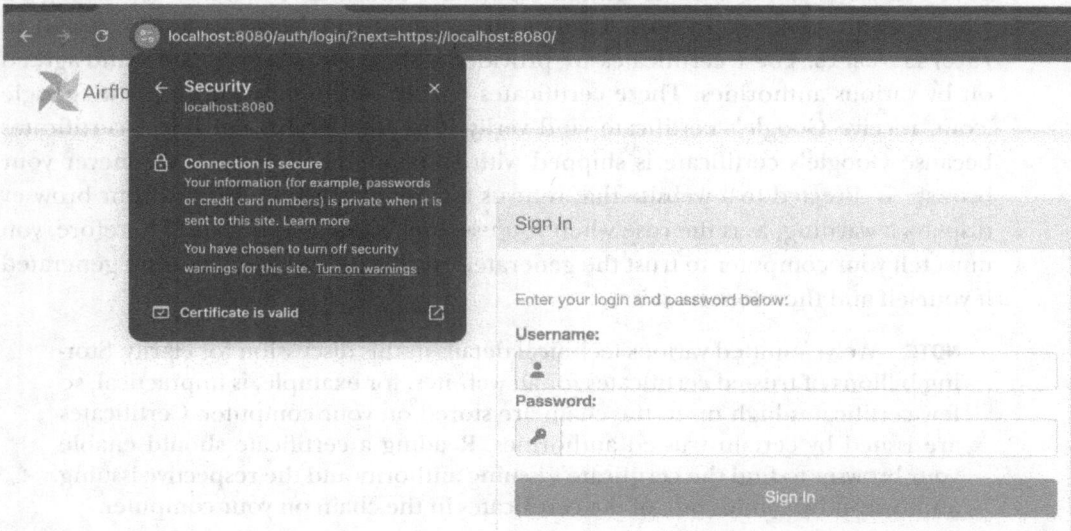

Figure 16.16 After you provide a certificate and private key, the UI is served on `https://localhost:8080`. No official certificate can be issued for localhost; therefore, it must be self-signed. Self-signed certificates are untrusted by default, so you must add such a certificate to your trusted certificates.

At this point, traffic between your browser and the Airflow web server is encrypted. Although an attacker can intercept the traffic, it's useless to them because the traffic is encrypted and therefore unreadable. Only the private key can decrypt the data, which is why it's important that you never share the private key and keep it in a safe place.

When using a self-signed certificate like the one shown earlier in listing 16.5, you initially receive a warning. Figure 16.17 shows the warning in Chrome.

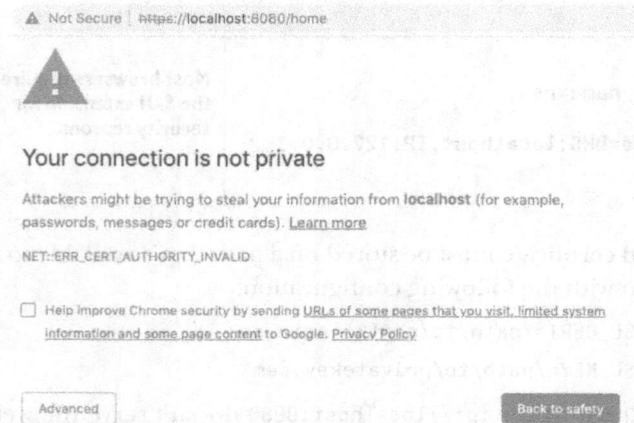

⚠ Not Secure | https://localhost:8080/home

Your connection is not private

Attackers might be trying to steal your information from **localhost** (for example, passwords, messages or credit cards). Learn more

NET::ERR_CERT_AUTHORITY_INVALID

☐ Help improve Chrome security by sending URLs of some pages that you visit, limited system information and some page content to Google. Privacy Policy

Advanced   Back to safety

Figure 16.17 Most browsers display warnings when you use self-signed certificates because their validity can't be checked.

Your computer holds a list of trusted certificates and their locations, depending on your operating system. In most Linux systems, the trusted certificates are stored in /etc/ssl/certs. These certificates are provided with your operating system and agreed on by various authorities. These certificates enable you to go to https://www.google .com, receive Google's certificate, and verify it in your pretrusted list of certificates because Google's certificate is shipped with your operating system. Whenever your browser is directed to a website that returns a certificate not in this list, your browser displays a warning, as is the case when you use a self-signed certificate. Therefore, you must tell your computer to trust the generated certificate, knowing that you generated it yourself and therefore trust it.

NOTE We've omitted various technical details in this discussion for clarity. Storing billions of trusted certificates for all websites, for example, is impractical, so few certificates high up in the chain are stored on your computer. Certificates are issued by certain trusted authorities. Reading a certificate should enable your browser to find the certificate's issuing authority and the respective issuing authority until it finds one of the certificates in the chain on your computer.

How you tell your computer to trust a certificate depends on your operating system. For macOS, for example, the process involves opening Keychain Access and importing your certificate into the System keychain (figure 16.18).

Select the System keychain.

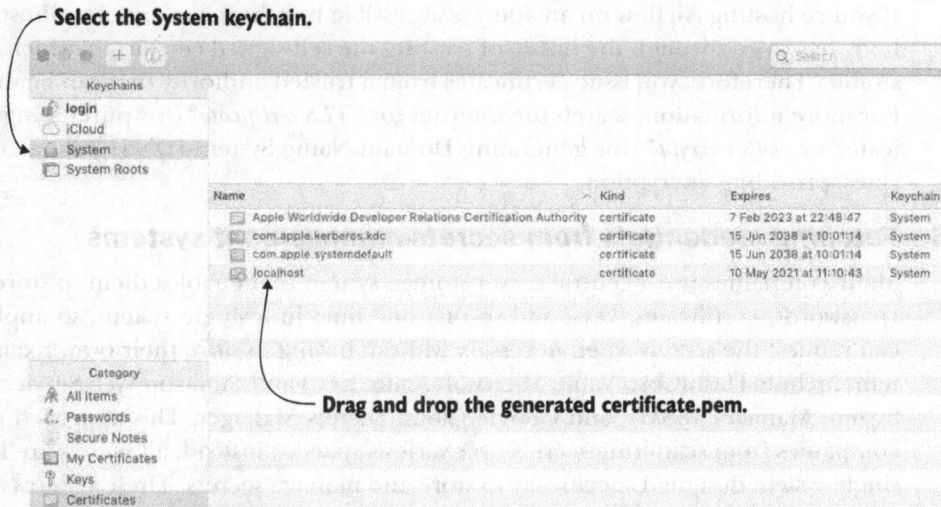

Drag and drop the generated certificate.pem.

Figure 16.18 Adding a self-signed certificate to the System certificates in macOS

Afterward, the certificate is known to the system but still not trusted. To trust it, you must explicitly trust SSL when encountering the self-signed certificate (figure 16.19).

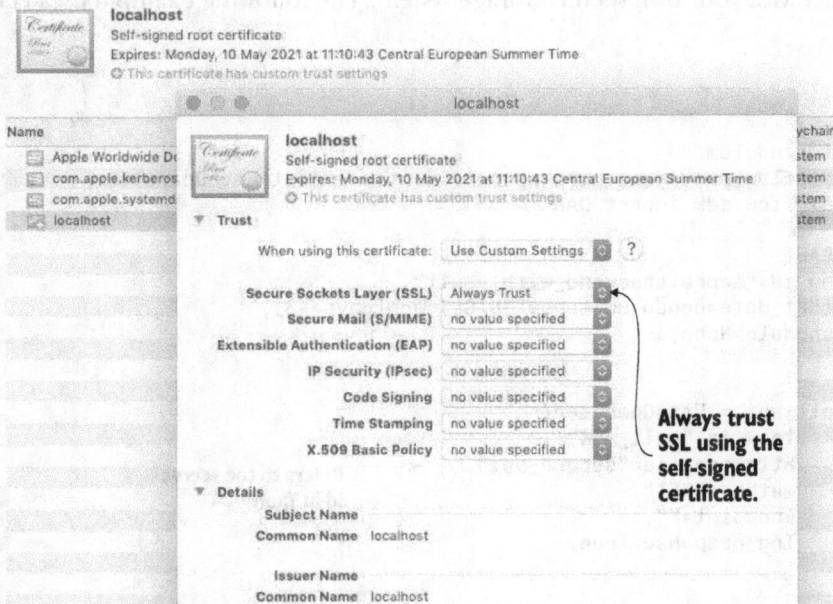

Always trust SSL using the self-signed certificate.

Figure 16.19 Trusting SSL using the self-signed certificate enables trust between your computer and the Airflow web server.

If you're hosting Airflow on an address accessible by others (i.e., not localhost), everybody has to go through the hassle of trusting the self-signed certificate, which is undesirable. Therefore, you issue certificates from a trusted authority that can be validated. For more information, search the internet for "*TLS certificate*" (for purchasing a certificate) or "*let's encrypt*" (for generating Domain Name System [DNS]–validated certificates, providing encryption).

16.5   *Fetching credentials from secrets-management systems*

Many companies use a central secret storage system that enables them to store secrets (passwords, certificates, keys, and so on) one time in a single system, so applications can request the secrets when necessary without having to store their own. Example systems include HashiCorp Vault, Microsoft Azure Key Vault, Amazon Web Services (AWS) System Manager (SSM), and Google Cloud Secrets Manager. This approach prevents companies from scattering secrets over various systems; instead, all secrets are kept in a single system designed specifically to store and manage secrets. These systems also provide features such as secret rotation and versioning, which aren't available in Airflow.

Secret values in Airflow can be stored in variables and connections. Wouldn't it be convenient and secure to connect with one of these secret storage systems instead of having to copy and paste secrets into Airflow? Airflow has a feature, the secrets backend, which provides a mechanism to fetch secrets from external secret storage systems while still using the existing variable and connection classes.

The secrets backend provides a generic class that you can subclass to implement and connect with your own secrets storage system. The following example uses HashiCorp Vault.

Listing 16.6   Fetching connection details from a configured secrets backend

```python
import pendulum
from airflow.providers.http.operators.http import HttpOperator
from airflow.sdk import DAG

with DAG(
    dag_id="secretsbackend_with_vault",
    start_date=pendulum.today("UTC").add(days=-3),
    schedule=None,
):

    call_api = HttpOperator(
        task_id="call_api",
        http_conn_id="secure_api",        ◄── Refers to the secret
        method="GET",                          id in Vault
        endpoint="",
        log_response=True,
    )
```

As you see in listing 16.6, there's no explicit reference to HashiCorp Vault in the DAG code. The `HttpOperator` makes an HTTP request, in this case to the URL set in the connection. Before the existence of secrets backends, you'd save the URL in an Airflow connection. Now you can save it in (among others) HashiCorp Vault. Keep a few things in mind when doing this, however:

- Secrets backends must be configured with `AIRFLOW__SECRETS__BACKEND` and `AIRFLOW__SECRETS__BACKEND_KWARGS`.
- All secrets must have a common prefix.
- All connections must be stored in a key named `conn_uri`.
- All variables must be stored in a key named `value`.

The secret name is stored as a path (this applies to all secret managers), such `secret/connections/secure_api`, where `secret` and `connections` can be folders used for organization and `secure_api` is the name that identifies the actual secret.

> **NOTE** The `secret` prefix is specific to the Vault backend. See the Airflow documentation for all details on your secrets backend of choice (https://mng .bz/152n).

The hierarchical organization of secrets in all secrets-management systems allows Airflow to provide a generic secrets backend to interface with such systems. In the Secrets Engines section of HashiCorp Vault (available at `localhost:8200` in our setup), the secret is stored as shown in figure 16.20.

Within a secrets engine in Vault, we create a secret with the name `connections/ secure_api`. Although the prefix `connections` isn't necessary, Airflow's secrets backend takes a prefix under which it can search for secrets, which is convenient for searching only one part of the secrets hierarchy in Vault.

Storing an Airflow connection in any secrets backend requires setting a key named `conn_uri`, which is the

Secrets Engines

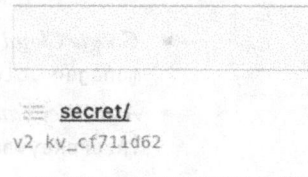

secret/
v2 kv_cf711d62

Figure 16.20 Secrets in Vault are stored in Secrets Engines, which can store secrets in various systems. By default, you get an engine named secret for storing key-value secrets.

key Airflow will request (figure 16.21). The connection must be given in URI format. The URI is passed internally to Airflow's `connection` class, where the proper details are extracted from the Uniform Resource Identifier (URI).

Suppose that we have an API running on hostname `secure_api`, port 5000; it requires a header with the name `token` and the value `supersecret` for authentication. To be parsed into an Airflow connection, the API details must be stored in URI format, as shown in figure 16.21: `http://secure_api:5000?token=supersecret`.

In Airflow, we must set two configuration options to fetch the credentials. First, we set `AIRFLOW__SECRETS__BACKEND` to the class reading the secrets:

- *HashiCorp Vault*—`airflow.providers.hashicorp.secrets.vault.VaultBackend`
- *AWS SSM*—`airflow.providers.amazon.aws.secrets. secrets_manager .SecretsManagerBackend`

< secret

Create secret

JSON

Path for this secret

connections/secure_api

Version data

| conn_uri | http://secure_api:5000?token=supersecret | 👁 | Add |

Save   Cancel

Figure 16.21   Saving Airflow connection details in Vault requires setting a key: `conn_uri`.

- *Google Cloud Secrets Manager*—`airflow.providers.google.cloud.secrets.secrets_manager .CloudSecretManagerBackend`
- *Azure Key Vault*—`airflow.providers.microsoft.azure.secrets.key_vault .AzureKeyVaultBackend`

Next, we must configure various details specific to the chosen secrets backend in `AIR-FLOW__SECRETS__BACKEND_KWARGS`. See the Airflow documentation for details on all secrets backends (https://mng.bz/152n). Take, for example, `BACKEND_KWARGS` for Vault:

```
{"url":"http:// vault:8200","token":"airflow","connections_path":"connections"}
```

Here, `"url"` points to Vault's URL, `"token"` refers to a token for authenticating against Vault, and `"connections_path"` refers to the prefix to query for all connections. In the Vault backend, the default prefix for all secrets (both connections and variables) is set to `secret`. As a result, the full search query, given a `conn_id` `"secure_api"`, becomes `secret/connections/secure_api`.

The secrets backend doesn't replace secrets stored in environment variables or the Airflow metastore; it's an alternative location to store secrets. The order of fetching secrets becomes the following:

1 Secrets backend
2 Environment variables (`AIRFLOW_CONN_*` and `AIRFLOW_VAR_*`)
3 Airflow metastore

With a secrets backend set up, you outsource the storage and management of secret information to a system developed specifically for that purpose. Other systems can connect to the secrets-management system, so you store a secret value only once instead of distributing it over many systems, each with the potential for a breach. As a result, your attack surface becomes smaller.

Technically, the number of possibilities for breaching your systems are limitless. But this chapter demonstrates various ways to secure data inside and outside Airflow—all with the goal of limiting the number of options for an attacker and safeguarding against some of the most common ways attackers gain unwanted access. As a final note, ensure that you keep up to date with Airflow releases, which sometimes contain security fixes or close bugs in older versions.

Summary

- In general, security doesn't focus on one item; it involves securing various levels of your application to limit the potential attack surface.

- The RBAC interface features a role-based security mechanism to allow certain actions by the groups in which users are organized.

- You can configure Airflow's RBAC to interface with your existing LDAP services to avoid having to perform user management in multiple places.

- You can make intercepted traffic between the client and the Airflow web server useless to an attacker by applying TLS encryption (also known as HTTPS).

- You make credentials in Airflow's database unreadable by an attacker by encrypting the secrets with a Fernet key.

- You can use a secrets-management system such as HashiCorp Vault to store and manage secrets so that secrets are managed in a single location and shared only when necessary with applications such as Airflow.

Airflow deployment options

This chapter covers

- Vendor-managed services for Airflow
- Rolling your own deployment in a Kubernetes cluster instead of using a managed service
- Deployment options when deploying in a Kubernetes cluster

Up to now, all our examples have run on Airflow deployed on your local machine using Docker Compose. This setup, however, is hardly production ready for running your pipelines outside a development setting.

In this chapter, we'll cover several options for deploying Airflow in production. We'll start by exploring the vendor-managed solutions available and discuss criteria for using a vendor-managed solution instead of deploying it yourself. Then we'll discuss how you can deploy Airflow on Kubernetes. In the process, we'll guide you through some choices you can make during such a deployment.

17.1 Managed Airflow

Rolling your own Airflow deployment can give you ultimate flexibility in the way you use it. Setting up and maintaining such a deployment can be a lot of work. One way to avoid this burden is to use a vendor-managed service, offloading most of the work to an external provider. This provider typically gives you tools that make it easy to create and manage new Airflow deployments without the hassle of managing them yourself. Usually, the provider also promises to maintain the underlying infrastructure so you don't have to worry about keeping your operating system and/or Airflow installation up to date with the latest security patches, monitoring the systems, and so on.

Three prominent managed Airflow services are Astronomer, Google Cloud Composer, and Amazon Managed Workflows for Apache Airflow (MWAA). The following sections provide a brief overview of these services and their key features.

17.1.1 Astronomer

While the public cloud hyperscalers such as Microsoft Azure, Amazon Web Services (AWS), and Google Cloud Platform (GCP) offer many products and services, Astronomer's DataOps platform and core expertise revolve around Airflow.

Astronomer employs many members of the Airflow PMC (Project Management Committee) and Airflow committers, is a big contributor to new Airflow version releases, and organizes community events. Astronomer has been significantly involved in both the planning and development of Airflow 3 and continues to provide substantial input to the project.

Astronomer provides a fully managed cloud service named Astro, which aims to abstract away the overhead and complexity of setting up, managing, and maintaining Airflow. Astro enables data engineering teams to focus on their core jobs (i.e., building effective and performant data pipelines that power critical data products) rather than manage the underlying infrastructure and maintain their Airflow environment. Astro also provides many additional benefits compared with open source Airflow that enable you to develop and build faster, deploy seamlessly to production, and track lineage with end-to-end data observability. This service is available on all three major clouds: Azure, AWS, and Google. Astronomer provides several options for creating and managing Airflow instances in Astro:

- Clicking in the UI
- Using the Astro command-line interface (CLI) via Astronomer's CLI
- Calling a REST API
- Using Terraform

When you've created these instances (called *deployments* in Astronomer), you can view and manage DAG run status, users, and more in the UI, shown in figure 17.1, which displays all your Airflow deployments in one overview. This enables a cloud offering such as Astro to provide additional details spanning all deployments, such as cost insights, which is convenient for multiteam organizations.

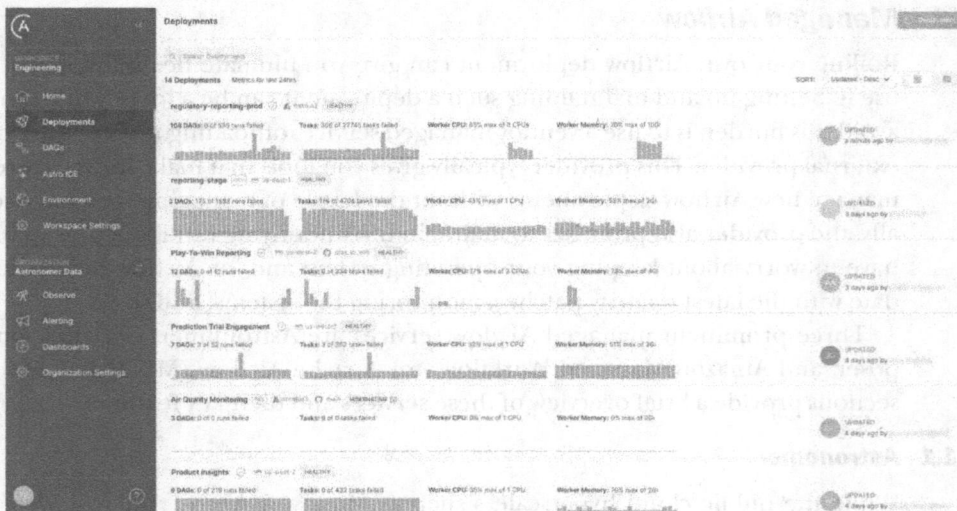

Figure 17.1   Astronomer UI overview of deployments

Astronomer also aims to make the lives of Airflow developers easier. Examples are the Astro CLI for local development; Astro IDE, an in-browser code editor for writing and deploying DAGs with optional assistance from a specialized AI agent; Astronomer Cosmos, for running dbt Core projects as Airflow DAGs (https://github.com/dbt-labs/dbt-core); and various monitoring and alerting capabilities, including alerts on events such as DAG failures, across all deployments. Your code is synced to version control, allowing pipeline development without a local setup. Some of these tools are also useful for Airflow developers who aren't using the managed service offering.

Astronomer adds its own specific tools, including Astro Observe, an orchestration-native observability solution built for teams using Airflow. Integrated into the Astro platform, it gives data teams unified visibility into pipeline health, real-time lineage, service-level agreement (SLA)performance, data quality, and data product–level costs in one place. By connecting observability directly to orchestration, Observe helps teams detect and resolve issues faster, reduce tool sprawl, and deliver reliable and cost-efficient data products.

Astronomer provides educational resources for all levels of Airflow users in its academy (https://academy.astronomer.io), tutorials (https://www.astronomer.io/docs/learn), and webinars (https://www.astronomer.io/events/webinars).

17.1.2 *Google Cloud Composer*

Google Cloud Composer is a managed version of Airflow that runs on top of GCP. It provides an easy, almost-one-click solution for deploying Airflow into GCP that integrates well with its services. GCP also takes care of managing the underlying resources; you pay only for the resources used. You can interact with Cloud Composer using the GCP CLI and/or monitor the state of your clusters from within the GCP web interface.

Like Astronomer, Cloud Composer is based on Kubernetes and runs on the Google Kubernetes Engine (GKE). A nice feature of Cloud Composer is that it integrates well with services within GCP (Google Cloud Storage, BigQuery, and so on), making it easy to access these services from within your DAGs. Cloud Composer provides a lot of flexibility with regard to how you configure your Kubernetes cluster in terms of resources so you can tune the deployment to your specific needs. As in Astronomer, you can install Python dependencies in your Airflow clusters using the web interface or the GCP CLI.

Cloud Composer charges a fee for the environment itself (number of nodes, database storage, network egress, and so on) in addition to costs for underlying services (GKE and Cloud Storage, which Cloud Composer uses to store DAGs, logs, and so on). For an up-to-date overview of these costs, see the GCP website (https://cloud.google.com).

As a strong proponent of open source software, Google contributes regularly to the Airflow open source project and has helped develop an extensive suite of operators for its services to enable their use from within Airflow. You don't need to use Cloud Composer to use these operators, however; they also function well from within Airflow (assuming that permissions are set up correctly).

17.1.3 Amazon Managed Workflows for Apache Airflow

Amazon Managed Workflows for Apache Airflow (MWAA) is an AWS service that makes it easy to create managed Airflow deployments in the AWS cloud; it's similar to Cloud Composer. When you use MWAA to run Airflow, the service manages the underlying infrastructure and scales your deployment to meet the demands of your workflows. Airflow deployments in MWAA integrate well with AWS services such as S3, Redshift, and SageMaker; Amazon CloudWatch for logging/alerting; and AWS Identity and Access Management (IAM) for providing a single login for the web interface and securing access to your data.

Like the other managed solutions, MWAA uses the `CeleryExecutor` to scale workers based on the current workload, with the underlying infrastructure managed for you. You can add or edit DAGs by uploading them to a predefined S3 bucket, where they will be deployed to your Airflow environment. You can use similar S3-based approaches to install additional Airflow plug-ins or Python requirements in the cluster as needed.

Pricing includes a base fee for the Airflow environment itself and an additional fee for each Airflow worker instance. In both cases, you have the option to choose small, medium, or large machines to tailor the deployment to your use case. The dynamic scaling of workers means that worker use should be relatively cost effective. There is an extra monthly storage cost for the Airflow metastore, as well as any storage required for your DAGs or data. See the AWS website for more details (https://aws.amazon.com).

17.2 Airflow on Kubernetes

To go from a proof-of-concept setup, as we've done up to now with our Docker Compose–based examples, to a Kubernetes-based production environment, we need access to a Kubernetes cluster. We won't describe how to set up such a cluster in the cloud or on a local machine. You can find good resources (https://kubernetes.io/ docs/tasks/tools) if you want to use minikube or kind to run a cluster on your local machine. In this chapter, we'll use https://k3s.io incorporated into Docker Compose to get started quickly. Setup for the Docker Compose–based Kubernetes setup is equivalent to setup in earlier chapters and is explained in appendix A.

We'll start by deploying Airflow with the provided Helm Chart to explore the deployed resources. Then we'll cover some of the deployment options discussed in chapter 15.

17.2.1 Preparing the Kubernetes cluster

To prepare for all the upcoming scenarios, we have to start the Kubernetes cluster and other services, such as an external metadata database and Docker image registry. Contrary to the earlier chapters of this book, we're not starting the Airflow components with the docker compose up command. We get a Kubernetes cluster with a master and agent node, a PostgreSQL database, and a Docker registry, which we'll use from section 17.2.6 and later in this chapter. The Airflow components we saw in previous chapters will be deployed inside the Kubernetes cluster later (figure 17.2).

Listing 17.1   Starting the Kubernetes cluster and other services

```
docker compose up -d
```

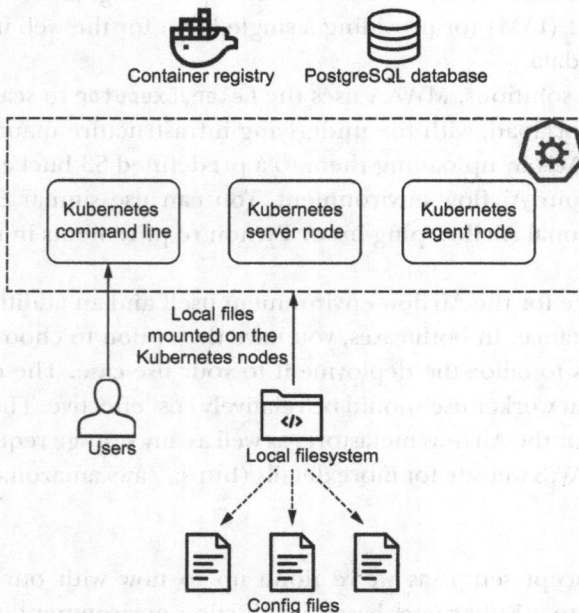

Figure 17.2   Kubernetes cluster and other services. Airflow components will be deployed inside the cluster.

17.2.2 *Connecting to your Kubernetes cluster*

For convenience, we're starting a separate container to interact with the Kubernetes cluster. This container is set up to use the config file provided by the cluster and connects to the cluster through its server name.

Listing 17.2   Starting the Kubernetes command-line container

```
docker exec -ti chapter17-k3s-cli-1 /bin/bash -l
```

For exploring the resources, we use `kubectl`, and for deployment, we use `helm` (https://helm.sh). Helm is a package manager for Kubernetes that helps you manage applications. Its charts help you define, install, and upgrade even complex Kubernetes applications. To connect these tools to our Kubernetes cluster, we provide the correct `kube-config` file with the `KUBECONFIG` environment variable. We can verify that the connection works as follows.

Listing 17.3   Verifying your connection

```
kubectl cluster-info

Kubernetes control plane is running at https://k3s-server:6443
CoreDNS is running at https://k3s-server:6443/api/v1/namespaces/
  kube-system/services/kube-dns:dns/proxy
Metrics-server is running at https://k3s-server:6443/api/v1/namespaces/
  kube-system/services/https:metrics-server:https/proxy

To further debug and diagnose cluster problems, use
  'kubectl cluster-info dump'.
```

17.2.3 *Deploying with the Apache Airflow Helm Chart*

We'll start with the default deployment provided with the Helm Chart from Airflow itself. We configure helm to use the `apache-airflow` repository that contains the official Helm Chart for Airflow and install that chart with the default configuration. The only change is configuring the `api-server` (which serves the Airflow UI) to have a `LoadBalancer` service type so that it's automatically exposed to outside the Kubernetes cluster and accessible from your local computer.

Listing 17.4   Deploying default Airflow with `helm`

```
helm repo add apache-airflow https://airflow.apache.org
helm upgrade --install airflow apache-airflow/airflow \
  --create-namespace \
  --namespace airflow \
  --set apiServer.service.type=LoadBalancer
  --set postgresql.image.repository=postgres
  --set postgresql.image.tag=16
```

We can verify the pods that are created. Next, we link the list of running pods to the architecture described in chapter 1. The pods in listing 17.5 correlate with the services in figure 17.3, where the Redis pod handles the queue functionality and the PostgreSQL pod handles the database.

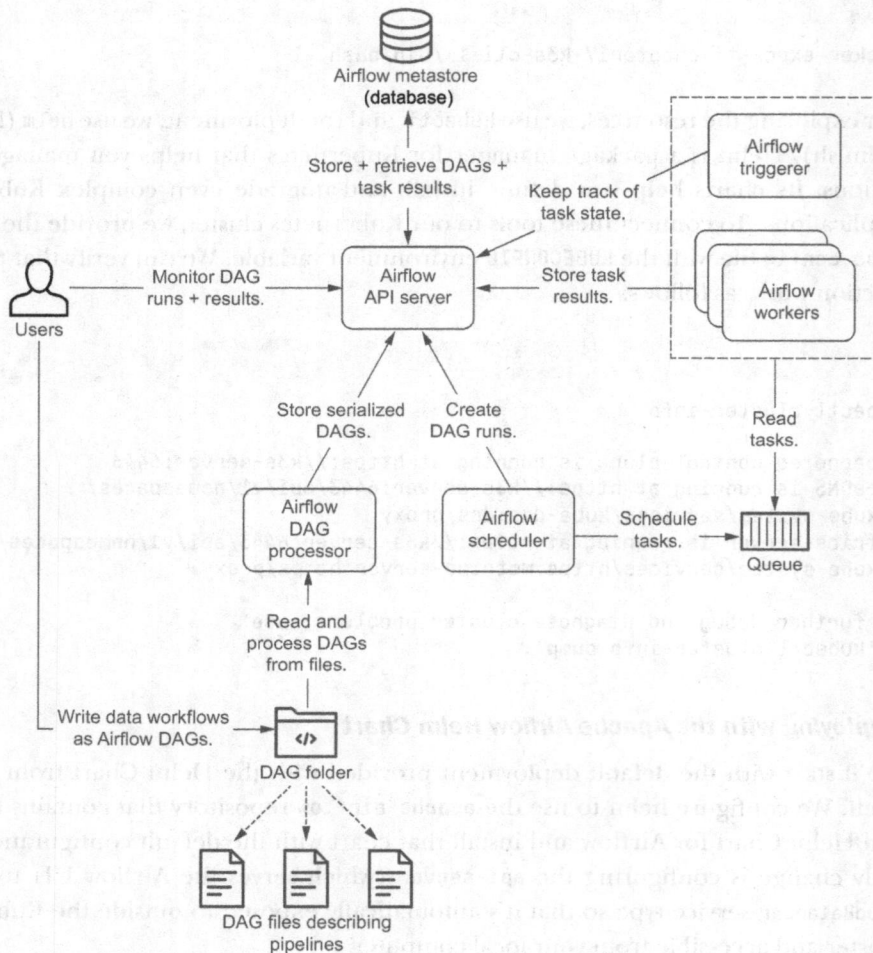

Figure 17.3   Airflow deployment with the `CeleryExecutor` architecture

Listing 17.5   Verifying pods

```
kubectl get pods --namespace airflow

NAME                                    READY   STATUS
airflow-api-server-78c766b59d-27zt7     1/1     Running
```

```
airflow-dag-processor-675587845c-h5h75    2/2        Running
airflow-postgresql-0                      1/1        Running
airflow-redis-0                           1/1        Running
airflow-scheduler-6f8f8c4df6-dzvh6        2/2        Running
airflow-statsd-75fdf4bc64-x49jh           1/1        Running
airflow-triggerer-0                       2/2        Running
airflow-worker-0                          2/2        Running
```

NOTE You can also access the UI with the username admin and password admin through `http://localhost:8080` (or `http://localhost:8081` if the api -server pod is running on the Kubernetes agent node).

17.2.4 Changing the default deployment configuration

Now that we're familiar with the default deployment of Airflow with the Helm Chart, we can see how to change this deployment to adhere to our wishes. Because there are a lot of moving parts, there are a lot of options to configure. In the rest of this chapter, we'll investigate some of these options.

Changing the default deployment options is done mostly by overriding the default values provided to the Helm Chart on install. (You can obtain the default values of the chart with the `helm show values apache-airflow/airflow` command.) The first change we'll make is creating a different admin user to use the same login as the other chapters and get an easy introduction to customizing an Airflow deployment. For this change, we provide a values-override config file: `/etc/helm/values/01-user-values.yaml`.

Listing 17.6   Overriding the initial user creation

```
webserver:
  # Create initial user.
  defaultUser:
    enabled: true
    role: Admin
    username: airflow
    email: airflow@example.com
    firstName: Airflow
    lastName: Second Edition
    password: airflow
```

To change the deployment, provide the values file to the `helm` command. You can verify that the change has been applied by logging into the UI as the new user with username airflow and password airflow. You may need to change the URL(port) because a redeployment could have switched the api-server pod from the master node to the agent node, or vice versa.

Listing 17.7   Changing the default user

```
helm upgrade --install airflow apache-airflow/airflow \
  --namespace airflow \
```

```
--set apiServer.service.type=LoadBalancer \
-f /etc/helm/values/01-user-values.yaml
```

Be aware that the old user still exists because we didn't destroy the deployment—only upgraded it with the new configuration. This depends on how the Helm Chart is developed and what type of change we're performing.

17.2.5 *Changing the apiserver secret key*

When deploying the Airflow release, you may notice the warning message printed to the console when the deployment finishes. The default Helm Chart generates a random key each time a deployment update is done, causing unnecessary restarts when updating the deployment.

Listing 17.8   Web server secret warning

```
###########################################################
#  WARNING: You should set a static   secret key #
###########################################################

You are using a dynamically generated webserver secret key, which can lead to
unnecessary restarts of your Airflow components.

Information on how to set a static webserver secret key can be found here:
https://airflow.apache.org/docs/helm-chart/stable/production-guide.
html#webserver-secret-key
```

The Helm Chart Production Guide reference provides an explanation and guidance on how to fix this problem (https://mng.bz/YZoe). We need to do two things: create a Kubernetes secret with the value (listing 17.9) and reference that secret in our configuration (listing 17.10; /etc/helm/values/02-apiserversecret-values.yaml).

Listing 17.9   Creating a Kubernetes secret

```
kubectl create secret generic my-apiserver-secret --namespace airflow
  --from-literal="api-secret-key=$(python3 -c 'import secrets;
  print(secrets.token_hex(16))')"
```

Listing 17.10   Referencing the secret

```
# 2 - Overriding the webserver secret reference
apiSecretKeySecretName: my-apiserver-secret
```

To change the deployment, provide the specific values file to the helm upgrade command:

```
helm upgrade --install airflow apache-airflow/airflow \
  --namespace airflow \
```

```
--set apiServer.service.type=LoadBalancer \
-f /etc/helm/values/02-apiserversecret-values.yaml
```

When deploying the changes, you can see that the warning is gone. Be careful here. This way of configuring the secret isn't secure enough for a production deployment. See the Kubernetes documentation (https://mng.bz/GwYV) for more secure options, like using the secrets stored in an external store such as Microsoft Azure Key Vault, HashiCorp Vault, or Google Secrets Manager.

17.2.6 Using an external database for Airflow metadata

Using an external database for Airflow's metadata is the best way to go in a production deployment. It enables the organization to configure the database correctly and control the authorization and access outside the Airflow deployment. Also, you can arrange backup and recovery according to the company's best practices.

When using an external database as Airflow's metastore, we have to do a couple of things. First, we need the connection details for the external database. In this case, we'll use the PostgreSQL database provided in the Docker Compose file. The hostname is `postgres`, the database name is `airflow`, and the username and password are airflow and airflow. Make sure that the script `/enable-external-dns.sh` is executed from within the Kubernetes command-line container to ensure that this database can be reached from within the Kubernetes cluster. We can provide these connection details to our Helm Chart deployment via a Kubernetes secret, as follows.

Listing 17.11 Creating the Kubernetes secret with the database connection details

```
kubectl create secret generic mydatabase \
  --namespace airflow \
  --from-literal=connection=postgresql://airflow:airflow@postgres:5432/airflow
```

Also, we need to configure the Helm Chart to use this secret and disable the PostgreSQL database config. Because we're going to use a different database, we have to make sure that we provide the previous changes, such as the different default user and the web server secrets key, because they were executed in the default metadata database, which we're going to replace. For convenience, we've combined all three changes in the config-override file `/etc/helm/values/03-externaldatabase-values .yaml`, shown in the following listing.

Listing 17.12 Using an external database

```
# Override default values in the Apache Airflow Helm Chart
#
# 3 - Using the external database
postgresql:
  enabled: false

data:
```

```
    metadataSecretName: mydatabase

# 2 - Overriding the webserver secret reference
apiSecretKeySecretName: my-apiserver-secret

# 1 - Overriding the default user since we use a different database
webserver:
  # Create initial user.
  defaultUser:
    enabled: true
    role: Admin
    username: airflow
    email: airflow@example.com
    firstName: Airflow
    lastName: Second Edition
    password: airflow
```

We change the deployment by providing the specific values file to the `helm upgrade` command:

```
/enable-external-dns.sh
helm upgrade --install airflow apache-airflow/airflow \
  --namespace airflow \
  --set apiServer.service.type=LoadBalancer \
  -f /etc/helm/values/03-external-database-values.yaml
```

When the deployment is finished, we can check the changes by logging in to the UI again. In this case, we don't have the admin user anymore because we started using the new external metastore, so we have to use the airflow user. To clean up, we can delete the PostgreSQL database used in the default deployment.

Listing 17.13   Cleaning up the database in Kubernetes

```
kubectl delete statefulset airflow-postgresql --namespace airflow
```

TIP If you're using PostgreSQL as your database, you'll likely want to enable PgBouncer (https://www.pgbouncer.org), a lightweight connection pooler for PostgreSQL. Airflow can open many database connections due to its distributed nature, and using a connection pooler can significantly reduce the number of open connections on the database. Some cloud databases already offer this feature as a built-in service, so we won't go into details here.

17.2.7 Deploying DAGs

Now that we have the infrastructure setup, we can get our DAGs deployed to our Airflow environment. We have a few options:

- Include the DAGs in the container image we use.
- Mount a Kubernetes volume and upload the DAG definitions there.

- Use a Git repository and synchronize the DAGs into Airflow using a Git synchronization.

PROVIDING DAGS IN THE IMAGE

The simplest way to provide the DAGs to all the components of Airflow that need access to them is to bake the files into the container image used in the deployment. Building the DAG files into the Airflow image is also a popular option for its immutability; any change to DAG files results in the build and deployment of a new Docker image, so you're always certain which version of your code you're running. (This is the same approach taken by Astronomer's managed service.) Another nice benefit is that upgrading Airflow is relatively easy: it involves bumping the base image tag. The following listing shows how this option works by extending the default Airflow image with a single COPY statement.

Listing 17.14   Extending the Docker image

```
ARG AIRFLOW_IMAGE_NAME=apache/airflow:3.1.3
FROM ${AIRFLOW_IMAGE_NAME}

COPY dags ${AIRFLOW_HOME}/dags/
```

With this Dockerfile, we need to build a new image containing the DAGs and provide that image to a container registry that can be reached from within our Kubernetes cluster. In our Docker Compose–based setup, we provide a registry and the following commands to build, tag, and push the custom image (part of publish-custom-images .sh) to that container registry.

Listing 17.15   Building the custom image

```
docker build -t manning-airflow/my-airflow:k8s
  -f Dockerfile.dags-in-image .

docker tag manning-airflow/my-airflow:k8s
  localhost:3632/manning-airflow/my-airflow:k8s

docker push localhost:3632/manning-airflow/my-airflow:k8s
```

It might seem a bit strange that we push the Docker image to localhost:3632. This local port is mapped in the Docker Compose file to the registry container's port 5000. We'll refer to registry:5000 in the Helm Chart values file. We're going to use multiple Docker images to explain more different setups going forward. A build script, which builds them all in one go, is provided for your convenience. The following listing shows how to run that script.

Listing 17.16   Building all Docker images

```
./publish-custom-images.sh
```

After we publish our custom image, we have to make sure our deployment will use that image. We can do that by overriding the `images.airflow.repository` and `images.airflow.tag` values. To prevent our previous changes from being reverted, we provide those values together with the new values, as shown in the following listing (/etc/helm/values/04-dags-in-image-values.yaml).

Listing 17.17   Using DAGs inside the Docker image

```
# Override default values in the Apache Airflow Helm Chart
#
# 4 - Dags baked inside custom image
images:
  airflow:
    repository: registry:5000/manning-airflow/my-airflow
    tag: k8s
    pullPolicy: Always

# 3 - Using the external database
postgresql:
  enabled: false

data:
  metadataSecretName: mydatabase

# 2 - Overriding the webserver secret reference
apiSecretKeySecretName: my-apiserver-secret

# 1 - Overriding the default user since we use a different database
webserver:
  # Create initial user.
  defaultUser:
    enabled: true
    role: Admin
    username: airflow
    email: airflow@example.com
    firstName: Airflow
    lastName: Second Edition
    password: airflow
```

We change the deployment by providing the specific values file to the `helm upgrade` command:

```
helm upgrade --install airflow apache-airflow/airflow \
  --namespace airflow \
  --set apiServer.service.type=LoadBalancer \
  -f /etc/helm/values/04-dags-in-image-values.yaml
```

When we log in to the UI after this upgrade, we should see that the `01_dag_in_image` in the UI is available (figure 17.4). We can execute it by unpausing the DAG.

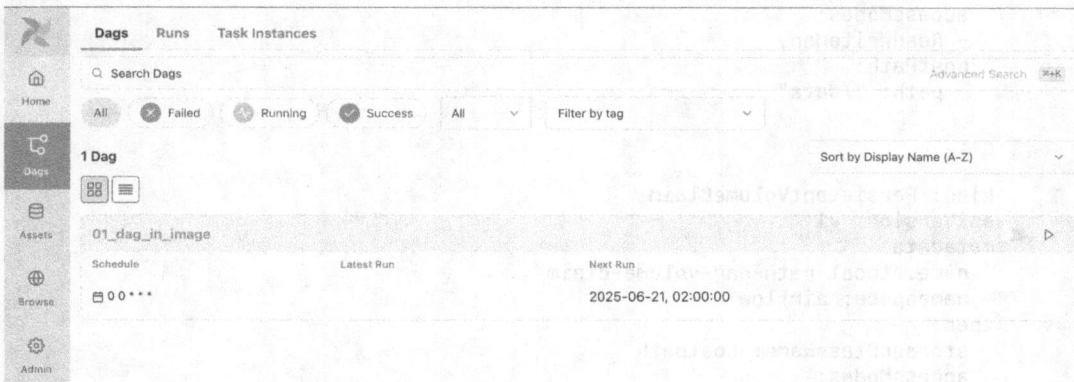

Figure 17.4 DAG from the default Docker image shown in the UI

USING A KUBERNETES VOLUME FOR DAGS

The preceding method works well if you have a single team responsible for writing DAGs but becomes cumbersome when you have multiple teams using the same Airflow environment. Another way to provide your DAGs is through a Kubernetes persistent volume.

Persistent volumes are Kubernetes's abstraction over storage, allowing you to mount shared volumes to containers without having to know the underlying storage technology. One of the trickiest parts is to set up a continuous integration/continuous delivery (CI/CD) pipeline in which DAG code is pushed to the shared volume, which typically doesn't provide out-of-the-box functionality for pushing directly to the shared volume. DAG code must be copied to the volume with a pushing method or a pulling method. The solution may depend on your chosen volume type, so see the Kubernetes documentation on volumes (https://mng.bz/z2vr) for more information. Because the correct implementation depends on the chosen persistent volume type, we won't get into the details here.

In this chapter's setup, we made sure that the DAGs from the local filesystem are available in the /data directory of the Kubernetes nodes. We'll use this directory for the persistent volume, as shown in the next listing (/etc/helm/values/dag-pvc.yaml).

Listing 17.18 Declaring a persistent volume

```
kind: PersistentVolume
apiVersion: v1
metadata:
  name: local-path-dag-volume
  namespace: airflow
spec:
  storageClassName: hostpath
  capacity:
    storage: 1Gi
```

```
    accessModes:
    - ReadWriteMany
    hostPath:
      path: "/data"


---


kind: PersistentVolumeClaim
apiVersion: v1
metadata:
  name: local-path-dag-volume-claim
  namespace: airflow
spec:
  storageClassName: hostpath
  accessModes:
  - ReadWriteMany
  resources:
    requests:
      storage: 250Mi
```

We deploy the persistent volume with the following Kubernetes command:

```
kubectl -n airflow apply -f /etc/helm/values/dag-pvc.yaml
```

When we've deployed the persistent volume, which uses the /data directory on the
Kubernetes hosts, we can change our Airflow deployment to use the persistent volume
instead of the custom image we used before, as shown in the next listing (/etc/helm/
values/04-dags-in-persistent-vol-values.yaml).

Listing 17.19   Using DAGs from a persistent volume

```
# Override default values in the Apache Airflow Helm Chart
#
# 4 - Dags in persistent volume
dags:
  persistence:
    enabled: true
    existingClaim: local-path-dag-volume-claim


# 3 - Using the external database
postgresql:
  enabled: false

data:
  metadataSecretName: mydatabase

# 2 - Overriding the webserver secret reference
apiSecretKeySecretName: my-apiserver-secret

# 1 - Overriding the default user since we use a different database
webserver:
  # Create initial user.
```

```
defaultUser:
  enabled: true
  role: Admin
  username: airflow
  email: airflow@example.com
  firstName: Airflow
  lastName: Second Edition
  password: airflow
```

We change the deployment by providing the specific values file to the `helm upgrade` command:

```
helm upgrade --install airflow apache-airflow/airflow \
  --namespace airflow \
  --set apiServer.service.type=LoadBalancer \
  -f /etc/helm/values/04-dags-in-persistent-vol-values.yaml
```

When we log in to the UI after this upgrade, we should see that the DAGs `02_teamA_dag_from_pvc` and `02_teamB_dag_from_pvc` are available, and we can execute them by unpausing the DAGs (figure 17.5).

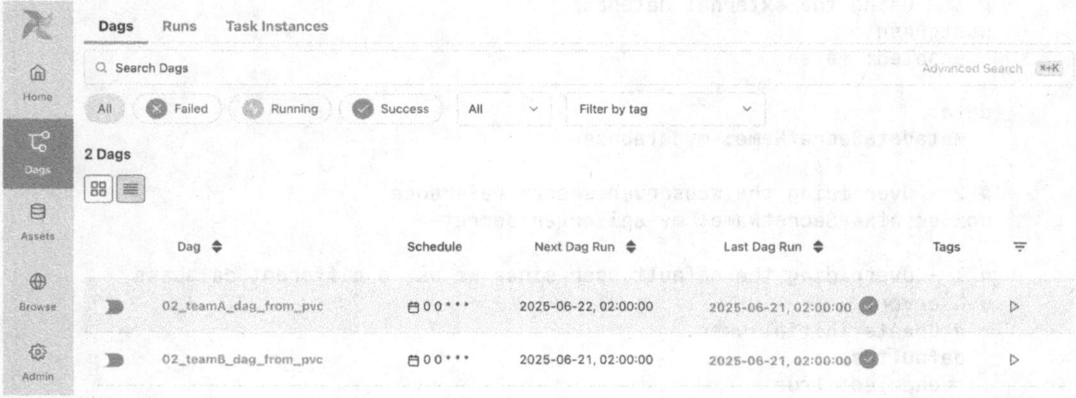

Figure 17.5 DAGs from persistent volume shown in the UI

USING A GIT REPOSITORY FOR DAGS

A third option for managing the DAGs in your Airflow deployment is synchronizing the DAG files from a Git repository. Airflow creates a sync container that pulls the code from the configured repository before starting a task (`/etc/helm/values/04-dags-in-git-values.yaml`).

Listing 17.20 Using DAGS from a Git repository

```
# Override default values in the Apache Airflow Helm Chart
#
```

```
# 4 - Dags in git repository
dags:
  persistence:
    enabled: false
  gitSync:
    enabled: true

    # git repo clone url
    # ssh example: git@github.com:apache/airflow.git
    # https example: https://github.com/apache/airflow.git
    repo:
  https://github.com/godatadriven/data-pipelines-with-airflow-2nd-ed.git
    branch: master
    rev: HEAD
    # The git revision (branch, tag, or hash) to check out, v4 only
    ref: master
    depth: 1
    # the number of consecutive failures allowed before aborting
    maxFailures: 0
    # subpath within the repo where dags are located
    # should be "" if dags are at repo root
    subPath: "chapter02/dags"


# 3 - Using the external database
postgresql:
  enabled: false

data:
  metadataSecretName: mydatabase


# 2 - Overriding the webserver secret reference
apiSecretKeySecretName: my-apiserver-secret


# 1 - Overriding the default user since we use a different database
webserver:
  # Create initial user.
  defaultUser:
    enabled: true
    role: Admin
    username: airflow
    email: airflow@example.com
    firstName: Airflow
    lastName: Second Edition
    password: airflow
```

We change the deployment by providing the specific values file to the `helm upgrade` command:

```
helm upgrade --install airflow apache-airflow/airflow \
  --namespace airflow \
  --set apiServer.service.type=LoadBalancer \
  -f /etc/helm/values/04-dags-in-git-values.yaml
```

If the deployment finishes successfully, we see the DAGs from chapter 2 in our Airflow UI. We also see that the `dag-processor` pod contains the extra `git-sync` container. This container will update the DAGs when a new version is available in the Git repository (figure 17.6).

Listing 17.21 Showing the extra `git-sync` container

```
kubectl -n airflow get pod -l component=dag-processor \
 -o jsonpath='{range .items[*].spec.containers[*]}{.name}{"\n"}{end}'

dag-processor
git-sync
dag-processor-log-groomer
```

Figure 17.6 DAGs from Git repository (`chapter02`) shown in the UI

17.2.8 *Deploying a Python library*

In many cases, you may need to install some additional Python libraries in your Airflow environment so your DAGs will work. These libraries could include pandas for data manipulation in Python as well as additional Airflow providers that you want to use. In this section, we'll look at how to ensure that these libraries are installed and available in your Airflow environment.

PROVIDING PYTHON LIBRARIES TO INSTALL ON STARTUP

In previous examples, we sometimes used the _PIP_ADDITIONAL_REQUIREMENTS environment variable to mention Python libraries that have to be installed on startup of the environment. This method is flexible and certainly usable in nonproduction environments, but isn't meant to be used in a production setup.

PROVIDING PYTHON LIBRARIES IN THE IMAGE

As with the DAG deployment in the image, the simplest way to provide the Python libraries you need is to install them in the container image used in the deployment. For this purpose, we can extend the default Airflow image with a couple of commands.

Listing 17.22   Extending the Docker image

```
ARG AIRFLOW_IMAGE_NAME=apache/airflow:3.1.3
FROM ${AIRFLOW_IMAGE_NAME}

COPY dags-dependencies ${AIRFLOW_HOME}/dags/

RUN pip install tensorflow
```

With this Dockerfile, we again need to build the new image and provide that image to a container registry that can be reached from within our Kubernetes cluster. In our Docker Compose–based setup, we provide a registry, and with the following commands, we can build, tag, and push the custom image (part of publish-custom-images .sh) to the container registry.

Listing 17.23   Building the custom image with dependencies

```
docker build -t manning-airflow/airflow-deps:k8s
   -f Dockerfile.deps-in-image .

docker tag manning-airflow/airflow-deps:k8s
   localhost:3632/manning-airflow/airflow-deps:k8s

docker push localhost:3632/manning-airflow/airflow-deps:k8s
```

When we publish our custom image, we must make sure that our deployment will use that image. We can do that by overriding the images.airflow.repository and images .airflow.tag values. To prevent our previous changes from being reverted, we provide them with the new values, as shown in the next listing (/etc/helm/values/05 -dependencies-in-image-values.yaml).

Listing 17.24   Using dependencies from a Docker image

```
# Override default values in the Apache Airflow Helm Chart
#
# 4 - Dags and dependencies baked inside custom image
images:
```

```
  airflow:
    repository: registry:5000/manning-airflow/airflow-deps
    tag: k8s
    pullPolicy: Always

# 3 - Using the external database
postgresql:
  enabled: false

data:
  metadataSecretName: mydatabase

# 2 - Overriding the webserver secret reference
apiSecretKeySecretName: my-apiserver-secret

# 1 - Overriding the default user since we use a different database
webserver:
  # Create initial user.
  defaultUser:
    enabled: true
    role: Admin
    username: airflow
    email: airflow@example.com
    firstName: Airflow
    lastName: Second Edition
    password: airflow
```

We change the deployment by providing the specific values file to the `helm upgrade` command:

```
helm upgrade --install airflow apache-airflow/airflow \
  --namespace airflow \
  --set apiServer.service.type=LoadBalancer \
  -f /etc/helm/values/05-dependencies-in-image-values.yaml
```

When we log in to the UI again after this upgrade, we should see that the DAG `01_dag_dependencies_in_image` is available (figure 17.7), and we can execute it by unpausing the DAG. The version task should succeed and print the TensorFlow version in the logs (figure 17.8).

The downside of this approach is that all the Airflow workers use the same set of dependencies. If you use the Airflow deployment with multiple teams, this soon becomes a bottleneck leading to conflicting dependencies for different use cases. One way to overcome this problem is to use multiple queues in the `CeleryExecutor` where you configure separate workers to pick up the tasks and set up each worker to use one of the available queues. For each worker/queue combination, you can configure a separate image and have full control of what Python libraries are installed where.

An example of such a setup is the `CeleryKubernetesExecutor`, which uses this mechanism in a slightly different way. It delegates not to a separate Celery worker but to the `kubernetes` queue, which executes the tasks through the `KubernetesExecutor`.

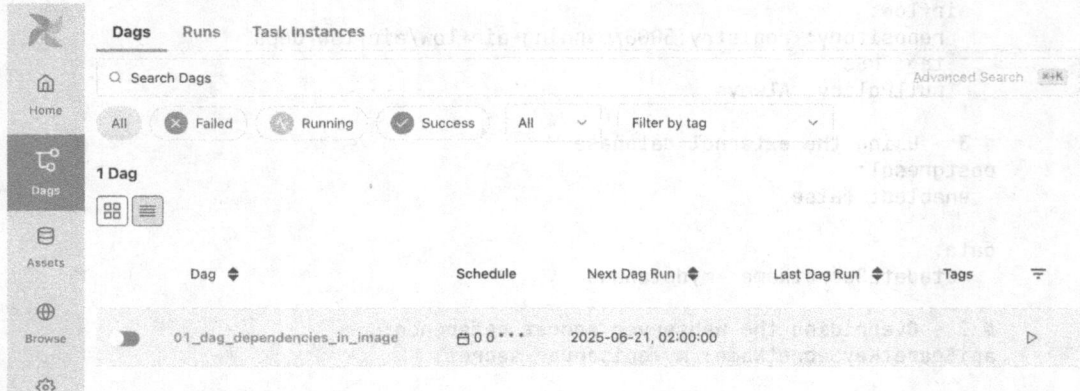

Figure 17.7   Dependencies in image shown in the UI

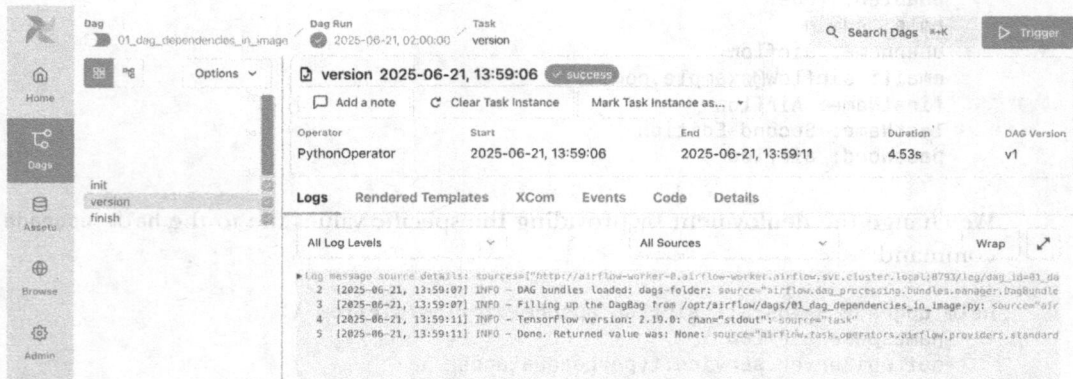

Figure 17.8   Version of dependency printed in the log of the task

This specialized executor, available in Airflow 2, has been deprecated in Airflow 3 and superseded by the ability to configure multiple executors (instead of a single one) with the option to specify which executor to use on a task-by-task basis. This feature is still marked experimental but currently is the best way to show by example.

17.2.9   Configuring the executor(s)

In this section, we configure the Airflow deployment with multiple executors and show you how this setup allows you to choose among a multitude of images when running your tasks. As mentioned earlier, you can choose which executor to use in your Airflow deployment. The options are covered in chapter 15, so we won't repeat them here.

This section focuses on configuring the default `CeleryExecutor` and the `Kubernetes-Executor` (/etc/helm/values/06-multiple-executors-values.yaml and the following listing). We'll deploy an example DAG with tasks that run on each executor, as well as tasks that use an image other than the default configured one in the `KubernetesExecutor` (part of `publish-custom-images.sh`) to showcase its flexibility.

Listing 17.25 Building the custom images used in the executors

```
docker build -t manning-airflow/airflow-executors:k8s
    -f Dockerfile.executors_default_image .
docker build -t manning-airflow/airflow-executors-tf:k8s
    -f Dockerfile.executors_tensorflow .
docker build -t manning-airflow/airflow-executors-tf-old:k8s
    -f Dockerfile.executors_tensorflow_old .

docker tag manning-airflow/airflow-executors:k8s
    localhost:3632/manning-airflow/airflow-executors:k8s
docker tag manning-airflow/airflow-executors-tf:k8s
    localhost:3632/manning-airflow/airflow-executors-tf:k8s
docker tag manning-airflow/airflow-executors-tf-old:k8s
    localhost:3632/manning-airflow/airflow-executors-tf-old:k8s

docker push localhost:3632/manning-airflow/airflow-executors:k8s
docker push localhost:3632/manning-airflow/airflow-executors-tf:k8s
docker push localhost:3632/manning-airflow/airflow-executors-tf-old:k8s
```

We use the three built images as follows:

- The `manning-airflow/airflow-executors:k8s` as the default image used in the tasks executed with the `CeleryExecutor`
- The `manning-airflow/airflow-executors-tf:k8s` as the default image used in tasks executed with the `KubernetesExecutor`
- The `manning-airflow/airflow-executors-tf-old:k8s` image from within the config override provided from the task definition in the DAG

Listing 17.26 Configuring the executors

```
# Override default values in the Apache Airflow Helm Chart
#
# 6 - Multiple executors
executor: "CeleryExecutor,KubernetesExecutor"
config:
  kubernetes:
    worker_container_repository: '' # Needs to be empty to be
  overriden via pod_template_file
    worker_container_tag: '' # Needs to be empty to be overriden
  via pod_template_file
  kubernetes_executor:
    worker_container_repository: '' # Needs to be empty to be overriden
  via pod_template_file
    worker_container_tag: '' # Needs to be empty to be overriden via
```

```
pod_template_file

# 4/5 - Dags and dependencies baked inside custom image
images:
  airflow:
    repository: registry:5000/manning-airflow/airflow-executors
    tag: k8s
    pullPolicy: Always
  pod_template:
    repository: registry:5000/manning-airflow/airflow-executors-tf
    tag: k8s
    pullPolicy: Always

# 3 - Using the external database
postgresql:
  enabled: false

data:
  metadataSecretName: mydatabase

# 2 - Overriding the webserver secret reference
apiSecretKeySecretName: my-apiserver-secret

# 1 - Overriding the default user since we use a different database
webserver:
  # Create initial user.
  defaultUser:
    enabled: true
    role: Admin
    username: airflow
    email: airflow@example.com
    firstName: Airflow
    lastName: Second Edition
    password: airflow
```

We change the deployment by providing the specific values file to the `helm upgrade` command:

```
helm upgrade --install airflow apache-airflow/airflow \
  --namespace airflow \
  --set apiServer.service.type=LoadBalancer \
  -f /etc/helm/values/06-multiple-executors-values.yaml
```

When we log in to the UI again after this upgrade, we should see that `01_dag_dependencies_in_image` is available, and we can execute it by unpausing the DAG. The DAG will run three tasks. The `version_celery` task is expected to fail (see figure 17.9) because the `tensorflow` dependency is missing in the default image. Both the `version_k8s` and `version_k8s_old` tasks should succeed, as shown in figure 17.10. While the tasks in the DAG are running, we see that the `KubernetesExecutor` is spawning new pods to execute the two Kubernetes tasks (listing 17.27).

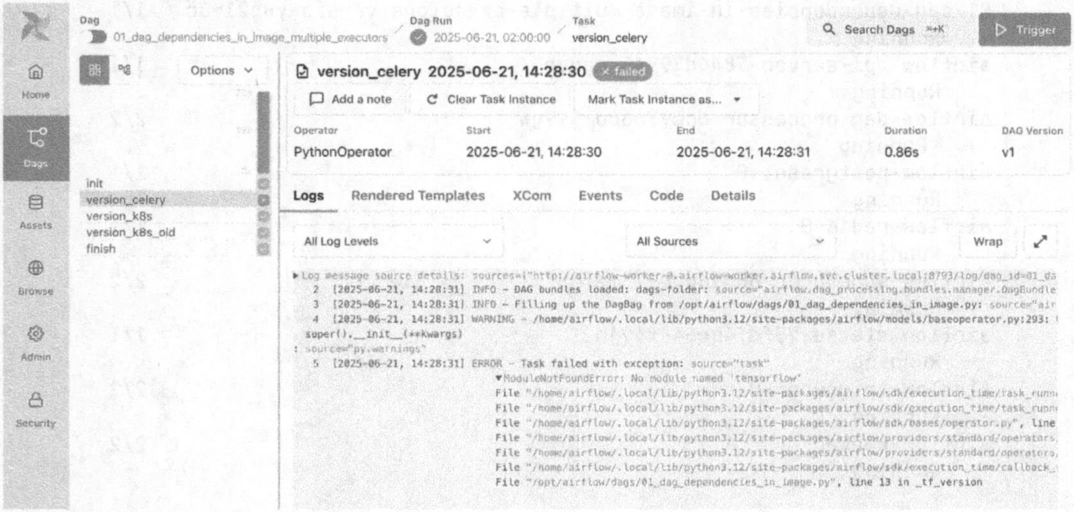

Figure 17.9 Module not found in the default worker image executed by the `CeleryExecutor`

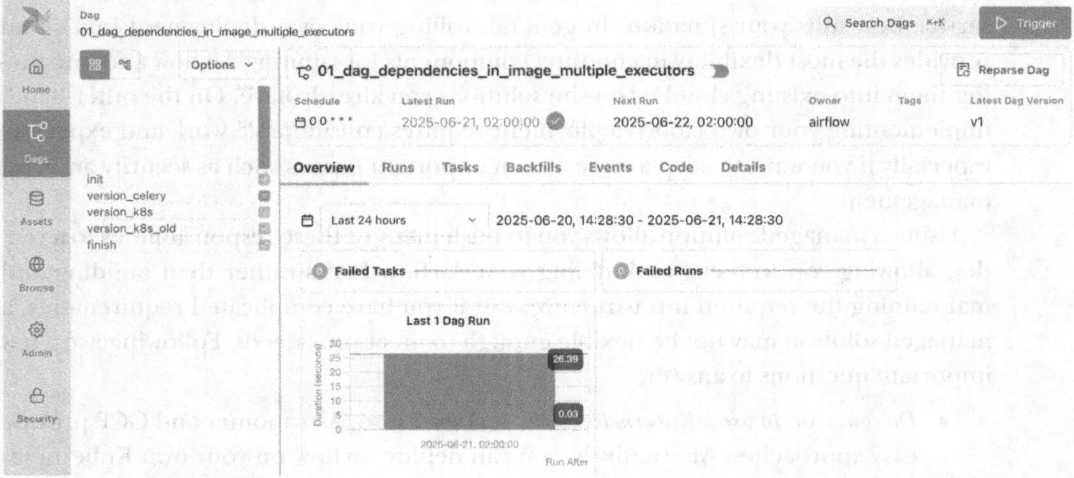

Figure 17.10 The `KubernetesExecutor` executes two tasks with images containing different versions of tensorflow

Listing 17.27 The Kubernetes executor pods running tasks

```
kubectl -n airflow get pods
NAME                                                        READY
    STATUS
01-dag-dependencies-in-image-multiple-executors-versio-kveshcz2   1/1
    Running
```

```
01-dag-dependencies-in-image-multiple-executors-versio-yuc21m6c    1/1
⇒  Running
airflow-api-server-7844d79945-cg6vr                                1/1
⇒  Running
airflow-dag-processor-6cc9766cd-j99gw                              2/2
    Running
airflow-postgresql-0                                               1/1
⇒  Running
airflow-redis-0                                                    1/1
⇒  Running
airflow-scheduler-65d96dc497-42fc8                                 2/2
⇒  Running
airflow-statsd-75fdf4bc64-x49jh                                    1/1
⇒  Running
airflow-triggerer-0                                                2/2
⇒  Running
airflow-worker-0                                                   2/2
⇒  Running
```

17.3 *Choosing a deployment strategy*

When you pick a platform for running your Airflow workloads, we recommend examining the detailed features of the offerings (and their prices) to determine which service best suits your situation. In general, rolling your own deployment in a cloud provides the most flexibility in choosing components for running Airflow and integrating them into existing cloud or on-site solutions you already have. On the other hand, implementing your own cloud deployment requires considerable work and expertise, especially if you want to keep a close eye on important factors such as security and cost management.

Using a managed solution allows you to push many of these responsibilities to a vendor, allowing you to focus on building your Airflow DAGs rather than building and maintaining the required infrastructure. But if you have complicated requirements, a managed solution may not be flexible enough to meet your needs. Following are a few important questions to answer:

- *Do you want to use a Kubernetes-based workflow?* If so, Astronomer and GCP provide easy approaches. Alternatively, you can deploy Airflow on your own Kubernetes cluster, perhaps using the Helm Chart from Astronomer.
- *Which services do you want to connect to from your DAGs?* If you're heavily invested in GCP technologies, using Cloud Composer may be a no-brainer due to its easy integration with other GCP services. But if you're looking to connect to on-site services or those in other clouds, running Airflow in GCP may make less sense.
- *How do you want to deploy your DAGs?* Astronomer and Cloud Composer provide easy ways to deploy DAGs using the CLI (Astronomer) or a cloud bucket (Cloud Composer). But consider how you want to tie this functionality into your CI/CD pipelines for automated deployments of new DAG versions and the like.

- *How much do you want to spend on your Airflow deployment?* Kubernetes-based deployments can be expensive due to the costs of the underlying cluster. Other deployment strategies using other compute solutions in the cloud or Software-as-a-Solution (SaaS) solutions like Astronomer can be cheaper options. If you already have a Kubernetes cluster, you may want to consider running Airflow on your own Kubernetes infrastructure.

- *Do you need more fine-grained control or flexibility than managed services provide?* In this case, you may want to use your own deployment strategy (at the cost of more effort in setting up and maintaining the deployment, of course).

As this short list demonstrates, you have many factors to consider when choosing a solution for deploying your Airflow cluster. Although we can't make this decision for you, we hope that this list gives you some pointers to consider when choosing a solution.

Summary

- Vendor-managed services provide an easy alternative to creating your own deployment by managing many details for you.
- Deploying your own Airflow installation on Kubernetes with Helm gives you full flexibility.
- You have many configurations to choose among when handling your own Airflow deployment.
- A common pattern emerges from the example configurations: providing a custom values override file and a specific `helm upgrade` command.
- The choice between using a vendor-managed service and creating your own cloud deployment depends on many factors, with managed solutions providing greater ease in deployment and management at the expense of less flexibility and (possibly) higher running costs.

appendix A
Running code samples

This book comes with an accompanying code repository on GitHub (https://mng
.bz/Ow82). The repository holds the code used in this book, along with easy-to-
execute Docker environments that enable you to run all the examples yourself. This
appendix explains how the code is organized and how to run the examples.

A.1   Understanding the code structure

The code is organized by chapter, and each chapter is structured the same way. The
top level of the repository consists of several chapter directories (numbered 01–17),
which contain self-contained code examples for the corresponding chapters. Each
directory contains at least the following files/directories:

- dags—Directory containing the DAG files demonstrated in the chapter
- compose.yaml—File describing the standard Airflow setup needed to run the
  DAGs
- compose.override.yaml—File with chapter-specific overrides and extra
  services
- .env—Chapter-specific environment variables
- README.md—Readme file introducing the chapter examples and explaining
  any chapter-specific details on how to run the examples

Where possible, code listings in the book refer to the corresponding file in the chapter directory. For some chapters, code listings shown in the chapters correspond to individual DAGs. In other cases (particularly for more complex examples), several code listings are combined into a single DAG file.

Other than DAG files and Python code, some examples later in the book require extra supporting resources or configuration. The extra steps required to run these examples are described in the corresponding chapters and their readme files.

A.2   *Running the examples*

Each chapter comes with a Docker environment that you can use to run the corresponding code examples.

A.2.1   *Starting the Docker environment*

To start running the chapter examples, run the following inside the chapter directory:

```
$ docker compose up --build
```

This command starts a Docker environment with several containers required to run Airflow, including the following:

- Airflow API server
- Airflow scheduler
- Airflow DAG processor
- Airflow triggerer
- Airflow workers
- PostgreSQL database for the Airflow metastore
- Redis queue for the executors

To avoid seeing the output of all the containers on your terminal, you can start the Docker environment in the background by using

```
$ docker compose up --build -d
```

Some chapters create additional containers that provide other services or APIs required for the examples. Chapter 15, for example, uses the following monitoring services, which are created in Docker to make the examples as realistic as possible:

- Grafana
- Prometheus
- Flower
- Redis

Fortunately, the `compose.override.yaml` file takes care of the details for you. But don't hesitate to dive into the specifics of this file if you're interested.

A.2.2   *Inspecting running services*

After an example is running, you can check out which containers are running by using the docker ps command:

```
$ docker ps
CONTAINER ID    IMAGE                   ... NAMES
d7c68a1b9937    apache/airflow:3.0.3    ... chapter02_airflow_scheduler_1
557e97741309    apache/airflow:3.0.3    ... chapter02_airflow_apiserver_1
742194dd2ef5    postgres:13             ... chapter02_postgres_1
```

By default, Docker Compose prefixes running containers with the name of the containing folder, meaning that you should be able to recognize containers that belong to a chapter by their names. You can also inspect the logs of the individual containers using docker logs:

```
$ docker logs -f chapter02_airflow_scheduler_1
[2024-11-08T21:36:13.966+0000] {executor_loader.py:254} INFO –
  Loaded executor: CeleryExecutor
[2024-11-08T21:36:14.009+0000] {scheduler_job_runner.py:935} INFO –
  Starting the scheduler
[2024-11-08T21:36:14.009+0000] {scheduler_job_runner.py:942} INFO –
  Processing each file at most -1 times
[2024-11-08T21:36:14.013+0000] {manager.py:174} INFO –
  Launched DagFileProcessorManager with pid: 55
[2024-11-08T21:36:14.014+0000] {scheduler_job_runner.py:1847} INFO –
  Adopting or resetting orphaned tasks for active dag runs
```

We hope that these logs will provide valuable feedback if things go awry. Some chapters spin up additional services that require a lot of memory and CPUs or so many extra services that we advise giving your Docker runtime enough available resources. In our case, 4 CPUs, 16 GB of memory, and 80 GB of disk space worked for all examples. The examples in early chapters, which are less complex, require fewer resources.

A.2.3   *Tearing down the environment*

When you're done running an example, you can exit Docker Compose by pressing Ctrl-C. (Note that this step isn't necessary if you're running Docker Compose in the background.) To fully tear down the Docker environment, run the following command from the chapter directory:

```
$ docker compose down -v
```

In addition to stopping the various containers, this command should remove any Docker networks and volumes used in the example. To check whether all containers have indeed been removed, use the following command:

```
$ docker ps -a
```

The command may show a list of unrelated containers that you'll want to remove. To remove containers one by one, use the following command,

```
$ docker rm <container_id>
```

where the `container_id` is obtained from the list of containers shown by the `ps` command. Alternatively, you can use the following shorthand to remove all containers:

```
$ docker rm $(docker ps -aq)
```

Finally, you can remove any unused volumes previously used by these containers with this command:

```
$ docker volume prune
```

> **WARNING** We urge you to use caution with this command, however. It may result in inadvertent data loss if you end up discarding the wrong Docker volumes.

appendix B
Prometheus metric mapping

This appendix contains a mapping for converting metrics from StatsD format to Prometheus format, as explained in chapter 15. This mapping is also provided in the book's GitHub repository (https://mng.bz/Ow82), where it's demonstrated using the Prometheus StatsD exporter. The StatsD exporter takes StatsD metrics provided by Airflow and exposes them in a format Prometheus can read. Some conversions, however, aren't efficient or in line with Prometheus's naming conventions, so this mapping explicitly maps Airflow's StatsD metrics to Prometheus metrics. Because Airflow is an open source project, this mapping is subject to change.

Listing B.1 Prometheus StatsD exporter mapping for Airflow metrics

```
mappings:

- match: "airflow.dag_processing.total_parse_time"
  help: Number of seconds taken to process all DAG files
  name: "airflow_dag_processing_time"

- match: "airflow.dag.*.*.duration"
  name: "airflow_task_duration"
  labels:
    dag_id: "$1"
    task_id: "$2"

- match: "airflow.dagbag_size"
  help: Number of DAGs
```

```
    name: "airflow_dag_count"

- match: "airflow.dag_processing.import_errors"
  help: The number of errors encountered when processing DAGs
  name: "airflow_dag_errors"

- match: "airflow.dag.loading-duration.*"
  help: Loading duration of DAGs grouped by file. If multiple DAGs are found
    in one file, DAG ids are concatenated by an underscore in the label.
  name: "airflow_dag_loading_duration"
  labels:
    dag_ids: "$1"

- match: "airflow.dag_processing.last_duration.*"
  name: "airflow_dag_processing_last_duration"
  labels:
    filename: "$1"

- match: "airflow.dag_processing.last_run.seconds_ago.*"
  name: "airflow_dag_processing_last_run_seconds_ago"
  labels:
    filename: "$1"

- match: "airflow.dag_processing.last_runtime.*"
  name: "airflow_dag_processing_last_runtime"
  labels:
    filename: "$1"

- match: "airflow.dagrun.dependency-check.*"
  name: "airflow_dag_processing_last_runtime"
  labels:
    dag_id: "$1"

- match: "airflow.dagrun.duration.success.*"
  name: "airflow_dagrun_success_duration"
  labels:
    dag_id: "$1"

- match: "airflow.dagrun.schedule_delay.*"
  name: "airflow_dagrun_schedule_delay"
  labels:
    dag_id: "$1"

- match: "airflow.executor.open_slots"
  help: The number of open executor slots
  name: "airflow_executor_open_slots"

- match: "airflow.executor.queued_tasks"
  help: The number of queued tasks
  name: "airflow_executor_queued_tasks"

- match: "airflow.executor.running_tasks"
  help: The number of running tasks
  name: "airflow_executor_running_tasks"
```

index

www.ingramcontent.com/pod-product-compliance
Lightning Source LLC
Chambersburg PA
CBHW010805150126
38204CB00003B/3